WEAPONS & WARFARE

WEAPONS & WARFARE

REVISED EDITION

Volume 2

MODERN WEAPONS AND WARFARE (SINCE C. 1500)

Editor
JOHN POWELL
Oklahoma Baptist University

SALEM PRESS
Pasadena, California   Hackensack, New Jersey

Editorial Director: Christina J. Moose
Acquisitions Manager: Mark Rehn
Acquisitions Editor: Steven L. Danver/Mesa Verde Publishing
Editorial Assistant: Brett S. Weisberg
Research Supervisor: Jeffry Jensen
Photo Editor: Cynthia Breslin Beres
Production Editor: Joyce I. Buchea
Graphics and Design: James Hutson
Layout: Mary Overell

Cover images: The Granger Collection, New York; Library of Congress;
©iStockphoto.com/(Craig DeBourbon, Ian Ilott, Melissa Madia, Adam James Kazmierski)

Library of Congress Cataloging-in-Publication Data

Weapons & warfare / editor, John Powell. — Rev. ed.
   p. cm.
Includes bibliographical references and index.
   ISBN 978-1-58765-594-4 (set : alk. paper) — ISBN 978-1-58765-595-1 (v. 1 : alk. paper) — ISBN 978-1-58765-596-8 (v. 2 : alk. paper) — ISBN 978-1-58765-597-5 (v. 3 : alk. paper)
1. Military weapons—History. 2. Military art and science—History. I. Powell, John, 1954-
II. Title: Weapons and warfare.
   UF500.W48 2010
   623.409—dc22

2009050491

PRINTED IN CANADA

Contents
Modern Weapons and Warfare Since c. 1500

List of Illustrations, Maps,
and Time Lines xxxix
Alphabetized Index of Essays xli
Categorized Index of Essays xlv

Weapons and Forces

Swords, Daggers, and Bayonets 393
Pole Arms 398
Gunpowder and Explosives 403
Small Arms and Machine Guns 408
Artillery. 418
Tanks and Armored Vehicles 427
Aircraft, Bombs, and Guidance
Systems 435
Rockets, Missiles, and Nuclear
Weapons. 451
Chemical and Biological Weapons. 467
Modern Fortifications 473
Sieges and Siege Techniques. 479
Armies and Infantry 484
Cavalry. 490
Naval Development: The Age of Sail 499
Naval Development:
The Age of Propulsion 508

Western Warfare in the Age of Maneuver

European Wars of Religion. 519
The Era of Gustavus Adolphus. 525
The Era of Frederick the Great. 532
The Era of Napoleon Bonaparte 539
The Crimean War. 548
The American Civil War 559

Warfare in the Age of Expansion

Colonial Warfare 577
The Ottoman Empire 587
The Mughal Empire 599
African Warfare 611
Iran 623
Japan 632
China 640
Imperial Warfare 652

Warfare in the Industrial Age

The Age of Bismarck. 663
The "Great" War: World War I 670
The Spanish Civil War 685
World War II: United States, Britain,
and France. 692
World War II: The Soviet Union. 703
World War II: Germany and Italy 710
World War II: Japan 720

Warfare in the Political Age

China 731
The Cold War: The United States,
NATO, and the Right 741
The Cold War: The Soviet Union,
the Warsaw Pact, and the Left 750
Israeli Warfare 759
The Cold War: The Nonaligned States. 765
Colonial Wars of Independence 771
Warfare in Vietnam 781
Warfare in Afghanistan: The Soviet-
Afghan Conflict 791

WARFARE IN THE GLOBAL AGE

Warfare in Iraq 799

Warfare in Afghanistan:
  The United States 806

The War on Terror 813

Warfare and the United Nations 821

Global Military Capabilities 828

LIST OF ILLUSTRATIONS, MAPS, AND TIME LINES
Volume 2

Afghanistan: The Soviet-Afghan Conflict *(time line)* 792
Aircraft, Bombs, and Guidance Systems *(time line)* 441
American Civil War *(time line)*. 562
American Civil War: Confederate and Union Territories *(map)* 560
American Civil War, 1861-1865 *(map)*. 565
Armies and Infantry: Modern *(time line)* 485
Artillery *(time line)* 420
Bayonets *(drawing)* 395
British India at the End of the Nineteenth Century *(map)* 608
Catholic and Protestant Territories, 1590-1598 *(map)* 521
Cavalry: Modern *(time line)* 492
Chemical and Biological Weapons *(time line)* 468
China: Modern Warfare *(time line)* 733
China Under the Qing Dynasty, c. 1697 *(map)* 641
Chinese Civil War, 1926-1949 *(map)*. 734
Chinese Expansion in the Eighteenth Century *(map)*. 642
Cold War Era: Nonaligned States *(time line)*. 767
Cold War Era: Soviet Union, Warsaw Pact, and the Left *(time line)*. 752
Cold War Era: United States, NATO, and the Right *(time line)* 743
Crimean War *(time line)* 552
Crimean War, Battle Sites, 1853-1856 *(map)*. 549
Fortifications, Modern *(time line)*. 475
Frederick the Great's Era *(time line)* 532
Gettysburg, 1863 *(map)*. 564
Germany, Unification of, 1863-1871 *(map)* 664
Gulf War, 1991 *(map)*. 800
Gunpowder and Explosives *(time line)* 406
Gustavus Adolphus's Era *(time line)* 528
Imperial Holdings in Africa as of 1914 *(map)* 653
Japan, c. 1615 *(map)* 634
Japan: Modern *(time line)*. 632
Mughal Empire *(time line)* 600
Mughal Empire in the Seventeenth Century *(map)*. 603
Napoleonic Battle Sites *(map)* 541
Naval Development: The Age of Propulsion *(time line)* 508
Naval Development: The Age of Sail *(time line)*. 499
Ottoman Empire *(time line)*. 589

Ottoman Empire, c. 1700 *(map)* 590
Ottoman Expansion Under Süleyman the Magnificent *(map)* 588
Pole-Arms *(time line)* 399
Rockets, Missiles, and Nuclear Weapons *(time line)* 455
Ṣafavid Iran in the Seventeenth Century *(map)* 627
Sieges and Siege Techniques: Modern *(time line)* 480
Sixteenth Century, World Exploration *(map)* 578
Small Arms and Machine Guns *(time line)* 410
Spain, Division of, 1936 *(map)* 686
Spanish-American War, Caribbean Theater *(map)* 654
Spanish Civil War *(time line)* 687
Swords, Daggers, and Bayonets *(time line)* 393
Terror, War on *(time line)* 814
Thirty Years' War: Battle Sites *(map)* 526
Turkey, Republic of, 1923 *(map)* 593
United Nations, Warfare and the *(time line)* 822
Vietnam Conflict, 1954-1975 *(map)* 782
Vietnam, Warfare in *(time line)* 785
World War I: Offensives on the Western Front, 1918 *(map)* 680
World War I: The "Great" War *(time line)* 671
World War I: Western Front, 1915-1917 *(map)* 672
World War II: Germany and Italy *(time line)* 712
World War II: Japan *(time line)* 721
World War II: Japan and the Pacific Theater *(map)* 722
World War II: Normandy Invasion, 1944 *(map)* 696
World War II: The European Theater *(map)* 706
World War II: The Soviet Union *(time line)* 704
World War II: United States, Britain, and France *(time line)* 693

ALPHABETIZED INDEX OF ESSAYS

African Warfare (c. 1500-1935) 611

The Age of Bismarck (1863-1890). 663

Aircraft, Bombs, and Guidance Systems
(since 1900) 435

The American Civil War (1861-1865) 559

Ancient Fortifications (to c. 500 C.E.) 40

The Anglo-Saxons (c. 500-1100 C.E.) 240

Armies and Infantry: Ancient and
Medieval (c. 2500 B.C.E.-1400 C.E.) 60

Armies and Infantry: Modern
(since c. 1500). 484

Armies of Christendom and the Age
of Chivalry (c. 918-1500 C.E.). 260

Armies of Muḥammad and the Caliphate
(622-1060 C.E.) 281

Armies of the Seljuk Turks
(c. 900-1307 C.E.) 288

Art and Warfare 851

Artillery (since c. 1500) 418

The Assyrians (c. 1950-612 B.C.E.) 94

Berber Warfare (c. 1000 B.C.E.-1000 C.E.) . . . 179

Biology, Chemistry, and War 947

Bows and Arrows (to c. 1500 C.E.) 12

Byzantium (312-1453 C.E.). 221

Carthaginian Warfare (814-202 B.C.E.). 149

Cavalry: Ancient and Medieval
(to c. 1500 C.E.). 65

Cavalry: Modern (since c. 1500) 490

Celtic Warfare (c. 500 B.C.E.-900 C.E.). 174

The Chaldeans (626-539 B.C.E.) 100

Chariots (to c. 400 B.C.E.) 31

Chemical and Biological Weapons
(since c. 1500) 467

China: Ancient (c. 1523 B.C.E.-588 C.E.) 191

China: Medieval (581-1644 C.E.). 311

China: Modern Warfare (since 1912) 731

China: The Qing Empire (1644-1911) 640

City-States and Empires Through
Old Babylon (c. 3500-1595 B.C.E.) 83

Civilian Labor and Warfare 897

Clubs, Maces, and Slings
(to c. 1500 C.E.) 3

The Cold War: The Nonaligned States
(since 1955) 765

The Cold War: The Soviet Union,
the Warsaw Pact, and the Left
(1945-1991) 750

The Cold War: The United States, NATO,
and the Right (1945-1991) 741

Collaboration in War. 965

Colonial Warfare (1420-1857). 577

Colonial Wars of Independence
(1935-1991) 771

Commemoration of War 856

Counterinsurgency 901

The Crimean War (1853-1856). 548

Crossbows (to c. 1500 C.E.) 17

Crusading Armies of the West
(1095-1525 C.E.). 272

Cryptography 1001

Diplomacy. 1008

Education, Textbooks, and War 905

The Egyptians (c. 3000-30 B.C.E.) 111

The Era of Frederick the Great
(1712-1786) 532

The Era of Gustavus Adolphus
(1609-1697) 525

The Era of Napoleon Bonaparte
(1789-1815) 539

Ethiopia (c. 300-1543 C.E.) 304

European Wars of Religion
(c. 1517-1618). 519

Film and Warfare. 861

Financing War. 1013

Firearms and Cannon (to c. 1500 C.E.) 35

The Franks and the Holy Roman Empire
(482-918 C.E.) 231

Galleys to Galleons (to c. 1600 C.E.) 386
Genocide 969
Geography, Weather, and Warfare 837
Global Military Capabilities (2010) 828
The "Great" War: World War I
   (1914-1918) 670
Greek and Hellenistic Warfare from
   Alexander to Rome (336-30 B.C.E.) 140
Greek Warfare to Alexander
   (c. 1600-336 B.C.E.) 129
Gunpowder and Explosives
   (since c. 1500) 403

Handarms to Firearms
   (c. 1130-1700 C.E.) 375
The Hebrews (c. 1400 B.C.E.-73 C.E.) 105
The Hittites (c. 1620-1190 B.C.E.) 89

Ideology and War. 868
Imperial Warfare (1857-1945) 652
The Incas (c. 1200-1500 C.E.) 359
India and South Asia: Ancient
   (c. 1400 B.C.E.-500 C.E.) 209
India and South Asia: Medieval
   (c. 500-1526 C.E.) 336
Intelligence and Counterintelligence 1018
International Arms Trade 1024
Iran (c. 1500-1922) 623
Israeli Warfare (since 1948) 759

Japan: Medieval (c. 600-1600 C.E.) 321
Japan: Modern (c. 1600-1930) 632

Knights to Cavalry (c. 1000-1600 C.E.) 380
Knives, Swords, and Daggers
   (to c. 1500 C.E.) 21

Literature and Warfare 873
The Lombards (c. 500-1100 C.E.) 245

The Magyars (c. 500-1100 C.E.) 248
The Maya and Aztecs
   (c. 1500 B.C.E.-1521 C.E.) 351
Medicine on the Battlefield. 952
Medieval Fortifications
   (c. 500-1500 C.E.) 47

Mercenaries. 976
Military Organization 1029
Modern Fortifications (since c. 1500) 473
The Mongols (c. 600-1450 C.E.) 328
The Mughal Empire (1526-1858) 599
Music and Warfare 878

Naval Development: The Age of
   Propulsion (since c. 1850). 508
Naval Development: The Age of Sail
   (c. 1500-1850). 499
Nomadic Warriors of the Steppe
   (to c. 500 C.E.). 202
North American Indigenous Nations
   (c. 12,000 B.C.E.-1600 C.E.) 364

The Ottoman Armies (1299-1453 C.E.) 293
The Ottoman Empire (1453-1923) 587

Paramilitary Organizations 911
Peace Movements and Conscientious
   Objection to War 981
The Persians (to 651 C.E.) 118
Picks, Axes, and War Hammers
   (to c. 1500 C.E.) 8
Pole Arms (c. 1500-1900) 398
The Press and War 915
Prisoners and War 989
Propaganda 921
Psychological Effects of War 957

Religion and Warfare. 883
Revolt, Rebellion, and Insurgency 929
Rockets, Missiles, and Nuclear Weapons
   (since c. 1200). 451
Roman Warfare During the Empire
   (27 B.C.E.-476 C.E.) 165
Roman Warfare During the Republic
   (753-27 B.C.E.). 157

Sieges and Siege Techniques: Modern
   (since c. 1500). 479
Sieges and Siegecraft: Ancient and
   Medieval (c. 7000 B.C.E.-1500 C.E.) 55
Small Arms and Machine Guns
   (since c. 1500). 408

Southeast Asia (c. 500-1500 C.E.) 344
The Spanish Civil War (1936-1939) 685
Spears and Pole Arms (to c. 1500 C.E.) 26
Strategy 1033
Swords, Daggers, and Bayonets
    (c. 1500-1900). 393

Tactics. 1037
Tanks and Armored Vehicles
    (since 1898) 427
Television and Warfare. 889
Tribal Warfare in Central and Eastern
    Europe (c. 500 B.C.E.-800 C.E.) 183

The Vikings (c. 700-1066 C.E.). 253
Violence in the Precivilized World
    (to c. 4000 B.C.E.). 77

War Crimes and Military Justice 994
The War on Terror (since 1988) 813

Warfare and the United Nations
    (since c. 1990). 821
Warfare in Afghanistan: The Soviet-
    Afghan Conflict (1979-1989) 791
Warfare in Afghanistan: The United
    States (since 2001) 806
Warfare in Iraq (since 1990) 799
Warfare in Vietnam (1945 1975) 781
War's Impact on Economies 933
Warships and Naval Warfare
    (to c. 1200 C.E.). 70
West African Empires (400-1591 C.E.). 298
Women, Children, and War 938
World War II: Germany and Italy
    (1933-1945) 710
World War II: Japan (1931-1945) 720
World War II: The Soviet Union
    (1939-1945) 703
World War II: United States, Britain,
    and France (1939-1945) 692

CATEGORIZED INDEX OF ESSAYS

AFRICA

African Warfare 611
Berber Warfare 179
Carthaginian Warfare 149
The Cold War: The Nonaligned States 765
Colonial Wars of Independence 771
The Egyptians 111
Ethiopia 304
Geography, Weather, and Warfare 837
Imperial Warfare 652
Roman Warfare During the Republic 157
The War on Terror 813
Warfare and the United Nations 821
West African Empires 298

AIR FORCES

Aircraft, Bombs, and Guidance Systems . . . 435
Military Organization 1029
Rockets, Missiles, and Nuclear Weapons . . . 451

AMERICAS

The American Civil War 559
The Cold War: The United States,
    NATO, and the Right 741
Colonial Warfare 577
Colonial Wars of Independence 771
Geography, Weather, and Warfare 837
Imperial Warfare 652
The Incas 359
The Maya and Aztecs 351
Naval Development: The Age of Sail 499
North American Indigenous Nations 364
The War on Terror 813
Warfare and the United Nations 821
World War II: United States, Britain,
    and France 692

ANCIENT WORLD (TO C. 500 C.E.)

Ancient Fortifications 40
Armies and Infantry: Ancient
    and Medieval 60
The Assyrians 94
Berber Warfare 179
Bows and Arrows 12
Byzantium 221
Carthaginian Warfare 149
Cavalry: Ancient and Medieval 65
The Chaldeans 100
Chariots 31
China: Ancient 191
City-States and Empires Through
    Old Babylon 83
Clubs, Maces, and Slings 3
Crossbows 17
The Egyptians 111
Ethiopia 304
Geography, Weather, and Warfare 837
Greek and Hellenistic Warfare from
    Alexander to Rome 140
Greek Warfare to Alexander 129
The Hebrews 105
The Hittites 89
India and South Asia: Ancient 209
Knives, Swords, and Daggers 21
The Maya and Aztecs 351
Nomadic Warriors of the Steppe 202
North American Indigenous
    Nations 364
The Persians 118
Picks, Axes, and War Hammers 8
Roman Warfare During the Empire 165
Roman Warfare During the Republic 157
Sieges and Siegecraft: Ancient
    and Medieval 55
Spears and Pole Arms 26
Violence in the Precivilized World 77
Warships and Naval Warfare 70

ASIA: CENTRAL AND STEPPES

The Cold War: The Nonaligned States 765
The Cold War: The Soviet Union,
   the Warsaw Pact, and the Left 750
Colonial Wars of Independence 771
Geography, Weather, and Warfare 837
Imperial Warfare 652
The Mongols 328
Nomadic Warriors of the Steppe 202
The War on Terror 813
Warfare and the United Nations 821
Warfare in Afghanistan: The Soviet-
   Afghan Conflict 791
Warfare in Afghanistan:
   The United States 806
World War II: The Soviet Union 703

ASIA: EASTERN

China: Ancient 191
China: Medieval 311
China: Modern Warfare 731
China: The Qing Empire 640
Colonial Wars of Independence 771
Geography, Weather, and Warfare 837
Imperial Warfare 652
Japan: Medieval 321
Japan: Modern 632
The Mongols 328
Southeast Asia 344
The War on Terror 813
Warfare and the United Nations 821
World War II: Japan 720

ASIA: INDIA AND SOUTH

The Cold War: The Nonaligned States 765
Colonial Wars of Independence 771
Geography, Weather, and Warfare 837
Imperial Warfare 652
India and South Asia: Ancient 209
India and South Asia: Medieval 336
The Mughal Empire 599

The War on Terror 813
Warfare and the United Nations 821
Warfare in Afghanistan:
   The United States 806

ASIA: SOUTHEASTERN

The Cold War: The Nonaligned States 765
Colonial Wars of Independence 771
Geography, Weather, and Warfare 837
Imperial Warfare 652
The War on Terror 813
Warfare and the United Nations 821
Warfare in Vietnam 781

AUXILIARY FORCES

Civilian Labor and Warfare 897
Collaboration in War 965
Medicine on the Battlefield 952
Mercenaries 976

BIOCHEMICAL WEAPONS

Biology, Chemistry, and War 947
Chemical and Biological Weapons 467

COLONIALISM AND IMPERIALISM

Colonial Wars of Independence 771
Counterinsurgency 901
Genocide 969
Imperial Warfare 652
Paramilitary Organizations 911
Revolt, Rebellion, and Insurgency 929
Warfare in Vietnam 781

CULTURE AND WARFARE

Art and Warfare 851
Commemoration of War 856

Film and Warfare 861
Ideology and War 868
Literature and Warfare 873
Music and Warfare 878
Propaganda 921
Religion and Warfare 883
Television and Warfare 889

CUTTING WEAPONS

Knives, Swords, and Daggers 21
Picks, Axes, and War Hammers 8
Swords, Daggers, and Bayonets 393

ECONOMICS AND TRADE

Civilian Labor and Warfare 897
Financing War 1013
International Arms Trade 1024
War's Impact on Economies 933

EIGHTEENTH AND NINETEENTH CENTURIES (1700'S AND 1800'S)

African Warfare 611
The Age of Bismarck 663
The American Civil War 559
Armies and Infantry: Modern 484
Artillery 418
Cavalry: Modern 490
Chemical and Biological Weapons 467
China: The Qing Empire 640
Colonial Warfare 577
The Crimean War 548
The Era of Frederick the Great 532
The Era of Napoleon Bonaparte 539
Geography, Weather, and Warfare 837
Gunpowder and Explosives 403
Imperial Warfare 652
Iran 623
Japan: Modern 632
Modern Fortifications 473
The Mughal Empire 599

Naval Development: The Age
   of Propulsion 508
Naval Development: The Age of Sail 499
The Ottoman Empire 587
Pole Arms 398
Sieges and Siege Techniques: Modern . . . 479
Small Arms and Machine Guns 408
Swords, Daggers, and Bayonets 393
Tanks and Armored Vehicles 427

EUROPE AND MEDITERRANEAN

The Age of Bismarck 663
The Anglo-Saxons 240
Armies of Christendom and
   the Age of Chivalry 260
Byzantium 221
Carthaginian Warfare 149
Celtic Warfare 174
The Cold War: The Nonaligned States . . . 765
The Cold War: The Soviet Union,
   the Warsaw Pact, and the Left 750
The Cold War: The United States,
   NATO, and the Right 741
Colonial Wars of Independence 771
The Crimean War 548
Crusading Armies of the West 272
The Era of Frederick the Great 532
The Era of Gustavus Adolphus 525
The Era of Napoleon Bonaparte 539
European Wars of Religion 519
The Franks and the Holy Roman Empire . . 231
Galleys to Galleons 386
Geography, Weather, and Warfare 837
The "Great" War: World War I 670
Greek and Hellenistic Warfare from
   Alexander to Rome 140
Greek Warfare to Alexander 129
Imperial Warfare 652
Knights to Cavalry 380
The Lombards 245
The Magyars 248
The Ottoman Armies 293
The Ottoman Empire 587
Roman Warfare During the Empire 165

Roman Warfare During the Republic 157
The Spanish Civil War 685
Tribal Warfare in Central and
    Eastern Europe 183
The Vikings. 253
The War on Terror 813
Warfare and the United Nations 821
World War II: Germany and Italy 710
World War II: The Soviet Union. 703
World War II: United States, Britain,
    and France. 692

EXPLOSIVE WEAPONS

Aircraft, Bombs, and Guidance Systems. . . . 435
Artillery. 418
Firearms and Cannon 35
Gunpowder and Explosives 403
Rockets, Missiles, and Nuclear Weapons . . . 451

GLOBAL ISSUES

Chemical and Biological Weapons. 467
The Cold War: The Nonaligned States. 765
The Cold War: The United States,
    NATO, and the Right 741
Colonial Wars of Independence 771
Geography, Weather, and Warfare. 837
Global Military Capabilities 828
The "Great" War: World War I 670
Imperial Warfare 652
Rockets, Missiles, and Nuclear
    Weapons. 451
The War on Terror 813
Warfare and the United Nations 821
World War II: United States, Britain,
    and France. 692

GUERRILLA AND INSURGENT FORCES

Counterinsurgency 901
Paramilitary Organizations 911
Revolt, Rebellion, and Insurgency 929

HANDARMS

Firearms and Cannon 35
Handarms to Firearms 375
Small Arms and Machine Guns 408

INTELLIGENCE AND ESPIONAGE

Cryptography 1001
Intelligence and Counterintelligence 1018

INTERNATIONAL RELATIONS

Diplomacy. 1008
Prisoners and War 989
War Crimes and Military Justice 994

LAND FORCES

Armies and Infantry: Ancient
    and Medieval 60
Armies and Infantry: Modern 484
Cavalry: Ancient and Medieval 65
Cavalry: Modern 490
Knights to Cavalry 380
Military Organization 1029

MIDDLE AGES (C. 500-C. 1500 C.E.)

The Anglo-Saxons 240
Armies and Infantry: Ancient
    and Medieval 60
Armies of Christendom and
    the Age of Chivalry 260
Armies of Muḥammad and the Caliphate . . . 281
Armies of the Seljuk Turks. 288
Berber Warfare 179
Bows and Arrows 12
Byzantium 221
Cavalry: Ancient and Medieval 65
Celtic Warfare 174
Chariots 31

China: Medieval 311
Clubs, Maces, and Slings 3
Crossbows 17
Crusading Armies of the West 272
Ethiopia. 304
Firearms and Cannon 35
The Franks and the Holy Roman Empire . . . 231
Galleys to Galleons. 386
Geography, Weather, and Warfare 837
Handarms to Firearms 375
The Incas 359
India and South Asia: Medieval 336
Japan: Medieval 321
Knights to Cavalry 380
Knives, Swords, and Daggers 21
The Lombards 245
The Magyars 248
The Maya and Aztecs 351
Medieval Fortifications 47
The Mongols 328
North American Indigenous Nations 364
The Ottoman Armies 293
The Ottoman Empire 587
Picks, Axes, and War Hammers 8
Sieges and Siegecraft: Ancient
    and Medieval 55
Southeast Asia 344
Spears and Pole Arms 26
Tribal Warfare in Central and
    Eastern Europe 183
The Vikings. 253
Warships and Naval Warfare 70
West African Empires 298

Crusading Armies of the West 272
The Egyptians 111
Geography, Weather, and Warfare 837
Greek and Hellenistic Warfare from
    Alexander to Rome 140
Greek Warfare to Alexander 129
The Hebrews 105
The Hittites 89
Imperial Warfare 652
Iran 623
Israeli Warfare 759
The Mongols 328
The Ottoman Armies 293
The Ottoman Empire 587
The Persians 118
Roman Warfare During the Empire 165
Roman Warfare During the Republic 157
The War on Terror 813
Warfare and the United Nations 821
Warfare in Iraq 799

MILITARY THEORY

Collaboration in War 965
Counterinsurgency 901
Cryptography 1001
Intelligence and Counterintelligence 1018
Military Organization 1029
Revolt, Rebellion, and Insurgency 929
Strategy 1033
Tactics 1037

MIDDLE EAST

Armies of Muḥammad and the Caliphate . . . 281
Armies of the Seljuk Turks. 288
The Assyrians 94
Byzantium 221
The Chaldeans 100
City-States and Empires Through
    Old Babylon 83
The Cold War: The Nonaligned States. . . . 765
Colonial Wars of Independence 771

MORALITY, ETHICS, AND JUSTICE

Collaboration in War 965
Genocide 969
Ideology and War. 868
Mercenaries. 976
Peace Movements and Conscientious
    Objection to War 981
Prisoners and War 989
Religion and Warfare. 883
War Crimes and Military Justice 994

NAVAL FORCES

Galleys to Galleons. 386
Military Organization 1029
Naval Development: The Age
   of Propulsion 508
Naval Development: The Age of Sail 499
Warships and Naval Warfare 70

SCIENCE AND WARFARE

Biology, Chemistry, and War 947
Medicine on the Battlefield. 952
Psychological Effects of War 957

SHOCK WEAPONS

Clubs, Maces, and Slings 3
Picks, Axes, and War Hammers 8

SIEGECRAFT AND DEFENSIVE WEAPONS

Ancient Fortifications 40
Medieval Fortifications 47
Modern Fortifications 473
Sieges and Siege Techniques: Modern. 479
Sieges and Siegecraft: Ancient
   and Medieval 55

SIXTEENTH AND SEVENTEENTH CENTURIES (1500's AND 1600's)

African Warfare 611
Armies and Infantry: Modern 484
Artillery. 418
Cavalry: Modern 490
Chemical and Biological Weapons. 467
China: The Qing Empire 640
Colonial Warfare 577
The Era of Gustavus Adolphus. 525
European Wars of Religion. 519
Geography, Weather, and Warfare 837

Gunpowder and Explosives 403
Iran 623
Japan: Modern 632
Modern Fortifications 473
The Mughal Empire 599
Naval Development:
   The Age of Sail 499
The Ottoman Empire 587
Pole Arms 398
Sieges and Siege Techniques: Modern. 479
Small Arms and Machine Guns 408
Swords, Daggers, and Bayonets 393

SOCIAL IMPACT OF WARFARE

Civilian Labor and Warfare 897
Counterinsurgency 901
Education, Textbooks, and War 905
Genocide 969
Paramilitary Organizations 911
Peace Movements and Conscientious
   Objection to War 981
The Press and War 915
Prisoners and War 989
Propaganda. 921
Psychological Effects of War 957
War Crimes and Military Justice. 994
War's Impact on Economies 933
Women, Children, and War 938

THROWING AND SHOOTING WEAPONS

Bows and Arrows 12
Clubs, Maces, and Slings 3
Crossbows 17
Spears and Pole Arms 26

THRUSTING WEAPONS

Knives, Swords, and Daggers 21
Pole Arms 398
Spears and Pole Arms 26
Swords, Daggers, and Bayonets 393

TWENTIETH AND TWENTY-FIRST CENTURIES (1900'S AND 2000'S)

African Warfare 611
Aircraft, Bombs, and Guidance Systems 435
Armies and Infantry: Modern 484
Artillery 418
Cavalry: Modern 490
Chemical and Biological Weapons 467
China: Modern Warfare 731
China: The Qing Empire 640
The Cold War: The Nonaligned States 765
The Cold War: The Soviet Union,
     the Warsaw Pact, and the Left 750
The Cold War: The United States,
     NATO, and the Right 741
Colonial Wars of Independence 771
Geography, Weather, and Warfare 837
Global Military Capabilities 828
The "Great" War: World War I 670
Gunpowder and Explosives 403
Imperial Warfare 652
Iran 623
Israeli Warfare 759
Japan: Modern 632
Modern Fortifications 473
Naval Development: The Age
     of Propulsion 508
The Ottoman Empire 587
Rockets, Missiles, and Nuclear Weapons . . . 451

Sieges and Siege Techniques: Modern 479
Small Arms and Machine Guns 408
The Spanish Civil War 685
Tanks and Armored Vehicles 427
The War on Terror 813
Warfare and the United Nations 821
Warfare in Afghanistan: The Soviet-
     Afghan Conflict 791
Warfare in Afghanistan:
     The United States 806
Warfare in Iraq 799
Warfare in Vietnam 781
World War II: Germany and Italy 710
World War II: Japan 720
World War II: The Soviet Union 703
World War II: United States, Britain,
     and France 692

VEHICLES OF WAR

Aircraft, Bombs, and Guidance Systems 435
Chariots 31
Galleys to Galleons 386
Naval Development: The Age
     of Propulsion 508
Naval Development: The Age of Sail 499
Rockets, Missiles, and Nuclear Weapons . . . 451
Tanks and Armored Vehicles 427
Warships and Naval Warfare 70

WEAPONS AND FORCES

SWORDS, DAGGERS, AND BAYONETS

Dates: c. 1500-1900

NATURE AND USE

Edged weapons, such as swords, daggers, and bayonets, are the oldest and most basic instruments of warfare in continuous use since prehistoric times. The use of edged weapons, such as the combat knife, is still taught in basic military training, and the sword, though rendered a military anachronism after the introduction of the repeating rifle, retains a place of honor in formal military dress and ceremony. Both Western and Eastern sword-fighting techniques continue to be studied as martial art forms.

The dagger is arguably the oldest form of edged weapon, being simply a utilitarian knife adapted for service in combat. In its most basic form the dagger consists of a pointed blade, most often of forged metal, although stone, antler, bone, and hardwood have also been used, usually measuring between 6 and 20 inches in length, set into a handle and sharpened to a cutting edge along one or both sides. From this elemental form evolved, by simple extension of the blade length, the various forms of short sword and, later, the long sword. After the introduction of practical firearms in the late seventeenth century, an adaptation of the dagger resulted in the creation of the bayonet, which allowed an empty or fouled musket to be quickly and easily transformed into a serviceable pike by the simple expedient of ramming the dagger's round handle into the muzzle.

Among the most familiar forms of dagger is the bowie knife, named for the American frontiersman Colonel James Bowie of Alamo fame (1796-1836), but actually designed by Bowie's brother, Rezin. The bowie knife's distinctive straight-backed blade is clipped along the top edge into a shallow concave curve at the end, thus imparting a double cutting edge to the point. Equally distinctive is the Sykes-Fairbairn commando dagger, widely used by British paratroopers during World War II; its elegant symmetrical blade was inspired by an ancient Egyptian pattern. Also developed during World War II, the Ka-Bar combat knife, known also as the Mark II in the U.S. Navy and as the Mark III in the U.S. Army and U.S. Marines, employs a variant of the clipped bowie blade. In hand-to-hand fighting, the Ka-Bar is gripped like a hammer in the right hand, while the splayed left hand is held pressed against the chest to protect the heart.

Distinctive non-Western dagger forms include the Malay kris, with a long slender blade, often ground to a wavy edge along its length, that widens to an asymmetrical spur near the handle; the *kukri*, a general-purpose long dagger in use by the Gurkas of Nepal since the nineteenth century with an obtuse "bent" blade that is sharpened along its inner edge; and the East Indian *katar*, a triangular punching dagger with a handle that is mounted at right angles to the long axis of its blade.

TURNING POINTS

c. 1200	As forged steel processes are refined, several European cities, including Sheffield, Brussels, and Toledo, emerge as swordmaking centers.
1450-1700	Sword blades become lighter, narrower, and longer, gradually evolving into the familiar rapier design.
c. late 16th cent.	Japanese swordmaking techniques reach a peak of sophistication, with a variation of the hammer-welding process.
1846-1848	Although military swords have entered a period of decline, cavalry sabers prove decisive during the Mexican-American War.

The earliest forms of sword are virtually indistinguishable from long daggers, a case in point being the ancient Roman *gladius*, a standard weapon of the Roman legions, which measured a modest 2 feet in length.

DEVELOPMENT

Blades of great antiquity, such as those from Mesopotamian and Egyptian cultures dating from 3000 B.C.E., are often short in length, a characteristic necessitated by the use of bronze, which lacks the material strength to produce long serviceable blades. Following the development and subsequent refining of forged steel processes around 1200 C.E., several European cities emerged as respected centers of sword blade production during the late medieval era. Principal among these were the smiths of Sheffield, Brussels, Paris, Nuremberg, Augsburg, and, most respected of all, those of Toledo.

The whitesmith, as the sword maker was known, created a blade from a mass of smelted wrought iron, called a "bloom," by repeatedly heating it and hammering it flat upon an anvil. Through successive repetitions of this procedure, particles of carbon were mixed with the iron, turning it into hardened, carburized steel. Early sword blades were steeled only along their cutting edges, their inner cores composed of the relatively softer and more flexible iron. A technique called pattern welding was later devised to combine the advantageous flexibility of the soft iron core with the harder, but also more brittle, edge-taking quality of hardened steel.

In the pattern-welding process, slender rods of iron are twisted together, heated, and hammer-welded into flat bars of harder carburized iron, which are then sharpened to form the cutting edge. The pattern-welded blade reveals a characteristic serpentine effect upon its surface that persists even in the polished blade. Pattern welding was known to Roman sword makers of the Pax Romana, or Roman Peace (c. 27 B.C.E.-180 C.E.), as well as to the later Vikings. The word "damascene," literally "of Damascus," is often incorrectly used as a synonym for the pattern-welding technique; more properly the term refers to the mottled surface characteristic of blades from Syria and Persia, common after the tenth century. The metal in these blades was repeatedly heated and folded during the hammer-welding process, creating laminated layers of alternating high and low carbon content metal.

Weapons of superior quality bore recognized trademarks, such as that of a running wolf for the arms makers of Solingen (in the Ruhr Valley), which were sometimes fraudulently copied by lesser craftsmen. The legendary Spanish blades of Toledo especially inspired many German and Italian emulations.

Until the mid-1400's, most swords were straight-bladed, double-edged weapons, widely thought to have been too heavy and poorly balanced to allow for the development of elaborate fencing techniques. However, it has been noted that many of these older swords are surprisingly well balanced and of sufficiently light weight—most averaging around 3 pounds—to allow a well-conditioned hand to wield them with surprising dexterity. During the period from 1450 to 1700 blades gradually became lighter, narrower, and longer, developing into the familiar rapier design associated with the musketeers of Louis XIII (1601-1643). These rapiers eventually evolved into the light, fast-dueling swords of the seventeenth and eighteenth centuries, whose basic form still survives in the fencing foil and the épée: slender pointed swords of, respectively, rectangular and triangular cross-section that feature shorter blades, typically 32 inches or less in length.

The shape of the sword's blade dictates the type of attack for which it is used. The curved Persian scimitar, introduced to Europe by the Turks during the Crusades and widely emulated in the European cavalry saber, was more suited for a downward hewing attack or a forward cut-and-thrust motion. In contrast, the narrow thrusting blade typical of most sixteenth century dueling swords was thought to provide a distinct tactical advantage, because the linear thrust is a quicker and more direct motion than the curving slash. Moreover, the thrusting blade was regarded as more lethal, because piercing wounds to the torso were more likely to prove fatal than slash wounds to the same area. Blades ground to a wavy *flamberge* edge, which increased the length of the actual cutting edge, were thought to inflict more damaging and more painful wounds.

In its most general form the sixteenth century sword was cruciform in shape and consisted of a straight or curved steel blade, designed principally for cutting and sharpened along one or both edges. Along the length of the blade might be a narrow groove, technically called a fuller but more popularly known as a "blood groove," intended to reduce the overall weight of the blade and, at the same time, impart to it added strength and flexibility. The sword's cutting edge extended forward from the *ricasso*, that portion of the blade just beyond the cross guard. Extremely long swords, such as the *espadon* or the Scottish claymore (or *claidheamh-mor*, literally, "great sword"), often feature a longer ricasso, blunted, or wrapped with a partial leather sheath, to allow the handler's grip on the blade to be shortened for quicker action. The hilt, or heft, of the sword typically consisted of a simple bar-shaped cross guard or slender rodlike *quillons* bent into a basket-shaped enclosure surrounding and protecting the handle, into which was inserted the blunt spike-shaped end, or tang, of the blade. The metal pommel that capped the end of the tang might be formed into any number of shapes, including multilobed forms, wheels, ovals, or more complex "perfume-stopper" designs, intended to counterbalance the weight and length of the weapon.

It is a historical irony that the golden age of the sword, the sixteenth and seventeenth centuries, was also the period during which gunpowder came into widespread use. As the military popularity of the sword began to wane, the fashion of carrying a sword became increasingly common among male civilians, inspired in no small measure by the rise of dueling

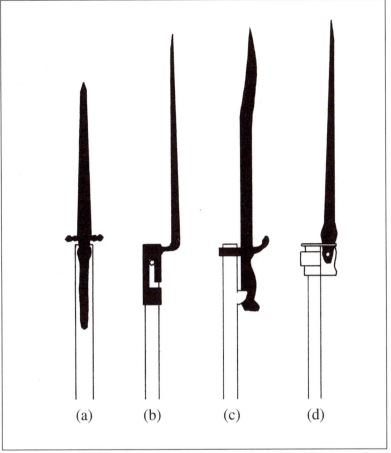

Kimberly L. Dawson Kurnizki

Bayonets enabled firearms to be quickly and easily transformed into serviceable pikes and could be attached by (a) plugging into the muzzle, (b) fitting as a sleeve over the muzzle, (c) locking into a slot on the muzzle, or (d) attaching permanently to the muzzle and folding down when not in use.

among the nobility. Lighter weapons, such as the rapier, became especially popular. The épée, with its slender, three-edged blade pointed only at the tip, and the dueling saber, sharpened along one of its three edges, evolved as various schools of fencing became formalized, each with its own distinctive, nationalistic flavor.

Among the principal developments of this period was the introduction of the *main gauche*, a specialized form of long dagger wielded in the left hand, designed as a shorter twin of its full-length companion sword. The main gauche allowed a swordsman to bring his free hand into play to menace or parry the thrusts of an attacker. A popular variant from around 1600 was the sword breaker, with comblike notches along one edge that enabled a defender to ensnare and, with sufficiently developed strength of the wrist, even break his opponent's blade. A rarer form of sword breaker featured blades designed to spring open from either side of the dagger's blade at the touch of a button, although oddities such as this were probably more formidable in appearance than useful in actual combat.

The seventeenth century dueling sword was a stiff, straight-edged weapon whose development owes much to the simplified and widely adopted French school of fencing. Its narrow blade was designed primarily for thrusting attacks, but it was also quite capable of delivering cuts to the arms or face. Imported Spanish, Italian, or German blades, fitted

with a fashionable "swept" hilt after delivery, were especially popular. The ricasso of the blade was often imprinted with spurious trademarks and signatures, often misspelled, of famous bladesmiths. Guards became increasingly complex, often featuring elaborately curved quillons or tines intended to ensnare an enemy's blade or rings to guard a finger hooked over the cross guard for better control.

By the end of the eighteenth century, the military sword had entered into its period of decline. The cutlass-like infantry short sword used by Napoleon's Grande Armée, which evolved from the huntsman's sword, was more useful as a bivouac tool than as a weapon. The cavalry saber, however, retained a vestige of its authority and was used decisively as late as the Mexican-American War (1846-1848) in actions at Palo Alto and Resaca de las Palmas (1846) and Contreras-Churubusco (1847), as well as in numer-

Library of Congress

The cavalry saber was used decisively as late as the Mexican War (1846-1848) in the Battle of Palo Alto.

ous campaigns of the so-called American Indian wars of the nineteenth century. In fact, cavalry troopers regularly practiced with sabers as part of their customary tactical evolutions well into the second half of the nineteenth century.

In Japan the development of an elaborate and sophisticated dueling cult fueled the evolution of the single-edged samurai sword, more properly known as the *katana* (sword) or *daito* (long sword). Intended to be wielded with two hands, the katana was worn tucked into the waist sash along with a companion sword, identical to it but shorter in length, called the *wakizashi*. A short dagger, called the *tanto*, was generally worn by women and tradesmen for their personal protection. Practice in the art of Japanese fencing was facilitated by the use of a more forgiving bamboo "sword," called a *shinai*, or a wooden *bokken*.

Samurai swordsmithing techniques, which reached a peak of sophistication during the late sixteenth century, constitute a variation of the hammer-welding process. A bar of hardened steel is sandwiched between softer iron, heated, hammered, and folded successively dozens of times to produce a fine cutting edge with a temper that is regulated by sheathing the blade in a fine clay slip. Heat treating of the exposed edge produces a visible pattern along the temper line that is categorized according to its resemblance to certain naturalistic forms. Military officers' swords bearing serial numbers on the blade, mass-produced during World War II, are of considerably less value than are authentic handmade blades. Blades prized too highly for use in battle were often kept in an unadorned white wood storage scabbard, called a *shira saya*, resembling a simple pinewood cane.

BOOKS AND ARTICLES

Burton, Richard Francis. *The Book of the Sword*. 1884. Reprint. New York: Dover, 1987.

Childs, John. *Warfare in the Seventeenth Century*. London: Cassell, 2001.

Diagram Group. *The New Weapons of the World Encyclopedia: An International Encyclopedia from 5000 B.C. to the Twenty-first Century*. New York: St. Martin's Griffin, 2007.

Evangelista, Nick, and William M. Gaugler. *The Encyclopedia of the Sword*. Westport, Conn.: Greenwood Press, 1995.

Jörgensen, Christer, et al. *Fighting Techniques of the Early Modern World, A.D. 1500-A.D. 1763: Equipment, Combat Skills, and Tactics*. New York: Thomas Dunne Books, 2006.

Talhoffer, Hans. *Medieval Combat*. Translated by Mark Rector. London: Greenhill, 2000.

Thompson, Leroy. *Combat Knives*. London: Greenhill, 2004.

Thompson, Logan. *Daggers and Bayonets: A History*. Staplehurst, England: Spellmount, 1999.

Warner, Gordon, and Donn F. Draeger. *Japanese Swordsmanship*. New York: Weatherhill, 1993.

Yumoto, John M. *The Samurai Sword*. 1958. Reprint. Rutland, Vt.: Charles E. Tuttle, 1991.

FILMS AND OTHER MEDIA

Modern Marvels: Axes, Swords, and Knives. Documentary. History Channel, 2002.

Reclaiming the Blade. Documentary. Galatia Films, 2008.

Larry Smolucha

POLE ARMS

Dates: c. 1500-1900

NATURE AND USE

The generic term for any type of thrusting or cutting weapon mounted on a long handle is pole arm. These weapons have been in use since the time of primitive humankind, and they persist to this day in vestigial form as bayonets affixed to the muzzles of rifles. Because pole arms allow both thrusting and cutting, many types have evolved over the centuries under a wide variety of names. Generally those pole arms designed for thrusting only have been called spears, or since the fifteenth century, pikes, after the French word *pique*. The lengths of pikes varied greatly, though they commonly measured between 15 and 21 feet. Such lengths made pikes unwieldy and awkward for use in individual combat. To be effective in battle, pikes had to be used en masse, because a single pike could be blocked or evaded, allowing the enemy to attack in close. The best use of pikes was a dense formation in which overlapping rows of pike heads threatened the enemy.

Because of the pike's limited utility in close combat, pole arms with shorter shafts and cutting edges were developed. Typically such weapons were mounted on shafts of about 4 to 6 feet in length. In Europe the most common forms of cutting-edged pole arms featured either ax-heads or swordlike cutting blades. A bewildering variety of names in many languages were created to describe weapons whose appearances and uses were often quite similar. An early pole arm popular with knightly combatants was the poleaxe, which combined a short, hammer-shaped head and a strong pike-head with a spike on the back of the head. The halberd combined an ax-head with a pike point and a spike on the back of the head. Another common weapon was the glaive, which featured a swordlike cutting edge and some form of spike set at an angle to the head. The spikes on the backs of these weapons generated great penetrating power and could also be used to drag mounted combatants from their saddles.

To ensure that the heads were not cut off their shafts, most of these pole arms featured steel shanks called *langets* that extended part way down the shaft. The langets were usually riveted to the shafts. By putting cutting heads on the ends of long shafts, infantry gained not only reach over their adversaries but also weapons capable of penetrating the increasingly common plate armor of the late Middle Ages and Renaissance. Another common feature of early pole arms was a small steel roundel mounted at the base of the blade. This roundel deflected blows sliding down the blade away from the user's hands. These weapons were very popular among infantry forces throughout the Renaissance. Other pole arms featured wide-bladed heads in the shape of exaggerated spear points. These weapons probably derived from civilian boar spears, but the edges on these heads also allowed slashing attacks. Such weapons included the partisan and the spontoon.

DEVELOPMENT

Spears have been in use as weapons since ancient times. The dense pike formations favored by the ancient Greeks and Macedonians were called phalanxes. Phalanxes were very daunting to face but could seldom maintain formation integrity when moving across rough ground. More mobile sword-armed foes such as the Romans defeated the pike-armed phalanxes by attacks to the flanks and rear. During the Middle Ages, battles were usually decided by shock delivered by a cavalry charge. The best antidote to the cavalry proved to be a steady, pike-armed infantry. Overlapping ranks of pikes deterred the horses and gave the infantryman a weapon long enough to strike his mounted foe. The best-known and most effective infantry of the Middle Ages was that of the Swiss pikemen. Threatened by the Burgundians in the fourteenth century, the Swiss cantons defended themselves with militia forces using pikes. Since the militiamen could not afford the expensive armor of the day, most went into battle with little or no armor. Without the weight of armor these foot soldiers could travel easily across even the roughest terrain. Their formations could therefore move with unprecedented speed. When facing cavalry forces, the rapid Swiss infantry charges usually overwhelmed the enemy before it could properly deploy for battle. At battles such as Morgarten (1315) and Sempach (1386) the Swiss caught mounted knights in restricted terrain and inflicted horrendous casualties with their pikes. The Swiss also found that if the front of their formations became disordered or if mounted knights penetrated into the pike phalanx, the pike's awkward length made the pikemen vulnerable and resulted in many casualties. To protect the pikemen, the Swiss began to include a number of halberd-armed men in every pike column. The halberd's shaft still allowed it to reach a mounted man, but its shorter length allowed it to be swung within the confines of the phalanx's inner ranks. In addition, the length of the shaft allowed a great momentum to be imparted into the weapon's head, thus creating the great percussive power necessary to penetrate or crush the plate armor of the day.

By the beginning of the sixteenth century, disciplined pike-armed infantry had become the backbone of Europe's increasingly professional armies. At the same time, firearms had become lighter and convenient enough to be used by infantry in battle. Such handheld firearms could inflict heavy casualties upon pike-armed forces arrayed for battle but suffered from the very serious shortcoming that the harquebusiers were vulnerable while performing the slow and complicated steps involved in reloading their weapons. Under El Gran Capitán, the Spanish commander Gonzalo Fernández de Córdoba (1453-1515), Spanish forces began to combine blocks of pike men with blocks of harquebusiers. Such formations, called *tercios*, were successful combined-arms units. The harquebusiers deployed outside the pike square and fired into the enemy lines. If the enemy charged, the harquebusiers could retreat into the pike formation for protection. Thus a tercio combined continuous fire with the shock power of the pike. The devastating potential of these tactics was demonstrated at the Battle of Cerignola (1503). A French force of cavalry and Swiss mercenaries attacked Fernández de Córdoba's Spanish forces deployed behind a ditch. The fire of the harquebusiers was so severe that the French formations broke apart, whereupon Fernández de Córdoba's pikemen charged. The disordered French were overwhelmed and suffered heavy casualties. These tactics put a premium on the pikes and handguns but reduced the need for cutting weapons such as halberds and glaives.

By the beginning of the seventeenth century the need for pikes was further reduced by the military reforms introduced by the military innovator Maurice of Nassau (1567-1625). Maurice's reforms reduced the size and depth of formations to facilitate maneuverability and increased the number of muskets in units. Adopted throughout the continent, these re-

TURNING POINTS

1315	Swiss pikemen begin a string of victories against mounted knights by defeating the Austrians at Morgarten, leading to their fourteenth and fifteenth century dominance of infantry warfare.
1503	The first effective use of the combination of firearms and pikes, a formation called the "Spanish Square," is made at the Battle of Cerignola.
c. 1600	The military reforms of Maurice of Nassau reduce the size and depth of pike formations to facilitate maneuverability and increase the number of muskets in units.
1688	Sébastien Le Prestre de Vauban introduces the socket bayonet, which fits over a musket's muzzle and allows the musket to be loaded and fired with the bayonet attached. As the socket bayonet replaces the pike, specialized pike troops disappear from use.

An engraving by Hans Holbein the Younger showing Schlechten Krieg, or "bad war," the result of tangled pole arms (here, pikes wielded by Swiss pikemen, or Landsknechte) in an early sixteenth century battle.

forms saw mixed pike and gun formations with the ratio of guns to pikes increasing; for example, by the end of the English Civil War of 1642-1651 the forces of the New Model Army of military leader Oliver Cromwell (1599-1658) averaged two or three guns per pike.

As the need for dense pike formations decreased due to the increasing reliability and firepower of handguns, the use of pole arms such as the halberd and glaive underwent a great change. The potency of pike- and gun-armed forces was tied directly to their ability to hold formation. Disordered ranks proffered openings that invited an enemy charge; once a formation was breached, individuals were vulnerable. In a

pike formation, though, a halberd was too short to be of use except in extreme circumstances. Thus halberds were increasingly relegated to use by officers and line sergeants. For junior officers, the shaft of a halberd was a good tool for aligning ranks, pushing against the backs of men who were slow to advance. If a unit disintegrated, such a weapon could also be useful in a melee. As a result, varieties of pole arms such as spontoons and partisans saw increased usage as badges of rank, especially for noncommissioned officers. As these weapons became less necessary in the battle line, they became more ornate and ostentatious. Halberds and spontoons of this period, for example, often featured embossed coats of arms on their blades. These weapons were especially evident at parades and other formal occasions. By the end of the eighteenth century such weapons had largely disappeared from battlefield use, but they remain in ceremonial use to this day. England's ceremonial guards, the Beefeaters, and the Papacy's Swiss Guard, for example, still serve at their posts with halberds in hand.

As the proportion of pikes in a formation continued to decline, a simple solution to the need for pike protection for the musketeers was the introduction of the bayonet. A bayonet was a cutting weapon that could be affixed to the muzzle of a musket to turn it into an emergency pike. Bayonets ranged in length from oversized knives to short swords. The earliest bayonets were plug bayonets, which were probably introduced in the early 1600's, though the earliest accounts of their use date from the 1640's. These were typically double-edged daggers whose handles fit into the muzzle of a musket or harquebus. The difficulty of a plug bayonet was that while it was being used, the harquebus could not fire. In 1688 this problem was solved when the French field marshal Sébastien Le Prestre de Vauban (1633-1707) introduced the socket bayonet, a bayonet mounted on a socket so that the blade was offset to the side. The socket fitted over a musket's muzzle and onto a lug located near the muzzle. This allowed the musket to be loaded and fired with the bayonet attached. Although it was not as long as a pike, the bayonet offered the soldier a pike-like weapon for close-quarter fighting. With the bayonet at hand, there was no longer a need for specialized pike troops, and pikes disappeared from use. Since Vauban's introduction of the socket bayonet, bayonets have been in continuous use throughout the world. Changes in the shape of the socket or the size of the bayonet have not altered the weapon's basic function. Although many military thinkers praised the bayonet charge as the ultimate moment in battle, statistics show that by the nineteenth century bayonet combats were very rare. Indeed, the diaries and accounts of soldiers indicate that bayonets were used far more often for utilitarian purposes such as opening cans, cooking food over a fire, or chopping brush than for battle. In the late twentieth century bayonets increasingly became more of a utility tool than a weapon. Many Soviet bayonets, for example, featured a lug on the scabbard and a matching hole near the bayonet's tip to allow the blade to fit over the lug and be used with the scabbard as wire-cutter with the bayonet's back edge as the cutter. Although this innovation enhanced the bayonet's usefulness, it removed it yet further from its roots as a pike.

Although pole arms ceased to be realistic weapons of war by the end of the 1600's, their simplicity has made them useful in conditions of extreme need. For example, while planning for his slave insurrection, the abolitionist John Brown (1800-1859) forged pikes with which to arm runaway slaves. In the final days of World War II, Japanese civilians, including women, trained with bamboo pikes as part of the planned last-ditch resistance to an American landing.

BOOKS AND ARTICLES

Anglo, Sydney. *The Martial Arts of Renaissance Europe*. New Haven, Conn.: Yale University Press, 2000.

Colby, C. B. *Revolutionary War Weapons: Pole Arms, Hand Guns, Shoulder Arms, and Artillery*. New York: Coward-McCann, 1963.

Diagram Group. *The New Weapons of the World Encyclopedia: An International Encyclopedia from 5000 B.C. to the Twenty-first Century*. New York: St. Martin's Griffin, 2007.

Grant, R. G. *Warrior: A Visual History of the Fighting Man*. New York: DK, 2007.

Miller, Douglas. *The Landsknechts*. Illustrated by Gerry Embleton. Botley, Oxford, England: Osprey, 1979.

Snook, George A. *The Halberd and Other European Pole Arms, 1300-1650*. Bloomfield, Ont.: Museum Restoration Service, 1998.

Stone, George Cameron. *A Glossary of the Construction, Decoration, and Use of Arms and Armor in All Countries in All Times*. New York: Jack Brussel, 1961. Reprint. Mineola, N.Y.: Dover, 1999.

Tarassuk, Leonid, and Claude Blair. *The Complete Encyclopedia of Arms and Weapons*. New York: Bonanza Books, 1979.

FILMS AND OTHER MEDIA

Ancient Discoveries: Death Weapons of the East. Documentary. History Channel, 2008.

Kevin B. Reid

Gunpowder and Explosives

Dates: Since c. 1500

Nature and Use

An explosive is a stable substance or device that upon detonation produces a volume of rapidly expanding gas that exerts sudden pressure on its surroundings. In general, explosives are divided into two general types: propellants and detonators. Propellants, such as gunpowder and jet fuel, are used to accelerate projectiles, particularly bullets and rockets. Detonators, such as dynamite (trinitrotoluene, or TNT), are often used to ignite propellants. Detonators that can be touched off only by a high-energy source are termed high explosives.

Explosives are further classified as blasting explosives and military explosives. Blasting explosives are typically used in mining, construction, and tunnel building. Military explosives are used in bombs, explosive shells, torpedoes, and missile warheads. Military explosives must be physically and chemically stable over extreme ranges of temperature and humidity for long periods of time. They must also be insensitive to impacts, such as those experienced by an artillery shell when it is fired from a gun or penetrates steel armor. Military explosives are used for a wide range of purposes: They are fired in projectiles and dropped in aerial time bombs without premature explosion. Raw materials necessary to manufacture such explosives must be readily available for high rates of production during wartime.

Another classification of explosives separates them into chemical, mechanical, and nuclear types. Chemical explosives, such as gunpowder and dynamite, are the most commonly used and explode through chemical reactions. Mechanical explosives involve physical reactions, such as a container's being overloaded with compressed air. Nuclear explosives produce a sustained nuclear reaction and are the most powerful explosives.

The first known explosive was black powder, also known as gunpowder. It was developed in China during the tenth century or possibly earlier. The initial purpose was for use in fireworks and signals. The first European mention of gunpowder was by thirteenth century scientist and educator Roger Bacon (1220-1292), who recorded a recipe in 1267. His term, "fire for burning up the enemy," suggests that Bacon regarded gunpowder as an incendiary, not a propellant. The composition he suggested endured for more than three hundred years and consisted of 75 percent potassium nitrate (saltpeter), 15 percent charcoal, and 10 percent sulfur. The charcoal and sul-

A hand grenade.

403

fur constitute the fuel of the powdered mixture, whereas the saltpeter acts as the oxidizer.

Black powder revolutionized warfare and played a significant role in the development of European patterns of living up until modern times. The Chinese first used black powder as a gun propellant as early as 1130, placing it in bamboo tubes that were reinforced with iron to propel stone projectiles and arrows. When used in war, gunpowder was often more successful in creating fear in the enemy ranks than in inflicting actual damage. Chinese records indicate that the Chinese used black powder in bombs for military purposes. Torches, glowing tinder, or heated iron rods were used to ignite the powder, and usually, a trail of the powder led to the main charge in order to give the firer time to reach safety.

Firearms that use gunpowder are frequently mentioned in fourteenth century manuscripts from many different countries. By the end of the fourteenth century, many countries were using gunpowder as a military aid to breach the walls of castles and cities. Although black powder remained the standard gun propellant until the late nineteenth century, it is now used only in igniters, safety fuses, and fireworks.

DEVELOPMENT

In 1425 the mixing process for the ingredients of black powder was greatly improved when the corning, or granulating, process was developed in England. Heavy wheels ground and pressed the fuel and oxidizer into a solid mass that was subsequently broken down into smaller grains. The first gunpowder mill was erected near Nuremberg, Germany, in about 1435. Corned gunpowder was used for small guns and hand grenades during the fifteenth century.

By 1540 the French had become the first people to control explosive pressure in wheeled cannons by using relatively large, slow-burning powder grains of uniform size. In the seventeenth century, the English and Dutch militaries developed the howitzer, a short cannon firing explosive shells in a high arc to hit a distant target. Large muskets were used in America with some success during the French and Indian War (1754-1763). Shorter, lighter muskets were the most widely used weapon in the American Revolution (1775-1783). If the French had developed more fieldworthy muskets, they might have had more success in the Napoleonic Wars (1793-1815).

In the 1790's Henry Shrapnel (1761-1842), an English artillery officer, developed the "shrapnel shell," consisting of a spherical shell packed with a small charge of black powder and several musket balls. These single-shot multiple explosives were effective against concentrations of enemy troops. By using batteries of many guns, massed artillery fire was employed to destroy attacking enemy formations or to disrupt defending forces before they could launch an attack. During the early 1800's, mobile artilleries, including horse-drawn units, were used to shift explosives from one strategic location to another on the battlefield.

In 1805 English artillerist Sir William Congreve (1772-1828) used gunpowder to develop rockets for warfare and launching tubes to greatly improve the rockets' accuracy. Congreve's inventions expanded the use of rockets for military purposes, greatly changing the way war was waged in Europe. Hand-to-hand combat with specific implied rules of chivalry became outdated, as more powerful gunpowder weapons that produced a higher number of casualties and more serious wounds were adopted. Congreve's rockets were used to bombard Boulogne, Copenhagen, and Danzig in the Napoleonic Wars and in the British attack on Fort McHenry (1814), near Baltimore, Maryland, during the War of 1812 (1812-1815).

The development of different types of guns to propel explosive charges became critical in warfare. In the Crimean War (1853-1856), Russian troops armed with smoothbore muskets were no match for the British, with their more advanced musket rifles. The deadly effect of rifled muskets was clearly demonstrated during the American Civil War (1861-1865). Because individual soldiers could hit their enemies with accurate fire out to 250 yards, frontal attacks, in which soldiers advanced in ordered ranks across open fields, had to be abandoned. By 1862 both Union and Confederate troops had built field entrenchments and barricades to provide protection from artillery explosives. During the Battle of König-

F. R. Niglutsch

During the Battle of Königgrätz, Prussian soldiers were able to overwhelm the Austrians by firing six shots from their high-powered rifles for every shot discharged by the Austrian muzzle-loading rifles.

grätz in the Seven Weeks' War (1866), Prussian soldiers were able to overwhelm the Austrians by firing six shots from their high-powered rifles for every shot discharged by the Austrian muzzle-loading rifles.

Until the discovery of fulminating gold in the early 1600's, gunpowder was the only known explosive. Gunpowder remained in wide use until the mid-1800's, when the first modern explosives, nitroglycerin and dynamite, were invented. Nitroglycerin was discovered by an Italian chemist, Ascanio Sobrero (1812-1888), in 1847. Its value for blasting was later demonstrated by Swedish inventor Alfred B. Nobel (1833-1896), who also invented dynamite in 1866. Stable ammonia dynamites began to appear in the late 1880's, followed by low-freezing dynamites after 1925.

Since black powder is relatively low in energy, leaves a large proportion of corrosive solids after explosion, and absorbs moisture readily, it was succeeded in the late 1800's by smokeless gunpowder and picric acid. The first smokeless powder, known as cordite, was invented by English chemists Sir James Dewar (1842-1923) and Sir Frederick Augustus Abel (1827-1902) in 1889. It was made in two forms: a gelatinized nitrocellulose and a mixture of nitrocellulose and nitroglycerin, with a small quantity of petroleum jelly to act as a stabilizer. Smokeless powder soon became the primary ammunition used in pistols.

As early as 1873 picric acid was detonated to produce explosions, and it was found in 1885 to be a suitable replacement for black powder. From 1888 into World War I, it was used as the basic explosive for

TURNING POINTS

c. 1300	The Chinese first use black powder to propel projectiles through bamboo tubes, revolutionizing warfare.
c. 1425	The corning, or granulating, process is developed to grind gunpowder into smaller grains.
c. 17th cent.	The howitzer is developed by the English and Dutch for use against distant targets.
1754-1763	Large muskets are first used successfully by Americans in the French and Indian War.
1790's	British artillerist Henry Shrapnel invents the "shrapnel shell," packed with gunpowder and several musket balls and designed to explode in flight.
1805	British artillerist William Congreve develops first warfare rockets and launching tubes.
1904-1905	Trinitrotoluene (TNT) is first used as a military explosive during the Russo-Japanese War.
1944	Germany launches the first long-range ballistic missiles, the V-1 and V-2, against England during World War II.
1945	The United States drops the first atomic bombs, whose huge explosive impact derives from nuclear reactions, on the Japanese cities of Hiroshima and Nagasaki, effectively ending World War II.

military purposes. Because it required prolonged heating at high temperatures in order to melt, and because it also caused shells to corrode in the presence of water, an active search for better explosives continued.

During the twentieth century, TNT was the most commonly used conventional military explosive. Although it had been used extensively in the dye industry during the late 1800's, it was not adopted for use as a military explosive until 1902, when the German army used it to replace picric acid. TNT was first used in warfare during the Russo-Japanese War (1904-1905). The U.S. Army began using it in 1912. After an economical process was developed for nitrating toluene, TNT became the chief artillery ammunition in World War I (1914-1918). The most valuable property of TNT is that it can be safely melted and cast alone or with other explosives as a slurry.

During World War I, all of the major powers adopted smokeless powder, bolt-action, magazine-fed repeating rifles. These rapid-fire weapons rendered the battlefield a "no-man's-land." Massed artillery explosive fire denied both sides the ability to maneuver forces, a condition that led to trench warfare, such as at the Battle of the Marne (1914), where the Allies stopped the Germans from advancing farther into France. As a result, gas shell projectiles loaded with chlorine and mustard gas were employed against the enemy. The Germans also made wide use of liquid oxygen explosives during World War I.

With the advent of tanks, World War II (1939-1945) saw a return to maneuver tactics, with artillery explosives continuing to provide the most destructive force on the battlefield. Nitroguanidine, referred to as Gudol Pulver, was a primary explosive used during World War II. It produced very little smoke, had no evidence of a muzzle flash on firing, and also increased the lifetime of the gun barrel. Pentaerythitol tetranitrate (PETN) and cyclotrimethylene trinitramine (RDX) were developed for use as detonators and for filling hand and antitank grenades. A mixture of TNT, RDX, and wax was used to detonate bombs. A mixture of PETN and TNT was used for detonating demolition charges. Torpedo warheads were often made of cast mixtures of RDX, TNT, and aluminum.

Some of the most effective weapons used during World War II were missiles, consisting of a rocket that delivered an explosive charge called a warhead. The first successful long-range ballistic missile was the German V-2 that was principally developed by Wernher von Braun (1912-1977), a pioneer of German rocketry. These missiles were launched into England from German-occupied countries in Europe. Most ballistic missiles, aircraft munitions, and artillery use solid rocket propellants.

The atomic bomb was the first nuclear weapon to be developed, tested, and used. Developed under the direction of American physicist J. Robert Oppenheimer (1904-1967), it was implemented near the end of World War II. On August 6, 1945, an atomic bomb was dropped by an American B-29 bomber, the *Enola Gay*, over Hiroshima, Japan, instantly killing more than 70,000 people. On August 9, the United States dropped a second atomic bomb, killing some 40,000 people in Nagasaki, Japan. Due to such devastation, this explosive device has never again been used in a war.

In more recent conflicts, such as the Korean War (1950-1953) and the Vietnam War (1961-1975), artillery explosives provided most of the fire support for ground forces. Laser-guided projectiles were developed to destroy tanks. During this period the United States began using medium-sized howitzers capable of firing chemical and nuclear explosives. Grenade launchers saw a great deal of action in Vietnam, and search-and-destroy air explosives razed numerous Vietnamese villages.

During the 1990's advances in onboard computer systems and self-locating capabilities enabled modern cannons and missile launchers to move independently around the battlefield, stopping to fire explosives and then quickly moving to a new firing position. Some modern artillery cannons and launchers can deliver "smart" explosives. These projectiles and warheads use sophisticated seekers and sensors to locate and home in on stationary or moving targets.

BOOKS AND ARTICLES

Akhavan, Jacqueline. *The Chemistry of Explosives*. Cambridge, England: The Royal Society of Chemistry, 1998.

Brown, G. I. *The Big Bang: A History of Explosives*. Stroud, Gloucestershire, England: Sutton, 1998.

Buchanan, Brenda J. *Gunpowder: The History of an International Technology*. Bath, England: Bath University Press, 1996.

_____, ed. *Gunpowder, Explosives, and the State: A Technological History*. Burlington, Vt.: Ashgate, 2006.

Cooper, Paul W., and Stanley R. Kurowski. *Introduction to the Technology of Explosives*. New York: Wiley-VCH, 1996.

Guilmartin, John Francis, Jr. *Gunpowder and Galleys: Changing Technology and Mediterranean Warfare at Sea in the Sixteenth Century*. Rev. ed. Annapolis, Md.: Naval Institute Press, 2003.

Kelly, Jack. *Gunpowder—Alchemy, Bombards, and Pyrotechnics: The History of the Explosive That Changed the World*. New York: Basic Books, 2004.

Neiberg, Michael S. "The Emergence of Gunpowder Weapons, 1450 to 1776." In *Warfare in World History*. London: Routledge, 2001.

Partington, James R. *A History of Greek Fire and Gunpowder*. Baltimore: Johns Hopkins University Press, 1998.

Wilson, Clay. *Improvised Explosive Devices in Iraq: Effects and Countermeasures*. Washington, D.C.: Congressional Research Service, Library of Congress, 2005.

FILMS AND OTHER MEDIA

Deadly Explosives. Documentary. Paladin Press, 1997.

High Explosives. Documentary. History Channel, 1998.

Modern Marvels: Bombs. Documentary. History Channel, 2005.

Tactical Use of Explosives. Documentary. Spy Tech Agency, 1996.

Alvin K. Benson

SMALL ARMS AND MACHINE GUNS
Dates: Since c. 1500

NATURE AND USE

Small arms are firearms that are designed to be carried and fired by individual soldiers. A machine gun is a firearm that continues to fire automatically as long as the operator keeps the trigger depressed. Medium and heavy machine guns are technically not small arms, because they are designed as crew-served weapons.

Firearms are weapons in which a projectile, normally made of lead, is propelled by confined gas generated by the rapid burning of some kind of gunpowder. Firearms have, at every stage of their development, repeatedly revolutionized the tactics and strategy of warfare, and they are universally the weapons of individual soldiers.

All modern firearms trace their lineage back to the small cannon of the thirteenth century. From this clumsy beginning all varieties of modern firearms have developed: the rifle, a shoulder-fired weapon supported with both hands; the pistol, designed to be held and fired with one hand; and the machine gun, models of which vary enormously in power, weight, and complexity.

A light machine gun fires a rifle cartridge and is effective up to 600 yards. A medium machine gun fires a similar cartridge but is normally mounted on a tripod and served by a crew. A heavy machine gun fires a much more powerful cartridge—usually about 0.5 inch (12.5 millimeters) in caliber—and can be used effectively to up 2,000 yards. Heavy machine guns are not only infantry weapons; they are also found mounted on tanks, helicopters, and fixed-wing aircraft. Submachine guns ordinarily fire pistol cartridges and are designed to be easily carried and operated by one person. The useful aimed-fire range of such a weapon might be from 75 to 100 yards.

The general pattern of firearms development has been to increase their portability, power, accuracy, and speed of operation. By 1500 the cart-mounted small cannon of the Middle Ages had evolved into the hand cannon, which had become, by the late sixteenth century, the musket—a smoothbore shoulder-fired weapon that would dominate military tactics and strategy until the mid-nineteenth century.

DEVELOPMENT

Black powder, the earliest form of gunpowder, is a mixture of potassium nitrate, sulfur, and charcoal. When ignited by a flame, it burns rapidly and generates a great deal of gas. This gas, expanding in a gun barrel, can drive a bullet or shell at high velocity. Gunpowder is believed to have originated in China, during the tenth century or possibly earlier. The earliest firearms were extremely cumbersome; they had to be carried in carts or set on wooden trestles and were more like small cannons. It was not until the mid-fourteenth century that portable hand firearms loaded from the muzzle end were introduced. In muzzle-loading weapons, a powder charge is poured into the barrel and a projectile is pressed down upon the charge. The powder is ignited by a lighted match, a cinder, or a hot wire. Access to the powder charge is through a small hole drilled in the breech of the gun, and when the match or hot wire is placed against the touch hole, the charge is lit. Although such guns had a range of several hundred yards, they were not very accurate. A less skilled soldier could be expected to hit a stationary man-sized target consistently at only 40 or 50 yards.

In the early years of firearms development neither the rates of fire nor the accuracy of handheld weapons was equal to those of the longbow or crossbow. Consequently the cannon, whose range, striking power, and relative ease of manufacture made it superior to the catapult, had an earlier impact on military tactics and strategy. Like the longbow and crossbow, handheld firearms did have the ability to penetrate armor. Indeed, firearms were superior to longbows and crossbows in striking force, thereby accelerating the disappearance of the armored mounted knight in battle. Troops using firearms were vulnerable to cavalry or mass infantry shock attacks and consequently required the protection of pike formations or entrenchments. Their usefulness was limited to harassing fire and skirmishing preliminary to the main action. Before firearms could become universally practical weapons of war, a number of difficult technical problems had to be solved. These problems fall into the general categories of ignition, accuracy, and speed.

IGNITION

Until the mid-nineteenth century nearly all firearms, including artillery, were loaded from the muzzle end. Neither the metallurgy nor the manufacturing techniques of gun making lent themselves to the invention of a breech closure that could be consistently sealed against the escape of powder gases during firing. Not only would propellant gases escape with each shot, endangering the shooter, but heat and gas resulting from continued firing quickly eroded and destroyed the breech mechanism. Consequently, technical progress focused on refining the method of ignition. The inconvenience of carrying a separate match or hot wire was first surmounted by the matchlock device, which was developed around 1450. In the matchlock a curved piece of metal called a cock, for its resemblance to a rooster's neck, held a lighted "match," usually a cord of hemp fiber that had been soaked in a solution of saltpeter. To fire, the match was pressed against a small pan placed alongside the touch hole into which a few grains of powder acting as a priming

charge had been placed. The cock was moved by means of a mechanically linked trigger. The matchlock's advantage was immediately appreciated, and its development was rapid. The Spanish harquebus, a matchlock weapon, was successfully and decisively used at the Battle of Pavia in 1525. In this battle, the decisive military engagement of the war in Italy between Francis I (1494-1547) of France and the Holy Roman emperor and Spanish king Charles V (1500-1588), the French army of 28,000 was virtually annihilated by a Spanish force of 7,500, which included 1,500 harquebusiers firing volleys into the rear of the French cavalry and utterly routing them.

Nineteenth century sailors operating the hand-cranked Gatling gun, which utilized a system of barrels rotating around a central axis, each firing in turn.

TURNING POINTS

1690   The Brown Bess flintlock musket is developed, and its variations
        remain in use by all European nations until the mid-nineteenth
        century.
1700   The introduction of rifling and patched-ball loading increases the
        accuracy of firearms.
1848   The Sharps carbine, a single-shot, dropping-block breechloader
        firing paper and metallic cartridges, is developed.
1873   Colt single-action Army revolver issued.
1884   Hiram Maxim invents the first practical machine gun.
1898   The Mauser Model 1898 is produced, the culmination of military
        bolt action design.
1908   The Luger P.08 is adopted as the official German service pistol.
1936   The M1 Garand rifle is the first standard-issue semiautomatic
        military rifle.
1947   The Kalashnikov AK-47 becomes the first widely deployed
        modern assault rifle.

Because matchlocks required the use of a lighted match, they were not only cumbersome but also particularly susceptible to failure in wet weather. To remedy this problem, the wheel lock was invented in 1517. This mechanism used a revolving serrated wheel to strike sparks into the priming charge from a piece of iron pyrite. The wheel, which was spring powered, had to be wound up with a key. Although wheel locks were extremely expensive to manufacture, they were used extensively, because they could be managed by mounted troops on horseback. The wheel lock was also the first practical firearm for use in hunting, because it did not require a constantly lighted match.

The next great advance in firearms technology was the flintlock. The earliest flintlock was the *snaphaan*, or snaphance, developed in Scandinavia and Holland from about 1550 to 1570. This was the first ignition system to introduce the striking action of the cock, which was driven against a metal frizzen by a spring. The cock, with a piece of flint clamped in its jaws, struck a glancing blow against the frizzen, producing sparks to fire the priming charge. Flintlocks, in various forms, were used for nearly 300 years. Flintlock guns were manufactured for military purposes in England as late as 1842. In the most advanced flintlocks, the frizzen and pan cover were made in one piece that was moved by the action of the cock, thus simultaneously exposing the priming pan and firing the gun. This innovation was a great aid in protecting the priming charge from moisture.

In 1807 Alexander Forsyth (1769-1843), a Scottish clergyman and inventor, discovered that potassium chlorate could be detonated by a blow and used to ignite a powder charge. This discovery became the basis of all later percussion and self-contained cartridge development. Forsyth's first design used small pills of priming compound in existing flintlocks. Later experiments with tape and disk primers and the use of fulminate of mercury as the detonating compound brought about the development of the percussion cap, a small copper cap containing a bit of fulminate of mercury. The cap was placed over a hollow tube or nipple leading to the main powder charge. When struck by the descending hammer, the fulminate exploded to fire the gun. Similar caps became the basis of internally primed self-contained cartridges: the pinfire cartridge, invented by Casimir Lefaucheux (1802-1852) around 1828; the rimfire cartridge, developed by Louis Nicholas Flobert in 1845; and the center-fire cartridge, developed by American artist and inventor Samuel F. B. Morse (1791-1872) and first manufactured in 1858. Percussion caps made firearms far less susceptible to ignition malfunctions due to wet weather or mechanical problems. They brought about a substantial increase in the rate of fire. The old infantry tactic of charging the enemy to get within bayonet range became much riskier as rates of fire increased.

ACCURACY

Most military firearms from the fifteenth century to the end of the nineteenth century fired a round lead ball of caliber 0.40 to 0.60. (In England and the United States "caliber" is usually reckoned in tenths or hundredths of an inch; in most of the rest of the world the metric system is used.) Such a ball, weighing about one-half ounce, would be fired from a smoothbore barrel. The best such weapons could be loaded and fired two or three times per minute and provided a fair chance of hitting an enemy at 75 to 100 yards.

During the eighteenth and nineteenth centuries new tactics for such weapons evolved. Armies lined up in rows, and one rank would fire while another was reloading. For close combat, when there was insufficient time to reload, soldiers could fix swords or bayonets to the end of the rifle.

Greater accuracy and range could be achieved by cutting spiral grooves, or rifling, into the barrel and thus spinning the bullet or ball like a gyroscope. The bullet must fit the bore tightly to take the rifling, and consequently it is much more difficult to muzzle-load a rifle than a smoothbore weapon. The nineteenth century developments of patched balls and hollow-base cylindrical bullets were early attempts to overcome this difficulty. A hollow-base bullet is smaller than bore diameter so that it may be easily loaded. When the rifle is fired, the expanding gas presses the base of the bullet outward, forcing it into the rifling. The Minié ball, used extensively in the American Civil War (1861-1865), was such a bullet. With a rifled barrel and slow, careful loading, a sharpshooter might be able to hit a stationary enemy at 400 or 500 yards.

By the mid-nineteenth century, although few military leaders had yet perceived it, the combination of the rifled musket, percussion cap, and cylindrical bullet had made the old tactics obsolete. Battles in

which soldiers stood out in the open to load and fire resulted in immense casualties, even with rifles that could be fired three times per minute. The heavy casualties suffered by both sides in the American Civil War demonstrated the need for new tactics.

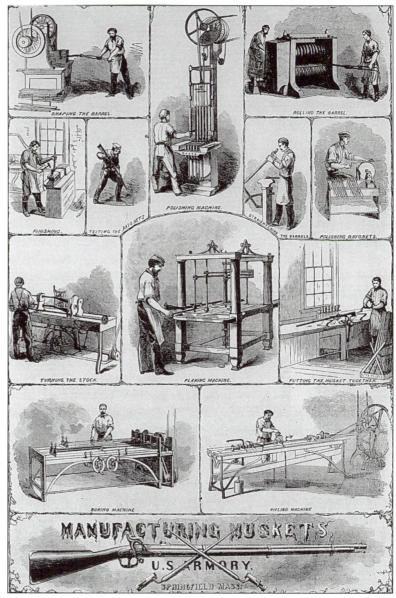

An engraving from an 1861 issue of Harper's Weekly *describes the Springfield Armory's manufacture of single-shot, muzzle-loading rifles, widely used weapons during the American Civil War.*

PROPELLANTS

Until 1885 the term "gunpowder" referred exclusively to black powder. Afterward, it came to refer to both black powder and smokeless powder. The nineteenth century discovery that treating cellulose with nitric acid and sulfuric acids produces nitrocellulose, or guncotton, an explosive compound, led to the development of smokeless gunpowder. Combustible substances such as glycerin, wood pulp, cotton, and cotton wastes are all used as sources of cellulose. The strength of the explosive compound depends on the degree of nitrification; unless the residual acid is carefully neutralized, these compounds can deteriorate and explode spontaneously. By the 1880's scientists had discovered ways of stabilizing nitrocellulose compounds to slow their combustion. These propellants are far more powerful than black powder and also far more efficient, in the sense that 90 percent of their weight becomes gas, leaving fewer solid particles to become smoke.

Smokeless powders offered immense military advantages. The effective range of small arms increased from 200 to perhaps 800 yards. The effective range of the largest cannons increased to more than 20 miles. Indeed, a few guns were deployed that could actually hurl a shell more than 75 miles. Moreover, there was no longer the immense amount of smoke that had shrouded battlefields where black powder weapons were used. Many battlefields, such as that at Waterloo (1815), were so obscured by the smoke of musketry that command and control became impossible. Smokeless powder also left far less residue in the barrel of a gun. The accuracy of a black powder gun declined quickly as the barrel became fouled. Modern small arms and machine guns do not fall off in accuracy with extensive firing. The superiority of smokeless powder was so obvious that nearly all of the world's armies abandoned black powder cartridges within just fifteen years after the first use of smokeless powder.

Smokeless powders are classified by their content. Single-base powders consist of nitrocellulose compounds only; double-base powders also contain nitroglycerin. Although the latter tend to contain more energy, they also tend to be more erosive in gun barrels, a significant factor for military weapons, par-

ticularly machine guns. Triple-base powders, which came into use in the late twentieth century, use nitroguanidine as an additional primary ingredient. These offer higher energy still and are also less erosive.

The burning rate and energy content of contemporary powder is controlled not only by the chemical composition of the powder but also by the size and shape of the grains. For example, the powder used in 16-inch naval rifles has grains of nearly an inch in diameter and 2.44 inches in length. By contrast, rifle and pistol powders have grains that can be less than 0.03 inch in both length and diameter.

SPEED

A further revolution in warfare resulted from the development of breech-loading repeating arms firing self-contained cartridges. Once it was discovered that a cartridge could be made of drawn brass, it became possible to design efficient breech-loading guns. When a brass cartridge is fired, the case is expanded by the pressure of the gases, sealing off the breech end of the mechanism. The first firearms of this sort were single shots that used hinged or dropping blocks to close the breech, but soon a variety of actions were developed to permit rapid repeat fire. Although the Spencer repeating lever-action rifle was used in the United States as early as the American Civil War (1861-1865), most military development focused on bolt-action magazine rifles. A bolt-action weapon is one in which a turning bolt locks a loaded cartridge in place and then extracts the fired case. An operating handle attached to the bolt gives the operator great leverage for the extraction operation. The first usable bolt-action weapon was the so-called needle gun, invented by Johann von Dreyse (1787-1867). Although not a very successful design, it was briefly adopted by the Russian and Prussian armies in the mid-nineteenth century and showed itself far more effective than the single-shot rifles used by Prussia's adversaries. The development of smokeless nitrocellulose-based powders in 1885 encouraged further bolt-action development. Smokeless powder rifles utilize a smaller bore diameter than black powder weapons. Although the fixed setting of the "battle sight" is normally for about 200 yards—

well within the point-blank range of the cartridges—the high-velocity metal-jacketed bullets they fire remain dangerous at 1,800 yards. Trained soldiers can fire ten aimed shots per minute. By 1890 every major army in the world, with the exception of the U.S. Army, was armed with bolt-action magazine rifles. The seminal design for these rifles was produced by Peter Paul Mauser (1838-1914), the German arms inventor and manufacturer. This became the basic infantry weapon of the German army in 1898, and its bolt action was widely, almost universally, copied around the world. The 7.92-millimeter cartridge used by the Germans fired a pointed 154-grain bullet at 2,880 feet per second. Because of its excellent ballistic qualities, this cartridge became nearly as influential for future designs as Mauser's rifles.

The American 1903 Springfield rifle is a modification of Mauser's 1898 model; for manufacturing rights, the United States government paid Mauser $200,000. Another notable twentieth century bolt-action military rifle design was the British Short Magazine Lee-Enfield (SMLE) .303, which was used in both world wars. All of these bolt-action rifles could be loaded very rapidly with cartridges from "stripper clips" that could be placed into slots in the receiver. A full magazine's worth of cartridges could be pressed into the rifle in just a second or two.

Some armies appreciated the impact of the increase in lethality of infantry weapons that resulted from rifling and breech-loading. For example, by 1870 the Prussians had dropped the close-order bayonet charge from their tactics. Prussian combat formations spread into "open order" so that all infantrymen acted as skirmishers, a technique informally developed by U.S. infantrymen from the middle of the American Civil War onward. Most general staffs did not fully understand until finally the combination of these rifles and the deployment of the machine gun produced the static trench system of World War I. The firepower that entrenched defenders could produce completely over-whelmed offensive action until the development of armored vehicles after World War I.

AUTOMATIC WEAPONS

An automatic weapon is one that continues to fire as long as the trigger is held back. Although assault rifles and a few light machine guns are carried by soldiers as individual weapons, most machine guns are crew-served weapons.

All four of the great pioneers of automatic weaponry—Richard Gatling (1818-1903), Sir Hiram Maxim (1840-1916), John M. Browning (1855-1926), and Isaac Lewis (1858-1931)—were Americans.

The hand-cranked Gatling gun, invented in 1862, utilized a system of barrels rotating around a central axis, each firing in turn. The first truly fully automatic gun, however, was invented by Maxim in 1884. It used the recoil energy of the gun itself to extract and eject the fired cartridge case and to load a fresh cartridge. Although machine guns may be recoil- or blowback-operated, the most common method of firing is by tapping a bit of the propellant gas from the barrel. The expanding gas presses against a piston linked to the mechanism of the gun. In 1890 the first gas-operated gun was developed by Browning. A third important gas-operated machine gun design was provided by Lewis; Lewis's gun was later the first machine gun used in aerial combat. The Browning, manufactured by Colt, and the Lewis gun,

North Wind Picture Archives via AP Images

The Maxim field gun, the first fully automatic gun, invented in 1884.

manufactured by Vickers and Savage, were the mainstays of Allied armies in World War I. The German MG08 machine gun, known as the Spandau, was a redevelopment of Maxim's design.

Of the different magazine-feed systems developed for machine guns, the belt of cartridges became the most dominant. In this method, cartridges are tied together by spring clips in long "belts" that feed into the gun during firing and are ejected on the other side. Modern military machine guns have cyclic rates of 500 to 1,000 rounds per minute.

Hulton Archive/Getty Images

Sir Hiram Maxim explains to his grandson how his machine gun works.

The use of machine guns during World War I completely changed the face of war. During the British attack on entrenched German positions at the Somme in July, 1916, the attackers suffered 60,000 casualties on the first day, of whom 20,000 were killed. Most of these casualties were inflicted by machine guns. The military establishments of the warring powers had been unable to conceive of the firepower of the machine gun and the magazine rifle and seemed unable to adjust their tactical thinking. In effect the war became a siege punctuated by occasional vast slaughters as troops were forced again and again to attack in the open. As the lesson sank in, it resulted in the disappearance of cavalry from the world's armies and the development of armored vehicles to punch through infantry emplacements.

SEMIAUTOMATIC RIFLES

A semiautomatic weapon is one that fires a shot for each pull of the trigger, as opposed to a machine gun, which continues to fire for as long as the trigger remains depressed. Semiautomatic rifles are much harder to design than are machine guns, because the latter tend to be crewserved weapons; their added weight and bulk are less significant than for rifles. The first semiautomatic rifle deployed as a standard infantry weapon by a major power was the M-1, designed by John C. Garand (1888-1974) and adopted by the United States in 1936. This gasoperated .30-caliber weapon weighed less than 10 pounds. It was the best military rifle of World War II and was widely copied by other designers.

ASSAULT RIFLES AND SUBMACHINE GUNS

In the decade following World War II most countries designed or built full-caliber rifles similar to the

M-1; many of these were "selective-fire" weapons, which could be fired either automatically or semiautomatically. The U.S. M-14 rifle is an example. The M-14 was similar to the M-1, but it loaded from a twenty-round box magazine. A skilled soldier could fire fifty aimed shots per minute with this weapon. Partly as a result of studies showing that relatively few infantrymen in combat actually fired their weapons and that even fewer aimed them, the major powers began to concentrate on designing lighter rifles for intermediate-range cartridges. At the end of the twentieth century the world's two most common military rifles were the U.S. M-16, a selective-fire .22-caliber assault rifle, and the Russian AK-47, a selective-fire rifle of similar weight that shoots a short .30-caliber cartridge. The cartridges for such rifles are normally carried in twenty- or thirty-round magazines, giving soldiers great firepower. Although the M-16 is capable of great accuracy, the AK-47's sights are very rudimentary; these rifles were designed primarily for "suppressing fire," or large amounts of fire whose primary purpose is to force the enemy to keep their heads down. Infantry tactics have been adjusted accordingly: Flanking rather than frontal assaults are the rule, while the high volume of fire forces the defenders to lie low until they have been enveloped and overwhelmed by close-range automatic weapons fire.

Submachine guns have a similar role in close-range fire. The first submachine gun used in combat was the 9-millimeter Bergmann, introduced by Germany in 1918 at the end of the World War I. During World War II most of the major powers issued submachine guns of various kinds. The best-known and most influential were the British Sten gun, the American Thompson submachine gun, and the German Schmeisser MP40. All of these fired pistol cartridges. Submachine guns made the pistol obsolete as a practical offensive weapon: They cost less than pistols to produce, and they produce a tremendous volume of fire that is directable at longer ranges. They were considered particularly useful for street fighting in cities and towns. The newest models of submachine guns add a "burst" mode to the common selection of semi-automatic or full-automatic fire. In burst mode the weapon will fire three shots for each pull of the trigger.

In most armies submachine guns are issued only for special operations in which close-range engagements are expected. Moreover, because submachine guns normally use subsonic pistol cartridges, they can be effectively silenced for stealth attacks.

PISTOLS

Pistols have gone through most of the same developmental patterns as heavier weapons. In military use the pistol was considered especially useful for mounted cavalry because it could be fired with one hand. A military flintlock pistol weighed 2 to 3 pounds and was about 12 inches long. A seventeenth century cavalryman would normally be armed with two or three loaded pistols as well as a sword or lance.

With the development of percussion caps and self-contained cartridges, pistol design forged ahead rapidly. Because pistols are low-powered weapons, compared with rifles, it is easier to design repeating mechanisms for them. In the days of black powder and percussion caps, revolvers were designed with a cylinder containing multiple chambers. The first successful design was patented by Samuel Colt (1814-1862) in 1835. With this weapon, the soldier could shoot six or more shots before reloading. Some designs made it possible to carry several loaded cylinders, thus permitting relatively quick reloading. Percussion revolvers were widely used as short-range weapons, particularly by officers during the American Civil War. Revolvers continued in military service after the development of metallic cartridges; although the first adopted in the United States was the Smith and Wesson 1869 .44 American, the most famous was the .45-caliber Colt single-action Army model of 1873, known as the Peacemaker. With a hiatus or two, this weapon has been in production since 1873.

Semiautomatic pistols were first built in Germany and Austria. Design work there culminated in the adoption of the Luger pistol as the official sidearm of the German military forces from 1908 to 1932. The American designer John M. Browning devised a dropping-barrel, locked-breech design, the best-known example of which is the .45-caliber Colt 1911 A1. Browning's locking system is used in nearly all military pistols built around the world.

Modern military pistol designs utilize the double-

Library of Congress

Samuel Colt with the Colt pistol.

action principle. The chamber of the weapon may be loaded while the hammer is uncocked. The gun may be fired either by a long straight through-pull on the trigger or by an initial cocking of the hammer, which gives a lighter trigger pull. After the first shot, the hammer remains cocked. The M9 Beretta 92 SB, the present American service pistol, operates in this fashion.

Statistics compiled by American military authorities during the course of World War II and the Vietnam War (1961-1975) show that the number of actual casualties inflicted upon the enemy with pistols was so small that it may not be worthwhile to spend any time or money on handgun design or procurement. However, because soldiers have always felt some comfort in the possession of a sidearm, their demand continues whether or not they are actually effective. Even though pistols are close-range weapons, they are extremely difficult to shoot accurately even at short range without a great deal of training and practice. The cartridges fired by modern military pistols generate 300 to 400 foot-pounds of energy, only a fraction of the energy produced by a rifle cartridge. Pistols have not had an effect on military tactics for many years.

BOOKS AND ARTICLES

Chase, Kenneth. *Firearms: A Global History to 1700*. New York: Cambridge University Press, 2003.

Gluckman, Arcadi. *United States Martial Pistols and Revolvers*. Harrisburg, Pa.: Stackpole, 1956.

Greener, W. W. *The Gun and Its Development*. 9th ed. New York: Bonanza Books, 1967.

Hall, Bert S. *Weapons and Warfare in Renaissance Europe: Gunpowder, Technology, and Tactics*. Baltimore: Johns Hopkins University Press, 1997.

Haskew, Michael E. *The Sniper at War: From the American Revolutionary War to the Present Day*. New York: Thomas Dunne Books/St. Martin's Press, 2005.

Hogg, Ian V. *The Story of the Gun*. New York: St. Martin's Press, 1996.

Hughes, B. P. *Firepower: Weapons Effectiveness on the Battlefield, 1630-1850*. New York: Scribner, 1975.

Jones, Richard D., and Leland S. Ness, eds. *Jane's Infantry Weapons, 2009-2010*. 35th ed. Surrey, England: Jane's Information Group, 2009.

McNab, Chris, ed. *Gun: A Visual History*. New York: DK, 2007.

North, Anthony, Charles Stronge, and Will Fowler. *The World Encyclopedia of Pistols, Revolvers and Submachine Guns: An Illustrated Historical Reference to Over Five Hundred Military, Law Enforcement, and Antique Firearms from Around the World*. London: Lorenz, 2007.

Otteson, Stuart. *The Bolt Action: A Design Analysis*. New York: Winchester Press, 1976.

Pauly, Roger. *Firearms: The Life Story of a Technology*. Westport, Conn.: Greenwood Press, 2004.

Pegler, Martin. *Sniper: A History of the U.S. Marksman*. Botley, Oxford, England: Osprey, 2007.

Smith, Anthony. *Machine Gun: The Story of the Men and the Weapon That Changed the Face of War*. London: Piatkus, 2002.

Walter, John. *Guns of the Elite Forces*. London: Greenhill, 2005.

_____. *The Modern Machine Gun*. New York: Greenhill Books/Lionel Leventhal, 2000.

Zhuk, A. B., and John Walter. *The Illustrated Encyclopedia of Handguns: Pistols and Revolvers of the World, 1870 to the Present*. London: Greenhill Books, 1995.

FILMS AND OTHER MEDIA

Early Machine Guns: Advent of Rapid Firepower. Documentary. History Channel, 1998.

Glory. Feature film. Columbia Tri-Star, 1989.

History of Firearms. Documentary. History Channel, 2000.

Robert Jacobs

ARTILLERY
Dates: Since c. 1500

NATURE AND USE

Broadly defined, the term "artillery" refers to machines designed to propel missiles or projectiles of any kind. Since the Middle Ages, however, the term has described crew-served weapons using the combustion of a propellant charge to propel a projectile toward an enemy at ranges greater than those attainable with small arms. Artillery weapons are traditionally divided into categories based on their use in battle. Hence, naval artillery is deployed on ships, coastal artillery includes all guns designed for defending coastlines, and field artillery is utilized on land for support of battlefield operations. Within each of these categories are specific classes of weapons. The most common classes include guns, referring to artillery firing along a flat trajectory; howitzers, describing weapons firing along an angled trajectory between that of a gun and mortar; and mortars, referring to weapons firing at very high angles over relatively short distances. At one time armies also utilized siege artillery, designed to batter down city walls; garrison artillery, used to protect fixed installations; and various versions of horse artillery. These types of weapons have been replaced in the modern era by antitank, antiaircraft, atomic, and self-propelled artillery. The first two terms are self-explanatory, the third refers to artillery firing atomic warheads, and the fourth describes artillery fitted to motorized—usually tracked and armored—carriages capable of independent movement. In contrast, non-self-propelled artillery is moved by vehicles and usually called towed artillery. Finally, artillery can be separated into tube (or cannon) and rocket artillery. The former utilizes a tube and pressure projection to drive a missile forward, while the latter uses jet propulsion to drive a warhead toward a target.

On the battlefield, artillery is used to provide either direct (when the target can be seen) or indirect (when the target is not visible to the firing weapon) fire against enemy troops, vehicles, or installations. Artillery may also be used for general bombardment, the interdiction of supply routes, illumination via flares and other pyrotechnic devices, the screening of friendly forces via smoke rounds, the delivery of atomic warheads, and defense against enemy air attack. At sea or in a coastal defense role, specialized artillery serves to destroy enemy ships or aircraft and to bombard land targets. Artillery units use a wide variety of specialized ordnance, including antipersonnel, antiarmor, nuclear, chemical, high-explosive, and proximity fuse.

DEVELOPMENT

FIELD ARTILLERY

Although modern artillery dates to the Battle of Crécy (1346), most armies before 1500 used their guns in sieges rather than on the battlefield. Great bombards battered down the walls of Constantinople in 1453, for example, and the French successfully used artillery to conduct sieges during the Hundred Years' War (1337-1453).

However, the promise of battlefield artillery could hardly be denied. Cannon already positioned for sieges proved crucial to French victories over the English at Formigny (1450) and Castillon (1453). Hussite leader Jan Žižka (c. 1376-1424) successfully used artillery carried on wagons during the Hussite Wars (1419-1434). The most prescient demonstration of field artillery was by French king Charles VIII (r. 1483-1498), who brilliantly used lightweight bronze artillery in campaigns against Italy in the 1490's and in a dramatic victory over the Spanish at Ravenna (1512).

These victories stimulated considerable innovation in ordnance, and throughout the 1500's experts tinkered with a wide variety of ammunition. Most cannon fired solid cast-iron round shot, or solid iron balls; bombs, iron shells filled with explosive gunpowder; canisters, cans filled with small projectiles; and grape shot, a cluster of iron balls. The ordnance used depended on the target. Solid shot proved effective at long range and against fortifications, bombs were valuable against troops and horses in the open, and canister and grape shot were deadly at close range. Unfortunately, ammunition remained severely limited in most armies, and explosives were unreliable. Worse, the diverse experimentation of inventors created so many different types of guns and ammunition that consistent supply in many armies became almost impossible.

Artillery took a great leap forward in 1537, when Italian mathematician Niccolò Fontana Tartaglia (1500-1557) published the first scientific treatise on gunnery. Tartaglia's pioneering work discussed the basic principles of ballistics, proving that guns reached their greatest range when fired at an angle of 45 degrees and that all trajectories are curved. Tartaglia also developed the first gunner's quadrant and laid the foundation for the systematic scientific study of artillery. When Spanish scholars built upon Tartaglia's work in the 1590's and computed the first firing tables, artillery moved into a new age.

It was an age characterized by arms races between designers of guns and fortifications and between leaders seeking ways to use field artillery more effectively. Holy Roman Emperor Maximilian I (1459-1519) classified artillery in the 1490's as either siege or field and ordered the general use of iron shot by his gunners to simplify logistics. He also increased the amount of training his gunners received and placed his artillery men in a separate branch of the army to enhance their prestige. These efforts were followed by Holy Roman Emperor Charles V (1500-1558) and King Henry II (1519-1559) of France, who also standardized their artillery. The two rulers instituted, between them, a system of classification and battlefield use that lasted in Europe for almost three hundred years. The system defined three basic types of artillery pieces: long-barreled, thick-walled pieces designed for accuracy and long range, called culverin; lighter, shorter-barreled pieces that sacrificed range and accuracy to fire heavier projectiles shorter distances, called cannon; and short-barreled, thin-walled weapons firing very heavy projectiles at high angles called *pedrero*. The names of these weapons varied among nations, but the fundamental system of organization endured into the modern era, in which culverin are known as guns, cannons are known as howitzers, and the early pedrero are known as mortars. Most armies followed this system, reducing the number of calibers and standardizing ammunition and generally abandoning experiments with dangerous breech-loading artillery that loaded from the rear. Breechloaders had a tendency to explode when gases leaked from the breech during firing, a problem known as *obturation*. They became commonplace only in the nineteenth century, after technological advances had allowed gunners to seal breeches consistently.

Another quantum leap in artillery organization took place in the early 1600's, when King Gustavus II Adolphus of Sweden (1594-1632) established the foundations of modern field artillery. Adolphus ordered the development of a small, truly mobile leatherbound gun; made all gunners into soldiers subject to army discipline; and abandoned the widespread practice of hiring unreliable civilian gun crews. The king organized his new guns into regiments and assigned his artillery specific battlefield roles based on the weight of the projectile they fired: 24-pounders were for siege work, 12-pounders for field artillery, and 4-pounders for assignment to individual regiments. Later, Adolphus added 9-pound guns and organized them into batteries of five to ten guns behind his infantry. These changes were revolutionary. Adolphus used artillery en masse, rather than piecemeal, concentrating firepower at the decisive place on the battlefield. He was the first to allow artillery and infantry to fight together as interdependent supporting arms. Previously, artillery units had typically been placed in front of infantry, because the guns were unreliable and could not fire safely over the heads of friendly forces. Once battle was joined these guns were usually overrun by the general engagement and could not be fired again. In contrast, Adolphus's system allowed the guns to be fired continuously and to move from point to point as needed.

Adolphus's army also pioneered the use of cartridge ammunition, which consisted of properly measured bags of gunpowder bound to different types of projectiles. Cartridge ammunition made loading much faster and also increased the consistency of shot, because powder loads were measured out in advance instead of being thrown into guns in the heat of battle. Adolphus used these innovations to smash the Catholic League at the Battle of Breitenfeld in 1631. Other nations quickly moved to duplicate his powerful, mobile artillery.

Louis XIV (1638-1715) of France further advanced the nature and use of artillery when he organized the first permanent artillery regiment in 1671 and established a school of artillery in 1690. At his direction, French engineers perfected an elevating screw that simplified the process of raising and lowering barrels and developed a system of ropes, known as a *prolonge*, for pulling gun carriages. Most important, they refined the elongated priming tube, which was filled with powder and inserted into the touchhole of an artillery piece in order to ignite the charge inside the breech. Priming tubes made the process of firing both safer and more reliable and allowed gunners to reload faster than ever before.

These advances spurred even more improvements in artillery. In the 1690's the Dutch fielded the first true howitzers, and Swiss inventor Jean de Maritz (1680-1743) revolutionized cannon production in 1740 by casting them as solid pieces and then drilling out the bore. This proved far more precise than casting cannon around a hollow centerpiece, and it soon became standard practice throughout Europe. In England, Benjamin Robins (1707-1751) published *New Principles of Gunnery* in 1742, proving the value of elongated projectiles and rifled barrels and refining ballistic principles.

This explosion of new ideas and technology encouraged battlefield innovation, and Frederick the Great of Prussia (1712-1786) introduced the first horse artillery units in 1759. Gunners in these units rode the horses that pulled their gun carriages, and Frederick separated them from foot artillery formations, in which the gunners walked alongside their pieces. Horse artillery proved much faster than foot artillery and gave gunners the chance to stay abreast of advancing infantry and cavalry formations. They proved crucial to Prussian military successes in the mid-eighteenth century.

In France, Inspector General of Artillery Jean-Baptiste Vacquette de Gribeauval (1715-1789) designated artillery as field, siege, garrison, or coastal, and standardized all cartridges, limbers, ammunition chests, and tools. He then divided artillery pieces into battalion, brigade, and army guns; decreased their weight by as much as 50 percent; and began harnessing horses in pairs to move artillery more quickly. Gribeauval also introduced a calibrated rear sight and a graduated tangent sight to improve aiming, and he refined the manufacture of cannon and ammunition

TURNING POINTS

1346	The first definitive use of gunpowder artillery on a battlefield takes place at the Battle of Crécy.
1420	Hussite leader Jan Žižka makes innovative and effective use of artillery, with the *Wagenburg*, a defensive line of wagons and cannons.
1759	Frederick the Great of Prussia introduces the first true horse artillery units, which, because of their unprecedented mobility and firepower, are quickly adopted by other European nations to become a staple of most eighteenth and nineteenth century armies.
1873	German arms manufacturer Alfred Krupp invents one of the first practical recoil systems for field artillery pieces.
1904-1905	The effective use of indirect fire during the Russo-Japanese War spurs American and European leaders to adopt it for their own armies in order to defend their guns against counterbattery and infantry weapon fire.
1978	The United States begins production of the first precision-guided artillery munitions.

to reduce windage, or the space between ammunition and the walls of a cannon through which explosive gases can escape, by one-half. Gribeauval's modifications greatly increased the range and power of French guns, and when combined with reorganized gun crews and additional training upon its complete adoption in 1776, his system made French artillery the finest in Europe.

Chevalier Jean Du Teil (1738-1820) developed a theory for the employment of these weapons, which he articulated in his *De l'usage de l'artillerie nouvelle dans la guerre de campagne connoissance néccessaire aux officiers destinés a commander toutes les armes* (1778). Du Teil argued for the massed employment of mobile artillery on the battlefield and advocated the use of artillery to open breaches in enemy lines at close range. He also suggested the avoidance of counterbattery fire, because it held little hope of disabling enemy guns. These tactics were used with distinction by French emperor Napoleon Bonaparte (1769-1821), who massed artillery in grand batteries with great effect over the course of his career. Perhaps the finest example of Napoleon's use of mobile artillery came at the Battle of Friedland in 1807, in which aggressive French gunners pushed to within 60 yards of the Russian lines to support cavalry and infantry attacks.

Across the Channel, Englishman John Muller (1699-1784) called for lighter British field pieces in his *A Treatise of Artillery* (1757). Sir William Congreve, another Englishman, developed the famous block trail carriage in 1792. A single piece of wood with a center of gravity moved forward and a handspike at the rear, Congreve's carriage dramatically improved artillery mobility. Congreve also designed an accompanying limber and ammunition wagon, which seated gunners and, when joined with the new carriage, increased the speed of artillery movement. Henry Shrapnel's (1761-1842) spherical shell filled with lead bullets and surrounded by explosives increased the effectiveness of artillery systems. Shrapnel's invention allowed artillery units to fire antipersonnel rounds at long range against troops in the open. The charges exploded in the air, showering troops with lead bullets, or shrapnel, as they came to be called. All of these changes made the standard

smoothbore black powder cannon, with a bronze barrel and a range of between 500 and 1,000 yards, more important than ever on the nineteenth century battlefield.

That importance was threatened by the growing prominence of rifled infantry weapons in the early 1800's. Rifling, or spiral grooves cut into the bore of a weapon, dramatically increased range. Although it made reloading more difficult, it also allowed infantry units greater range than did artillery and ultimately made smoothbore cannon obsolete. To compete, an Italian developed the first practical rifled, breech-loading cannon in 1846. Loading at the breech, or rear, of the cannon took less time than loading at the muzzle, and rifling allowed artillery to once again outreach infantry weapons. By the 1860's modern armies had incorporated rifled artillery with ranges of up to 4,000 yards, dramatically expanding the battlefield and making infantry assaults in the open practically impossible.

Most armies, however, were slow to adopt rifled artillery and infantry weapons on a large scale, and smoothbore weapons dominated the inventories of European and American armies well into the nineteenth century. This resistance to change stemmed from the fact that rifled weapons took longer to load and required more training to operate, and from a stubborn attachment to tradition among officers who did not understand how the greater range of rifled weapons demanded fundamental changes in battlefield tactics.

That understanding finally came after the Franco-Prussian War (1870-1871), in which Prussian forces equipped with rifled steel breech-loading artillery decisively defeated the French. This new artillery, manufactured by the legendary arms maker Alfred Krupp (1812-1887), utilized steel and advanced gun design to produce weapons with range far greater than that of any others in the world. Its pivotal role in the Franco-Prussian War forced other nations to play catch-up, and by the 1890's Krupp's steel breech-loaders were the dominant artillery weapons worldwide.

These new guns fired extremely heavy shells, demanding more research into the problem of recoil, the rearward movement of guns caused by their firing. Scientists experimented with hydraulic cylinders attached to gun barrels to reduce recoil on field artillery but with mixed results. Trail spades and brakes were still required on field guns to keep them from moving too far out of position when fired, until the French developed the revolutionary M-1897 75-millimeter field gun in the 1890's. The French "Seventy-five" had a long recoil cylinder capable of reducing recoil to a fraction of its former strength and could fire thirty rounds a minute to a maximum range of 8,000 yards. It represented a quantum leap in artillery technology, driven by the shame of French defeat in the Franco-Prussian War.

Other late nineteenth century improvements in artillery included the development of smokeless powder, high explosive rounds, better fuses, and, by the 1890's, the widespread use of metallic cartridges for ammunition. Each invention represented an enormous leap forward in destructive power and range for artillery weapons, and armies struggled to develop new ways to utilize them. Most organized their big guns into a separate artillery branch and placed them at the disposal of division- or corps-level commanders, because the great range of artillery prohibited its use too close to the battlefield. That distance, however, required gunners to learn how to use artillery in an indirect role, supporting units by firing at targets they could not see, and the limited communication technology of the period made such a role difficult at best.

Karl G. Guk (1846-1910) of Russia laid the foundation for effective indirect artillery fire in 1882, calling for forward observers equipped with compasses and utilizing aiming points to direct artillery fire, and gunners soon abandoned the idea of independent aiming and fired at targets as a battery to maximize their chances of hitting a target. Ironically, Guk's own army suffered the first effective battlefield use of indirect aiming when Japanese forces destroyed Russian artillery with counterbattery fire during the Russo-Japanese War (1904-1905).

These events set the stage for World War I (1914-1918), in which artillery played a decisive role in almost every theater of operation. Commanders desperate to break the stalemate of trench warfare ordered long, sustained bombardments of enemy positions, using larger and larger guns and more powerful ordnance. Field commanders pioneered the use of aircraft as observation platforms for indirect fire and used sound and flash ranging to spot enemy batteries at long range. Because observers could not always see enemy positions or contact friendly artillery, they developed rolling barrages that moved fire forward in front of advancing infantry on a preset timetable. Some units also practiced unobserved firing, using their guns to hit areas in which enemy activity was suspected, and predicted fire, in which units aimed without spotting rounds and unleashed surprise barrages on enemy positions. During World War I artillery units used poison gas shells on a large scale, began using vehicles and railway cars instead of horses to move their heavy guns, and experimented with the first self-propelled artillery.

During the interwar years refinement of the radio finally allowed forward observers to call in accurate indirect fire at great range. In the United States these efforts culminated in the development of the Fire Direction Center (FDC) during the 1930's. A centralized command post connecting multiple batteries, the FDC could by 1941 mass four battalions of artillery on one target within five minutes. This ability to quickly mass artillery fire against various targets gave the United States a tremendous advantage on the battlefield and served as a model that other countries quickly sought to emulate.

In World War II (1941-1945), artillery again proved decisive, accounting for more casualties than any other family of weapons. Combatants used thousands of guns, towing them with horses and moving others with vehicles or on self-propelled carriages. These guns grew progressively in size and destructive power. The Germans, for example, developed an 88-millimeter gun that served throughout the war as an antiaircraft, antitank, and artillery weapon. The British fielded their famous 25-pounder, which fired a 3.45-inch projectile 13,000 yards, and the United States developed a towed and self-propelled version of the 155-millimeter gun and howitzer. To observe fire from these new weapons, armies added aircraft to artillery units and promoted widespread use of the radio, allowing close battlefield support for ground forces. Artillery units also diversified, as the threat from enemy tanks and aircraft demanded specialized weapons to defeat them. Antitank artillery units fired hollow charges or discarding sabot rounds through tapered barrels to destroy tanks with high velocity rounds. Some armies even fielded self-propelled antitank guns called tank destroyers or guns as large as 240 millimeters, called assault guns, for close support of infantry. These guns were joined by antiaircraft artillery designed to defend against enemy air attack. A revolutionary new technology in this field was the variable time (VT) fuse, which was fielded by the United States in 1941. The VT fuse allowed gunners to detonate rounds at a preset range, throwing shrapnel in the path of enemy aircraft rather than hitting them directly. It was especially important in defending U.S. ships against Japanese air attack in the Pacific.

After World War II, artillery units struggled to adjust to the nuclear age. Tactical nuclear artillery became a reality in 1953, when the United States fired an atomic warhead from a 280-millimeter gun named Atomic Annie in Nevada. The United States eventually fielded atomic warheads for 155-millimeter howitzers as well, and the Soviet Union quickly followed suit.

Within conventional artillery, the United States found that during the Korean War (1950-1953) many units were handicapped by guns that could not traverse 360 degrees. By the 1960's the United States had developed a new family of self-propelled guns. These new guns, with fully enclosed crew shelters, could fully traverse and elevate to 75 degrees. In response, the Soviet Union also revamped its artillery, fielding a 203-millimeter field gun with a 31,900-yard range, a 152-millimeter field howitzer, and new self-propelled guns.

Library of Congress

The Krupp arms manufacturing company's exhibit of a massive cannon at the 1893 Chicago World's Fair.

The United States also found a need for lighter pieces that could be carried by aircraft to support airborne and air mobile forces. In the 1950's it therefore developed a 75-millimeter pack howitzer and 105-millimeter and 155-millimeter towed howitzers suitable for air transport. These guns were used with great effect during direct American involvement in the Vietnam War from 1965 to 1973, when they were often repositioned with helicopters.

As the Vietnam conflict ended, the 1973 Israeli-Arab October War saw the first widespread use of remotely piloted vehicles (RPVs) for battlefield obser-

Army Times Publishing Co.

A gun crew of the Sixty-fourth Artillery Battalion, Twenty-fifth Infantry Division, fires a 105-millimeter howitzer on North Korean positions in 1950.

All of these advances, along with the use of next-generation RPVs and sophisticated fire-control computers, were validated during the Gulf War (1990-1991). In this conflict U.S. artillery units devastated Iraqi positions with advanced and traditional munitions that fired with unprecedented accuracy and played a key role in keeping Allied casualties low, speeding coalition forces to victory.

As armies evolve into the twenty-first century, artillery promises to play a vital role on conventional battlefields, with computers and advanced ordnance producing faster rates of fire over greater ranges with astonishing accuracy. Like their counterparts in centuries past, however, the artillery of the future will have to balance performance with speed of movement, lest it find itself unable to deploy to trouble spots around the world in a timely manner.

vation and artillery spotting, and spurred yet another outburst of technological innovation. Advanced armies had already experimented with ordnance that separated into a greater number of individual warheads called submunitions and with rocket-assisted warheads that gave traditional artillery greater range. During the 1970's they also moved into the realm of laser-guided projectiles when the United States fielded the Copperhead 155-millimeter cannon-launched guided weapons system. The Copperhead gave the United States unprecedented targeting accuracy and paved the way for the development of "fire-and-forget" artillery shells in the 1980's. These "smart" munitions carried onboard target-seeking sensors that allowed individual warheads to seek out and destroy enemy tanks, a capability desperately needed by outnumbered U.S. forces in Europe. From the 1960's onward the United States also pioneered the use of radar for counterbattery artillery fire and developed the means to detect the exact location of enemy artillery by computing the trajectory of their shells backward to the point of origin.

COASTAL ARTILLERY

From their inception cannons have been used to defend coastal installations against naval attack. The English, for example, placed guns in Dover as a protection against the French in 1370, and Henry VIII (1491-1547) ordered fortifications and coastal guns positioned in all major English coastal towns from 1538 onward. These coastal guns generally evolved in tandem with field artillery, with the important exception of their size. Because coastal guns were not required to move, they were designed to be the largest and most technically advanced artillery weapons in the world. Guns as large as seventeen tons protected the Dardanelles from attack as early as the 1400's, and around the world coastal guns ranged from standard sizes to leviathans that would be impossible to deploy on land or aboard ship.

By the nineteenth century, most advanced countries boasted coastal fortifications equipped with these cannons in brick and stone emplacements. The United States joined in this effort by building twenty-four forts equipped with more than 750 guns along the Atlantic coast between 1806 and 1811. By the late 1800's, breech-loading guns were dominant, with guns placed in disappearing barbette carriages and hidden behind or beneath concrete walls.

World War I prompted yet another burst of coastal gun emplacements, with guns as large as 12, 14, and 16 inches finding their way into the arsenals of the world's armies and navies. These large guns were necessary to defeat heavily armored warships, and designers went to great lengths to find ways to minimize their great recoil and to develop mountings to support their enormous weight. Others extended the range of these large guns by using longer barrels and experimented with rail-mounted guns that moved from one coastal position to another. In the long run these guns proved expensive and far less effective than ship-mounted artillery, and their vulnerability to air attack led most nations to abandon them after World War II.

NAVAL ARTILLERY

At sea cannons had, by the mid-1400's, become vital weapons in the navies of the world. Like their cousins in coastal artillery, shipboard cannons developed roughly in parallel with guns on land. The one exception to this rule was the gun carriage. Early cannons were attached to the ship itself, but by the 1500's designers introduced wheels to carriages that supported guns and allowed sailors to move them. These truck carriages were held in place by breeching ropes that constrained the cannon but still allowed recoil to move them backward. They therefore spared the hull of the ship the full force of recoil and presented gunners with a means to maneuver the gun back into position for firing. This simple technology prevailed until well into the nineteenth century and helped smoothbore muzzle-loading cannon to dominate naval warfare for three centuries.

These cannon were arranged along the gun decks on both sides of sailing ships and fired through ports in the side of the hull, which could be closed in inclement weather. Naval architects designed several classes of ships to carry cannon, from small and fast frigates to enormous ships of the line, which boasted as many as one hundred or more guns. These ships generally fired standard artillery rounds and sought

to deliver them simultaneously in great broadsides, when all guns on one side of a ship fired at the same target. Although ordnance changed relatively little prior to the 1850's, the Scottish did introduce a specially designed carronade in 1778, which sacrificed range to fire a large-caliber round from a light gun. The British Royal Navy adopted the carronade for close-quarter action in the late 1700's, and many other nations quickly followed suit.

The relative stasis in naval gun design was shattered in 1858, when the French launched *La Gloire*, the world's first ironclad warship. The British responded by building their own armored warship, the HMS *Warrior*. In the 1860's they proved that armor-piercing shells fired at high velocity were far superior in defeating armor to much heavier solid shot traveling at slower speeds. This discovery induced navies around the world to adopt spherical shells tipped with metal, known as armor-piercing rounds, and the days of round shot were finally over.

Naval designers then had to decide where to place their armor-piercing guns and how best to protect them with armor plate. Some chose to place their guns at either the front or rear of their ships, while others adopted the sponson, a semicircular platform that allowed guns a 180-degree traverse both fore and aft. The ultimate solution came when designers produced revolving turrets that allowed guns to fire in almost any direction. These turrets, first deployed on the Danish *Rolf Kraki* in 1861, freed ships from linear tactics and allowed attacks from a variety of directions. When coupled with steam power, which freed ships from reliance upon the wind, they completely revolutionized naval warfare.

By 1874 the English were deploying ships with 12.5-inch muzzle-loaders in turrets weighing as much as 750 tons, and the growing size of turrets required hydraulic and mechanical power to rotate them. As breech-loading guns became dominant in the late 1800's, designers sank turrets down into the hulls of ships and used compressed air and water to cleanse gun barrels, interlocking doors to separate ammunition storage from firing compartments, and pressurization to reduce the risk of accidental explosion. They also developed machines to take over the process of loading ammunition, and by World War I battleships carrying guns as large as 15 inches were recognized as the dominant weapons of their era.

These ships required sophisticated targeting systems to account for the great range of their guns, as well as for their own movement and the movement of their targets. Naval designers therefore placed fire-control centers high up in the masts and control towers of ships to allow a good view of targets and gave these centers control over the firing of guns in all turrets. During and after World War I these fire-control centers were aided by observation aircraft and fired at such great range that they had to account for the curvature of the earth in their firing computations.

During World War II battleships reached their zenith, when the United States and Japan utilized ships with guns as large as 16 and 18 inches, respectively. Rather than playing a primary role in the naval battles of the era, however, these great ships were eclipsed by aircraft as the dominant weapon on the high seas. They served primarily as antiaircraft and shore bombardment platforms and were retired after the war as aircraft and guided missiles replaced them. Although U.S. battleships were brought out of retirement so their great guns could bombard distant land targets during the Korean War (1950-1953), the Vietnam War (1961-1975), and the Gulf War (1990-1991), as of 2000 there were no battleships in the active inventory of any world navy. Ships that continue to mount heavy guns generally do so as a means of self-defense against small ships or aircraft, and the guns are usually no larger than 5 inches. They are, however, guided by radar and boast extremely fast rates of fire, seemingly indicating that naval artillery will endure well into the twenty-first century.

BOOKS AND ARTICLES

Bailey, Jonathan B. A. *Firepower and Field Artillery*. 2d ed. Annapolis, Md.: Naval Institute Press, 2004.

Dastrup, Boyd L. *The Field Artillery: History and Sourcebook*. Westport, Conn.: Greenwood Press, 1994.

Halberstadt, Hans. *The World's Great Artillery: From the Middle Ages to the Present Day*. Rochester, Kent, England: Grange, 2002.

Hazlett, James C., Edwin Olmstead, and M. Hume Parks. *Field Artillery Weapons of the Civil War*. 2d ed. Newark: University of Delaware Press, 1988. Reprint. Urbana: University of Illinois Press, 2004.

Hogg, Ian V. *Anti-Aircraft Artillery*. Marlborough, England: Crowood, 2002.

_____. *Artillery 2000*. London: Arms and Armour, 1990.

_____. *Twentieth-Century Artillery*. New York: Sterling, 2000.

Kinard, Jeff. *Artillery: An Illustrated History of Its Impact*. Santa Barbara, Calif.: ABC-CLIO, 2007.

McKenney, Janice E. *The Organizational History of Field Artillery, 1775-2003*. Washington, D.C.: Center of Military History, United States Army, 2007.

Mehl, Hans. *Naval Guns: Five Hundred Years of Ship and Coastal Artillery*. Translated by Keith Thomas. Annapolis, Md.: Naval Institute Press, 2002.

Norris, John. *An Illustrated History of Artillery*. Stroud, Gloucestershire, England: Sutton, 2001.

Rogers, H. C. B. *A History of Artillery*. Secaucus, N.J.: Citadel Press, 1975.

FILMS AND OTHER MEDIA

Artillery: Arms in Action. Documentary. A&E Home Video, 2000.

Weapons at War: Artillery. Documentary. History Channel, 2001.

Lance Janda

TANKS AND ARMORED VEHICLES
Dates: Since 1898

NATURE AND USE

Although primitive designs for horse-powered, armored combat vehicles date back to the fifteenth century, it was not until the nineteenth century that they actually took a cohesive shape. As early as 1898 the U.S. Army had designed and built a motorized gun carriage, which, although fitted with only an armor shield, is considered to be one of the world's first armored cars. This steam-propelled vehicle, equipped with a .30-caliber Colt machine gun, continued to be built on a small scale into the twentieth century. During the Second Boer War in South Africa (1899-1902), the British army also employed armored trailers and steam traction engines, notably Fowlers, for hauling supplies and guns. These original armored vehicles were obviously limited and were not recognized by the military authorities of any nation until the outbreak of World War I (1914-1918).

Colonel Ernest Swinton (1868-1951), who originated the tank in 1915 and fought in the Boer War, saw the potential for modern firepower and its devastating effect on men in the open. As an officer of the Royal Engineers, he was familiar with mechanical transport, including petrol-engined, Caterpillar-tracked vehicles such as those that had been developed previously in both England and the United States. In October, 1914, Swinton recognized that the line of fortified trenches, which stretched from the North Sea to the Swiss frontier, was unlikely to be breached by conventional means of attack by infantry and cavalry. Barbed wire entanglements, secured by intensive fire from artillery and automatic weapons, made a war of movement impossible and precluded any decisive action. Swinton sought a radical solution to the trench deadlock and used the American Holt tractor design, then being used in France, as a starting point. The track was the key, he believed, as it made cross-country movement on rough ground

easier. Swinton encountered a great deal of opposition, however, from military authorities who were skeptical about untried methods. The Royal Naval Air Service had sent armored car squadrons to the Calais area as early as September, 1914, to protect the advanced improvised landing strips they had set up for their air squadrons supporting the Naval Brigade. These vehicles were not intended for offensive use, however, and they were largely confined to roads.

In July, 1915, Swinton was sent back to London from his post in France to become secretary of the Dardanelles Committee of the Cabinet. He stood at the center of the group of politicians, officials, soldiers, and technicians whose aim was to create what became known as the tank. Perhaps more important than Swinton's contribution to production of the tank was his original document outlining tank tactics that were used for years to come. His memorandum described the characteristics, capabilities, and limitations of tanks and defined their basic use, in conjunction with infantry and artillery, to crush enemy wire, to cross trenches, to destroy machine guns, and finally to advance so deeply into enemy defenses that their guns could also be tackled. Swinton also envisaged the need for tanks to communicate by telephone or wireless both with each other and with their supporting arms. In Swinton's opinion, tanks were merely an auxilliary to infantry, and their independent operation was, in his mind, inconceivable.

The first tanks ran trials in January, 1916; they first entered battle in September of the same year, at Flers-Courcelette, in northern France, where forty-nine vehicles were used to add impetus to a flagging infantry action. Success was limited, however, due to the limited number of tanks available, the lack of crew experience, and the vehicles' inherent mechanical limitations. However, some of the British army staff were convinced of the tank's value, and orders increased. The tank's real, or perhaps more famous, introduction came in November, 1916, at Cambrai, in northern France. For the first time, a joint tank-infantry operation had been carefully planned to fit the strengths and limitations of armored vehicles. The attack was made on a seven-mile front, and the tanks attacked in three waves; each tank worked with the tank behind it to cross the three lines of the German defensive system. Smoke shells were fired to camouflage the tanks' arrival, and, when the smoke cleared, the Germans were greeted by the large metal vehicles, emerging from the morning fog with guns blazing. So complete was the surprise that some of the German units panicked and fled; however, Cambrai was not an absolute victory for armored vehicles. After the first objective had been achieved, the infantry began to lose contact with the tanks. The tank units were left alone to face a German artillery battery, and many tanks were destroyed. Even though the tanks kept breaking through enemy lines, because there was no infantry there to hold the ground, their gains were useless. The armored attack on Cambrai was significant in that, in one day, it opened a large hole in the German defense system. Only 4,000 British soldiers died at Cambrai, a greater achievement than the 1917 Passchendaele Offensive, which took four months and 400,000 casualties. Although the tank restored mobility to the battlefield and was touted as the answer to the stalemate caused by the machine gun, barbed wire, and entrenchments, many skeptics remained to be convinced of the advantages of armored warfare.

DEVELOPMENT

The first tank prototype was called Mother. The lozenge-shaped frame was such that the lower run of the track in contact with the ground approximated the shape and radius of a wheel with a 60-foot diameter. It was calculated that this shape would comfortably cross a 5-foot trench or run up a 4.5-foot vertical parapet. It was in 1916 that the term "tank" first came into use to describe what had hitherto been described as a "landship." Mother's success led to the first tank, known as the Mark I, which was identical to Mother

except that it was constructed with armor plate instead of boiler plate. The Mark I, used at Flers-Courcelette, was armed with a 6-pounder (pdr) gun and three Hotchkiss machine guns. Improvements to the Mark I followed in subsequent models: Wider track shoes were fitted at every sixth link, armor was slightly increased, and a raised manhole hatch was placed on top to protect the driver. The wheeled cart that trailed the earlier model was also discarded, because it was ineffective on the muddy battlefield.

TANKS IN WORLD WAR I

The first tanks had crews of eight. In these vehicles, steering and gear changing were cumbersome and tiring operations that placed considerable strain on the vehicle's transmission. By the time the Mark V model had been developed, four-speed gearboxes were used, and the gears could then be changed by one man. The Mark V's engines were much more powerful, and once they were made to be air-cooled, they became immune to frost. The extreme weight of the early Mark models made it impossible to control the steering and braking by hand power alone; hydraulic lines were introduced to allow control of the massive vehicles. Its armor was also increased, and a rear-firing machine gun was added.

When the United States entered World War I, it jointly produced the Mark VIII with the British. Prior to this time, however, French Renault light tanks and British Mark V tanks were used. German tank projects met with the same type of skepticism that had been prevalent in Britain. Although the tank was used in army exercises, its value in battle was not appreciated by the German General Staff, who considered tanks suitable only for secondary tasks, such as frontier patrol work, gun transport, and reconnaissance. A German infantry force mounted in trucks did execute a lightning strike as part of General Erich von Falkenhayn's (1861-1922) offensive against Romania in 1916, and the lessons were not lost on the German General Staff.

THE INTERWAR YEARS

In the post-World War I era, the development and organization of mechanization was viewed as a possible decisive factor in warfare. Military mechanized vehicles could be divided into the following types: armored fighting vehicles, armored carriers, and armored tractors. The tracks themselves were still of a very primitive type, no more than a series of plates joined together by hinge pins. These tracks were laterally rigid, so that steering was accomplished by skidding the tracks in contact with the ground. The pins and plate wore out very rapidly. However, the tracks were effectively sprung in 1922, increasing the life, as well as the expense and difficulty of manufacture, of the track. Despite these innovations, by the 1930's the British army had returned to traditional dogma and entered World War II with a defensive doctrine.

The British military thinkers J. F. C. Fuller (1878-1966) and Sir Basil Henry Liddell Hart (1895-1970) restored the strategic emphasis on mobility and the use of armor in war. In 1919 Fuller asserted that the tank could completely replace the infantry and cavalry, and that artillery, in order to survive, should be developed along the lines of the tank. Military perfection, he believed, no longer could be based on numbers of soldiers: Technological advances such as the internal combustion engine had rendered human masses insignificant in the age of modern warfare, negating the need to literally destroy the enemy's armies in the field. As Fuller argued, armored forces could paralyze, demoralize, and cause the disintegration of armies by striking at their rear communications and command systems. With slaughter and destruction reduced, he believed, war would become both more humane and more rational. Fuller's work soon attracted attention, and he acquired a faithful disciple in Hart, who in 1922 was converted to Fuller's vision of armored warfare.

By the late 1920's the British government had become increasingly concerned about the dilapidated

Hulton Archive/Getty Images

A tank of the type the British used successfully against the Germans at Cambrai in 1917.

condition of its army, resulting in experimental trials with mechanized and mixed units, held between 1927 and 1931. On the Salisbury Plain in August, 1927, exercises were conducted with an incongruous force of armored cars, various-sized tanks, and cavalry and infantry units. Although problems such as constant congestion at bottlenecks were ubiquitous, the trials demonstrated the mobility advantages inherent in mechanized strategy. In 1931 an exercise was conducted by the First Brigade Royal Tank Regiment. The force was composed entirely of tracked vehicles, and, using a combination of radios and colored flags for communication between the tanks, they functioned in unity and precision. This period of experimentation and development soon lost impetus, however, as the army's leadership became increasingly conservative. This fear of change discouraged further innovation and experiment in armor. Even after the rise of Adolf Hitler (1889-1945) and British recognition of the German continental threat, little was done to improve land forces, as such action was politically unpopular and financially difficult to reconcile with expenditure on the British navy.

Germany had always believed war to be a useful instrument to ensure national security and to foster Germany's higher status in Europe. Therefore, although antiarmor elements existed in Germany, it was on the whole a more conducive environment for armored warfare. Mechanization of the army was part of a more encompassing program, and the creation of tank formations was initially a subordinate element in improving overall mobility. Tank warfare became increasingly important and by 1929 formed the main thrust of army modernization. The turning point had come in 1927, when Germany concluded that the principles of tank warfare would need to be reconsidered, embracing the concept of decision-oriented, operationally independent armored warfare.

With the rise of National Socialism in the 1930's, the party's leader, Hitler, guaranteed rearmament, and his new government immediately began to fulfill this promise. Armor doctrine found fertile ground, and supporters in the government backed the development of armored forces against the skepticism of more conservative officers. Light- and medium-model armored vehicles equipped with machine guns, an armor-piercing gun, and radios, and capable of speeds of up to 25 miles per hour, began to appear in 1938 and 1939 as the Panzer III and Panzer IV. At the outbreak of World War II in September, 1939, six Panzer divisions existed and were being trained in the technique of the Blitzkrieg, literally "lightning war," the violent and surprise offensive by which Poland was overwhelmed in 1939.

The Spanish Civil War (1936-1939) set the stage for the armored warfare of World War II. The Republicans, supported by France and the Soviet Union, followed French armor doctrine and distributed their tanks within the infantry formations. They employed the tanks in support of infantry frontal attacks, forcing the vehicles to move at walking pace and providing lucrative targets for the Nationalist antitank gunners. The Germans, who supported the Nationalists,

persuaded them to concentrate their armor, group it with motorized infantry and mobile artillery, and deploy it where the enemy was weak, in fast-moving attacks on narrow fronts. This strategy was effective and played a significant role in the success of the Nationalist offensives of 1938-1939 that led to their victory. The French and the Russians both drew false conclusions about tank strategy after the war. Both nations believed that the antitank gun had mastered the tank and that tank formations could not play an independent operational role in future waging of war. The Germans quickly proved them wrong.

TANKS IN WORLD WAR II
On August 1, 1939, Germany invaded Poland, beginning the conflict that evolved into World War II. By this time the German army understood that tank forces could not act alone. They prepared their tank force for penetration, but then attached to it a motorized support of infantry, artillery, and engineers. Germany used the same tactic of rapid, self-supporting mobility after defeating Poland, attacking France in May, 1940. In France the German army was also aided by air support, which proved to be another effective strategy. It is significant to note that, although France had more tanks than Germany, the defensive doctrine that the French applied to their use failed to hold out against the lightning offensive movements of the German Panzer divisions. France was defeated in June of 1940. Germany then turned and attacked Russia in June, 1941. After the initial German success of rapid, armored pincer movements, the Russians developed the T-34 tank. It was armed with a long, high-velocity 76-millimeter gun, which shredded the German armor. The T-34 itself seemed immune to the Panzer's own shells. Their top speed of 33 miles per hour, over the Panzer's 25 miles per hour, on a wider-tracked base was also indispensable in the mud and snow of the eastern front. After gaps had been created in the front, the Russians sent in their tank forces, composed mostly of the formidable T-34, to enlarge and expand the breakthrough. Once the Americans joined the battle on the western front, the most commonly used vehicle was the Sherman tank, which helped turn the tide on the Germans in North Africa and later in France.

M-1A1 Abrams tanks in Iraq during Operation Desert Storm.

TANKS IN MODERN CONFLICTS

The Israeli-Arab October War (1973) displayed a new style of armored warfare. The Israeli army charged into the Suez Canal area in small groups of tanks, unsupported by reconnaissance, infantry, artillery, or air forces. The Egyptians, who were armed with RPG-7 rocket launchers and Sagger antitank guided missiles (ATGM), soundly defeated the Israeli forces. This initial defeat, however, did not, as many thought, portend the end of the heavy, slow-moving tank. After the first disastrous days, the Israelis restored the mobility of their tank formations; their ultimate success was primarily due to the reintroduction of all arms cooperation. Infantry was vulnerable to artillery and machine-gun fire. Artillery was vulnerable to attack by tanks and infantry. Tanks also were vulnerable to a variety of antiarmor weapons. When used together, however, each force compensated for the weakness of the other. The tanks destroyed enemy armor and machine guns; infantry cleared antiarmor weapons and held ground; and artillery, secure behind the armor and infantry, neutralized enemy antiarmor weapons and artillery. The ef-

fective use of tanks, therefore, had to be adapted to the changing technologies of armor and antiarmored warfare.

There have traditionally been two methods of defeating the thick, rolled homogeneous armored steel that has generally protected tanks. Kinetic energy (KE) attack involves firing a high-velocity projectile from a large-caliber gun. In flight, the light outer jacket, or sabot, of the projectile falls off, and the remaining kinetic energy is concentrated in its smaller-diameter core, made up of high-density material. The core then forces its way through the armored plate. Chemical energy (CE) attack uses an explosive charge to create energy to defeat the armor plate. The shell's explosive charge creates and directs a narrow, high-pressure jet that forces its way through the armor plate.

In the mid-1970's and early 1980's, three new developments in armor technology appeared to counter traditional antitank weapons. It had been known for some time that some materials, such as ceramic or glass, severely degraded shaped charge jets. The Soviets thus developed simple laminate armor for protection against both KE and CE attack; the T-72, for example, was fitted with this armor as well as with ceramic inserts in cavities within the cast turret armor. Another development was explosive reactive armor, developed by the Israelis and consisting of small panels bolted to the exterior of the tank. When struck by a high explosive antitank (HEAT) projectile, the explosive detonated, driving the plates apart and disrupting the shaped charge jet. The most significant of the new armors was Chobham armor, a complex laminate developed by the British and first publicly shown in 1976. It was composed of spatial layers of various materials, such as steel ceramic and aluminum, and was reported to give significantly better protection than any other armor against multiple attacks by KE and CE warheads. Other innovations included the fitting of tanks with explosion-suppression systems and the substition of combustible hydraulic fluids for electronic systems. As shell penetration of armor caused possible ruptures in hydraulic lines, internal catastrophic explosions from hydraulic vapor became common. Moreover, ammunition was placed in separate, protected bin compartments. The latter two concepts were practiced by the British. In the Middle East wars during 1970's and 1980's, British-designed tanks proved difficult to ignite.

Soviet revisions in operational doctrine at this time saw the evolution of Operational Maneuver Group (OMG) concept. This involved the employment of self-contained, highly maneuverable, heavily armored formations early in an offensive. OMGs would, theoretically, attempt to punch their way through the defenses of the North Atlantic Treaty Organization (NATO) before they were fully developed and strike deep into the NATO rear, with the intent of causing chaos and the rapid collapse of the defense. The OMG concept evolved from the Soviets' experience in World War II, but the Israelis in the 1956, 1967, 1973, and 1982 wars used a similar doctrine most successfully. Soviet tanks, such as the T-64, T-72, and T-80, had 125-millimeter guns, automatic loaders, and integrated fire-control systems to permit rapid, accurate, and lethal fire. These tanks also had multi-barreled grenade dischargers, which were capable of firing smoke grenades that degraded the performance of the new thermal imaging sight technology. Although the So-

AP/Wide World Photos

Armored vehicles are towed into the former Yugoslavia by British Chinook helecopters during the 1999 Kosovo crisis.

viet threat soon subsided with the disintegration of the Soviet Union in 1989, a new threat quickly took its place.

The Gulf War (1991) saw the most technologically advanced ground combat of the century. The American M-1A1's, British Challengers and Chieftains, and French AMX-30's were shipped in to combine the best old-fashioned hardware with modern targeting computer software. The American M-1A1 is a rolling fortress that radiates a menacing power. The four-man tank weighs 63 tons and measures 26 feet long. The tank's primary weapon is a 120-millimeter M68E1 smoothbore cannon that fires M-728 armor-piercing shells up to a distance of 2.5 miles while moving at 20 miles per hour. Other armament includes two 7.62-millimeter M-240 machine guns and one .50-caliber Browning M-2HB machine gun. With its powerful 1,500 horsepower gas turbine engine, the M-1A1 has a top speed of about 42 miles per hour and consumes fuel at the rate of 6 gallons per mile. The M-1A1 has a range of about 288 miles. It carries forty rounds and is equipped with an advanced carbon dioxide laser rangefinder, thermal viewing for night fighting, and a better suspension than earlier versions. The M-1A1 is considered the most sophisticated and capable main battle tank in the world. Even the Iraqi use of the Soviet T-72, a generation behind the M-1A1 in development, could not make the battle any real test for the coalition forces. Although the preceding air campaign created highly favorable conditions for the ground forces to accomplish their mission, it was ultimately the ground forces and their tactical air support that destroyed the Iraqi army.

With the growing emphasis on airpower in the 1990's, particularly in Bosnia and Kosovo, the true potential for armored warfare remained unrealized. As in the first tank battles, it remains clear that there must also be an armed force to hold any ground that is gained. Tanks and armor, therefore, will always have their place in the waging of war.

BOOKS AND ARTICLES

Alexander, Arthur J. *Armor Development in the Soviet Union and the United States*. Santa Monica, Calif.: RAND, 1976.

Chamberlain, Peter, and Chris Ellis. *Tanks of the World: 1915-1945*. London: Cassell, 2002.

Citino, Robert. *Armored Forces*. Westport, Conn.: Greenwood Press, 1994.

Estes, Kenneth W. *Marines Under Armor: The Marine Corps and the Armored Fighting Vehicle, 1916-2000*. Annapolis, Md.: Naval Institute Press, 2000.

Foss, Christopher F., ed. *The Encyclopedia of Tanks and Armored Fighting Vehicles: The Comprehensive Guide to Over Nine Hundred Armored Fighting Vehicles from 1915 to the Present Day*. San Diego, Calif.: Thunder Bay Press, 2002.

Fuller, J. F. C. *Machine Warfare: An Enquiry into the Influences of Mechanics on the Art of War*. London: Hutchinson, 1941.

Guderian, Heinz. *Achtung-Panzer! The Development of Armoured Forces, Their Tactics, and Operational Potential*. Translated by Christopher Duffy. London: Brockhampton Press, 1999.

Gudmundsson, Bruce I. *On Armor*. Westport, Conn.: Praeger, 2004.

Hogg, Ian V. T*he Greenhill Armoured Fighting Vehicles Data Book*. London: Greenhill Books, 2000.

Koch, Fred. *Russian Tanks and Armored Vehicles, 1946 to the Present: An Illustrated Reference*. Atglen, Pa.: Schiffer, 1999.

Macksey, Kenneth. *Tank Warfare: A History of Tanks in Battle*. London: Rupert Hart-Davis, 1971.

Pugh, Stevenson. *Armour in Profile*. Surrey, England: Profile, 1968.

Spielberger, Walter J. *Panzer II and Its Variants*. Vol. 3 in *The Spielberger German Armor and Military Vehicles*. Atglen, Pa.: Schiffer, 1993.

Stone, John. *The Tank Debate: Armour and the Anglo-American Military Tradition*. Amsterdam: Harwood Academic, 2000.

Wright, Patrick. *Tank: The Progress of a Monstrous War Machine*. London: Faber, 2000.

FILMS AND OTHER MEDIA

Hell on Wheels. Documentary. History Channel, 1998.

The Tanks Are Coming. Short film. Warner Bros., 1941.

Aaron Plamondon

Aircraft, Bombs, and Guidance Systems

Dates: Since 1900

Nature and Use

Aircraft possess great mobility and firepower, which enable them to affect tactical or strategic situations decisively. They can circumvent both enemy and environmental obstructions to army and naval movement. Their speed and range can render any enemy position vulnerable to surveillance or attack. Even slower aircraft such as helicopters move with a speed and agility that ground vehicles cannot match. Technological progress and military developments have created or eliminated various aircraft types. These factors made it necessary that some aircraft design features be optimized in order to produce the best machines to fly specific air missions. Furthermore, although aircraft have grown increasingly important to any military endeavor, like all weapons they are tools whose effectiveness depends on the situation and combat objective.

Types of Aircraft

Airships, also called dirigibles, existed at the beginning of the twentieth century. These large, specially built balloons had propeller engines and small wings at their stern that allowed controlled flight. In 1900 Germany's Count Ferdinand von Zeppelin (1838-1917) introduced cigar-shaped, metal-framed versions called rigid dirigibles or, after the builder himself, zeppelins. Already in operation were more sausage-shaped airships with less rigid frames, later nicknamed blimps. Since airships could remain airborne for long periods, they served best in observational roles. However, their expense, large size, support demands, slow speed, clumsy handling, and hydrogen interiors combined to make them unsuitable for direct combat.

The airplane first flew in 1903, and by 1911 primitive models were flying in combat. Airplanes have been the most prevalent and successful type of military aircraft, reaping the windfall of successive technological advances and serving in a wide variety of roles. Improvements in thrust allowed for the evolution of piston engines and propellers to jet engines with afterburners. Aerodynamic design advanced from fabric biplanes to titanium and composite-alloy swept-wing planes. The exigencies of World War I (1914-1918) determined the basic airplane types and design philosophies for air combat: fighter, attack, and bomber.

Fighters, Attack Planes, and Bombers

Fighters enabled an air arm to meet its most important mission, air superiority, by shooting down aircraft and thus defeating the enemy's air effort. As daytime fighters evolved from World War I, the best designs possessed an optimum compromise of speed, climbing ability, acceleration, and maneuverability. Further, they required the best air-to-air weaponry, whether that was powerful machine guns or guided missiles. Thus, sheer performance and hitting power enabled fighters to outperform and shoot other planes, especially in the maneuvering duels against other fighters known as dogfights. Expanding requirements and technological developments bred variations. Radar drove the creation of night fighters, which, during World War II (1939-1945), were often planes lacking optimum fighter performance but possessing room for electronic gear and the extra crew to operate it.

The Cold War's technology developments and military conditions bred more fighter variants. Interceptors such as the U.S. F-106 and the Soviet MiG-25 stressed speed and climb over maneuverability because they required the potential to attack incoming nuclear-armed bombers quickly. Anticipating the

The German Zeppelin airship LZ-3 in 1909.

effect of higher speeds, onboard radars, and guided air-to-air missiles upon aerial warfare, the leading air arms reduced emphasis upon traditional air fighting skills such as dogfighting and gunnery. Further, because fighters had during previous wars performed well in other missions, such as ground attack, air leaders pursued a more versatile, cost-effective force by building multipurpose fighters, "fighter-bombers," or fighters adapted to other missions. Although planes such as the U.S. F-4 achieved some success in this regard, they were still not the best at all missions. Indeed, conflicting mission requirements, jet performance extremes, and radar-guided missiles' space and cockpit task demands rendered impossible the optimization of traditional day fighter, interceptor, and attack plane needs in one design. Further, this produced very expensive planes. The United States, which most assiduously pursued this aim, built cheaper planes with more traditional air combat

strengths, such as the F-16, to supplement its forces. Even so, the U.S. Navy and Air Force also expanded these planes' roles.

Attack planes required similar characteristics, but not at the expense of extra range, ruggedness, and bomb delivery prowess. Beyond these specifications, attack plane designers faced choices in meeting a variety of force application missions. Attack planes supported the fighters' air control mission by flying offensive counterattacks against enemy airfields. They conducted interdiction campaigns against enemy ground forces by attacking reserve units, supply lines, and command or communications facilities. They flew close air support missions against enemy troops at or near the battle front, and they supported naval actions by attacking ships and dropping mines. Finally, attack planes hit strategic targets such as cities, command centers, and industries if their range allowed it. Specific targets were widely varied and included runways, buildings, ships, troops, bridges, fortifications, and tanks. Target variety and diverse attack environments created different carriage specifications for bombs, torpedoes, missiles, guns, and nuclear weapons. Day, night, bad weather, and low- or high-altitude attacks also required design changes and different onboard equipment.

Through World War II, attack planes usually carried two crew members, a pilot and gunner, and they were powered by either one or two engines. Many possessed the structural strength and aerodynamic stability necessary to conduct dive-bombing attacks, which offered greater bombing accuracy. Others carried torpedoes. During both world wars, fighter planes also flew attack missions; and in World War II, several types, such as the U.S. P-47, excelled in this role.

However, the ever-widening performance spectrum often necessitated greater specialization to handle different nations' specific power projection needs. Jet fighters were also adapted to fly attack missions, including defense suppression raids against surface-to-air missile (SAM) and antiaircraft artillery (AAA) sites. Strike planes such as the North Atlantic Treaty Organization's (NATO's) Panavia Tornado emphasized speed and bomb carriage for deep interdiction attacks. Also, they often carried two crew members to handle the increasingly complex array of radars, computers, infrared sights, and guided bombs required for day, night, and all-weather attacks. Other attack planes such as the U.S. A-7 also carried more sophisticated avionics but were single-seat, jet-age dive-bombers. Finally, army air support demands generated propeller and jet planes that flew more slowly, carried special armament, remained airborne longer, or operated from austere surroundings. The United States even modified cargo planes to serve as orbiting attack gunships.

Because bombers carried more weapons and flew farther than attack planes, they delivered a bigger punch at longer distances when flying conventional interdiction missions or strategic raids against targets within an enemy nation. Thus, they usually had at least two crew members and two or more engines. For protection, bomber designers wanted speed, but only if it did not sacrifice the other needs. Because

they were usually slower than fighters, most bombers through World War II carried many defensive guns. The greater aircraft speeds and long-range, air-to-air missiles seen afterward dictated that bombers carry fewer guns, if any at all. Later designs relied upon speed, electronic countermeasures, or "stealth" anti-radar design for protection.

EARLY USES OF MILITARY AIRCRAFT

Although World War I produced basic air combat designs, the airplane's earliest and most obvious military missions were observation and reconnaissance. World War I observation planes carried weapons and usually did not differ from attack or fighter types, though the Germans specially designed their Rumpler planes to fly at high attitudes. World War II air arms modified fighters and fast bombers such as England's Mosquito to carry camera gear and use performance to evade defenders. This practice continued afterward, but the Cold War's explosive improvements in jet fighter and SAM performance forced the creation of special models. The U.S. U-2 and SR-71 were capable of either or both great speed and ultra-high altitude.

Post-World War I military needs and technological innovations created more airplane types to meet force enhancement and support requirements. Although primitive resupply operations occurred in World War I, postwar transport plane advances opened military air supply opportunities. Cargo planes obviously required long-range and load carriage ability to support aerial logistic and army paratroop operations. The subvariants split between those with exceptional capacity and range, such as the U.S. C-5, and smaller, rugged types able to operate from short, unimproved airfields, such as the U.S. C-130. The U.S. Air Force led other air arms in modifying large planes, usually transports, to accomplish various electronic support missions. These included airborne early warning—radar at high altitude allowed greater surveillance coverage—and electronic intelligence-gathering. Later models tracked ground vehicular traffic. Also, the leading national air arms modified transports and other types to fly airborne tanker missions. These tankers had a decisive effect upon airplane endurance and striking distance. Finally, the Vietnam War (1961-1975) and later conflicts witnessed the use of remotely piloted planes, or "drones," for surveillance and decoy purposes.

HELICOPTERS

After their first appearance in World War II, helicopters made great strides. Initially, piston engines' limited thrust restricted helicopter missions to small-scale logistics. Jet-powered helicopters appearing from the 1950's onward enjoyed expanded opportunities. Big cargo helicopters conducted large-scale airmobile troop transfers, and smaller, faster, and more agile attack helicopters flew traditional scouting missions as well as immediate firepower support for either airmobile or antiarmor activities. Attack helicopters' navigation and fire control avionics nearly matched those of jet planes.

AIRCRAFT WEAPONS

From almost their first appearance in battle, aircraft have used these basic weapons types: guns, missiles, and bombs. Although each weapon's fortunes fluctuated throughout the twentieth century, by the century's end, all three remained in active use, meeting specific combat demands served by each weapon's individual strengths.

The machine gun has been an aircraft weapon since World War I, though early airplane designs limited its impact. Most fighters were too small to carry many guns or much ammunition. The thin wings of these aircraft meant that one or two fuselage-mounted, forward-firing guns shot either above the propeller or through it via a synchronization mechanism. Other planes fired guns toward the rear against attackers or, in early rear-engine planes, from the very front. World War II fighters' more substantial wings mounted up to eight machine guns or fewer guns of high 20-millimeter caliber. A few planes carried small cannon for use against hardened targets.

In the 1950's some U.S. fighters lacked guns, because air leaders believed that high aircraft speeds and guided missiles rendered these weapons useless. However, guns reestablished their worth during close-in dogfight combats of various 1960's wars, and later U.S. fighters carried guns. Gun caliber, muzzle velocity, and rate of fire also dramatically improved during this time, reaching its zenith when the Americans introduced the Gatling rotary cannon technology featuring phenome-

Hulton Archive/Getty Images

World War I "ace" Eddie Rickenbacker, standing beside one of the fighter planes he piloted. Fighter action was the best-known action of World War I air combat.

nal firing rates—thousands of rounds per minute. The U.S. A-10 was built around a car-sized, 30-millimeter Gatling gun designed for antiarmor attack missions. The U.S. Air Force's transports-turned-gunships carried small artillery. Helicopters carried guns for both antipersonnel and antiarmor operations.

During World War I, airplanes used rockets to attack observation balloons. World War II featured more widespread rocket use. The Americans and especially the British used rockets against both ships and tanks. German fighters fired rockets against Allied bomber formations. As the war ended, the Germans used radio-controlled missiles against ships and bridges. They were also developing a wire-guided air-to-air missile.

GUIDED MISSILE SYSTEMS

After World War II, air-launched missile performance greatly improved. Guided missiles affected air-to-air combat tactics, especially regarding firing positions against a target. Heat-seeking missiles such as the U.S. Sidewinder tracked strong heat contrast and allowed greater firing distance and less precise aiming than did guns. Early heat-seeking missiles tracked aircraft exhaust, requiring that a fighter pilot maneuver toward an opponent's tail to shoot. Later versions even sensed an airplane's engine section, which allowed all-aspect shots. Radar missiles could also shoot a target from any direction and even from beyond visual range (BVR). However, both early and later radar-guided missiles required the pilot to fly forward, illuminating the target with radar so the missile could hit it. Late-twentieth century radar missiles did not even require this action, but their target identification and launch procedures remained more cumbersome than those of heat-seeking missiles. Thus, in spite of their intimidating air-control potential, BVR shots were often prohibited during combat to prevent accidentally shooting one's own planes. Even so, radar missiles became so effective that the United States developed the F-22 stealth fighter in the 1990's to counter them.

Air-to-ground missile capability also increased in the 1990's. Attack planes and helicopters continued to use rockets either as weapons or as target markers for other aircraft. As for guided air-to-ground missiles, initial designs such as the U.S. Bullpup required that the pilot continually guide the missile toward the target. Indeed, the laser-guided, antitank missiles used by helicopters through the twentieth century's end also required continual laser illumination. However, more lethal air defenses made self-guided missiles ever more attractive. In the 1970's, the United States introduced Maverick tactical missiles that tracked video or infrared image contrast. Additionally, considering radar-guided SAMs and AAA, the United States and other nations built missiles that were guided by radar transmissions.

However, the best air-to-ground guided missiles were long-range, or cruise, missiles. The primary worth of these jet- or rocket-powered weapons was standoff capability: hitting targets while avoiding air defenses. As early as the 1960's, both U.S. and Soviet bombers carried cruise missiles for standoff strategic attacks. In the 1980's efficient engines, along with vastly improved navigation and targeting gear, gave these weapons remarkable speed, range, and accuracy. Navies equipped attack planes with antiship cruise missiles, and these achieved spectacular success in the 1982 Falkland Islands War. In the 1990's, U.S. bombers used cruise missiles in various wars and punitive air strikes. These achieved the desired politico-military impact with little threat to the attackers.

BOMBS

However, bombs were the most common method for achieving the airpower payoff. Although the earliest bombs were grenades and modified shells, from World War I through the twentieth century's end their outward appearance remained essentially the same: that of a cigar-shaped metal cylinder with tail fins. They achieved explosive destruction of ground targets, and even by World War I's end, aircraft carried bombs of more than 1,000 pounds in weight. Additionally, the war introduced bomb variants designed for specific destructive effects. Some achieved basic blast impact, others inflicted fragmentation damage upon people and thinly protected facilities, and still others featured incendiary effects. In World War II, bomb size increased to over 20,000 pounds, and different variations continued. Hardened bombs pierced armor, air-dropped mines blocked shipping lanes, and still others intensified incendiary damage by carrying jellied gasoline (napalm) or phosphorus. Most significant not only for airpower but also for warfare overall were atomic bombs, which achieved cataclysmic destructive effects.

The Cold War witnessed the rise of other bomb types, such as the conventional cluster bomb and the nuclear hydrogen bomb. Cluster bombs used a bomb-shaped shell that opened while airborne and released many smaller bombs designed for either antipersonnel or antiarmor effects. Hydrogen bombs' nuclear fusion achieved unlimited blast and radioactive impact.

The most significant development in bomb technology came with the widespread use, at least by the United States, of precision-guided bombs. These weapons first appeared in World War II, but conventional war demands, particularly in Vietnam, accelerated development of bombs with laser or television seekers, along with controllable fins for steerage. Most required that a crew member guide them to the target. Their most significant impact was a virtual revolution in precision, in which fewer planes were needed to destroy a given target.

DEVELOPMENT

War and technological progress created fluctuations in the fortunes of general aircraft types. In World War I, airships and airplanes both executed war missions, but by World War II, the airship's combat use had faded, as the airplane became the preeminent combat air machine. By the 1960's the helicopter had joined the airplane as part of the modern air arsenal.

At the beginning of the twentieth century military balloons already existed, having been used in previous wars for observation. At this time dirigibles offered the best hope for more aggressive combat airpower projection, because they possessed the controlled mobility that balloons lacked. Indeed, some military observers feared airship attacks in future wars. However, despite the better range and load capacity of airships compared to those of the earliest

airplanes, airships' weaknesses limited enthusiasm for their combat use even among the Germans, who were their strongest proponents.

On October 11, 1911, during the Italo-Turkish War, an Italian pilot flew the first combat mission, using his plane for reconnaissance. Afterward, Italy used airplanes and dirigibles for bombing attacks. The Turks protested but, foreshadowing future aerial arms races, then procured their own aircraft.

World War I effected a swap in the dirigible and airplane's combat fortunes. Early in the war, a few nations used airships for scouting and army attack missions. The latter soon ended due to losses to the armies' guns. In 1915, as other nations ceased airship attacks, German zeppelins flew night raids on England to disrupt morale and military industry. These raids disturbed the British, but they neither induced a morale collapse nor destroyed industrial or military targets. Airships were too inaccurate, too susceptible to adverse winds, and, as England's defenses improved, too vulnerable. Although zeppelin raids continued through 1918, they became ever more sporadic after 1916 as losses mounted.

THE INCREASING ROLE OF AIRPLANES

The airplane replaced the airship in various roles. In early battles at the Marne (1914) and Tannenberg (1914), observation planes' information helped the winning armies make decisive moves. Indeed, the airplane's most visible impact in the war came via spotting activities that made western front army surprise attacks and breakthroughs extremely difficult. Wireless radios were too primitive and insecure to allow easy air-to-ground communication, but spotter crews eventually combined rudimentary radio use with other signaling means to direct artillery fire and report enemy dispositions.

Airplanes offered more flexibility and striking power in naval operations, despite the initial promise of airships as observer craft. British naval planes conducted one of the first offensive counterattacks when they bombed German zeppelin hangars in late 1914. Their sustained attacks cost the Germans more zeppelins and sparked a small-scale air superiority struggle between British and German seaplanes. By 1915 airplanes had helped direct naval gunfire against ships and shore targets. Although planes' small bomb loads and inaccuracy usually prevented their sinking capital ships, a British plane sank a Turkish transport with a torpedo in August, 1915. Later, German bombers also sank ships with torpedoes. By 1918 Allied long-range seaplanes patrolled so well that German submarines used sky-search periscopes.

However, ships' mobility made air-to-ship communications unreliable. Further, seaplanes required that ships stop for launch and recovery. These problems surfaced in the 1916 Battle of Jutland, when scout aircraft for both sides delivered only belated reports. In 1917 the British converted a cruiser, the HMS *Furious*, into an aircraft carrier that launched and recovered airplanes while under way. Carrier-based fighters better enabled the Royal Navy to defeat German seaplanes and zeppelins.

Airplanes also surpassed zeppelins in attack and strategic bombing, though bomb load limitations and poor accuracy also hindered their effect. By 1915 all western front air arms had attempted interdiction missions. The aggressive flying policy England's Royal Flying Corps commander General Hugh Trenchard (1873-1956) included striking airfields and supply lines. However, its impact was reduced by dispersed attacks, limited destructive capacity, inaccuracy, and German repair efforts. Trenchard's close air support missions involving trench attacks achieved some morale effect, but these uncoordinated raids by fighters and attack planes suffered high losses and forever soured the British on the mission. The British achieved better army air support results in the Middle East against the Turks than on the western front, thanks to arid terrain and dispersed ground forces. These conditions better allowed British planes to disrupt enemy ground efforts, and in September, 1918, they trapped and

destroyed two Turkish divisions in a narrow pass. In the Germans' 1918 western front offensive, dedicated air support units in purpose-built Halberstadt attack planes flew concentrated strikes against Allied troops at or near the front. They enjoyed better success than that seen in previous British efforts, though British planes materially assisted their army's counterattack via interdiction and attacks upon antitank defenses.

Early in the war, the Russians and Italians produced large bombers for long-range attacks, but they lacked the resources to sustain deep bombing operations. In 1917 the Germans fielded huge multi-engine planes that continued the attack that zeppelins had started against England. Like airships, they were inaccurate and failed to cause significant damage. Although British defenses soon forced them to attack

TURNING POINTS

Oct. 11, 1911	After an Italian pilot flies the first combat mission, using his plane for reconnaissance, during the Italo-Turkish War, Italy begins using airplanes and dirigibles for bombing attacks.
May 10, 1940	The German Luftwaffe conducts the first combat parachute and glider troop landings to open Germany's western front attack.
Nov. 10, 1940	The British Royal Navy produces a decisive aerial victory at Taranto Harbor, Italy, crippling the anchored Italian fleet with nighttime bomb and torpedo attacks.
Dec. 7, 1941	The Japanese navy launches a morning surprise air raid against the U.S. fleet at Pearl Harbor, Hawaii, sinking or damaging several U.S. battleships and affirming airpower's military importance.
Aug. 6, 1945	In the first nuclear air strike, an American B-29 bomber drops an atomic bomb on Hiroshima, Japan, hastening Japan's surrender and the end of World War II.
June 5, 1967	The Israeli Air Force (IAF) launches devastating surprise counter-air raids against threatening Arab nations.
Oct. 6, 1973	The IAF suffers heavy losses against densely packed Arab missiles in the first day of the Arab-Israeli October War.
Jan. 17, 1991	A U.S.-led U.N. coalition leads a well-orchestrated air attack against Iraqi dictator Saddam Hussein in an effort to oust his forces from Kuwait.

only at night, German planes still mounted a bombing campaign that caused public outcry and forced the British to divert fighters from the front.

THE EVOLUTION OF THE FIGHTER PLANE

The fighter plane was created to stop the enemy from flying these emerging missions, as well as to protect friendly missions from enemy fighters. Fighter designs evolved especially quickly, in part because of their fiercely competitive purpose. Initially, rear-engine "pusher" planes with forward-mounted guns represented the fighter ideal. However, the appearance of Germany's Fokker E-III's in the summer of 1915 heralded the first major fighter technology advance. The E-III synchronized machine-gun fire through its front-mounted propeller and, flown by a great aerial tactician such as the German ace Oswald Boelcke (1891-1916), it became an aerial scourge. Escalations in technology encouraged disciplined formation flying for protection. Improved Allied fighters such as France's Nieuport countered the E-III, until Germany introduced the Albatross series in 1917. This development and massed German fighter sweeps inflicted high air losses. The Allies permanently regained the technological and numerical edge later that year with such planes as England's Sopwith Camel and France's SPAD.

Fighter action was the best-known aspect of World War I air combat. The top pilots received national adulation, and those who downed at least five planes (actually, the number varied by country) were dubbed "aces." Fighters helped end the zeppelin threat and forced attack and bomber planes to fly at night or in formations escorted by their own fighters. Boelcke's air fighting principles remained valid through the century's end.

The war established more than fighter aces. Naval air war, attack, and strategic bombing concepts emerged. Germany's bombing of England stirred a public uproar and spurred the creation of the Royal Air Force (RAF) in 1918. Although airplanes were relatively primitive, good production required dedicated organization and advanced industrial capacity. Russia and Italy's internal problems stifled bombing's promise. The United States lacked the time to produce competitive designs. Industrial strength and

desperate wartime struggle made the western front combatants air warfare leaders. The Allies partially owed their final air superiority to their two-to-one airplane production lead over the Germans. Finally, air fighting required skill, and at times the British and Germans experienced training difficulties that incurred even higher losses.

EARLY AIRPOWER ADVOCATES

World War I inspired postwar airpower advocacy in certain countries. Its bloody ground stalemate appalled Italian air officer Giulio Douhet (1869-1930), who believed that airplanes could surmount traditional obstacles and break this condition. Douhet asserted that bombers could use poison gas bombs, if necessary, to strike an enemy nation and induce an internal collapse similar to Germany's downfall in 1918. Although Douhet overestimated the bomber's destructive power and underestimated air defenses and national will, he affected thinking in other areas through his writings.

Royal Air Force commander Hugh Trenchard did not publish his ideas as Douhet did, but his policies reflected similar thinking. Trenchard wanted bombers that could strike any nation that attacked Britain, and he also aimed to justify his newly independent service's existence. Ironically, it already had done so as it executed the government's postwar desire to police its colonies by air.

U.S. Army Air Service general William "Billy" Mitchell (1879-1936) reacted not only to trench slaughter but also to drastic postwar budget cuts. His unsuccessful but outspoken advocacy of a separate air force including naval and land-based air units stemmed from his opinion that only experienced aviators understood airpower. Influenced somewhat by Douhet, he also believed that bombers could induce a national collapse.

All these men experienced varying degrees of controversy expressing themselves, because even the victorious nations' military budgets stifled rapid air development. Many advances came from civilian sources. Germany developed a metal attack monoplane at war's end, but airline companies and other civilian organizations produced innovations that increased speed and bad weather capability: retractable landing gear, pressurized cockpits, voice radio, and instrument navigation. In 1931 the Boeing B-9 introduced variable-pitch propellers, which helped acceleration and climb. In 1932 the Martin B-10 featured enclosed cockpits and improved bomb capacity. The 1920's Schneider and Thompson Trophy air race winners were streamlined monoplanes that influenced later fighter designs, such as England's Spitfire.

The military contributed to aviation developments where possible, especially after the leading nations rearmed in the late 1930's. Military pilots set distance and altitude records using boosted engines, another innovation. Americans improved high-altitude bombing accuracy with the Norden sight. The Soviet Union introduced paratroop operations.

Despite relatively slow advancement, aircraft improvements between the two world wars were significant. World War I's fabric biplane fighters with 250-horsepower engines flying at 100 knots changed to metal monoplanes with 1,000-horsepower engines and 300-knot speeds. New monoplane bombers were smaller but faster and carried more bombs. Modified airliners such as the U.S. C-47 transformed logistical considerations.

Army Times Publishing Co.

A P-47 fighter plane, which during World War II also excelled as an attack plane, making bombing runs.

AIRPOWER IN WORLD WAR II

At the beginning of World War II, the most advanced and determined nations again had the best air arms, though technological complexity and organizational demands vexed some of them. The now independent German Air Force (Luftwaffe) appeared to be the strongest, with standout planes such as the Messerschmitt-109 fighter and the Junkers-87 dive-bomber. However, bombsight and aircraft developmental problems combined with leadership changes to stifle the production of heavy bombers, producing a more tactical orientation. Bombers such as the Heinkel-111 seemed adequate for strategic bombing against European targets, but Luftwaffe leaders ruined other bomber designs by demanding dive-bomb capability for even big planes. The Luftwaffe's Spanish Civil War (1936-1939) experience apparently supported its air policy choices.

Motivated by American bomber technology advances, the U.S. Army Air Corps—later renamed the Army Air Force, anticipating its future independent status—emphasized strategic bombing. The British upgraded their fighter defenses in response to heavy bomber development problems, the rising German air threat, and their own radar advances. Rapid industrialization formed the foundation for a large Soviet air force, which produced some promising designs, but the 1930's purges of Joseph Stalin (1879-1953) hindered development. France and Italy lagged behind because of incoherent national defense policy and lack of resources.

Aircraft carriers demanded even more resources and intent, and only three powers used them: the United States, Japan, and England. Under Admiral William Moffett's (1869-1933) leadership, American naval air resisted Billy Mitchell's threats to its own status and, exploiting arms treaty conditions, built new aircraft carriers. Admiral Joseph Mason Reeves (1872-1948) led tactical innovations that gave the carrier force an aggressive fighting style. Japan developed a similar carrier doctrine, and both navies fielded planes that delivered a knockout blow or defeated air threats, such as the U.S. Dauntless dive-bomber and Japan's Zero fighter. England's navy anticipated facing many European land-based planes and built smaller, more rugged carriers. Small carrier size and the RAF's control and neglect of naval aircraft development meant that British carriers lacked the aerial punch of other navies' carriers.

World War II began with Germany's 1939 Poland invasion and 1940 Western Europe offensives. The Luftwaffe was an important part of what became known as Blitzkrieg warfare. It simultaneously stifled enemy air defense and attacked any direct or resupply effort impeding rapid tank advances. On May 10, 1940, it conducted the first combat parachute and glider troop landings to open Germany's western front attack.

The Luftwaffe embarked upon more independent action in the summer, 1940, Battle of Britain, the first air-dominated major battle in history. The Germans' pre-invasion daylight air campaign failed for many reasons. Their leaders established an unrealistic campaign timetable, their attacks did not destroy the radar sites that gave British fighters a decisive edge, and they ceased attacking airfields just when these missions began hurting the RAF. Downed German fliers fighting over the RAF's homeland could not fly again as could their British opponents. Meanwhile, British industry recouped fighter losses. On September 15, 1940, the Germans suffered a mauling that convinced them of their campaign's failure.

Germany's bombers also had insufficient defensive armament, and its fighters lacked sufficient range to escort them. However, these deficiencies also existed in other air forces. The British had earlier encountered similar problems when they lost many bombers during unescorted daylight raids. After the Battle of Britain, both sides reverted to nighttime bombing and daylight fighter sweeps. Bombing accuracy was atrocious, and both sides justified the raids as a way to destroy industrial workers' morale, if not the workers themselves.

The European air war assumed an electronic character. German bombers used intersecting radio beams as an approximate bomb-release point, and the British tried to jam the beams. Both sides' search radars guided radar-equipped night fighters against enemy bombers. Later, bombers dropped foil strips to muddle radar returns.

Given the western front aerial deadlock, the Royal Navy produced a decisive aerial victory at Taranto Harbor, Italy, on November 10, 1940. Carrier-based Swordfish biplanes crippled the anchored Italian fleet through nighttime bomb and torpedo attacks. Apart from eliminating a Mediterranean naval threat, the Taranto raid impressed Japanese naval leaders, whose carriers launched a morning surprise air raid against the U.S. fleet at Pearl Harbor, Hawaii, on December 7, 1941. The Japanese sank or damaged several U.S. battleships, indelibly affirming airpower's military importance.

The U.S. entry into World War II introduced a combatant with unlimited resources, organizational prowess, and aroused willpower. The Soviets, already at war, also mass-produced warplanes, but they concentrated upon designs, such as the Shturmovik attack plane, that provided army air support. The United States, however, produced abundant outstanding planes for all missions.

U.S. airpower first established itself in two decisive Pacific theater naval victories. The spring, 1942, Battles of Coral Sea and Midway featured no surface engagements, as carrier planes decided the outcome. Both sides launched massed raids to sink the enemy's carriers and eliminate the primary naval threat. Vast distances and ships' mobility still made reconnaissance and communications difficult. Thus, carrier battle victory could be terrifyingly random.

Pacific air fighting up through the Solomon Islands campaign (1942-1944) ensured further U.S. success through attrition of Japanese warships and, most important, experienced Japanese pilots. Japan's pilot training setup failed to produce the abundant replacements that the Americans enjoyed. In the Atlantic, the U.S. Navy increasingly used aircraft carriers and long-range patrol planes to avert the German U-boat threat.

North African fighting against the Germans in 1943 helped U.S. Army Air Force leaders establish doctrinal and command setups that endured through the century's end. A single air leader controlling all of a war theater's air assets would ensure unity of air command and a coherent air campaign, which followed the tactical mission priority of air superiority, interdiction, and then close air support.

From 1942 onward, the Army Air Force pursued a bigger goal with its daylight strategic bombing campaign against Germany. Its leaders believed that their B-17 and B-24 bombers possessed ample defensive armament and bombing accuracy to withstand defenses and win the war by inducing Germany's internal collapse. In the meantime, England would continue night attacks with its new heavy bombers.

The Americans dismissed earlier British and German day bombing failures as irrelevant, but by autumn, 1943, their campaign staggered under heavy losses and targeting decisions that sometimes negated intended effects. The installation of drop tanks on the superb U.S. P-47 and P-51 fighters saved the campaign. This adjustment allowed long-range escort, which reduced losses and decimated German fighter forces. The latter effect helped guarantee air superiority for the 1944 Normandy landings. It also enabled paratroop assaults and ample air support for the Allied armies' sweep across Europe.

The Pacific war's concluding years witnessed complete U.S. air superiority, backed by such outstanding naval fighters as the Hellcat and the Corsair. The Japanese carrier threat disappeared, and amphibious assaults enjoyed lavish air support. The Japanese introduced one late-war air menace when they launched a morbid form of guided weapon, land-based kamikaze suicide missions, against American ships. On August 6, 1945, in the first nuclear air strike, an American B-29 bomber dropped an atomic bomb on Hiroshima, Japan. Another bomb hit Nagasaki three days later. These raids hastened Japan's surrender.

The atomic bombs' effect upon Japan's surrender did not completely vindicate visionaries such as Billy Mitchell. Although the bombs ended the war's fighting sooner, they also struck a nation reeling from other military disasters. Debate over their necessity and impact continued through the century's end and involved issues beyond airpower's capabilities.

The European strategic bombing campaign failed to win the war single-handedly, as its proponents had hoped. However, more concentrated attacks in the war's final year demolished Germany's oil production and transportation facilities. Bombing crippled Germany's war effort through overall damage, reduced worker output, and massive defense and industry diversions. It also facilitated the accomplishment of other air missions.

LESSONS OF WORLD WAR II

Western European air warfare involved the most advanced air combatants, but its conduct and lessons were not universally applicable. In some theaters, strategic bombing was not relevant and air arms did not follow tactical priorities that the U.S. Army Air Force confirmed while fighting the Germans. The Russian front was so vast, and Soviet resources were so abundant, that a strategic bombing campaign was neither possible nor desirable for either side. This situation existed in the Pacific war's early years, when

Hulton Archive/Getty Images

A "Fat Man" atomic bomb. The first such bombs, "Fat Man" and "Little Boy," were dropped from B-29 bombers on the Japanese cities of Hiroshima and Nagasaki, effectively ending World War II.

Japan was too distant for sustained bombing. In both theaters, tactical campaigns featuring tank battles, carrier battles, or amphibious landings were themselves decisive, and required that attack planes execute their missions even as fighters struggled for air superiority. In some amphibious landings, no air threat and no rear area existed to justify fighters or an interdiction campaign, but air support missions were very important.

Other results echoed World War I's lessons. As it evolved, airpower demanded tremendous resources, and the American war effort understandably overwhelmed its opponents. Under great pressure, given their many well-armed opponents, the Germans and Japanese made critical airplane procurement and pilot training errors that helped them to lose the air war. Indeed, insufficient resources and incoherent application hampered Germany's introduction of Messerschmitt-262 jet fighters at war's end. The Soviet air force suffered frightful losses but possessed ample resources and people with which to overcome them.

Above all, airpower demonstrated its decisive impact upon modern war. Strategic bombing accelerated national defeat. Airplanes were integral to the Blitzkrieg-style armored offensives that many armies came to favor. For example, Army Air Force planes literally provided flank security as U.S. armies raced across France. The aircraft carrier replaced the battleship as the most important naval unit. Transports enabled paratroop assaults and long-range supply.

POST-WORLD WAR II AIRPOWER

The atomic bomb and jet technology seemed to guarantee airpower's combat primacy in the postwar years, but troubling times lay ahead. Nuclear-armed bombers gave any nation possessing them a compelling military trump card, and superpower nuclear parity helped prevent a third world war through deterrence. Indeed, throughout the 1950's, the newly independent U.S. Air Force's Strategic Air Command, with its B-52 bombers and KC-135 tankers, received most of the U.S. defense budget. However, nuclear weapons were otherwise militarily ineffective, because their actual use was unthinkable.

Further, airpower's expense skyrocketed with aviation technology progress, as only the superpowers could afford a full air arsenal and associated training and support costs. Jet-powered bombers were extremely expensive, and by century's end, one American B-2 stealth bomber cost nearly one billion dollars. Air combat's evolution bred even more diverse types, which incurred great expense in electronic gear if not aircraft design: drones, early warning planes, special reconnaissance planes, and tankers. Cold War rivalry sustained a swift evolution cycle of aircraft design, as six fighter generations created more expense via increasingly exotic engines, airframes, and weapons. The

Army Times Publishing Co.

Two F-4 Phantom IIs, often employed as multipurpose fighter-bombers, in flight over a coastline.

late 1940's saw straight-wing jets. The early 1950's saw transonic swept-wing planes such as the U.S. F-86 and Soviet MiG-15 used in the Korean War (1950-1953); the mid-1950's, afterburner-engine supersonic planes such as the U.S. F-100; and the late-1950's, Mach-2 radar-equipped fighters, such as the U.S. F-4, the Soviet MiG-21, and France's Mirage series, all of which fought in many wars. In the 1970's superfighters such as the U.S. F-14 and F-15 combined speed, maneuverability, and sophisticated fire control. By century's end stealth fighters had been developed.

Expense incurred great procurement risk and occasional embarrassing failures, as England's TSR2 attack plane and U.S. F-111 multipurpose fighter programs revealed. Unexpected threat advances and high program costs sometimes sparked controversy, as when U.S. leaders canceled the B-70 and debated procuring the B-1. The widening airpower performance and task spectrum forced hard choices about aircraft design strengths. Fighter-bombers such as the U.S. F-105 lacked maneuverability for dogfighting as well as endurance and bomb carriage for close air support. Their cost and training demands also discouraged their use in diverse missions. Thus, air arms had to tailor designs for certain fighting styles and situations. The Soviet Union mass-produced relatively simple fighters capable of quick attacks and escapes. The United States fielded many attack planes, such as the A-4 and the A-10, for tactical support. The British and U.S. Marines chose the AV-8 Harrier attack plane because its vertical takeoff-and-land performance promised deployment flexibility.

Above all, post-World War II combat revealed that a remarkably wide spectrum of conventional war situations remained possible, driving combat plane design variations. In the Korean War U.S. jet fighters outfought Soviet MiGs to maintain air superiority. Attack planes thus became critical factors in stopping two communist offensives and maintaining the lines until the 1953 cease-fire. The U.S. A-1 and other propeller-driven attack planes remained useful, given that they were more maneuverable, carried more weapons, or flew longer than the available jets. U.S. air arms ignored Korea's results and emphasized nuclear warfare training through the 1950's.

U.S. AIRPOWER IN THE VIETNAM WAR

However, similar conditions arose in the U.S. war in Vietnam. U.S. airpower was omnipresent, providing on-call fire support, transportation, and surveillance. Indeed, it significantly supported the defeat of the Communists' 1968 Tet Offensive and was primarily responsible for thwarting North Vietnam's 1972 offensive.

However, Vietnam warfare exposed problems in U.S. air strategy. U.S. planes could not completely disrupt North Vietnam's war effort due to jungle concealment, political restrictions, and the Communists' determination despite severe air-inflicted losses. Oriented toward bomber interception and nuclear strikes, U.S. fighters and attack planes and their crews performed less well than expected against North Vietnam's Soviet-supplied fighters and SAMs. Indeed, these defenses forced the Americans to use special radar jamming and attack planes.

Vietnam's ground war and relatively light air defenses brought forth special attack planes, some of which defied air progress notions. The AC-130 transport-turned-gunship and maneuverable, Korean War-vintage A-1 were two examples. Their weapons capacity and endurance made them excellent close air support machines.

Helicopters confirmed their worth during the ground war in Vietnam. They had first been used by the United States in 1944 for light logistics duties in Burma, and they performed similarly in subsequent small wars. Before Vietnam, U.S. Army generals and other officers developed helicopter organizational setups that, combined with the capabilities of jet-powered helicopters such as UH-1 transports and AH-1 gunships, gave unprecedented mobility and immediate firepower to Army troops in South Vietnam. Despite their utility, however, helicopters remained vulnerable to ground fire, as the Soviet Union's helicopter misfortunes in its Soviet-Afghan War (1979-1989) also revealed.

Across the world, airpower proved more decisive when the Israeli Air Force's (IAF) June 5, 1967, surprise counter-air raids crippled the Arab nations threatening Israel. After destroying their opponents' air forces, Israeli jets spent the rest of the Six-Day War pummelling Arab army units, who could not hide in the desert. Despite its outstanding reputation, even the IAF suffered heavy losses against densely packed Arab SAMs and AAA in the Israeli-Arab October War's first day, October 6, 1973.

The Israelis recovered and did well in that and later conflicts, but airpower difficulties in the Vietnam and October Wars sparked technological and tactical innovation. Stealth technology and standoff precision weapons promised better fortunes against SAMs. Western air arms conducted more realistic training, such as the U.S. Air Force's Red Flag exercises.

AIRPOWER IN THE 1990's

Refinements allowed U.S. airpower to rebound in wars of the 1990's. The Cold War's end removed Soviet sponsorship from other American enemies. These nations' leaders lacked military expertise and valued their internal power more than military victory.

Throughout late 1990, Iraqi dictator Saddam Hussein let a U.S.-led U.N. coalition mass against him in their effort to oust his forces from Kuwait. On January 17, 1991, these forces opened the Gulf War (1990-1991) with a well-orchestrated air attack that quickly immobilized the Iraqis. Surveillance planes reported all Iraqi ground and air movements. Fighter and defense suppression missions, including surveillance and decoy drones, stifled air defenses. Attack planes battered army positions. Stealth planes attacked deep interdiction targets, such as command and communications centers, with no losses. Precision-guided weapons destroyed targets with minimum risk and attack-force size. After several weeks of aerial bombardment, U.N. ground forces liberated Kuwait with limited Iraqi opposition.

In spring, 1999, U.S.-led NATO air forces compelled Serbian dictator Slobodan Milošević to remove troops from Kosovo province. Overwhelming U.S. air strength, including B-2's, cowed Serb air defenses and delivered accurate deep strikes with precision weapons. Losses were minimal.

Although air-only threats and actions had been made in the past, the Kosovo war was the first conflict in which airpower alone forced a nation to withdraw its troops from a contested area. Milošević's internal concerns and a threatened ground invasion apparently also influenced his decision. Kosovo proved that in warfare's wide situational spectrum, cases exist where airpower alone can win wars.

Each war determines the types of weapons that will best serve one's ends, and most late-twentieth century combat conditions did not favor strategic airpower as much as Kosovo's did. U.S. political limitations in the 1993 Somalia skirmishes inhibited airpower's full play. Different situations allowed more tactical airpower units, such as aircraft carriers, significant influence. In conflicts where conditions prevented nearby basing, such as the Falkland Islands War, the 1983 invasion of Grenada, the 1988 U.S.-Iran naval fights, and 1999 Desert Fox punitive raids against Iraq, carrier-based airplanes provided most if not all of the airpower's punch.

AP/Wide World Photos

An F-22 Raptor, developed in the 1990's and called the most sophisticated fighter plane ever, flies over California.

A B-2 Spirit bomber over the Pacific in 2006.

Increasing air weapon expense meant that nearly all nations could not address all of the air warfare scenarios seen after World War II, or even the ones they would most likely encounter. The combatants in the Israel-Arab Wars, the Iran-Iraq War (1980-1988), and the Indo-Pakistani Wars were all limited by their lack of airpower resources. By century's end, economic constraints forced even the United States to review how much of the widening airpower spectrum—stealth fighters, close air support planes, attack helicopters, advanced drones, surveillance planes—it could afford.

BOOKS AND ARTICLES

Boyne, Walter J., ed. *Air Warfare: An International Encyclopedia.* Santa Barbara, Calif.: ABC-CLIO, 2002.

Boyne, Walter J., and Philip Handleman, eds. *Brassey's Air Combat Reader.* Washington, D.C.: Brassey's, 1999.

Buckley, John. *Air Power in the Age of Total War.* Bloomington: Indiana University Press, 1999.

Cooling, Benjamin, ed. *Case Studies in the Achievement of Air Superiority.* Washington, D.C.: Air Force History and Museums Program, 1994.

_____. *Case Studies in the Development of Close Air Support.* Washington, D.C.: Air Force History and Museums Program, 1990.

Cox, Sebastian, and Peter Gray, eds. *Air Power History: Turning Points from Kitty Hawk to Kosovo*. Portland, Oreg.: Frank Cass, 2002.

Everett-Heath, John. *Helicopters in Combat*. Poole, England: Arms and Armour, 1992.

Gates, David. *Sky Wars: A History of Military Aerospace Power*. London: Reaktion, 2003.

Hall, R. Cargill, ed. *Case Studies in Strategic Bombardment*. Washington, D.C.: Air Force History and Museums Program, 1998.

Higham, Robin. *Air Power*. New York: St. Martin's Press, 1972.

Hone, Thomas, Norman Friedman, and Mark Mandeles. *British and American Aircraft Carrier Development*. Annapolis, Md.: Naval Institute Press, 1999.

Meilinger, Phillip, ed. *The Paths of Heaven*. Maxwell Air Force Base, Ala.: Air University Press, 1997.

Musciano, Walter. *Warbirds of the Sea*. Altglen, Pa.: Schiffer, 1994.

Nordeen, Lon O. *Air Warfare in the Missile Age*. 2d ed. Washington, D.C.: Smithsonian Institution Press, 2002.

Olsen, John Andreas, ed. *A History of Air Warfare*. Dulles, Va.: Potomac Books, 2009.

Spick, Mike, ed. *The Great Book of Modern Warplanes: Featuring Full Technical Descriptions and Battle Action from Baghdad to Belgrade*. Osceola, Wis.: MBI, 2000.

Stephens, Alan, ed. *The War in the Air, 1914-1994*. American ed. Maxwell Air Force Base, Ala.: Air University Press, 2001.

Yanushevsky, Rafael. *Modern Missile Guidance*. Boca Raton, Fla.: CRC Press, 2008.

FILMS AND OTHER MEDIA

Black Hawk Down. Feature film. Columbia, 2001.

Bombs, Rockets, and Missiles. Documentary. History Channel, 1997.

Dr. Strangelove: Or, How I Learned to Stop Worrying and Love the Bomb. Feature film. Columbia, 1964.

Enola Gay and the Bombing of Japan. Documentary. Brookside Media, 1995.

Fail Safe. Feature film. Columbia Pictures, 1964.

Memphis Belle. Feature film. Enigma, 1990.

Smart Bombs. Documentary. History Channel, 1998.

Douglas Campbell

ROCKETS, MISSILES, AND NUCLEAR WEAPONS

Dates: Since c. 1200

NATURE AND USE OF ROCKETS AND MISSILES

Although the terms "rocket" and "missile" are sometimes used interchangeably, when speaking of weapons the term "rocket" generally refers either to the means of propulsion or to a relatively small rocket projectile, and the term "missile" usually refers to a more complex weapon. A ballistic missile follows a ballistic trajectory—the path a thrown rock would take—for most of its flight and is guided only during or shortly after launch.

At its most basic, a rocket motor is simply a chamber with a nozzle at the rear. Fuel is burned in the chamber to produce hot, pressurized gases that then are exhausted through the nozzle. In accordance with Isaac Newton's third law of motion, which states that for every action there is an equal and opposite reaction, the rocket is pushed forward by expelling these exhaust gases backward out of the nozzle. The rocket is not pushed forward by the exhaust gases pushing against the air behind the rocket, as is sometimes supposed. In fact, because a rocket carries its fuel along with an oxidizer to burn it, a rocket does not need air and can operate in the vacuum of space.

Although it is not known exactly when the first rocket was invented, its origins likely lie with the fire-arrow, a tube filled with burning powder attached to an arrow. Gases escaping from the tube helped propel the arrow, and sparks from the burning powder conveniently started fires. Thirteenth century Mongol leader Genghis Khan (r. 1206-1227) used fire-arrows in battle, and in 1429, French troops under Joan of Arc (c. 1412-1431) used rockets in the defense of Orléans. Improvements led eventually to the war rockets of Tipu, Sultan of Mysore in the south

of India (r. 1782-1799), who used them in 1792 to terrorize British soldiers.

Colonel William Congreve (1772-1828) at London's Woolrich Arsenal was assigned to study Tipu's rockets and to develop a rocket for the British artillery that could be made in large numbers. The product of his research, the Congreve rocket, had a range of 2.7 kilometers and consisted of an iron case filled with black powder. The case was attached to a long stabilizing stick, and air drag on the stick kept the rocket pointed forward. A chamber on the front of the rocket held either an incendiary or an explosive that was ignited by a fuse.

Congreve considered rockets to be ideal weapons for ships, because there is no recoil, as there is with cannons. In 1806, during the Napoleonic Wars, the British navy fired two thousand Congreve rockets at the French in Boulogne, setting several buildings ablaze. In 1807 thirty thousand rockets were fired into Copenhagen and set much of that city on fire. Inspired by the barrage of Congreve rockets fired by the British against Fort McHenry during the War of 1812, Francis Scott Key wrote his poem "The Star-Spangled Banner," which became the U.S. national anthem.

Later, William Hale of Britain dispensed with the clumsy guide stick and spin-stabilized the rocket by placing three slanted metal vanes in the rocket's exhaust. The Hale rocket was used by the United States during the Mexican War. However, as artillery evolved in accuracy, rockets were employed less frequently, except for special uses, such as carrying lightweight lines from rescuers to stranded ships.

Rockets and missiles can be divided roughly into three groups, depending upon their ranges. Battlefield weapons are used in a local area, with the combatants often within sight of each other. Theater mis-

A U.S. Air Force TM-76 B Mace tactical range ballistic missile in a 1961 test launch at Cape Canaveral.

siles have ranges of 160 to 3,200 kilometers, whereas intercontinental missiles have longer ranges. Both theater weapons (except low-flying cruise missiles) and intercontinental missiles rise through the atmosphere and coast through space before reentering the atmosphere to strike their targets.

DEVELOPMENT OF ROCKETS AND MISSILES

After military interest in rocketry declined, progress depended upon the efforts of a few indefatigable individuals, such as American physics professor

Robert H. Goddard (1882-1945), who took a practical engineering approach. Goddard began by experimenting with solid-fuel rockets and developed a portable rocket, the forerunner of the bazooka, for the military. He became the world pioneer in the development of liquid-fuel rockets, but his work was eventually surpassed by that of Wernher von Braun (1912-1977) and his associates, who were working for the German military.

WORLD WAR II
With Germany leading the way, World War II saw the reemergence of the rocket as a useful weapon. The post-World War I Treaty of Versailles (1919)

had limited the number of artillery pieces Germany could possess but had not mentioned rockets. Germany exploited this loophole and began rocket research and development in earnest during the 1930's. Battlefield rockets were used by several nations during World War II, but only Germany used theater weapons: the V-1 and V-2. Germany also had begun design work on an intercontinental missile before the end of the war.

World War II battlefield rockets included barrage rockets, antitank rockets, and rockets fired from aircraft. Although barrage rockets were not extremely accurate, they could be fired by the hundreds to saturate an area. The German Nebelwerfer, or "fog thrower," began as a weapon used to lay down a smoke screen but was adapted to fire barrage rockets. The Nebelwerfer, a towed 6-tube launcher, was nicknamed Moaning Minnie by the Allies because of the eerie sound made by its incoming rockets. Its range was up to 6,000 meters. U.S. barrage rockets could be fired from the Calliope, a 60-tube launcher mounted on the turret of a Sherman tank. When fired in massive numbers, the rockets were ripple-fired, or fired in rapid succession, to minimize one rocket destroying another in the air. The Soviets launched Katyusha rockets from the Stalin Organ, a launcher with 16 to 48 tubes mounted on a gun carriage. The British navy equipped some landing craft with Mattress Projectors, which could fire about 1,000 rockets in 45 seconds. Two such craft could deliver 27,000 kilograms (60,000 pounds) of explosives in less than a minute. The rockets had a range of 3 to 6 kilometers and were used for heavy coastal bombardments prior to landings.

U.S. troops took the Germans by surprise in North Africa with the introduction of the bazooka, a rocket-powered grenade. The rocket, launched from a shoulder-held tube, could disable a moving tank up to 200 meters away and knock out stationary targets up to 700 meters away. The Germans soon answered with antitank rockets of their own: the *Panzerfaust* and the *Panzerschreck*.

Germany worked on several air-launched missiles, but the most successful were the radio-controlled glide bombs Henschel HS 293 and the Fritz-X, also known as the Ruhrstahl SD-1400. When launched, a flare mounted on the missile's tail ignited, and the bombardier watched the flare while using radio-controlled flaps and spoilers to guide the missile to its target. Glide bombs were quite successful when they were first deployed in the summer of 1943. The rocket-powered HS 293 was used against convoy escort ships. The armor-piercing Fritz-X sank or disabled a number of warships, including battleships and cruisers. These missiles would have been even more successful, but they were subject to radio jamming. The controlling aircraft also were vulnerable, and, after the Allies gained air superiority, German bombers could no longer get close enough to their targets to use these missiles.

Russian aircraft successfully used unguided salvos of RS-82, and later, RS-132, rockets against ground troops and armor. British aircraft used their "60-pounder" to decimate German tanks. The 60-pounder was named for the weight of its high-explosive warhead. General-purpose rockets, such as the U.S. 4.5-inch (114-millimeter) HE M8 rocket, were used against vehicle convoys, tanks, trains, fuel and ammunition depots, airfields, and barges. In mid-1944, the M8 was upgraded to the 5-inch (127-millimeter) High Velocity Air Rocket (HVAR), also known as the Holy Moses because of its impressive destructive effect.

THE V-1

The Allies had no counterpart to the German theater missiles, the V-1 and V-2. The V-1 was a cruise missile with a maximum range of about 260 kilometers and a top speed of 645 kilometers per hour. Launched from the Pas de Calais area of France, it could reach London in twenty-two minutes. It carried 850 kilograms of high explosives and could have carried nerve gas, but German leader Adolf Hitler was under the mistaken impression that the Allies also had nerve gas and would have used it. Hitler launched the V-1's in retaliation for the Allied bombing of Germany, hence the name *Vergeltungswaffen Einz*, meaning Retaliation Weapon One. This translation quickly evolved to the pithier Vengeance Weapon One, or V-1.

The V-1's motor was a surprisingly simple pulse jet: a long stovepipe with shutter strips across the air intake at the front end. Air mixed with fuel was exploded by a spark plug. The explosion closed the shutter strips, forcing the exhaust gases out the back end. Incoming air opened the strips, and the process repeated forty-two times a minute, making a characteristic low rumble or buzzing sound that inspired the name "buzz-bomb." The motor only worked at high speeds, so the V-1 was flung into the air at 400 kilometers per hour (250 miles per hour) from a 48-meter-long ramp equipped with a steam catapult.

Beginning in June, 1944, more than 8,000 V-1's were fired at London. Many failed, many were shot down, but about 2,400 arrived. When a timing mechanism indicated that the missile was over its target, the flight control surfaces put the missile into a dive that normally extinguished the engine. Londoners learned to dread hearing the buzzing stop. Over six thousand people were killed and another forty thousand were wounded by V-1's. The bombs destroyed 130,000 British homes and damaged an additional 750,000. The Germans sent 9,000 V-1's against various cities in Europe, including 5,000 against the Belgian port city, Antwerp.

THE V-2

V-2's were about twenty times as expensive to build as V-1's, but both weapons carried enough explosives to destroy a large building. V-1's were developed by the German air force, whereas V-2's were developed by Wernher von Braun and his associates for the German army. Both weapons were manufactured by forced laborers working under deplorable conditions. The V-2 burned liquid oxygen and ethyl alcohol mixed with water, and it weighed about 12,300 kilograms at launch. Although powered flight lasted only seventy seconds, by then the rocket's speed was nearly five times the speed of sound. It had a 320-kilometer range and could reach England in about five minutes. Because it traveled so quickly, there was no defense against it. Furthermore, the V-2's mobile launch facilities were difficult to find and destroy.

More than 1,100 V-2's fell in southern England beginning in September, 1944, killing about 2,700 people and injuring over twice that number. About half of these V-2's hit London. Between December,

1944, and the end of March, 1945, when all V-2 operations ceased, about 2,100 V-2's were fired at Antwerp. Seventeen percent of these exploded on the launch pad, 18 percent failed in the air, but 65 percent reached Antwerp, often striking within several hundred meters of their targets. A total of 7,000 people were killed by V-2's. The V-1 killed about two people per launch, and the V-2 killed about five people per launch. Had either weapon been used in sufficient numbers two or three years earlier, the course of the war might have been different. Although neither weapon ultimately had much effect on the war, the development of the V-2 led directly to the missiles and spaceships that followed it.

DEVELOPMENT OF MODERN BATTLEFIELD MISSILES

Great improvements in missile accuracy required the development of better sensors and of sophisticated electronics based on integrated circuits. Integrated circuits became available in the early 1960's and grew progressively more complex and more reliable.

ANTITANK MISSILES

On the day after the Soviet Sagger antitank missile was introduced in the Vietnam War in 1972, the Americans introduced its counterpart, the TOW missile. TOW is an acronym for tube-launched, optically tracked, and wire-command-link-guided. During the brief 1973 Israeli-Arab October War, TOW and Sagger missiles together destroyed more than 1,500 Israeli, Jordanian, Iraqi, and Syrian tanks.

After a TOW is launched, the gunner must keep the crosshairs of the launch tube sight centered on the target until the missile impacts. As the missile flies at half the speed of sound, a thin wire unreels behind it. A small beacon on the missile's tail sends an infrared signal to a sensor on the launch tube, and a computer in the launch tube sends flight corrections back to the missile through the connecting wire and guides the missile to the target. The TOW can be fired from the ground using a tripod-mounted tube or from launchers mounted on vehicles, including the high-mobility multipurpose wheeled vehicle (HMMWV) and the

Cobra helicopter. There have been five major upgrades to the TOW, which is used by forty-three Allied countries.

Antitank missiles such as the TOW and the Sagger often use a shaped charge that explodes on impact and focuses the explosive energy into a small jet that can penetrate the tank armor. In defense, sandwich armor consisting of an outer steel plate and a thick inner steel plate was developed. Three types of sandwich material have been used: honeycomb ceramic that flows under impact and disrupts the projectile's explosive jet; depleted uranium that retards the projectile's momentum with its massive inertia; and a layer of explosive that detonates and pushes back against the impacting projectile. The latter is called Explosive Reactive Armor (ERA).

The nose of the TOW 2A has an extended probe and a small disrupter charge. The probe and the disrupter charge detonate the reactive armor, and after its protective effect is expended, the main shaped charge explodes and penetrates the main armor. The TOW 2A can penetrate any armor currently in use. The TOW 2B flies over the top of the targeted tank, which is less protected than the sides. When laser and magnetic sensors alert the missile that it is above the tank, two tantalum penetrator projectiles are explosively formed. One is fired directly downward, and the other is fired slightly off to the side to increase the hit probability. The projectile material is designed to start fires within the target. The TOW 2B is expected to be effective against any tank developed in the near future. The TOW FF, a wireless TOW fire-and-forget missile allowing gunners to dive for cover or engage other targets, is under development.

AIR DEFENSE MISSILES

Just as TOW missiles enable soldiers to stop tanks, surface-to-air missiles (SAMs)—man-portable air defense systems (MANPADS) in their smallest versions—enable troops to counter high-speed, low-level, ground-attack aircraft, or bring down high-flying aircraft. After World War II, German rocket technology was adapted to Cold War needs, though it was not until the late 1950's that it proved to be effective. The Soviet Union was in the forefront of SAM development, adapting German models to the new battlefield climate. One of the most notable achievements of this emerging technology came on May 1, 1960, when the Soviet Union downed a U-2 spy plane, piloted by Gary Powers, with an SA-2 surface-to-air missile. After that time, several generations of SAMs and MANPADS were developed, leading to greater precision and portability. Older technologies are widely available and relatively inexpensive, while more so-

TURNING POINTS

1792	War rockets are used by the sultan of Mysore to terrorize British soldiers.
1805	British artillerist William Congreve develops the first warfare rockets and launching tubes.
1846-1848	Hale rockets, an improvement on Congreve rockets with metal vanes in the rockets' exhaust, are used in the Mexican-American War.
1926	Robert Goddard achieves the first free flight of a liquid-fueled rocket.
1945	The world's first atomic bomb is exploded near Alamogordo, New Mexico.
1952	The world's first hydrogen bomb is exploded at Enewetak Atoll in the Pacific Ocean.
1983	U.S. president Ronald Reagan announces plans to pursue a Strategic Defense Initiative (SDI) designed to provide space-based defense against nuclear missile attacks.
1987	U.S. president Ronald Reagan and Soviet general secretary Mikhail Gorbachev sign the Intermediate-range and shorter-range Nuclear Forces (INF) treaty, the first arms treaty to actually reduce the numbers of nuclear weapons instead of merely limiting their growth.
2002	The United States withdraws from the Anti-Ballistic Missile (ABM) Treaty.
2009	U.S. president Barack Obama is awarded the Nobel Peace Prize, with special reference to his "work for a world without nuclear weapons."

A Soviet surface-to-air missile being deployed in Egypt.

phisticated versions are readily available to organizations or individuals with sufficient funding. As a result, MANPADS became a characteristic weapon of the late Cold War and in the practice of terrorism.

One of the most widely used systems, the FIM-92 Stinger, was developed by the United States and provided to Islamic guerrilla fighters, the Mujahideen, in Afghanistan for use in their defense against Soviet invasion during the 1980's. It is estimated that more than 270 Soviet aircraft were shot down with Stingers. When the gunner sights an aircraft, he can send an electronic signal to identify whether it is friend or foe. The Stinger is another fire-and-forget weapon: Once it has been launched, the gunner can dive for cover or engage another target. The Stinger uses both infrared and ultraviolet sensors to home in on the target and can approach it from any aspect. Its speed is supersonic, and its maximum range is 8 kilometers. As global terrorism expanded following the attacks of September 11, 2001, military planners recognized the danger of MANPAD attacks, particularly against civilian aircraft, but no cost-efficient countermeasure could be found.

MISSILES IN THE GULF WAR

Several modern missiles were put to the test during the 1991 Gulf War. The start of the air war came during the dark early morning hours of January 17, 1991, when eight Apache helicopters launched laser-guided Hellfire missiles and Hydra-70 rockets against two Iraqi early-warning ground control radar sites. The Iraqi air defense system was so extensive that only Moscow was judged to be better defended than Baghdad. Because of this, only unmanned cruise missiles and the nearly invisible Stealth aircraft penetrated deeply into Iraq at first. The first goal was to create gaps in the Iraqi air defense and open the way for more conventional aircraft. F-4G Wild Weasel aircraft broadcast strong radar jamming signals and also recorded Iraqi radar signals, playing them back with various delays to clutter Iraqi radar displays with floods of false targets.

DEVELOPMENT OF MODERN CRUISE MISSILES

Cruise missiles are theater weapons. Early cruise missiles, such as the Snark, the Matador, and the Hound Dog, deployed in the 1950's and 1960's, suffered from various problems, especially unreliability and inaccuracy. However, as bombers found it ever more difficult to penetrate improved air-defense systems, stand-off, unmanned weapons became increasingly attractive. Eventually improvements in engine technology and guidance systems led to the modern cruise missiles originally deployed in the 1980's and used during and after the Gulf War.

The Tomahawk cruise missile is launched from surface ships and submarines with a solid propellant rocket that burns for twelve seconds, after which a small turbofan motor takes over and propels the missile at 880 kilometers per hour (550 miles per hour). The Tomahawk is not easy to shoot down, because it is difficult to track. Detection by radar is difficult, because the missile is small and cruises at only 15 to 30 meters above the ground. Detection by infrared sensors is also difficult, because the turbofan motor puts out very little heat.

All versions of the Tomahawk use an inertial navigation system (INS) while over water. The INS has four crucial elements: gyroscopes, inertial masses, a computer, and an accurate clock. By measuring the magnitude and duration of the forces on the inertial masses and by using the gyroscopes to establish direction, the computer can calculate the missile's acceleration, velocity, and position. If the computer finds that the missile is not where it should be, commands can be sent to the flight control surfaces to correct its course.

The Tomahawk BGM-109B is a ship-to-ship weapon with a range of 470 kilometers. When it reaches its target area, it circles until it locks onto the enemy ship's radar or locates the ship with its own radar. It carries a 450-kilogram semi-armor-piercing warhead and can either strike the target broadside or pop up and dive down on the target. A ground-launched Tomahawk, the BGM-109A, was briefly deployed in Europe but was removed under a provision of the 1988 Intermediate-range and shorter-range Nuclear Forces (INF) treaty. The Tomahawk has a range of 2,500 kilometers and carries a 200-kiloton nuclear warhead. In addition to INS, the Tomahawk has a Terrain Contour Matching System (TERCOM), which, at selected checkpoints, scans the terrain with radar, comparing topographical features against stored data and correcting its flight path as necessary. To avoid detection, the radar remains off most of the time. The accuracy of the Tomahawk's TERCOM system was such that 50 percent of the missiles would hit within 45 meters of their targets, close enough for the 200-kiloton nuclear warheads to destroy the targets.

The Tomahawk BGM-109C and Tomahawk BGM-109D have ranges of 1,600 kilometers. Both weapons use, in addition to INS and TERCOM, the Global Positioning System (GPS). When they near their targets, they also employ a Digital Scene Matching Area Correlator (DSMAC) that compares images from an electronic camera in the missile nose against stored data. The DSMAC system makes these weapons exceptionally accurate, reducing their error probability to 10 meters. The missile can hit the target

horizontally, pop up and dive down on the target, or fly over and burst above the target. The 109D is similar to the 109C but dispenses 166 BLU-97/B Combined Effect Munitions (CEM). Each CEM is about the size of a soft-drink can, weighs about 1.5 kilograms, and consists of three types of submunitions: fragmentation, incendiary, and shaped-charges that can penetrate 13 to 18 centimeters of armor. The 109D can dispense the CEMs in batches on several targets.

The air-launched cruise missile (ALCM) AGM-86 uses INS, TERCOM, and GPS guidance systems. It originally carried a 200-kiloton nuclear warhead but has been converted to carry a massive 900-kilogram (2,000-pound) blast-fragmentation warhead that sprays a cloud of ball bearings. The ALCM is designed to destroy dispersed, soft targets such as surface-to-air missile batteries. B-52G and B-52H bombers can carry twelve missiles in external racks, and some B-52H bombers can carry eight more missiles internally.

On January 17, 1991, at the start of the Gulf War, 297 Tomahawks were prepared to be launched from ships, but nine failed prelaunch tests. Of the 288 actual launches, 6 failed to cruise and 242 (81 percent of those launched) hit their targets. At about the same time, high-flying bombers launched thirty-five ALCMs at targets in Iraq. Television reporters watched in amazement as missiles streaked past their hotel and made right turns into the next street on their way to their targets.

In January, 1993, forty-five Tomahawks were launched against Iraqi nuclear development facilities and similar targets. In September, 1995, thirteen Tomahawks hit surface-to-air missile sites in Bosnia. As a response to Iraqi harassment of Western aircraft patrolling the no-fly zone, 13 ALCMs were fired from B-52Hs and thirty-one Tomahawks were fired from ships in the Persian Gulf in September, 1996. In response to the terrorist bombings of U.S. embassies in Kenya and Tanzania, thirteen Tomahawks destroyed a suspected chemical weapons factory in the Sudan, and sixty-six Tomahawks hit guerrilla training camps in Afghanistan in August, 1998. Striking against weapons of mass destruction and Iraqi air-defense sites in December, 1998, the United States and Britain attacked about one hundred targets in central and southern Iraq. They used fighters, bombers, ninety ALCMs, and 330 Tomahawks. In March, 1999, NATO (North Atlantic Treaty Organization) forces struck targets in Yugoslavia and Kosovo with fighters, bombers, and one hundred cruise missiles.

Cruise missiles seem to have become the weapon of choice in many situations. Although laser-guided bombs can be up to ten times more accurate and are significantly less expensive to build, they put pilots at risk. Even though a few cruise missiles do go astray and cause unintended damage, they have proven accurate enough and reliable enough to be used against targets surrounded by civilians. Future upgrades will cut the production costs of cruise missiles in half by discontinuing the capability to launch them from torpedo tubes, including a small television camera for tracking the target, replacing mechanical gyroscopes with laser-ring gyroscopes, and giving them the ability to be redirected to new targets while in flight.

DEVELOPMENT OF INTERCONTINENTAL BALLISTIC MISSILES

After World War II, the United States and the Soviet Union experimented with captured German V-2 rockets and worked to develop intercontinental ballistic missiles (ICBMs). In 1957 the Soviets launched an SS-6 Sapwood multistage ballistic missile and also put the first two artificial satellites, Sputnik 1 and Sputnik 2, into orbit. (A multistage rocket has the advantage that the excess weight of spent stages can be discarded.) The United States suddenly perceived a "missile gap" and reinvigorated its own missile program. The first U.S. satellite, Explorer 1, was lifted into orbit by a Juno 1 rocket atop a Jupiter C on January 31, 1958. The Jupiter ICBM was declared operational in 1958 and deployed in Italy and Turkey, while the Thor missile became operational in 1959 and was deployed in the United Kingdom. Both missiles were liquid fueled, with ranges of 3,200 kilometers. They had inertial guidance systems and carried 1.5-megaton nuclear warheads.

The Soviet SS-6 had a range of about 5,600 kilo-

meters (3,500 miles) and had to be launched from northern latitudes in order to reach the United States, but the bitter northern cold often rendered the missile inoperable. Perhaps in response to the failure of the SS-6 and to the deployment of the Thor and Jupiter, the Soviet Union attempted to base SS-4 Sandal missiles in Cuba, thereby precipitating the Cuban Missile Crisis of 1962. The SS-4 carried a 1-megaton warhead and had a range of about 1,600 kilometers. After coming to the brink of nuclear war, the Soviets withdrew these missiles. Not long afterward, the Jupiter and Thor missiles were retired from service in 1964 and 1965, respectively.

Missiles deployed in the homeland are not subject to the consent of other nations. The Atlas and Titan I missiles were both deployed in the United States in 1959. These were liquid fueled, carried 2- to 4-megaton warheads, and had inertial or radio-inertial guidance systems. The Atlas had a range of about 16,000 kilometers and used liquid hydrogen. The Titan I was a two-stage missile with a range of about 10,000 kilometers. It used liquid oxygen, a cryogenic (supercold) liquid that had to be pumped onboard during a lengthy procedure during launch preparation. The Titan II used storable liquid fuels that could remain in the missile so it could be launched more quickly. It weighed 148 metric tons (325,000 pounds) at liftoff and was the largest missile ever deployed by the United States. More than 30 meters long and 3 meters in diameter, it had a range of 14,500 kilometers and a throw weight of 3.6 metric tons. It delivered a 9-megaton nuclear warhead, so it did not matter that its CEP was 1.6 kilometers.

SOLID-FUEL ROCKETS
Because a Soviet ICBM could reach the United States in thirty-five minutes, the United States needed antiballistic missiles (ABMs) that could be fired in minutes, so solid-fuel rockets were developed. Solid fuels are more stable than liquid fuels and do not require heavy pipes and pumps. Although they were always ready to fire, they made flight control more difficult, because solid-fueled rockets could not be throttled back nor use gimbal-mounted motors to steer. The Minuteman I became operational in 1962 and was the first U.S. solid-fueled missile. It

was held ready in a underground silo and had a range of 10,000 kilometers.

In the mid-1960's, the Soviets, the British, and the United States equipped some of their missiles with multiple reentry vehicles (MRVs), warheads that separated before the missile returned into the atmosphere. Several warheads from the same missile striking the target area made it more likely that the target would be destroyed. In 1982 the British used MRVs to incorporate penetration aids such as decoys, radar-reflecting chaff, and electronic jammers in missiles designated to attack Moscow, which was protected by an antiballistic missile shield. The United States took the next step and developed multiple independently targetable reentry vehicles (MIRVs) to penetrate the nationwide antiballistic missile system that it feared the Soviets would build. The missile payload was now a bus that could maneuver in space and send its warheads to different targets. It had to be liquid fueled so that it could repeatedly start and stop its rocket motors. The United States deployed its first MIRVed missile, the Minuteman III, in 1970. Its first three stages were solid fueled, with a range of 13,000 kilometers and a CEP of 365 meters. That was close enough because it carried three 200- to 350-kiloton nuclear warheads.

The United States feared that not enough Minuteman missiles in its silos would survive a Soviet preemptive strike and decided to build a mobile missile, the MX Peacekeeper. It carried up to ten 300-kiloton nuclear warheads, with a range of 11,000 kilometers and a CEP of 90 meters. Because no satisfactory mobile basing plan was found, the MX was housed in Minuteman silos. Its radically improved accuracy was due to a new inertial guidance system in which the gyros and accelerometers

were housed in a floating ball. It also updated its position by sighting stars or certain satellites. Many consider the MX to be a first-strike weapon, because it is accurate enough to destroy missiles in their silos.

The Strategic Arms Reduction Treaty II (START II, 1993-2000) required the United States to remove MIRV capability from its ICBMs. Although the treaty was never formally put into force, both the United States and Russia generally followed its provisions. MX missiles were retired and Minuteman III missiles were refitted with single 300-kiloton warheads. Their updated guidance systems have a CEP of 100

U.S. Department of Defense

A Minuteman III missile being launched from Vandenberg Air Force Base in California.

meters. Trident submarine missiles were allowed to continue to carry up to eight warheads. Russia was required to make corresponding reductions.

NATURE AND USE OF NUCLEAR WEAPONS

When a conventional explosive is detonated, it takes but a tiny fraction of a second for chemical reactions to turn the explosive into high-pressure gases. The subsequent rapid outward expansion of these super-hot gases is the explosion. Rapidly occurring nuclear reactions can do the same thing, but because nuclear forces are one million times stronger than chemical forces, the energy released is one million times greater.

Nuclear explosive devices are difficult to make and involve two basic kinds of nuclear reactions: fission and fusion. The bombs dropped on Hiroshima and Nagasaki were fission weapons. In a fission chain reaction, neutrons strike nuclei of plutonium or uranium 235, causing them to split roughly in half. In doing so, they release two to three new neutrons, along with a great deal of energy. Uranium 235 is the isotope of uranium that has 92 protons and 143 neutrons in its nucleus. It fissions, or splits, more readily than the more common uranium 238, which has 92 protons and 146 neutrons. Isotopes that readily fission and sustain a chain reaction are said to be fissile. The most common fissile isotopes are uranium 235, which must be painstakingly separated from the far more abundant uranium 238, and uranium 233 and plutonium, which must be made in nuclear reactors.

For a nuclear explosion to occur, the chain reaction must be supercritical; that is, each fission must lead to more than one new fission. For example, suppose that each fission produced two neutrons and that each of these two neutrons produced two new fissions. If there were two fissions in the first generation, there would be four in the second, eight in the third and 2^N in the Nth generation. At this rate, every nucleus in 17 kilograms of uranium could fission in fewer than 85 generations. This would take less than two-millionths of one second.

The minimum amount of uranium required to produce an explosion is called the critical mass. Critical mass depends not only on the amount of material present but also on its shape and on the materials surrounding it. If there is less than a critical mass, too many neutrons escape from the uranium without producing fissions, and the process fizzles out. The critical mass of weapons-grade uranium-235 metal is 17 kilograms, if it is surrounded by a good neutron reflector. The critical mass of weapons-grade plutonium metal is only 4 kilograms, but that increases to 10 kilograms without a neutron reflector. A critical mass cannot be assembled before it is intended to explode, because a stray neutron produced by a cosmic ray could initiate an untimely explosion.

The atomic bomb dropped on Hiroshima on August 6, 1945, weighed 4.4 metric tons (9,700 pounds) and had a yield equal to 14.5 kilotons of the high explosive TNT. The yield was about 1.3 percent of the maximum possible yield for the amount of fissile material used. The core contained 60 kilograms of uranium 235, surrounded by 900 kilograms of uranium 238 to serve as a tamper and neutron reflector. The inertia of the tamper briefly slows the core's expansion and allows a few more generations of fission to occur. To keep it below critical mass, a large segment of the uranium-235 core was removed and placed into a short cannon. When the Hiroshima bomb fell to 680 meters above the ground, the cannon fired the missing segment into the core. That action also mixed a small amount of beryllium and radioactive polonium 210, a combination that produced a flood of neutrons. Two-thirds of the city was destroyed in the explosion, and about 140,000 people were killed, either immediately or within a few months from injuries they sustained during the explosion.

The bomb that was dropped on Nagasaki on August 9, 1945, used plutonium, primarily plutonium 239. When plutonium is made in a nuclear reactor by adding neutrons to uranium 238, plutonium 240 and plutonium 242 are also formed. The latter two isotopes can spontaneously fission and produce too many neutrons to make gun assembly predictable. The Nagasaki bomb used 6.1 kilograms of plutonium in a noncritical configuration. This plutonium core was surrounded by 2,300 kilograms of high explosives. When the explosives were detonated simultaneously from all sides, the resulting implosion compressed the plutonium core to twice its normal density, thereby achieving critical mass. The resulting nuclear explosion had a yield of about 23 kilotons of TNT, 17 percent of the maximum possible yield for that amount of plutonium. About 70,000 people were killed either immediately or within a few months.

For several years weapons scientists speculated about building "the super," in which light elements would be fused into heavier elements and give off a great deal of energy in the process. After the Soviets exploded their first atomic bomb in 1949, work on the hydrogen bomb, as it is now called, began in earnest. Edward Teller (born 1908) and Stanislaw M. Ulam (1909-1984) had the key insight of how to use an atomic bomb to create the high temperature and pressure necessary for fusion.

Inside a 300-kiloton hydrogen warhead may be a uranium-238 cylinder about 1 meter long and 0.5 meter in diameter. Inside the cylinder at one end there is a small fission bomb about the size of a soccer ball that serves as a nuclear trigger. A fat rod of lithium deuteride (LD) lies along the cylinder's axis with a slab of uranium 238 (the pusher) between it and the trigger. Deuterium is heavy hydrogen, and its nucleus is a proton-neutron pair. A thin plutonium rod (the spark plug) lies along the center of the LD rod, and the outside of the LD rod is covered with a uranium-238 tamper. The space around the rod is filled with plastic foam. The exploding trigger creates a pressure of 1 billion atmospheres and a temperature of 100 million Kelvins. X rays turn the foam into plasma while the outer uranium cylinder momentarily channels the energy and pressure onto the LD rod. As the rod and its plutonium core compress, neutrons cause the spark plug to fission, and then lithium fissions into tritium, a proton linked to two neutrons, and helium. Tritium and deuterium now fuse, releasing a tremendous amount of energy along with high-energy neutrons. These neutrons cause part of the outer uranium cylinder to undergo fission as it disintegrates. Hence this is a fission-fusion-fission weapon.

By 1964, the Soviet Union (1949), the United

Kingdom (1952), France (1960), and China (1964) had all developed nuclear weapons. In an attempt to prevent further expansion, the Non-Proliferation Treaty (NPT) was negotiated in 1968. Although it was generally effective in discouraging further development of nuclear weapons, India, Israel, and Pakistan failed to sign the treaty and later acquired nuclear capability. Iran, North Korea, and Syria are widely regarded as supporting programs that might lead to the development of nuclear weapons.

During the Cold War, Warsaw Pact nations equipped and maintained an army twice the size of that of the defending North Atlantic Treaty Organization (NATO) forces. In an effort to make up for this imbalance, the United States deployed many tactical nuclear weapons with yields of about 10 kilotons or fewer. The most notorious of these was the neutron bomb, or Enhanced Radiation Weapon (ERW). One version was a projectile for an 8-inch howitzer (artillery gun) with a range of about 17 kilometers. A second version was a warhead for the Lance missile with a range of about 130 kilometers. These warheads were fission-fusion devices, small plutonium bombs containing tritium, with a 1-kiloton yield. The blasts of such warheads would destroy buildings within a radius of 760 meters (0.5 mile), and the neutron radiation would kill unshielded people at about twice that distance. Strategists argued that because these weapons caused less collateral damage than larger weapons, the Warsaw Pact nations would believe that they were more likely to be used and would be deterred from attacking. These weapons were kept ready for use for about ten years, after which they were included in the nearly 7,000 nuclear warheads and bombs retired at the end of the Cold War.

DEVELOPMENT OF NUCLEAR STRATEGIES

World War II military strategists used the Nagasaki bomb to show that the Hiroshima bomb had not been a fluke and that more such bombs would be used if necessary. This ploy was partially a bluff, given that the next bomb would not have been ready to deploy until the end of August, 1945. However, the Japanese initiated surrender negotiations the day after Nagasaki was destroyed. Most historians agree that the use of these nuclear weapons probably saved more lives than they took, because they ended the war quickly and without the necessity of invading the Japanese homeland. Even as World War II ended, the Cold War with the Soviet Union had already begun. As the only nation with nuclear weapons, the United States could threaten to use them without fear of retaliation in kind. As the West disarmed, nuclear weapons were seen as a relatively cheap substitute for maintaining a large military force, and the United States began building a large nuclear stockpile.

Several years before the Western Allies believed it would happen, the Soviets exploded a plutonium bomb on August 29, 1949. In response, the United States developed the hydrogen bomb, first testing it in 1952. The Soviets tested a hydrogen bomb only one year later. To contain communism, the United States threatened "massive retaliation" if the Soviets committed unspecified aggression anywhere in the world. The Soviets could have been attacked from bomber bases in Europe or, after 1948, by intercontinental bombers based in the United States.

After the Soviets had developed a large number of nuclear weapons and its own intercontinental bomber force in 1955, the doctrine became "mutual assured destruction" (MAD). With each country able to destroy the other, neither could afford to try anything foolish. MAD required that the United States be able to absorb a nuclear attack by the Soviets and still deliver a devastating response. It was seriously proposed that nuclear missiles be placed on the Moon, because missiles aimed at the Moon would take days to arrive, and during that time, U.S. bombers could hit the Soviet Union. If, instead, the Soviets first targeted the continental United States, missiles from the Moon could be launched at the Soviet Union. A more practical course was taken by building up a triad of nuclear bombers, ICBMs, and submarine-launched missiles. It was judged that the Soviets could not destroy enough of the triad in a preemptive strike to escape overwhelming retribution.

Intercontinental bombers might take fifteen hours to reach their targets, and they could be recalled in case of a false alarm. ICBMs put a hair trigger on

MAD, because they take only thirty minutes to reach their targets and, once underway, cannot be recalled. Missiles launched from nearby submarines might take only seven to fifteen minutes to reach their targets. As missiles became more accurate, warhead yield was reduced from multimegatons to between 100 kilotons and 475 kilotons, and a "counterforce" doctrine was introduced, in which the enemies' armed forces, particularly their nuclear weapons, were targeted. In the belief that the Soviets were less likely to try something if they were more sure that the United States would not hesitate to respond, the doctrine of "flexible response" was advanced in the early 1980's. This meant that, in place of MAD, the U.S. response would be commensurate with the scope of the enemy attack. Many found flexible response to be a very disturbing policy, because it made the use of nuclear weapons no longer unthinkable. They feared that any limited nuclear war would escalate into full-scale nuclear war. Fortunately, perhaps because of MAD, the nuclear powers have gone to great lengths to avoid directly fighting each other, and there has been no further use of nuclear weapons.

The nuclear stockpile of weapons in the United States peaked in 1966 at about 32,000, more than four times the number possessed by the Soviet Union. Soviet stockpiles peaked in 1986 at about 41,000. As a result of a series of agreements that began with the Strategic Arms Reduction Treaty I (1991), by 2009 those numbers had been reduced to about 10,000 in the United States (with 6,700 in reserve or waiting dismantlement) and 13,000 in Russia (with 8,100 in reserve or waiting dismantlement). These numbers tell only part of the story, however, as different types of nuclear weapons have varying yields of power.

With the election in the United States of President Barack Obama in 2008, new impetus was given to the reduction of nuclear arsenals. Speaking in Prague in April of 2009, Obama argued that the United States had "a moral responsibility to act" and committed America to "a world without nuclear weapons." Among the steps he planned to pursue were negotiation of a new strategic arms reduction treaty with Russia, ratification of the Comprehensive Test Ban

Treaty, and a new treaty ending production of weapons grade nuclear materials. Although none of these had been achieved by the end of 2009, his efforts gained worldwide attention and widespread international support. In bestowing on Obama the 2009 Nobel Peace Prize, the committee "attached special importance" to his "vision of and work for a world without nuclear weapons."

DEVELOPMENT OF MISSILE DEFENSE AND ANTIBALLISTIC MISSILES

Thirty-six nations possess ballistic missiles of some type, and fifty-two nations have antiship cruise missiles. Doubtless, defenses against missiles have been sought ever since missiles became effective weapons. British fighter planes were able to shoot down some V-1's, and the more daring pilots flew alongside, slipped a wing under the V-1, and then tipped it, confusing the V-1's primitive autopilot and sending the missile into a dive. There was no defense against the V-2's. In the 1982 Falkland Islands War, there was no defense when the HMS *Sheffield* was lost to a French Exocet cruise missile launched by the Argentinian air force. An Iraqi air force pilot flying a French-built Mirage fighter mistakenly launched two Exocets at the USS *Stark* in 1987. Thirty-seven sailors died, and twenty-one others were wounded. The *Stark* was protected by a Phalanx close-in weapon system (CIWS), but it failed to fire because of a tragic mistake: Because France was an ally, Exocets were tagged as friendly.

The Phalanx system is deployed on nearly all U.S. Navy ships and in the navies of several allied nations. The Phalanx is a fast-reaction, rapid-fire 20-millimeter gun system. First deployed in 1978, current models fire 4,500 rounds per minute, although the magazine holds only 1,550 rounds. The rounds are hard and dense—they were originally made from depleted uranium but are now made of tungsten—and they fly at very high speeds. Their muzzle velocity is 1,113 meters per second, more than three times the speed of sound. The system uses radar and a forward-looking infrared (FLIR) detector to locate and track targets automatically. The FLIR is the ship's last line of defense against incoming missiles and aircraft, and a recent upgrade allowed it also to engage small, fast-moving surface craft during both day and night.

The Avenger Pedestal-Mounted Stinger system can shoot down cruise missiles. It is mounted on a heavy high-mobility multipurpose wheeled vehicle (HMMWV). A gyro-stabilized turret gives it a shoot-on-the-move capability. The gunner's turret has a .50-caliber (12.7-millimeter) machine gun and eight Stinger missile launch pods. It has a forward-looking infrared sensor, laser range finder, and a video autotracker. It can also receive tracking cues by radio from a nearby radar set, if one is available.

The Patriot missile was originally an antiaircraft weapon but was hurriedly modified in the mid-1980's to defend against ballistic missiles. A phased-array radar locates the target and directs the missile to it. As it nears the target, the missile homes in on radar waves reflected from the target, then a proximity fuse detonates a 90-kilogram, high-explosive warhead. At first the Patriot missile seemed to be very successful at stopping Iraqi Scud missiles during the Gulf War (1990-1991). Later analysis showed that many of the Scuds simply broke apart as they hit the lower atmosphere at high speed, and that the Patriot usefully destroyed some of the debris. Other Scuds were only knocked off course by Patriot explosions, but certainly the Patriot missile was at least a partial success. The Patriot missile and radar, upgraded to the Patriot Advanced Capability-3 (PAC-3), was scheduled to deploy alongside earlier Patriot missiles in 2012. Although slower than some earlier models, it has hit-to-kill capabilities, and can protect five times the area.

In March, 1983, U.S. president Ronald Reagan gave dramatic impetus to the development of missile defenses with announcement of his Strategic Defense Initiative (SDI), with the "ultimate goal of eliminating the threat posed by strategic nuclear missiles." This spawned a series of expensive and technologically unproven initiatives, including the creation of laser defenses, that led critics to dub the program "Star Wars," after the fantasy film series of the same name. By 1993, the program was renamed Ballistic Missile Defense Organization (BMDO), and the emphasis had shifted from national to regional defense. Although a comprehensive global defense system was never developed, a number of the technologies emanating from the SDI were pursued and eventually deployed.

Testing of weapons using high-energy lasers has demonstrated the technology's battlefield potential for combating missile attacks. Israel and the United States collaborated in developing a Tactical High Energy Laser (THEL) system, which was expected to be useful against short-ranged (20-kilometer) Katyusha rockets frequently employed against Israel by Hizbullah units. The system's weakness against medium- and long-range missiles led to interest in various mobile systems (MTHEL), including the creation of a prototype of airborne units, unveiled in 2006. With funding for the MTHEL discontinued by the United States in 2004, its deployment became unlikely in the short term. The first generation of lasers required chemical reactions to produce high amounts of energy in a short period of time, usually burning ethylene with nitrogen trifluoride before adding deuterium. Studies suggested that effective MTHEL systems would require electrically produced lasers, which likely could not be deployed until the 2010's.

The Navy Area Theater Ballistic Missile Defense (TBMD) system was developed to protect U.S. and Allied forces and areas of vital national interest against theater ballistic missiles. The lower-tier defense uses Aegis cruisers and destroyers, which have phased-array radars and battle management computers that can simultaneously detect and track more than one hundred targets. Incoming enemy missiles are intercepted with the Standard Missile (SM)-2, which has a range of 185 kilometers. Missiles slipping through that defense are then engaged by the Phalanx system. As a result of massive cost overruns in perfecting radar and SM-2 Block IVA capabilities, the Department of Defense canceled the program in December, 2001, though upper-tier defense uses the Terminal High Altitude Area Defense (THAAD) system's long-range, hit-to-kill interceptor, which was first activated in 2008. Surviving enemy missiles aimed at ground targets are then engaged by the Patriot (PAC-3) system. Arrow-2 is a two-staged interceptor developed jointly by the United States and Israel. It uses a blast-fragmentation warhead to destroy enemy missiles and has a range between those of the Patriot and the THAAD interceptor. It could be employed by the United States if deemed necessary.

The lower tier of the theater missile defense systems seems to be well founded. The upper-tier THAAD interceptor is less well developed, and the National Missile Defense (NMD) system is even further from deployment. The first attempt at an NMD was the Safeguard antiballistic missile system. It used longer-ranged (748 kilometers) Spartan missiles with 5-megaton warheads and shorter-ranged (40 kilometers) Sprint missiles with low-kiloton yield warheads. The Sprint warheads were enhanced-radiation devices intended to cripple incoming warheads with neutron radiation. Unfortunately, they had a fatal flaw—the first few nuclear explosions destroying incoming missiles would have blinded the acquisition and tracking radar. The system was built despite the known flaw, but it remained active for only four months in 1976.

An ABM system can attack missiles as they rise through the atmosphere (boost phase) and are most vulnerable; as they coast through space (mid-course phase), when decoys are the most effective; or as they plunge back into the atmosphere over the target (terminal phase), when time is short. The boost phase lasts from three to five minutes; the mid-course phase, up to 20 minutes; and the terminal phase, about 1 minute. To maintain enough assets in orbit to destroy a massive attack during launch would be prohibitively expensive. In fact, since MIRVed warheads and decoys are cheaper than antiballistic missiles and their support system, it is cheaper to overcome an ABM system with a massive attack than it is to build an ABM system extensive enough to stop a massive attack.

However, it might be practical to stop a limited attack. Such an attack might be a missile, or a few missiles, launched by a renegade military commander or by a rogue nation. Although none of these scenarios seems likely, any of them could kill thousands of people or many more. This fact makes it worthwhile to at least consider a defense against them. In the quarter century since the development of the Safeguard system, technology has advanced to the point that it is now possible "to hit a bullet with a bullet";

however, current systems are more effective against shorter-ranged missiles than they are against longer-ranged missiles.

If built, the National Missile Defense system would have several elements. Large, phased-array surveillance radars would detect and track missiles aimed at the United States. X-band radar has a shorter wavelength than normal radar and can therefore see finer detail. Ground-based X-band radar would be used to track targets and discriminate against decoys. Infrared sensing satellites already in orbit monitor the Earth to detect the hot exhaust gases of missile launch. This system was used to detect Scud launches during the Gulf War. The Space-Based Infrared System (SBIRS) would be an expanded and modernized version of the current system. It would acquire and track the missiles shortly after launch and provide the greatest warning. The system's weapon component is the Ground-Based Interceptor (GBI), a missile always kept ready to launch a Kill Vehicle (KV) into space. The KV would have its own sensors, propulsion, communications, and guidance systems and would maneuver to the target, distinguish decoys, and destroy the target in a high-speed collision. Concern over the possibility of attacks from rogue states and terrorist groups led to continued government funding of SBIRS, despite its prohibition by the Anti-Ballistic Missile (ABM) Treaty signed by the United States and Russia in 1972. The United States unilaterally withdrew from the treaty in 2002.

BOOKS AND ARTICLES

Alexander, Brian, and Alistair Millar, eds. *Tactical Nuclear Weapons: Emergent Threats in an Evolving Security Environment.* Washington, D.C.: Brassey's, 2003.

Baker, David. *The Rocket: The History and Development of Rocket and Missile Technology.* New York: Crown, 1978.

Berhow, Mark. *U.S. Strategic and Defensive Missile Systems, 1950-2004.* Illustrated by Chris Taylor. Botley, Oxford, England: Osprey, 2005.

Boyne, Walter J., ed. *Air Warfare: An International Encyclopedia.* Santa Barbara, Calif.: ABC-CLIO, 2002.

Busch, Nathan E. *No End in Sight: The Continuing Menace of Nuclear Proliferation.* Lexington: University Press of Kentucky, 2004.

Chayes, Abram, and Jerome B. Wiesner, eds. *ABM: An Evaluation of the Decision to Deploy an Antiballistic Missile System.* New York: Harper and Row, 1969.

Delgado, James P. *Nuclear Dawn: The Atomic Bomb, from the Manhattan Project to the Cold War.* Botley, Oxford, England: Osprey, 2009.

Denoon, David B. H. *Ballistic Missile Defense in the Post-Cold War Era.* Boulder, Colo.: Westview Press, 1991.

Ehrlich, Robert. *Waging Nuclear Peace: The Technology and Politics of Nuclear Weapons.* Albany: State University of New York Press, 1985.

Gruntman, Mike. *Blazing the Trail: The Early History of Spacecraft and Rocketry.* Reston, Va.: American Institute of Aeronautics and Astronautics, 2004.

Hallion, Richard P. *Storm over Iraq: Air Power and the Gulf War.* Washington, D.C.: Smithsonian Institution Press, 1992.

"Homeland Security: Protecting Airliners from Terrorist Missiles." Congressional Research Service Report for Congress RL31741, February 16, 2006.

Levine, Alan J. *The Missile and Space Race.* Westport, Conn.: Praeger, 1994.

Quinlan, Michael. *Thinking About Nuclear Weapons: Principles, Problems, Prospects.* New York: Oxford University Press, 2009.

Rhodes, Richard. *Arsenals of Folly: The Making of the Nuclear Arms Race.* New York: Alfred A. Knopf, 2007.

_____. *The Making of the Atomic Bomb*. New York: Simon and Schuster, 1986.

Tsipis, Kosta. *Arsenal: Understanding Weapons in the Nuclear Age*. New York: Simon and Schuster, 1983.

Van Riper, A. Bowdoin. *Rockets and Missiles: The Life Story of a Technology*. Westport, Conn.: Greenwood Press, 2004.

Yanarella, Ernest J. *The Missile Defense Controversy: Technology in Search of a Mission*. Rev. and updated ed. Lexington: University Press of Kentucky, 2002.

FILMS AND OTHER MEDIA

Bombs, Rockets, and Missiles. Documentary. History Channel, 1997.

The Day After. Television miniseries. ABC, 1983.

Fail Safe. Feature film. Columbia Pictures, 1964.

History of Nuclear Weapons: The Ultimate Weapons. Documentary. Tapeworm Video, 2005.

On the Beach. Feature film. Kramer, 1959.

Trinity and Beyond: The Atomic Bomb Movie. Documentary. VCE Inc., 2006.

War Machines of Tomorrow. Documentary. Nova/WGBH Boston, 1996.

Charles W. Rogers

CHEMICAL AND BIOLOGICAL WEAPONS

Dates: Since c. 1500

NATURE AND USE

Both chemical and biological weapons are considered "silent weapons of mass destruction." The distinction between chemical and biological warfare is important because of differences in the scientific research and technological development that have influenced their use in war.

Chemical weapons are inanimate substances, usually gaseous or liquid, that can rapidly cause death or disability. Since antiquity, poisons have been used as a fatal means of settling interpersonal conflict. Thus, knowledge of poisons must be considered the precursor to chemical weapons development. Poison science emerged as soon as humans developed a consistent technique for recognizing the detrimental properties of natural plant, animal, or mineral extracts. However, large-scale production of artificial chemicals required substantial technological advancements to facilitate both mass production and the safe deployment of dangerous chemicals against opponents in war. Chemical weapons have also been targeted against plants and animals for the purpose of debilitating agriculture and food resources; such chemicals are more adequately categorized by the familiar labels of herbicides and pesticides.

Biological weapons are preparations of live microorganisms that can rapidly cause debilitating disease and death in exposed populations. Pathogenic bacteria, viruses, and fungi with low infectious doses and high environmental survival rates are the primary components of biological weapons. Inanimate microbial products, such as fungal toxins, have also been developed as weapons, but these are better labeled as chemical weapons. By definition, biological weapons include pathogens targeted at domesticated plants and animals as a strategy for starving agricultural productivity. The use of biological weapons predates both the establishment of the germ theory of disease and the scientific understanding of the discrete nature of pathogens.

DEVELOPMENT

CHEMICAL WEAPONS

Three distinct classes of chemical weapons have existed throughout the developmental history of chemical warfare. The first, lethal agents, cause death at various degrees of potency, depending on the biochemical properties of the components. The second, incapacitating agents, are used to render soldiers incompetent for battle, and they generally do not kill more than 2 percent of exposed populations. The third, irritating agents, such as lachrimators, or tear gases, make it difficult for soldiers to fight without wearing cumbersome protective gear, such as face masks and respirators. Irritating agents are generally nonlethal to all except individuals with preexposure conditions, such as asthma.

There have been at least five generations of chemical weapons since the 1500's. The first generation predated the development of the large-scale industrial production facilities that facilitated the first concerted use of chemicals during World War I. Second-generation chemical weapons, mostly respiratory impairment gases, were developed for use during World War I. Third-generation agents, mostly nerve gases, were developed after World War I. Fourth-generation agents include psychoactive chemicals capable of inducing hallucinations in exposed individuals. Fifth-generation chemical weapons include new combinations of previously known chemical weapons, combinations of chemical and biological agents, or binary chemical weapons, which are endowed with innovative modes of delivery and action.

The first generation of chemical weapons in the

modern era is traced to artist and inventor Leonardo da Vinci's (1452-1519) description of shells loaded with very fine sulfur and arsenic dust. There is no evidence that Leonardo da Vinci's chemical weapon was actually used, so it is impossible to judge its effectiveness, but the description clearly marks the development of a weapon based on the coupling of specific chemicals with propelled contraptions. The second notable development after Leonardo da Vinci was the unsuccessful proposal developed between 1811 and 1855 by Thomas Cochrane (1775-1860),

TURNING POINTS

CHEMICAL WEAPONS

1500-1855	Toxic smoke weapons include arsenical compounds.
1845-1920	Asphyxiating gas weapons include the industrial-scale production of chlorine and phosgene.
1920-1960	Nerve gases, such as tabun and sarin, are developed to inhibit nerve function, leading to respiratory paralysis or asphyxia.
1959-1970	Psychoactive chemical weapons are developed to produce hallucinations in exposed individuals.
1970-present	Binary chemical weapons, stored and shipped in their component parts, are developed to increase quantities that can be safely transported to deployment sites.

BIOLOGICAL WEAPONS

300 B.C.E-1763 C.E.	During the miasma-contagion phase, environments are deliberately polluted with diseased carcasses and corpses.
1763-1925	During the fomites phase, specific disease agents and contaminated utensils are introduced as weapons, with smallpox, cholera, and the bubonic plague as popular agents.
1925-1940	During the cell culture phase, biological weapons are mass-produced and stockpiled; Japan's research program includes direct experimentation on humans.
1940-1969	During the vaccine development and stockpiling phase, there are open-air tests of biological dispersal in urban environments in the United States.
1969-present	During the genetic engineering phase, recombinant DNA biotechnology opens new frontiers in the design and production of biological weapons.

British naval officer and tenth earl of Dundonald, to use smoke from burning coal tar and carbon disulfide against French and Russian opponents.

The second generation of chemical weapons, developed toward the end of the nineteenth century, includes chlorine and phosgene. Chlorine was discovered and used as a bleaching agent before the end of the eighteenth century, and phosgene was discovered in 1812 as a product of the reaction between chlorine and carbon monoxide. Prohibition of poisonous gases was on the agenda of the first Hague Peace Conference, convened in 1899 by Czar Nicholas II (1868-1918). Although detailed knowledge of the manufacture and use of chemical weapons was limited, the U.S. delegation to the 1899 conference took a lone position in refusing to ratify an agreement to abstain from the use of "asphyxiating or deleterious gases." The second Hague Peace Conference, convened by President Theodore Roosevelt in 1907, expanded the prohibition to include "poison or poisoned weapons." The Hague conference agreements remained in force until April 22, 1915, when Germany used chlorine tear gas in Ypres, Belgium, against Franco-Algerian soldiers during World War I.

Although hundreds of chemicals have been tested for military purposes since 1915, fewer than 5 percent of them proved to be of significance to weapons development. The Geneva Protocol, signed by several countries on June 17, 1925, for the "prohibition of the use in war of asphyxiating, poisonous, or other gases and of bacteriological methods of warfare," did little to deter the development of new chemical weapons or the improvement of delivery of old ones. Among the chemicals mentioned were organophosphorus nerve agents, which constitute the

British soldiers wear gas masks to protect against respiratory-impairment gases as they wield a Vickers machine gun at the Battle of the Somme, July, 1916.

third generation of chemical weapons. Nerve gases inhibit certain cholinesterase enzymes that affect nerve function and lead to excessive sweating, uncontrollable vomiting and defecation, and, finally, death from respiratory paralysis or asphyxia. Tabun and sarin were discovered by chance in 1936 and 1938, respectively, by the German scientist Gerhard Schrader (1903-1991), who was conducting research on pesticides for the company I. G. Farbenfabriken. Tabun persists in the environment, whereas sarin dissipates rather quickly. Tabun was the first nerve gas to be manufactured on a large scale, and it was stockpiled by Germany during World War II.

Nazi Germany's use of lethal gas and other countries' capacity to develop and manufacture chemical weapons led to a post-World War II emphasis on defense strategies against chemical weapons. Sophisticated military reconnaissance strategies for chemical weapons included automatic detection systems such as the Nerve Agent Immobilized Enzyme Alarm Detector, which responds to small concentrations of nerve agents and cyanide. Similarly, equipment for personal and collective protection was rapidly developed, as were methods of environmental decontamination and medical treatment for exposed individuals.

Psychoactive chemicals, the fourth generation of chemical weapons, were developed between 1959 and 1965. The incentive was to calm the growing public distaste for the use of lethal chemicals. The

U.N. workers prepare Iraqi rockets, reportedly filled with sarin, a chemical weapon that affects nerve function, for destruction after the Persian Gulf War.

best-known psychoactive chemical weapon is quinuclidinyl benzilate, known as BZ, a relative of the psychedelic drug lysergic acid diethylamide (LSD), which induces altered states of consciousness. In the United States, BZ was advertised in a publicity campaign known as Operation Blue Skies, intended to reduce public anxiety about chemical warfare. The campaign promoted the drug as one that caused only temporary insanity and paralysis of the will to fight, thereby pacifying violent individuals. However, BZ was too expensive for large-scale manufacture, and the dose required for effect was unpredictable.

Binary weapons are representatives of the fifth generation of chemical weapons. Binary artillery projectiles were developed in the United States in response to growing tensions during the Cold War era (1945-1991) and to the apparent superiority of Soviet chemical weapons. Between 1978 and 1985, research was intensified on the development of binary projectiles designed for deployment in war crises. In 1987 the United States designed a binary system to increase the quantity of sarin that could be trans-ported to areas where it was required. The two chemicals that react to form sarin would be stored and shipped separately and then brought together at the gun site, where mixing and deployment could proceed rapidly and safely.

BIOLOGICAL WEAPONS

The development of modern biological weapons occurred in four distinct phases based on scientific advancements in the understanding of infectious diseases and the manipulation of microorganisms and ensuing technological innovations. The "contagion and miasma" phase (300 B.C.E.-1763 C.E.) occurred before the causative microbial origin of diseases was fully understood. During this period biological weapons consisted of attempts to contaminate the environment with actual bodies of diseased animals or humans. The second phase of biological weapons development (1763-1925) was marked by the use of fomites, or materials that have been in contact with diseased persons, used as weapons. The third, the "culture and stockpile" phase, involved the development of technical capacity to cultivate large quantities of microorganisms and vaccines. This period lasted from 1925 to 1969. The fourth phase, beginning in 1969, no less than a biological-science revolution, is marked by the development of genetic engineering, or recombinant DNA, facilitating the construction of organisms with new pathogenic traits.

Until the seventeenth century diseased corpses and carcasses were used as biological weapons by the Greeks, Romans, and Persians to contaminate drinking water and spread disease. Modern biological weapon development was initiated in 1763 when American military officers contemplated the use of smallpox-contaminated blankets against Native Americans in the French and Indian War; however, there is no concrete evidence that the proposal was implemented.

The discoveries of French chemist and microbiologist Louis Pasteur (1822-1895) greatly influenced the trajectory of biological weapons development in the nineteenth and twentieth centuries. During World War I, Germany allegedly used the plague and cholera against opponents in Russia and Italy, respectively. Anton Dilger (1884-1918), a German secret agent working in the United States, is credited with the development of batch culture techniques for producing large quantities of *Bacillus anthracis*, the causative agent of anthrax, and *Pseudomonas mallei*, the causative agent of glanders. Germany used these biological weapons to target horses and cattle in 1916 and was accused of dropping plague bombs and inoculating toys and candy in Romania.

The Geneva Protocol of 1925 condemned the use of biological and chemical weapons but did not restrict their development, research, or stockpiling. The U.S. Congress did not ratify the Geneva Protocol until 1975 and did so only after several reservations were added to the provisions relating to the use of banned agents against nonsignatory nations or violators of the protocol. The first dedicated biological warfare research program was established by the Soviet Union in 1929. Japan and the United Kingdom initiated similar programs in 1934, and the U.S. Army joined the race in 1941. Japan's biological weapons development program was particularly notable, because it involved tests and experimentation on human subjects.

During the Cold War period, intensive research and development on biological weapons was made. In 1943 the United States had established Fort Detrick in northern Maryland as the main center of biological weapons research. Canada, the United Kingdom, and the United States collaborated on modeling biological weapons dissemination, including the release of pathogens in the Caribbean Sea and open-air experiments in urban centers within the United States. By 1950 experiments on the aerial dispersal of pathogens had been conducted with *Serratia marcescens* and *Bacillus globigii* in San Francisco, California, and Norfolk, Virginia. Urban locale experiments to aid the development of biological weapons were conducted in the transportation subways of New York City in the 1960's. Nevertheless, the U.S. military concluded around 1969 that the potential usefulness of

biological weapons was severely limited under battlefield conditions. This policy reversal led to the relaxation of international research and development programs on biological warfare. Consequently, there was widespread support for the 1972 Biological Weapons Convention on the "prohibition of the development, production and stockpiling of bacteriological (biological) and toxin weapons and on their destruction."

The fourth phase of biological weapons development effectively began in 1969, with the invention of recombinant DNA techniques. These new biotechnology techniques created endless possibilities of recombining pathogen attributes from a variety of sources to produce more potent biological weapons than those isolated directly from nature. An outbreak of anthrax in Sverdlovsk, in the Soviet Union, killed at least sixty-four people in 1979. By 1982 several reports had been published in Western news media on the use of genetic engineering in the Soviet biological weapons development program. In 1988 the potential impact of U.S. biological weapons testing in Utah's Dugway Proving Grounds was publicized. During the 1980's and 1990's, attention became focused on the relatively easy access that developing nations have to genetic engineering techniques for producing potent pathogens. Moreover, belief in the boundless potentials of recombinant DNA created the fear that it is virtually impossible to develop effective defense technology against biological weapons.

There were allegations that biological weapons were used during the Iran-Iraq War (1980-1988). In 1998 the defunct apartheid regime of South Africa was accused of developing and using biological weapons. The involvement of developing countries worldwide, and African countries in particular, in the development and use of biological weapons is particularly troublesome because the continent harbors some of the most deadly pathogens, including viruses such as the Ebola virus. The increasing incidence of antibiotic-resistant strains of pathogenic bacteria has been a relatively recent cause for alarm in the development of biological weapons. Antibiotic resistance traits can evolve naturally in microbial populations, but the dangerous traits can also be manipulated to render the defense strategies based on known medications ineffective.

BOOKS AND ARTICLES
Bowman, Steve. *Biological Weapons: A Primer.* Huntington, N.Y.: Novinka Books, 2001.
Cirincione, Joseph. *Deadly Arsenals: Nuclear, Biological, and Chemical Threats.* 2d ed. Washington, D.C.: Carnegie Endowment for International Peace, 2005.
Cole, Leonard A. *The Eleventh Plague: The Politics of Biological and Chemical Warfare.* New York: W. H. Freeman, 1997.
Croddy, Eric, Clarisa Perez-Armendariz, and John Hart. *Chemical and Biological Warfare: A Comprehensive Survey for the Concerned Citizen.* New York: Copernicus Books, 2002.
Dando, Malcolm. *Biological Warfare in the Twenty-first Century: Biotechnology and the Proliferation of Biological Weapons.* London: Brassey's, 1994.
Drell, Sidney D., Abraham D. Sofaer, and George D. Wilson, eds. *The New Terror: Facing the Threat of Biological and Chemical Weapons.* Stanford, Calif.: Hoover Institution Press, 1999.
Harris, Robert, and Jeremy Paxman. *A Higher Form of Killing: The Secret History of Chemical and Biological Warfare.* New York: Random House Trade Paperbacks, 2002.
Langford, Roland E. *Introduction to Weapons of Mass Destruction: Radiological, Chemical, and Biological.* Hoboken, N.J.: Wiley-Interscience, 2004.
Spiers, Edward M. *Chemical and Biological Weapons: A Study of Proliferation.* New York: St. Martin's Press, 1994.
Tucker, Jonathan B. *War of Nerves: Chemical Warfare from World War I to Al-Qaeda.* New York: Pantheon Books, 2006.
_____, ed. *Toxic Terror: Assessing Terrorist Use of Chemical and Biological Weapons.* Cambridge, Mass.: MIT Press, 2000.
Wheelis, Mark, Lajos Rózsa, and Malcolm Dando, eds. *Deadly Cultures: Biological Weapons Since 1945.* Cambridge, Mass.: Harvard University Press, 2006.
Wright, Susan, ed. *Preventing a Biological Arms Race.* Cambridge, Mass.: MIT Press, 1990.

FILMS AND OTHER MEDIA
Plague War. Documentary. Public Broadcasting Service/WGBH, 1998.
Spying on Saddam: Investigation of the UN's Dramatic, Thwarted Effort to Uncover Iraq's Chemical, Biological, and Nuclear Weapons. Documentary. Public Broadcasting Service/WGBH, 1999.
Terrorism: Biological Weapons. Documentary and information guide. Emergency Film Group/Detrick Lawrence Corporation, 2000.
Terrorism: Chemical Weapons. Documentary and information guide. Emergency Film Group/Detrick Lawrence Corporation, 2000.
Toxic Agents: Viruses and Chemical and Biological Warfare. Documentary. History Channel, 2008.

Oladele A. Ogunseitan

MODERN FORTIFICATIONS

Dates: Since c. 1500

MEDIEVAL FORTIFICATIONS

NATURE AND USE

The fortifications of the sixteenth century differ little from those of medieval and ancient times with regard to key features such as moats, towers, and walls. In the field of strategic use, as they had in the past, fortifications provided protection for key positions and served a strategic role as part of greater defensive lines. This role became more dominant in the twentieth century. However, such continuous lines of defense were not unknown before the modern period, as attested by the Great Wall of China, built in the third century B.C.E. and spanning almost 1,500 miles, and Hadrian's Wall, built in the second century C.E. and extending more than 100 miles across Great Britain. The Romans also created hundreds of miles of less solid fortifications, known as the Limes, to close off other parts of their empire. During the Middle Ages, continuous obstacles forming a defensive line were found from England to as far east as Russia.

During the modern era, new forms of fortifications supplanted the castle and fortified cities in Europe. However, medieval-style fortifications remained in use in most of Asia, Africa, and the Americas. Thus, the major fortified sites of Japan, China, and the Indian subcontinent are more reminiscent of medieval cities than modern ones. Many fortifications in the Americas were also built in the more archaic style, with some notable exceptions, such as the sixteenth century Inca fortress of Sacsahuamán, overlooking Cuzco, and the easily defendable complexes of the Pueblo Indians of southwestern North America.

DEVELOPMENT

It has long been assumed that the cannon brought about the demise of the castle in Europe. However, this is not totally true. Although castles with weak, high walls did indeed succumb to the cannon, others continued in service for centuries. In the 1970's a castle used by terrorists in Lebanon was able to resist the modern ordnance launched from Israeli jets. What did bring a major change to fortifications was the need to create positions that could more effectively mount cannons and resist cannon fire. Cannons mounted on high fortification walls proved less effective than those that were placed lower down, because they lacked "grazing fire," or the field of fire in which a projectile is able to strike any object within its path above a certain height. As a result, the walls of many fortifications were lowered and made wider to accommodate large artillery pieces. At the same time, they became smaller targets by presenting a lower profile.

The first of these "improved" fortifications were built in western Europe. Italian engineers initiated some of the first significant changes in the 1480's. The Sangallo family of architects designed new forts in the Italian peninsula in the late fifteenth and the sixteenth century and in 1493 added bastions to Rome's Castel Sant Angelo, originally built in 135-139 by the emperor Hadrian (76-138) as a mausoleum for himself and his successors. In the 1490's a member of the Sangallo family built Sarzanello, a hilltop fort of triangular shape that included rounded bastions and a triangular *ravelin*, or V-shaped outwork, to protect the entrance. The transition from medieval to Renaissance styles also appears in city fortifications during the end of the fifteenth century in places such as Civita Castellana, north of Rome, and the Greek island of Rhodes, where bastions were added and the walls were modified.

At Salses, in modern-day southwestern France, a modernized fortification was built in 1498, improving on the Italian designs. Salses proved too weak to resist French cannons at close range, however, and in 1503 it was redesigned with thicker walls, the height of which was already mostly concealed in a large ditch that protected them from direct artillery fire. The guns mounted atop the walls of the fort were close to ground level, allowing grazing fire.

At the end of the 1530's, King Henry VIII (1491-1547) of England, facing the threat of invasion from the European continent, protected his coastline with a series of new forts designed to mount artillery and muskets. These forts, located near the beaches, consisted of a series of rounded bastions surrounding a central circular keep and sitting in a deep and wide dry moat. The best known of these forts are Deal, Walmer, and St. Mawes.

During the Renaissance, new forts built to secure key positions were large enough to resist the increasingly large armies that moved across Europe. When the Europeans arrived in America, they secured their hold on the land whenever possible with the newest type of stone fortifications. Otherwise, they relied on wooden stockades not much different from those used in the Middle Ages. The most interesting transfer of technology occurred in the sixteenth century, when the Portuguese helped the Ethiopians build castle-like fortifications at Gonder in northwestern Ethiopia. The influence of the new Renaissance techniques began in Africa with Portuguese forts from Ceuta (1415) to Mozambique (1506) and in Asia from Goa (1510) to Malaca (1511).

SEVENTEENTH AND EIGHTEENTH CENTURIES: VAUBAN AND BASTIONED FORTS

The seventeenth and eighteenth centuries marked the great age of "scientifically designed" fortifications. The masters of the art perfected their designs based on mathematical calculations, only modifying final plans to match the terrain. During this period, the bastion, with two fronts and two flanks attached to the curtain walls, became the dominant feature. Additional outworks were added for protection. The wide, deep moat acquired additional protective positions, low walls rose from its base, and a *glacis*, or gentle slope, was created to provide clear fields of fire.

During the sixteenth century the Italians lost their dominance in the field of military architecture and were replaced by the Germans, the Dutch, and the French, who developed their own schools of fortifications. The Dutch mathematician Simon Stevin (1548-1620) wrote a treatise on defenses, emphasizing the use of water features.

The French school included such masters as Jean Errard de Bar-le-Duc (1554-1610), who built a number of fortifications and in 1600 published a treatise on design in which he warned against reliance on geometrical calculations over design to suit the terrain. In 1640, Blaise François, comte de Pagan (1604-1665), emphasized the importance of the bastions and the use of detached bastions and outworks, including listening galleries to deter mining operations against the walls. Sébastien Le Prestre de Vauban (1633-1707), considered a genius of military engineering, emerged in the age of French domination, during the reign of Louis XIV (1638-1715).

Vauban based much of his work on that of Pagan but also emphasized the use of detached bastions, claiming that their fall would not result in the loss of the entire fort. One of the best examples of Vauban's first system of fortification is the citadel of Lille, in northern France. Vauban later refined his first system with a second and a third, and an example of the latter can be seen in Neuf Brisach, built in 1699 in northeastern France. One of Vauban's contemporaries, the Dutch solider and military engineer Baron Menno van Coehoorn (1641-1704), developed a system in the Netherlands that was adapted to water defenses and was much more economical to build than were fortifications of Vauban's second and third systems. Although they designed many fortifications, Coehoorn and Vauban were masters of the siege and knew that no fortification was impregnable.

Some of the important features of the bastioned fortifications of the Vauban era included the bastion, *bonette*, *caponier*, casemate, counterguard (a ravelin with a redoubt), counterscarp, covered way, crown work, detached bastions, glacis, hornwork, *lunette*, ravelin, and *tenaille*, which were used to protect the curtain.

The new fortifications in France and some other countries also defended key ports, forming coastal defenses; others guarded mountain passes; others still were incorporated in a loose line covering the exposed frontier. There were no solid lines of defenses, but an army of the period would have had either to eliminate these positions or to leave its lines of communications exposed. Many older fortifications still remained in service, and some played a prominent role in conflicts such as the English Civil War of 1642-1651.

The eighteenth century did not bring any major changes in fortifications design. In the mid-eighteenth century, John Muller (1699-1784) published in England *A Treatise Containing the Practical Part of Fortification* (1755), which explained the design elements of Vauban's and Coehoorn's systems, among others. French military engineer Marc-René de Montalembert (1714-1800) emphasized the use of artillery for defense of fortifications and insisted that protecting the guns in casemates was the best policy.

NINETEENTH CENTURY TRANSITION

A transitional phase began late in the eighteenth century when the threat of French invasion lent a new importance to coastal defenses in England. Naval action against a strong tower in Corsica in 1793 led the British to create similar towers to defend their vulnerable coastline. More than one hundred of these circular brick Martello towers were completed between 1805 and 1812. With thick walls at the base and rising to a height of about 10 meters, they held an artillery piece protected by a parapet on the roof. Martello towers were also built in North America and South Africa.

Interesting innovations appeared in the first half of the nineteenth century. Walls were made slightly higher to add more positions for cannons at different levels. Some examples include the Maximilian towers built at Linz, Austria, in 1830 and later near Verona, Italy, which consisted of three floors and eleven mounted guns. The Malakov Tower of Sevastopol,

TURNING POINTS

c. 1480   Fortifications begin to undergo design changes, such as lower, wider walls, to accommodate the use of cannons.

c. 1530   King Henry VIII of England builds series of forts on southern coastline to guard against European invasion.

c. 1660   Sébastien Le Prestre de Vauban emerges as a genius of military engineering, designing bastioned fortifications.

1793   Circular brick Martello towers are built in Corsica, and their design is copied as far away as North America.

1880's   The French develop high-explosive artillery, rendering all existing forts obsolete.

1930's   As the building of extensive fortified lines begins, the French complete the Maginot line along eastern border of France.

Ukraine, mounted guns on two floors and the roof, and the pentagonal Fort Sumter in the harbor of Charleston, South Carolina, accommodated artillery on two floors and the roof.

The Prussian school of fortifications adopted the earlier ideas of Montalembert, opting for a polygonal design and replacing bastions with caponiers that protected the ditches and became essential in covering the faces of the forts. The masonry forts of the nineteenth century proved inefficient in the American Civil War (1861-1865) when Forts Sumter and Pulaski proved vulnerable to rifled artillery. The Americans soon came to rely on wood and earthen forts, such as Fort Wagner in Charleston harbor, South Carolina, to withstand heavy bombardment. After the Franco-Prussian War (1870-1871) both the French and Germans also reconsidered their designs.

LATE NINETEENTH CENTURY

Raymond Adolphe Seré de Rivières (1815-1895) initiated new polygonal designs with surrounding ditches to secure France's borders, forming an almost continuous line defended by fortress girdles and barrier forts in restricted terrain. German military strategists did the same for Germany's borders, emphasizing the use of detached polygonal forts to form a fortress girdle around key cities. These forts served as artillery platforms and were located well beyond the town's perimeter to keep modern long-range artillery out of range. By the mid-1880's, the French had developed a new high-explosive shell that rendered all existing forts obsolete. All masonry forts had to be reinforced with concrete. Many of the newly outdated German forts and exposed artillery positions were replaced with detached battery positions. Interval works were created to fill the gaps in the rings. The new forts were built with concrete instead of bricks and reinforced with armor.

Both France and Germany adopted armored galleries and turrets for their artillery in the 1870's, but it was not until the 1890's that these became the essential artillery positions of key forts. The German Gruson Works, founded in 1869 and later absorbed by Krupp, became a primary supplier of armored turrets to Germany and other countries, such as Switzerland. The French used turrets built at Saint-Chamond in southeast-central France. The new French forts also included armored observation positions and machine-gun turrets with Bourges casemates designed for flanking fire and mounting 75-millimeter guns. Belgian military engineer Henri-Alexis Brialmont (1821-

1903) created a fortified ring at Antwerp, and more modern rings, with forts that included a central citadel with artillery turrets enclosed by a moat, at Namur and Liège. In the last decade of the century, the Germans created a new type of fortification called the *Feste*, which included large garrison areas and artillery blocks mounting several turreted guns. The first Feste was built at Mutzig. Several more were built around Metz and Thionville, but none saw combat until World War II. Across the border, the French continuously modernized their forts, forming fortress "girdles" at Verdun, Toul, Épinal, and Belfort. During World War I the Germans based their strategy on maintaining their defensive positions in France, going through Belgium, avoiding the French fortifications, and using their new super-heavy 420-millimeter artillery to smash the weaker Belgian forts built by Brialmont. In 1916 a change in strategy led the Germans into a disastrous campaign against the heavily defended Verdun forts, which had a telling effect on postwar considerations.

TWENTIETH CENTURY

In the 1930's, influenced by the Verdun experience, the French built the Maginot line, a line of defensive fortifications covering the eastern border of France. The new forts, known as *ouvrages*, reflected not only the lessons learned at Verdun but also the influence of the German Feste, now located in France. These ouvrages mounted medium artillery in turrets and casemates in individual blocks and had a subterranean service and garrison area linked to the combat area by a main gallery of up to 1 kilometer in length. The forts, with concrete roofs of up to 3.5 meters high on subterranean positions up to 30 meters deep, could resist rounds of up to 420 millimeters.

The Germans also built subterra-

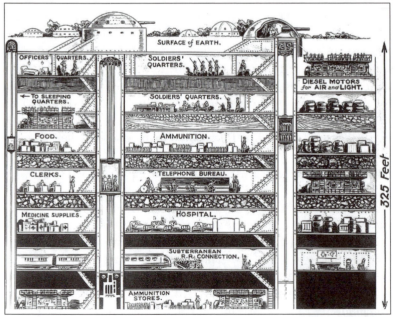

Hulton Archive/Getty Images

A sectional diagram of the Maginot line, defensive fortifications built along France's eastern border to protect against German invasion.

nean forts on their East Wall in the 1930's, but after 1936 they created a new type of fortified line, the West Wall, which used smaller bunkers deployed in depth and protected by massive minefields. The Italians created a new line of Alpine fortifications known as the Vallo Alpino, and the Swiss created similar, smaller positions to defend their National Redoubt with only a few modern, smaller versions of Maginot-style forts on the border. The Czechs, with French assistance, created a line of fortifications to encircle their vulnerable border, one section of which included Maginot-style ouvrages. Even the Belgians built a series of new forts to defend Liège from German attack. The Soviets created the Stalin line, with numerous positions similar to those on the Swiss and Czech lines, but abandoned it in 1940 for another line that was not completed. The Finns built a line of small fortifications called the Mannerheim line, with small bunkers and obstacles, and, after its loss, built a stronger position called the Salpa line. The longest defensive line, the Atlantic Wall, was created by the Germans between 1941 and 1944. It stretched from the Spanish border along the coast through Norway. This was not a continuous line but included many "fortress zones" built around ports with smaller strongpoints. Bunkers, mines, artillery positions, and other obstacles defended possible landing sites. In addition, the Germans built special concrete positions for heavy artillery on coastal sites, huge fortified submarine pens, command posts, and shelters in the lands they occupied. Their opponents built similar positions before and during World War II, from the English coast to Gibraltar and Singapore and from the American coast to the entrance to Manila Bay.

After World War II, the heavily defended gun-bearing fortifications forming continuous defensive lines were largely abandoned in favor of smaller strongpoints and lighter border defenses. The Cold War led to a new generation of fortifications that were created largely to protect command centers, such as the U.S. Air Force command center at Cheyenne, Wyoming. Some older fortifications, such as a few Maginot ouvrages, were restored for that purpose. Underground missile silos were constructed to protect nuclear missiles. However, when conventional war broke out most armies relied upon fortified lines consisting of field fortifications, fortified strongpoints, and even trenches. Such was the case in the Korean and Vietnam Wars, and in the 1990's, when the Iraqis built defenses on the border of occupied Kuwait.

BOOKS AND ARTICLES

Brice, Martin Hubert. *Forts and Fortresses: From the Hillforts of Prehistory to Modern Times, the Definitive Visual Account of the Science of Fortification*. New York: Facts On File, 1990.

Chartrand, René. *The Forts of New France in Northeast America, 1600-1763*. Illustrated by Brian Delf. Botley, Oxford, England: Osprey, 2008.

Clements, W. H. *Towers of Strength: The Story of the Martello Towers*. South Yorkshire, England: Leo Cooper, 1999.

Duffy, Christopher. *Fire and Stone: The Science of Fortress Warfare, 1660-1860*. London: David and Charles, 1975.

Dunstan, Simon. *Israeli Fortifications of the October War, 1973*. Illustrated by Steve Noon. Botley, Oxford, England: Osprey, 2008.

Field, Ron. *American Civil War Fortifications: Mississippi and River Forts*. Illustrated by Adam Hook. Botley, Oxford, England: Osprey, 2007.

_____. *Forts of the American Frontier, 1820-91: The Southern Plains and Southwest*. Illustrated by Adam Hook. Botley, Oxford, England: Osprey, 2006.

Griffith, Paddy. *The Vauban Fortifications of France*. Illustrated by Peter Dennis. Botley, Oxford, England: Osprey, 2006.

Hogg, Ian. *The History of Fortification*. New York: St. Martin's Press, 1981.

Hughes, Quentin. *Military Architecture*. London: Hugh Evelyn, 1974.

Kaufmann, J. E., and Robert Jurga. *Fortress Europe*. Conshohocken, Pa.: Combined, 1999.

Kaufmann, J. E., and H. W. Kaufmann. *Fortress America: The Forts That Defended America, 1600 to the Present*. Illustrated by Tomasz Idzikowski. Cambridge, Mass.: Da Capo Press, 2004.

Stephenson, Charles. *The Fortifications of Malta, 1530-1945*. Illustrated by Steve Noon Botley, Oxford, England: Osprey, 2004.

Weaver, John R. II. *A Legacy in Brick and Stone: American Coastal Defense Forts of the Third System, 1816-1867*. McLean, Va.: Redoubt Press, 2001.

FILMS AND OTHER MEDIA

Last of the Mohicans. Feature film. Morgan Creek Productions, 1992.

Modern Marvels: Atlantic Wall. Documentary. History Channel, 1999.

Modern Marvels: Forts. Documentary. History Channel, 1999.

Modern Marvels: The Maginot Line. Documentary. History Channel, 2000.

Vincennes. Feature film. Chronicles of America Pictures, 1923.

J. E. Kaufmann

SIEGES AND SIEGE TECHNIQUES
MODERN
Dates: Since c. 1500

NATURE AND USE

A siege is an operational method used by armies to capture heavily fortified or defended areas, including cities and castles. The process begins when the besieging force cuts off access and egress to the besieged area. The purpose of this action is to prevent resupply or reinforcement of or escape from the garrison, compelling the garrison to surrender with minimal loss to the attacking force. If the besieged force does not surrender once it is surrounded, the siege continues until the attacker gives up or storms the fortifications using its military capabilities. Against a determined defense, the latter option could result in significant casualties to one or both sides.

DEVELOPMENT

In the early modern period, siege warfare closely resembled siege warfare of the earliest recorded times. In general, once the line of circumvallation, or wall that denied the besieged city any outside contact, was completed, the opposing forces sat and waited for one side or the other to run out of supplies. The ability to create a breach in the defenses was extremely limited, and going over the defenses was extremely costly in lives.

Cannons were used by the English during the Siege of Calais (1346-1347). The cannons of the day were direct-fire weapons with limited range and power. It was not until the Siege of Constantinople (1453) that a mortar was able to lob artillery fire over the walls and into the defenses behind them. Although these new weapons made it a little easier to breach some defenses, they did not alter the way sieges were conducted. It was not until Charles VIII

(1470-1498) of France invaded Italy in 1494, with what is considered the first modern artillery train, that artillery became a significant part of siege warfare. The first major impact of this development was the change in the design of city and castle defenses from high, narrow walls to low, thick walls that were more resistant to artillery fire.

In the early part of the sixteenth century as the Turks expanded their empire throughout the Mediterranean, there were few forces standing in their way. By 1565 the only obstacle to complete Turkish domination of the region was the fortress of the Knights Hospitallers on the island of Malta. This fortress was commanded by Jean Parisot La Valette (1494-1568), whose strenuous defense, coupled with timely help from outside forces, prevented the Turks from seizing the fortress and blocked the westward expansion of the Ottoman Empire.

Gradually, over time, the art of fortification developed beyond the capacity of attacking forces to overcome. Many books were written on the subject, the first by the Italian Jacomo Castriotto (c. 1530-c. 1570) in 1564 and later by the Frenchman Blaise François, comte de Pagan (1604-1653) in 1541 and Chevalier Antoine de Ville (1596-1657) in 1625. However, no one took the time to write about capturing these great new fortifications. The weapons of the day were incapable of overcoming building technology, so sieges remained a waiting game.

The waiting game continued well into the seventeenth century. It was at Stenay (1654) where a little known French engineer, Sébastien Le Prestre de Vauban (1633-1707) first made his presence felt. Vauban succeeded in taking the fortress by siege, resulting in his becoming the king's engineer. Over the next fifty years, Vauban would revolutionize the art of siege warfare. He became the greatest military engineer of his day and changed the way sieges would be fought for generations to come. In fact, his fortress at Maubeuge would stand against German assaults for nearly two weeks in 1914. It was said that there was no fortification Vauban could not take and that no fortification built by Vauban would fall. Of course, there were several occasions on which Vauban was forced to lay siege to his own work.

In his lifetime Vauban constructed more than one hundred fortified locations and conducted dozens of sieges. During this period he made two major contributions to the art of siege warfare. At the Siege of Maastricht (1673), he first employed the system that became known as "saps and parallels" to capture the city in thirteen days. The saps and parallels system would be the standard method for besieging fortresses for the next 160 years, culminating in the last of the great classical sieges, the Siege of Antwerp in 1832.

Vauban's system was simple and elegant. Once the fortress or city was cut off, a trench was dug around the target. This trench, dug at long range for cannons of the day, was called the first parallel. Once the first parallel was complete, a series of saps were dug toward the fortifications. These saps were also trenches, dug in a zigzag manner to prevent the defending force from getting a clean shot at the engineers doing the work. At approximately medium range for cannons, a second parallel that circled the enemy positions connected these saps. Along this second parallel, artillery positions were prepared, so that the attacker's cannonfire could achieve better results.

Once the supporting troops were in place, another set of saps was dug toward the enemy positions. This second set of saps was connected by a third parallel, constructed at close range for the cannons. Again, the parallel would contain artillery positions. From the third parallel the final assault would be conducted. Vauban was able to develop the system to the point where he was able to predict the time until the successful completion of the siege before it even started. The entire process was codified in his book, *De l'attaque et de la défense des places* (1737-1742; attack and defense).

The second of Vauban's innovations dealt with effective use of cannons during sieges. The cannons of the day were low-trajectory, direct-fire weapons that were used to batter away at the enemy defenses but which could do little else. It was during the Siege of Philippsburg (1688-1697) that Vauban developed the concept of ricochet fire, making the cannons more useful. He determined a method that allowed the cannonball to bounce off the fortification walls and into the area behind it, causing damage and disruption to previously protected activities. Ricochet fire remained an artillery technique until the development of the howitzer in the 1830's ended the need for it.

The seventeenth century would showcase a number of great engineers who left their mark on siege warfare. After Vauban, perhaps the second most significant was the Dutch engineer Baron Menno van Coehoorn (1641-1704). Coehoorn is known for two significant contributions to siege warfare. The first was his advocacy of the direct method of resolving sieges. He felt that one should look for shortcuts, trading lives for time if necessary, and that storming the defenses was preferable to starving the defenders. His second contribution was the Coehoorn mortar. Like other mortars, it had a short range and a high trajectory, useful for lobbing shells over

TURNING POINTS

1494	Charles VIII introduces the modern siege train.
1565	The Siege of Malta ends the Turkish advance across the Mediterranean.
1673	The use of saps and parallels is introduced by Sebastién Le Prestre de Vauban at the Siege of Maastricht.
1696	Ricochet fire is introduced by Vauban at the Siege of Philippsburg.
1781	The Siege of Yorktown ends the American War of Independence.
1832	The last of the classical sieges occurs at Antwerp.
1942	The use of aerial resupply is introduced at Stalingrad.
1968	The last major sieges of the period occur at Hue and Khe Sanh, Vietnam.

walls. The major difference was that his mortar was designed to be lightweight and easily transportable and to lob small, antipersonnel grenades with a high rate of fire. The high rate of fire would keep the enemy pinned down while his forces could storm the works.

The fortifications constructed in the French, Dutch and, later, German styles, as developed by Vauban, Coehoorn, and others during the late seventeenth and early eighteenth centuries, changed the face of warfare in Europe for the next one hundred years. During the period from 1749 to 1815 a total of 289 major sieges were conducted throughout Europe, representing more than one-third of the total major engagements during the period. Even in North America sieges played a key role; the Siege of Yorktown (1781), for example, ended the American Revolution (1775-1783).

By the middle of the nineteenth century, the science of artillery had overtaken the science of fortifications. Advancements in gunpowder technology, forging, and projectile design changed the face of siege operations. New gunpowder mixes and better metallurgy increased the range of the weapons, and rifling and shell aerodynamics improved accuracy. It was no longer necessary to dig saps and parallels close to the defenses. They could be attacked more effectively, and safely, from longer ranges. The development of the howitzer made indirect fire much more effective as well. Expensive fixed fortifications became obsolete except at large cities.

As the role of permanent fortifications declined, the value of field, or temporary, fortifications increased. The field fortification of choice was the

North Wind Picture Archives via AP Images

George Washington and the comte de Rochambeau at the Siege of Yorktown, which effectively ended the American Revolutionary War.

trench. Most of the sieges over the later part of the nineteenth century involved rings of trenches on both sides, rather than those constructed by the attackers. In North America, key examples were the Sieges of Vicksburg (1863) and Petersburg (1864-1865), both during the American Civil War (1861-1865). In Europe, despite the presence of major permanent fortifications, the same was true. Both sides fought from trenches during the Siege of Paris (1870) during the Franco-Prussian War (1870-1871). This trend continued through the end of World War I. To some extent, combat across the entire western front of that war had devolved to siege warfare techniques by early 1915.

The introduction of the tank to the battlefield late in World War I began the move away from trenches and toward strongpoints. Defensive works soon became a series of individual strongpoints or fortifications, linked by fields of fire and communications lines but fighting independently. This change would also affect the way sieges were conducted. It was no longer possible to create one breach and force the defender to surrender; each strongpoint had to be dealt with individually. However, some fundamental rules still applied. The first objective of a besieging force remained the isolation of the defender from resupply and reinforcement. This was no longer done with lines of circumvallation, however, but with strongpoints and patrols. Once that had been accomplished, the attacker then sought to create weaknesses in the defense. Finally, if surrender was not obtained, storming was necessary.

Each of these steps became more difficult to make as technology advanced. As weapon lethality increased, so did troop dispersion. It became more difficult to concentrate forces to cut off the defender. Too many holes existed and small units could escape by avoiding the besieger's patrols and fixed positions. Besiegers were further hindered by the increased use of aircraft for resupply. It was no longer

necessary to move through the sieges. Instead, supplies and reinforcements could be brought in over the top of the lines. There were limitations, however, as the Germans found out during World War II at Stalingrad (1942-1943). The number of aircraft sorties required to resupply the army was beyond the capability of the German air force, and eventually the surviving 91,000 men of the German Sixth Army were forced to surrender to the Russians. Similarly, in Vietnam at Dien Bien Phu (1954), the French attempted to supply their defending force by air. Although they were successful for some time, the attacking Vietnamese inflicted enough damage to the runway that flights in and out became impossible. The introduction of the helicopter diminished the need for runways and made aerial resupply more practical, but limited lift capacity was a problem. At Khe Sanh (1968) American forces were able to successfully resupply their forces in this manner and were able to break the siege.

The introduction of the atom bomb (1945) and other weapons of mass destruction have provided a possible means to overcome any strongpoint but also present tremendous risk to the entire environment. Since the late 1960's, advances in conventional weapons technology have also greatly reduced the need to conduct sieges. Precision strikes, remote imagery, and other tools make the work of assaulting defended positions so much easier that attacking armies in the most recent large-scale conflicts have not had to resort to sieges in order to clear enemy positions.

BOOKS AND ARTICLES

Bruce, Robert B., et al. "Artillery and Siege Warfare." In *Fighting Techniques of the Napoleonic Age, 1792-1815: Equipment, Combat Skills, and Tactics*. New York: Thomas Dunne Books/St. Martin's Press 2008.

Burke, James. "Siege Warfare in Seventeenth Century Ireland." In *Conquest and Resistance: War in Seventeenth-Century Ireland*, edited by Pádraig Lenihan. Boston: Brill, 2001.

Duffy, Christopher. *Siege Warfare: The Fortress in the Early Modern World, 1494-1660*. 1979. Reprint. London: Routledge, 1996.

_____. *Siege Warfare: The Fortress in the Age of Vauban and Frederick the Great, 1660-1789*. London: Routledge and Kegan Paul, 1985.

Eltis, David. "The New Siege Warfare and Its Implications." In *The Military Revolution in the Sixteenth Century*. London: I. B. Tauris, 1995.

Haskew, Michael E., et al. "Siege Warfare." In *Fighting Techniques of the Oriental World, A.D. 1200-1860: Equipment, Combat Skills, and Tactics*. New York: Thomas Dunne Books/St. Martin's Press, 2008.

Jörgensen, Christer, et al. "Siege Warfare." In *Fighting Techniques of the Early Modern World, A.D.1500-A.D.1763: Equipment, Combat Skills, and Tactics*. Staplehurst, England: Spellmount, 2005.

Melegari, Vezio. *The Great Military Sieges*. London: New English Library, 1972.

Showalter, Dennis E., and William J. Astore. "Gunpowder Cannons, New Fortresses, and Siege Warfare." In *The Early Modern World*. Westport, Conn.: Greenwood Press, 2007.

Watson, Bruce Allen. *Sieges: A Comparative Study*. Westport, Conn.: Praeger, 1993.

FILMS AND OTHER MEDIA

Masada. Television miniseries. Arnon Milchan Productions, 1981.

The Messenger: The Story of Joan of Arc. Feature film. Gaumont, 1999.

Soldiers: A History of Men in Battle, Engineer. Documentary. Churchill Films, 1990.

Yorktown. Documentary. Colonial Williamsburg Foundation, 2006.

Jacob P. Kovel

ARMIES AND INFANTRY
MODERN
Dates: Since c. 1500

NATURE AND USE

Modern infantry warfare began in the sixteenth century with the advent of the pike, which transformed the concept of the infantry. The pike was utterly useless when used alone, but when used together with hundreds of other pikes, it was harder to stop and harder to attack than was any other hand weapon. However, for thousands of pikemen to work together, they had to learn to march in time to the beat of the drum, and they had to learn to respond simultaneously and uniformly to a series of clearly understood commands. The effectiveness of the pike was utterly dependent on order, and disorder spelled disaster. The solution was drill, or marching exercises.

The Swiss, who revolutionized the employment of the pike, and were quickly copied by every other nation in Europe, had developed a system of drill that allowed for rapid movement in good order, instant changes of facing, wheeling, opening, and closing of the intervals between ranks and files and the merging of ranks and files. They had also developed a series of standard motions for individual pikemen, so that when the command was given to "Port your pike," all pikemen knew exactly what posture to assume.

Although the Swiss did not invent drill, they created a degree of emphasis and elaboration that had not been seen since the days of the Roman legions. In the sixteenth century, if one wanted to be an effective pikeman, one had to learn and practice, and then continue to practice. Every man, from front to rear, had to be a professional. Amateur militia could and did attempt to master the drill and weapons of the professionals, but they were nearly always swept aside if they got in the way of professional pikemen.

In the sixteenth century, the word "professional" was generally synonymous with "mercenary," and the armies of sixteenth century Europe were composed of mercenaries from all over Christendom. Because these mercenaries required payment, failure to pay could result in strikes, mutinies, desertions, or even outright betrayal. It could even lead to disasters such as the Sack of Rome in 1527, in which an imperial army stormed and brutally pillaged the Holy City, even though the emperor had made peace with the pope. In another disaster, known as the Spanish Fury (1576), an unpaid Spanish army that had been sent to the Netherlands to crush a revolution rekindled it by sacking the pacified city of Antwerp.

The pike alone was inadequate for battle; pikemen were at a serious disadvantage against missile weapons. At Bicocca (1522), an unsupported Swiss pike formation was shot to pieces by Spanish and imperial harquebusiers after they were stalled behind a sunken road. These same harquebusiers gave a similar treatment to the French cavalry at Pavia (1525) when they hid behind hedges to blast the armored knights from their horses.

The successes of the harquebusiers, ironically, highlighted their weakness: They were able to bring their full power to bear only when they had an obstacle between them and their targets, which kept their enemies just out of reach. Essentially, the "shot," a generic term for firearm troops, was strong where pikes were weak, and pikes were strong where the shot was weak. When combined, the pikes could defend the shot from cavalry and other pikes, while the shot could kill from a distance. When combined, these forces were formidable.

Despite its flaws, the firearm killed as had no weapon that previously had been seen on any battlefield. It smashed through armor, it crushed bone, and it tore through soft tissue. It had what modern soldiers call "lethality," and it behooved sixteenth century commanders to develop tactical systems that optimized its strengths and mitigated its weaknesses. Part of this strategy was combining firearms with pikes, the other was developing a firing drill as elaborate as those of the pikes.

The most common method was to arrange the shot in a formation of eight to twelve ranks. The first rank would fire and fall away to the rear of the formation to reload. The next rank would then step up and fire, followed by the next, followed by the next. The commander could time his shots to regulate the expenditure of ammunition or intensify his fire as needed. An eight-rank formation could sustain a rate of fire of one volley every five seconds. These formations could advance or retire while firing and deliver aggressive, point-blank attacks at a jog or run. They could also double their ranks to the front, thus turning eight ranks into four, and deliver a single smashing volley in the face of an enemy charge.

This formidable combination of firepower and shock effect made infantry the anchor of any battle formation. Ironically, however, the infantry's limited mobility meant that it was not usually the decisive force in battle. A common scenario would be for the infantry to plod ahead and lock its opposite numbers in prolonged "push of pike" and point-blank musketry, while the cavalry battled on the flanks. The cavalry that was victorious would then ride around the rear of the enemy infantry. Most infantry would break and run at this point, while the best soldiers, such as the Spanish *tercios* at Rocroi (1643), would form squares and patiently wait to die.

DEVELOPMENT

For most of the sixteenth century, pikes favored extremely deep formations of as much as a hundred ranks depth. At the core of these formations would be the colors and the "double-pay men," who would issue forth through the intervals between the files to smash a stubborn enemy with halberds or two-handed swords. The shot, in massive formations, would form blocks on the wings. The advantage of such formations, often called "battles," were their tremendous staying power; there was always someone to take the place of the man who fell. Such formations could also form a 360-degree defense in seconds by facing every man to the outside. They could also provide a place of relative safety in the rear ranks, where new recruits could be seasoned. They almost certainly provided a huge morale boost, assuring each soldier that he was part of something massive and invincible. They were, however, also tremendously wasteful of manpower. The Dutch commander Maurice of Nassau (1567-1625) had to make much more frugal use of limited resources in his rebellion against the Spanish, so he developed a system where the "battles" were reduced to "battalions"

TURNING POINTS

1503	The first effective use of the combination of firearms and pikes, a formation called the "Spanish Square," is made at the Battle of Cerignola.
1522	Spanish harquebusiers slaughter Swiss pikemen in the service of the French at the Battle of Bicocca.
1525	Spanish harquebusiers slaughter French cavalry at the Battle of Pavia, hiding behind hedges to blast the armored knights from their horses.
c. 1600	The military reforms of Maurice of Nassau reduce the size and depth of pike formations to facilitate maneuverability and increase the number of muskets in units.
1688	Sebastién Le Prestre de Vauban introduces the socket bayonet, which fits over a musket's muzzle and allows the musket to be loaded and fired with the bayonet attached.
1792-1815	French armies develop attack column formations with light infantry "screens."
1914-1918	The French develop the "fire and maneuver" system of small-unit tactics.
1939-1945	The use of tanks becomes crucial to infantry operations during World War II.

of twelve ranks depth in the pikes and eight in the shot.

The battalion formation, with pikes in the center and shot on the flanks, allowed every man to use his weapon, and provided for much greater tactical flexibility. Conversely, it meant that every man needed to pull his weight, and that there was no "safe" place to keep the less reliable men.

INFANTRY AROUND THE WORLD

The firearm spread rapidly and was adopted from Japan to Morocco. The Japanese, under the influence of the Portuguese, developed a balanced infantry force that combined harquebuses with blocks of well-drilled spearmen.

Outside Japan and western Europe, the adoption of the firearm did not bring with it a parallel adoption of pikes, a development of drill, or an improvement in the status of the infantry. In India's Mughal Empire, Persia, and Muscovy, infantry remained at best old-fashioned and at worst rabble. The cavalry was the place of honor and the key to victory. In China it was said that one should not use good iron to make a nail, nor a good man to make a soldier, emphasizing long-term strategy over tactical efficiency.

Only in the Ottoman Empire was there a large and efficient corps of professional infantry, known as the janissaries. They were armed primarily with firearms and relied on friendly cavalry and wagons to protect them from enemy cavalry. Unlike European shot, they were freely engaged in close combat and carried both swords and shields. They would deliver a close-range blast at their enemies, draw their swords, and charge. They did not employ rigid formations or precise drill. Although the Turkish janissaries were the best in the world in the fifteenth century, they generally found themselves outclassed by pike and shot formations on level ground in the sixteenth.

Interestingly, while Europe continued to develop increasingly more deadly and efficient ways of making war, the armies of the East changed little until they found themselves the objects of European imperial ambitions in the eighteenth and nineteenth centuries. They then either adapted to a European model or were conquered.

THE AGE OF THE BAYONET

The invention of the socket bayonet at the end of the seventeenth century combined with several ongoing developments to reinvent warfare for the eighteenth century. The socket bayonet, meant that a soldier could both shoot a musket and defend himself. When formed shoulder-to-shoulder, a row of bayonets did as well as a row of pikes at warding off a cavalry attack, but this same impenetrable wall of steel points could also deliver a deadly hail of lead. At the end of the seventeenth century, the shot had dominated the field, with a small contingent of pikes waiting only to chase off cavalry. With the advent of the bayonet, the pike was instantly discarded.

The simultaneous adoption of the flintlock and the later introduction of the steel ramrod also served to increase the soldier's rate of fire from one to two or even three to four shots a minute. Warfare became a process of massing one's firepower in the decisive point, delivering an effective volley, and charging home with the bayonet. With high rates of fire and universal use of muskets, formations quickly went from the eight ranks of the Dutch system to four, to three, and then to two ranks.

Drill also changed. The focus became one of making the soldier a nonthinking cog in a machine whose purpose was to march in a steady and orderly manner, close within a few yards of an enemy, deliver an orderly and smashing volley, and charge home with the bayonet—or to stand its ground against an enemy trying such an attack. Drill took on the jerky, precise, and rapid form now associated with drill teams, and soldiers were, for the first time, forced to stand absolutely still when at "attention." In fighting the natural tendency to fidget and look around, the soldier was distracted from the natural tendency to flinch and to feel fear.

In the eighteenth century, these well-drilled lines of infantry dominated military operations. Cavalry could still deliver a decisive blow, and artillery was getting more mobile and more deadly, but most battles were being settled by steadiness, discipline, and the effective use of infantry firepower.

The French Revolutionary Wars (1792-1802) and the Napoleonic Wars (1803-1815) saw one major change in the idea of infantry effectiveness. The

French revolutionary armies could not match the royal armies of Europe in drill and precision, but they could outmatch them in numbers and motivation. Although the infantry of France still learned to march in step and fire on command, their favored formations—attack columns with loosely formed "light infantry" screens—were designed to complement the idea of massing overwhelming force at the decisive point and using that force aggressively.

THE INDUSTRIAL AGE

Following the Napoleonic Wars, infantry formations became more loose, and drill became less rigid. Attacks became less about marching mechanically into the face of the foe, and more about enthusiastic bayonet charges, supported by massed artillery. The nineteenth century conscript and reservist armies had to be more motivated by nationalism and belief in a cause than by drill and iron discipline.

The introduction of the breech-loading rifle accelerated this development when it doubled the infantryman's rate of fire, and made him capable of firing just as well, if not better, from the prone position as he did standing. The infantry line was reduced from two ranks to one, and commanders emphasized spirit and speed in the attack and rapid, accurate fire in the defense.

As formations became more loose, and men tended to seek cover, officers became concerned about losing control of men whom they could not see and who could not see them. They worried about soldiers panicking and wasting ammunition in blind firing or finding a hole and staying there.

During World War I, infantry operated in even looser formations than had been seen previously, but the Napoleonic notion of success based upon massed force and will to win remained strong. The futility of human wave assaults is well known, but it should be mentioned that if these attacks had always failed—if the combination of machine guns, barbed wire, artillery, and rifle fire had stopped the infantry dead, then they would not have been employed as they were for so long. The fatal problem was that these bayonet attacks did work or at least achieved limited success a fair amount of the time.

While casualties increased at Verdun (1916), the Somme (1916), and Vimy Ridge (1917), there were developments taking place that would point the way toward the future of the infantry. The French were developing a system for small-unit operations that involved some units providing covering fire, while others maneuvered to new firing positions, whence they would provide covering fire in their turn. They had perfected the "fire and maneuver" system that is the key to all modern small-unit infantry tactics.

The Germans formed elite corps of heavily armed and well-trained shock troops called *Sturmtruppen*, or storm troopers, who would slip forward and probe for weaknesses in the line. When they found one, they would attack with grenades and other close combat weapons to punch a hole in the enemy's trench lines. While the main body of the infantry widened the holes and eliminated strongpoints, teams of storm troopers would work their way deep into enemy territory, disrupting communications, ambushing reinforcements, and attacking supply and command centers.

The most significant development for the infantryman in World War I was not tactical but technological. The British solution to the trench warfare problem was the tank. The massive iron war machines of World War I were crude in nature, but by World War II, they had come to be the decisive force on the battlefield.

In World War II, infantry without tanks were no better off than had been the infantry in the trenches of World War I. However, if tanks without infantry encountered enemy infantry, they had to "button up" and blindly crash around until immobilized and killed by infantrymen they could not see. Therefore, by the twentieth century, tanks and infantry had developed a symbiotic relationship similar to that of the sixteenth century pikes and shot. Each needed the other to survive and win.

The twentieth century infantryman became a member of a combined arms team that balanced the strengths and weaknesses of foot soldiers, tanks, artillery, and to an increasing degree, aircraft. He also became accustomed to operating more autonomously than ever before. The modern battlefield is an alarmingly empty place. Friends and foes alike are concealed, and all are disbursed. The infantryman

U.S. soldiers from the 289th Infantry make their way down a snowy road in Belgium in January, 1945.

can see only a few friends and can usually glimpse the enemy for only a few fleeting moments. Modern infantrymen must be able to work in small and often unconnected groups toward a common goal. Soldiers are made to understand the plan and their place in it and should be willing to continue to carry out the mission even when out of the sight of leaders. Many infantries have not met this standard, and large numbers of soldiers in any operation spend the whole time isolated and paralyzed by uncertainty, but success in modern combat depends on some significant number of soldiers continuing to carry on, despite uncertainty.

In World War II, infantrymen who had been as-

signed to tank formations frequently rode in armored personnel carriers that provided enough mobility to keep up with the tanks, as well as some protection. The armored personnel carrier evolved into the tanklike armored fighting vehicle (AFV), and the modern mechanized infantry commander is constantly faced with the decision of when or if to dismount his infantry. If they are dismounted too soon, they get left behind or slow down the advance; if they are dismounted too late, the tanks may be destroyed by enemy antitank weapons, incinerating the infantry in their vehicles.

At the end of the twentieth century, infantry remained central to operations in Vietnam and Korea, and in counterinsurgency operations in Northern Ireland. In large-scale, conventional wars such as the Gulf War (1990-1991), however, infantry was primarily defined by its relationship to the armored vehicle. In modern U.S. Army parlance, an infantryman, on foot, doing what an infantryman has always done, is called a "dismount," as if to suggest that his natural place is inside an armored vehicle, and his existence as an infantryman is a temporary and transitory state of affairs.

BOOKS AND ARTICLES

Addington, Larry H. *The Patterns of War Since the Eighteenth Century*. 2d ed. Bloomington: Indiana University Press, 1994.

Army Historical Foundation. *U.S. Army: A Complete History*. Arlington, Va.: Hugh Lauter Levin Associates, 2004.

Carver, Michael. *Britain's Army in the Twentieth Century*. London: Macmillan, 1998.

Duffy, Christopher. *The Military Experience in the Age of Reason, 1715-1789*. New York: Barnes and Noble Books, 1987.

English, John A. *Marching Through Chaos: The Descent of Armies in Theory and Practice*. Westport, Conn.: Praeger, 1996.

English, John A., and Bruce I. Gudmundsson. *On Infantry*. Westport, Conn.: Praeger, 1994.

Griffith, Paddy. *Battle Tactics on the Western Front: The British Army's Art of Attack, 1916-1918*. New Haven, Conn.: Yale University Press, 1994.

House, Jonathan M. *Combined Arms Warfare in the Twentieth Century*. Maps by George Skoch. Lawrence: University Press of Kansas, 2001.

Keegan, John. *The Face of Battle*. New York: Barnes and Noble Books, 1989.

Killingray, David, and David Omissi, eds. *Guardians of Empire: The Armed Forces of the Colonial Powers, c. 1700-1964*. Manchester, England: Manchester University Press, 1999.

Mackenzie, S. P. *Revolutionary Armies in the Modern Era: A Revisionist Approach*. New York: Routledge, 1997.

Marshall, S. L. A. *Men Against Fire: The Problem of Battle Command in Future War*. New York: William Morrow, 1947.

Oman, Sir Charles. *A History of the Art of War in the Sixteenth Century*. 1937. Reprint. Mechanicsburg, Pa.: Stackpole Books, 1999.

Osgood, Richard. *The Unknown Warrior: An Archaeology of the Common Soldier*. Stroud, Gloucestershire, England: Sutton, 2005.

Ross, Steven T. *From Flintlock to Rifle: Infantry Tactics, 1740-1866*. Rutherford, N.J.: Fairleigh Dickinson University Press, 1979. Reprint. Portland, Oreg.: F. Cass, 1996.

Smith, Digby George. *Armies of 1812: The Grand Armée and the Armies of Austria, Prussia, Russia, and Turkey*. Staplehurst, England: Spellmount, 2002.

Tsouras, Peter G. *Changing Orders: The Evolution of the World's Armies, 1945 to the Present*. New York: Facts On File, 1994.

FILMS AND OTHER MEDIA

Band of Brothers. Television miniseries. Home Box Office, 2001.

The Big Red One. Feature film. Lorimar, 1980.

Kelly's Heroes. Feature film. Avala Film, 1970.

Weapons at War: Infantry. Documentary. History Channel, 1999.

Walter Nelson

CAVALRY
MODERN
Dates: Since c. 1500

NATURE AND USE

Cavalry are defined as horse-riding warriors. There are at least eighty-four different species of horses in the world, and the rider always seeks to find a size of horse that matches the classification of duty. Because a trained cavalry horse and rider can be four to five times more expensive to equip and train than an infantryman, only about one-fourth of the large national armies from the sixteenth to nineteenth centuries were composed of cavalry.

The types of cavalry used since 1500 are classified as heavy, light, and medium. Heavy cavalry are large, armored men on large horses who forcefully charge into and through an enemy's line of battle or position. Light cavalry are smaller men on smaller and faster horses, whose mobility allows them to serve a variety of battle and nonbattle duties. Medium cavalry are expected to perform any of the duties of the heavy or light cavalries but are uniquely trained to dismount and use firearms as infantry. Cavalry who carry spears or lances are classified mostly as light or medium, being able to perform light nonbattle duties and to perform medium duties on the battlefield against infantry and cavalry.

Cavalry reached the height of its use and development during the Napoleonic Wars (1803-1815). In large European armies, cuirassiers who wore upper body armor and metal helmets were the most common heavy cavalry; dragoons were the most common medium cavalry; and a variety of riders, including hussars, lancers, cossacks, and chasseurs, formed the light cavalry. Heavy and medium cavalry could be expected to advance against infantry, cavalry, and artillery, whereas light cavalry typically fought other cavalry, artillery positions, and smaller groups of infantry. The light cavalry's mobility suited them

for a variety of noncombat duties, including observing or searching for the enemy, carrying and intercepting messages, escorting officers and dignitaries, protecting or plundering supplies and equipment, and gathering food and supplies from local settlements.

A horse was mature enough for cavalry duty at about age four, was at the height of its power by age nine, and was useful until age eighteen. On the march at about 4 miles per hour, 20 to 25 miles per day was a horse's reasonable limit. A military cavalry horse was trained to the sights and noises of the battlefield; therefore, training exercises might include mock battles with drumbeats, gunshots, artillery, waving colors, and drills in crossing and jumping obstacles without hesitation.

During battle, cavalry were typically positioned on the flanks of the line to protect the sides and rear of infantry and to be located outside the infantry and artillery lines of fire. Cavalry formations also were positioned behind infantry to stop deserters, to reinforce weak sectors of the battle line, and to wait for the proper moment to deliver the final thrust to finish a weak or shaken enemy. If the battle was won, the light cavalry was used to pursue a retreating enemy and capture prisoners.

DEVELOPMENT

The sixteenth century is significant in the development of cavalry warfare; technical and strategic advances in weaponry and the formalization of full-time national professional armies took place during that time. Gunpowder weapons such as muskets, pistols, and artillery could penetrate a knight's armor and could kill from beyond the reach of swords, axes,

Friedrich Wilhelm von Seydlitz leads the decisive cavalry charge at the Battle of Rossbach (1757) during the Seven Years' War.

or spears. Significant increases in population, commerce, and trade enabled political leaders to build large national treasuries from taxes and to pay, train, and equip professional armies and officers. The French Wars of Religion (1562-1598), the Thirty Years' War (1618-1648), and the English Civil War (1642-1651) resulted in the development and sharing of new skills, tactics, weapons, and equipment.

The Hundred Years' War (1337-1453) influenced the decline of the armored knight. The English longbows and steel-tipped arrows used in that conflict could penetrate the heavy armor of French knights from 100 yards and could be shot four to five times per minute. This scenario repeated itself at the Battles

of Crécy (1346), Poitiers (1356), and Agincourt (1415). French advances in artillery technology and use was a factor in their eventually driving the British out of France.

Steel-tipped arrows and the longbow were made obsolete by the development and use of the harquebus, which was the first primitive form of musket firearm. The development of artillery also contributed to the decline of the bow and arrow, and mounted archers had disappeared by the mid-1500's. In addition to swords, cavalry were armed with a shorter version of the harquebus and two or more pistols.

During the French Wars of Religion, a new tactic called the caracole was used by cavalry in battle.

TURNING POINTS

1415	English archers and infantry inflict a major defeat upon mounted French knights at the Battle of Agincourt, initiating the decline of the heavily armored cavalry knight.
c. 1500	The development of gunpowder muskets, pistols, and cannons forces tactical and strategic changes in the use of spears, bows and arrows, swords, cavalry, and armor.
mid-1500's	European cavalries begin to appear armed with short muskets that can be fired from both mounted and dismounted positions.
1642-1649	During the English Civil War, the Royalist Army is the first to use horse artillery in the form of a small brass cannon mounted onto a horse-drawn cart.
1712-1786	Frederick the Great of Prussia is the first to use Jägers, or "huntsmen," expert mounted marksmen.
1804-1815	French emperor Napoleon Bonaparte develops his cavalry to the height of its quantity and quality, making it as significant as infantry in the outcomes of battles and campaigns.
1854-1871	Cavalry comprises a significant portion of the armies of late nineteenth century wars, but unacceptably high casualty rates occur against large bodies of infantry. The only significant successes of cavalry in these wars are when cavalry fight cavalry, dismounted as dragoons, and when performing light-horse nonbattle duties.
1914-1918	The World War I armies form large cavalry components, which are converted into infantry as the war evolves into stagnant trench warfare and high casualty rates occur.

Cavalry were tightly formed several lines deep, and each line in turn would ride to within ten paces of the enemy, fire their pistols, and quickly wheel away to reload in the rear, while the next rank rode forward to shoot. The harquebus and pistol were more accurate if fired while dismounted, but in close-contact fighting the pistol was light and left the cavalryman's other hand free to control the horse. If a cavalryman shot his pistol and had no opportunity to reload, he would then use his sword to attack and defend. One tactical use of the sword was to cut the reins of enemy cavalry so they would lose control of their horses. Due to the possibility of misfiring, each cavalryman carried several loaded pistols and a sword into battle. At this time horse armor disappeared, and the cavalry

soldiers reduced their own armor, adopting a body armor called a cuirass.

King Gustavus II Adolphus of Sweden (1594-1632), whose armies were very successful in the Thirty Years' War, is recognized by military historians as the first expert to develop and use modern concepts of technology, logistics, strategy, and tactics on the battlefield. He spent half of Sweden's national budget on the army and formalized the processes of payment, clothing, supplying, feeding, and medical care for his soldiers. He increased the power of his army through the use of conscription, mercenaries, and a system of training and discipline reminiscent of that of the ancient Roman legions. He also directed his technological experts to significantly improve the effectiveness and reliability of pistols, muskets, and lighter mobile cannon.

Gustavus is also credited as the first military leader since Alexander the Great (356-323 B.C.E.) to use tactical flexibility in the training and organization of his army and its usage on the battlefield. His army had various types of infantry and cavalry, which were given specific tactical duties and then trained as disciplined masters of those duties. Relative to the large masses of enemy formations, Gustavus used smaller units strategically spaced so that they could quickly and aggressively respond to the opportunities of a battle.

Gustavus also revolutionized the use of firearms in battle. In recognition of the fact that firearms such as the pistol and musket were inaccurate, unreliable, and time-consuming to reload, Gustavus forbade the use of the caracole and decided that cavalry would attack quickly, in large numbers, primarily with swords. He trained his cavalry to attack in three lines. The first line would fire a pistol volley, then all three lines would charge with the sword. The pistol was used only during the ensuing close-contact melee fight. Each regiment of his cavalry was supported in its attack by medium, musket-armed cavalry, known as musketeers, and two light 4-pound cannons, each drawn by one horse or three men.

A regiment in the Swedish cavalry of 1620 consisted of about one thousand men divided into eight squadrons; each squadron had a support staff of ten or more individuals who served as quartermaster, muster clerk, chaplain, provost, barber, medical orderly, ferrier, and trumpeter. By the 1630's, to increase maneuverability, a regiment was reduced to 560 men in eight squadrons. At the Battle of Breitenfeld (1631), 10,000 Swedish cavalry clashed with 16,000 Imperial cavalry with great success, and light Swedish cavalry pursued the beaten foe for four days afterward.

During the Thirty Years' War the grenadier cavalry made its first appearance in the French army. Grenadiers were a few brave select men chosen from musketeer units to attack enemy fortifications in small groups using hand bombs, or grenades. Grenadiers wore a different type of headgear called a *colpack*, which allowed them to sling their muskets over their heads onto their backs, freeing both hands to light the grenade fuse and throw it. In some parts of Europe, colpacks became more elaborate, resembling a bishop's miter.

Historians believe that during the English Civil War, Prince Rupert (1619-1682) of the king's Royalist army was the first to have his cavalry use mobile horse artillery. Called a "galloping gun," it was a small brass cannon mounted on a horse-drawn cart. The gunners accompanied the cart on horseback. A cavalry regiment serving the king's Royalist army consisted of three hundred to five hundred men organized into six troops. Historians agree that the cavalry, who fought mostly from a dismounted position, decided the Battles of Marston Moor (1644) and Naseby (1645).

In the army of the French king Louis XIV (1638-1715), a French cavalry regiment varied in size from 300 to 450 men and formed 20 to 30 percent of the army. Louis XIV had four types of horsemen: the Household Cavalry, who were the smartly uniformed chosen elite used during special ceremonies and for royal escorts; the armored heavy cavalry, known as cuirassiers; the medium foot cavalry, known as carabineers and dragoons, so called for their carbine or dragon musket weapons; and the line cavalry, lighter, more mobile lancers, hussars, and mercenary Russian cossacks.

Frederick the Great (1712-1786) of Prussia is credited with the first use of a select group of expert, mounted shooters or marksmen, called *Jägers*, or "huntsmen." These huntsmen were typically from the rural countryside and had developed expert skills in riding, shooting, and the hunting of select targets. Frederick is credited also with increasing the number of light cavalry and giving some of them the task of military policing and preventing desertion. Frederick's forces used horse artillery in greater numbers than had been used previously. A horse artillery team consisted of three drivers on six horses pulling the cannon, and eight gunners, who accompanied on horseback. By 1786 Frederick's total

F. R. Niglutsch

Russia's Cossack Imperial Guard advance into Turkey in 1877 during the Third Russo-Turkish War.

horse artillery consisted of six troops of nine cannons each.

Cavalry warfare reached its historical peak during the reign of Napoleon Bonaparte (1769-1821), military commander and later emperor of France. Under Napoleon's great cavalry leaders, Antoine Charles Lasalle (1775-1809), Joachim Murat (1767-1815), and François Christophe Kellermann (1735-1820), the French cavalry of the era became known for its aggressive audacity on the battlefield and its flamboyant lifestyle off it.

In 1805 Napoleon created a Cavalry Reserve Corps of 22,000 men commanded by Marshal Murat. However, during battle, this corps was under the direct control of Napoleon himself. In that first organization, the Cavalry Reserve had two heavy divisions consisting primarily of cuirassiers and five medium divisions consisting of dragoons. The individual infantry corps was assigned the use of light cavalry regiments.

An important component of the Cavalry Reserve Corps was the Imperial Guard regiments, whose soldiers were promoted to that elite status based on proven experience, bravery, and loyalty to Napoleon. Especially in the cavalry, Napoleon's soldiers were expected to dress according to a strict uniform code, and individual regiments even had a distinct color of horse. Napoleonic soldiers of different types wore uniforms of various colors to make themselves distinct on both parade grounds and battlefields.

Cavalry made up approximately one-fourth of an army during the Napoleonic era, and the largest numbers of cavalry in battle were at Eckmühl (1809) and Borodino (1812). At Eylau in 1807, Marshal Murat led eighty squadrons of French cavalry in a massive column charge against the Russian center of infantry, thereby saving the French from defeat. The confrontation took place on a cold, snowy day, the low temperatures allowing the French cavalry to gain an irresistible speed over the frozen ground and causing the Russian muskets to misfire.

Napoleon's army was defeated at the Battle of Leipzig in 1813 by a large allied force that included 60,000 cavalry. Because the allies had their cavalry assigned to the direct control of various infantry corps, there was no effective pursuit of the French, thus allowing them to reorganize. By contrast, after the French victory over the Prussians at Jena in 1806, Murat's light cavalry pursued the beaten foe 22 miles per day for several weeks.

During Napoleon's last battle at Waterloo on June 15, 1815, his cavalry totaled 14,000 of the army's 85,000 soldiers. During the late afternoon, middle phase of the battle, five thousand to eight thousand French cavalry repeatedly charged the British and allied army under Arthur Wellesley, the duke of Wellington (1769-1852). The French cavalry were slowed by the muddy ground and were resisted by the bayonets of Wellington's infantry, which was securely formed in twenty large square formations, four to six lines deep. The approaching French cavalry were blasted by British artillery fire and, when the French became disarrayed between the squares, were countercharged by British cavalry. Toward the end of the battle, the British and Prussian light cavalry successfully drove the defeated French army from the field, and the Prussians pursued the French for several days back to France.

After the Napoleonic Wars cavalry remained a sizable portion of most national armies. In the wars that followed, cavalry were slaughtered when they charged firmly placed infantry and artillery. During the Crimean War (1853-1856) the disciplined rifle fire from the "Thin Red Line" of the Ninety-third Scottish Highlanders turned away a large body of charging Russian cavalry at Balaklava on October 25, 1854. Later that day the Heavy Brigade of the British cavalry was successful in a charge against a larger group of Russian cavalry. At this battle the Heavy Brigade consisted of the Scots Greys, the Inniskilling squadrons, and the Fifth Dragoons squadron.

The most famous Crimean War battle was the Charge of the Light Brigade, which occurred at Balaklava on October 25, 1854, at 11:00 A.M. The British Light Brigade consisted of 673 men representing the Eighth and Eleventh Hussar Regiments, the Fourth and Thirteenth Light Dragoons, and the Seventeenth Lancers. Fitzroy James Henry Somerset, the Baron Raglan (1788-1855), the British commander, wanted the Light Brigade to retake some Turkish cannon captured by the Russians earlier in the day. Due to mistaken orders, the Light Brigade charged a different, more heavily defended artillery position and suffered severe casualties of 113 men killed and 134 men wounded.

During the American Civil War (1861-1865), cavalry acted as medium-weight dragoons, fighting with carbines, shot guns, pistols, and sabers. Away from the battlefield they performed a multitude of light-horse duties, primarily serving as the army's "eyes and ears." In 1862 the cavalry of Confederate general Jeb Stuart (1833-1864) rode entirely around the Union army, disrupting communications and creating fear and panic among the Northern population and army alike. In 1863 the largest cavalry-versus-cavalry battles took place at Brandy Station (June 9) and at Gettysburg (July 1-3).

On July 1, at the Battle of Gettysburg, Union general John Buford's (1826-1863) dismounted cavalry held back the initial Confederate infantry attacks long enough for Federal infantry to arrive and fight a daylong delaying action. Ultimately, this delaying tactic enabled the Union infantry to consolidate a defensive position on the high ground along Cemetery Hill and Cemetery Ridge and hold back General Robert E. Lee's (1807-1870) invasion of the north. Buford's cavalry used carbine rifles from behind hastily constructed field fortifications of fence rails, rocks, and dirt. When General John Reynold's Union First Corps infantry relieved them, Buford's remaining men remounted and rode to protect the army's open left flank.

The Franco-Prussian War (1870-1871) was the last major conflict involving large forces of cavalry, and it marked the end of offensive heavy cavalry attacks. In almost every instance of cavalry charges against breech-loading rifles there were few positive results and severe casualty rates. Mars-la-Tour (1870), the largest cavalry battle of the war, included five thousand French and Prussian cuirassiers and large numbers of other cavalry types.

One innovative cavalry tactic of the war involved the Prussian high command reversing traditional policy by ordering all the cavalry ahead of the army. This resulted in a massive screen between the opposing armies, blinding the French and keeping the Prussians completely and accurately informed of every French move.

At the Battle of the Little Bighorn (1876) during the Second Sioux War, the U.S. Seventh Cavalry

North Wind Picture Archives via AP Images

A cavalry duel during the American Civil War.

At the Battle of the Little Bighorn in 1876, the U.S. Seventh Cavalry was almost entirely wiped out by a superior number of Sioux.

under the leadership of George Armstrong Custer (1839-1876) was almost entirely wiped out by a superior number of Sioux and Cheyenne American natives. Custer's plan was to surprise the natives' village by dividing his force to attack from several sides at one time. Custer and most of his entire regiment were killed when the natives, on horseback and on foot, counterattacked, chased, and surrounded Custer's separate units, finishing off the soldiers, who had not been issued sabers, after their ammunition and numbers became low.

During the Spanish-American War (1898) future U.S. president Lieutenant Theodore Roosevelt was mounted when he led his First United States Cavalry Regiment "Rough Riders" in a successful charge on foot up the San Juan Heights of Cuba. The Americans suffered 20 percent casualties from Spanish and Cuban rifle, artillery, and machine-gun fire.

On September 2, 1898, at the Battle of Omdurman in the Sudan, the four hundred troopers of the British Twenty-first Lancers, which included future prime minister Lieutenant Winston Churchill (1874-1965), successfully defeated a formation of 3,000 Dervish infantry. The British charged a smaller group of Dervish visible in open ground but were surprised by a couple of thousand Dervish hidden in a depression. The British charged into the large body of Dervish infantry with lances and swords, engaged them for a short time in a close-contact melee, rode through the Dervish, dismounted, and then forced the Dervish to retreat with concentrated carbine and pistol fire. The Lancers suffered casualties of 70 men and 119 horses in that battle.

At the beginning of World War I (1914-1918) most of the European national armies initially raised large numbers of cavalry. After a short time, however, most of the cavalry were converted into infantry in response to manpower needs and the defensive style of trench warfare. Horses were used mostly to transport supplies, equipment, and artillery. The communication and reconnaissance duties of light cavalry were taken over by the use of airplanes, zeppelins, bicycles, motorcycles, and automobiles. The most active and numerous cavalry units were Russian cossacks positioned on the eastern front of Europe. A few British Lancers and German Uhlan units on the western European front were stationed in the rear of their armies to serve light cavalry duty, prevent desertion, and as a possible rear guard in the event retreat was necessary.

Two significant cavalry actions occurred in the Middle East (Arab) sector of the war, where British and Australian forces were fighting mostly Turkish forces. On October 31, 1917, at the Gaza-Beersheba Line, the Fourth Australian Light Horse Brigade charged in loose order across an open, sandy plain and defeated two entrenched lines of Turkish infantry who used rifles and machine guns. Analysts believe that Australian horse artillery support and the audacity and speed of the charge enabled the horsemen to close faster then the Turks could lower the sights of their guns to shoot accurately.

At the Battle of Megiddo, Palestine (September 19-21, 1918), a large force of General Allenby's British and allied cavalry successfully rode around the Turkish-German flank, cut their communications, and caused much confusion as the enemy forces retreated. In several instances where the retreating forces were attempting to establish a new line of resistance, they were attacked and dispersed before they became too strong.

There were no cavalry battles during World War II (1939-1945), but there are several accounts of Polish lancer cavalry being slaughtered by German tank columns in 1939 as Hitler invaded Poland. One account describes the Polish cavalry as being falsely led to believe the German tanks were fake cardboard versions. During World War II, armored tank development permanently replaced cavalry in warfare.

BOOKS AND ARTICLES

Barthorp, Michael. *Heroes of the Crimea: The Battles of Balaclava and Inkerman*. New York: Sterling, 1991.

Bielakowski, Alexander. *U.S. Cavalryman, 1891-1920*. Illustrated by Raffaele Ruggeri. Botley, Oxford, England: Osprey, 2004.

De Quesada, Alejandro. *Roosevelt's Rough Riders*. Illustrated by Stephen Walsh. Botley, Oxford, England: Osprey, 2009.

Ellis, John. *Cavalry: The History of Mounted Warfare*. New York: G. P. Putnam's Sons, 1978. Reprint. Barnsley, England: Pen and Sword, 2004.

Elting, John R. *Swords Around a Throne*. New York: Da Capo Press, 1997.

Fowler, Jeffrey T. *Axis Cavalry in World War II*. Illustrated by Mike Chappell. Botley, Oxford, England: Osprey, 2001.

Hollins, David. *Hungarian Hussar, 1756-1815*. Illustrated by Darko Pavlovic. Botley, Oxford, England: Osprey, 2003.

Jarymowycz, Roman Johann. *Cavalry from Hoof to Track*. Westport, Conn.: Praeger Security International, 2008.

Lawford, James, ed. *The Cavalry: Techniques and Triumphs of the Military Horseman*. Indianapolis: Bobbs-Merrill, 1976.

Livesey, Anthony. *Battles of the Great Commanders*. London: Tiger Books, 1987.

Morton, Matthew Darlington. *Men on Iron Ponies: The Death and Rebirth of the Modern U.S. Cavalry*. DeKalb: Northern Illinois University Press, 2009.

Sinclair, Andrew. *Man and Horse: Four Thousand Years of the Mounted Warrior*. Stroud, Gloucestershire, England: Sutton, 2008.

Smith, Gene. *Mounted Warriors: From Alexander the Great and Cromwell to Stewart, Sheridan, and Custer.* Hoboken, N.J.: Wiley, 2009.

Spring, Laurence. *The Cossacks, 1799-1815.* Illustrated by Philip Haythornthwaite and Adam Hook. Botley, Oxford, England: Osprey, 2003.

Urwin, Gregory J. W. *The United States Cavalry: An Illustrated History, 1776-1944.* Poole, Dorset, England: Blandford Press, 1983. Reprint. Norman: University of Oklahoma Press, 2003.

Vuksic, V., and Z. Grbasic. *Cavalry: The History of a Fighting Elite, 650 B.C.-A.D. 1914.* New York: Sterling, 1993.

Wittenberg, Eric J. *The Union Cavalry Comes of Age: Hartwood Church to Brandy Station, 1863.* Washington, D.C.: Brassey's, 2003.

FILMS AND OTHER MEDIA

The Charge of the Light Brigade. Feature film. Warner Bros., 1936.

First in Battle: The True Story of the Seventh Cavalry. Documentary. History Channel, 2006.

Henry V. Feature film. BBC/Curzon/Renaissance, 1989.

Horse Warriors. Documentary. Worldwide Pictures/The Learning Channel, 1998.

Alan P. Peterson

NAVAL DEVELOPMENT
THE AGE OF SAIL
Dates: c. 1500-1850

NATURE AND USE

The period from 1500 to 1850 saw dramatic developments in naval warships. Although the first effective gun-armed sailing ships had appeared around 1500, these ships were little more than converted merchant ships, not designed to make the most effective use of artillery. Nonetheless, they allowed Europeans to display maritime power on a global scale for the first time, as evidenced by the creation of the Spanish and Portuguese empires in Asia and the Americas, and also in parts of Africa, in the early sixteenth century. The first type of sailing ship designed around gun armament was the galleon, which appeared in approximately 1550. Although galleons were still used by the Spanish as cargo carriers, warships became increasingly differentiated from merchant ships. By 1600 the principal missions of warships were fairly well defined: to seize command of the sea in order to facilitate or prevent invasion; to attack and defend maritime commerce; and also to attack onshore targets. These basic missions continued throughout the age of sail, and into the age of propulsion.

In the sixteenth century, galleons became the principal fighting ships. They were supported in the early seventeenth century by ships known as pinnaces, smaller vessels that were especially useful in coastal waters too shallow for galleons. Because all warships of the sailing era were constructed of wood, they were vulnerable to fire. Fireships were designed to be set on fire with the intention of crashing into enemy ships; and pinnaces often defended against fireships. Oared vessels, or vessels with auxiliary oar power, increasingly played only a supporting role to sailing ships, especially in the Mediterranean and Baltic Seas.

By the late seventeenth century, further refinements had appeared. Navies increasingly classified their warships. Ships of the highest rating came to be called ships of the line, because they were considered powerful enough to fight in the line of battle, which became the characteristic fleet tactic. Ships of lesser ratings fulfilled the roles of the pinnaces and fireships. Shore attack was not forgotten; by the 1680's vessels known as bomb ketches had been built for this purpose. The frigates, sloops, and corvettes of the eighteenth and nineteenth centuries developed from ships of these lesser rates. These smaller ships were used as the pinnaces had been, to scout for enemy fleets, to attack and defend commerce, and to

TURNING POINTS

1501	The development of gunports allows a ship's heaviest guns to be mounted on its lowest decks, stabilizing its center of gravity.
1571	The Battle of Lepanto II, fought between the Ottoman Turks and the Christian forces of Don Juan de Austria, is the last major naval battle to be waged with galleys.
1588	The English employ galleons to individually attack the larger ships of the formidable Spanish Armada, defeating the Spanish and revolutionizing naval tactics.
1653	The line of battle, allowing for more effective use of broadside firepower, is developed.
1700-1815	Naval battles are fought by ships of the line.
1850	Most navies have converted their sailing ships to steam propulsion.

carry messages and repeat flag signals from senior commanders to subordinates.

In general, warships became more standardized and more specialized as the age of sail progressed. The distinction between warships and merchant ships became more sharply drawn, especially after the mid-seventeenth century, when the line of battle was developed. Ships grew in size, and also in number. Fleet actions were increasingly decided by shipboard artillery, leaving little scope for the boarding and hand-to-hand combat that had characterized earlier battles. Improvements in ship design, rigging, seamanship, and techniques of food preparation led to further developments in the eighteenth century. For example, large-scale fleet actions occurred in the waters of the New World as well as those of Europe. Year-round operations also became more common, whereas earlier ships had rarely gone to sea in winter. Because fleets could stay at sea longer, navies could blockade their enemies, stationing a fleet off an enemy's port and preventing its forces from leaving.

By 1800 sailing warships were providing the great naval powers, particularly England, with weapons of tremendous power, versatility, and range. However, by the end of the 1850's the tremendous technological developments in steam propulsion, iron working, and ordnance had rendered sail-powered wooden warships obsolete.

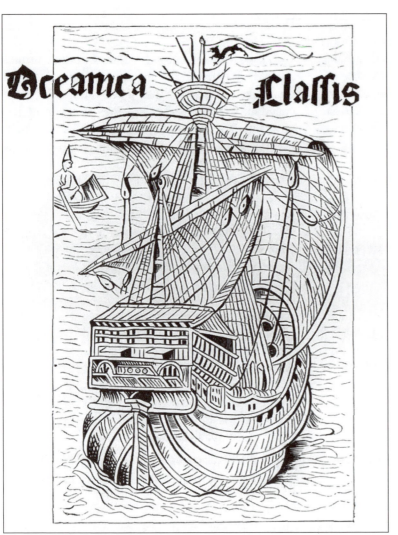

Frederick Ungar Publishing Co.

A caravel like the one depicted here, based on a drawing attributed to Christopher Columbus, was used by explorers of Africa and Asia during the fifteenth and early sixteenth centuries.

DEVELOPMENT

ARTILLERY

One of the dominant themes in the development of sailing warships was the effort to make shipboard artillery more effective, which characterized both ship design and naval tactics. Although guns had been mounted on warships as early as the fourteenth century, they tended to be small because they had to be fitted to shoot over the bulwarks that lined the sides of the upper decks. The fitting of too many heavy guns in this manner would have endangered the stability of ships, because the guns would be placed comparatively high above the waterline. Around 1500 the major Atlantic maritime powers— England, Spain, Portugal, Scotland,

F. R. Niglutsch

Peter the Great, czar of Russia, made a trip to Western Europe, including a highly anticipated visit to Holland in the Dutch Republic to learn the art of shipbuilding.

and France—began to cut ports for guns to be fired through the sides of ships. These gunports could be closed in heavy weather, so the guns could be mounted lower in the ship with less risk of their firing affecting the balance of the ship. In turn, because they were mounted lower, guns could be heavier without endangering the ship's stability. The introduction of the gunport therefore represented an important step forward in warship firepower.

SHIP STRUCTURE

Other than strengthening the hull structure to resist the forces exerted in firing the guns, few modifications were made to early sixteenth century warships. They tended merely to be versions of existing merchant vessels, typically carracks and caravels, with high forecastles—superstructures at the bow, or front, of the ship. The high forecastles facilitated

boarding attacks, the dominant form of naval action at the time. Boarding involved sending armed parties from one's own ship to attack the enemy's ship. Thus the towering forecastles acted almost as medieval siege towers. At the same time forecastles and aft castles, those in the rear of the boat, could be defended as strongholds against enemy boarders. However, because of these high forecastles, few guns could be brought to bear at the bow of the ship, which was a significant limitation. Traditionally, navies had attacked in line side-by-side, a method derived from Mediterranean galley tactics. Because galleys needed to leave room for the rowers, they could carry only heavy guns at the bow. They were thus highly effective in coastal waters, even in northern Europe, because they were able to attack "bows on," a maneuver to which the sailing ship could not effectively respond.

INTRODUCTION OF THE GALLEON

To solve the problems of gun placement, Portugal, England, Spain, and Denmark invented a new type of ship around 1550: the galleon. Galleons had a lower bow structure, like that of a galley (hence, perhaps, the name), so a heavier armament could be mounted in the bow. This proved effective at the Battle of Lepanto in 1571. The lower bow also lessened wind resistance, facilitating maneuverability. This design culminated in the so-called race-built galleons, developed by the English in the 1580's. These ships had comparatively fine lines and carried a relatively heavy gun armament. The increase in armament was important: The English navy believed it would have to rely on shipboard artillery to defeat the Spanish, their major rivals, who carried many more soldiers on their ships. In contrast the Spanish intended to use artillery mainly to weaken their opponent before boarding, which they believed was the decisive tactic. A test of these theories came in 1588, when the Spanish Armada was unable to force a boarding battle on the English fleet. Although the English had little success in sinking outright Spanish ships by gunfire, they did inflict sufficient casualties to demoralize the Spanish fleet, much of which was destroyed on its way home. The defeat of the Spanish Armada prevented Spain from invading England.

Even after the decisive defeat of the Spanish Armada, naval experts remained divided on the issue of guns versus boarding. Although wooden ships could be wrecked by gunfire, causing many casualties, they proved difficult to sink. Indeed, the English fleet nearly ran out of ammunition defeating the Spanish Armada. Therefore it is not surprising that the Dutch, the foremost naval power of the early seventeenth century, continued to advocate the importance of boarding. They used this tactic to win spectacular victories against the Spanish, such as the Battle of the Downs (1639). The Dutch, in relying so heavily on boarding tactics, may have been merely making a virtue out of necessity, initially lacking the relatively plentiful supply of artillery possessed by the English.

The bows-on attacks favored by all navies from the introduction of the galleon down to the mid-seventeenth century also limited the effectiveness of shipboard artillery. For obvious hydrodynamic reasons, a ship's hull must be longer than it is wide; but attacks with lines abreast were seen at Malta in 1565, when the Turks used ships to bombard Fort St. Elmo. In a naval battle the major use of cannons in massed formation with lines abreast was undoubtedly the Battle of Lepanto in 1571, although paintings of the battle show that some of the guns were mounted on the side for broadsides. This shift occurred because, obviously, there was more space for mounting guns along the ship's side than across either its bow or stern.

Consequently, even the galleon, with its significant forward-firing armament, mounted most of its guns along the side, or broadside. This gun placement led to the development of a turning movement that became standard in all naval tactics. The ship fired its forward guns, then turned its side toward the enemy, in order to bring its heaviest armament to bear. That motion also permitted the ship to turn away from the enemy that part of its armament which needed to be reloaded. At that time, guns could not always be withdrawn into the ship for reloading, as crews tended to be too small to push the guns back into firing position. Instead, gunners had to climb out onto the barrel to reload, a dangerous activity under fire. Turning the rearming side of the ship away from the enemy allowed reloading with greater safety. However, with each ship turning to shoot and reload at its own pace, fleet actions tended to become disorganized melees.

BROADSIDE FIREPOWER AND THE LINE OF BATTLE

It was the English, who continued to build ships of exceptional gun power, who started adopting broadsides with their turning tactic. The most notable of these was HMS *Sovereign of the Seas*, the first one-hundred-gun warship, launched in 1637 and measuring 1,500 tons—about double the size of the galleons of 1588. The English navy was the first to develop a style of fighting at sea that maximized the importance of broadside firepower. This new style was the line of battle, developed in the First Anglo-Dutch War (1652-1654) by the English navy under the joint command of Robert Blake (1599-1657), George Monck (1608-1669), and Richard Deane (1610-1653). In the line of battle, also known as the line ahead, a fleet was arrayed in a single line of ships, one behind the other: the most effective arrangement for deploying broadside firepower. The ships in the line of battle no longer turned to reload their guns, because gun crews were larger, so that in-board loading became the rule. At the Battles of Gabbard Shoals (June 2-3, 1653) and Scheveningen (July 31, 1653), the English fleet in the line of battle won lopsided victories over the Dutch, who sought to fight in the old manner. Indeed, Dutch admiral Maarten Tromp (1598-1653) was killed in the latter battle, and the Dutch were forced to sue for peace.

By the time of the Third Anglo-Dutch War (1672-1674) the line of battle had been adopted by the major naval powers of the period, which included England, France, and the Netherlands. Only powerfully armed and constructed ships could hope to stand up to the type of punishment dealt out by the line of battle.

Hence an increasingly sharp differentiation arose between those ships fit to fight in the line of battle and those that were not. This differentiation was defined by a rating system based on the number of guns a ship carried. By the 1670's, first-rates carried one hundred or more guns, second-rates carried sixty to ninety guns, and so forth. Only ships of the first four rates ranked as ships of the line. A ship required multiple decks in order to carry as many as seventy to one hundred guns; in the English and French navies first-rates always had three decks. The gun batteries became heavier, as navies increasingly used cheaper cast-iron guns instead of the more expensive, if slightly more reliable, bronze guns. The use of iron guns was another technological development pioneered by England.

The huge fleets—containing as many as one hundred ships—amassed for the great sea battles of the late seventeenth century rendered command and control nearly impossible for the admirals of the period. No matter where they placed their flagships, part of

P. F. Collier and Son

Ships of the line were considered powerful enough to fight in the line of battle, which became the characteristic fleet tactic.

their line of battle, which could stretch for 10 miles or more, would likely be out of visual range. This problem would be compounded by the vast clouds of smoke given off by black powder weapons and by atmospheric conditions such as fog. Naval commanders were also hampered by inadequate signaling systems. For all these reasons, late seventeenth century lines of battle often disintegrated into melees.

Moreover, naval tactics in the age of sail suffered from the fundamental problems associated with relying on the wind for propulsion. Winds could die down or suddenly shift direction. Furthermore, the square rig—the most common rig on Western warships—did not permit ships to sail directly into the wind. Neither was sailing highly efficient with the wind directly behind.

By the eighteenth century, fleets had become easier to control. Although navies were larger, individual fleets tended to be smaller. This paradox arose because the major navies—those of England, France, and Spain—now operated over a much larger area of the globe, using multiple fleets. Smaller fleets had less difficulty maintaining the line formation. Navies also developed better signaling techniques, involving not only signal flags but also night signaling by use of lanterns. The increasing adoption of professional officer corps by eighteenth century navies brought the line of battle under better control.

However, these very improvements in the line of battle, in some ways, worked against its decisiveness. If fleets arrayed in the line of battle were relatively equal in numbers of ships and guns, it was difficult for either side to win a clear-cut victory. Such was the case, for example, at the Battle of Málaga (1704) in the War of the Spanish Succession (1701-1714), fought between an Anglo-Dutch fleet and the French. In addition, fireships, previously an effective tool, were difficult to use against the better-controlled fleets. To regain the advantage, navies turned to the finer points of naval tactics. Much attention was paid to the relative advantages of being to windward of the enemy fleet, possessing the "wind gauge," or having the enemy fleet to windward, possessing the "lee gauge." Although it was easier to withdraw from the lee gauge, it was generally easier to shoot from the wind gauge, in part because the

smoke from firing would blow away toward the enemy. However, because ships could heel, or incline, away from the wind, in severe weather, it might be dangerous to open the gunports on the lowest deck if firing from the windward.

The best way to win a victory between evenly matched forces was to take advantage of an enemy's error. This proposition is well illustrated by the Battle of Quiberon Bay (1759) during the Seven Years' War. In that battle, an English fleet under Admiral Sir Edward Hawke (1705-1781) fought a French fleet of about equal strength. The French commander, believing the weather too rough for a sea battle, decided to bring his fleet into coastal waters, where he doubted that the English would follow for fear of wrecking their ships on unfamiliar shores. However, in its haste to gain shelter, the French fleet became disordered. Hawke, seeing this, immediately attacked. In the ensuing battle, the English sank or captured seven ships, with no losses of their own. The English fleet won not only a great tactical victory but also a strategic one, because the French fleet had been intended to escort an invasion convoy.

Superior proficiency in seamanship and gunnery also permitted a navy to win without possessing greater numbers. For example, England was able to win a string of victories during the French Revolutionary Wars (1792-1802) and the Napoleonic Wars (1793-1815). English sailors were more skilled, and English gun crews shot faster than all of their opponents except the Americans. Conversely, the French navy, hitherto the most formidable opponent of the English, had been weakened by the loss of experienced officers brought about as a result of the French Revolutionary Wars. The most spectacular of the English victories were those won by Admiral Horatio Nelson (1758-1805), including the Battle of Trafalgar (1805), where the English fleet of twenty-seven ships attacked in a two-column formation designed to split the Franco-Spanish fleet of thirty-three ships and force a close-quarters gunnery action. The tactic was exceedingly risky and possible only for a commander who had confidence that his men could outfight the enemy. The English won decisively, capturing nearly twenty ships, the majority of which later sank, owing to the combined effects of heavy battle damage and bad weather. Although no English ships were lost, Nelson himself was killed during this battle, considered his greatest victory.

From 1700 to 1815 the greatest fleet actions were fought by ships of the line carrying between 60 and 131 guns with a maximum shot weight of 32 to 42 pounds, arranged on at least two decks. During this period, ships were still classed by rate. First-rates carried more than 100 guns and weighed up to 3,000 tons; they were generally used as flagships and as strong points in the line of battle. The most common line-of-battle ship came to be a two-decked, third-rate vessel of 74 guns and around 1,500 tons. This size offered the best compromise between firepower and sailing capability. Ships had become much larger: This third-rate ship was approximately the size of a first-rate of the seventeenth century.

INCREASING IMPORTANCE OF FRIGATES

Whereas the ship of the line dominated fleet actions, frigates played a major role in scouting and in the attack and defense of commerce. Frigates carried between 30 and 50 guns firing 18- to 24-pound shot usually arranged on only one complete gun deck. Frigates were usually faster than ships of the line; they were also much smaller, generally less than 1,000 tons before 1780. However, by 1800, a number of navies, including that of the United States, had built very large frigates, such as the famous USS *Constitution*, launched in 1797 with 44 guns and weighing 1,500 tons. The French even cut decks off ships of the line in an effort to combine the greater resistance to gunfire and heavier guns of the ship of the line with the greater speed of the frigate. These ships were called *razées*. All navies employed smaller

F. R. Niglutsch

Admiral Horatio Nelson's brilliant naval strategy overwhelmed Napoleon's forces during the Battle of the Nile in 1798.

The French bombard Algiers during a naval battle in 1830.

ships, such as sloops and corvettes, to perform roles similar to those of frigates.

Many English officers considered French ships to be better and faster than English ships. French ships did tend to be slightly larger, but they may have been more weakly built. Furthermore, the English inaugurated most of the technical innovations of the period, including the use of copper bottoms on ship's hulls, which reduced the loss of speed caused by marine growth, and carronades, thin-walled cannons that fired a heavy shot to deadly effect at short range. Both of these innovations appeared during the American Revolution (1775-1783), where they played a major role in the English victory at the Battle of Les Saintes (1782). This victory, however, in some ways came too late for the English, whose inability to maintain control of the seas earlier in the war had led directly to their failure to defeat the American colonists.

The period from 1815 to 1850 marked the swan song of the sailing warship. Wooden ships had reached unprecedented sizes, due to the system of diagonal bracing developed in 1811 by the English naval constructor Robert Seppings (1767-1840). However, the new technology of the steam engine provided the possibility of maneuver independent of the wind and conferred a decisive tactical advantage. By the 1850's most navies had converted their sailing ships to use steam propulsion, although sails were retained for cruising. Naval guns had become more destructive as well, with the introduction of explosive shells and heated cannonballs, known as "red-hot shot," beginning in the 1820's. These developments in ordnance doomed the wooden warship, which was increasingly replaced by metal-hulled and metal-armored ships in the 1860's.

BOOKS AND ARTICLES

Crowdy, Terry. *French Warship Crews, 1789-1805*. New York: Osprey, 2005.

Fremont-Barnes, Gregory. *The Royal Navy, 1793-1815*. New York: Osprey, 2007.

Gardiner, Robert, ed. *Cogs, Caravels, and Galleons: The Sailing Ship, 1000-1650*. London: Conway Maritime Press, 1992.

_____. *The Line of Battle: The Sailing Warship, 1650-1840*. London: Conway Maritime Press, 1992.

Hopkins, T. C. F. *Confrontation at Lepanto*. New York: Tom Doherty Associates, 2006.

Konstam, Angus. *Lepanto, 1571*. New York: Osprey, 2003.

_____. *The Pirate Ship, 1660-1730*. New York: Osprey, 2003.

_____. *Renaissance War Galleon, 1470-1590*. New York: Osprey, 2002.

_____. *Spanish Galleon, 1530-1690*. New York: Osprey, 2004.

_____. *Tudor Warships (1): Henry VIII's Navy*. New York: Osprey, 2008.

Lardas, Mark. *Ships of the American Revolutionary Navy*. New York: Osprey, 2009.

Lavery, Brian. *Nelson's Navy: The Ships, Men, and Organization, 1793-1815*. London: Conway Maritime Press, 1989.

Rodger, N. A. M. *The Safeguard of the Sea: A Naval History of Britain, 660-1649*. New York: W. W. Norton, 1998.

Stilwell, Alexander. *The Trafalgar Companion*. New York: Osprey, 2005.

Tunstall, Brian. *Naval Warfare in the Age of Sail: The Evolution of Fighting Tactics, 1650-1815*. Edited by Nicholas Tracy. London: Conway Maritime Press, 1990.

FILMS AND OTHER MEDIA

Master and Commander. Film. Twentieth Century Fox, 2003.

The Great Ships: Ships of the Line. Documentary. History Channel, 1996.

Mark S. Lacy

NAVAL DEVELOPMENT
THE AGE OF PROPULSION
Dates: Since c. 1850

NATURE AND USE

Warships have proliferated since the 1850's, in size, number, and type. In the mid-nineteenth century, steam-powered warships replaced sailing ships as the main element of naval forces, screened by smaller frigates. The battleship emerged as iron replaced wood in the 1860's, and large-caliber guns were increasingly employed. Battleships and cruisers dominated late nineteenth century naval warfare. In the twentieth century, the development of submarines, torpedo boats, destroyers, aircraft, aircraft carriers, nuclear power, and guided weapons influenced naval warfare.

DEVELOPMENT

NAVAL TECHNOLOGY PRIOR TO 1850
The 1850's marked a turning point in the development of naval warfare technologies. Up until this time wood had remained the building material of choice, and most warships relied on sail power. The few steam-powered vessels in existence were propelled by fragile and vulnerable side paddle wheels. Although they improved upon sailing vessels, paddle wheel steamers had several problems. The externally mounted paddle wheels were susceptible to battle damage, and their drive machinery, high above the waterline, was vulnerable. The side paddles also took up a large portion of the side space, limiting the number of broadside weapons a vessel could carry. Also, only the portion of the paddle wheel that was in the water provided drive, wasting a large portion of the available power.

MID-NINETEENTH CENTURY NAVAL INNOVATIONS
Within a decade, however, several technical developments transformed naval warfare. First, improved machinery was built to move new, propeller-driven ships. Propellers offered several advantages over paddle wheels. The propellers, below the waterline, were out of the line of direct enemy fire, as were the engines and boilers. Without large side paddles, steam-powered ships could carry additional broadside guns. In contrast to that of the partly submerged paddle wheel, all of the propeller's turning motion moved the ship.

Second, iron began to replace wood in ship construction. Iron offered additional protection against ever-increasing gun calibers while allowing the construction of larger vessels than wood permitted. The use of iron as a building material stemmed from British and French

TURNING POINTS

1860   England launches HMS *Warrior*, its first ironclad warship.

1862   The first battle between two armored warships, the USS *Monitor* and the CSS *Virginia*, is fought in Hampton Roads.

1906   HMS *Dreadnought*, the first all-big-gun battleship, is launched at Portsmouth, England.

1923   HMS *Hermes*, the first purpose-built aircraft carrier, is commissioned.

1942   The Battle of the Coral Sea is the first naval battle fought entirely by carrier-based aircraft.

1954   The USS *Nautilus*, first nuclear-powered submarine, is commissioned.

experiments during the Crimean War (1853-1856), when both countries built floating armored batteries to bombard Russian positions. The shift from wood to iron as a construction material occurred in 1860, when the French commissioned *La Gloire*, a traditional wooden ship with an armored exterior, considered the world's first seagoing ironclad. Concerned for its naval supremacy, the British in the same year launched HMS *Warrior* and HMS *Black Prince*, frigates constructed entirely of iron, and also converted several wooden ships of the line into ironclads. A year later, the outbreak of the American Civil War (1861-1865) promoted the use of ironclads. The Confederacy utilized many ironclad ships in an attempt to break the Union blockade, beginning with the CSS *Virginia*, a casement monitor built upon the burned hulk of a Union warship. The *Virginia*'s initial success was countered by the arrival of the USS *Monitor*, the U.S. Navy's first ironclad. Fighting to a draw, the March 9, 1862, clash between the *Monitor* and the *Virginia* was the first between armored warships. Union ironclads appeared in increasing numbers throughout the war, as monitors to control southern rivers, as larger coastal ironclads, and as a single attempt at an ocean-going iron warship, the USS *New Ironsides*. The Confederacy, with limited resources, produced few ironclads but used them with good effect to block many Union naval efforts.

F. R. Niglutsch

The CSS Alabama, *during a battle with the USS* Kearsage, *was sunk off the coast of Cherbourg, France, in 1864 at the height of the U.S. Civil War.*

CAPITAL SHIPS AND CRUISERS

Between 1865 and the end of the nineteenth century, naval warfare changed relatively little. With few naval battles to test technological developments, all the major navies followed a similar line of development. The dimensions and displacement of capital ships, or the most powerful ships in world navies, continued to grow at a generally even pace as armor grew thicker to defeat larger and larger naval guns. By the 1880's, navies generally consisted of two types of ships: capital ships, which formed the main battle line, and cruisers, which policed overseas colonial holdings. Both types of ship had generally similar characteristics. Battleships with heavy armor typically carried four main-battery guns, generally in the 10- to 13-inch caliber range, backed by a secondary battery in the 4- to 6-inch caliber range. Some battleships, particularly the early American vessels, carried an 8-inch-caliber intermediate battery. The profusion of guns resulted from a shortcoming in fire control. The only means to estimate range on the featureless ocean was to observe the splash caused when shells landed in the ocean. Because shell splashes of various calibers looked the same at long range, ships had to be relatively close before accurate shooting from the main-caliber guns could begin. At these close ranges, the smaller guns came into play. Cruisers, optimized for long range, carried only light armor and a main battery in the 5- to 6-inch caliber category. Both types of warships used increasingly complex reciprocating machinery, with steam created in boilers forced through a piston engine to turn the propeller shaft, a noisy, complex, and relatively fragile means of propulsion.

Among the major navies, only the French followed a separate policy. Clearly unable to match England's industrial capacity, the French navy opted for a wartime strategy of *guerre de course*, or preying upon an enemy's seaborne commerce in lieu of a major fleet action. This strategy emerged from the success enjoyed by the small number of Confederate commerce raiders during the American Civil War (1861-1865). Although they were few in number, the Confederate raiders sank many Union merchant ships, drove up insurance rates, and diluted Union seapower. Unable to match the British in a building contest, the French followed the Confederate example to combat English numerical superiority. To achieve its wartime objectives, the French navy relied not on battleships but on large numbers of commerce-raiding cruisers.

LATE NINETEENTH CENTURY NAVAL INNOVATIONS

At the end of the nineteenth century, however, additional technological advances further changed warship development. The creation of advanced optical range finders vastly increased the accuracy of large-caliber guns, dramatically increasing the expected battle range. The demand for additional speed led to

the adoption of turbine machinery that replaced the large piston engines with fan blades attached directly to the drive shaft, eliminating tons of machinery while increasing reliability. Although they were initially coal-fired, boilers of turn-of-the-century dreadnoughts burned fuel oil with the advantage of better fuel economy and ease of transfer. Lastly, armor plate became smaller and stronger when alloy steel, especially the carbon steel developed by the German Krupp firm, replaced wrought iron.

In a revolutionary leap in capital ship development, all of these developments were combined in HMS *Dreadnought*, launched by the British in 1906. The *Dreadnought* featured ten 12-inch guns, aimed by newly advanced rangefinders and backed only by a few light weapons. Unburdened by smaller guns, *Dreadnought* carried extensive side belt and interior deck armor. It was the first capital ship to be fitted with turbine propulsion, enjoying a significant speed advantage over its foreign rivals. In theoretical war-games, British officers believed the *Dreadnought* to be the equal of three mixed-caliber battleships. *Dreadnought* represented such a huge leap forward in technology that the ship gave its name to its own type of warship: All subsequent battleships became

C. A. Nichols & Company

In 1862, the American Civil War witnessed the first battle of armored warships: the Union's Monitor *(right), the U.S. Navy's first ironclad, and the Confederacy's* Virginia.

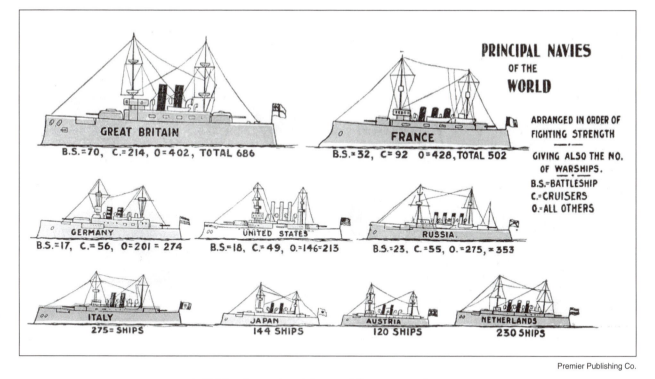

PRINCIPAL NAVIES OF THE WORLD

ARRANGED IN ORDER OF FIGHTING STRENGTH
GIVING ALSO THE NO. OF WARSHIPS.
B.S.=BATTLESHIP
C.=CRUISERS
O.=ALL OTHERS

GREAT BRITAIN
B.S.=70, C.=214, O=402, TOTAL 686

FRANCE
B.S.=32, C=92 O=428, TOTAL 502

GERMANY
B.S.=17, C.=56, O=201 = 274

UNITED STATES
B.S.=18, C.=49, O.=146=213

RUSSIA.
B.S.=23, C.=55, O.=275, =353

ITALY
275= SHIPS

JAPAN
144 SHIPS

AUSTRIA
120 SHIPS

NETHERLANDS
230 SHIPS

Premier Publishing Co.

A 1902 schematic of the world's principal navies.

known as dreadnoughts, and all previous capital ships were termed pre-dreadnoughts. The firepower concentrated in these ships prompted a building spree throughout the industrialized world, as navies sought an edge in military power and national prestige in the form of dreadnought battleships. German dreadnought construction triggered a naval arms race with Great Britain that led directly to World War I (1914-1918). Even small navies, such as those of Austria-Hungary, Argentina, and Chile, emptied their national treasuries to build dreadnoughts. Technological advances also allowed for a different type of capital ship in 1907, when the British unveiled HMS *Invincible*, the first battle cruiser. Designed to operate as a reconnaissance force for the dreadnought battle fleet, battle cruisers were dreadnoughts that sacrificed armor protection for additional speed. In practice, however, a few knots of speed could not protect the battle cruisers from other capital ships, and the British lost three battle cruisers within a few hours on May 31, 1916, at the Battle of Jutland.

NAVAL WEAPONS DEVELOPMENT

At the same time that technology accelerated capital ship development, other technical breakthroughs threatened the battleship's dominance in naval warfare. Naval mines, first used in large numbers during the American Civil War, increased in explosive power and sophistication. The development of aircraft led to the use of battleships as reconnaissance platforms, with some early theorists speculating that airpower had rendered battleships obsolete. The torpedo, however, emerged as the biggest threat to the capital ship, while causing a proliferation in warship types. A single, well-placed torpedo could sink the largest battleship, and swarms of small, cheap torpedo boats threatened the existence of large battle fleets. The torpedo was even more of a threat when delivered by the submarine. First perfected in the United States, the submarine approached its target by stealth, defeating all defensive measures. Submarines also proved outstanding commerce hunters, and hundreds of British merchant ships fell victim to German submarines, the dreaded U-boats, during World

Hulton Archive/Getty Images

The British ship HMS Dreadnought in *1909.*

tool, aircraft developed into offensive weapons thanks to new weapons such as the airdropped torpedo and bombs delivered by horizontal dive-bombers. The significance of naval airpower increased when several navies introduced the aircraft carrier in the 1920's. The United States, Great Britain, and Japan began with makeshift vessels such as the USS *Langley*, converted from a collier, or coalship, and progressed to larger, dedicated carrier construction, beginning with HMS *Hermes* in 1923. Carrier construction also benefited from the 1922 Washington Treaty by permitting the United States and Japan to convert battle cruisers canceled under the terms of the treaty, such as the USS *Lexington* and the *Akagi*, into aircraft carriers. These large ships, capable of carrying more than one hundred aircraft, gave the United States and Japan operational experience in large-scale carrier operations that both nations used to devastating effect in World War II.

War I. The answer to the torpedo boat and submarine threat was the destroyer. A small, multipurpose warship, the destroyer was fast enough to hunt down and destroy torpedo boats while delivering its own torpedo attack to enemy capital ships. The destroyer's maneuverability and speed also suited it to hunt submarines.

POST-WORLD WAR I NAVAL INNOVATIONS

After World War I, naval technology expanded into wider fields, particularly after a naval limitation treaty signed at the Washington Naval Conference in 1922 restricted capital ship construction. Unable to build new battleships, the major navies applied advances in technology to update existing capital ships: converting them to fuel oil, adding exterior bulges to counter torpedoes, and mounting antiaircraft guns to ward off attacking airplanes. Although they were denied new battleships, navies faced no restrictions on other types of warships. Improved torpedoes fired from larger submarines greatly enhanced the impact of both weapons. Intended for fleet reconnaissance, the larger submarines with greater range developed into deadly commerce raiders in World War II (1939-1945). Technology also promoted the use of aircraft in naval warfare. From their origin as a reconnaissance

WORLD WAR II NAVAL INNOVATIONS

Naval warfare changed dramatically in World War II, as the stresses of war pushed technology to its limit. The most significant operational change caused by the war was the shift in emphasis as the aircraft carrier replaced the battleship as the primary capital ship. The range and flexibility of aircraft, coupled with the high-profile loss of many battleships early in the war, forced the combatants to rely on carrier airpower in lieu of battleships. This is especially true in the Pacific, where fast, wide-ranging carriers, with their ability to destroy both naval targets and inland enemy positions, proved a much more useful weapon. Airpower also benefited from the American capacity to mass-produce warships. Although the Americans and British had mass-produced small antisubmarine vessels in World War I, the rapid production of all types of warships in World War II transformed the scale of naval warfare. In addition to smaller ships, American shipyards churned out hundreds of destroyers, dozens of cruisers, and a plethora of aircraft carriers. These carriers ranged in size from the 35,000-ton Essex-class fleet carriers and the 15,000-ton Independence-class light carriers to the more than one hundred small escort carriers in the 10,000- to 12,000-ton category. In comparison, the British and Japanese produced only a fraction of America's naval output, while Germany, France, and Italy produced relatively few ships in wartime. The one exception was Germany's submarine production. The German navy's reliance on U-boats to combat British naval supremacy led to the production of approximately 1,100 submarines during the war, most of which were destroyed by the Allies. Although the primary German fleet submarine was little more advanced than its World War I counterpart, late-war U-boats contained many advanced features. These advanced submarines featured advanced hull forms for high underwater speed, advanced peroxide fuel cells, and snorkels for submerged recharging of the batteries. Fortunately for the Allies, these vessels emerged too late in the war to change its outcome.

In response to the German U-boat threat, the Allies promoted the use of electronic warfare to detect the submarines. The British development of sonar between the wars proved invaluable during World War II, as did other detection methods. High-frequency direction finding (HFDF, often called "huff duff") allowed the Allies to exploit the large amount of radio traffic needed to coordinate the massed German submarine attacks, the famous "wolf packs." The Allies were able to divert convoys away from danger areas and to attack the U-boats with antisubmarine aircraft by triangulating the wolf packs' radio transmissions to find their locations. Radar, usually associated with land-based air defense, also permitted aircraft to become potent antisubmarine weapons. Because they ranged over a much wider area than did slower surface ships, aircraft could use ra-

dar successfully, even at night, to detect and attack surfaced U-boats. The Germans attempted to counter Allied radar with a radar-detecting device known as Metox, a primitive form of electronic countermeasure that proved ineffective against more advanced British radar sets.

GUIDED WEAPONS DEVELOPMENT

The major German weapons development of World War II was guided weapons. The Germans developed the first effective acoustic homing torpedo, which guided itself to its target, a ship, by the sound the ship generated. The weapon had little influence because it proved easy to decoy, and the Allies captured an example of the weapon and soon produced their own antisubmarine version. The German-developed antiship missiles, however, had a much bigger impact. Carried into the battle area by a German bomber, the FX-1400 missile flew under command guidance to its target, with an observer in the launch aircraft maneuvering the missile via joystick controls. The weapon menaced the Allied landings at Anzio in September of 1943, damaging the British battleship HMS *Warspite* and the U.S. cruiser USS

Library of Congress

The USS Scorpion, *a nuclear submarine, surfaces at Portsmouth, England.*

Savannah. Italian battleships, steaming out to surrender to the Allies on September 9, came under attack from the missile; the battleship *Roma* was sunk, and the *Italia* was severely damaged. The Allied development of electronic jamming, however, reduced the later impact of the weapon.

NAVAL AIRCRAFT AND PERSONNEL CARRIERS

Specialized amphibious warfare ships represented the final major development during World War II. The conflict marked the first time that large-scale invasions came from the sea, and specialized landing craft emerged to carry troops onto enemy shores. The craft ranged from small personnel carriers to the utilitarian landing ship tank (LST), often referred to by their crews as "large slow target," which came directly onto the beach. The immense landing ship dock (LSD) was capable of carrying other landing craft into the invasion area. In dozens of landings in the Pacific and Europe, the Allied navies perfected their ability to mass and deliver thousands of men and tons of matériel. During the Normandy landings of June 6, 1944, D day, the Americans and British landed 100,000 men. Operation Olympic, the anticipated American invasion of Japan, envisioned the landing of more than one-half million men in the opening attack.

In the postwar era, navies struggled to incorporate many of the technological advances and weapons introduced during World War II. With the exception of the United States, the world navies relegated their battleships to the scrap yard as the aircraft carrier maintained its position as the primary capital ship. Two requirements caused a surge in the size of new American carrier construction. First, heavier jet aircraft, introduced at the end of the war, needed longer takeoff and landing spaces than wartime carriers permitted. Second, wary of losing its influence to the new U.S. Air Force, the U.S. Navy demanded larger carriers capable of accommodating large carrier-based nuclear bombers. The first of these postwar carriers emerged in 1954 when USS *Forrestal*, the first of the supercarriers, was launched. Specially designed to operate jet aircraft, with British-developed steam catapults, arresting gear, and an angled landing deck, *Forrestal* and subsequent supercarriers formed

the backbone of American naval strength. The massive supercarriers, more than 1,000 feet long and displacing more than 80,000 tons, pushed the limits of fuel-oil propulsion, leading to the construction of several nuclear-powered carriers: USS *Enterprise* in the 1960's and the Nimitz class of the 1980's and 1990's. Nuclear power freed the carriers from any real speed constrictions and reduced the amount of logistic support needed by obviating the need for oilers.

Nuclear power, however, had the biggest impact on submarine construction, beginning with the first nuclear submarine, USS *Nautilus*, in 1954. Nuclear power plants permitted the construction of the first true submarines. Non-nuclear submarines are properly submersibles—vessels capable of submerging that actually spend most of their time on the surface, recharging their electrical batteries. Nuclear-powered submarines, however, can stay submerged indefinitely, limited only by crew fatigue, because water and oxygen are two of the by-products of their nuclear reactors. The postwar development of guided weapons led to two classifications of nuclear submarines. Attack submarines perform the traditional submarine missions: attacking surface ships and hunting other attack submarines. The threat of fast attack submarines became so acute, postwar surface vessels incorporated helicopter facilities into their design, as only aircraft could hope to counter the faster submarines. Ballistic-missile submarines, carrying long-range guided ballistic missiles armed with nuclear warheads, act as a last line of nuclear deterrence. The first ballistic-missile submarine, the USS *George Washington*, was commissioned in 1959. The Soviet, British, French, and Chinese navies followed suit with their own ballistic-missile submarines. One type of these submarines, the Russian Typhoon, is, at 26,000 tons displacement, the largest submarine in the world.

POSTWAR NAVAL INNOVATIONS

In the postwar era, electronic systems continued to proliferate, and modern warships were festooned with antennas and radar dishes. Contemporary warships feature electronic radar, sonar, electronic countermeasures, communications, fire control, and intelligence-gathering facilities, all considered necessary for modern naval warfare. The miniaturization of electronics also led to the replacement of guns with missiles as the main naval armament in the postwar era. Antishipping missiles, with a far greater range than that of the largest battleship battery, began to replace naval guns in the 1960's. The Soviet Union in particular embraced antiship missiles fired from swarms of small attack boats and long-range bombers to counter the United States' massive naval presence. Many smaller navies acquired inexpensive antiship missiles, such as the French Exocet or the American Harpoon, to offset numerical deficiencies.

For defense against this threat, warships acquired radar-guided, rapid-fire guns. In the air defense role, surface-to-air missiles replaced massed batteries of antiaircraft guns beginning in the late 1950's, when the guns could no longer defeat the fast-moving jets.

A final feature of naval development in the postwar era is the proliferation of the multipurpose ship. Due to the high cost of new technology, most navies can no longer afford specialized warships, and small, cheap, multipurpose frigates have come to form the backbone of most navies. Only major navies can afford such expensive items as aircraft carriers, amphibious warships, and dedicated antiaircraft cruisers.

BOOKS AND ARTICLES

Baer, George W. *One Hundred Years of Sea Power: The U.S. Navy, 1890-1990.* Palo Alto, Calif.: Stanford University Press, 1994.

Friedman, Norman. *The Postwar Naval Revolution.* Annapolis, Md.: Naval Institute Press, 1986.

Gardiner, Robert, ed. *The Eclipse of the Big Gun: The Warship, 1906-1945.* Annapolis, Md.: Naval Institute Press, 1992.

_____. *Navies in the Nuclear Age: Warships Since 1945.* Edison, N.J.: Chartwell Books, 2001.

_____. *Steam, Steel, and Shellfire: The Steam Warship, 1815-1905.* Annapolis, Md.: Naval Institute Press, 1992.

Henry, Mark R. *The U.S. Navy in World War II.* Illustrated by Ramiro Bujeiro. Botley, Oxford, England: Osprey, 2002.

Hutchinson, Robert. *Jane's Submarines: War Beneath the Waves from 1776 to the Present Day.* New York: HarperCollins, 2001.

Mindell, David A. *War, Technology, and Experience Aboard the "USS Monitor."* Baltimore: The Johns Hopkins University Press, 2000.

Polmar, Norman. *Historic Naval Aircraft: From the Pages of "Naval History" Magazine.* Washington, D.C.: Brassey's, 2004.

Poolman, Kenneth. *The Winning Edge: Naval Technology in Action.* Annapolis, Md.: Naval Institute Press, 1997.

Roberts, John. *The Battleship Dreadnought: Anatomy of a Warship.* Annapolis, Md.: Naval Institute Press, 1992.

Rose, Lisle Abbott. *Power at Sea.* 3 vols. Columbia: University of Missouri Press, 2007.

Schultz, Richard H., Jr., and Robert L. Pfaltzgraff, Jr., eds. *The Role of Naval Forces in Twenty-first Century Operations.* Washington, D.C.: Brassey's, 2000.

Sondhaus, Lawrence. *Navies in Modern World History.* London: Reaktion, 2004.

_____. *Navies of Europe: 1815-2002.* Harlow, England: Longman, 2002.

Tangredi, Sam J., ed. *Globalization and Maritime Power.* Washington, D.C.: National Defense University Press, 2002.

Wertheim, Eric. *The Naval Institute Guide to Combat Fleets of the World: Their Ships, Aircraft, and Systems.* 15th ed. Annapolis, Md.: Naval Institute Press, 2007.

FILMS AND OTHER MEDIA

Air Power at Sea. Documentary. National Syndications, 1998.

Battleships. Documentary. A&E Television Networks, 1998.

Carrier: Fortress at Sea. Documentary. Discovery Channel, 1996.

The Ironclads. Documentary. A&E Home Video, 1997.

Sea of Honor: The U.S. Navy Story, 1775-1945. Documentary. Entertainment Distributing, 1996.

Seapower: The History of Naval Warfare from Ancient to Modern Times. Documentary. Cromwell Productions, 2000.

Struggle for the Seas. Documentary. Films for the Humanities and Sciences, 1995.

Steven J. Ramold

WESTERN WARFARE IN THE AGE OF MANEUVER

EUROPEAN WARS OF RELIGION

Dates: c. 1517-1618

POLITICAL CONSIDERATIONS

In the sixteenth century, Europe experienced a period of civil strife, rebellions, and conflicts that came to be called the European Wars of Religion. The Protestant Reformation fueled strife between the Catholic and Protestant churches and led to changes in weapons and war across the subcontinent. Christendom divided into camps willing to fight and die for their versions of the religion. Roman Catholics, Lutherans, Calvinists, Eastern Orthodox, and members of other sects became polarized around the reformist ideas of Desiderius Erasmus (1466[?]-1536) and Martin Luther (1483-1546). Luther's 1517 publication of his Ninety-five Theses ignited the Wars of Religion. Peasant revolts along with the separation of nobility and clergy from the papacy followed. French, German, and east European territories fell into a century of civil turmoil. European political powers became embroiled in the debate even as the Renaissance, absolutism, mercantilism, and the scientific revolution changed Europe from within.

Challenges outside Europe also fueled change. The Islamic Ottoman Turks under Süleyman the Magnificent (1494/1495-1566) captured the medieval city of Constantinople in 1453, opening Europe to invasion by powerful Turkish sultans who challenged the emerging Habsburg line and Holy Roman Empire. The Eastern Orthodox Church of Constantinople was exiled to Russia as the Russian state grew across Eurasia under Ivan IV "the Terrible" (1530-1584). Early modern states struggled to emerge through political and economic consolidation amid these external pressures. Simultaneously, seafaring advances helped extend European political power across the seven seas, providing an outlet for and from the religious wars. The conquest of the Americas and the opening of trade routes into the Indian, Atlantic, and Pacific oceans led to global changes

known as the Columbian Exchange, which saw both Protestant and Catholic European states emerge as international powers even as the chaotic Wars of Religion racked Europe.

MILITARY ACHIEVEMENT

European states from 1517 to 1618 achieved military successes abroad but only mixed results within Europe, owing to civil conflict and the gunpowder revolution, which created equilibrium among larger states. Warfare was revolutionized, from naval and land battles to fortifications and logistics. Several of the great debates in history center on if and when Europe experienced a "Military Revolution" and what relationship any such revolution had to "the rise of the West" in global affairs.

The formation of the Catholic Spanish Habsburg Empire (1518-1648) under Charles V (1500-1558) and the rise of a number of Protestant states—including England, Sweden, and the Dutch Estates General—spread civil revolts into state conflicts. Northwestern Europe moved toward Protestantism, while Mediterranean and central Europe remained in league with the Roman Catholic Papacy. Eastern Europe, especially Russia, emerged as the new home of Eastern Orthodox Christianity. Europe became a mosaic of territories where identity was based on a blend of religious beliefs, ethnicity, and political state.

The Spanish Habsburg Empire became the most powerful in Europe as Charles V developed the first global empire with holdings on all the major continents, taking the title of Holy Roman Emperor in alliance with Catholic Europe. Charles used military and political means to control much of Europe, the Americas, and parts of coastal Africa and Asia. Conquests of the Aztec (1521) and Inca empires (1535) helped fund the Military Revolution of gunpowder in Eu-

The Ottoman Turks besieged the old Habsburg capital of Vienna in 1529 and formed an alliance with France's King Francis against the Habsburgs in the 1530's and 1540's.

rope and European expansion by sea across the globe. An uneasy competition and eventual alliance (1580) with neighboring state Portugal meant the empire controlled both the best land military units in Europe (Spanish *tercios*) and the best seafarers (Portuguese mariners). However, the Spanish Habsburg Empire was obligated to suppress the Protestant Reformation, defend against the Turkish expansion, and expand globally to fund the gunpowder revolution. Bankruptcy resulted four times from 1518 to 1644. The Turkish threat, armadas against Protestant England, religious wars with Netherlands and German rebels, and conflicts in the Indian and Pacific oceans ensured the high cost of empire.

The Ottoman Turks conquered much of southeast Europe, even besieging the old Habsburg capital of Vienna in 1529 and forming an alliance with Fran-

cis I of France against the Habsburgs in the 1530's and 1540's. Turkish victories on land at Mohács (1526) and at sea at Preveza (1538) were eventually reversed as the reigns of Süleyman the Magnificent and Charles V ended. Habsburg victories included breaking the Siege of Malta in 1565 and destroying the Ottoman navy at Lepanto in 1571. By 1618, the role of the Turks in Europe was on the decline because of Habsburg military successes. However, the high cost of global empire left the Habsburgs vulnerable to other European states, such as England, France, and the Netherlands, which took over global sea trade from Spain and Portugal in the seventeenth century. In addition to military changes and religious strife, mercenaries on land and pirate privateers at sea were a large part of the chaotic sixteenth century.

WEAPONS, UNIFORMS, AND ARMOR

The sixteenth century saw gunpowder transform weapons and warfare in Europe. Originally from Asia, gunpowder weapons were combined with European metallurgical skills, especially bell making, to create two kinds of weapons that changed warfare and thus global power. These were bronze and iron cannon (siege, ship, and field artillery cannon) and firearms (harquebus, musket, and pistol). The changes to land warfare were greatest in two areas: sieges and battles. Siege artillery and mines destroyed the medieval castle walls and led to complex star-shaped fortifications of earth, timber, and stone. Sieges became protracted affairs requiring enormous resources on both sides. On the battlefield, firearms led to professional soldier units of volley-fire infantry. Medieval land warfare had been dominated by tall stone castles, armored knights, and cavalry, spear, pike, and sword on land. In the sixteenth century these were supplanted by complex earth fortifications, pike and shot infantry, harquebuses, muskets (after 1550), pistols, giant siege cannon, and field artillery with wheeled carriages.

Uniforms moved away from armored protection made obsolete by guns toward regularized clothing units to identify specialized groups of professional soldiers. Matchlocks and wheel locks developed as firing mechanisms for firearms. Metal projectiles replaced stone, and weapons moved from breech-loaded to muzzle-loaded. Siege artillery, such as the mons meg (1449), Turkish bombards (1450), and the tsar pushka, or czar cannon (1586), weighed from fifteen to forty tons and fired five-hundred-pound metal or fifteen-hundred-pound stone shot over several miles.

The ships involved in naval warfare changed from lightweight, clinker-built (with overlapping sideboards), rowed, ram-and-board galleys with few guns to heavy-timber (often oak) sailing ships, carvel-built (with flush sideboards for strength), bristling with gunpowder weapons, side gun ports, and complex rigging. Under Henry VIII (1491-1547), English warships such as the enormous *Mary Rose* and *Great Henry* were built with skeletons of keel and ribs and could hold up to two hundred gunpowder weapons and 400 crew. The man-of-war, the first purpose-built warship for fleet duty, by 1540 carried 200 sailors, 185 soldiers, 30 gunners, powder boys, several pilots and cartographers, and a captain. Cannon included fifty-pound cannon, thirty-two-pound demicannon, long-range culverin of small poundage, and many antipersonnel hand cannon, such as demiculverins, sakers, falcons,

CATHOLIC AND PROTESTANT TERRITORIES, 1590-1598

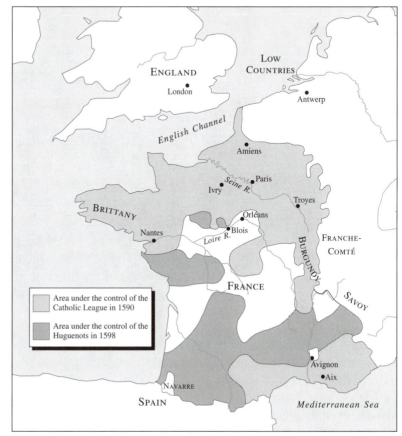

Area under the control of the Catholic League in 1590

Area under the control of the Huguenots in 1598

and robinets. The gun carriage, consisting of wooden side brackets, trunnions, and transoms, held the gun through recoil. By 1550 the English had sixteen naval cannon sizes, the Spanish twelve, and the French six. Shot could be canister, grape, chain, double, exploding, or even heated, depending on the situation. Powder was refined from the ground powder of land siege cannon to a "corned" variety of coarse grain that allowed for uniform firing across a broadside volley.

MILITARY ORGANIZATION

In sixteenth century Europe, the Wars of Religion and the emergence of gunpowder weapons disrupted state development and the ability of rulers to field large-scale, well-organized military units. Funding and loyalty were the two main variables to be overcome, thus mercenaries hired by private contractors on behalf of states formed the bulk of all military systems during war. Armies rarely exceeded thirty thousand, and naval forces usually consisted of small flotillas, with exceptions at Lepanto in 1571 and the Armada of 1588. Ethnic groups became associated with particular weapons and military units, such as English (Welsh) longbowmen, Swish and German pikemen, Spanish sword and bucklers or harquebusiers, and French heavy cavalry and musketeers. Sir Francis Drake (c. 1540-1596) was perhaps the best-known maritime mercenary, hired as a privateer by Queen Elizabeth I (1533-1603), or, as King Philip II of Spain (1527-1598) labeled him, a pirate.

Frederick Ungar Publishing Co.

An engraving of the St. Bartholomew's Day Massacre of 1572, in which Huguenot leaders and thousands of other Protestants were killed by French Catholic nobles in Paris.

Maurice of Nassau (1567-1625), as well as his brother and cousin, moved the Dutch forces toward permanent mercenary units by providing year-round training and state pensions as part of the Dutch Protestant revolt against the Spanish Empire. However, it was the advent of the printing press that led to the popularization of such ideas as manuals on military changes, from the infantry training system to projectile ballistics, spread throughout Europe. Scientific specialists such as artillery and siege engineers like Leonardo da Vinci (1452-1519), aristocrats turned officers and leaders such as Maurice's cousin John, and merchants turned sea commanders such as Ferdinand Magellan (c. 1480-1521) organized their troops and sailors around ethnic and religious companies and brigades that varied greatly in size and loyalty, owing primarily to the disruptions of the Wars of Religion.

Unit clothing and constant fighting did identify professional mercenary groups, but irregular state funding and loyalty issues often resulted in confusing conflicts and fluctuating levels of military organization. The main exceptions were the Spanish square tercio, or regiment of 3,000 regionally recruited men, and the Dutch linear battalion of 550 musketeers. On warships, powder boys of ten to fourteen years old became crucial, but their numbers varied largely depending on recruitment tactics, some of which resulted in near slavery for these boys. Pilots and ship's captains were often chosen for their expertise on particular regions or types of expeditions, but it was not uncommon to find Portuguese pilots on a Dutch ship captained by an Englishman with sailors recruited from around the globe, especially if it was a pirate ship.

DOCTRINE, STRATEGY, AND TACTICS

Niccolò Machiavelli, in his influential work *Il principe* (1532; *The Prince*, 1640), argues that the first work of rulers is war and that "there is no wall, whatever its thickness that artillery will not destroy." Employing the gunpowder revolution in military systems thus became a major doctrine informing the strategy and tactics of religious, state, and dynastic powers. Religious doctrine could affect the use of guns (sometimes labeled the devil's weapon). Dynastic rivals among Habsburgs, Tudors, Valois, Osmans, and Bourbons often struggled to fund the Military Revolution while building states, so the economic doctrine of creating wealth became key. Turkish, Russian, and Spanish Habsburg gains on land and Portuguese, Dutch, and English gains at sea often came as internal turmoil racked rival states in France, Hungary, the Italian peninsula, or Poland, thus indicating that opportunism was perhaps the most successful doctrine.

Strategy and tactics were transformed in the sixteenth century by the emergence of gunpowder weapons and large sailing ships. Strategy became dominated by expensive siege warfare on land and control of lucrative global sea trade. Armies lived off the land and the work of peasants, who were often unpaid, leading to revolt, mutiny, and worse. Tactically, pike and shot dominated, and musketeers (after 1550) became as common as pikemen in the seventeenth century. Training manuals and drill made it easy, inexpensive, and fast to train peasants into sailors, pikemen, or volley-fire infantry. Expensive cavalry adopted the tactic of *caracol*, or riding forward and firing pistols en masse before wheeling in reverse, but this was ineffective and their numbers declined. Steady rates of infantry volley fire were achieved by the Dutch using the "countermarch" system of six to twelve lines of infantry. After the soldiers in the first line fired, they would retreat to the rear to go through the complex reloading process.

At sea, the expense of naval seafaring again was key. The Portuguese alone had a variety of ships, including *naus, caravels, gales,* and *bergantim*. All served as both merchant ships and warships. Only the English man-of-war was utilized mainly for war fleet activity. The Portuguese caravel, English man-of-war, and Spanish galleon led to these nations' domination of naval battles abroad but to stalemates at home. The Habsburg Holy League owed its victory over the Turkish Empire at the naval Battle of Lepanto in 1571 (in which more than 100,000 men were involved) mainly to gunpowder weapons, while the defeat of the Spanish Armada of 1588 owed more to storms than to gunpowder. Europe thus remained deadlocked into the seventeenth century at home but was expanding successfully abroad.

CONTEMPORARY SOURCES

The popularization of the European printing press in the sixteenth century meant that works on militarism and religion became widely influential in Europe. Christians became polarized around the ideas of moderate reformer Desiderius Erasmus, whose works accounted for 20 percent of all print sales by 1530. Erasmus was in communication with most European scholars of the period, and his five editions of critical analysis and discussion of language translation issues concerning the Bible were most influential. The third and fourth editions of his *Testamentum* (1527; *The Essential Erasmus*, 1964) relied on Hebrew, Greek, Latin Vulgate, and his own Latin texts in parallel columns. Erasmus also produced works on the role of princes and Christian soldiers of the time. Martin Luther, with his publication of the Ninety-five Theses (originally known as the "Disputation of Martin Luther on the Power and Efficacy of Indulgences") in 1517, spurred on the Reformation in local languages. In the influential work *The Prince*, Machiavelli discusses leadership strategy in the early modern world, and he also produced works on war. Jacob de Gheyn II's book of engraved prints *The Exercise of Armes* (1607) was a military drill book that could be used to train peasants in volley firearm tactics regardless of their language.

BOOKS AND ARTICLES

Black, Jeremy. *Cambridge Illustrated Atlas of Warfare: Renaissance to Revolution*. New York: Cambridge University Press, 1996.

De Souza, Philip. *Seafaring and Civilization*. London: Profile Books, 2001.

Knecht, Robert. *The French Religious Wars, 1562-1598*. New York: Osprey, 2002.

Konstam, Angus. *The Spanish Armada*. New York: Osprey, 2009.

Lynn, John. *Battle: A History of Combat and Culture*. Boulder, Colo.: Westview Press, 2003.

Parker, Geoffrey, ed. *Cambridge Illustrated History of Warfare*. New York: Cambridge University Press, 1995.

Rogers, Clifford, ed. *The Military Revolution Debate*. Boulder, Colo.: Westview Press, 1995.

FILMS AND OTHER MEDIA

Battlefield Britain: Spanish Armada. Documentary. DD Home Entertainment, 2005.

History's Mysteries: Drake's Secret Voyage. Documentary. A&E Home Video, 2006.

The Return of Martin Guerre. Feature film. Arrow Films, 1982.

Christopher Howell

THE ERA OF GUSTAVUS ADOLPHUS

Dates: 1609-1697

POLITICAL CONSIDERATIONS

Religious division, dynastic ambition, and national rivalry were all parts of the political context of warfare in the seventeenth century. These factors overlapped, often in complex ways. For example, the Thirty Years' War (1618-1648) began as a revolt by Protestant Czechs against the German Catholic Habsburg Dynasty. Later, France and Spain, the two leading European powers, joined the war on opposite sides. Although both countries were ruled by Catholic dynasties, the Bourbons and the Spanish branch of the Habsburg family, respectively, they and their ruling houses were also vying for European hegemony.

As religious passions cooled after 1630, national rivalry moved to the forefront. Whereas European princes in the sixteenth century had looked upon war as a private affair, they now increasingly viewed it as a public affair involving the whole state. This change in attitude led to higher military spending, not only for wartime expenditures but also for the funding of large peacetime military establishments, which appeared for the first time since the fall of the Roman Empire. Thus, a new political attitude toward war does much to explain how European military burdens rose dramatically in a century of generally low or even stagnant economic growth.

In the Netherlands and England, higher military spending and standing armies came at the price of granting political control to representative institutions. More commonly, enhancing the political power of the monarch seemed the best way to promote the strength and stability of the state. Strong monarchies of this sort became known as absolute monarchies, and the seventeenth century is known as the Age of Absolutism. It must be remembered, however, that the federal republic of the Netherlands set the pattern for large peacetime militaries later copied by the absolutist states.

MILITARY ACHIEVEMENT

The Netherlands forced Spain to grant a truce in 1609, which tacitly recognized Dutch independence

Library of Congress

Gustavus II Adolphus is mortally wounded in battle at Lützen in 1632.

THE THIRTY YEARS' WAR: BATTLE SITES

after over thirty years of revolution of Dutch Protestant provinces against Spanish occupation. The ability of the tiny Dutch republic, with a population of only 1.5 million, to fight to a standstill what was then the strongest military power in Europe represents one of the greatest military achievements of the century. The Dutch army, commanded by Maurice of Nassau (1567-1625), became the wonder of Europe.

The Swedish king Gustavus II Adolphus (1594-1632), who ruled an even less populous and much poorer country than the Netherlands, copied and improved upon the Dutch model. By defeating the hith-

erto unbeaten Catholic armies of Bavaria (Battle of Breitenfeld, 1631) and the Austrian Habsburgs (Battle of Lützen, 1632) during the Thirty Years' War, he established Sweden as one of the greatest military powers in Europe, a position the nation would hold until its defeat by the Russian army at Poltava in 1709. Furthermore, Sweden replaced the Netherlands as the military model for Europe.

France, the most populous and wealthiest country in Europe, proved to be a military underperformer in the first part of the century due to aristocratic and religious factionalism. Matters began to improve only in the 1630's and 1640's, thanks to the efforts of the statesman Armand-Jean du Plessis, cardinal et duc de Richelieu (1585-1642) and commanders such as Louis I de Bourbon, prince de Condé (1621-1686), known as the Great Condé, whose victory over the main Spanish army at the Battle of Rocroi (1643) marked the end of Spanish claims to European hegemony. However, it was not until after 1660, when French king Louis XIV (1638-1715) consolidated absolute monarchy, that the French army became the most powerful and admired in Europe. By the 1680's, France had also amassed the largest navy in Europe. French military and naval ascendancy, coupled with Louis's aggressive use of his military forces, stimulated the formation of powerful military coalitions led by England, the Netherlands, and Austria, which fought France to a standstill in the War of the Grand Alliance (1688-1697) and again in the War of the Spanish Succession (1701-1714).

These wars also established England as the principal rival to France. The foundations of England's naval and military power had been laid during the First English Civil War (1642-1646), which saw the creation of the English Republic (1649-1660). The army and navy of the Republic briefly became the terror of Europe, defeating the powerful Dutch navy and savaging the decaying Spanish Empire. However, not until after the War of the Glorious Revolution (1689-1692), which established the principle of parliamentary sovereignty, could the English government harness its country's commercial wealth and thereby establish its military strength on a firm foundation. During the 1690's, the English navy surpassed the French navy as the strongest in Europe, a position it would hold into the twentieth century.

WEAPONS, UNIFORMS, AND ARMOR

For much of the seventeenth century, the heavy matchlock musket and the long pike were the dominant infantry weapons. By the end of the century, both had been largely replaced by a single weapon system: the flintlock musket fitted with a socket bayonet.

Although the matchlock musket was effective against body armor, it was unreliable, with a misfire rate of about 50 percent. Its operation depended on a continuously burning "slow" match, which could easily be extinguished by rain and wind. Furthermore, the rate of fire was slow. Soldiers could fire about one shot every two minutes, even after the development of drills to teach loading. Although more sophisticated ignition systems, such as the wheel lock and the flintlock, were available, they were often prohibitively expensive. In addition, the wheel lock, although widely used in cavalry pistols, proved too fragile for infantry use.

The sturdier flintlock began to be issued in musket form to elite infantry units around the middle of the seventeenth century, by which time flintlock pistols

F. R. Niglutsch

A skirmish before the Battle of Poltava in 1709. Only after the Russian forces had maneuvered into a favorable position did the entire army engage in battle.

had largely replaced the wheel lock among cavalry-men. By 1700, flintlock muskets had become the most common infantry firearm, allowing a significant improvement over the matchlock in both rate and reliability of fire.

Plug bayonets, so named because they were inserted directly into the muzzle, were used throughout the century but were never very popular, because, when mounted, they blocked the gun from being fired. In 1687 French military engineer Sébastien Le Prestre de Vauban (1633-1707) invented the far superior socket bayonet. Because the socket bayonet fitted around, not inside, the muzzle, the gun could be both loaded and fired with the bayonet attached. Socket bayonets were soon adopted throughout Europe. By effectively converting every musket into a spear, socket bayonets also rendered the pike obsolete.

Steel armor, widely worn by infantry into the mid-seventeenth century, was largely abandoned by the 1690's, because it offered too little protection against gunfire to justify its weight and cost. Only heavy cavalry continued to wear armor, but only breastplates and backplates, and not the helmets or the arm and thigh protection that had been carried into the 1640's.

Grenades became popular in the waging of siege warfare, and special units of infantry known as grenadiers appeared. Although the grenade was their main weapon, the term "grenadier" soon came to be used as a general designation for elite troops.

Standardized uniforms became increasingly common in the seventeenth century. Early in the century, colonels often outfitted their regiments with uniforms of a single color, but the English adopted the first armywide standard uniform color when they introduced their famous red coat in 1645. By the end of the century, uniforms of a single color for whole armies had become the norm, with individual regiments distinguished by different-colored lapels and cuffs.

Artillery also tended to become standardized around weapons of a few calibers rather than the miscellaneous collection of guns that had characterized sixteenth century artillery. Artillery also became lighter and more mobile during the seventeenth century.

MILITARY ORGANIZATION

Although sixteenth century peacetime standing armies were small, consisting chiefly of royal guards and fortress garrisons, the seventeenth century was characterized by large standing armies and navies. The Dutch republic set the example, keeping some 30,000 men under arms after its truce with Spain in 1609. In contrast, France, with ten times the population of the Netherlands, had only 10,000 soldiers at that time. The Dutch, and later the Swedes, also pioneered the creation of a professional, long-service officer corps. The Dutch also led the way in creating a professional navy, although the English had surpassed them by the 1650's.

Standing forces with professional officers could be far more effectively drilled and disciplined than forces raised, or hired as units under the contract system, for a single conflict. The dangers of mercenaries are well illustrated by the career of Count Albrecht Wenzel von Wallenstein (1583-1634). Wallenstein's position as a military contractor on a grand

TURNING POINTS

1600	The Battle of Nieuwpoort is the first battlefield test of Maurice of Nassau's linear infantry tactics.
1609	The Netherlands forces Spain to grant a truce tacitly recognizing Dutch independence after over thirty years of revolution of Dutch Protestant provinces against Spanish occupation.
1631	The Battle of Breitenfeld is successful test of Gustavus Adolphus's military reforms.
c. 1687	Sébastien Le Prestre de Vauban invents the socket bayonet, which attaches to the musket barrel and allows simultaneous use of the musket.
1697	The European balance of power is shifted at the end of the War of the Grand Alliance.

scale allowed him to pursue policies so at odds with those of his nominal employers, the Austrian Habsburgs, that they felt compelled to assassinate him. By the end of the century, all major powers maintained standing armies, divided into regiments, the basic military administrative unit. Some countries, notably Sweden, even began to employ conscription as a means of raising armies.

Standing forces, whether composed of volunteers or conscripts, were expensive. The creation of new military agencies was required to administer and supply these standing armies. Bureaucratic development reached a peak in France in the second half of the century, as the nation's peacetime army expanded to around 165,000 men, with a maximum wartime strength of nearly 400,000 men. France also established the first professional military engineering corps in Europe and created a huge military support structure, featuring a system of supply depots or "magazines," hospitals, barracks, and naval arsenals, which provided a model soon copied by the other powers.

DOCTRINE, STRATEGY, AND TACTICS

The seventeenth century was an age of sieges. Fortresses played a critical role in the domination of territory. If a hostile fortress were in the area, a substantial body of troops would be required to surround it fully. Otherwise, units sallying out of the fortress could disrupt supply lines and foraging parties, preventing offensive operations. A fortress could completely block the use of a river on which it was stationed, a crucial defensive factor, because rivers were far and away the best lines of supply, given the poor state of roads throughout Europe in the 1600's. A fortress built on hostile territory could serve as a supply magazine and a secure jumping-off point for offensive operations.

It is not surprising that much effort went into the design of better fortresses and siege techniques. From the 1660's onward, the French, under the guidance of Vauban, led the way in fortification design and siegecraft. Vauban devised a new system of advancing in successive parallel trenches, which sealed

off the fortress and allowed the relatively secure deployment of devastating artillery fire against the fortress walls.

If the assault and defense of fortresses increasingly ruled strategy, it by no means eliminated battles between field armies. Interest in the improvement of battlefield tactics remained high throughout the century. Infantry were traditionally deployed in squares of pikemen, fifteen ranks deep, surrounded on all sides by musketeers. Although this formation was defensively effective, it was inefficient in the use of manpower. Beginning in the 1590's, Maurice of Nassau replaced these square formations of around 1,500 men with a more linear formation of about 800 men as the basic tactical building block. The new formation was still composed of pikemen and musketeers, but these were now deployed in only five ranks, with the pikemen in the center and the musketeers on the wings. Because the formation was more shallow, it could actually occupy a longer front and bring more muskets to bear to the front. To make this musketry effective, Maurice developed elaborate drills to allow some men to reload while others fired, permitting a continuous fire. These new tactics required almost mechanical discipline, something best achieved by professional forces.

Successfully tested at the Battle of Nieuwpoort (1600), Maurice's new "linear" formations were copied and improved upon by Gustavus II Adolphus, beginning in the 1620's. By the end of the century infantry formations had become increasingly linear, typically only three ranks deep.

As infantry formations became less capable of all-around defense, cavalry played increasingly decisive roles in battle. The mark of a superior tactician, such as the Great Condé, came to be in timing the launch of a decisive cavalry charge. Cavalry required reforms to become truly effective in this newly decisive role. At the beginning of the century, most cavalry in Western Europe had abandoned the heavy lance and adopted the pistol as their principal weapon. Instead of charging in lines, they attacked in a snakelike formation, the caracole, designed to facilitate the reloading of pistols.

Influenced by his experience fighting the Poles, Gustavus II Adolphus, who had never abandoned the traditional cavalry charge, trained his cavalry to charge in lines, using their swords instead of pistols. Another of Gustavus's pioneering military reforms was his use of more mobile field artillery, which assisted cavalry shock action by softening up infantry formations in preparation for the cavalry assault. Gustavus based his revolutionary battle tactics on mobility and firepower, arranging his infantry in more shallow formations to fire heavy volleys on command. As successful commanders increasingly came to agree with Gustavus, firepower increasingly dominated infantry tactics, while shock increasingly dominated cavalry tactics.

Naval tactics also evolved throughout the seventeenth century, with the development of the line of battle by the English navy in the 1650's. The line of battle formation, which had become universal by the 1670's, maximized the importance of broadside firepower and allowed for more effective deployment of shipboard artillery.

CONTEMPORARY SOURCES

Although the seventeenth century witnessed an enormous outpouring of military treatises, memoirs, and histories, only a few are available in modern editions. Robert Monro's *Monro, His Expedition with the Worthy Scots Regiment Called Mac-Keys* (1637) is an excellent account of the Thirty Years' War from the perspective of a Scottish soldier of fortune. The works of the Habsburg general Count Raimondo de Montecuccoli (1609-1680) are generally regarded as the most penetrating of the military treatises written during the seventeenth century.

Sébastien Le Prestre de Vauban wrote a number of military works, especially on siege warfare, of which he was probably the greatest practitioner of all time.

BOOKS AND ARTICLES

Asch, Ronald G. "Warfare in the Age of the Thirty Years' War, 1598-1648." In *European Warfare, 1453-1815*, edited by Jeremy Black. New York: St. Martin's Press, 1999.

Brauer, Jurgen, and Hubert van Tuyll. "The 1600's: Gustavus Adolphus and Raimondo de Montecuccoli." In *Castles, Battles, and Bombs: How Economics Explains Military History*. Chicago: University of Chicago Press, 2008.

Brzezinski, Richard. *The Army of Gustavus Adolphus (1): Infantry*. Illustrated by Richard Hook. Botley, Oxford, England: Osprey, 1991.

_____. *The Army of Gustavus Adolphus (2): Cavalry*. Illustrated by Richard Hook. Botley, Oxford, England: Osprey, 1993.

Chandler, David. *The Art of Warfare in the Age of Marlborough*. 2d ed. Staplehurst, England: Spellmount, 1990.

Duffy, Christopher. *The Fortress in the Age of Vauban and Frederick the Great, 1660-1789*. London: Routledge and Kegan Paul, 1985.

Frost, Robert I. *The Northern Wars: War, State and Society in Northeastern Europe, 1558-1721*. New York: Longman, 2000.

Guthrie, William P. *Battles of the Thirty Years' War: From White Mountain to Nordlingen, 1618-1635*. Westport, Conn.: Greenwood Press, 2002.

Lynn, John A. *Giant of the Grand Siècle: The French Army, 1610-1715*. Cambridge, England: Cambridge University Press, 1997.

Parker, Geoffrey, ed. *The Thirty Years' War*. 2d ed. London: Routledge and Kegan Paul, 1997.

Rothenberg, Gunther E. "Gustavus II Adolphus." In *The Reader's Companion to Military History*, edited by Robert Cowley and Geoffrey Parker. Boston: Houghton Mifflin, 1996.

Van der Hoeven, Marco, ed. *Exercise of Arms: Warfare in the Netherlands, 1568-1648*. Leiden, Netherlands: E. J. Brill, 1998.

Wedgwood, C. V. *The Thirty Years' War*. London: J. Cape, 1938. Reprint. New York: New York Review Books, 2005.

Weigley, Russell Frank. "The Return of the Legions: Gustavus Adolphus and Breitenfeld." In *The Age of Battles: The Quest for Decisive Warfare from Breitenfeld to Waterloo*. 1991. Reprint. Bloomington: Indiana University Press, 2004.

FILMS AND OTHER MEDIA

Alatriste. Feature film. Estudios Picasso, 2006.

The Last Valley. Feature film. ABC Pictures, 1970.

Marston Moor. Documentary. Cromwell Productions, 1999.

Mark S. Lacy

THE ERA OF FREDERICK THE GREAT

Dates: 1712-1786

POLITICAL CONSIDERATIONS

Military and naval combat in the 1700's, the era that came to be dominated by King Frederick II of Prussia (or Frederick the Great, 1712-1786), saw changes in the style, organization, tactics, and strategy of engagement. These modifications were, in part, political and economic, according to needs of the states in question, but they were also taught by generals in the field or by independent military reformers who sought to contribute their observations and experience.

Between 1667 and 1713, King Louis XIV (1638-1715) committed France to various wars, seeking first to expand his nation and then to take the throne of Spain. Austria, England, and the Netherlands resisted until Louis's armies finally began to falter. Between 1704 and 1709 France's most able generals were defeated, and the way was opened for a compromise peace in 1713.

More than forty years of war, however, had seriously undermined the strength and financial stability of most European governments. As a result, these nations had trouble operating at prewar budgetary levels and were unable to field armies that were equipped and trained as they had been during the late 1600's. France, whose army had been the largest and best in Europe for nearly a century, was bankrupt, and Austria was deep in debt. Sweden had exhausted itself in its fight with Russia for control of the Baltic area. Russia, Sweden's foe, now secure in its outlet to the Baltic Sea and, after 1725, free of Czar Peter I (1672-1725), wished to reexamine its involvement in Europe. England, drained, but somewhat better off than its allies, desired to shift its resources elsewhere.

The passing of the best generals of the early eighteenth century influenced European states to curtail their aggressive policies. European rulers lacked sufficient finances to fund costly wars and were hesitant to trust poorly equipped armies to leaders with limited experience. In the Seven Years' War (1756-1763), for instance, only one of six French commanders was competent. Consequently mid-eighteenth century Europe found itself in a military void that the small state of Prussia was quick to exploit. Frederick II, Prussia's ruler, took advantage of his opponents' limits, seizing Silesia from Austria in 1740 and holding it until 1763 despite attacks from France, Austria, and Russia. This triumph, which made Frederick famous, also elevated Prussia to the status of a great state.

France's military humiliation by Prussia, coupled with its financial distress and with absolutism's inability to function properly under the regimes of Louis XV (1710-1774) and Louis XVI (1754-1793), made political change in that nation inevitable. A revolution in 1789 was followed

TURNING POINTS

mid-1700's	Advances in cannon technology allow smaller guns to shoot farther with less powder.
1757	Frederick the Great wins renown and respect with his masterful use of the oblique attack at Leuthen.
1778-1779	Frederick the Great begins deploying semi-independent detachments during the War of Bavarian Succession, foreshadowing use of independent army divisions.
1782	British commander George Rodney defies prevailing military wisdom by attacking weak points in the French line at Les Saints.
1798	British admiral Horatio Nelson abandons traditional line tactics in victory over French at Abū Qīr Bay.

by a continental war that introduced technical, tactical, and strategic innovations to the military arena.

MILITARY ACHIEVEMENT

Warfare in the age of Louis XIV had been a product of the 1600's. Professional soldiers and sailors sought to disengage, rather than to engage. To fight meant to risk both reputation and army. To win without fighting, commanders largely ignored mobility and methodically maneuvered for the best position. Battle was offered only when the advantage was theirs and pursuit, in the event of victory, was generally refused as an unnecessary risk. Further, to buttress this basically defensive posture, the Dutch, the Austrians, and the French built massive interlocking fortresses and supply depots that were designed to protect the frontier and either to slow or to halt an advancing enemy. It was an age in which Sébastien Le Prestre de Vauban (1633-1707) and Baron Menno van Coehoorn (1641-1704) were the premier fortress builders on the continent and defined the war that military leaders such as Claude-Louis-Hector de Villars (1653-1734), François de Neufville, marquis de Villeroi (1644-1730), and Louis-François de Boufflers (1644-1711) practiced.

Still, not everyone conformed to the expected defensive norm. Austrian general Eugène of Savoy (1663-1736), for one, was noted for his forced marches, surprise attacks, and flank movements. His rapid victory at Turin (1706) was decisive and helped to reduce French forces in Italy. He was supported by his friend and fellow soldier John Churchill, first duke of Marlborough (1650-1722), who preferred night marches and interior lines of movement. Churchill's opinion that a single victory was "of far greater advantage to the common cause than the taking of twenty towns" was reinforced by that of Eugène. During the War of the Spanish Succession

King Frederick the Great reviews his troops.

(1701-1714), unbeknownst to the enemy, the two friends unexpectedly combined against a French army at Blenheim (1704), turned its flank, and dispersed it, capturing most of the survivors. Two years later Churchill accomplished the identical feat at Ramillies-Offus. In 1708 the men reunited, through forced marches, at Oudenarde, turned both flanks of an unprepared French army, and drove it from the field. Unfortunately, a similar linkup at Malplaquet in 1709 was met and badly repulsed, hindering a fuller acceptance of the doctrine of mobility.

It remained for the young king of Prussia, Frederick II, to undercut the doctrine of defense, impressing all of Europe with his concept of movement and attack. For Frederick the objective was not to hold territory but to force the enemy to give ground. Through experience, he learned to avoid costly sieges and set battles and instead sought short wars to maximize his limited resources. He also utilized rapid movement, interior lines of march, and the element of surprise to keep his multiple enemies off balance. "I have so many enemies that I have no choice but to attack," he

F. R. Niglutsch

The duke of Marlborough leads his troops during the Battle of Blenheim (1704).

wrote in 1759. "I have only kept going by attacking whenever I can and by scoring little advantages which add up." He surprised and routed the Austrians at Hohenfriedberg (1745) in the War of the Austrian Succession and ambushed the French flanking column at Rossbach (1757) during the Seven Years' War. Yet it was his masterful use of the oblique attack at Leuthen (1757), Zorndorf (1758), and Torgau (1760) that won Frederick fame and respect.

Ships, like armies, were expensive and were not intended to be chanced to the fortunes of war. A commander should, in the words of a seventeenth century writer, "keep his ship and his men out of danger." Vessels and fleets were expected to maintain lines of supply by sea, blockade enemy ports, and, whether engaged in single-ship or fleet action, to remain on the defensive and not to risk vessels' giving chase to defeated foes. Fleet commanders were further re-

quired by their permanent orders to avoid, whenever possible, engaging in battle, but if forced, to take "a line of battle [parallel to that of the enemy as] the basis and formulation of all discipline in sea fights." From these lines each side would fire at the other from a distance, each with the hope that the other would make a mistake or lose the wind. During the War of the Grand Alliance (1688-1697) the French did not pursue defeated Dutch and English forces at Beachy Head (1690), and at La Hogue (1692) the English were not permitted to follow up on significant French losses. In each case a continued engagement could have meant the destruction of the fleeing ships. It remained for Lord George Rodney (1718-1792) to challenge convention at the Battle of Les Saintes (1782). He took advantage of breaks in the French line caused by the wind and sent his ships through them to wreak havoc. Rodney gained great acclaim but was deprived of his command for exceeding his instructions. Even more unfortunate was Sir John Byng (1704-1757), who in 1757 was court-martialed and shot for failing to comply with his instructions. In 1798 Horatio Nelson (1758-1805) followed up on Rodney's work by abandoning traditional line tactics and capturing all but two French ships at Abū Qīr Bay, off Egypt. As a result Nelson was given a better command and made a baron.

WEAPONS, UNIFORMS, AND ARMOR

Military equipment remained reasonably standard during the 1700's. European armies adopted similar-caliber flintlock muskets between 1692 and 1705, and this weapon, despite the introduction of the more accurate but less durable rifle, became the primary infantry arm of the century. Although heavy and cumbersome, it decidedly improved its user's killing efficiency. Firearms, rather than swords, daggers, and pole arms, now decided battles. The centuries-old pike was replaced by a bayonet that locked onto the end of the musket, allowing the musket to be used simultaneously as both a firearm and a shortened pike.

Of all weaponry, artillery displayed the most noticeable improvements. At the beginning of the century, cannons were divided into two categories: defensive for fortress use and offensive for regimental and siege work. The latter accompanied the army in long artillery trains and were heavy, cumbersome, and slow to move, hindering the offensive movements so important to men such as Eugène, Churchill, and Frederick the Great.

Change, however, followed the War of the Spanish Succession. Jean de Maritz (1680-1743) revolutionized the casting of cannon, allowing for smaller guns to fire a projectile farther and use less powder. This development enabled Europeans to make lighter, smaller artillery pieces, often 4-, 8-, and 12-pound guns, and to increase their maneuverability on the battlefield.

Uniforms, standard by 1700, changed little until the French Revolution of 1789, but armor was almost totally discarded. Only in the heavy cavalry, and especially among the French, was armor retained. Deflective chest plates were worn on the front and the back, but they were unable to withstand direct musket fire. Regimentals remained much the same until the *levée en masse*, a French draft of sorts, mandating large numbers of new battalions, including light infantry and cavalry. At this point, and especially under Napoleon, different uniform designs and colors would proliferate.

Naval ships of the period changed little. The ships of most nations were similar in design; the vessels of individual navies differed only in construction techniques, quantity, and quality. France, for example, built a better ship and used fewer, but heavier, guns, whereas England, whose vessels sailed better, used sturdier construction. Yet, all nations divided their major capital ships into categories with the top three categories carrying more than 100 guns, more than 80 guns, and from 74 to 80 guns. The last, a third-class ship of the line, was generally the workhorse of every fleet.

R. S. Peale and J. A. Hill

Austrian soldiers captured at the Battle of Hohenfriedberg (1745) are marched past an army of the Quadruple Alliance.

MILITARY ORGANIZATION

Over the course of the century, organizational change brought larger armies, smaller but better-armed battalions, fewer cavalries, and a more effective use of artillery. In response to the strategies of military leaders such as Swedish king Gustavus II Adolphus (1594-1632), Churchill, and Eugène, continental states gradually decreased the number of men in a battalion, the primary building block of the regiment. By 1720 most armies had reduced their battalions to 500 to 700 men and had improved their deployment, thereby increasing firepower. Artillery, lighter and more numerous, was advocated by the late 1700's as a weapon to prepare the way for an assault. Massed cannons were used to good effect at Valmy (1792) and at Jemappes (1792) during the French Revolutionary Wars, but it was not until 1796

at Castiglione della Stivere during the Napoleonic Wars that guns were decisive in breaking an enemy line. In 1809, a hundred or more cannons paved the way for Napoleon's success at Wagram.

Due, in part, to the rise of nationalism, armies slowly increased in size. During the Thirty Years' War (1618-1648), they had averaged 20,000 to 30,000 men. By the time the War of the Spanish Succession began in 1701, armies frequently had from 60,000 to 80,000 soldiers per side. By 1805 to 1812 Napoleon Bonaparte was directing armies of 180,000 to 600,000 soldiers. The doctrine of attack and the increased size of forces now obliged generals to discard the seventeenth century concept of supply storehouses and to force traveling armies to live largely off the land. Although there was no division of an army into independent commands, divisions, or corps, the concept had already been foreshadowed in

F. R. Niglutsch

King of Prussia Frederick II made masterful use of the oblique attack at the Battle of Leuthen in 1757.

the writings of the French general Maurice, comte de Saxe (1696-1750) and Jean Du Teil (1738-1820). It became a reality when Frederick the Great, during the War of the Bavarian Succession (1778-1779), required his units to march to battle by separate routes, acting as semi-independent detachments. These precedents were absorbed by men such as Napoleon, who would later employ independent divisions successfully at Marengo (1800), Ulm (1805), Austerlitz (1805), and later battles.

While armies were increasing in numbers and units were being independently deployed, cavalry as a whole was being reduced, because it was less effective than infantry as a striking and killing force. Yet, light cavalry, like light infantry, was becoming increasingly popular. Such units were seen as useful in shielding maneuvering formations, artillery, and attacks.

A new formation, the column, was also emerging in French thought and training. It was created by Jean-Charles de Folard (1699-1752), who sought to save time in battle by using the marching column as a direct vehicle of attack, substituting shock for traditional firepower. His work was furthered by François-Appollini de Guibert (1744-1790), an organizer of France's citizen army of 1789-1790. Guibert recommended a restricted use of the column with an attack upon a narrow front or a salient. Massed artillery fire and sharpshooters could pin down the defenders as the attacking column, hopefully shielded by terrain, advanced. Folard and Guibert's work, intended as an option for traditional line tactics, soon became the standard for French revolutionary armies.

DOCTRINE, TACTICS, AND STRATEGY

The art of war evolved over the course of the eighteenth century. Tactics were no longer a matter of preserving an army, preparing and fighting a set battle, or using fortresses in order to remain on the defensive. By 1795 armies were expected, whenever possible, to seize and hold the offensive and to avoid sieges and fortresses. According to Napoleon, the best form of defense was attack. Strategically, European armies were beginning to understand that the defeat and destruction of the opposing force formed the object of warfare and that the loss or gain of territory was a secondary consideration. Gustavus, Eugène, Churchill, and Frederick were at last making their point.

CONTEMPORARY SOURCES

The best accounts of the eighteenth century are to be found in the memoirs, papers, and instructions of the chief soldiers of the era. Sébastien Le Prestre de Vauban's *Mémoire, pour servir d'instruction dans la conduite des sièges et dans la défense des places* (1740; *A Manual of Siegecraft and Fortification*, 1968), John Churchill's *Memoirs of John, Duke of Marlborough* (1818-1819), Prince Eugène's *Feldzüge gegen die Türken* (1876-1892), and Maurice, comte de Saxe's *Les Réveries: Ou, Mémoires sur l'art de la guerre* (1757; *Reveries: Or, Memoirs upon the Art of War*, 1757) are all highly informative as to the actions and lives of the principals. Among the best and the most explicit, however, is *Die General-Principia vom Kriege* (1747; *The Instruction of Frederick the Great for His Generals*, 1985), by Frederick II. Alfred T. Mahan's *The Influence of Sea Power upon History, 1660-1783* (1890), despite its publication date, is the best available source for naval service.

BOOKS AND ARTICLES

Almond, Mark. "Frederick the Great and the Era of Limited War." In *Revolution: Five Hundred Years of Struggle for Change*. New York: De Agostini, 1996.

Brauer, Jurgen, and Hubert van Tuyll. "The 1700's: Marlborough, de Saxe, and Frederick the

Great." In *Castles, Battles, and Bombs: How Economics Explains Military History*. Chicago: University of Chicago Press, 2008.

Chandler, David. *The Art of Warfare in the Age of Marlborough*. London: Oxford University Press, 1976.

Duffy, Christopher. *The Military Life of Frederick the Great*. New York: Atheneum, 1985.

Dupuy, Trevor. *The Harper Encyclopedia of Military Biography*. New York: HarperCollins, 1992.

Dwyer, Philip G., ed. *The Rise of Prussia, 1700-1830*. New York: Longman, 2000.

Luvaas, Jay, ed. *Frederick the Great on the Art of War*. New York: Da Capo Press, 1999.

Millar, Simon. *Zorndorf, 1758: Frederick Faces Holy Mother Russia*. Westport, Conn.: Praeger, 2005.

Pois, Robert A., and Philip Langer. "Frederick the Great at Kunersdorf, August 12, 1759." In *Command Failure in War: Psychology and Leadership*. Bloomington: Indiana University Press, 2004.

Schieder, Theodor. *Frederick the Great*. Translated by Sabina Berkeley and H. M. Scott. New York: Longman, 2000.

Showalter, Dennis. *The Wars of Frederick the Great*. New York: Longman, 1996.

Szabo, Franz A. J. *The Seven Years' War in Europe, 1756-1763*. New York: Pearson/Longman, 2008.

Thackeray, Frank, and John Findling. *Events That Changed the World in the Eighteenth Century*. Westport, Conn.: Greenwood Press, 1998.

Weigley, Russell Frank. "The Battles of Frederick the Great." In *The Age of Battles: The Quest for Decisive Warfare from Breitenfeld to Waterloo*. 1991. Reprint. Bloomington: Indiana University Press, 2004.

FILMS AND OTHER MEDIA

Barry Lyndon. Feature film. Warner Bros., 1975.

Last of the Mohicans. Feature film. Morgan Creek Productions, 1992.

The War That Made America: The Story of the French and Indian War. Documentary. Public Broadcasting Service, 2006.

Louis P. Towles

THE ERA OF NAPOLEON BONAPARTE
Dates: 1789-1815

POLITICAL CONSIDERATIONS

Eighteenth century warfare prior to the 1789 French Revolution had been shaped by the political, social, and economic conditions of the day. Wars were fought over narrow dynastic issues by small professional armies. These armies were composed of soldiers from the lowest levels of society, commanded by aristocratic officers. Casualties were kept to a minimum, because each soldier represented a major investment of state resources, and battles fought using rigid linear tactics were seldom decisive. However, the French Revolution dramatically altered the basis of eighteenth century warfare. The revolution opened the way for an era of mass armies and full national mobilization and set in motion the transformation of France from a royal kingdom to a modern nation-state. The revolution enabled France to institute the *levée en masse*, a draft of citizen soldiers that supplied unprecedented levels of manpower for military service. To support this enlarged French army, the revolutionary government was compelled to mobilize the economic resources of the nation fully. After 1792, faced with the threat of internal counterrevolution and foreign intervention, France became a nation at arms; a full national response was needed to save the revolution from its many enemies. Armies increased dramatically in size, higher casualty rates became acceptable, and war became more decisive and total.

Revolutionary France could afford neither the expensive professional armies that were the hallmarks of the old style of warfare nor the time needed to train rough conscripts in the ways of rigid eighteenth century linear warfare. The revolution served to undermine the traditional aristocratic officers' corps. In the place of the old royal army, a new national army was formed, composed of conscript citizen-soldiers commanded by officers who advanced through their talent rather than their titles. The poor economic condi-

tions in France produced armies that had to survive on the fruit of the countryside rather than depend on long baggage trains with overstretched lines of communication. The benefit of this otherwise unfortunate sitation was that the French army gained greater speed and mobility. The new armies of revolutionary France dominated the battlefields of Europe and won victory after victory. It took the military genius of Napoleon Bonaparte (1769-1821), emperor of France from 1804 to 1814, to realize the full potential of this new type of warfare.

Between 1792 and 1815 seven anti-French coalitions were formed by Great Britain, Russia, Austria, and Prussia. France's dynastic opponents had little choice but to follow the French military example or face defeat. With the exception of Great Britain, all the great powers copied the French military system to a greater or lesser degree. With its chief reliance on sea power, Britain remained conservative in its military thinking and committed to linear warfare fought by a small professional army. This system proved remarkably successful against the French in Spain and later against Napoleon at Waterloo. The combination of British financial resources and command of the sea made Britain the central power in the resistance to France's imperial ambitions. In the end, Napoleon's goal of achieving European mastery proved beyond the resources of France in the face of determined resistance by the other great powers.

Following Napoleon's downfall, the armies of Europe largely reverted to the traditional pattern of long-service professional armies. The conservative political and social order reasserted itself across Europe. While the nobility continued to dominate the ranks of the officers' corps in many armies, they did so to a lesser degree. With the reduction of foreign troops so widely employed in the armies of the eighteenth century, the rank-and-file soldiers of the nineteenth century chiefly served in the armies of their re-

F. R. Niglutsch

The foundations for the age of Napoleon were laid by the French Revolution, which is widely considered to have begun with the storming of the Bastille prison on July 14, 1789.

spective nations. A period of relative peace settled over Europe after Napoleon's defeat. No wars on the scope and scale of the French Revolutionary Wars (1792-1802) or the Napoleonic Wars (1803-1815) were waged. Nevertheless, the rise of modern nationalism and the spread of industrialization in the nineteenth century laid the foundations for the total world wars of the twentieth.

MILITARY ACHIEVEMENT

The Napoleonic Era ushered in a revolution in warfare: No longer was military power limited by the economic, political, and social conditions of the eighteenth century. The French Revolution produced the age of national warfare, in which the near-total re-

sources of a nation were placed into pursuit of victory. Not only were large pools of manpower mobilized, but civilian resources were also tapped. War became more mobile, more destructive, and more decisive. To a large degree, the elements of this new type of warfare were in place prior to Napoleon's rise to power. Prerevolutionary military thinkers in the French royal army had published writings advocating change, and the various revolutionary governments of France had swept away the old army, opening the way for new military innovations. Apart from substantially improved artillery, the weapons used by armies of the Napoleonic period had changed little since the start of the eighteenth century. Key to the changes in warfare were the overall changes produced by an age of revolution. France's opponents had little choice but to adopt the new way of war or face defeat. The armies of Britain, France, Austria, Prussia, and Russia would decide the fate of Europe on the battlefield.

Considered one of the most gifted generals in history, Napoleon dominated this period in the history of warfare. The French Revolution provided him with the tools of success and opened the way for his rise to power. Napoleon personally embodied the motto of careers open to talent. He fought nearly fifty pitched battles and won most of them. More than one hundred years after Napoleon's defeat at Waterloo, generals were still trying to copy his achievements. The stress on offensive operations became the accepted road to victory for all military establishments

with the goal of quick decisive victories on the battlefield. It should be noted that the Napoleonic era also produced a number of capable generals other than Napoleon, including Louis-Nicolas Davout (1770-1823) and André Masséna (1758-1817), two of Napoleon's own marshals, as well as Arthur Wellesley, the duke of Wellington (1769-1852), Archduke Charles of Austria (1771-1847), and Russian prince and field marshal Mikhail Illarionovich Kutuzov (1745-1813). This period, with the introduction of systematic military education, ushered in the beginning of military professionalism. In 1802 the Royal Military College was opened at Sandhurst, England; West Point was es-

SELECTED BATTLE SITES IN THE NAPOLEONIC WARS

tablished in the United States in the same year; in 1808 St. Cyr opened in France; and Prussia's war academy, the Allgemeine Kriegsschule, was created in 1810.

WEAPONS, UNIFORMS, AND ARMOR

The battles of Napoleonic era were noisy, smoky affairs with the discharge of a great deal of black powder. Battlefields were often covered in dense, black smoke that limited visibility. A soldier in combat could rarely see much beyond the few yards in front of him as a battle unfolded. The primary infantry

North Wind Picture Archives via AP Images

French uniforms during the Napoleonic period (from left): for infantry, grenadiers, and cavalry.

weapon of the period was the smoothbore, muzzle-loading, flintlock musket. The most famous muskets of the period were the British Brown Bess and French Model 1777. These weapons had changed little from the beginning of the eighteenth century; all were highly inaccurate and unreliable, with an effective range of 300 yards. The caliber of the weapons varied widely, and their low rate of accuracy made a high rate of volley fire essential. Army manuals of the day often stressed that soldiers should concentrate on rapid fire over aim. A well-trained soldier could produce a rate of fire of three shots per minute. Misfires in battle were common. Each soldier carried an angular sleeve bayonet that varied between 15 and 18 inches in length. The bayonet was used for shock on the battlefield and rarely for hand-to-hand combat. In addition to the smoothbore musket, soldiers were equipped with muzzle-loading rifles. Rifles had greater accuracy than muskets but had a substantially reduced rate of fire of ten shots in ten minutes. Muskets were the chief weapon of the line infantry. Rifles were employed chiefly by light infantry units for skirmishing.

Cavalry relied upon the saber and, to a limited extent, the lance. Cavalry units were divided into light and heavy formations. Light cavalry was used for reconnaissance and security and carried curved swords for cutting. Heavy cavalry was used to break the line of enemy infantry and carried longer and straighter sabers.

The lance was most effective against infantry or retreating cavalry. Short carbines and pistols supplemented the sabers, swords, and lances. Little armor was used in the Napoleonic era. Heavy cavalrymen known as cuirassiers were equipped with partial body armor that covered the upper part of the torso. They also wore helmets, gauntlets, and heavy leather boots. The evidence would suggest that such body armor offered its wearer little protection.

Artillery during the Napoleonic era was, along with the infantry and the cavalry, one of the three main combat branches of the army. The effective use of artillery could often decide the outcome of a battle. Guns were divided into siege and field cannons. Prior to the French Revolution, artillery improvement had stood as the most important single advance in military technology. During this time, artillery pieces were made lighter and more mobile, so that they could be quickly concentrated on the battlefield wherever they were most needed. Artillery varied from the largest pieces, weighing more than 2,000 pounds and shooting 12-pound balls with ranges up to 900 yards, to smaller and lighter howitzers with ranges of more than 500 yards. Teams of draft horses were used to pull artillery pieces into action. Six horses were required to pull a heavy 12-pounder. Teams of four horses were required for the smaller 8- and 4-pounders. Three different projectiles were used. Round shot composed of a solid iron ball was the most widely used type of projectile. It was particularly effective against men lined up in dense formations. Explosive shells were fired by howitzers. For close work, canisters composed of many smaller iron balls in a metal casing were used to great effect against infantry. The British also used shrapnel or spherical cases packed with balls in an exploding shell. A unique artillery weapon was the Congreve rocket, invented by British artillerist Sir William Congreve (1772-1828) in 1808. The rocket, weighing between 5 and 32 pounds, produced much noise but proved highly inaccurate and unreliable in battle.

After the Napoleonic Wars, the percussion cap replaced the flintlock in firearms. The percussion cap allowed for a much greater rate of fire and fewer misfires. By 1849 Claude-Étienne Minié (1804-1879) of the French army had invented a conical-pointed cylindrical bullet called the Minié ball for muzzle-loading rifles, which provided increased rates of fire, accuracy, and range. With the Minié ball, killing range on the battlefield went from 100 to 400 yards. The rifled musket came to replace the smoothbore musket as the chief infantry weapon by the time of the American Civil War (1861-1865).

The advance of industrialization in the first half of the nineteenth century had a significant impact on military affairs. Introduction of the system of interchangeable parts made the mass production of weapons possible. Industrialization and the development of the steam locomotive had given rise to the development of the railroad by the 1820's. Railroads revolutionized warfare by providing armies with greater mobility and speed. The shift in military technology from smoothbore muskets to rifled muskets was not accompanied by a similar change in tactics on the battlefield. The consequences would be the heavy casualty rates of the American Civil War. Technological developments began to shift the battlefield advantage from offensive to defensive operations.

Although the Napoleonic period is often remembered for its elaborate uniforms, the reality was frequently far from ideal. Most troops, except for certain elite groups such as guard formations, had to make do with whatever clothing they could get. Few soldiers were ever fully outfitted in regulation uniforms. The scope of Napoleonic warfare placed great strain on governments' abilities to produce enough clothing for the needs of European armies. At times, even in the best-regulated armies, soldiers wore civilian gear.

MILITARY ORGANIZATION

Prior to the French Revolution, innovators in the old royal army introduced the practice of organizing armies into divisions that contained both artillery and infantry. Later, after the revolution, the divisional organization that contained infantry, cavalry, and artillery was introduced. Each division was capable of independent operations, greater speed, and increased mobility. In effect, each division functioned as a mini-army combining all three combat arms. By the time of Napoleon, with larger armies reaching numbers of 200,000 or more soldiers, divisions were grouped into corps for administrative purposes and for better command and control. Each division was organized into two or three infantry brigades of two regiments each and one brigade of artillery composed of two batteries. Corps were made up of two to

Napoleon, mounted on a white horse, at the Battle of Austerlitz in 1805.

four divisions under a single commander. Most armies followed the French organizational pattern. Nevertheless, the British army was still organized into independent brigades until 1807, when they followed the French model and adopted divisional organization. For the ill-fated Russian campaign, Napoleon organized his vast army into three army groups composed of two to three corps each.

DOCTRINE, STRATEGY, AND TACTICS

Prior to the French Revolution, warfare had focused on avoiding costly, uncertain battles. The object of war was not to destroy the enemy but to achieve limited objectives with limited means. The French Revolution ushered in an era of total warfare, in which the objective became the destruction of the opposing force. With the advent of mass armies and the con-

cept of the nation-at-arms, war grew in scope and scale. Military doctrine, strategy, and tactics reflected this change. The emergence of new military formations, especially the division and army corps, and the old concept of combined arms, or blending infantry, artillery, and cavalry together on the battlefield, made Napoleonic warfare possible.

Inspiration also came from the campaigns of King Frederick the Great (1712-1786) of Prussia, who stressed speed and mobility in war. Many of the ideals applied in the Napoleonic era were rooted in the writings of prerevolutionary French military thinkers such as Maurice of Saxony (1696-1750), Pierre-Joseph de Bourcet (1700-1780), and François-Appollini de Guibert (1744-1790), among others. Although many of the elements of Napoleonic warfare had been present prior to the French Revolution, they were not fully realized until the time of the French Revolution and the Napoleonic Wars.

Napoleonic warfare stressed quick decisions and decisive battles achieved by destruction of enemy field forces. The goal was to destroy the opponent's state of balance and will to fight while achieving economy of force in the pursuit of particular political goals. Better roadways and the combined arms divisional formation made this type of warfare feasible. Prior to the beginning of a campaign, detailed planning was conducted in order to leave little to chance. Alternative plans were also made to allow for the accommodation of changing circumstances. Flexibility, mobility, and opportunity were stressed. Once the campaign was under way, efforts were made to maintain good field security to conceal the intentions of the attacker from the enemy. Deception was often used. A cavalry screen was placed forward to disguise the line of operations and the makeup of the army. Each unit would march in self-contained divisions by different routes, staying within one or two days' marching distance from each other. Once contact was made with the opposing army, rapid, concerted effort took place, with the goal of achieving superior force on the battlefield and a quick victory. At this tactic, Napoleon stood out as the greatest strategist of the time; no other commander equaled his abilities.

Limitations of the weapons of the day determined battlefield tactics. From the onset of the French Revolutionary Wars, France relied on the column for attack. The often poorly trained citizen soldiers of France initially lacked the discipline and training to fight in the linear formation that was the standard for all other European armies. At first, large numbers of skirmishers would be placed in front of the attacking column. Napoleon came to rely increasingly on huge attack columns with a reduced number of skirmishers out front. One by one, except for the British, the other European powers followed the French example. Britain retained the line that was often formed into two ranks. The combination of steady troops, well trained in rapid musket fire, and the greater firepower offered by the line over the column accounts for the Duke of Wellington's victories over the French in Spain and at Waterloo. The British soldiers were noted for their ability to load and fire quickly on the battlefield. Wellington usually preferred to fight on ground, the reverse slope, which offered the best protection from artillery fire and masked portions of his army from the enemy. Confident in the steadfastness of his troops and in the superiority of the line that offered greater firepower over the attack column, Wellington was perhaps the only general of the era not intimidated by the new French tactical system.

The advances in artillery allowed for greater battlefield mobility and concentration. Light cavalry units were used in scouting and skirmishing roles. Heavy cavalry was used on the battlefield for its shock impact. The chief defenses against cavalry were concentrated artillery fire and the formation of infantry units into squares such as those employed by the British at Waterloo.

Napoleon (center) examines a group of French soldiers at the Battle of Jena in 1806.

CONTEMPORARY SOURCES

The two most influential military thinkers of the period were Swiss soldier Antoine-Henri de Jomini (1779-1869) and Prussian army officer Carl von Clausewitz (1780-1831). Each of these men provided influential interpretations of Napoleonic warfare. Jomini had served on the military staff of Napoleon and that of Russian czar Alexander I (1777-1825) as well. His most influential work, *Précis de l'art de la guerre* (1838; *Summary of the Art of War*, 1868), came to be widely used by all Western armies. In it Jomini sought to identify what he saw as the unchanging principles of war by studying the conduct of military campaigns. He laid great stress on seizing the opponent's lines of communication. Once that had been achieved, a successful battle would follow, because the victorious army would have the overall strategic advantage as well as superior manpower and matériel. Jomini's writing, with its stress on unalterable principles of war, tended to prevent a careful review of the changing circumstances of nineteenth century warfare.

Clausewitz served in the Prussian army against Napoleon and went on to become the head of the Allgemeine Kriegsschule, the Prussian war college. His famous philosophical reflections on war were published after his death under the title of *Vom Kriege* (1832-1834; *On War*, 1873). Clausewitz argued that war was in fact a political act in which the chief goal was total victory. Unlike Jomini, Clausewitz rejected the ideal of unchanging principles of war. He argued that the conduct of war always changed due to new technological advances and altered circumstances. He contended that the main objective in war should be the destruction of the enemy's military forces. The ideals of Clausewitz had their greatest impact in the last quarter of the nineteenth century. Napoleon, the greatest soldier of the era, never wrote in a systematic way about his art of war. His writings and remarks were formed into a collection of a little more than one hundred maxims that served as the closest expression of his ideals of tactics and strategy.

BOOKS AND ARTICLES

Addington, Larry H. *The Patterns of War Since the Eighteenth Century*. 2d ed. Bloomington: Indiana University Press, 1994.

Bell, David A. *The First Total War: Napoleon's Europe and the Birth of Warfare as We Know It*. Boston: Houghton Mifflin, 2007.

Black, Jeremy. "Revolutionary and Napoleonic Warfare." In *European Warfare, 1453-1815*, edited by Black. New York: St. Martin's Press, 1999.

Bruce, Robert B., et al. *Fighting Techniques of the Napoleonic Age, 1792-1815: Equipment, Combat Skills, and Tactics*. New York: Thomas Dunne Books/St. Martin's Press, 2008.

Chandler, David. *On the Napoleonic Wars*. London: Greenhill Books, 1999.

Doughty, Robert A., and Ira Gruber. *Warfare in the Western World: Military Operations from 1600 to 1871*. Lexington, Mass.: D. C. Heath, 1996.

Esposito, Vincent J. A., and John R. Elting. *Military History and Atlas of the Napoleonic Wars*. New York, Praeger, 1964. Reprint. Mechanicsburg, Pa.: Stackpole Books, 1999.

Gates, David. "The Napoleonic Era and Its Legacy." In *Warfare in the Nineteenth Century*. New York: Palgrave, 2001.

Isemonger, Paul Lewis, and Christopher Scott. *The Fighting Man: The Soldier at War from the Age of Napoleon to the Second World War*. Stroud, Gloucestershire, England: Sutton, 1998.

Keegan, John. *Intelligence in War: Knowledge of the Enemy from Napoleon to Al-Qaeda*. London: Hutchinson, 2003.

McNab, Chris, ed. *Armies of the Napoleonic Wars: An Illustrated History*. Botley, Oxford, England: Osprey, 2009.

Muir, Rory. *Tactics and the Experience of Battle in the Age of Napoleon*. New Haven, Conn.: Yale University Press, 1998.

Paret, Peter, ed. *Makers of Modern Strategy from Machiavelli to the Nuclear Age*. Princeton, N.J.: Princeton University Press, 1986.

Pois, Robert A., and Philip Langer. "Napoleon in Russia, 1812." In *Command Failure in War: Psychology and Leadership*. Bloomington: Indiana University Press, 2004.

Rothenberg, Gunther E. *The Art of Warfare in the Age of Napoleon*. Bloomington: Indiana University Press, 1980.

Weigley, Russell Frank. "The Climax of Napoleonic War: To Austerlitz and Jena-Auerstadt." In *The Age of Battles*. 1991 Reprint. Bloomington: Indiana University Press, 2004.

Weller, Jac. *On Wellington: The Duke and His Art of War*. London: Greenhill Books, 1998.

FILMS AND OTHER MEDIA

Biography: The Great Commanders: Napoleon Bonaparte. Documentary. Biography Channel, 1998.

The Duellists. Feature film. Enigma Productions, 1977.

Foot Soldier: The Napoleonic Soldier. Documentary. A&E Home Video, 1998.

Horatio Hornblower. Television series, Meridian Productions, 1998-2003.

Master and Commander. Film. Twentieth Century Fox, 2003.

Napoleon and Wellington. Documentary. A&E Home Video, 1999.

Waterloo. Feature film. Paramount Pictures, 1970.

Van Michael Leslie

THE CRIMEAN WAR

Dates: 1853-1856

POLITICAL CONSIDERATIONS

The Crimean War (1853-1856), fought by Britain, France, and the Ottoman Turks against Russia, took place in an era during which the major European powers were in heavy competition over trade and territory as they sought to build their empires. This quest served to spur the technological innovations that would alter the shape of warfare in the nineteenth century. The invention of the telegraph meant, for instance, that field commanders were in close contact with government officials throughout military campaigns and that information about the campaigns could reach civilians on the home front much more quickly. The building of railroads meant that people and freight could be carried over large distances at faster speeds than ever before and that much land transport was no longer affected by the vagaries of weather. The invention of steam-powered ships similarly revolutionized naval warfare. The nineteenth century also saw early experiments with chemical warfare and the development of mines designed to affect shipping. Individual weaponry changed quite dramatically as well, as long-range rifles made muskets and bayonets obsolete. The most successful European powers were the ones that adopted new technologies, the fastest of which left others struggling to modernize their industries and armies.

MILITARY ACHIEVEMENT

The Crimean War was sparked by rivalries between the great European powers. Russia had long coveted access to the Mediterranean Sea through the straits of the Dardanelles and the Bosporus, both of which remained in Turkish hands in the 1850's. Because Russia, France, and Britain were competing for trade with the Ottoman Empire, any Russian expansion into the Mediterranean could threaten the interests of Britain and France as well as the territorial integrity of the Ottoman Empire itself. The relationship between Britain and Russia was further complicated by each country's rival desires for influence in India and the Middle East. France was willing to block Russian expansion into Turkish territory but had its own interest in territorial expansion at the expense of the Turks in Egypt and other parts of North Africa.

In July, 1853, Russian soldiers marched into the principalities of Moldavia and Wallachia, then under Turkish control, and continued to advance east toward the Danube River. In early October, Turkey declared war on Russia and sent its armies toward the Danube and the Caucasus Mountains. During the winter of 1853-1854, France and Britain watched from the sidelines; their only action was to send some troops to stations in the Mediterranean. However, at the end of March, 1854, the Crimean War officially began when Britain and France declared war on Russia. The major military goal of the Allied forces was to invade the Crimean Peninsula and eventually to capture the Russian naval base at Sevastopol. Once that fortress finally fell in 1855, the war's major fighting ended and peace negotiations soon began.

WEAPONS, UNIFORMS, AND ARMOR

During the Crimean War, the British and the French used much more modern weaponry than did either the Turks or the Russians. Every French infantryman was armed with a new Minié rifle. Although some British regiments still used the Brown Bess, a brown-stocked, 12-pound, .753-caliber flintlock musket with a range of only 100 yards, the vast majority of British soldiers were equipped with the American-made 1852 Enfield rifle. An improved version of the Minié rifle, the Enfield rifle used a .577-caliber bullet

MAJOR SITES IN THE CRIMEAN WAR, 1853-1856

Major battles in Crimean War

RUSSIAN EMPIRE

AUSTRIAN EMPIRE

Inkerman
Nov. 5, 1854

Sevastopol
October, 1854-
September, 1855

Sea of Azov

Balaklava
Oct. 25, 1854

SERBIA

Black Sea

OTTOMAN

MONTENEGRO

Sinope
Nov. 30, 1853

EMPIRE

GREECE

Dardanelles

Gallipoli
April, 1854

Mediterranean Sea

with a range of 1,600 yards. It was deadly accurate at 800 yards. The Allied rifles could be loaded twice as quickly as could muskets. Allied cavalrymen were armed with sabers, steel-tipped lances, and carbines. Colt revolvers were also given to British cavalry soldiers but were seldom used, because they had a short range and were difficult to manage on horseback.

By contrast, only 6,000 Russian infantrymen were equipped with modern rifles; the remainder went into battle armed with smoothbore muskets. Turkish infantry also used the now-outdated smoothbore muskets. Turkish cavalry soldiers were issued short sabers and carbines that did not always work properly. The Turkish cavalry also tended to be poorly equipped with horses that were too small and old to compete with those of the other Allied armies. In addition, the saddles used by the Turks were often in poor condition and their spurs were rusty. The irregular cavalry, known as the Bashi-Bazouks, used any weapon possible, including bamboo spears. The Russian cavalry also tended to have smaller mounts, and its mobility was hampered because these smaller animals were expected to carry heavier packs than those borne by the horses of the other armies.

The armies that fought in the Crimean War were clearly unconcerned with camouflaging themselves from the enemy, wearing a variety of colorful uniforms and headgear. For instance, Sardinian riflemen wore light blue overcoats, blue turtleneck tunics, dark blue pants tucked into black leather boots, and wide-brimmed black hats with black rooster feathers. Other Sardinian troops were outfitted in green. Green was also used by the African-Egyptian troops from the Sudan who were part of the Turkish force. In this case, they wore bright green jackets and white trousers. Because the Turks did not have standardized uniforms, some of their other troops wore dark blue uniforms, gray woolen socks, and sheepskin sandals. Members of the Turkish irregular cavalry wore whatever they liked. The uniforms of the French and British troops were more standardized. French officers wore all blue, whereas the soldiers wore blue tunics, red trousers, and red caps. The Zouaves—elite French infantry troops who were originally Algerian tribesmen but now mostly European in ethnic origin—used the same color scheme, but their trousers were baggy and their red caps were so floppy that they resembled nightcaps. The British infantry was equipped with scarlet tunics and white leather cross-belts. Trousers were dark blue for the majority of the troops. The exceptions were the Scottish highland regiments, who wore kilts, and the light cavalry of James Thomas Brudenell, the seventh earl of Cardigan (1797-1868), who wore cherry-colored trousers.

A cartoon by John Leech decries the wretched conditions British soldiers faced in the Crimea. One soldier says to the other, "Well, Jack! Here's good news from home. We're to have a medal," and the other replies, "That's very kind. Maybe one of these days we'll have a coat to stick it on!"

The artillery forces wore blue uniforms. All soldiers wore stocks: tight leather collars that kept their heads erect. The headgear varied greatly among the British forces. Both brass and leather helmets were worn, as were black bearskin hats called busbies. Russian soldiers sported gray greatcoats over green or blue jackets and blue pants with a red stripe down the side. They also wore leather cross-belts and leather boots. Russian soldiers were all issued white linen undergarments in addition to the rest of their uniforms. Three types of headgear were used by the Russian army during the Crimean War: a black leather helmet with a brass spike on top; a tall shako, a stiff hat with a high crown and a plume; and a flat, visorless forage cap.

Typically, the soldiers who fought during the Crimean War were issued only one uniform, which was to be worn in all weather and on all occasions. It was intended that soldiers would receive a new uniform each year but would keep their greatcoats for a longer period of time. For instance, British soldiers were given a new greatcoat once every three years. Supply routes to the Crimea were poorly organized, however, and at one point, a freak winter storm destroyed some of the ships carrying new uniforms to the Allied forces. Many soldiers ultimately had to scavenge for their uniforms. Only the Russian soldiers seem to have carried extra shirts, socks, trousers, and leather boots with extra soles in their knapsacks. Muslim members of the Turkish army each carried a prayer rug as part of their equipment.

The Crimean War featured the heaviest artillery bombardments the world had seen to that point. Soldiers were able to fire 200-pound explosive shells over a distance of several miles. These massive shells were specifically designed to destroy heavy fortifications. Smaller 32- or 68-pound shells could, similarly, be launched over great distances. Some cannonballs were made from solid iron so they would smash through anything in their path. Other balls were purposely heated so they would start fires on impact. Most shells, however, were explosive and timed to explode either in the air or just after impact. Some shells hurled only the metal from their casings, whereas others contained other, smaller shells or grenades to cause a chain of explosions.

The Turkish military engineers proved to be the best in battle. Their artillery was excellent and accurate, and their soldiers were equipped with modern British cannons. The British Royal Horse Artillery was equipped with the same 6-pound cannons, but the British troops were less well trained in this area than were the Turks. The heavier siege guns of the British were not as good as those of the French or Russians. During the Crimean War, the Russian army proved particularly innovative in this area and pioneered the use of rockets, horse-drawn artillery, and heavy siege guns.

Mines were used by both the French and the Russians during the Siege of Sevastopol. The French tried to put mines under the defenses of the city, but their mines had conventional fuses that sometimes went out before detonating. The Russians were more successful. They would tunnel under the French tunnels and set off mines that detonated electronically.

The Crimean War involved naval power as well as artillery and mines. At the time, Britain had the world's best navy, with more total ships, more steam-powered ships, and better long-range guns than any other power. The French navy was weaker than that of the British but was stronger than those of the Russians and Turks. In total, the British and French fielded a combined eight triple-decked battleships, twenty-two double-decked battleships, seven frigates, thirty paddle-driven warships, and several hundred troop transports. By comparison, the Turkish navy had only six, severely outgunned battleships in the Black Sea and almost no steam-powered ships. Similarly, the Russian navy had yet to convert its ships to steam power, and its naval forces are best remembered during the Crimean War for the role they played in the defense of Sevastopol, sinking six ships to block the entrance to the city's harbor and then removing the guns from their ships for use on land.

MILITARY ORGANIZATION

The armies that fought the Crimean War were similar in structure but different in composition. Each army had infantry and cavalry divisions. The cavalry was usually split between light and heavy brigades with the heavy brigades featuring larger men and horses. The Russian Cossack units and the Turkish Bashi-Bazouks served as irregular cavalry. The French also had a group of elite infantrymen, called the Zouaves.

Russia relied on an army of serfs. The recruits were chosen by their owners or by village councils and saw their twenty-five-year terms as death sentences. Few of these soldiers were literate, and they received no further education during their time in the army; thus, they had little incentive to fight. For infringements of discipline, the Russian troops were subject to physical punishments such as punching or flogging. Soldiers typically formed "artels," groups of ten men who shared food and supplies and looked after one another. These were not official army groupings but functioned similarly to the artels, or craftsmen's and workers' cooperatives, formed in Russia.

One-sixth of officers came from the nobility, and promotion was often based on family connections and wealth rather than on merit. Since the czar was the ultimate commander, he made decisions about promotion and could intervene in any aspect of the running of the armed forces. The remaining officers were "junkers," the sons of petty nobles who had not succeeded in secondary school and could find no career other than the armed forces. The junkers served in the ranks for six years before earning their commissions. Corruption was widespread in the Russian army, and the officers frequently stole money allocated for arms and supplies. Russian officers who wanted to evade the dangers of battle could buy medical certificates asserting they were wounded and no longer capable of active service.

TURNING POINTS

1807	American inventor Robert Fulton invents the first steamship, which by the time of the Crimean War has largely replaced the sail-powered ships in British, French, and American navies.
1834	Turkey creates its first military academy.
1840's	The telegraph becomes widely used and links governments with field commanders.
1847	The first use of anesthesia during a battlefield operation.

The vast majority of British troops were volunteers: Only 1 percent were criminals and vagrants being punished by the legal system. Wages were a shilling a day. Infantryman signed on for a ten-year period, whereas cavalryman served twelve-year terms. Irishmen had flocked to the British army during the Great Potato Famine of 1845; by the time of the Crimean War, fully one-third of the British troops were Irish. Although the British also hired mercenaries from parts of Germany, Sardinia, Switzerland, and the United States, these men were sent home before seeing action in the Crimean War. Almost all of the officers in the British army came from society's elite. One-third were from titled or landed families, and the rest came from families associated with the so-called gentlemen's professions, such as the clergy and the law. British officers tended to be well educated but had little formal military training. Since both commissions and promotions were sold, the wealthy dominated the higher ranks of the armed forces, and British officers could sell their commissions and go home whenever they wished.

The French army emphasized merit rather than birthright. Few officers were from the nobility. Instead, they had to earn their promotions and to live on their military salaries. Consequently, they had more sympathy and understanding for the men under their command. Whereas British officers spent little time with their soldiers, French officers would more frequently share the living and dining quarters of their men. French soldiers were conscripted by lottery for six-year terms, and during their service they were given rudimentary education in hygiene, history, and the meaning of morale and military spirit. They were not subject to flogging or other forms of corporal punishment.

After a series of defeats in the eighteenth century, the Turks began to reform their army along French and Russian lines. By the start of the Crimean War, these reforms had seen some success: Junior officers were literate and had received some military training. However, they were resented by many senior officers who remained illiterate. Corruption affected the Turkish army's ability to supply itself, because officers often siphoned off money allocated for provisions in order to pay the bribes needed for promotions. The Turkish force was multinational in its composition: Some officers were Hungarians, Italians, and Poles who had fled their homelands, and the infantry had come from all over the empire. Desertion was a problem among the infantry, because conscripted peasants from Armenia, Tunisia, Romania, and Egypt felt little loyalty to the Ottoman Empire that had conquered their homelands. Even if the troops did remain with the army, they fought with little enthusiasm.

The Granger Collection, New York

An engraving depicting the famous Charge of the Light Brigade, at the Battle of Balaklava (1854).

Women and children were also part of the Crimean War. All sides had female nurses, and children served as buglers and drummers. Roughly 10 percent of the Allied soldiers were legally married and, according to regulations, four wives per company of one hundred men were allowed to go with the troops in order to cook and do the laundry. Wives who already had children were not eligible to accompany the army. The wives frequently served as nurses in field hospitals as well. In the field they carried all of their belongings on their backs and, if they were widowed in the course of a campaign, they were left to fend for themselves by sleeping in ditches or dugouts. Because widows' pensions did not exist at the time, it was difficult for widows to return to their native countries. However, it was also economically challenging for a wife to remain in her native country while her husband left to fight overseas. Governments and armies made no provisions for the economic survival of women and children left behind, so women were sometimes forced to rely upon their needlework skills, prostitution, or charity. It was not unheard of for women to stow away on troop ships, or even to commit suicide, after their husbands' departure for the Crimea. The wives of Allied officers seldom accompanied their husbands, although a handful of aristocratic women did visit the Crimea in the summer to offer social amusements to the commanding officers. The wives of Russian soldiers remained behind in their native villages. Few Russian officers' wives chose to join their husbands during the war.

DOCTRINE, STRATEGY, AND TACTICS

In most armies at the time of the Crimean War, there was a clear division between the officers and the enlisted men. The officers tended to be aristocrats who were schooled from childhood about honor and glory. There was a sense among many officers that there was no glory in a death other than in combat and that cowardice meant certain disgrace. The quest for glory led to several actions during the war that can only be labeled military follies, the most stunning example being the infamous Charge of the Light Brigade (1854), commemorated in a poem by Alfred, Lord Tennyson (1809-1892). Rank-and-file troops often had a perspective on the war that was different from that of their commanders and were motivated by appeals to national pride, regimental pride, or a sense of competition between regiments.

In the 1850's army officers were not typically

trained to think about supplies or to plan ahead. This lack of emphasis on strategic planning meant that the Allied armies entered the Crimean War without any knowledge of battlefield terrain. The commanders were also ignorant of the local climate and the size of the forces they would face. For instance, the British commander Fitzroy James Henry Somerset, the Baron Raglan (1788-1855), assumed that fresh water supplies and horses would be available. The British took neither medical supplies nor their hospital wagons with them during the invasion of the Crimea and, in fact, made no provisions at all to care for wounded soldiers. The supply base built by the British was at Balaklava, at times more than 9 miles from the front lines. The only way to the base was along a dirt road that ran uphill and became a river of mud when it rained. The situation was made worse by the lack of pack animals; all supplies had to be carried to the front by the soldiers themselves. Only at the end of April, 1855, was a rail link completed between the British supply base at Balaklava and the front.

The British were not alone in these oversights, however; the Turks had little transport to speak of and had made an agreement with the British to supply them. Because the Turks did not organize their own supply trains and the British were not in a position to fulfill the agreement, Turkish soldiers were forced to live off the land. The French were closer to their supply base and were accompanied by *viviandières*, young women who acted as provisioners for the French troops. Because the French had brought pack animals to use for the transportation of material, they transported food and ammunition for all of the Allied armies. The situation was equally bad for the Russian soldiers. Their officers frequently stole the funds allocated to purchase food, and supply conveys were often delayed by poor weather.

The officers who served during the Crimean War were no better at planning battles than they were at organizing their forces. Despite the creation of a Turkish military academy in 1834, many senior Turkish officers remained illiterate. British officers received little formal military training, and the vast majority had not studied maps, topography, or military tactics. Moreover, in peacetime these officers spent little time with their regiments and preferred to

leave the day-to-day management to their sergeants. Similarly, Russian officers were not required to have any formal knowledge of military tactics. Only the French officers received a solid military training at several military academies. They were expected to study map reading, tactics, fortification, and topography. Their grasp of the material was tested through regular examinations and regiment inspections, but the training of the French officers was nullified once the campaign in the Crimea began. British senior officers did not get along well with the French commanders, who tended to come from less distinguished and less wealthy families. Because the Allies needed to coordinate their forces in battle, it was imperative for the commanders to agree on a strategy. However, as the war began the Allies could agree upon no coordinated plan. Joint command quickly broke down amid personal rivalries between the commanders. The lack of coordination was most evident during the Siege of Sevastopol. The original plan was for the Allied armies to attack the city from the north, destroy the city's docks, and sink the Russian fleet. However, this plan was eventually abandoned in favor of a joint British and French attack from the south. The Turks took no direct part in the Siege of Sevastopol. A strong assault as soon as the British forces were in place would most likely have succeeded in taking the city, but the French commanders insisted on waiting for the arrival of their siege guns before the engagement began. In the end, the Allies camped nearby and waited for almost a month before firing any weapons at the city's defenders. The reprieve gave the general in charge of Sevastopol's defenses time to build a series of fortifications and await reinforcements. By the time the British and French commanders agreed to attack the city, it was virtually impregnable. It ultimately took almost a year for the Allies to take Sevastopol.

The Crimean War saw two distinct types of warfare: land battles and sieges. The tactics used by the armies varied depending on the situation and on their national traditions. During land battles, the British infantry would advance in a line, unhurriedly and silently, toward the enemy fire. In contrast, the French commanders encouraged individual initiative and had trained their troops in athletics, hand-to-hand combat, and mountain climbing. French soldiers rushed to the attack as quickly as possible, in part because their officers believed they would retreat otherwise. Both the French and the Russians would scream and shout as they advanced. The Russian army's main infantry tactic was to have the troops advance in densely packed columns at the same time as the enemy approached and to fire at the enemy as the Russians advanced. The troops were told that aiming was not important, and few of the bullets found their mark, because target practice was not part of a Russian soldier's normal training. After using their firearms, the Russians would then charge with their bayonets. The types of advances used by all of the armies in the Crimean War actually made it easier for the enemy to kill the advancing soldiers. Troops were often under fire for more than a mile before they engaged the enemy in hand-to-hand combat. Moreover, in their brightly colored uniforms, soldiers could be seen so far away that advances lacked any element of surprise. Joint maneuvers also proved difficult during the war. No army would agree to deviate from its tactics in order to better synchronize an attack. In-

stead, for instance, the British soldiers were told to maintain the discipline of their advance and not to try to match the pace set by the French. Commanders, often within the same army, proved reluctant to communicate with one another during a battle.

Should an infantryman survive the initial advance and meet the enemy, hand-to-hand combat would begin. All types of weapons would be used: bayonets, swords, stones, even feet and teeth for kicking and biting. Rifle butts frequently served as clubs. All troops were trained to rely on their bayonets more than any other weapon.

The cavalries were also part of land battles during the Crimean War. Both the British and the French successfully used cavalry charges against the enemy. They benefited because Russian infantrymen were not instructed on how to defend themselves against enemy cavalry charges. In contrast, Russian dragoons would ride into battle but fought on foot, and the regular Russian cavalry did not demonstrate the iron discipline needed for a successful charge. Things were even more difficult for the Turks; the Bashi-Bazouks, although clearly the most superb of

P. F. Collier and Son

British troops at the Battle of Balaklava in 1854.

F. R. Niglutsch

The final assault by the allied forces at Sevastopol in 1855.

the Turkish horsemen, refused to fight against regular cavalry and had to be used to terrorize enemy civilians instead.

Infantry advances and cavalry charges continued to be used during the Siege of Sevastopol but were supplemented with several other tactics as well. Before the soldiers would attack, the Allied armies would pound the city with heavy artillery bombardments and try to tunnel under the Russian fortifications. New long-range rifles meant that sharpshooting emerged as an effective tactic during the

Crimean War. Under the cover of darkness, a sniper would crawl toward the enemy lines and dig a foxhole. Then he would wait until daylight revealed a target. Other nighttime activities developed during the Siege of Sevastopol, in which the Russians engaged in nighttime raids on enemy trenches in order to kill sleeping soldiers and capture prisoners who could supply them with information. Indeed, all sides relied on spies to obtain information about the enemy. Suspected spies, however, would be shot if they were captured.

CONTEMPORARY SOURCES

A variety of contemporary sources are available to readers who wish to know more about the Crimean War. British newspaper correspondents accompanied the British army and telegraphed their stories to London, where the items would be published without censorship. *The Times* had a circulation of 40,000 copies per issue at the time of the Crimean War. The French were also accompanied by correspondents, but their stories were subject to strict censorship and, consequently, are not as accurate as those that appeared in British newspapers.

Many participants in the Crimean War wrote accounts of their experiences both immediately after the war and for many years following it. Some of the English-language memoirs and diaries include those of George Higginson, *Seventy-one Years of a Guardsman's Life* (1916); John Richard Hume, *Reminiscences of the Crimean Campaign with the Fifty-fifth Regiment* (1894); Frederick Robinson, *Diary of the Crimean War* (1856); and Humphry Sandwith, *A Narrative of the Siege of Kars* (1856). Many Russian, Sardinian, and French soldiers also wrote memoirs, but their works have not been translated into English. Due to the low literacy rate among the Turkish troops, few of their firsthand accounts exist. All of the memoirs reflect the age in which they were written, conveying the attitudes, beliefs, and prejudices of the 1850's and omitting certain elements that a modern reader would expect from accounts of contemporary warfare. For instance, because it was not fashionable to discuss emotions, particularly those experienced during battle, the authors describing their Crimean War experiences rarely discuss topics such as combat fatigue.

In addition to the various memoirs, there were travel accounts written by people with first-hand views of the Crimean War. These books were not necessarily written by regular soldiers or even by military personnel. Among the most useful is George Palmer Evelyn's *A Diary of the Crimea* (1954), which describes the role he played as a British mercenary in the Crimean War. Evelyn's account is particularly informative about the layout of the battlefields. Sir Henry Clifford's *Henry Clifford, VC: His Letters and Sketches from the Crimea* (1956) provides another firsthand account of the war, focusing on the period from September 18, 1854, to April 18, 1856. George B. McClellan's *The Armies of Europe Comprising Descriptions in Detail of the Military Systems of England, France, Russia, Prussia, Austria, and Sardinia: Adapting Their Advantages to All Arms of the United States Service and Embodying the Report of Observations in Europe During the Crimean War, As Military Commissioner from the United States Government, 1855-1856* (1861) provides a great deal of information about the organizations of the armies of most combatants in the Crimean War. Drawings and charts illustrate the information.

Letters Home from the Crimea (1999) is a collection of letters by Temple Goodman, a cavalryman who saw action in the Battle of Balaclava as well as the Siege of Sevastopol. Other published collections of letters include *"Little Hodge": Being Extracts from the Diaries and Letters of Lt.-Colonel Edward Cooper Hodge Written During the Crimean War, 1854-1856* (1971), written by Edward Cooper Hodge and edited by George Paget, the marquess of Anglesey; *Letters from the Army in the Crimea, Written During the Years 1854, 1855, and 1856* (1857), by Sir Anthony Coningham Sterling; *Life, Letters, and Diaries of Lieutenant-General Sir Gerald Graham with Portraits, Plans, and His Principal Despatches* (1901), by R. H. Vetch; and *Crimean Diary and Letters of Lieutenant-General Sir Charles Ash Windham, K.C.B., with Observations upon his Services During the Indian Mutiny* (1897), by Sir C. A. Windham.

Finally, special mention should be made of Leo Tolstoy's (1828-1910) fictional account of the Siege of Sevastopol, entitled *Sevastopolskiy rasskazy* (1855-1856; *Sebastopol*, 1887), as well as his published diaries covering the years of the Crimean War. As a young man, Tolstoy served as an artillery officer during the war and was stationed in Sevastopol at the time of the siege. His work is more readily available than many of the other primary sources discussed above and provides a Russian view of the war.

BOOKS AND ARTICLES

Almond, Ian. "The Crimean War, 1853-6: Muslims on All Sides." In *Two Faiths, One Banner: When Muslims Marched with Christians Across Europe's Battlegrounds.* Cambridge, Mass.: Harvard University Press, 2009.

Baumgart, Winfried. *The Crimean War, 1853-1856.* New York: Oxford University Press, 1999.

Curtiss, J. S. *The Russian Army Under Nicholas I, 1825-1855.* Durham, N.C.: Duke University Press, 1965.

Edgerton, R. *Death or Glory: The Legacy of the Crimean War.* Boulder, Colo.: Westview Press, 1999.

Fletcher, Ian, and Natalia Ishchenko. *The Crimean War: A Clash of Empires.* Staplehurst, Kent, England: Spellmount, 2004.

Fuller, W. C., Jr. *Strategy and Power in Russia, 1600-1914.* New York: Free Press, 1992.

Grainger, John D. *The First Pacific War: Britain and Russia, 1854-1856.* Rochester, N.Y.: Boydell Press, 2008.

Griffith, P. *Military Thought in the French Army, 1815-51.* Manchester, England: Manchester University Press, 1989.

Harris, Stephen. *British Military Intelligence in the Crimean War, 1854-1856.* London: Frank Cass, 1999.

Lambert, A. D. *The Crimean War: The British Grand Strategy, 1853-56.* Manchester, England: Manchester University Press, 1990.

Small, Hugh. *The Crimean War: Queen Victoria's War with the Russian Tsars.* Stroud, Gloucestershire, England: Tempus, 2007.

Sweetman, John. *Balaclava, 1854: The Charge of the Light Brigade.* Botley, Oxford, England: Osprey, 1990. Reprint. Westport, Conn.: Praeger, 2005.

_____. *The Crimean War.* Botley, Oxford, England: Osprey, 2001.

Thomas, R., and R. Scollins. *The Russian Army of the Crimean War, 1854-56.* Botley, Oxford, England: Osprey, 1991.

Troubetzkoy, Alexis S. *A Brief History of the Crimean War: The Causes and Consequences of a Medieval Conflict Fought in a Modern Age.* New York: Carroll and Graf, 2006.

FILMS AND OTHER MEDIA

Balaclava, 1854. Documentary. Cromwell Productions, 1996.

The Charge of the Light Brigade. Feature film. Warner Bros., 1936.

Combat Camera. Documentary. A&E Home Video, 1992.

The Crimean War: A Clash of Empires. Documentary. Direct Cinema Limited, 1996.

Florence Nightingale and the Crimean War. Filmstrip. Multi-Media Productions, 1980.

Trumpets and Typewriters: A History of War Reporting. Documentary. ABC, 1983.

Alison Rowley

THE AMERICAN CIVIL WAR

Dates: 1861-1865

POLITICAL CONSIDERATIONS

Long considered a watershed in American history, the American Civil War (1861-1865) was also a turning point in the execution of warfare. Although it did not begin as a radically new kind of war, this conflict developed into the first total modern war, in which farmers, artisans, and businessmen played as important a role as soldiers and sailors. It was the first time that a nation, having passed through the Industrial Revolution, put to large-scale military use new scientific discoveries and modern technological advances. Breech-loading rifles replaced smoothbore muskets, ironclads replaced wooden ships, and the telegraph replaced dispatch bearers. Military leaders made use of such new weapons as land and naval mines, machine guns, armored railroad cars, submarines, and aerial reconnaissance from anchored balloons. The American Civil War was the first conflict to be extensively photographed, the first to combine weapons technologies with mass production, and the first to transport large numbers of men and equipment over long distances via railroad.

The Civil War was rooted in the political paradoxes of the American Revolution (1775-1783), which had been a civil war as well as a war for independence. The American Revolution created the world's leading democracy, which was also a slave-based republic. Founding fathers such as George Washington (1732-1799) and Thomas Jefferson (1743-1826) established a union of states in which white liberty and black slavery coexisted. In the decades following the Revolution, Northern states instituted programs of emancipation, whereas Southern states, spurred by the productivity of the cotton gin and the demands of European textile factories for raw cotton, promoted the expansion of slavery.

According to many scholars, the increasing political, economic, and cultural tensions between North-ern and Southern states made violent conflict between these antagonistic civilizations inevitable. Others see the Civil War as a constitutional or moral struggle, pitting libertarians against abolitionists. Still others see the crisis in terms of technological history. The Northern business class, friendly toward the technology that had made it wealthy and powerful, was hostile toward a Southern plutocracy wedded to an outdated agricultural society that resisted industrialization.

Although the war was ultimately decided by both military and technological achievements as well as by industrial and agricultural production, the political context influencing these developments was also important. In terms of international politics, both the North and South had strong ties of economic interdependence with European countries. For example, both Britain and France relied on raw cotton from the South to keep their textile mills productive, but these countries also had extensive investments in Northern land and railroads. In terms of domestic politics, the North and South, though claiming to be equally dedicated to the principles of the Declaration of Independence and the United States Constitution, had significant political differences that would influence military developments. The Confederate leaders may have seen themselves as the true heirs to the founding fathers of the United States, but the South's material and military weaknesses forced Confederate president Jefferson Davis (1808-1889) to reduce the rights of the seceded states in order to expand the power of his central government. For example, he forced through the Confederate Congress laws that resulted in the continent's first draft, the impressment of goods and labor, and the suspension of certain civil and economic liberties—all to help secure the new republic.

For Northerners, the relative unanimity that followed the outbreak of hostilities in 1861 quickly dissolved as leaders debated a series of controversial war measures, including conscription and emancipation. The military became enmeshed in politics when soldiers were required to capture and imprison influential "Copperheads," Northerners who sympathized with Southern secession. Following the instructions of Republican politicians, some state militia arrested draft dodgers and dissenting newspaper editors. Particularly troublesome to many was the brutal suppression of the 1863 Irish-immigrant riots against the draft in New York City. Because the wealthy could buy substitutes to serve in their place, many less advantaged Irish felt that the federal government was failing to live up to its egalitarian ideals.

President Abraham Lincoln (1809-1865) did try to engage an important group of Americans in the war effort when, in March, 1863, he signed an Act of Congress creating the National Academy of Sciences (NAS). The Academy's charter required its members, whenever called upon by government agencies, to investigate and report on any subject of science or technology. During its first year and a half the NAS had committees studying such important military matters as magnetic deviation on iron ships, the protection of iron vessels from corrosion, the preparation of accurate wind and current charts, and the development of efficient steam engines. Although the NAS did much to encourage the invention and production of weapons that amplified the abilities of Northern armies to inflict damage on Southern soldiers, it failed to improve significantly medical techniques and facilities, with the result that disease

CONFEDERATE AND UNION TERRITORIES

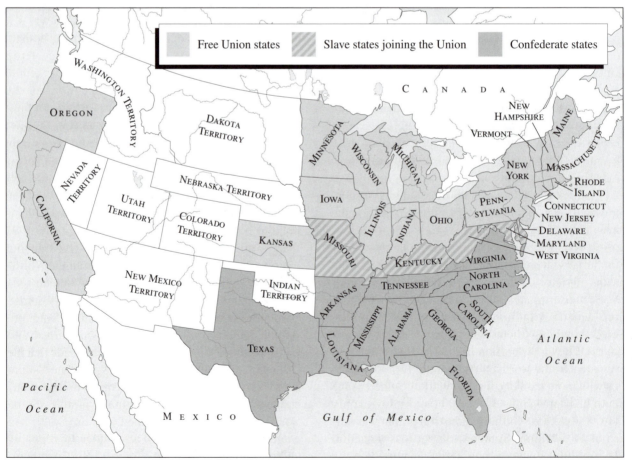

Gay Brothers and Company

Confederate forces fire on Fort Sumter in 1861.

killed twice as many Union soldiers as Confederate weapons did.

The Civil War began with the attack on Fort Sumter in April, 1861. At this time, the Union possessed overwhelming superiority in both manpower and material resources needed to conduct war in an industrial age. Although neither the South nor the North had made any special preparations for a prolonged war, Northerners had many advantages over Southerners, which politicians tried to turn into the means of victory. The North, exclusive of the border and far western states, surpassed the South in population, with 18.5 million Northerners to 5.5 million Southern whites (there were also 3.5 million black slaves). The disproportion in industrial strength was even greater: the North had more than 100,000 factories with more than one million workers, whereas the South had approximately 20,600 factories with only 111,000 workers. Northern industrial output was valued at $1.5 billion; Southern output was valued at $155 million. Because the Civil War would be the

first modern war, iron and steel would become the basic material for the production of munitions, railroads, bridges, and other equipment and structures. The total output of pig iron in the United States in 1860 was about 860,000 tons, of which the South produced only 26,000 tons, or 3 percent. Pennsylvania alone manufactured 560,000 tons of iron, which helps to explain Southern raids into this state. In 1860 there were 30,500 miles of railroad track in the United States, 72 percent of which lay in the North.

In sum, political decisions and developments affecting technology, industry, and the military helped shape the course of the Civil War and its resolution. Although the South was outmanned, outgunned, and outproduced by the North, a case can be made that the Confederacy's initial success and ultimate failure owed much to such intangibles as moral and religious concerns and civilian and military morale. Some Southern sympathizers claimed that the South had waged this war in defense of an aristocratic republic, and only the overwhelming force of Northern num-

TURNING POINTS

Apr. 12, 1861	Confederate forces attack Fort Sumter, South Carolina, initiating the Civil War.
Mar. 9, 1862	The Battle of Hampton Roads between the ironclads USS *Monitor* and CSS *Virginia* revolutionizes naval warfare.
May 5, 1862	Confederate General Gabriel J. Rains uses the first land mines to cover his retreat from Williamsburg, Virginia.
May 31-June 1, 1862	At the Battle of Seven Pines (Fair Oaks), Virginia, a machine gun is used for the first time in war.
Feb. 17, 1864	The Confederate submarine CSS *H. L. Hunley* becomes the first underwater vessel to sink an enemy ship, the USS *Housatonic*, near Charleston, South Carolina.

bers and arms had defeated it. Certain Northern sympathizers saw the war primarily as a moral crusade against slavery. Lincoln himself believed that he was using the men, matériel, and weapons at his disposal to save the Union. Even his Emancipation Proclamation, which became effective January 1, 1863, actually freed no slaves but declared that only slaves in rebellious states would be freed. After the war, emancipation reshaped American race relations, but during the war Lincoln's political actions resulted in increased federal power over civilians and the military.

The significance of the Civil War for the military has been a central concern to scholars. Some have emphasized the role of traditional weapons and techniques during most of the war, whereas others have located the center of this war's modernity in its evolution into a total war. Both of these views came under criticism in the 1980's, when some scholars argued that technology, in the form of new rifles and other weapons, actually made little difference on small-scale Civil War battlefields. Others questioned the notion of the Civil War as the first total war, claiming that military leaders rarely destroyed civilian lives and property in any systematic way. During the 1990's there were some comparisons with the War of the Triple Alliance in South America (1864-1870) where the Paraguayans fought even more bitterly than the Confederates in the U.S. Civil War,

leaving their country even more devastated than the southern states. Similarly that conflict was seen as a contest between the martial spirit of one country against the industrial power of its enemies. These interpretations and reinterpretations of a war that has been so extensively studied and so charged with moral, religious, and political meaning are likely to continue.

MILITARY GOALS AND ACHIEVEMENTS

The military goals of both the Confederacy and the Union can be simply stated. The South was fighting for independence, the North for restoration of the Union. The Confederacy was thus forced into a war whose ultimate goal was the defense of its own territory. Although it did occasionally expand the war into the enemy's territory in the west and north, that was a matter of operational strategy rather than national policy. The North's goals were different from those of the South and far more difficult to accomplish. In order to restore the Union, Lincoln had to destroy the Confederacy. To force a new country of several million people to cease to exist is a much more daunting task than to protect such a country from external attacks. At the start of the war, slavery's abolition was not one of the North's military goals. Both Lincoln and the Congress were explicit in asserting that they wanted to restore the Union without interfering with slavery.

Military aims guided military achievements. To preserve its independence, the Confederacy built an army but did not want to use it: It wanted only to be left alone. In contrast the North had to be aggressive. Unless Lincoln could compel the rebellious states to return to the Union, he would lose the war. The Union was initially successful in achieving some of its goals. With the aid of military force it was able to keep the border states of Maryland, Missouri, and Kentucky in the Union, but because of the small number of Union sympathizers in the eleven seceded states, Northern armies eventually had to invade the Confederacy's territory to destroy its armies and government.

Despite the North's manpower and material advantages, the initial military achievements in the Civil War were primarily Southern. The Confederates won several early battles, helped by their excellent generals and the introduction of new weapons. After the Battle of Antietam in September of 1862, Union leaders shifted to a defensive strategy in the East, accepting a temporary stalemate in Virginia, but became more aggressive in the West. By 1863 the Union had achieved control of the Mississippi River, effectively dividing the Confederacy. Confederate general Robert E. Lee (1807-1870) then embarked on an invasion of the North by crossing into Pennsylvania. After his defeat at Gettysburg (July 1-3, 1863), however, the rebel army had to return to Virginia. Whether there might have been a peace agreement had Lee won the battle, is now hotly debated. The Union achieved a second major military goal in 1863 with its occupation of East Tennessee. In early 1864 Ulysses S. Grant (1822-1885) was promoted to general-in-chief of the Union forces, and he embarked on a war of attrition to subdue Lee's army. General William Tecumseh Sherman (1820-1891), Grant's replacement in the West, was able to capture Atlanta in the summer of 1864 and then march through Georgia to the sea, effectively splitting the Confederacy into still smaller pieces. By April 9, 1865, the war was over.

The benefit of spies to both sides has now become a new field of research in itself, partly sparked by the major role ascribed to Henry Thomas Harrison (1832-1923) at Gettysburg in the 1993 film on the battle. Much recent scholarship has also been devoted to the nature of the possibility of foreign involvement in the war. Certainly the war in Mexico between Emperor Maximilian and the supporters of Bentio Juárez meant that the French were, for a while at any rate, distracted from the American Civil War. The British, however, had divided loyalties and certainly viewed the naval aspect of the war with contentment. Although initially an attempt by the Confederacy to internationalize the war, the net result of this aspect of the war was that Confederate raiders destroyed much of the U.S. merchant navy, leaving Britain supreme in trade until 1914. That the British later had to pay compensation for their help (unwitting or otherwise) to the South shows at least a level of complicity.

WEAPONS, UNIFORMS, AND ARMOR

Despite its reputation as the first modern war, the Civil War was actually fought with both old and new weapons. During the war's early years many soldiers were issued old flintlock or smoothbore muskets. In 1860 American arsenals held more than 500,000 small arms, and when the war started, 135,000 of these were confiscated by the South. Only 10,000 of these guns, however, were modern rifles. The two great government armories were at Harpers Ferry, Virginia, and Springfield, Massachusetts. The North

The battlefield at Gettysburg yields up carnage, 1863.

GETTYSBURG, 1863

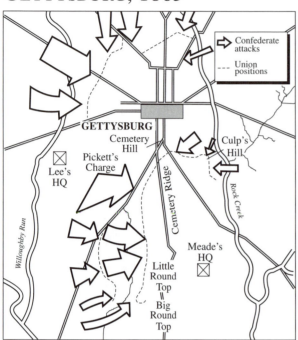

and South exchanged control of Harpers Ferry numerous times during the conflict, and so its production of weapons was hampered, whereas the Springfield armory was able to produce about two million rifles during the four years of the war. These Springfield rifles, single-shot muzzle-loaders, became the most widely used weapon of the U.S. Army.

The Confederacy found weapons to be in short supply, particularly early in the war. In 1861 the weapons collected from citizens and confiscated from federal armories were insufficient to arm the increasing numbers of recruits. The South's output of small arms measured in the hundreds rather than the thousands, hence the need for European purchases. However, lack of funds, competition from the North, and difficulty of shipping through the Northern blockade handicapped the South's attempts to acquire arms for its troops. Only 50,000 arms had reached the South from Europe by August of 1862. The situation improved later in the war, and by the war's end the South's Ordnance Bureau had imported some 330,000 arms, mostly Enfield rifles, through the blockade.

The North was in a much better position than the South to arm its troops. The federal government was able to acquire arms from several private armories, such as the Colt Arms Works at Hartford, Connecticut, in addition to the arsenal at Springfield. The North also possessed supplies of saltpeter for gunpowder, lead for cartridges, and copper for percussion caps. Furthermore, three cannon factories were located in the North: at South Boston, Massachusetts; West Point, New York; and Pittsburgh, Pennsylvania.

The war created a demand for improved and efficient weapons, which were supplied by American inventors. The basic infantry weapon of both North and South was the rifled musket, and although it resembled the muskets of earlier wars, it actually incorporated several modifications that transformed its performance. Smoothbore muskets had a killing range of about 50 yards, whereas rifled muskets could kill at 500 yards. Most of these rifles were muzzle-loaders, but a French officer, Claude-Étienne Minié Claude-Étienne Minié (1804-1879), had devised a bullet with a hollowed base that allowed it to expand when fired, forming a tight fit as it left the barrel. This Minié ball, so named despite its cylindrical shape, vastly increased the range and accuracy of the new rifled muskets. The Minié ball and rifled musket were responsible for over 80 percent of battlefield casualties during the American Civil War.

The South produced about 600,000 rifles during the war; the North imported about 400,000 and manufactured another 1,700,000. Although a single-shot, breech-loading rifle had been developed at the Harpers Ferry armory just before the war, large numbers of these breech-loading weapons became available only late in the war. Repeating rifles, used mainly by the cavalry, were also developed. Percussion caps, which were reliable in all kinds of weather, improved the rate of fire and added to the range and accuracy of the rifles. These improved weapons had the effect of extending the killing zone in front of a line of soldiers.

Just as small arms were at a transitional stage at the beginning of the war, so, too, was artillery. Cannons were both smoothbore and rifled, with rifled cannon barrels becoming more widely adopted. During the four years of the conflict, nearly one-half of the Union cannons, but only one-third of Confederate cannons, were rifled. Rifled barrels gave projectiles greater distance, velocity, and accuracy. Cannons were muzzle-loaded with various projectiles, including solid shot and explosive shells such as canisters. These canisters, which killed more men than all other artillery rounds combined, were metallic cylinders packed with musket balls, nails, or metal scraps that, when explosively propelled from cannons, scattered their lethal pellets over a wide area.

At the start of the war, the U.S. Army had about 4,200 cannons, most of which were heavy pieces in coastal fortifications; only 167 were field artillery. The Union army used 7,892 cannons in the war, compared with more than four million small firearms. These data imply that the Civil War was basically an infantry war, in which artillery played a supporting role. Numbers can be deceiving, however; artillery,

MAJOR SITES IN THE CIVIL WAR, 1861-1865

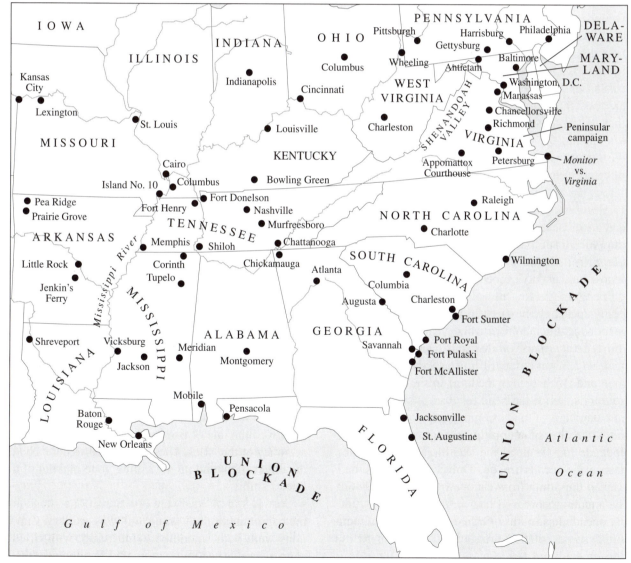

when properly used, was often highly effective. Union artillery was superior to its Confederate counterpart in terms of numbers, quality, maintenance, and skilled use.

If hit in the head or chest by bullets or shrapnel, infantry soldiers often died. The Minié ball shattered bones, shredded tendons, and mangled major organs beyond repair. Arm and leg wounds frequently required amputation. Soldiers wounded but not killed on the battlefield frequently succumbed to infections in camp hospitals. On the Northern side, the total medical casualties recorded from May 1, 1861, to June 30, 1866, were 6,454,834. Of this number, at least 195,627 died. If the 425,274 cases due to battle wounds and injuries (and the subsequent 38,115 deaths) are subtracted from the total medical casualties, the remainder, constituting the diseases, numbered 6,029,560 cases, and 157,512 deaths. Southern casualties exhibited a similar pattern, but Confederate medical data are so incomplete and disordered that it is impossible to be specific. With more research into the developments of military medicine during the war, the large numbers of casualties in battles and elsewhere has been better able to be analyzed.

Because of its weaknesses in small arms, artillery, and medical care, the South had greater incentives than the North to develop new weapons. For example, early in the war a Confederate general introduced land mines, and a Confederate captain invented a machine gun. The first use of land mines in war took place during a delaying action that the Confederate army fought near Williamsburg, Virginia, on May 5, 1862. To cover his withdrawal to Richmond, General Gabriel J. Rains ordered 10-inch shells to be buried in the road, with strings attached to the fuses. Union cavalry set off these buried shells, causing casualties and panic.

A breech-loading machine gun, invented by Confederate captain R. S. Williams, was first used at the Battle of Seven Pines, or Fair Oaks (May 31-June 1, 1862). This unwieldy weapon, weighing 275 pounds, with an ammunition box of 600 pounds, was pulled by one horse and was operated by three men. Operators turned a crank that fed bullets from a hopper into the breech, and the gun fired these at the rate of twenty to forty per minute, with a range of 2,000 yards. When, in October of 1863, the Confederates brought six of these machine guns into action at the Battle of Blue Springs, Tennessee, the torrent of bullets caused mass confusion in the opposing Union army. However, the Williams machine guns were prone to malfunction and saw little action in the remainder of the war. The same was true of a similar machine gun invented in 1862 by Dr. Richard Gatling (1818-1903) of Indiana. The multibarreled Gatling gun could fire 250 shots a minute, but its unreliability meant that it was used only minimally by the North, and there have even been suggestions that as it was being produced at Cincinnati, Ohio (the original drawings being lost in a fire), Gatling might have had mixed sympathies in the war, and the finished products could easily have been captured by the Confederate forces.

A new weapon that did have significant use in the Civil War was the ironclad. The ironclad's advent came at a time of rapid naval transition—from sail to steam, side-wheel to screw propeller, and thick wood sides to iron armor. The first Confederate ironclad, the CSS *Virginia*, quickly proved its effectiveness. This experimental craft was built from the scuttled USS *Merrimack*, which was raised, armored with two layers of thick iron plates, armed with six 9-inch guns, and fitted with a heavy cast-iron prow for ramming. The renamed *Virginia* was designed to break the Union blockade at Hampton Roads, Virginia, and on March 8, 1862, it sent four large Union warships to the bottom of the channel without sustaining any damage.

Union spies had alerted Northern officials to the construction of the CSS *Virginia*, and Secretary of the Navy Gideon Welles (1802-1878) engaged Captain John Ericsson (1803-1889), a brilliant engineer, to construct an ironclad in response to this Southern threat. The USS *Monitor*, which was less than one-third the size of the *Virginia*, had a distinctive revolving turret containing two 11-inch guns. (Some of its details were also published in the *Scientific American*.) On March 9, 1862, it confronted the *Virginia* in one of the most famous naval battles in history. For three hours, each ship fired at the other, neither able to inflict any serious damage on the other. The *Vir-*

ginia had shown that wooden ships were helpless when attacked by an ironclad, and now the *Monitor* had shown that an ironclad could neutralize another ironclad. Ironclads clearly represented the future of naval warfare, consequently dooming wooden navies. Within a week of the battle, Welles ordered six new ironclads, called "monitors" after their prototype. Many others followed, to be used on western rivers and to support the blockade of Southern ports.

Less successful than the ironclads was the submarine. Because Southern ports were desperate to break the blockade, private citizens contributed to financing the CSS *H. L. Hunley*, a nine-man underwater vessel designed to approach blockaders undetected and to sink them with explosives. On February 17, 1864, the *Hunley* was able to attach an explosive charge to the USS *Housatonic* by means of a long wooden spar. The explosion sent this 1,800-ton, 23-gun corvette to the bottom of the sea just outside the entrance to Charleston Harbor. However, the *Hunley* also sank, drowning its crew. Naval mines, which were used by both North and South, proved to be more effective than submarines in sinking enemy ships.

Uniforms, as well as weapons, evolved over the course of the Civil War. In the early months of the conflict, individual states provided uniforms, which led to a motley of styles and colors. For example, some Union soldiers wore uniforms patterned after those of the Zouaves, French colonial soldiers in Algeria: baggy red breeches and brief blue coats with yellow sashes. Some Union regiments were initially attired in gray, and some Confederate soldiers wore blue, leading to tragic confusion on early battlefields. The Confederate government soon adopted cadet gray as the official color for its uniforms, but it was never able to clothe its soldiers consistently. Confederate officers were expected to provide their own uniforms, and these often did not conform to the standards set by the War Department in 1861. Coats were of many different cuts and materials, but after the first year of the war, they were generally a shade of gray. Not until 1862 were Union soldiers consistently

Courtesy of the U.S. Navy Art Collection, Washington, D.C.

A new weapon during the Civil War was the ironclad gunboat, such as the CSS Virginia. *The ironclad arrived at a time of a rapid naval transition from sail to steam and from thick wood sides to iron armor.*

uniformed in blue. As with weapons, the North had an advantage over the South, because their uniforms were made by the newly invented sewing machine, which had helped create a highly developed Northern clothing industry. Northern textile mills were converted to war production, and the factories of Lowell and Lawrence, Massachusetts, were soon turning out thousands of pairs of blue trousers and dark blue fatigue jackets.

Underneath their uniforms many Union volunteers wore body armor to protect themselves against enemy bullets. At least three New England firms manufactured and aggressively marketed the "soldier's bulletproof vest." This vest, containing large pockets into which steel plates were inserted, weighed 3.5 pounds. In some regiments more than half the soldiers used these steel-plated vests, but, as the war progressed, enthusiasm for this uncomfortable body armor waned, especially when enemy sharpshooters chose to aim at soldiers' heads instead of their chests. These bulletproof vests were far less common among Confederate soldiers, because steel was in very short supply in the South.

MILITARY ORGANIZATION

Because many officers of both the Union and Confederate armies had been trained at West Point, both armies were similar in military organization. The regiment was the basic unit. It was led by a colonel, with a lieutenant colonel as second and a major as third in command. A regiment, which initially had about 1,000 men, was divided into 10 companies, each officered by a captain and 2 lieutenants. There were three kinds of regiments: infantry, artillery, and cavalry. Infantry regiments were the nucleus of both the Union and Confederate armies. Artillery regiments were of two basic kinds: heavy artillery positioned in fortifications and light or field artillery attached to mobile armies. Cavalry regiments were organized in the same way as infantry, but the South expected its cavalrymen to provide their own horses, whereas the Union supplied its troops with horses. During the Civil War the Union raised 2,046 regiments: 1,696 infantry, 272 cavalry, and 78 artillery.

The number of regiments in the Confederacy is unknown because of the loss of relevant records, but estimates range from 750 to 1,000.

Military regiments were organized into increasingly larger units: brigades, divisions, corps, and armies, each commanded by a brigadier or major general. Union armies were normally named after rivers in the area of their command (for example, the Army of the Potomac), whereas Confederate armies often took their names from a state or part of a state (for example, the Army of Northern Virginia). Although regimental organization and numbers varied from army to army, time to time, and place to place, overall structures tended to remain constant. As the war continued, however, both the North and the South failed to maintain the strengths of existing regiments in the face of attrition due to casualties, deaths, and desertions. States preferred to set up new regiments rather than re-man old ones. Thus, as the war proceeded, the number of regiments became a very unreliable guide to the actual strength of armies.

DOCTRINE, STRATEGY, AND TACTICS

Throughout history, soldiers have performed according to their and their leaders' understanding of the nature of war itself. This understanding, which is an important component of military doctrine, is concerned with the beliefs that drive soldiers to fight and the methods by which they actually fight. These doctrines are also related to the means by which leaders establish military standards and how, in battle, they determine the balance between offense and defense, individual and group action, and traditional and modern technologies. Theoretically, a nation's founding principles help to shape its military doctrines, which, in turn, influence its military strategies and tactics. Practically, military doctrines determine how wars are fought.

At the start of the Civil War, the military doctrines of both North and South were guided by French military ideas about the organization and use of large numbers of soldiers. For Napoleon, a military campaign was an orderly sequence of informed decisions leading to a clear objective. American soldiers of

C. A. Nichols & Company

Union troops retreat at the First Battle of Bull Run (First Manassas) in 1861.

both Northern and Southern armies entered the Civil War prepared to fight a version of war more than fifty years old. However, technological progress modified military doctrines, even though conservative leaders often fought a new war with the techniques from an old one. Some Civil War officers were aware of the disjunction between old doctrines and new realities. For example, they realized the folly of lines of troops advancing into areas enfiladed by highly accurate small-arms and artillery fire. Some officers believed that the only way to conserve their troops during such an assault was to disperse them, even though this meant surrendering strict control of troop movements. This tactic generated controversy, since tight formations caused heavy casualties, but dispersed formations led to dangerously purposeless actions as

seen with the British and French forces in the Crimean War in the previous decade.

Like military doctrine, strategy has evolved in meaning over time. Initially strategy meant the military leader's art of war, but by the American Civil War its sense had become generalized to mean the science of war, or the use of reason to achieve national goals by military means. For example, the overall grand strategy of the Union was to reconquer and reoccupy all original U.S. territory and to restore federal authority throughout. The grand strategy of the Confederacy was to defend its political independence and territorial integrity.

The Northern strategy of preserving the Union at first seemed to require a military strategy of limited war: first suppress the insurrection in the eleven seceded states, then arrest Confederate leaders, and finally put Unionists in control. On May 3, 1861, General-in-Chief Winfield Scott (1786-1866) presented an offensive plan to bring the rebels to accept these terms with as little bloodshed as possible. He proposed economically strangling the Confederacy by blockading its ocean and river ports and gaining military control of the border states. Several newspapers contemptuously called this the Anaconda Plan, because it would take an interminably long time for the strangulation to become effective. Meanwhile, public opinion was clamoring for an immediate invasion to crush the rebellion.

By 1862 Union military strategy had evolved, under pressure from public opinion and President Lincoln, to a policy of conquest of Confederate territory. This new plan succeeded in Tennessee and the lower Mississippi Valley but was stalemated by Lee's victories in the East. Consequently, Northern military strategy changed yet again, in 1863, to a conviction that the Confederate armies would have to be destroyed. However, despite a significant Northern victory at Gettysburg, Lee's army survived and the Confederacy continued to resist. Thus, by 1864, Union strategists realized that it was inadequate to conquer territory and cripple armies. They had to destroy the capacity of the Southern people to wage war. Sherman's march of conquest and destruction through Georgia and South Carolina in 1864 contributed significantly to weakening the will of Southerners to continue to fight. To many, the Civil War had become, by 1865, a total war, and this fact finally led to the Confederacy's capitulation.

Although the Confederacy's national strategy of preserving its independence remained constant throughout the four years of the war, the military strat-

C. A. Nichols & Company

Richmond falls to Union troops in April, 1865; the war is effectively over.

egies devised to achieve this goal continually shifted. Initially Confederate leaders sparsely spread their troops around the circumference of their new country to repel potential invaders, but this tactic proved to be an unwise use of the South's limited manpower. Another unwise military strategy was the political decision to move the Confederacy's capital from Montgomery, Alabama, to Richmond, Virginia, about 100 miles from Washington, D.C. This move turned northern Virginia into one of the war's principal battlegrounds. The concentration of Confederate forces in the East weakened the West, allowing Union forces to gain control of the Mississippi River and divide the Confederacy.

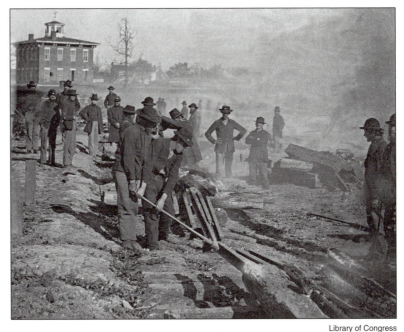

Library of Congress

Sherman's troops pulling up railroad tracks in Atlanta, Georgia.

However, the Confederacy proved more adept than the Union expected at countering the Anaconda Plan; Southern blockade runners were successful in bringing much-needed military supplies from Europe. Lee was also successful in convincing Confederate leaders to modify the "dispersed defensive" strategy into an "offensive-defensive" strategy. This meant that, although the national strategy remained the protection of the Confederacy, this goal could sometimes best be achieved by attacking the enemy in Confederate territory or by attacking the enemy's territory itself. Lee thus sought to break the Union's will to reunite the country by defeating its armies. However, in the end Lee's army could not withstand the unremitting pressure of the large, well-armed, and amply supplied Union armies.

The strategies of North and South were implemented by various tactics. In military terminology, tactics is the management of soldiers on a battlefield. The tactical systems of the Civil War were modifications of deployments in eighteenth century battles. Under the traditional system, soldiers in several long lines advanced toward enemy positions while exchanging controlled volleys. This continued until either the offensive or defensive lines broke down. Although military leaders on both sides continued to use this old tactic, the long range and high accuracy of such new weapons as rifled muskets and cannons, and, later, rapid-fire breechloaders, made its use extremely costly on the attackers. As the war evolved, some commanders developed new tactics that allowed infantry formations to be flexible, even to the point of granting individual soldiers free-handed initiative to achieve their mission.

Improved weapons also brought about the end of the classical cavalry charge, because Minié bullets and raking artillery fire easily downed horses and cavalrymen long before they could reach enemy positions. In the latter part of the war, military leaders used cavalry strictly for reconnaissance and the capture of critical road junctions. Because of the failures of traditional assault tactics, both Union and Confederate leaders used, during the campaigns of 1864 and 1865, a new technique that came to be called trench warfare, in which defensive lines were protected by forts with artillery, pits with riflemen, and elaborate breastworks of logs and dirt piles.

The Civil War was also the first American conflict in which the tactic of the rapid movement of men and matériel by railroad played a major role. However, during the initial phases of the war, railroads were used primarily to transport supplies, not troops, although reinforcements did arrive at the First Battle of Bull Run by railroad during the course of the fighting, changing the outcome. By the summer of 1862, when thousands of Union troops were transported to Washington, D.C., by rail to prevent Lee's army from capturing the capital, the advantages of train over foot and horse transport became obvious. The South, too, quickly realized the military significance of railroads, and Southern raiders destroyed Northern tracks, bridges, and locomotives. These tactics led to the creation of a special corps in the Union army to repair torn-up tracks and destroyed bridges. This corps used standardized, interchangeable parts and made a science of track and bridge reconstruction. This construction corps was also a destruction corps, because its men developed new ways of destroying enemy rails and bridges. For example, they both bent and twisted heated rails to render them irreparable and useless. The armored railroad car was yet another contribution to military transport technology that made its first appearance during the Civil War. These bulletproof cars were used to patrol important railroads, protecting key supply and troop-transport lines for Union armies.

Finally, naval tactics, like land tactics, experienced radical changes during the Civil War. Before the war naval tactics had involved the effective detection of enemy ships and the countermeasures to neutralize or destroy them. Guns were a fleet's decisive weapons, and a tightly spaced line of ships was its most advantageous formation. The tactical aim was to bring the maximum amount of firepower to bear on the enemy. The Battle of Hampton Roads changed all this. In terms of strategy, the mission of the *Monitor* was to protect the Union warships that had not yet been destroyed by the *Virginia*. Because the *Monitor* did this, the battle was a strategic victory for the North. From a tactical viewpoint, both the *Monitor* and the *Virginia* left the battle in almost the same condition as when they entered it, with the *Monitor* a bit more damaged than the *Virginia*. As for how the battle affected the strategic situation in Virginia, the battle was also a draw, because the Union still controlled Hampton Roads while the Confederates held the rivers.

Like this battle between the *Monitor* and *Virginia*, the military doctrines, strategies, and tactics of the Civil War helped to change the nature of warfare throughout the world. The First Battle of Bull Run (1861) would have been familiar in its weapons and tactics to a veteran of the Napoleonic Wars (1793-1815), whereas the trench warfare around Petersburg (1864-1865) and Richmond (1865) was a harbinger of World War I. Furthermore, Sherman's march through Georgia was an early intimation of the Nazi Blitzkrieg of World War II. The North's emphasis on outproducing rather than outfighting the South also had a profound influence on future strategic and tactical military thinking. Thus, in its weapons, strategies, and tactics, the Civil War may have begun with an eye to the past, but it ended as a portent of the future.

CONTEMPORARY SOURCES

The American Civil War has generated an immense and ongoing literature, with new books and articles are constantly appearing. An extensive introduction to the first hundred years of these writings is provided by the two-volume *Civil War Books: A Critical Bibliography* (1967-1969), edited by Allan Nevins, James I. Robertson, and Bell I. Wiley. A good way to keep up with new books and articles is through the bibliographies published annually by such periodicals as *Civil War History*.

Several multivolume histories of the Civil War provide excellent coverage of the conflict as well as a critical selection of primary and secondary sources. Alan Nevins's eight-volume *The Ordeal of the Union* (1947-1971) is both scholarly and significant, with the final four volumes emphasizing the war itself, largely from a Northern social, political, and military perspective. A history that emphasizes the Southern point of view is Shelby Foote's three-volume *The Civil*

War: A Narrative (1958-1974). An older account by an esteemed historian is Bruce Catton's three-volume *The Centennial History of the Civil War* (1961-1965). A short version of Catton's story, updated by the Pulitzer Prize-winning author James M. McPherson, is *The American Heritage New History of the Civil War* (New York: Viking, 1996), which includes an extensive set of maps, photographs, paintings, sketches, and other illustrative material. James M. McPherson's *Battle Cry of Freedom: The Civil War Era* (1988) is widely regarded as the best single-volume history of the war.

Official records of the Civil War were collected and published at the turn of the century by the U.S. Army and the U.S. Navy, respectively, as *The War of the Rebellion: Official Records of the Union and Confederate Armies* (1882-1900) and *The War of the Rebellion: Official Records of the Union and Confederate Navies* (1894-1922). These vast works of correspondence and official reports are excellent sources for scholars, but two primary sources that are accessible to general readers are *Personal Memoirs of U. S. Grant* (1885) and *Memoirs of W. T. Sherman* (1891). These memoirs emphasize the Union point of view. Jefferson Davis's two-volume *The Rise and Fall of the Confederate Government* (1881) provides a Confederate point of view. For Lee's view of the war the best source is the classic biography by Douglas Southall Freeman, *Robert E. Lee* (1935-1942), but this work should be supplemented by such later assessments as Alan T. Nolan's *Lee Considered: General Robert E. Lee and Civil War History* (1991).

BOOKS AND ARTICLES

Beringer, Richard E., et al. *Why the South Lost the Civil War*. Athens: University of Georgia Press, 1986.

Bruce, Robert V. *Lincoln and the Tools of War*. Indianapolis: Indiana University Press, 1956.

Connelly, Thomas L., and Archer Jones. *The Politics of Command: Factions and Ideas in Confederate Strategy*. Baton Rouge: Louisiana State University Press, 1983.

Engle, Stephen. *The American Civil War: The War in the West: 1861-July 1863*. New York: Osprey, 2001.

Gallagher, Gary W. *The American Civil War: The War in the East, 1861-May 1863*. New York: Osprey, 2001.

Gallagher, Gary W., Robert Krick, and Stephen Engle. *The American Civil War: This Mighty Scourge of War*. New York: Osprey, 2003.

Glatthaar, Joseph T. *The American Civil War (4): The War in the West, 1863-1865*. New York: Osprey, 2001.

Hattaway, Herman, and Archer Jones. *How the North Won: A Military History of the Civil War*. Urbana: University of Illinois Press, 1983.

Jones, Archer. *Civil War Command and Strategy: The Process of Victory and Defeat*. New York: Free Press, 1992.

Konstam, Angus. *Seven Days Battles: Lee's Defense of Richmond*. New York: Osprey, 2004.

Krick, Robert. *The American Civil War: The War in the East, 1863-1865*. New York: Osprey, 2001.

McWhiney, Grady, and Perry D. Jamieson. *Attack and Die: Civil War Military Tactics and the Southern Heritage*. Tuscaloosa: University of Alabama Press, 1982.

Smith, David. *Sherman's March to the Sea, 1864: Atlanta to Savannah*. New York: Osprey, 2007.

FILMS AND OTHER MEDIA

The Civil War. Documentary series. Public Broadcasting Service, 1990.

Cold Mountain. Feature film. Miramax, 2003.

Gettysburg. Feature film. Mayfair Turner, 1993.

Glory. Feature film. Columbia Pictures, 1989.

Gods and Generals. Feature film. Warner Bros., 2003.

Gone with the Wind. Feature film. The Selznick Studio, 1939.

Guns of the Civil War. Documentary. Monterey Home Video, 1993.

North and South. TV miniseries. ABC, 1985-1994.

The Outlaw Josey Wales. Feature film. Malpaso, 1976.

The Red Badge of Courage. Feature film. MGM, 1951.

Shenandoah. Feature film. Universal, 1965.

Smithsonian's Great Battles of the Civil War. Documentary series. Easton Press Video, 1992/ 1993.

Robert J. Paradowski

WARFARE IN THE AGE OF EXPANSION

COLONIAL WARFARE

Dates: 1420-1857

POLITICAL CONSIDERATIONS

Significant political, economic, and cultural changes in Europe during the fifteenth and sixteenth centuries allowed for extensive European colonial expansion to Asia, Africa, and the Americas. The medieval order was in a state of collapse; the concept of Christendom, a Europe united by the force of Christianity, was giving way to the rise of humanism and secularism. As Christian Europe split into ideological factions, nation-states emerged. France, England, Spain, and, for a brief period, Portugal all developed extra-European colonies and extended their historic rivalries in armed conflicts overseas.

The development of nation-states paralleled the rise of capitalism. Characterized by the ownership of private property, the emphasis on competition and profit, and the institution of bank credit, capitalism contributed to the hostilities among nations when expressed in the variation of mercantilism. Mercantilism, which was not fully articulated until the late seventeenth century, advanced a static view of wealth: If one nation increases its reserves of gold and silver, the reserves of other nations must decrease. Because there was, essentially, a fixed amount of gold and silver in the world, there was a race to obtain as much as possible; this economic philosophy resulted in a perpetual state of economic warfare among the European states.

Another factor that contributed to the beginning of colonial warfare was the technological revolution that made possible the commercial revolution. Europeans had ships and navigational instrumentation that made possible the acquisition of colonial outposts; they also possessed more sophisticated weaponry than did the native populations that they encountered in their overseas expansions. It was not surprising that the earliest colonial wars were struggles between the English, French, Spanish, and Portuguese, given the proximity of these nations to the Atlantic Ocean. France and England previously had been involved in the Hundred Years' War (1337-1453), fought over opposing dynastic claims to territory in northwestern France. These two nations continued their national rivalry in the colonies throughout the colonial and imperial periods.

When Britain acquired the Cape Colony, cartoonist Linley Sambourne drew colonial administrator and financier Cecil Rhodes straddling the continent in a symbolic depiction of British power in Africa.

World Exploration in the Sixteenth Century

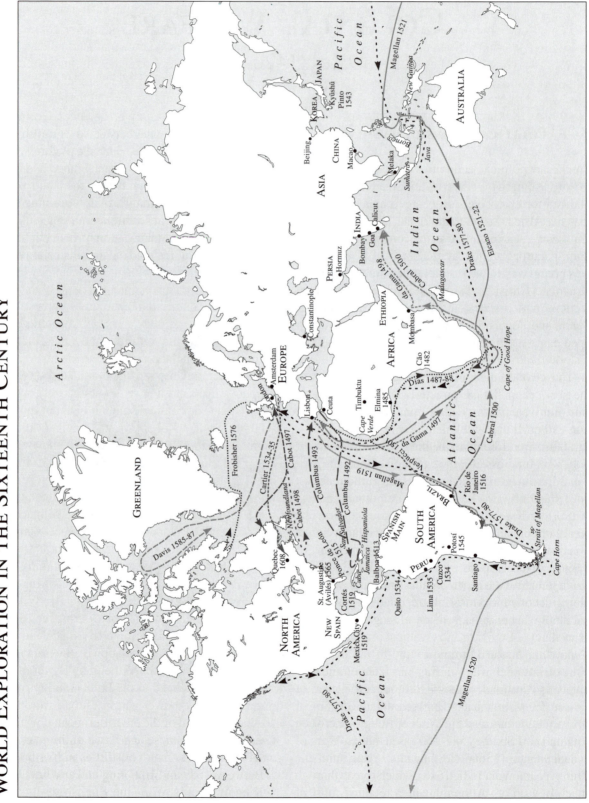

Under the leadership of Prince Henry the Navigator (1394-1460), Portugal during the 1420's was the first nation to establish colonial outposts in the Madeira and Azores islands. Henry recognized the capabilities of new navigational devices and sailing ships that were then being constructed. The early Portuguese penetration of coastal African and Indian Ocean locales was cut short by the emergence of Spain in 1492, when the kingdoms of Aragon and Castile combined to unite most of the Iberian Peninsula. In 1580, two years after an unsuccessful colonial war in Morocco, where the young Portuguese king was killed (the country briefly being ruled by his childless great-uncle), Portugal was incorporated into Spain for the next sixty years.

Throughout the sixteenth century, colonies in the Americas, Africa, and Asia were viewed as fiscal resources from which great wealth could be obtained. The native populations were viewed as pagans who should be Christianized; nonetheless, there was little if any sympathy for the native populations. The Europeans exploited the colonies and brought them into the network of the national policies and controversies. European wars, rivalries, and perceptions were also extended to the colonies.

Spain, the dominant colonial power in the sixteenth century, developed a global network of colonies in the Americas (Central and South America), Asia (the Philippine Islands), and numerous colonies in North Africa and along the route to India. The wealthiest power in Europe, Spain extended its interests into the areas now known as Belgium and eastern France. At the same time, the nation was identified as the defender of the Roman Catholic Church, its ruler taking the title His Most Catholic Majesty. In this capacity, Spain became an enemy of Anglican England as well as the Lutheran and Calvinist principalities in Central and Eastern Europe.

A variety of conflicts during the sixteenth and seventeenth centuries witnessed the rising power of France, the resurgence of England, and the decline of Spain. These included the Wars of Religion between England and Spain (1587-1601), the Dutch Wars of Independence (1566-1648) against Spain, and the Thirty Years' War (1618-1648), which spread through much of Europe. Although Spain retained most of its overseas empire and Portugal reassumed control of its empire after 1640, the major colonial forces through the remainder of the century were France, England, and the Netherlands. In the sixteenth century the French established colonial claims and settlements in Canada, the West Indies, and Africa. The English were active in North America, establishing significant colonies there in the seventeenth century. The Netherlands established centers of trade on territories in the West Indies, the Indian Ocean, and the Pacific. From the outset, the geopolitical conditions, combined with the tradition of continuing national conflicts, created an environment that lent itself to the probability of colonial wars.

In the seventeenth and eighteenth centuries, France emerged as the preeminent European power. Historians have frequently interpreted seventeenth and eighteenth century diplomacy as a contest between the absolutist regimes of France, Austria, Prussia, and Russia and the constitutional, representative governments of England and the Netherlands. One should be very careful in extending this general explanation. In most instances it provides an accurate context for European wars at home and abroad, but the particulars of many crises appear to have had little if anything to do with the concept of government.

Under the influence of King Louis XIV (1638-1715), France launched four major European wars: the War of Devolution (1667-1668), the Dutch War (1672-1678), the War of the Grand Alliance (1688-1697), and the War of the Spanish Succession (1701-1714), all of which were reflected in the colonies. England and the Netherlands, an important colonial power with trade routes and significant financial resources, combined under William III; William led the Netherlands against France during the 1670's and 1680's and became William III of England in 1689. In the context of European power, the principal issue at this time was the overwhelming power of France; the question related to the French ability to destroy the balance of power within Europe—the independence of action of the other European powers was at risk. In the colonies the last two of the wars of Louis XIV resulted in major hostilities in North America. Between 1689 and 1697 England and France fought King William's War—the English designation for the struggle. The French and English were assisted by their respective Native American allies and fought to a stalemate; when the war ended, all territories were returned (*status quo ante bellum*). While the Europeans fought the War of the Spanish Succession, which resulted in containing French power and ambitions, the English successfully fought the French and their Spanish allies in Florida, Acadia, and the Caribbean.

The Anglo-French rivalry was the primary cause for colonial wars in the eighteenth century. In 1739 the War of Jenkins's Ear broke out between Spain and England; it included an unsuccessful English attempt to take Cuba and Florida from the Spanish. This struggle was submerged by a larger European war, the War of the Austrian Succession (1740-1748), that once again pitted the French and English against each other; in addition to the Anglo-French contest, this war was significant because of the impact it had on the development of Central European political history. Austria, allied with France, and Prussia, partnered with England, fought to gain a dominant position in Central Europe. While that issue was not resolved in the eighteenth century, the Prussian and English victories destroyed the reality of Habsburg hegemony throughout Central Europe. After a brief interlude of peace the colonial war between France and England was renewed in both America (the French and Indian War, 1754-1763) and India. In 1756 the Seven Years' War (1756-1763) began in Europe. Both European and colonial wars were concluded by the 1763 Treaty of Paris, through which Britain gained French territory in Canada and India. However the war had been costly for all powers. Britain's relations with its American colonists declined over the issues of increased taxation and also representation in the British Parliament, as well as sharing the cost of defense. In July, 1776, the Americans declared their independence and were later joined by the French and the Dutch in the struggle with England. In the 1783 Treaty of Paris, England recognized the independence of the United States but retained Canada and its colonies in the West Indies.

At the close of the eighteenth century, the ideology of the Enlightenment challenged many basic notions on government, citizenship, and liberty. In 1789 the French Revolution broke out, and it served to be a cataclysmic force in European and world affairs. By 1798 the French Revolution was being led by Napoleon Bonaparte (1769-1821); a serious but practical reformer, Napoleon restored absolutism but tempered it with revolutionary sentiments. The American and French revolutions provided historic examples and motivation for Latin Americans who wanted to be free of Spanish control.

It was the great wealth that could be made in the colonies that attracted many young men to serve in the British East India Company, its French or Dutch counterparts, or elsewhere in the world. Disease in most of these places took its toll, but for those who survived, many could return to their own countries with massive wealth. Examples in Britain were the Pitt family, which went on to produce two prime ministers, and that of Robert Clive.

There was also an ability, through joint-stock companies, for many people who were not prepared to risk going to the colonies to profit by buying shares in companies involved in such trade. The trading in shares in these companies essentially led to the emergence of the European stock exchanges when traders would buy and sell stock based on information they held, or on speculation. In spite of some notable collapses, such as in the tulip market in the Netherlands in the 1630's and the South Sea Company in 1720 (known as the South Sea Bubble), many investors and speculators were still prepared to put their savings into similar ventures.

The desire for profit by company directors led to many instances of gross exploitation of the native peoples. The worst instances surrounded slavery, with many millions of Africans shipped to the Americas to work on plantations where many died through overwork or from disease. The tropical diseases held back development of plantations in Africa until the late nineteenth century, but many were also established in Asia with bonded laborers and convict labor rather than traditional forms of slavery.

During the early decades of the nineteenth century, European interest in colonial acquisitions declined. Nonetheless, European states continued to retain their colonial holdings, and England and France continued their respective interests in Australia, New Zealand, and Africa. In 1857 the British were confronted in India by the Sepoy Rebellion, precipitated by the introduction of a new rifle that required soldiers to bite off a cover lubricated with pig grease. Muslim soldiers refused to comply and mutinied against their British officers. In 1859 Charles Darwin's *On the Origin of Species by Means of Natural Selection* was published; the concept of social Darwinism quickly followed, and the notions of "survival of the fittest" and the natural conflicts in human and international relations became acceptable. These ideas paved the way for the emergence of a new colonialism, imperialism, which was advanced in the New Imperialism of British Prime Minister Benjamin Disraeli (1804-1881).

MILITARY ACHIEVEMENT

The major military achievements in the age of colonial warfare included the conquest, suppression, or dislocation of the native populations of North and South America; the triumph of Britain in the French and Indian War (1754-1763) in both North America and India; the success of the Americans in their war of independence against Britain; the initial military success and ultimate strategic failure of Napoleon's Egyptian Campaign of 1798 and 1799; and the expansion of Britain and France into Africa during the first half of the nineteenth century.

The Spanish advance in the New World was extensive and based upon the strength of the Spanish military. As well as their own military power, it re-

Hulton Archive/Getty Images

Spanish conquistador Francisco Pizarro captures Inca king Atahualpa in 1532. By 1600 Spain controlled all of the land from New Mexico and Florida in the north to Chile and the Río de la Plata in the south, with the exception of Portugal's Brazil.

lied on tactical alliances with some of the people in the Americas, with Hernán Cortés managing to get much support from Native Americans who were angered by the rule of the Aztecs. This policy of divide and rule had been practiced by the Romans in the building up of their empire and was quickly adopted by the European colonial powers.

By 1600 Spain controlled all of the land from New Mexico and Florida in the north to Chile and the Río de la Plata in the south, with the exception of Portugal's Brazil. The oppressive Spanish Conquest rested on a continued military presence and the suppression of the native populations; it was aggravated by the introduction of slaves from Africa. The destruction of the Mayan civilization was achieved through military forces under Francisco de Montejo in the sixteenth century. Spanish colonization remained the most active near seaports; the development of the interiors required extensive time and effort.

In the mid-eighteenth century Great Britain and France fought several wars. From the perspective of colonial wars, the most significant was the French and Indian War. During this struggle both powers were supported by the colonists and opposing Indian tribes. During the early years of the war, each side encountered victories and defeats; Britain was defeated at Fort Duquesne (1754) but prevailed at Lake George (1755). The turning point occurred in the campaign of 1759, when the British defeated the French at Quebec. Both Quebec and Montreal then came under British control, and by the end of September, 1760, Canada was British territory. This acquisition was ratified in the 1763 Treaty of Paris, which ended the war. In the same treaty Britain received Martinique, Grenada, St. Lucia, St. Vincent, and other French islands in the West Indies.

Without doubt the most significant colonial war of the era was the American Revolution against Britain. British forces prevailed militarily in almost every encounter during the war. However, at Yorktown (1781), a combined American-French force defeated the British army under the First Marquess Cornwallis (1738-1805). With traditional tactics, commander in chief of the Continental army George Washington (1732-1799) succeeded in forcing a British surrender. The British effort was doomed from the outset.

As a colonial power under King George III (1738-1820), the British were unwilling to reach a political settlement with their colonists. That error was compounded when they failed to recognize the resources that would be necessary to suppress a general rebellion with a battle line extending from Massachusetts to Georgia. The arrival of the French at Yorktown was also decisive; the French blocked any possible British retreat by sea and contributed troops and artillery for the Siege of Yorktown. This revolution led directly to the French Revolution and that to the Wars of Independence in Latin America.

In 1798 Napoleon Bonaparte led a military expedition to Egypt to attack the British position in India. Although Napoleon enjoyed a number of victories over Turkish and native forces, such as the Battles of the Pyramids (1798) and Aboukir (1799) and the Sieges of Alexandria (1798) and Jaffa (1799), he was overwhelmed by the brilliant naval strategy of Admiral Horatio Nelson (1758-1805) in the Battle of the Nile (1798). The French fleet was destroyed and Napoleon was forced in the next year to abandon his army and return to France.

WEAPONS, UNIFORMS, AND ARMOR

From the fourteenth to mid-nineteenth centuries, gunpowder weapons gradually replaced older medieval shock weapons. Although the wide range of medieval weapons continued to be employed in combat, they were increasingly replaced by the products of the gunpowder revolution. The development of corned powder resulted in more predictable and powerful detonations and led to advances in ballistics. Artillery advances were achieved with iron and bronze cannons; the matchlock, wheel lock, and flintlock firing mechanisms improved rifle and pistol accuracy, reliability, and safety. In the eighteenth century musket powder was developed for use in cannons, muskets, and pistols.

During the same century the English mathematician Benjamin Robins (1707-1751) invented the ballistic pendulum, a device that measured muzzle velocity. This instrument opened a new phase in the history of ballistics. Further advances in powder and

F. R. Niglutsch

Bengali mobile cannons are shown being pulled by oxen during the Battle of Plassey (1757).

firing were achieved in the early nineteenth century by Alexander Forsyth (1769-1843), a Scottish clergyman and inventor who assisted in the development of percussion ignition, and Joshua Shaw (1776-1860), an American who is credited with inventing the percussion cap in 1815. The British Long Land musket was known in the American colonies as the Brown Bess during the French and Indian War. After its weight was recognized as a problem in the colonies, it was shortened. The Brown Bess was the standard weapon used against Britain during the American Revolution. The 45-inch French Model 1763 and Model 1777 were significantly improved muskets. Rifling technology developed throughout the nineteenth century, and by the end of the American Civil War (1861-1865), rifles had replaced muskets. Advances in artillery paralleled those in rifling, with im-

proved accuracy and firepower. By the time of the Civil War, artillery could deliver explosive shells that devastated lines of march as well as fixed targets.

During the colonial era, Europeans wore their standard uniforms in combat. Brightly colored uniforms were ready targets for the opposing forces. Officers were easily identified. Colonial militias were uniformed as well; only native peoples in the service of a European power were not uniformed. This did, however, led to many native people being killed after battles with the colonial powers claiming that as they were not in uniform they were, in effect, spies. This was particularly true in counterinsurgency campaigns.

From the fifteenth through the late seventeenth century, Europeans continued to use some of the personal armor associated with the medieval period.

Although the use of such armor in colonial wars was less frequent, breastplates and helmets continued to be used. The protection associated with armor was based on personal hand-to-hand battlefield combat. With the increased use of gunpowder weapons, however, the armor of the time was ineffective and hindered the movements of the soldiers. Mobility was emphasized by Sir John Churchill, first duke of Marlborough (1650-1722) and Prince Eugène of Savoy (1663-1736), the leaders of the coalition forces against France during the War of the Spanish Succession (1701-1714). Likewise, armor was more of a detriment than an advantage in the colonial wars of the period. Armor for weapons was considered and adopted by the European armies during the eighteenth and nineteenth centuries. Coastal gun emplacements frequently provided armored protection for the guns and the personnel.

MILITARY ORGANIZATION

The design of the military organizations of the European colonial powers differed from those states that were not involved in colonial struggles. The two most evident differences were their reliance on colonial militias and their reliance on strong naval forces to transport troops and supplies. Britain's success in colonial wars resulted in large part from its superior navy and from the large numbers of colonial militiamen that could be brought into combat.

During the early centuries of the era of colonial war, the medieval notion that the landed aristocracy would provide the officer class continued. It was not until the eighteenth century, with its emphasis on professionalism, that the officer corps was opened to talented men from other classes. Once again, the British were more advanced than others. The French army during the French Revolution (1789-1793) and the ensuing Napoleonic period was accessible but reverted to the aristocracy after Napoleon's defeat (1815).

The colonial militias consisted of gentlemen farmers and merchants and their men. Although Washington had served in the French and Indian War, he was basically a farmer without any formal military training. The militias were armies of citizen soldiers; they fought colonial wars for specific reasons that they understood. In both America and France, these militias were the beginnings of "national" armies, unlike the armies that fought either for their monarch or for payment.

In addition, chartered companies such as the British East India Company, the Dutch East India Company (Vereenigde Oost-Indische Compagnie, or VOC), and the Compagnie Françoise des Indes (French Company of the Indies) were able to raise their own armies, which served as forms of paramilitaries, sometimes alongside national forces, and sometimes on their own. These quasi-military forces were often later integrated into national armies often directly with a regiment in one being transformed into a regiment in the other.

It was often these quasi-military forces which were able to prove the most effective in colonial wars. These often included officers from Europe, and then local recruits, as well as auxiliary units, the latter modeled on their Roman counterparts (the study of the Roman Empire became extremely popular during the eighteenth and nineteenth centuries). These chartered companies were able to draw up treaties with local rulers and were often provided soldiers by them, such as the Sikh units who fought alongside the British East India Company.

DOCTRINE, STRATEGY, AND TACTICS

Colonial conflicts between European rivals were fought using both traditional continental battle tactics of organized ranks facing one another in exchanges of gun and cannon fire and the less predictable guerrilla warfare tactics used by native and colonial populations. Native populations in America, Africa, and South America taught the European powers the importance of speed in combat, forcing them to adapt to local conditions. The uncertainty of geographical considerations was another factor that impacted colonial warfare. The major powers were dependent upon local sources for intelligence about the land, rivers, streams, crossings, resources, routes, emplacements, and concentrations of people. In North

America, it was not until the nineteenth century that this information was generally known and published; in South and Central America, Africa, and Asia, this information was not categorized until the mid-twentieth century. Finally, European military doctrines and strategy failed to appreciate fully the nature of colonial rebellions. Americans, Zulus, Chinese, and other local revolutionaries entered struggles to expel Europeans, not simply to gain a victory or to prevail in one of a series of wars. This raison d'être for colonial revolts provided an ideological motivation that was not recognized fully during the colonial wars.

CONTEMPORARY SOURCES

From the fifteenth to the mid-nineteenth centuries, with the expansion of printing and transportation, military strategists had increasing access to the strategic and tactical thoughts of others. In most instances, the strategy and tactics employed in Europe were extended and adapted in colonial wars. Among the earliest sources were Hernán Cortés's (1485-1547) description of the Siege of Tenochtitlán in 1529 and Francisco de Jerez's (born 1504) analysis of the capture of the last Incan emperor, Atahualpa (c. 1502-1533), in 1533.

More widely disseminated sources include Niccolò Machiavelli's (1469-1527) *Il principe* (1532; *The Prince*, 1640), *Discorsi sopra la prima deca di Tito Livio* (1531; *Discourses on the First Ten Books of Titus Livius*, 1636), *Dell'arte della guerra* (1521; *The Art of War*, 1560), and *Istorie fiorentine* (1525; *The Florentine History*, 1595). Although Machiavelli's works provided many insights into the Renaissance concepts of war, they clearly indicate that Machiavelli did not understand the value of artillery.

Two contemporary sources on naval strategy and tactics were Richard Hakluyt's (c. 1552-1616) description of the destruction of the Spanish Armada in *The Principall Navigations, Voiages, and Discoveries of the English Nation* (1589, 1598-1600) and Armand Jean du Plessis, duc de Richelieu's (1585-1642) thoughts on sea power, published in his *Testament politique* (1645; *Political Testament*, 1961). Military organization and formations were studied in Jean-Charles de Folard's (1669-1752) *Traité de la colonne et de l'ordre profond* (1730; treatise on the column) and *Nouvelles découvertes sur la guerre* (1724; new developments in warfare). Two other significant eighteenth century sources were Maurice, comte de Saxe's (1696-1750) *Les Rêveries: Ou, Mémoires sur l'art de guerre* (1756-1757; *Reveries: Or, Memoirs Concerning the Art of War*, 1776) and King Frederick the Great (1712-1786) of Prussia's *Instructions militaires du roi de Prusse pour ses généraux* (1765; *Military Instructions for His Generals*, 1944). The era of warfare associated with the French Revolution and Napoleonic Wars produced many significant works by its participants. Horatio Nelson's "The Trafalgar Memorandum" (1805) is a classic and clear statement of naval strategy, and Napoleon Bonaparte's views on strategy and tactics were published in his *Maxims de guerre de Napoléon* (1827; *Military Maxims of Napoleon*, 1831), which were included in several books published after his death in 1821. Finally, the experience of Prussian Carl von Clausewitz (1780-1831) in the wars against Napoleonic France led him to work to reform the Prussian army. His classic study, *Vom Kriege* (1832-1834; *On War*, 1873), was published after his death in 1831 and influenced military planners for generations.

As well as books on strategy and military science, there were countless books published that were written by participants in various conflicts. Many of these had a ready audience in their home countries, and some were translated and sold elsewhere. There was also coverage, from the 1790's, in newspapers and later in weekly and monthly magazines.

BOOKS AND ARTICLES

Black, Jeremy, ed. *War in the Early Modern World*. Boulder, Colo.: Westview Press, 1999.

Chaliand, Gérard. *The Art of War in World History: From Antiquity to the Nuclear Age*. Berkeley: University of California Press, 1994.

Chartrand, René. *British Forces in the West Indies, 1793-1815*. New York: Osprey, 1996.

Cipolla, C. M. *Guns, Sails, and Empires: Technological Innovation and the Early Phase of European Expansion, 1400-1700*. New York: Minerva Press, 1965.

Creveld, Martin van. *Technology and War: From 2000 B.C. to the Present*. New York: Free Press, 1989.

Downing, Brian M. *The Military Revolution and Political Change: Origins of Autocracy in Early Modern Europe*. Princeton, N.J.: Princeton University Press, 1992.

Dupuy, Trevor N. *The Evolution of Weapons and Warfare*. New York: Da Capo Press, 1984.

Fremont-Barnes, Gregory. *The Indian Mutiny, 1857-58*. New York: Osprey, 2007.

_____. *The Wars of the Barbary Pirates*. New York: Osprey, 2006.

Harrington, Peter. *Plassey 1757: Clive of India's Finest Hour*. Westport, Conn.: Praeger, 2005.

Haythornthwaite, Philip J. *The Colonial Wars Source Book*. London: Arms and Armour Press, 1995.

Heath, Ian. *The Sikh Army, 1799-1849*. New York: Osprey, 2005.

Keegan, John. *History of Warfare*. New York: Alfred A. Knopf, 1993.

Lynn, John A., ed. *Tools of War: Instruments, Ideas, and Institutions of Warfare, 1445-1871*. Urbana: University of Illinois Press, 1990.

McNeill, William H. *The Pursuit of Power: Technology, Armed Force, and Society Since A.D. 1000*. Chicago: University of Chicago Press, 1982.

Parker, Geoffrey. *The Military Revolution: Military Innovation and the Rise of the West, 1500-1800*. 2d ed. New York: Cambridge University Press, 1996.

Reid, Stuart. *Armies of the East India Company, 1750-1850*. New York: Osprey, 2009.

FILMS AND OTHER MEDIA

The Battle of Algiers. Feature film. Magna, 1966.

Lapu-Lapu. Feature film. Calinauan Cine Works/EDL Productions, 2002.

The Last of the Mohicans. Feature film. Twentieth Century Fox, 1992.

The Opium War. Feature film. Golden Harvest, 1997.

The Patriot. Feature film. Columbia Pictures, 2000.

Zulu. Feature film. Paramount Pictures, 1964.

Zulu Dawn. Feature film. American Cinema, 1979.

William T. Walker

THE OTTOMAN EMPIRE
Dates: 1453-1923

POLITICAL CONSIDERATIONS

The Ottoman Empire, founded by Osman I (r. 1290-1326), dominated much of southeastern Europe, the Middle East, and North Africa between the fourteenth and early twentieth centuries. Ottoman military superiority in the Balkans in the fifteenth and sixteenth centuries stemmed from the use of new modern armaments integrating infantry and cavalry with innovative tactics. The Ottomans borrowed methods from their adversaries and even used Christian and Jewish soldiers and officers in their campaigns. In addition to a magnificent army, they had a navy that was among the best in the Mediterranean area. However, one aspect of the early Ottoman success has been greatly exaggerated—that of the Ottomans' superiority in numbers. The Ottomans' rapid conquest of the Christian, Greek-speaking, Eastern Roman Byzantine Empire, as well as the other Balkan states in the years from 1290 to 1453, came not from larger forces but from essentially waiting for their Christian rivals to destroy each other in battle and then moving in and taking over the remaining territory. The Ottoman sultans made alliances with

The Ottoman Turks seize Constantinople from the Byzantines in 1453 to establish the Ottoman Empire.

OTTOMAN EXPANSION UNDER SÜLEYMAN THE MAGNIFICENT

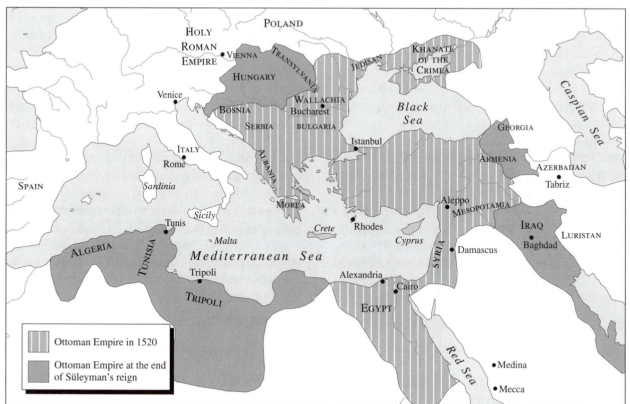

Ottoman Empire in 1520

Ottoman Empire at the end of Süleyman's reign

Christian states, and Turkish soldiers served as mercenaries in Christian armies, just as Christians fought in the Turkish armies.

National mythology has also greatly exaggerated the historical significance of key Ottoman victories before 1453, such as the defeat of the Serbs at Kosovo on June 15, 1389. In many ways the Ottomans inherited the Balkans by default, because the Byzantine army collapsed as a result of internal civil wars and external invasions by the Western European Christian Crusaders and other neighboring Christian states.

The decisive victory that established the Ottoman domination of the Balkans was the Siege of Constantinople in 1453. The Turks had prepared for this battle for fifty years. According to legend, the city was to fall to a sultan bearing the name of the prophet Muḥammad. Sultan Mehmed I (r. 1402-1421) initially appeared to be that man, but an internal contest for the throne and a war against Tamerlane in the east

made his attack on the Byzantine capital impossible. However, when his grandson Mehmed II (1432-1481) ascended the throne in 1451, both sultan and people were ready.

By 1453 Constantinople had become a shadow of its former self. The city's population, which had once exceeded one million people, had declined to only several tens of thousands. Constantinople was no longer a unified city but rather a series of villages behind walls. Mehmed II prepared his attack carefully, building fortresses on both sides of the Bosporus—Anadolu Hisari on the Asian side and Rumeli Hisari on the European side—the ruins of which still stand. He strengthened the janissary corps, raising their pay and improving the officer ranks. He constructed causeways over the Galati hill north of the old city, so that he could have his ships dragged up and over to the Golden Horn, the harbor of Constantinople, circumnavigating the chain and flotilla that protected the entrance to the city's vulnerable side. Mehmed's fleet of 125 ships and an additional number of smaller support craft was five times larger than that of the Greeks. With this fleet, Mehmed prevented the Byzantines from bringing supplies by sea as they had done in the past. The first Turkish troops to reach the walls of Constantinople in April, 1453, were a few knights, who were successfully met by the Byzantine soldiers in a brief skirmish. Ottoman reinforcements then drove the Greeks back behind the walls. Massive Turkish forces gathered over the next days, including cavalry, infantry, engineers, and naval forces. Most important were the cannons Mehmed had placed at the heretofore impenetrable walls; they began a constant bombardment that continued for seven weeks until they finally breached the wall.

Mehmed and his entourage of janissary soldiers, advisers, and imams, or religious leaders, took up their positions before the city. Mehmed offered the city either mercy if it surrendered without a fight, or pillage if it chose to fight. The Greeks chose to fight to the last.

After the fall of Constantinople the Ottomans continued to expand throughout the Muslim world in the Near East and North Africa. At the height of the empire under the sultan Süleyman I the Magnificent (1494 or 1495-1566) the European boundaries reached beyond the Danube River to the gates of Vienna. Süleyman's failure to take the Habsburg capital owed as much to the limitations of Ottoman military tactics, especially the definition of its campaigns by annual sorties lasting only from the spring to the fall, as it did to the defense of the Viennese. Süleyman also fought and lost to the naval forces of King Philip II of Spain (1527-1598) in the Mediterranean at the celebrated Battle of Lepanto (1571).

After Süleyman the Ottoman Empire went into a decline. Succeeding sultans rarely left their palaces and placed state matters in the hands of their ministers, most of whom were Christian slaves taken in the child tax from Balkan families. The Ottomans fought against Austria, Poland, the Papacy, and other European states for control of the Danubian plain for two hundred years. However, they found a European ally in France. In the late seventeenth century the grand viziers of the Albanian Köprülü family arrested the decline of the Ottoman Empire and spearheaded a revival of its former power. However, in 1664 at Szentgotthárd, on the Austrian-Hungarian border, the Ottomans suffered their first loss of land to the Christian powers. After the Thirty Years' War (1618-1648) the improved European armies surpassed the Turkish army in organization, tactics, training, armament, and even leadership. The Turks, whose advanced techniques and equipment had previously been their strong points, now found themselves falling behind their adversaries in these areas.

The Ottomans' failure to take Vienna in a second attempt (1683) began the loss of their territory to the European powers. In the eighteenth century the empire lost wars and land to both Austria and Russia. Inside the empire local warlords carved out virtually independent fiefdoms throughout the imperial provinces. The sultan's personal authority in reality did not extend beyond Constantinople. The grand janissary corps, which had gained the right to marry, were less an effective fighting force than a collection of sinecures. In 1792 Sultan Selim III (1761-1808) turned to France, the empire's old ally, for assistance in modernizing Ottoman armed forces, creating a modern corps in addition to the janissaries. However, the French Revolution (1789-1799) and the Napoleonic Wars (1793-1815) interrupted the partnership. The

TURNING POINTS

1453	With use of large cannons, the Turks capture Constantinople from the Byzantines, establishing the Ottoman Empire.
1571	The Battle of Lepanto II, fought between the Ottoman Turks and the Christian forces of Don Juan de Austria, is the last major naval battle to be waged with galleys.
1792	Modern French military techniques and arms are introduced into Turkey.
1826	The janissary corps are destroyed and the Turkish army is modernized.
1923	The Treaty of Lausanne creates the Republic of Turkey, bringing the Ottoman Empire to its official end.

THE OTTOMAN EMPIRE, C. 1700

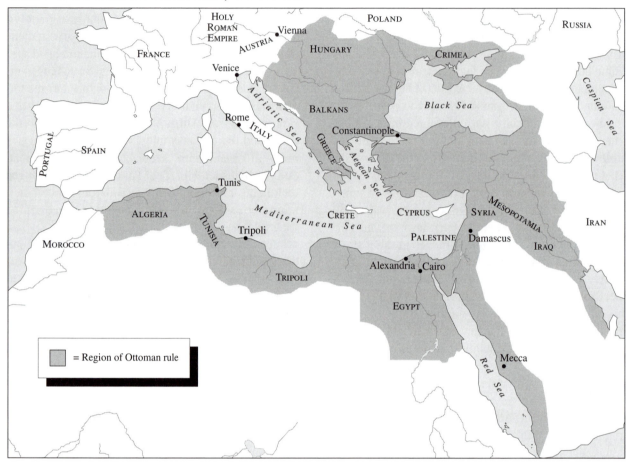

empire suffered from internal revolutions, such as those by the Serbs and the Greeks, and from uprisings by warlords and rogue pashas such as Ali Paşa (1741-1822), known as the Lion of Janina, in modern Albania, as well as wars with Russia and Persia. In a janissary revolt in 1806 Selim was dethroned and killed. His successor, Sultan Mahmud II (1785-1839), believed that the defeat of Napoleon would guarantee Ottoman territory at the Congress of Vienna (1814-1815), but when the Greek uprising of 1821 split the European alliance, Mahmud found himself at war against the combined forces of Russia, France, and England. In 1826, in order to modernize his forces, he did away with the janissaries.

Mahmud's successor, Abdülmecid I (1823-1861), allied himself to the powers by promising reforms in the treatment of his non-Muslim subjects. In the 1830's and 1840's the powers protected Abdülmecid from a vassal revolt. In the 1850's England and France joined Abdülmecid in the victorious Crimean War (1853-1856) against Russia. However, in 1877 Russia again went to war against the Turks to aid a Balkan uprising. Although the Russians defeated the Turks and liberated the Christian states of the region, England, Turkey's ally, prevented the Russian troops from taking Istanbul.

In the early twentieth century the Young Turk Revolution brought constitutional government and more westernization to the empire. However, Turkey lost wars to Italy (1911) and to a coalition of Balkan states (1912-1913), only managing to regain a modest amount of European territory around Edirne in the

Second Balkan War (May-June, 1913). After feeling betrayed by England and France, the Young Turk leaders turned toward friendship with Germany. After the outbreak of World War I in 1914, Turkey joined with the Central Powers in November of that year. Turkish troops faced the Russians in the Caucasus and the English in the Near East. The English had by then occupied Egypt and supported a revolt of the Arabs in Saudia Arabia and Palestine. With the collapse of Russia in 1917, the Turks received territory in the Caucasus, but the following year the Central Powers lost the war and the Allies divided up the territory of the empire among themselves.

However, while the Allies occupied Constantinople, Mustafa Kemal (1881-1938), later named Atatürk, or Father of Turks, raised the standard of revolt in Ankara, where he set up a rival government. Kemal led the army to victory over the Greeks (1920-1922) and renegotiated the Treaty of Sèvres (1920) to his advantage in the Treaty of Lausanne (1923), creating the Republic of Turkey and bringing the Ottoman Empire to its official end.

MILITARY ACHIEVEMENT

The Ottoman Empire in its early years successfully defeated the Christian powers of Europe and the Muslim states of the Near East. This success stemmed from the Ottomans' innovative use of tactics and strategy integrating cavalry and infantry. The Ottoman cavalry, or sipahi (rendered in English as "spahi"), was drawn from the noble free-born Muslim class, whereas the infantry, the janissaries, were slaves of the sultan forcibly recruited from the children of conquered European peoples, converted to Islam, and trained as fierce fighters. There were also irregular cavalry and infantry troops. The Ottomans also did not hesitate, when it served their purposes, to use Christian or Jewish commanders, as well as Christian allies and mercenaries.

The Muslims were among the first to effectively use cannon and gunpowder. Their success against European armies continued into the seventeenth century, when the decline of the empire began.

WEAPONS, UNIFORMS, AND ARMOR

In the early centuries the Ottomans effectively used siege weapons and artillery, such as mortars, catapults, and large cannons, that fired both iron and stone shot. Mehmed II, also called Mehmed the Conqueror, wished to have the most modern weapons and ordered a Hungarian gunsmith to build him large cannons, one of which was used at Constantinople, that could fire 1,200-pound cannonballs. Janissaries used scimitars, knives, stabbing swords, battle-axes, and harquebuses. The Turks were also skilled marksmen using muskets. Ottoman archers continuously rained arrows on the defenders of cities they attacked. The Ottomans were renowned for their sappers as well, who attacked the enemy's fortifications with axes. The spahi cavalry, true medieval warriors, carried bows, swords, lances, shields, and maces. The Ottoman navy consisted of corsairs and oared galleons.

The Turks established local janissaries and other regional corps in different parts of the empire, each with its own distinct uniforms, pennants, and standards. The traditional Ottoman uniforms consisted of short, loose pantaloons, a short shirt with a large sash, a high turban, stockings that reached above the hem of the pantaloons, and Turkish-style slippers. Janissaries also wore long, flowing robes and felt hats. The *akhis*, or officers, wore pantaloons, sashes, capes, red boots, long fur-trimmed robes, and tall, elaborately carved, large-plumed helmets whose height depended on the wearer's rank. Janissary food bearers wore black uniforms, sandals, pantaloons, short jackets with long sleeves, half-vestlike shirts, and conical hats. The sultans rode on caparisoned, or decoratively adorned, horses and carried bejeweled weapons.

The janissaries' standard was the scarlet crescent and double-edged sword symbol of Osman, the founder of the Ottoman dynasty. The akhis carried staffs with tails representing the sleeve of the sheik of the Bektashi dervishes, the janissaries' religious order. The number of tails on the akhi's staff depended on his rank. The janissaries' staff bore a spoon symbolizing their higher standard of living. The insignia of the janissary corps was the soup pot and the spoon.

Officers bore titles from the kitchen such as the First Maker of Soup, First Cook, and First Water-Bearer. The soup pot was the sacred object around which the janissaries gathered to eat or discuss events and policies. In rebellions they traditionally overturned these soup pots.

In the seventeenth and eighteenth centuries Turkish armament lagged behind the times. In 1796 the French ambassador General Jean-Baptiste Aubert-Dubayet brought to Turkey several pieces of modern armament and artillery as models for the Turks to copy and French engineers and artillery officers to teach the Turks modern methods. In the nineteenth and twentieth centuries the Ottoman Empire continued to modernize its forces and weaponry. Before World War I the Germans improved upon Turkish arms. German General Otto Liman von Sanders (1855-1929) came to Turkey to oversee the training of troops. During the war the Turks had excellent gunnery. However, two battleships ordered from England, which were to be the best of the fleet, had not been delivered before the Turks joined the Central Powers and were confiscated by the British. In the late nineteenth century the Turks adopted typical European khaki winter and summer army and blue navy uniforms. For officers, the fez—a brimless, flat-crowned hat—replaced the turban.

MILITARY ORGANIZATION

Within the Ottoman Empire the government and the military were closely linked. The empire was divided into two parts: European and Asian, each governed by *aghas*, area governors who administered the empire in the name of the sultan. Under the *aghas* stood the provincial governors, or *sanjak beys*. The sanjak, which has come to mean "province," was literally the standard of the governor, or bey. In 1453 there were twenty sanjaks in Asia and twenty-eight in Europe. The sanjak beys commanded troops, operated the policing powers in their provinces, and collected taxes. Within the sanjaks there were two types of agricultural estates: large *zaimets* and smaller *timars*. Ottoman theory held that all land belonged to God and was managed by the sultan; the managers of these es-

tates were free-born Muslim noblemen. The spahis, knights who served as the cavalry of the Ottoman armies, were the most numerous Ottoman warriors. The early sultans gave most of the land they conquered to these warriors, although a minor portion was reserved for government and diplomatic officials. The peasants, called *rayah*, literally "cattle," were the serfs who worked the land. The other governing functions were handled by the various Muslim, Christian, and Jewish religious authorities who ruled their own communities.

The Ottomans used both regular and irregular troops as police forces. The two most important regular land forces were the janissary infantry corps and the spahi knights. The Ottoman navy was a supplementary force that often carried janissary troops, as well as naval officers and sailors.

The janissaries were Christian and Jewish boys, as young as seven years old, periodically gathered in the Balkans through a child tax, called *devshirme*. Girls were also gathered to serve in various harems. Sultan Orhan (c. 1288-c. 1360) started the corps as a bodyguard, and Murad I (c. 1326-1389) developed it as a militia to guard the European territories. The boys were selected for the janissary corps based on their strength and intelligence. They were educated as Muslim Bektashi dervishes, the religious order favored by Ohran, and housed in barracks at Bursa. After the fall of Constantinople in 1453, Mehmed II moved the main janissary barracks to the sultan's palace in the capital. During battle, conquered fortresses served as their barracks, and local produce served as their food.

A minority, approximately 15 percent, of the most intelligent children were selected for government and diplomatic service, while the remainder were trained for the janissaries. The boys were educated in the palace school, where they studied subjects such as Turkish history, Muslim literature, and romantic and martial music. They practiced gymnastics and sports on both foot and horseback to increase their strength and agility. The students became expert in archery, swordsmanship, javelin throwing, and riding.

Early janissaries could not own property, marry, or perform other service, but they were armed and well paid and had a strong esprit de corps. They were the most respected infantry in Europe: fearless, well trained, dedicated troops with intelligent and cool-headed commanders. At the dedication of the corps, the sheik of the Bektashi, an officer of the corps, promised, "Its visage shall be bright and shining, its arm strong, its sword keen, its arrow sharp-pointed. It shall be victorious in every battle and will never return except in triumph." The janissaries were known for their military discipline, which rivaled that of the ancient Greeks and Romans.

In contrast to the "inside aghas," who were leaders of the government and palace service, the chief janissary officers held the title of "outside aghas." In the time of Mehmed II they numbered a force of ten thousand. They were unique in Europe, where most armies consisted almost completely of cavalry. The janissaries were commanded only by aghas, who had been appointed by the sultan, and the provincial beys and pashas had no authority over them.

When the Ottoman Empire went into decline, the janissary corps began to deteriorate. Muslims were recruited into the janissaries, affecting the traditional camaraderie. Janissaries also worked as artisans to supplement their income. During Süleyman's reign, they received the right to marry, and their sons began entering the corps, first through loopholes in the law and later through quotas. Nepotism grew rampant. Murad IV (1612-1640), recognizing the de facto practice, abolished the devshirme. Janissaries often paid others to serve in the field in their place, while still collecting their pay and enjoying their privileges.

The corps, if they disagreed with the imperial policies, would often mutiny in the field or in Constantinople. The janissaries began to influence politics as early as the fifteenth century, when they backed the sultan Mehmed I against his brothers, but in the seventeenth century the corps became stronger than the sultan. Sultans and ministers curried favor with the janissaries as well as the spahis through promotion and pay raises.

REPUBLIC OF TURKEY, 1923

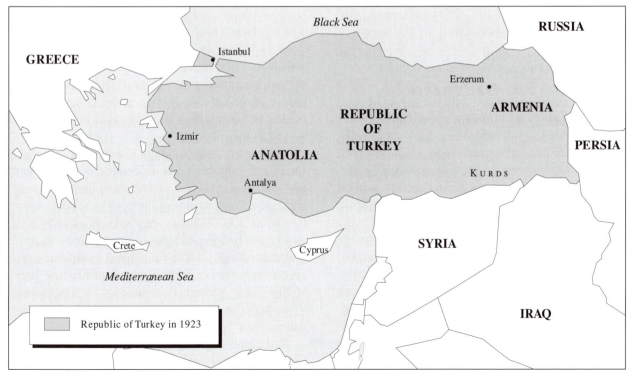

The vizier Köprülü Amca-zāde Hüseyin (died 1702) tried to reverse the downward trend by revising the muster roles of the janissaries, improving military equipment for both the janissaries and the navy, building new barracks, and refurbishing the imperial defenses, but the measures proved to be only temporary. The Ottoman forces also included renowned artillery and engineering units and highly skilled artisans who were supported through a guild system. These artisans supplied the Ottoman armies and maintained their morale and standard of living.

The Turkish sipahi cavalry were considered to be without peer. They were ready at any moment on the command of the sanjak beys to leave their fields and join in battle. Failure do so would mean loss of their position. Although the ranks were not hereditary, the son of a deceased spahi might be given a small amount of land for his needs. He would then have to prove himself in battle to earn a tamir or zaimet. There were also mounted soldiers at a lesser rank than spahi, and the spahis of the Porte in Constantinople, "the men of the sultan," who formed a separate corps. In the seventeenth century the number of feudal spahis dwindled, and, like the janissaries, the spahi also began to hire substitutes, some of whom were unscrupulous adventurers. Spahis were no longer suited for all-year duty against the modern European artillery. At the Battle of Mezö-Keresztes (1596) against Hungary they left the field en masse. The sultan dismissed thirty thousand spahis, turning a large group of nobles into landless malcontents and further increasing the problems of the empire.

In times of war the Ottoman Empire employed a supplemental irregular cavalry, the *akinjis*. Other irregular troops were the azab corps, a reserve infantry founded by Orhan. The sixteenth century governor of Bosnia used another irregular force to police his sanjak. These irregular troops did not receive regular pay but were rewarded with spoils of war. However, jealous of the pay and privileges of the regular forces, they sometimes rebelled.

In the seventeenth century the Ottoman Empire also fell behind in inventory and supply. While the great powers of Europe established modern professional armies in the sixteenth and seventeenth centuries, the sultans stubbornly held on to their antiquated

traditional techniques. They lacked modern financing procedures and an industrial system based on flexibility, free enterprise, and competition that was required for modern warfare. Pillaging and living off the land no longer sufficed. The haphazard Turkish system of taxes and economic restrictions held the empire's military behind while its European enemies forged ahead. Furthermore, the janissaries and artisan guilds joined together to protect their traditional privileges and maintain the military's traditional procedures.

In the eighteenth century all aspects of the army—training, discipline, armament, fortifications, field maneuvers—fell to a substandard state. Incompetence and ignorance ruled even in the most elementary matters. Open defiance and mutiny were rampant among the troops. Theft of supplies by both officers and soldiers was common. Janissaries often did not go on campaign but hired people in their stead. Janissaries would fight with their officers or demand privileges reserved for officers. The corps became a parasitic burden, a shadow of the unbeatable force it had been in its early days.

After a loss to the Russians in 1792, Sultan Selim III was anxious to reform his army. Although Selim's many reforms were not limited to military matters, an overhaul of the army played a key part in his plans. Selim looked to France, where the French Revolution of 1789 had brought about a new order. He sent special ambassadors to the courts of Europe and studied their detailed reports. He was particularly interested in guns and artillery, about which he himself had written a treatise. He was especially impressed with the revolutionary French army and requested help from Paris to improve the Turkish military. The French experts improved Turkish gun foundries, arsenals, and equipment. In both the army and navy they taught the Turks gunnery, fortifications, navigation, and related subjects. The Turkish engineering school was brought up to modern standards.

However, the sultan's advisers were divided. Some insisted on maintaining the old Turkish ways at any cost, whereas others advocated the Western techniques only to restore the past Turkish glory; still others called for a complete overhaul of the Turkish

F. R. Niglutsch

The British defeat of the Ottoman fleet at the Battle of Navarino Bay in 1827 effectively destroyed the Ottoman navy and paved the way for Greek independence.

military and society in the Western manner. Selim established the Topiji—a small force of prisoners, European deserters, and poor Muslims—and had them trained in the Western fashion as a prototype army. Impressed by the Topiji's superiority, Selim tried to introduce their methods and arms into the Turkish forces. The spahis accepted the new methods, but the janissaries continued to resist modernization. Selim thus enlarged the Topiji force, which by then included some of the French officers who had remained in Turkey. In 1805 he introduced a draft but was assassinated the following year in a janissary revolt. Mahmud II then ascended the throne.

The success of Mehmed Ali of Egypt in building a Western army with Muslims encouraged Mahmud to do away with the janissaries and rely solely upon the new army. Mahmud replaced the European officers

training the troops with Muslims and ordered 150 troops from each janissary battalion to join the new corps. On June 15, 1826, as expected, the janissaries revolted, overturning their soup pots and invading the palace. Mahmud was ready. He had increased his loyal artillery troops, placing them in strategic points in the streets. They drove the rebels back to their barracks, where they barricaded themselves and were destroyed by artillery in less then an hour. More than six thousand died in the shelling. Mahmud executed the surviving leaders, disbanded the corps, and outlawed the Bektashi dervish religious order. The remaining janissaries were exiled to Asia.

After the destruction of the janissaries, Mahmud reintroduced the old title *serasker*; originally held by a high commander of general rank, it was now given to the commander in chief who also served as minister of war and handled police duties in Constantinople. He paid special attention to the new army. Twelve thousand men were stationed at Constantinople and elsewhere in the provinces. Mahmud turned to England and Prussia for assistance training the new army. Officers were sent to England, and British officers came to Turkey. Prussia sent Lieutenant Helmuth von Moltke (1800-1891), who later became an architect of Prussia's renowned army, as a military adviser. Von Moltke helped to modernize the Ottoman Empire's defenses and to train and organize the new troops. He was dissatisfied, however, with Mahmud and the Ottoman army, who resisted instruction from foreigners. Turkey and Prussia exchanged cadets and officers as well, establishing a German tradition that would continue through the life of the empire.

In the 1840's the army was reorganized into active and reserve units, and the term of active service was reduced from twelve to five years. Soldiers who had actively served for five years would serve the balance of seven years in their home provinces as reserves. The military was further reorganized along Western lines, the number of troops was increased to 250,000, and military schools were established.

In 1808 the Young Turk Revolution brought German trained officers forward. Enver Paşa (1881-1922), one of the leaders of the revolt, had trained in German methods as a young officer and now went to Berlin as military attaché. The war minister Sevket Paşa (1858-1913) actually trained in Germany. Thus, the German influence that had existed since the time of Mahmud actually increased during the nineteenth century.

After the Young Turk Revolution, the use of officers in government positions reduced the efficiency of the army and navy in the field. Furthermore, capable officers opposed to the government were sent to distant posts. The defeats of the Italian and Balkan Wars impressed upon the new leaders the need for massive reform. Enver Paşa, who by that time had become one of the ruling triumvirate along with Mehmed Talât Paşa (1872-1921) and Ahmed Cemal Paşa (1872-1922) took this in hand. Much of the problem was the mistrust that the older officers had of the young military supporters of the revolution, a

situation that demanded a general purge of the senior officers. Sevket Paşa recognized the problem but refused to dismiss his friends in the officer corps. Therefore Enver Paşa took over the ministry and convinced the reluctant Sultan Mehmed V (1844-1918) to issue a decree retiring officers over fifty-five years of age. A new agreement with Berlin brought forty German officers to Turkey. They were led by Liman von Sanders, who was placed in charge of the first army in Constantinople.

DOCTRINE, STRATEGY, AND TACTICS

From the early days of the Ottoman Empire, the doctrine of warfare called for the conquest of Muslim and Christian land in the name of God. In fact, all of the empire's territory was seen to be God's land, administered by the sultan through aghas, beys, and pashas, military leaders as well as government officials. When the Ottoman sultans became the rulers of the Muslims of the Near East, they revived the old title of caliph, for the religious leader of Islam.

The Ottoman strategy was simple. On yearly campaigns, which, after 1453, began from Constantinople in a formal ceremonial military parade and lasted until late fall, their well-trained and courageous armies fought and conquered as much land and as many cities as they could. Victims who acquiesced were shown mercy. Those who resisted suffered a brief period of brutal pillage. In the fifteenth and sixteenth centuries the Ottomans managed the lands under their control well. Even non-Muslim communities had a great deal of autonomy. In the later centuries, inefficient government and arbitrary actions of virtually independent warlords, landlords, and local beys and pashas inflicted hardship.

The Ottomans learned from their adversaries, studying Western military forces and strategies. After the seventeenth century the viziers, more often than the sultan, marched on campaigns and sometimes participated in battles. Although the army was the main force, a flotilla of hundreds of boats accompanied the troops on the rivers of the region under attack.

A typical order of battle in the open field consisted

of three armies. For example, at Kosovo Field in 1389, Sultan Murad I commanded the center with his janissary corps and spahi knights. By tradition the army of the region where the battle was fought occupied the right flank. Thus Bayezid I (c. 1360-1403), the sultan's son and heir, led the army of Europe on his right. A younger son led the army of Asia on the left flank. At Kosovo an advance guard of two thousand archers began the attack. However, the standard Ottoman practice was to begin battle with an inferior line of irregulars. The janissaries would attack accompanied by drums and cymbals and exhorted by their non-janissary brothers of the Bektashi dervishes. If the enemy forces outnumbered the Turks, the strategy changed, and the Ottomans would wait in hiding for the battle to begin.

The Ottoman forces, well suited for siege warfare, used both cannons and mines. They dug trenches about 1,500 meters from the besieged city walls and set up their artillery behind the ridges. Archers then continually rained arrows on the city, while janissaries scaled the walls. The Turks were willing to continue a siege as long as it took for a city to surrender or fall. They often gave generous terms of surrender, allowing those who wished to leave the city to go freely.

CONTEMPORARY SOURCES

The best primary sources on the military history of the Ottoman Empire available in English and held in American libraries are memoirs and contemporary accounts of battles. Among the best of the former are the memoirs of Sir Edwin Pears (1835-1919), *Forty Years in Constantinople: The Recollections of Sir Edwin Pears, 1873-1915* (1916), Evliya Çelebi's (c. 1611-c. 1682) *Travels in Palestine* (1834), and Konstanty Michalowicz's (born c. 1435) *Memoirs of a Janissary* (1975), an account of a fifteenth century Turkish warrior found in the microform collection of the University of Michigan. The University of Michigan is the repository of numerous eyewitness accounts of Turkish-Western battle, a number of which have been published. Suraiya Faroqhi's *Approaching Ottoman History: An Introduction to the Sources* (1999) is a general survey of sources in Turkish and other languages.

BOOKS AND ARTICLES

Aksan, Virginia. "Ottoman War and Warfare, 1453-1812." In *European Warfare, 1453-1815*, edited by Jeremy Black. New York: St. Martin's Press, 1999.

_____. *Ottoman Wars, 1700-1870: An Empire Besieged*. Harlow, England: Longman/Pearson, 2007.

Almond, Ian. "Muslims, Protestants, and Peasants: Ottoman Hungary, 1526-1683." In *Two Faiths, One Banner: When Muslims Marched with Christians Across Europe's Battlegrounds*. Cambridge, Mass.: Harvard University Press, 2009.

Faroqhi, Suraiya. "The Strengths and Weaknesses of Ottoman Warfare." In *The Ottoman Empire and the World Around It*. New York: I. B. Tauris, 2004.

Gabriel, Richard A. *The Siege of Constantinople*. Carlisle, Pa.: U.S. Army War College, 1992.

Goodwin, Godfrey. *The Janissaries*. London: Saqi, 1992.

Guilmartin, John F., Jr. "Ideology and Conflict: The Wars of the Ottoman Empire, 1453-1606." In *Warfare and Empires: Contact and Conflict Between European and Non-European Military and Maritime Forces and Cultures*, edited by Douglas M. Peers. Brookfield, Vt.: Ashgate/Variorum, 1997.

Imber, Colin. *The Ottoman Empire, 1300-1650: The Structure of Power*. New York: Palgrave Macmillan, 2002.

Murphey, Rhoads. *Ottoman Warfare, 1500-1700*. New Brunswick, N.J.: Rutgers University Press, 1999.

Nicole, David. *Armies of the Ottoman Turks, 1300-1400*. Botley, Oxford, England: Osprey, 1985.

Reid, James J. *Crisis of the Ottoman Empire: Prelude to Collapse, 1839-1878*. Stuttgart, Germany: Steiner, 2000.

Turfan, M. Naim. *Rise of the Young Turks: Politics, Military, and Ottoman Collapse*. London: I. B. Taurus, 1999.

Turnbull, Stephen. *The Ottoman Empire, 1326-1699*. New York: Routledge, 2003.

Zorlu, Tuncay. *Innovation and Empire in Turkey: Sultan Selim III and the Modernisation of the Ottoman Navy*. New York: Tauris Academic Studies, 2008.

FILMS AND OTHER MEDIA

Lawrence of Arabia. Feature film. Columbia Pictures, 1962.

The Ottoman Empire: The War Machine. Documentary. History Channel, 2006.

The Ottoman Empire, 1280-1683. Documentary. Landmark Films, 1995.

Suleyman the Magnificent. Documentary. National Gallery and Metropolitan Museum of Art, 1987.

Frederick B. Chary

THE MUGHAL EMPIRE

Dates: 1526-1858

POLITICAL CONSIDERATIONS

Geographical features have played a critical role in the history of warfare in the vast subcontinent now called India. The snow-covered Himalayas in the north protected India from massive military invasions. The protective Himalayan barrier has allowed Indian civilization to develop in an unbroken historical tradition that goes back well beyond five thousand years. The Himalayas are also the source of India's great rivers, such as the Ganges, which were vital for food and water supply, transport, and trade and along the banks of which civilization from ancient times developed.

Lower in height than the Himalayas, the Vindhya Mountains run from west to east, dividing northern India from southern India, known as the Deccan. Southern India developed a complex and unique civilization rich in art, language, literature, music, and religious traditions. Conquest of the wealthy Deccan became the goal of many northern rulers intent on reviving the political and administrative unification of India first accomplished by the Maurya Dynasty (321-c. 185 B.C.E.).

The Western Ghats, the Eastern Ghats, and other ranges of hills compartmentalize the Deccan into small, easily defended sectors. Here, the inhabitants built vast self-sufficient forts to ward off intruders, and it was in these regions that an Indian variation of guerrilla warfare proved to be the ultimate challenge to Mughal supremacy, particularly during the reign of the later Mughal rulers. The political fate of the north hinged on great battles fought by conventional forces on fields such as Pānīpat. In the south, however, the numerous isolated states sometimes held their own, and the conquering armies were frequently at a disadvantage because of unfamiliar terrain, hostile populations, and impregnable defenses.

India's considerable wealth was amassed through the toil of its rural and urban peoples, the fertility of its lands, the emphasis on trade, and the abundance of food from the subcontinent's land and surrounding seas. Conquest of India or even a lucrative raid into its wealthy northern cities became a significant aspect of the military strategy of rulers in Central Asia, Afghanistan, and Persia.

From early times Indians favored a remarkable tolerance of diversity and religious and cultural variety. The country became a haven for foreign refugees from persecution, who brought traditions, ideas, and skills that enhanced the economy and the way of life. The prevailing tendency was for foreigners, whether refugees or invaders, eventually to settle in after some initial upheavals and to adopt the prevailing way of life while retaining features of their own cultural traditions. The assimilation process was not always smooth, and military engagements were a common feature of the initial contact between Indians and alien invaders.

The Mughals, a Muslim people, began their Indian adventure as alien military raiders in 1526 and concluded it in 1858 as the last acknowledged Indian imperial dynasty. Their story aptly illustrates the process of assimilation. Even as they conquered India politically and militarily, they absorbed, adopted, and made Indian culture their own.

From ancient times Indians had experimented with a variety of forms of government, ranging from democratic republics to vast unifying empires. Although Indian rulers fought each other in a bewildering array of military engagements over politics, land acquisition, and personal ambition, Indian society was generally more oriented to the arts of peace than those of war. Although Indian society had a warrior class and professional soldiers, it did not glorify war as a way of life, seeing war as merely a necessity to accomplish a political end. This crucial feature of Indian development meant that alien military forces frequently had enormous tactical advantages over defending Indian armies and frequently prevailed. The defenders, raised in a relatively nonviolent environment, fought with courage and valor but were frequently no match for the raiders. Hence India fell prey to frequent invasions that caused enormous turmoil until the process of civilizing and assimilating the outsiders took over. Occasionally, as with the Mughals, the invaders successfully utilized new military weaponry and innovative battle strategies in their bids to conquer India. In the process, they helped to change the methodology of warfare in the subcontinent.

As with most Indian governments, past and present, success and survival were largely dependent on the energy, determination, and dedication of a particular leader. The early Mughals produced a few outstanding rulers, the most prominent of whom was the emperor Akbar (1542-1605).

Pre-Mughal India

Pre-Mughal India consisted of a number of small states governed by a variety of Hindu and Muslim rulers. One of the most prominent of these kings was Ibrāhīm Lodī (died 1526), the Afghan sultan of Delhi from 1517. These kings, princes, and tribal chiefs fought incessantly to increase the size of their territories, to protect their kingdoms, to carve out trade routes to the ocean, to ensure the succession of their children, and even to unify the subcontinent. Because the Delhi sultanate had lost most of its political significance, power dissipated into the hands of numerous regional warlords, many of Afghan and Rajput origin. The absence of political unity could easily have been perceived as creating an ideal opportunity for a hardy foreign adventurer.

The Reasons for Mughal Warfare

After establishing a foothold in India in 1526, Mughal emperors continuously sought to unify the country. The conduct of warfare was regarded as the necessary business of rulers through much of the Mughal period. Where they encountered resistance to peaceful takeovers, warfare followed.

The Mughal emperors waged war against religious groups that resisted hated measures such as a tax on non-Muslims. The religious fervor of some later Mughal rulers such as ʿĀlamgīr incited violent opposition from the Hindu majority throughout India. The Mughals also fought against religious minorities such as the Sikhs. Fratricidal warfare was a marked feature of this dynasty, with princes warring against each other for control of the empire because there was no established tradition of primogeniture, or inheritance by the oldest son. Mughal imperial governors also fought against recalcitrant tribes and ethnic communities opposed to their rule.

As the power of the Mughal emperors declined, rebellious noblemen and governors sought to carve out their own kingdoms. Warfare was a significant element of Mughal India. The combination of ethnic wars, religious wars, dynastic wars, and civil wars ensured that there were few periods of peace during this period.

Turning Points

Apr. 20, 1526	Bābur makes effective use of artillery to defeat Sultan Ibrāhīm Lodī at the famous Battle of Pānīpat and establishes the Mughal Empire.
1527	The Mughals defeat the Rajputs at the Battle of Kanwa.
1529	The Mughals defeat the Afghans at the Battle of Ghāghara.
1556	Bābur's grandson Akbar is victorious at the second Battle of Pānīpat, against the Sur descendants of Shēr Shāh, and eventually conquers most of northern and eastern India, Afghanistan, and Baluchistan.
1632-1653	The fifth Mughal emperor, Shah Jahan, builds the Taj Mahal as a monument to his love for his wife Mumtaz Mahal.
1657	ʿĀlamgīr becomes the sixth Mughal emperor and ultimately expands the Mughal Empire to its greatest extent.
1739	Sack of Delhi by Persians.
1858	Mughals succumb to the British.

The wars of the later Mughal era were elaborate events involving thousands of soldiers, attendants, servants, camp followers, dancing girls, and vendors. The use of elephants, horses, oxen, and camels made for a uniquely Indian display of pomp and pageantry. The spectacle was enhanced with colorful costumes, decorative tents, and an impressive array of jewels and treasure chests.

MUGHAL INVASION OF INDIA

A descendant of both Genghis Khan (between 1155 and 1162-1227) and Tamerlane (1336-1405), Bābur (1482-1530) began as ruler of a small principality named Farghana, now located in Chinese Turkestan. By 1505 he had conquered the city of Kabul in Afghanistan, using it as a base for his ambitions on the wealth of India. Bābur's first raid into Punjab, in northern India, in 1524 was moderately successful. With the experience Bābur gained from this raid, he returned to India with a larger army and defeated Sultan Ibrāhīm Lodī at the famous Battle of Pānīpat on April 20, 1526.

Bābur's military successes were the product of his own expertise in the art of organizing a compact but well-trained, highly disciplined army for warfare in the plains of India. Bābur had additional advantages: His first-rate cavalry of Turkish troops was trained for quick maneuvers and sudden sallies and charges on opposing forces. Most important, Bābur made effective use of artillery, acquired from Turkey, in his Indian battles. The introduction of such weaponry played a decisive role in the Mughal victories. Although Indians had witnessed the use of large guns in sieges, the mobile artillery tactics of Bābur, using field guns and muskets, were a novelty.

OPPOSITION FROM INDIAN FORCES

Although Pānīpat was a significant battle that provided Bābur with control of Delhi and Agra, Bābur had to face stiff opposition from a variety of rulers. Fortunately for the Mughals, the Indians were unable to unite to defeat the invading army. The Rajputs and Afghans were separately and decisively defeated in the Battles of Kanwa (1527) and Ghāghara (1529). These victories were pivotal in the establishment of

the Mughal Empire, which now extended from Afghanistan in the north to Bengal in the east.

The defending Indian forces lost because their armies were unwieldy and undisciplined. These forces ranged from cavalry to infantry, some of whom were peasants armed only with bamboo sticks. A veritable city of servants, camp followers, and attendants hindered the mobility of the defending troops, which were unable to march more than a short distance each day. The cumbersome size of this force and the absence of effective communication between different wings of the army made cohesive fighting difficult.

Indian armies relied on the use of war elephants, which served a similar purpose to tanks in modern warfare. Elephants could push forward large guns, carry the commander into battle, act as a battering ram against a fort, or crush opposing infantry underfoot by rushing into the ranks. Equipped with an iron chain in its trunk and taught to wield it in all directions, an elephant could wreak havoc against an enemy force. Although these great animals were impressive and could frighten an enemy, they were also unpredictable and could retreat under attack into the ranks of panicked Indian foot soldiers. Frequently commanders rode on the elephants so that they had the best view of the battlefield; this high perch made the commanders prime targets for enemy arrows. If the commander was wounded, or if he felt the need to descend from the howda on top of his elephant, his troops often assumed that he was dead and scattered.

Although the Rajput Indians did not initially have firearms, they fought the Mughals with valor and determination. When all hope for victory was lost, they donned their traditional saffron garments and embarked on their final death ride, fighting the enemy with a ferocity that made them legendary in Indian history. Rajput women often committed mass suicide rather than surrender to the invaders. The Rajput ideals of chivalry and courage in the face of defeat have inspired generations of Indians.

MILITARY ACHIEVEMENT

Bābur's strategy at the Battle of Pānīpat became a model followed by his descendants in numerous battles throughout Indian history. Bābur's strategy in this battle was to provide as much protection to his forces as possible while allowing them the opportunity to act swiftly to take advantage of enemy weaknesses as the battle advanced. Bābur utilized ditches and jungle foliage to guard his left flank, protecting his right with control of houses in Pānīpat. The front of his force was shielded by 700 baggage carts tied together with ropes and interspersed with a screen of shields behind which he stationed the squadrons armed with new matchlock rifles to fire at the Indian troops. The use of this new weapon was decisive and successful against the densely packed ranks of defending forces.

One tactical technique Bābur utilized was the *taulqama*, a Turkish word referring to the horns of the crescent, in which the Mughals closed in on and destroyed the rear guard of the opponent. Each soldier in the thoroughly trained Mughal army knew his place, in either the vanguard, left wing, right wing, or the all-important center commanded by Bābur himself. The combination of good defenses and mobility ensured that Bābur's troops could take advantage of every weakness in the ranks of the defending force. First, a determined hail of arrows was directed at the Indian elephants, which panicked and turned to flee, killing many of the defending forces. The disorder in Indian ranks was as decisive a factor as the new Mughal weaponry. A lethal combination, this led to death for Sultan Ibrāhīm Lodī and thousands of his followers, slain on the battlefield and during the invaders' consequent plunder and devastation.

Pānīpat heralded a new age of warfare in India and ensured that future Mughal rulers would rely increasingly on firearms in battles. Although Bābur had utilized hand weapons and some light guns stationed on forks, the need for large mortars soon became evident. Large guns were cast for Bābur in Agra and first used during the Battle of Kanwa. These huge guns were transported on baggage carts from one battle to the next. Deceit was a favored tactic: Wooden dummy guns were mingled with the real guns to provide the appearance of a vastly more powerful arsenal than Bābur actually possessed. Bābur's determination and tactical expertise secured for him most of northern India.

Bābur's son and successor Humāyūn (1508-1556) utilized a large gun on a swivel that could fire a ball of more than 4 pounds of weight at a distance of up to 3 miles. Humāyūn's son and the greatest of the Mughal emperors, Akbar, improved on the technology by using more wheeled artillery carriages. He also lengthened the barrel of the hand musket and made various improvements to the firearms used by his vast army.

Bābur barely had the opportunity to consolidate his Indian kingdom before his death in 1530. His son, Humāyūn, inherited the new empire but lacked his father's dedication and military genius. Humāyūn conquered important regions such as Malwa and Gujerat in 1535 but could not retain control. He had to contend with the determination of Afghani soldier Shīr Shāh (c. 1486-1545), who defeated the Mughal emperor at the Battles of Chausa (1539) and Kanauj (1540). Humāyūn became a refugee at the Persian Court.

Shīr Shāh, as much of a military genius as Bābur, consolidated his empire with a series of military victories, dying in 1545 during a siege. Humāyūn eventually reconquered part of his empire in 1555 but died the following year, leaving the country to his son Akbar.

Although Akbar was young, was inexperienced, and lacked validity for his imperial title, he nevertheless showed determination and valor. At the age of thirteen, he was victorious at the Second Battle of Pānīpat (1556) against the Sur descendants of Shīr Shāh, who were led by an admirable Hindu general, Himu Bhargav, also known as Hemu (died 1556). It is significant that at this battle Himu girded his war elephants in plate armor and stationed both musketeers and crossbow archers on their backs. Clearly, the innovative changes of the Mughal invaders were being adopted and adapted to traditional Indian methods of fighting. Himu was mortally wounded on the battlefield, which led to a rout of his troops and victory for the hard-pressed Mughals. This battle gave the Mughals control of the Punjab, Delhi, and Agra. Five years later, Akbar conquered the Ganges and Yamuna river valleys, Gwalior, and parts of Rajasthan.

The consolidation of his empire and expanding

personal ambitions continually drove Akbar to warfare and conquest. His Rajput opponents had not, in those early stages, acquired the use of firearms. With these weapons and with the Turkish tactic of using archers on horseback, the Mughals were largely successful. At the Battle of Gogunda, also called the Bat-

tle of Haldighat (1576), Akbar and his opponent, the heroic Rānā Pratāp Singh, ruler of Mewār between 1572 and 1597, both used elephants in battle. Rānā Pratāp lost the battle but retreated strategically to the hills, later returning to regain some of his lost territory. His efforts to survive Mughal rule provided im-

THE MUGHAL EMPIRE IN THE SEVENTEENTH CENTURY

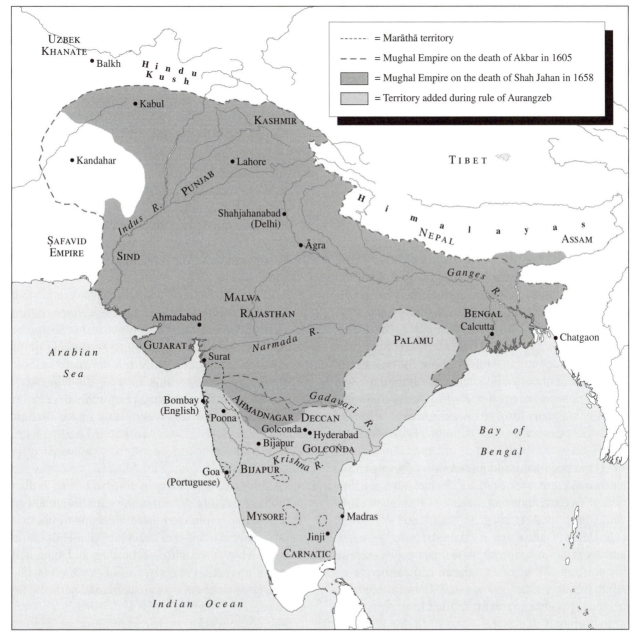

Akbar, the greatest Mughal emperor, was continually driven to expand his empire through warfare and conquest.

portant lessons to later rebels about the validity of fighting wars of attrition against the imperial giant. Rānā Pratāp never surrendered to Akbar, and this conflict was only resolved when Akbar's successor made peace with the Rānā's son, Amar Singh, in 1614.

Akbar eventually conquered most of northern and eastern India, Afghanistan, and Baluchistan and then turned his attention southward, fighting his final campaigns in Ahmadnagar (1600) and Khandesh (1601). He is now regarded as one of India's greatest emperors, not so much for his military prowess as for his policies of religious tolerance and deliberate assimilation of ethnic groups and his careful administrative methods. Nationalist Indians have gone so far as to portray Akbar as the founder of Indian national

consciousness, and this label reflects the admiration with which he is perceived.

Fratricidal conflict became a marked feature of Mughal political and military history with the rebellion from 1601 to 1604 of Prince Salīm (1569-1627), son and eventual successor of Akbar. Renamed Jahāngīr, Salīm took the throne upon Akbar's death in 1605 and ruled until his own death in 1627. Jahāngīr added Ahmadnagar and Kangra to the empire and subdued the Afghans in Bengal. Jahāngīr's encounters with the English and Portuguese failed to convince him of the need to take aggressive action to modernize his army; build a great fleet; and acquire the superior armaments, tactical knowledge, and training methods possessed by the English adventurers who sought to trade with his empire.

Jahāngīr's failure to appreciate the importance of modernization had devastating consequences for India, which eventually succumbed to the military might of the British and did not regain its independence until 1947. An absence of imperial concentration on Western military techniques, technology, and strategy resulted in long-term adverse political and economic consequences for India.

The fifth Mughal emperor, Shāh Jahān ruled between 1628 and 1658, when he was ousted from the throne by his son ʿĀlamgīr, and died a prisoner.

Shāh Jahān is famous mainly as the builder of numerous palaces, particularly the Taj Mahal (1632-1653), a monument to his love for his wife. Militarily, he succeeded to an extent in the Deccan but failed in his numerous attempts to oust the Persians from Qandahār. His illness in 1657 triggered a fratricidal war between his four sons, who all vied to capture the throne.

ʿĀlamgīr emerged the victor, becoming India's sixth Mughal emperor and ruling until his own death in 1707. Elephants were used with great effectiveness in this succession struggle. At the Battle of Khajwa (1659), ʿĀlamgīr's brother and opponent Prince Shuja (died c. 1660) utilized elephants swinging large iron chains from their trunks, wreaking havoc among ʿĀlamgīr's troops. ʿĀlamgīr, however, remained calm and emerged victorious.

ʿĀlamgīr expanded the Mughal Empire to its greatest extent, east to Assam, south to the land of the Marāṭhās, and beyond to Thanjavur and Tiruchchirappalli. The territorial expansion of the empire proved to be the undoing of the dynasty. Government at this time was personality-oriented, relying heavily for stability and prosperity on the energy and initiative of the emperor. India needed a ruler dedicated to the administration and government of its varied peoples. The fervently religious ʿĀlamgīr, however, was determined to convert India to the Muslim faith. He discriminated against and persecuted Hindus, provoking their opposition throughout the empire.

The Hindu Marāṭhās revolted against Mughal intolerance, under the banner of their leader Śivajī (1627-1680), who used a combination of surprise attacks, guerrilla warfare, reliance on nearly impregnable hill fortifications, and the plunder of rich cities such as Surat to finance these rebellious operations. Śivajī was a military genius, particularly in the use of cavalry. The Marāṭhā revolt, now legendary for its audacity against Mughal power, was somewhat successful in that Śivajī declared himself king of the Marāṭhās in 1674. The creation of this Hindu kingdom in defiance of the various Muslim rulers, including the Mughals, inspired the country's Hindu majority to stage other revolts. Śivajī is remembered for his ideals, his daring, and his administrative and military genius as one of India's greatest heroes.

Religious oppression also roused the Rajputs, the Sikhs, and the Jats against the increasingly unwieldy Mughal Empire. Rebellion flared up in various states such as Assam, Bundelkhand, Malwa, and Patiala. ʿĀlamgīr's success in ruthlessly suppressing these revolts generated widespread hostility to Mughal rule throughout India. Between 1681 and 1707, ʿĀlamgīr also fought a financially expensive war to subdue the Deccan, which drained the empire's once-wealthy treasuries.

ʿĀlamgīr's use of the Mughal army and his country's wealth to pursue a policy aimed at converting all of India to Islam was in stark contrast to the more pragmatic, self-interested liberal tolerance practiced by Akbar. India resisted the intolerant Mughals with determination, and the consequent warfare created dynastic insecurity, political instability, and a power vacuum that was energetically exploited by British adventurers seeking to expand the British Empire into the subcontinent.

ʿĀlamgīr was so obsessed with his persecution of the Hindu majority that he failed to grasp the significance of the European military threat and did not comprehend the need to build a strong Indian navy to match those of England and France. European nations controlled the oceans and this would be a fatal weakness for India.

This tactical error contributed to the loss of Indian independence, to its political takeover, and to its economic and financial degradation during European colonial rule. Unlike earlier invaders and conquerors, the British had no intention of assimilating into Indian civilization and saw India primarily as a source of wealth, raw materials, and markets for their homeland. This perception became more significant as Britain led the world in industrialization and India's wealth became vital to British economic survival, imperial expansion, and global wars with other European colonial powers. ʿĀlamgīr effectively destroyed loyalty to the Mughal Empire, and, after his death, weaker emperors could not recapture Akbar's earlier tradition of toleration. The Mughal Empire collapsed under a series of internal revolts, fratricidal conflicts, and determined pressure from the British East India Company, which was founded in 1600 as a trading agency and went on to acquire a vast empire in the subcontinent.

WEAPONS, UNIFORMS, AND ARMOR

The Battle of Talikota (1565), considered one of the most decisive battles in this period of South Indian history, demonstrated the importance of having well-armed, appropriately dressed troops in combat. The forces of the southern state of Vijayanagar commanded massive numbers but failed to equip their men with armor or even practical clothing. The Indian infantry, with their bamboo bows, short spears and swords, and foreign mercenaries wielding outdated artillery and muskets, were no match for the Deccan sultans who rode on Arabian horses, their armor-clad Iranian and Turanian soldiers carrying steel bows, metal javelins, and 16-foot lances. Additionally, the Muslims had mobile artillery carried on camels and elephants. Bābur's tactic of using supplies as a wall of protection for the front line of gunners was utilized once again. Historians estimate that the defeat of Vijayanagar resulted in the deaths of 16,000 troops. The great southern empire of Vijayanagar and its capital were destroyed by the invaders.

Indian warriors did not readily adopt the use of firearms during warfare. The Rajput ruler Maharaja Jaswant Singh (died 1678) would not use firearms in the Mughal War of Succession (1658-1659) against ʿĀlamgīr, because he felt such weaponry was not worthy of his heroic people.

During the Mughal era, the efficiency and range of firearms improved considerably. The rather crude primitive guns of Bābur's day were replaced by more accurate, sophisticated weapons, mounted on individual carriages pulled by bullocks. Indian artisans were able to copy the latest guns for their customers with a facility that would later amaze the Europeans. Shīr Shāh, recognizing the importance of the new technology, trained and used over 25,000 matchlock men in his army. Akbar took care to import and copy the latest weaponry from Europe, and eventually infantry were equipped with guns rather than spears. Indian commanders during the eighteenth century also used field glasses to survey the battlefield.

MILITARY ORGANIZATION

Although Bābur took over India with a brilliant combination of strategy, tactics, discipline, and innovative weaponry, his successors had to fight continuously to consolidate the empire he had founded. Constant warfare became a fixed feature of Mughal history, and there was accordingly a great emphasis on the organization of the military. Bābur's contribution to military organization lay in his introducing India to a new type of warfare that included significant reliance upon firearms. His emphasis on a highly mobile cavalry ensured victories in every major battle. His determination to protect his forces while enabling them to fight ensured that his archers and matchlock soldiers inflicted enormous casualties

from behind the defensive positions erected for them. His army, however, lived largely off the land in those early years of plunder and pillage.

Later emperors required a more constant and less controversial method of funding their military ventures. The six years of interlude in Mughal rule when Shīr Shāh governed India ironically provided the administrative foundations for the Mughal Empire. Now regarded as a genius in administration, Shīr Shāh divided the Indian Empire into districts for revenue purposes, established a sound currency, encouraged trade and commerce, constructed highways and ensured their safety with an elaborate police system, reformed the criminal justice system, and instituted direct recruitment of and regular payment to young men who joined the imperial army, thereby decreasing reliance on the cumbersome system of seeking military assistance from regional lords. Clearly, such reforms facilitated the recruitment, payment, and utilization of imperial armies to their maximum potential, a fact not lost on Akbar, who adopted many of these ideas.

Akbar is also credited with the *mansabdari* organization of the army, in which all military and civilian officials were classified on the basis of a salary scale and on their formal requirement to maintain and provide cavalry contingents for the emperor's wars. The recipients, called mansabdars, lived off the revenue of land grants called *jagirs*, which were not hereditary and were often transferred. Akbar encouraged Hindus to join both his armies and his government as bureaucrats and ministers. The emperor posted both a civilian governor and a military commander to each of the fifteen provinces of his empire. Military officials also participated in district government. With land grants, titles, and a variety of perquisites, Akbar created a multiethnic, multireligious nobility consisting of Central Asians, Iranians, Afghans, Rajputs, and Indian Muslims who were loyal to their emperor. Akbar was careful to ensure that no ethnic or religious group dominated his government.

During the early phase of this empire, the battle strategies of most Mughal engagements were quite similar. A strong, disciplined, well-equipped force handled the artillery. Archery from horseback created confusion and havoc in enemy ranks. The main

The Second Anglo-Sikh War (1848-1849) ended with British control of the Punjab and India's northwestern regions. Late Mughal intolerance of religious minorities, including the Hindus and Sikhs, deflected attention from the real threat: British colonialism.

army usually consisted of left, center, and right wings. The commander controlled the center. At the rear were commando-style reserve forces utilized to defend any wing that came under excessive pressure. Following initial resort to artillery, most of the engagement was by hand-to-hand combat.

The organizational methodology of the Mughals was borrowed from the Turks and was adapted to the prevailing situation of terrain, weather, and size of opposing forces in India. However, the sheer wealth of the Indian Empire and the complex diversity of its people eventually necessitated the creation of a vast military bureaucracy with noncombatants outnumbering soldiers ten to one. Although the Mughals had conquered India with compact, highly mobile, well-

equipped, and well-armed troops, as they settled in to govern India, each military action involved the transportation to the field of a growing retinue of baggage, suppliers, messengers, servants, dancing girls, clerks, spies, shopkeepers, money-lenders, and camp followers along with the soldiers who did the actual fighting.

A century after Bābur seized India, the Mughal army of combatants had grown sixfold. This enormous increase in size was partly a result of Akbar's policy. The growth in numbers of combatants required a corresponding increase in the number of servicing staff for the armed forces. However, what the Indian army gained in bureaucratic organization, it lost in maneuverability and the ability to strike suddenly at an unprepared opponent. So vast a crowd could not move more than a few miles per day.

Bābur used Asiatic Muslims and Persians to fire his large guns. Employment of European and Indo-European mercenaries to handle the gunnery work during battle became a significant feature of Mughal military tactics during Akbar's reign. No longer were Persians and Asiatic Muslims utilized as much. Hence the Mughals relied on outsiders in a critical aspect of their strategy. Although there were many European and Central Asian adventurers eager to work for the Mughal government, these mercenaries were detrimental to the welfare of the Mughal Empire, because they frequently changed sides, plotted constantly against their employers, and even deserted on the battlefield.

The spate of revolts fired by ethnic, religious, and other forms of oppression adversely affected state revenues by increasing the number of wars that had to be fought at the very moment when Indians were no longer contributing as generously to the Mughal treasury. As the empire declined, soldiers were not paid regularly and often revolted because they were hungry and their families were starving. The Mu-

BRITISH INDIA AT THE END OF THE NINETEENTH CENTURY

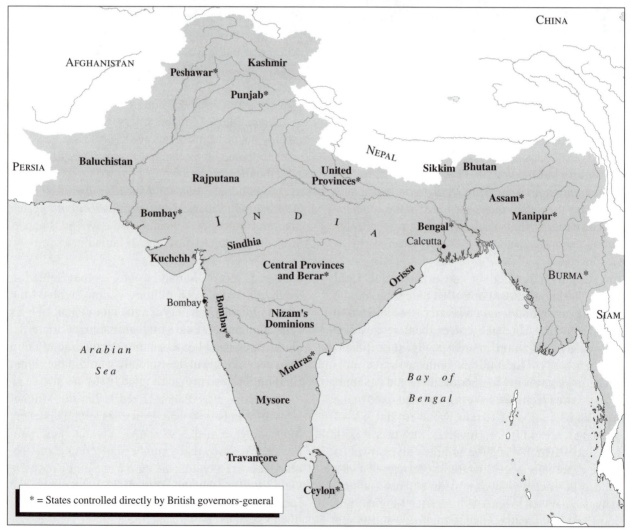

* = States controlled directly by British governors-general

ghals had retained the inherently feudal structure of their armed forces, which meant that the soldier's primary loyalty was to his own lord rather than exclusively to the emperor. This arrangement endangered cohesion in later conflicts and increased disorganization and a lack of discipline among the ranks. A number of scholars have suggested that the failures in the Deccan destroyed the reputation of the once-great Mughal army, the decline of which eventually led to the end of the Mughal Empire.

The Persian invasion of India by Nādir Shāh (1688-1747) in 1739 resulted in the Sack of Delhi, the slaughter of 30,000 Indians, and the transportation to Persia of vast booty. This was the low point of Mughal rule, and the dynasty finally ended in 1858 when the British, following the Indian revolt of 1857, imprisoned the nineteenth Mughal emperor Bahādur Shāh II (1775-1862) in Burma and shot and killed his two sons and grandson.

DOCTRINE, STRATEGY, AND TACTICS

Early Mughal leaders were committed to warfare as a means of conquering India and regarded the exercise of war as a normal activity of kings. Later Mughals did not match their doctrinal dedication to war with any great emphasis on ensuring that the army remained a tough, well-disciplined fighting force. The Mughal Dynasty, which had won a wealthy empire with a few thousand hardy followers, lost its military focus and dedication after succumbing to the luxury and opulence reaped from the resources of India.

Although most Mughal battles were fought on land and consisted of a variety of strategies and tactics suited to the particular terrain of the battlefield, the imperial fleet was occasionally utilized, as in the Battle of Daulambapur (1612). The Mughals won this battle with artillery and well-trained marksmen.

Warfare played a crucial role throughout the long history of Mughal India. It was the method by which the Mughals gained India and ironically it was their incompetence in warfare that cost them their empire. The Mughals were the product of a military tradition and utilized India's vast wealth to further their imperial ambitions to conquer the whole subcontinent. Their rule brought greatness to India politically and militarily and may have created a latent Indian consciousness among the hordes of Turkish, Afghani, Persian, Rajput, Sikh, Marāṭhā, and numerous other groups that had made India their homeland. In the end, the failure of Mughal rulers such as ʿĀlamgīr to appreciate the value of this cultural and religious pluralism doomed the Mughal Empire. The nascent national outlook fostered by Akbar would have to wait a few hundred years for Mahatma Gandhi (1869-1948) and Jawaharlal Nehru (1889-1964) to create a nation from the descendants of the Mughals and all the other peoples who came to India.

CONTEMPORARY SOURCES

The Bābur-nāmeh (early sixteenth century; *Memoirs of Bābur*, 1921-1922), the memoirs of the first Mughal emperor Bābur, are available in translation and provide a firsthand account of his perceptions. Additionally, numerous contemporaries of the Mughals wrote detailed accounts of the battles in both the Persian and Indian languages. Some of these records of military engagements have been translated or summarized into English and provide a vivid first-person view of warfare during this era.

BOOKS AND ARTICLES

Bidwell, S. *Swords for Hire*. London: John Murray, 1971.
Eraly, Abraham. *The Mughal World: India's Tainted Paradise*. London: Weidenfeld & Nicolson, 2007.
Gascoigne, B. *The Great Moghuls*. London: Jonathan Cape, 1971.

Gommans, Jos J. L. *Mughal Warfare: Indian Frontiers and Highroads to Empire, 1500-1700*. New York: Routledge, 2002.

Hallissey, R. C. *The Rajput Rebellion Against Aurangzeb*. Columbia: University of Missouri Press, 1977.

Kulkarni, G. T. *The Mughal-Maratha Relations: Twenty-five Fateful Years, 1682-1707*. Pune, India: Deccan College Post-Graduate Research Institute, 1983.

Nicolle, David. *Mughul India, 1504-1761*. Illustrated by Angus McBride. Botley, Oxford, England: Osprey, 1993.

Raj Kumar, ed. *Military System of the Mughals*. New Delhi, India: Ajay Verma for Commonwealth Publishers, 2004.

Reid, Stuart. *Armies of the East India Company, 1750-1850*. Illustrated by Gerry Embleton. Botley, Oxford, England: Osprey, 2009.

Sabahuddin, Abdul, and Rajshree Shukla. *The Mughal Strategy of War*. Delhi: Global Vision, 2003.

Sarkar, J. N. *The Art of War in Medieval India*. New Delhi, India: Munshiram Manoharlal, 1984.

———. *Military History of India*. Calcutta, India: M. C. Sarkar, 1960.

Wolpert, Stanley A. *A New History of India*. 6th ed. New York: Oxford University Press, 2000.

FILMS AND OTHER MEDIA

Warrior Empire: The Mughals. Documentary. History Channel, 2006.

R. K. L. Panjabi

AFRICAN WARFARE

Dates: c. 1500-1935

POLITICAL CONSIDERATIONS

From the sixteenth to the late nineteenth centuries, sub-Saharan Africa underwent drastic change, evolving from a continent of empires, kingdoms, states, and city-states to a continent under European domination. Although some sixteenth and seventeenth century African groups were living in stateless societies, most tended toward centralized states with significant military institutions. Powerful empires and kingdoms included those of Songhai, Oyo, Benin, and Bornu-Kanem in West Africa; Bunyoro, Buganda, and the Swahili city-states in East Africa; the kingdoms of the Kongo, Lunda, Luba, Changamire, and Mwanamutapa across Central Africa; the Funj Sultanate in the Sudan; and the Kingdom of Ethiopia.

Major causes of warfare were for the control of trade routes, including rivers and lakes, and of markets and agricultural and grazing land. Other causes were for the subjugation of peoples to serve as workers, soldiers, and taxpayers. There were hostilities along the west coast of Africa for control of international trade. Some wars were waged to consolidate power. Others, such as the Islamic jihads, or holy wars, in West Africa, involved religion, although most also had underlying economic or political considerations. In the nineteenth century African states warred against one another, but these confrontations soon were replaced by wars of resistance against European imperialism.

There is little consensus among historians concerning the relationship between the slave trade and warfare. During the 1500's Portugal expanded into Angola and Mozambique, disrupting existing states, seizing land and slaves, and initiating Africa into the Atlantic slave trade. Other European nations followed, and in the subsequent three hundred years, millions of Africans were enslaved or died in the Americas. An accurate assessment of the slave trade as a cause of war is difficult, because there are insufficient records. There were states, such as Dahomey, that went to war to obtain captives to sell to Europeans, but historians also have demonstrated regional and local causes for many African hostilities, such as the Yoruba civil wars of the nineteenth century. There is agreement on one point: In virtually all wars, regardless of their causes, captives were sold to Europeans as slaves, often in exchange for firearms.

In this environment of increased warfare, some kingdoms disappeared and others grew, as centralization emerged as a strategy for both expansion and defense. By the eighteenth century political and economic patterns had shifted. The savanna region of West Africa declined, as trade routes moved southward to forest states, such as Asante, Benin, and Dahomey, where commerce was linked with European merchants. In the nineteenth century there was a revival of state-building in the savanna region, as a series of jihads created new governments under Islamic law. The states of Futa Toro and Futa Jalon emerged in the west, and the Hausa city-states in northern Nigeria coalesced into the Sokoto caliphate. By mid-century the Tukulor Empire of 'Umar Tal (c. 1797-1864) and the Mandinka Empire of Samory Toure (c. 1835-1900) had also emerged as expansionist states with powerful military establishments. The Mossi states, significant since 1500, became more centralized and used their cavalry to resist Islamic expansion and avoid conquest. With the collapse of the Oyo Empire in the early 1800's, the Yoruba states underwent a series of civil wars that lasted almost to the end of the century. States, such as Ibadan, attempted to fill this power vacuum and adjust to changing economic conditions, as Europeans encroached along the coast.

In East Africa, Swahili economic and military

power grew as city-states were unified. Buganda remained a power in the lakes region. Ethiopia developed a more centralized monarchy and, with the aid of European firearms, began to expand and absorb its neighbors.

In Central Africa the Lunda, Kuba, Lozi, and Bemba kingdoms remained significant powers, as did the Ovimbundu kingdoms in Angola. The Luba kingdom in the central Congo became an expansionist state with a centralized administrative structure.

The Co-Operative Publishing Company

The British attempt to subjugate the Afrikaner settlers in southern Africa during the First Boer War, 1881.

There was violent competition for control of the long-distance trade routes that were used to transport slaves, ivory, copper, and salt. There was also competition for arable land. By the 1860's the decline of the Atlantic slave trade and the increased availability of firearms intensified the struggle for the remaining commerce.

Nineteenth century warfare was more intense in southern Africa than elsewhere on the continent. In the late 1700's population growth and a series of droughts had created a famine. Nguni chieftaincies began fighting over grazing land, initiating an era of great turmoil, the *mfecane*, or "crushing." Warfare and mass migration affected all of southern Africa, and small chieftaincies were integrated into larger entities. With its revolutionary military tactics, the Zulu kingdom emerged as the most significant African power in the region. Other groups, such as the Swazi and Sotho, consolidated chieftaincies into kingdoms for defensive purposes. Unable to resist the Zulu expansion, some Nguni groups fled northward. Mzilikazi (c. 1790-1868), an earlier ally of the Zulu, also fled north; engaging in Zulu-style warfare, he established the highly centralized Ndebele kingdom in present-day Zimbabwe. Wars continued through the nineteenth century, as the English and the Afrikaners, descendants of Dutch settlers, entered into a three-way struggle with the African states for control of South Africa, resulting in some of Africa's most famous battles: Blood River (1838), Isandhlwana (1879), and Ulundi (1879).

Throughout the nineteenth century, African kingdoms experienced a complex interplay of local, regional, and international forces. Economically, there was a dramatic shift

P. F. Collier and Son

British troops advance on the Zulus at the Tugela River in 1900.

away from the Atlantic slave trade toward the so-called legitimate trade, with a corresponding rearrangement of economic patterns and power balances. Politically, the process of centralization continued unabated in most parts of the continent. The integration of groups into larger, more centralized political entities provoked conflict and warfare, but in some cases promoted wider security and stability. The ending of the overseas slave trade, however, corresponded with the beginning of European imperialism. The development of African states and their subsequent increase in military prowess did not prevent the onslaught of European imperialism, but it did enable many African states to fight intense wars of resistance, such as the heroic efforts of the Mandinka and Dahomey kingdoms against France. The Zulu, Asante, and Benin kingdoms raised similar resistance to English imperialism. Ultimately futile, this resistance inspired subsequent generations, and in some instances, provided the basis for resistance to colonialism. Ethiopia escaped conquest

when its emperor Menelik II (1844-1913) defeated the Italian army at Adowa (1896). However, it later succumbed to the firepower and poison gas of Benito Mussolini's army in the second Italo-Ethiopian War (1935).

MILITARY ACHIEVEMENT

Between 1500 and 1900 the evolution of African warfare corresponded with the increasing centralization of African kingdoms, states, and empires. Centralization increased control of trade and resources that were used for further expansion. Conquest augmented the human and material resources for state formation, empire building, and consolidation of power. By the nineteenth century such consolidation had led to the economic integration of various regions of Africa.

West African states north of the rain forest were able to purchase horses for cavalry. Some smaller

F. R. Niglutsch

In 1896, the Mahdist state of ʿAbdullāh et Taʿāʾisha proclaimed a jihad and used extensive cavalry units to force Egypt out of the Sudan.

horses were bred locally, but the larger horses used by heavy cavalry had to be imported from North Africa. In many cases horses were obtained through trade of slaves. In the savanna regions cavalry became the most important aspect of their militaries, such as that of the Sokoto caliphate, which could put a cavalry of more than 25,000 on the battlefield. Neighboring Bornu-Kanem could field a cavalry of 7,000. In the central Sudan the Funj sultanate used cavalry to defeat the Christian kingdom of Alwa and maintain two centuries of control prior to Egypt's invasion (1820-1821). Later in the century the Mahdist state of ʿAbdullāh et Taʿāʾisha (1846-1899) proclaimed a jihad and used extensive cavalry units to force Egypt out of the Sudan. Cavalry dominated the military in the expansive region stretching from

western Senegal to the Sudan. Only the expanded use of firearms in the second half of the nineteenth century reduced its effectiveness.

The Islamic jihads of the nineteenth century transformed much of the savanna region of West Africa, not only by creating religious unity but also by politically integrating previously fragmented groups. Islam was spread widely throughout many of the region's rural populations. The implementation of Islamic law was accompanied by a significant spread of literacy, and in some cases, greater economic security. Trade linkages also were established with the wider Islamic world.

In both East and Central Africa consolidation of state power allowed for the exploitation of a wide range of natural and human resources. Local trade networks were linked to long-distance routes, bringing products from remote regions into a wider market arena connected to both the Atlantic and Indian Oceans. Along the East African coast, trade was dominated by the Swahili, who conducted armed caravans into the interior, developed long-distance commerce, and established Kiswahili as the lingua franca, or common language, of eastern Africa.

Although the consolidation of territory and governance and the expansion of economic relations were important accomplishments, two more overarching achievements of the African states and their militaries were realized in the years from 1500 to 1900. The first was the prevention of foreign occupation of African territory from 1500 to the 1870's. By the latter date only 10 percent of African territory, mostly in South Africa and Algeria, was under direct European control. Although diseases and other factors contributed to this state of affairs, the strength of African kingdoms and empires played a major role. Even during the era of the devastating slave trade, Africans were able to control the terms of trade and limit Europeans to small fortifications on the west coast.

The other important achievement was the powerful resistance of many African states to nineteenth century European imperialism. For many reasons, such as superior European military technology and logistical support, the use of African troops against each other, and the inability of African states to form alliances, the resistance was doomed to fail. Nevertheless, the era of resistance not only gave African people a sense of pride but also fostered the development of political and ethnic identities. Dahomey resisted French armies for four years. Although the massive, heavily armed British-Egyptian force defeated the Mahdist state at the Battle of Omdurman (1898), the foundations had been laid for Sudanese nationalism. In southern Africa political and economic turmoil also created broad-based ethnicities. Despite defeat by the English and exploitation by the Afrikaners, the concept of Zulu nationhood had been established; today, the Zulu are South Africa's largest ethnic group and a political force of considerable importance. The founder of the Sotho kingdom, Moshoeshoe (c. 1786-1870), used remarkable diplomacy and military acumen to develop armed mountain fortifications that survived Zulu and Afrikaner depredations; his kingdom emerged as the independent nation of Lesotho in 1966. With their defensive positions, diplomacy, and Zulu-style military organization, the Swazi consolidated chieftaincies into a kingdom that maintained its territorial integrity and emerged as the independent nation of Swaziland in 1968. These are but a few examples. The memory of the resistance survived in oral tradition and continues to play a large role in contemporary African historical writing. It provided a historical and psychological frame of reference in the nationalist struggles for freedom and established the foundation for future nationhood.

WEAPONS, UNIFORMS, AND ARMOR

In the period from 1500 to 1900, African weapons underwent slow, evolutionary development, until modern firearms were introduced in the mid-nineteenth century. In many African societies, weapons were part of a complex cultural system and were imbued with social, cultural, and religious, as well as military, significance. For example, amulets for spiritual protection were worn in leather pouches around soldiers' necks, were tied to uniforms, or were attached to weapons. Islamic soldiers wore small pouches with pieces of paper inscribed with verses from the Qur'ān.

African weapons types varied according to the geographical regions of their use. In the forest areas of West and Central Africa and the open veldt of southern Africa, infantries used throwing spears, multipointed throwing knives, and less common projectile weapons such as darts, slings, and throwing clubs. Infantry assault units carried shields and shock weapons: swords, clubs, axes, daggers, and spears.

Infantry units often were organized according to the weapons they carried. Typical examples were archer units, such as those of the Mossi and Luba. Archers provided long-range firepower, especially in open areas. Bows ranged in size from 2.5 to 5 feet in length, with a 40- to 50-pound draw and a general range of 75 yards. Arrows had iron-headed shafts that were sometimes dipped in poison.

Swords were among the most common weapons used by both infantry and cavalry units. These weapons had two-edged straight blades or curved blades. Most were manufactured locally, but the blades themselves were often imported. Swords used in the forest regions tended to be shorter in length. All cavalrymen carried a short sword for use after spears had been thrown or lost.

Infantries and cavalries made extensive use of the spear, which was the most commonly used weapon. Spears were differentiated by their functions: Lances were used for thrusting, whereas javelins were used for throwing. Six-foot lances were carried by heavy cavalry and used in shock assaults. Javelins were used by the more mobile light cavalry, with each rider carrying a supply of the weapons. The most sig-

nificant revolution in such weaponry occurred in South Africa, where the Zulu converted their long throwing spears into shorter, stabbing weapons; protected by heavy shields they advanced rapidly and engaged the enemy at close quarters.

Firearms were introduced into West Africa in the sixteenth century by North African Muslims and by Europeans on the coast. Early weapons were mostly flintlock muzzle-loaders, which became part of the trade cycle of guns, gold, and slaves. During the 1700's musket use spread among coastal and forest states, such as Dahomey, Benin, and Asante. Firearms helped these states dominate their neighbors. In the rest of Africa, firearms spread slowly until the 1850's when modern weapons were introduced.

The overall impact of the musket on African armies was limited. Guns and gunpowder of the eighteenth and early nineteenth centuries were poor and unreliable. Muskets were insufficiently maintained and were difficult to reload quickly without considerable training. They were inaccurate because they were shot from the hip. Coordinated firepower was rarely used. There is no evidence that the use of muskets increased the death rate, or that they were always decisive against enemies without firearms. In 1726 an Oyo cavalry without firearms defeated a Dahomian force armed with muskets. Despite these limitations, the intense sound of firearms created psychological terror in the enemy. In eastern and southern Africa and Ethiopia, firearms had even less impact on warfare than they had elsewhere. In Central Africa muskets were most often used by slave-raiding parties.

After 1850 modern firearms were made available in Africa, where obsolete European guns were sold as more effective weapons were produced on the European continent. Breechloaders such as the single-

Library of Congress

Uniforms of nineteenth century French soldiers in Algeria: infantry (left) and cavalry.

shot Snider were used in West Africa. Eventually, repeating rifles, such as the Winchester, were also used. Other firearms sold to African states included the Snider-Enfield, Martini-Henry, Chassepot, Mauser, French Gras, Lee-Enfield, and French Lebel models. Although Europeans sold these weapons by the thousands, they were reluctant to sell machine guns and artillery to African states, with the exception of Ethiopia. Some artillery was captured from European armies, but its availability and usage was limited. Overall, Africans failed to take advantage of modern firearms. Their courage and high morale allowed them to resist the European onslaught, but they could not prevail.

Throughout Africa soldiers wore distinctive uniforms for identification, protection, and mobility. The most elaborate uniforms belonged to the standing armies; the least formal were worn by the "citizens' armies." Soldiers of the Mandinka Empire wore conical straw hats, rust-colored trousers, and leather sandals; officers were identified by red turbans. Ethiopian soldiers wore trousers and knee-length tunics with bands tied around the waist. Cavalry troops wore long Islamic-style robes for lightweight protection from the sun. Throughout West Africa military jackets were common, as were long or short trousers with apronlike coverings. Troops in hot, dry regions usually wore sandals; in forest areas and in southern Africa, soldiers usually went barefoot.

Many African soldiers wore hats or helmets for protection and identification. Protective devices ranged from metal helmets in Benin and Ethiopia to strips of rolled cloth tied in turbans around the head. Other headgear was made of tightly woven palm fiber or heavily quilted cotton.

The shield served as the basic armor for the infantry and some light cavalry. Shields were made of animal hide, wood, or tightly woven grass. They varied in size and shape and sometimes reflected the social status of the user. Ethiopians placed high value on elaborately decorated shields. In southern Africa shield-making was a specialized craft. Oval-shaped Zulu shields, made from thick cattle hide, were 5 feet long. When infantry advanced in close order, shields were raised; when hitting the enemy line on the run, shields produced a shock effect on the enemy's de-

fenses. As the use of firearms spread, the use of shields declined.

Units of heavy cavalry, such as those of the Sudan, wore armor made of quilted cotton that was padded with fiber. Armor covered both man and horse. In some areas imported chain mail also was used. Not all heavy cavalry wore armor, as it was expensive, cumbersome, and reserved for the most elite units. Other armor included metal breastplates, padded jackets, and leather aprons worn around the waist.

MILITARY ORGANIZATION

Given the diversity of African civilizations, military organization took a wide variety of forms. Historian Bruce Vandervort describes four types of organization used by African states and empires. All were hierarchical systems. The first type included armies in which recruits were summoned locally or regionally to serve as discrete units within the military structure. In Ethiopia, for example, regions supplied military units that were under almost feudalistic local control; after 1855 the centralized monarchy commanded a more national army, with each unit representing its individual region. The armies of Dahomey, Benin, and Asante were similar in form. Some Islamic states, such as the Tukulor Empire, also had regional armies under central command; soldiers were under royal control but served under officers from their own regions.

In the second type of military organization, exemplified by that of the Zulu, individual soldiers from various regions were integrated into preexisting units. While under arms they lived, trained, and fought together, although they represented different regions or groups. Zulu kings Dingiswayo (c. 1770-c. 1818) and Shaka (c. 1787-1828) changed the military's traditional structure, transforming the Zulu age groups into military units. Age groups were composed of young men who underwent a common circumcision ceremony and initiation rite to enter adulthood. With growing military threats, the Zulu leadership did not want its young men to be far from home during this initiation. Instead, young unmarried men were placed in regiments with others of their age range. They were barracked in military settlements near royal households and became part of the Zulu standing army under direct control of the king. Additional youth were easily integrated into the units. They bonded by living and training together into a fighting force. The officers, or *indunas*, who replaced traditional territorial chiefs, were appointed by the king. The Ndebele instituted a similar system, in which soldiers served not under officers from their own region but under commanders who were part of a rigid hierarchy.

A third type of military organization was the "citizens' army," in which all physically able males were expected to bear arms during times of war. These levies commonly served as infantry under local officers and usually were required to bring their own weapons and provisions. Using this model, Mai Idris Alooma (r. 1571-1583) of Bornu-Kanem was able to put more than 100,000 soldiers in the field. This general call-up system was common throughout West Africa.

The fourth type of military organization was the standing army of professional soldiers. Earlier African armies had been loosely composed of units called up for specific purposes; by the nineteenth century there was a parallel development in the growth of centralized governments and the expansion of standing armies. Early examples were Bornu's standing unit of musketeers and Oyo's professional war chiefs. Later examples included Ethiopia and Dahomey and the Zulu, Tukulor, and Mandinka empires.

The roles of slaves in African armies varied. Because of the potential risk in arming slaves, many states used them only for transport. Most typically, slaves were used as soldiers in infantry units in the Islamic states of West Africa's savanna regions. The states of Bornu-Kanem and Sokoto made regular use of slave-soldiers, and Samory Toure integrated enslaved riflemen into Mandinka infantry units. In the nineteenth century some Yoruba states also used slaves as soldiers.

Military structure also varied in terms of balance between different types of units. In West Africa's open savanna regions the main force was cavalry, usually supported by infantry. The cavalry was an elite corps, sometimes forming a military aristocracy. The supply of horses and tack was shared by the king and the territorial leadership. Some cavalries were divided into light and heavy units, based on the type of horse and the military objective. Cavalry units tended to have more autonomy with territorial leadership, whereas infantries were more hierarchically structured under a centralized command.

In the forest areas of West Africa, armies relied primarily on infantry, because horses could not survive the sleeping sickness carried by the tsetse fly that was prevalent throughout the region. Infantries were divided into units of men wielding different weapons such as spears, swords, or bows and arrows. Some infantrymen carried muskets, but in the nineteenth century more modern firearms appeared. The use of firearms by infantry was most prevalent among the forest states.

In addition to land forces, some African states maintained fleets of war canoes and plank boats. They were used for transport and assault on rivers, lakes, and lagoons. Most were small and maneuverable, but larger canoes were 100 feet long, with a seating capacity of 100 soldiers. The Songhai made such extensive use of their Niger River canoe fleet that they appointed a naval commander. The Zambezi, Gambia, Senegal, and Congo Rivers were also sites of canoe warfare. The Buganda kingdom, known for its canoe fleet, was considered a naval power on Lake Victoria.

DOCTRINE, STRATEGY, AND TACTICS

The strategies of African militaries grew out of governmental policies and their long-term objectives. The causes of warfare and the development of strategic planning were interrelated. Strategic objectives included control of long-distance trade routes; access to cattle, horses, slaves, and food; creation of defensible borders; and ideological factors such as the establishment of Islamic theocracies. The achievement of strategic goals was based on the assessment of many variables, such as strength of the opposition, conditions at home, available weapons and manpower, perceptions of success, and the collection of intelligence.

Tactics included the conduct of the war, types of assaults or maneuvers, coordination of cavalry and infantry units, and use of weapons in the battle plan. Tactics varied widely from region to region. This was evident in the use of infantry. In late nineteenth century Ethiopia, for example, riflemen formed the core of the infantry. They were assault forces trained to maximize the effectiveness of their firepower, but they were also skilled in the techniques of ambush and skirmish. Infantry in the forest regions, however, relied primarily on the frontal assault supported by flanking movements. The armies of Asante and Dahomey had a standard marching formation: Advancing scouts preceded a main body with left and right wings, followed by a rear guard. Such infantries balanced units of archers, spearmen, swordsmen, and those armed with knives and clubs.

The integration of firearms into African infantries was a slow and uneven process. Firearms predomi-

nated only in Ethiopia, the Mandinka and Tukulor Empires, and the forest states of West Africa. Although muskets were available in the forest states after the sixteenth century, their increasing use generally did not revolutionize warfare. Even in the second half of the nineteenth century, when more effective breechloaders were introduced, there was little change in either military organization or tactics. Most states failed to develop a coordinated use of firearms.

Cavalry units dominated the armies in the western, central, and eastern Sudanic regions. Mounted units were composed of both light and heavy cavalry. Heavy cavalry carrying lances and swords were used as shock troops in direct assaults. Light cavalry rode small, fast horses that were used in flanking movements or surprise attacks; these horsemen carried lightweight spears and small javelins. Although most states had infantry units that exceeded cavalry in numbers, foot soldiers generally retained a support-

Associated Publishers, Inc.

Nineteenth century East African slavers march their captives to the coast. In virtually all African wars of the sixteenth through nineteenth centuries, captives were sold to Europeans as slaves, often in exchange for firearms.

ive role. Heavy cavalry were sometimes accompanied by archers; light cavalry often had footmen to carry extra javelins. Although 'Uthman dan Fodio (1754-1817) eschewed heavy cavalry in favor of light cavalry in his conquest of the Hausa states and establishment of the Sokoto caliphate, his cavalry tactics underwent few changes. Even the introduction of firearms had little impact on the Sudanic ideal of the warrior-horseman.

There were two significant exceptions to the traditional Sudanic cavalry and its associated military tactics. Nineteenth century Tukulor and Mandinka were Islamic states that incorporated large regions and diverse peoples. With the introduction of firearms, these states restructured their militaries. In establishing and expanding the Tukulor state, 'Umar Tal reduced the cavalry and relied more on infantry. He amassed large numbers of muskets and rifles. By mid-century he had assembled an infantry that coordinated firepower and tactical maneuvers with the shock element of the cavalry charge.

Samory Toure, often called the Bonaparte of the Sudan, was another military innovator. In building the Mandinka Empire he was renowned for both his diplomatic skills and his war tactics. He developed one of the only modernized armies in sub-Saharan Africa. He also reduced the cavalry and substituted large, well-armed, mobile infantry units. He acquired European artillery that supported infantry assaults. His army consisted of central units in the capital, with additional units in the outlying districts. Each district had a force of 5,000 that was organized around 300 highly trained professional soldiers called *sofas*. The standing army consisted of approximately 10 percent of all able-bodied men, but during wartime a conscription system called up 50 percent of the adult males. Samory adapted his strategy and tactics to those of his opponents. Against African enemies he used set-piece battles and direct assaults; against the French, with their artillery and rapid-fire weapons, he relied on guerrilla warfare. His infantry could employ guerrilla tactics because they traveled light, lived off the land, and attacked French supply lines. Each soldier had a firearm, often a repeating rifle, a saber, and a dagger. Samory combined firepower with rapid movement of troops. After fifteen years of resistance, French military power overwhelmed Samory's empire, but his memory remains a lasting legacy in the region.

Another example of outstanding tactical use of infantry was Shaka's Zulu army. Shaka had modified the long spear into a short-handled weapon used for stabbing

A political cartoon by John Tenniel warns the British against underestimating the indigenous peoples it was attempting to subjugate in southern Africa.

rather than throwing. The infantry advanced, sometimes running, in a tight line with shields raised to ward off enemy spears. With their stabbing spears they were able to engage the enemy at close quarters. To take full advantage of this new weapon, they developed an assault formation known as the "cow-horns." This consisted of three equal-sized regiments, with a fourth held in reserve, formed into a crescent shape. The center regiment was used as a shock force; the other units that flanked to the left and right extended forward. The center regiment initiated a furious assault on the opponent, while the "horns" enveloped the enemy from the sides and rear. Once in close quarters, the soldiers used their stabbing spears in hand-to-hand combat. Some Zulu shields had hooks on top, which were used to pull down an enemy's shield and expose part of his body. Zulu soldiers underwent extensive training and maintained a high level of fitness. Their highly mobile regiments sometimes traveled 50 miles in a day. Zulu tactics produced decisive victories and changed warfare throughout southern Africa, as Nguni groups carried the new developments northward into Mozambique, Zambia, Zimbabwe, and Malawi.

African military doctrine was influenced by the interrelationship of religion and warfare. Written documentation, oral tradition, and material culture indicate that virtually all armies engaged in pre- and postbattle ceremonies for purification, protection, and victory. Some kings and military leaders used divination to choose the best time for battle. In some societies the religious pantheon included a god of war who was usually associated with iron, such as Gu in Dahomey or Ogun in Yoruba territory. Invocation of the supernatural was considered essential in warfare.

CONTEMPORARY SOURCES

Primary sources for the study of African military history include African, Arabic, and European writings; African oral tradition; and local histories written by African authors. For the savanna regions of West Africa, there are many sources written in Arabic by African Muslims and North Africans. Two seventeenth century works are essential: *Tarikh al-Fattash* by Mahmud Kati (1468-1593) and *Tarikh as-Sudan* by Abd al-Rahman as-Sadi (1596-1656). Ibn Fartua (fl. 1582), the imam of Mai Idris Alooma, wrote an account of his experience. The "Kano Chronicle" is a native history of the Hausa people. There is a large body of contemporary Arabic documentation on nineteenth century Islamic states written by Fulani scholars. There is a similar collection of writing in Kiswahili on the history of the East African coast, among the most valuable being the "Kilwa Chronicle" and the "History of Pate."

Beginning in the 1500's European merchants made regular visits to the African coasts. Many left descriptions of wars, trade, and diplomacy. There are accounts by William Snelgrave, William Bosman, John Norris, Archibald Dalzel, Jean Barbot, O. Dapper, and many others. A plethora of Portuguese records exist, but these accounts, written before the mid-nineteenth century, deal almost exclusively with African coastal regions and contain little reliable information on events in the interior.

Many late-eighteenth and nineteenth century European sources were written by explorers, merchants, and missionaries. Some of the most important authors include Richard Burton, Hugh Clapperton, Henry Fynn, Heinrich Barth, Henry Stanley, John Duncan, Samuel Baker, René Caillié, J. S. Gallieni, John Speke, Mungo Park, and James Bruce. These works are valuable as sources but must be used carefully, as they contain ethnocentric observations and stereotypes, exaggerations, and misleading information. Nevertheless, they remain important sources for the study of African armies.

There are two other types of African sources. The first, oral tradition, is an integral part of African cultures and a rich source for military history. Given the connection between warfare and royal power, oral tradition must also be evaluated with caution, because it often reflects the viewpoint of the ruling elite. The second source includes local histories written by African authors. These are collections of oral traditions supplemented by the experiences of the authors and the memories of the local inhabitants. Examples are works by Nigerian authors Samuel Johnson and Jacob Egharevba. Historians should examine works of art, music, song, and dance for further insights into the role of the military. These sources become valuable when they are integrated and corroborated. Only then will one gain an understanding of warfare and society as it is reflected in the "new military history."

BOOKS AND ARTICLES

Akinjogbin, Adeagbo, ed. *War and Peace in Yorubaland, 1793-1893*. Ibadan, Nigeria: Heinemann, 1998.

Crowder, Michael, ed. *West African Resistance: The Military Response to Colonial Occupation*. New York: African, 1971.

Falola, Toyin, and Robin Law, eds. *Warfare and Diplomacy in Precolonial Nigeria*. Madison: African Studies Program, University of Wisconsin, 1992.

Inikori, J. E. "The Import of Firearms into West Africa, 1750-1807: A Quantitative Analysis." In *Warfare and Empires: Contact and Conflict Between European and Non-European Military and Maritime Forces and Cultures*, edited by Douglas M. Peers. Brookfield, Vt.: Ashgate/Variorum, 1997.

Lamphear, John. "Sub-Saharan African Warfare." In *War in the Modern World Since 1815*, edited by Jeremy Black. New York: Routledge, 2003.

Law, Robin. "Warfare on the West African Slave Coast, 1650-1850." In *War in the Tribal Zone: Expanding States and Indigenous Warfare*, edited by R. Brian Ferguson and Neil L. Whitehead. Santa Fe, N.Mex.: School of American Research Press, 1992.

Peers, C. J. *Warrior Peoples of East Africa, 1840-1900*. Illustrated by Raffaele Ruggeri. Botley, Oxford, England: Osprey, 2005.

Smaldone, Joseph P. *Warfare in the Sokoto Caliphate: Historical and Sociological Perspectives*. 1977. Reprint. New York: Cambridge University Press, 2008.

Smith, Robert S. *Warfare and Diplomacy in Precolonial West Africa*. 2d ed. Madison: University of Wisconsin Press, 1989.

Spring, Christopher. *African Arms and Armor*. Washington, D.C.: Smithsonian Institution Press, 1993.

Thornton, John K. *Warfare in Atlantic Africa, 1500-1800*. London: UCL Press, 1999.

_____. "Warfare, Slave Trading, and European Influence: Atlantic Africa, 1450-1800." In *War in the Early Modern World*, edited by Jeremy Black. Boulder, Colo.: Westview Press, 1999.

Vandervort, Bruce. *Wars of Imperial Conquest in Africa, 1830-1914*. Bloomington: Indiana University Press, 1998.

FILMS AND OTHER MEDIA

The Battle of Algiers. Feature film. Magna, 1966.
The British Empire in Color. Documentary. History Channel, 2008.
Shaka Zulu. Television miniseries. Harmony Gold, 1986.
Warriors: Zulu Siege. Documentary. History Channel, 2009.

Thomas C. Maroukis and Cassandra Lee Tellier

Iran

Dates: c. 1500-1922

Political Considerations

The names "Iran" and "Persia" are virtually synonymous. Iran is the name by which Iranians have always known their country. The name Persia, derived from the ancient Greek Persis, was used by outsiders until the twentieth century, when Reza Shah Pahlavi (1878-1944), the shah of Iran from 1925 to 1941, insisted that "Iran" should become the international usage.

Before the development of mechanized transport, the Iranian plateau was a singularly forbidding land in which to campaign. Its vast extent and prevailing aridity, its alternating landscape of desert and mountain, its virtual absence of navigable rivers, and its lack of roads and wheeled transport meant that it was best suited to the traditional warfare of pastoral nomadic tribesmen.

From 1500 to 1722 Iran was ruled by the Safavid Dynasty, one of the "gunpowder-empires" of the early modern period of Islamic history. The Safavids united the entire Iranian plateau and, at times, the adjacent regions of southern Iraq, Transcaucasia, and western Afghanistan under the rule of a single monarch—known as a *shah* (king) or *shahanshah* (king of kings)—and imposed a form of Shiism upon most of their subjects. Safavid rule eventually collapsed under assault from Ghilzay Afghans of the Qandahār region, thereby inducing czarist Russia and the Ottoman Empire to seize extensive areas of northern and western Iran.

Territorial integrity was restored by Nādir Shāh Afshari (1688-1747), a tribal leader of great military capacity, who expelled the invaders and launched successful campaigns far beyond the frontier of modern Iran, from Baghdad to Bukhara, and from the Caucasus to Delhi. Nādir Shāh was assassinated by rival tribesmen in 1747, and the Iranian plateau then reverted to tribal particularism and intertribal conflict. The eastern provinces of the former Safavid Empire (Khorāsān, Sistān, Herāt, and Qandahār), now passed into the hands of the Afghan Durrāni Dynasty established by Aḥmad Shāh Durrāni (c. 1722-1773) at the death of Nādir Shāh, while in the west internecine warfare prevailed. By the close of the eighteenth century, however, much of the plateau had been brought under the firm control of the head of the Qājār tribe, Aghā Muḥammād Khān (1742-1797). A cruel eunuch who had been castrated at the age of six by one of Nādir Shāh's nephews, Aghā Muḥammad Khān Qājār proved to be a brilliant and rejuvenating leader of tribal cavalry who was able to establish the frontiers that Iran continues to possess.

Aghā Muḥammad Khān Qājār bequeathed his conquests to a nephew whose descendants, the Qājār Dynasty, ruled Iran until 1925. Under this dynasty, Iran experienced humiliating military defeats at the hands of Russia (1804-1813 and 1826-1828) and Great Britain (1856-1857), a successful war with the Ottoman Empire (1821-1823), numerous internal uprisings, and an unsuccessful expedition against the Yomut Turkomans of the Gurgan region in 1889. The two wars with Russia led to the loss of substantial territory in Transcaucasia beyond the Aras River.

Throughout the nineteenth century, the government of Iran faced intense diplomatic pressure and threats to its national integrity from both Russia and Great Britain and confronted the challenges of Westernization and modernization. In 1906 popular protests against the ineptitude and corruption of the shah's government and its subservience to foreign interests led to the promulgation of a constitution and the establishment of a rather dubious parliamentary regime. However, the Anglo-Russian accord of 1907 divided Iran into spheres of influence between the two great powers, an arrangement that the government of Iran was powerless to prevent. During World

Reza Shah Pahlavi, who as a colonel modernized the Iranian army and in 1925 overthrew the Qajar Dynasty that had ruled Iran since the end of the eighteenth century.

background of these events that there occurred in 1921 the coup d'état that eventually brought to power the Cossack colonel Reza Khan, who from 1922 vigorously undertook the modernization of the Iranian army. In 1925 Reza Khan swept aside the moribund Qājār Dynasty and proclaimed himself Reza Shah Pahlavi. The Pahlavi Dynasty finally expired in the Islamic Revolution of 1979.

MILITARY ACHIEVEMENTS

The military history of the period from 1500 to 1922 falls into four broadly overlapping phases. First, under the rule of the Safavids (1500-1722) and of Nādir Shāh (r. 1736-1747), Iran was a formidable military power, confronting neighboring Ottomans, Mughals, and Central Asian Uzbeks. Iran relied mainly upon its superb tribal cavalry but increasingly adopted Ottoman and European weaponry and military organization. At first, the Iranians were no match against Ottoman artillery and well-disciplined infantry, the famous janissaries, as shown by their crushing defeat at Çaldiran (1514), but they were quick to learn, and early in the reign of Shah Ṭahmāsp I (1514-1576) the sources refer to the existence of gunners (*tupchiyan*) and musketeers (*tufangchiyan*). However, for most of the sixteenth century, the Safavids continued to rely upon their hardy and mobile cavalry, as in Ṭahmāsp's great victory over the Uzbeks at Jam (1528).

The dynamic ʿAbbās I the Great (1571-1629), who reigned from 1588 to 1629, introduced major innovations. His objectives were to enhance the power of the throne, to break the independence of the turbulent tribal leaders, and to win back the lands lost to

War I (1914-1918), despite its official neutrality, Iran found itself invaded by the forces of the belligerents and was later denied a voice at the Paris peacemaking in 1919. With Russia temporarily preoccupied with the Bolshevik Revolution (1917-1921), Great Britain attempted, without success, to impose upon the Iranian government a treaty that would have reduced Iran to a virtual British protectorate. It was against the

the Ottomans by previous shahs. His reforms, primarily the establishment of regular units personally loyal to and paid by the shah, some of whom were equipped with handguns and field artillery, soon produced the sought-for results. In 1598 Herāt was recaptured from the Uzbeks, and in 1605 the shah won a great personal victory over the Ottomans at Sufiyan, near Tabrīz. During protracted campaigning thereafter, the shah reoccupied Erivan and Nakhshivan, and in 1624 captured Baghdad, from which the Safavids had been expelled in 1534. In 1625, he took the great frontier-fortress of Qandahār from the Mughals, and in 1626 he showed outstanding generalship in foiling a massive Ottoman attempt to reconquer Baghdad. Both Baghdad and Qandahār were lost in 1638, but 'Abbās I's great-grandson, 'Abbās II (1633-1666), regained Qandahār in 1648 and beat back three Mughal attempts to retake it. Thereafter, however, inept rulers, flaccid government, and declining revenues led inevitably to the debacle of 1722, when Iran was conquered by Afghan raiders. The spectacular conquests of Nādir Shāh, who devoted himself to reestablishing Iran's former frontiers, made him the terror of neighboring lands. Nādir Shāh raised Iranian military prestige to unprecedented heights achieved at a dreadful cost of lives and revenues.

In the second phase of Iran's military history, from 1747 to 1797, Iran, exhausted by the loss of manpower and resources that was the price paid for Nādir Shāh's glory, seemed to have turned in upon itself. The country was wholly preoccupied with intertribal conflicts, cause and effect of the general economic decline, and paid little attention to developments beyond its frontiers. The forces involved were much smaller than those of the recent past, were probably less well equipped, and maintained themselves by plunder. The genius of Aghā Muḥammad Khān Qājār in large measure reconstituted the Iranian monarchy as it had been under the Safavids.

During the third phase, which spanned the greater part of the nineteenth century, Iran was forced to confront the reality of the overwhelming military superiority of Europe, specifically, of Russia and Great Britain. Threatened by Russia in the northwest, 'Abbās Mīrzā (1789-1833), the heir-apparent of the

second Qājār ruler, Fatḥ 'Alī Shah (1771-1834), who was also governor of Azerbaijan, became an enthusiastic reformer and variously sought the help of British and French advisers and equipment to defend his exposed province. The British and French presence was dependent upon the exigencies of those countries' relations with Russia, but 'Abbās Mīrzā also employed up to 88 Russian deserters and any other European mercenaries who came his way. During the First Russo-Iranian War (1804-1813), he possessed a force of 6,000 infantry trained by European officers and known as the Nizam-i Jadid, or the New Army. The infantry's numbers had grown to 8,000 by 1817 and to 12,000 by 1831. In addition, there was a corps of 1,200 gunners trained by European artillery officers and a single cavalry regiment, although where the cavalry were concerned, 'Abbās Mīrzā retained his faith in the esprit and mobility of traditional tribal levies. To meet the needs of these forces, he established, under European supervision, an arsenal with a cannon foundry and powder mill in Tabrīz and renovated the forts of Tabrīz, Ardabīl, and Khvoy.

Opinions varied considerably regarding the fighting capacity of the Nizam-i Jadid troops, and it was said that 'Abbās Mīrzā's rival for the throne, Muḥammad 'Ali Mīrzā, governor of Kermānshāh, had greater success against the Russians with his Kurdish tribal levies, armed and deployed as in the time of Aghā Muḥammad Khān. 'Abbās Mīrzā encountered opposition not only from military conservatives but also from the Shiite clergy, who opposed innovations of all kinds as likely to lead to the introduction of further infidel ways. Enthusiasm for further military reforms diminished after the Second Russo-Iranian War (1825-1828) and confirmed the permanent Russian occupation of the Transcaucasian provinces. The poor showing of Iranian troops during the Anglo-Iranian War (1856-1857), which had been designed to force the Iranian withdrawal from Herāt, only reinforced Iranian disillusion. It was quite apparent to the new ruler, Nāṣir al-Dīn Shāh (1831-1896), that his country lacked the ability to withstand foreign aggression. Merely employing more foreign advisers, a stream of which made their way to Tehran from Britain, France, Italy, and Austria, was not enough; a much more radical solution was called for.

Although the shah was not unintelligent, he found himself, in this, as in other aspects of the administration, pulled back and forth between reformers and reactionaries.

Nāṣir al-Dīn Shāh's first prime minister, Mīrzā Taqī Khān Amīr Kabīr (c. 1798-1852), vigorously initiated reforms, which came to nothing when, having provoked powerful enemies, the shah dismissed him in 1851 and later had him executed. In 1857 a ministry of war was created, and the reforming minister planned changes for the army between 1871 and 1881 that his capricious master would not allow him to implement.

The fourth phase, however, emerged after Nāṣir al-Dīn Shāh's European tour of 1878, during which he developed great enthusiasm for what he saw of the czar's Cossack regiments. As a result, on his return to Tehran, an Iranian Cossack Brigade was formed, with Russian officers, equipment, and drill. The Cossack Brigade possessed a professionalism that no previous unit of the Iranian army had possessed and by the close of the century was the most effective force in the country. Ironically, when a reactionary ruler, Muhammad Ali Shah (1907-1909) used it in an attempt to overthrow the newly granted constitution, it was a rebel army of Bakhtiyari tribesmen who marched on Tehran and saved the constitution. The success of the Cossack Brigade led to the creation of a Swedish-officered gendarmerie in 1910. During World War I, the British, concerned with German agents and recalcitrant tribes in eastern and southern Iran, formed the South Persian Rifles. Service in all these units exposed an ever-increasing number of Iranian officers, noncommissioned officers, and other ranks to European military discipline, drill, weaponry, and tactics. They would constitute the first generation of troops in Reza Shah's new model army.

WEAPONS, UNIFORMS, AND ARMOR

The tribal levies that constituted the bulk of Safavid forces carried the weaponry traditionally associated with fighting men on the Iranian plateau: a compound horn bow with a quiverful of arrows, a long spear that could be used like a lance or thrown like a javelin, a scimitar (*shamshir*), a mace (*piyazi*), and assorted daggers. There was no uniformity of equipment or dress: A tribesman brought to the campaign whatever he happened to possess, supplemented by what could be looted on the battlefield. For the elite, armor consisting of four iron plates covering chest and back and with a hole for the arms on the two side-pieces was an innovation of the Safavid period. It was known as *chahar aina* and worn over chain mail. In addition, vambraces, or armor for the forearms, known as *bazuband*, were worn, and the rider carried a round steel shield. The cone-shaped helmet (*khud*) was topped by a steel spike, with one or more tubes in front to hold a spray of heron or peacock feathers. Usually, chain mail was attached to the sides and back of the helmet to give some additional protection to the neck and shoulders. Iran had a reputation for manufacturing fine steel (*fulad*) and was especially famous for its swordsmiths (*shamshirgar*), with their finely watered and damascened blades. In the seventeenth century, the town of Qom was known for its manufacture of swords, but in the eighteenth century Khorāsān took its place. During the nineteenth century the manufacture of armor and swords died out in Iran, although it had formerly been among the most acclaimed mechanical arts.

Over the course of the Safavid period, an increasing number of soldiers carried harquebuses, carbines, or muskets, known collectively by the name *tufang*. To traditional mounted archers, such weapons seemed cumbersome and ineffective, and as did the Egyptian Mamlūks, Iranian cavalry long regarded firearms as unmannerly. At first, these weapons, along with more traditional arms and armor, were imported from abroad. During the reign of Muhammad Khudabanda (r. 1578-1588), a Russian envoy from Czar Ivan the Terrible (1530-1584) brought to Qazvin, then the Safavid capital, five hundred firearms and one hundred pieces of artillery.

The earliest cannons came from Russia or Western Europe. The Ottomans naturally would not allow artillery bound for Iran to pass through their territory, although the Iranians must occasionally have captured Ottoman field pieces. As early as 1539 Safavid sources mention the office of the *tupchi-bashi*, the officer in command of the artillery, who would later have overall responsibility for both the gunners and musketeers. Iranians would eventually manufacture their own cannon and handguns, and until 1922 the gunsmith (*tufangsaz*) was a respected and ubiquitous figure in the bazaars of larger towns such as Shīrāz, Kermānshāh, or Mashhad. However, the gunsmith's trade would end with Reza Shah's prohibition on the private possession of firearms.

The military revival under Nādir Shāh seems to have owed nothing to improved weaponry or technological innovation. Nādir Shāh was a superb com-mander in the field. His victories and the enormous booty he derived from them provided the revenues with which to maintain increasingly larger armies. These were composed of not only Iranians but also Caucasians, Uzbeks, Afghans, and Baluchis. After Nādir Shāh's death in 1747, no further changes oc-curred for the remainder of the eighteenth century. The revival of Iran under Aghā Muḥammād Khān Qājār, who reigned from 1779 to 1797, was based upon his skillful generalship, his astute balancing of tribal rivalries, and his ability to bring out the best in the fighting qualities of his followers.

ṢAFAVID IRAN IN THE SEVENTEENTH CENTURY

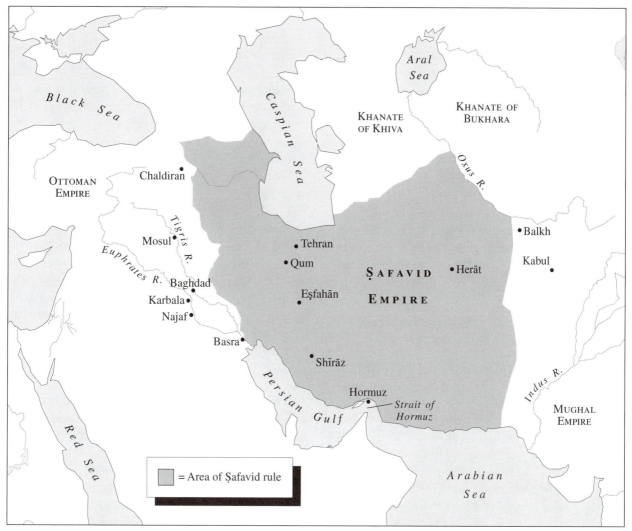

The most significant development during the nineteenth century was the employment of European military advisers, who introduced the Iranian military to European uniforms, drill, discipline, and tactics. These advisers were attached to the forces of not only the shah but also his sons, who were themselves provincial governors and who sought to improve the quality of their provincial levies in anticipation of the inevitable fratricidal struggle for the throne, which would occur at the shah's demise. Thus, Muḥammad ʿAlī Mīrzā, governor of Kermānshāh, enlisted French officers to train his Kurdish levies. Such officers, Napoleonic veterans unemployed since Waterloo, were en route for the Punjab to seek service with the Sikhs.

European units generally trained with weapons of European origin, typically redundant muzzle-loaders known as the Brown Bess. European observers commented unfavorably on the condition in which Iranian soldiers maintained their firearms, which were inadequately cleaned and were often allowed to rust. In the early decades of the nineteenth century, most cannons were of British or French origin, but later in the century there were imported Austrian muzzle-loaders, including 7-centimeter mountain guns for mule batteries. By the end of the century, the best artillery was of Russian manufacture. Again, European observers visiting the Tehran arsenal saw artillery pieces deteriorating from neglect, many with gun carriages that had been allowed to rot. Unquestionably, during the quarter-century prior to the 1921 coup, the best-armed unit of the Iranian army was the Cossack Brigade.

MILITARY ORGANIZATION

Throughout the Safavid period and down to the time of Aghā Muḥammad Khān Qājār, there was a minimum of military organization. In wartime, the shah summoned his vassal chieftains, who then, if they were so inclined, came to his summons with their followers, who thereafter continued to serve under their own hereditary leaders, who fought alongside those of the shah, or abandoned him, if self-interest required. For this reason ʿAbbās I the Great was determined to rely as little as possible upon the turbulent

and often insubordinate tribal levies, even while recognizing their advantages: speed, mobility, hardiness, and agility. With these benefits in mind, he formed two new units: the *shahisevan*, "those loyal to the shah," recruited from tribesmen willing to sublimate their tribal affinities in fanatic dedication to the service of the shah, and the *gullar* or *ghulams*, slave-soldiers similar to the Mamlūks of earlier Muslim armies in the Middle East. Iranian slave-soldier troops consisted of Christian slaves or prisoners of war, typically Armenians, Circassians, and Georgians. They became converts to Islam and were recruited to join what was, in effect, a kind of Safavid Praetorian Guard, properly known as the *ghulaman-i khassa-yi sharifa*, "Slaves of the Noble Household." These troops were paid for by revenues from the crownlands and were provided by the government with firearms. Their commander (*gullar-agasi*) enjoyed the prestige of being one of the greatest officers of state. Unfortunately, the later Safavids allowed this standing army to deteriorate to the point that little of it remained by the eighteenth century. The Qājārs had to begin anew, relying mainly upon foreign advisers in an international situation far less favorable than that enjoyed by their Safavid predecessors.

The military weakness of the Qājārs, and the pressure to initiate army reform that built up after 1921, is easily demonstrated by a glance at the Iranian army as it was in 1891. The total strength of 43,889 consisted of 12,427 irregular cavalry amassed through tribal levies; 2,493 European-style semiregular cavalry; 25,000 European-style regular infantry; 1,800 artillery troops, with a nominal 164 guns; 80 camel artillery, useless ceremonial relics of Safavid times; 169 Austrian Corps under the command of Austrian officers; and 2,000 militia.

Only a few of these units were significant. The irregular cavalry were recruited from the tribes that had formerly played so large a part in Iranian military exploits, among which the Kurds, Timuris, and Bakhtiyaris stood out prominently. Tribal units were commanded by tribal chieftains, who held the rank of general (*sartip*) or colonel (*sarhang*). The subordinate officers consisted of a "commander of one hundred" (*yuzbashi*), a "commander of fifty" (*panjbashi*), and a lieutenant (*naib*). On active service, officers received allowances but no pay. The common soldier (*sarbaz*) and his noncommissioned officers received a graduated scale of pay and rations: for the sarbaz, 6.5 pounds of barley for himself and 13 pounds of straw for his horse per diem. Both officers and men provided their own cavalry mounts. The latter were not more than 14.5 hands high but struck observers as possessing great strength, speed, stamina, and remarkable powers of endurance. Riders were extremely agile and could perform extraordinary feats of marksmanship at full gallop. One English officer, Sir Henry Creswicke Rawlinson (1810-1895), who trained tribal levies in southwestern Iran during the early nineteenth century, described his men as "the very *beau ideal* of military material, the men being athletic, strong, hardy and active." European conventional wisdom, however, held that the native officer corps were of deplorable quality and that Iranian soldiers would perform well only when commanded by European officers. The irregular cavalry were organized into approximately ninety squadrons of between fifty and seven hundred men drawn from all parts of the country, the majority coming from Khorāsān (24 squadrons), Azerbaijan (23), Tehran (6), Gīlān and Māzandarān (5), and Kermānshāh (5).

The semi-irregular cavalry were equipped, drilled, and trained in European style and consisted of three regiments, two cantoned in Tehran and one in Eşfahān. The two regiments in Tehran formed the Cossack Brigade, with officers and weapons provided by Russia, although both officers and men supplied their own horses. The government issued rifles, swords, saddles, and bridles. The government also provided barracks (*sarbazkhana*), accommodations facing an open square or courtyard, with stabling on the ground-floor, resembling a traditional caravansary. The regiment in Eşfahān was equipped and trained in imitation of Prussian uhlan light cavalry, a whim of the powerful governor Zil as-Sultan, a son of Nāşir al-Dīn Shāh. Taken as a whole, the semi-irregular cavalry, and especially the Cossack Brigade, were regarded as the most effective part of the army, thanks to the zeal of their Russian officers.

The regular infantry were conscripted province by province, under the command of the local governor. So grim was the life of the *sarbaz* held to be that re-

cruitment was by virtual impressment, local communities banding together to designate the unfortunate recruit or sometimes paying a sum of money to anyone who would volunteer freely. Service was for life, unless a soldier could raise enough money to buy a discharge from his colonel, and the age range in the regiments ran from adolescent boys to toothless graybeards. However, Christians, Jews, Zoroastrians, and cultivators on crown-lands were exempt from military service. A regiment ideally consisted of 10 companies of 100, both officers and men, making a total of 1,000 men per regiment, but the full complement of men was rarely achieved, and most companies were fixed at around 70. The pay and allowances of the common soldiers were pitiable and were further subject to various perquisites and bribes demanded by the officers. Uniforms, provided by the government, consisted of a tunic of coarse blue serge, trousers of the same material, a brown leather belt, and a black lambskin hat known as a shako, with a brass badge. Outside Tehran, however, most soldiers lacked a full uniform.

DOCTRINE, STRATEGY, AND TACTICS

There is no evidence of strategic thinking on the part of Iranian military leaders during the period from 1500 to 1922. Traditional tactics consisted of the cavalry charge en masse, performed with such great verve and dash that even better-disciplined opponents wavered and retreated. However, if the initial impetus of the massed charge failed to achieve its aim, Iranian cavalry quickly became demoralized and withdrew. At other times they practiced with great effect the ambuscade and the harrying of stragglers and supplies on the line of march. Over the vast expanse of the Iranian landscape, they were skilled at pursuing a "scorched-earth" policy against invading troops operating far from their bases, who were thereby deprived of the food and fodder that was normally obtained by living off the land. Both Ottomans and Russians found themselves hamstrung by such tactics, which were particularly skillfully employed by Aghā Muḥammād Khān Qājār.

During the nineteenth century Iranian officers, especially those stationed in Azerbaijan, acquired the rudiments of strategic thinking and battlefield tactics from their European military advisers, but for most of the century they received no formal military education. At the beginning of Nāṣir al-Dīn Shāh's reign, his first reforming prime minister, Mīrzā Taqī Khān Amīr Kabīr, founded a European-type academy, the Dar al-Funun, which included some classes in military instruction designed specifically for young officers. Later in the reign, the shah's favorite son and commander in chief, Naib as-Saltana, established a military academy. However, as late as 1891, the shrewd Lord George Curzon (1859-1925) could write of the officer corps: "Ignorant of military science, destitute of esprit de corps, selected and promoted with no reference to aptitude, they are an incubus under which no military system could do otherwise than languish." At the time Curzon wrote, however, a change was becoming apparent. Iranian officers were benefiting from Russian instruction in the Cossack Brigade and later from the Swedish officers in charge of the gendarmerie. A number would see service with the British-controlled South Persian Rifles during World War I. These would form a nucleus of experienced officers who would become the agents of Reza Khan's post-1922 reforms. It is surely no surprise that the architect of the modern Iranian army should have emerged from the ranks of the Cossack Brigade.

CONTEMPORARY SOURCES

Accounts of warfare under the Safavids and Qājārs are to be found in contemporary Persian-language chronicles. Two excellent examples are Iskandar Beg Munshi's (1560-1633) *Tarikh-i ʿAlamara-yi ʿAbaci* (c. 1571-1629; *The History of Shah ʿAbbās the Great*, 1978) and Hasan-e Fasai's (born c. 1821), *Farsnamah-ī Nasiri* (1895-1896; *History of Persia Under Qājār Rule*, 1972). Safavid military organization is described in an anonymous Safavid administrative manual, *Tadhkirat al-muluk* (c. 1137-1725; *A Manual of Safavid Administration*, 1943). Chapters 21, 23, and 26 of Sir John Malcolm's (1769-1833) two-volume *The History of Persia from the Most Early Period to the Present Time* (1815) provide material on the early Qājār army by an eyewitness. In addition to the official reports of foreign embassies in Tehran, European travelers in nineteenth century Iran frequently wrote down their subjective but insightful impressions of military matters. The most informative is that of Lord George Curzon, *Persia and the Persian Question* (1892). Brigadier-General Sir Percy Sykes (1867-1945), who commanded the South Persian Rifles during World War I, provides a personal account of wartime Iran in chapters 85 through 89 of *A History of Persia* (1915).

BOOKS AND ARTICLES

Atkin, M. *Russia and Iran, 1780-1828*. Minneapolis: University of Minnesota Press, 1980.

Axworthy, Michael. *The Sword of Persia: Nader Shah, from Tribal Warrior to Conquering Tyrant*. New York: I. B. Tauris, 2006.

Blow, David. *Shah Abbas: The Ruthless King Who Became an Iranian Legend*. New York: I. B. Tauris, 2009.

Chalabian, Antranig. "The Scorched-Earth Strategy That Shah Abbas I Used Against the Turks in Armenia." *Military History* 16, no. 6 (February, 2000): 22.

Cronin, Stephanie. *The Army and the Creation of the Pahlavi State, 1910-1926*. London: I. B. Tauris, 1997.

English, Barbara. *The War for a Persian Lady*. Boston: Houghton Mifflin, 1971.

Finkel, Caroline. "Battle of Çaldiran." In *The Reader's Companion to Military History*, edited by Robert Cowley and Geoffrey Parker. Boston: Houghton Mifflin, 1996.

Haneda, Masashi. "The Evolution of the Safavid Royal Guard." *Iranian Studies* 21 (1989): 57-86.

Kazemzadeh, Firuz. "The Origin and Early Development of the Persian Cossack Brigade." *American Slavic and East European Review* 15 (1956): 351-363.

Lockhart, Laurence. "The Persian Army in the Safavid Period." *Der Islam* 24 (1959): 89-98.

Matthee, Ruda. "Unwalled Cities and Restless Nomads: Firearms and Artillery in Safavid Iran." In *Safavid Persia: The History and Politics of an Islamic Society*, edited by Charles Melville. London: I. B. Tauris, 1996.

Savory, Roger. "The Sherley Myth." *Iran* 5 (1967): 73.

Ward, Steven R. *Immortal: A Military History of Iran and Its Armed Forces.* Washington, D.C.: Georgetown University Press, 2009.

FILMS AND OTHER MEDIA

Iran: The Forgotten Glory. Documentary. Mystic Films International, 2009.

The Persians. Documentary. History Channel, 2006.

Gavin R. G. Hambly

JAPAN
MODERN
Dates: c. 1600-1930

POLITICAL CONSIDERATIONS

In the years from 1600 to 1930, Japan underwent three major shifts in political leadership: The Tokugawa period was followed by the era of the Meiji Restoration, and then, shortly before 1930, the nation saw the triumph of military ultranationalism over constitutional government. The Tokugawa era, or "period of Great Peace," marked a turning point for Japan after centuries of civil war that had divided the archipelago as families struggled against one another for power around landed estates called *shoen*. After the military failures of two "pretend" shoguns (Oda Nobunaga and Toyotomi Hideyoshi), Japan was finally dominated by a powerful political daimyo lord named Tokugawa Ieyasu. The shogun used the alternate attendance system in order to "capture" rival daimyos by forcing each to maintain two residences, one at home and one in the new capital city of Edo (later called Tokyo). He also created an elaborate bureaucratic structure under a "tent" government called the *bakufu*, which helped to make policy and personnel decisions, and supervised the some 260 daimyos who still presided over feudal Japan. Daimyos were divided into inside (*fudai*) and outside (*tozama*), with the former receiving political favors for their loyalty to the government in Edo.

The emperor and the samurai remained two major feudal entities of the Tokugawa peace, but their power waned in the ensuing century as the daimyos jockeyed for influence in the new government, and landed estates required less protection from samurai armies than in previous periods. Challenges to the rule of the shogun were minimal as violence was restricted to small skirmishes in the streets, peasant rebellions, and the enforcement of maritime restrictions and the ban on Christianity imposed in the 1630's and 1640's. The spread of Christianity and the Portuguese Christian missionaries who arrived in Japan with Western and Chinese merchants were seen as threats to the unity and stability of the Tokugawa state. With some very particular exceptions (such as the Dutch), foreigners were banned from the interior parts of the Japanese archipelago, and Japanese Christians were persecuted. These actions, along with famines and other difficulties, later led to a number of rebellions and uprisings, the largest and most famous of which was the Shimabara Rebellion in 1637-1638.

The next major period of change for Japan did not arrive until the mid-nineteenth century, when the appearance of gunboat diplomacy forced the so-called opening of Japan by Western powers, underscoring the weaknesses of the shogunate

TURNING POINTS

1603	Tokugawa Ieyasu becomes shogun, marking the beginning of early modern Japanese history.
1867	The last Tokugawa shogun surrenders power to imperial forces, paving the way for the Meiji Restoration and Japan's reentry into world politics and culture.
1904	Japan attacks the Russian-controlled port of Lüshun, traditionally known as Port Arthur, beginning the Russo-Japanese War, fought between Russia and Japan for control over Korea and Manchuria.
1905	The Japanese navy wins a stunning victory at the Battle of Tsushima, devastating the Russian fleets and forcing Russia to surrender Korea and other territory to Japan.

and leading to its collapse. With the negotiation of treaties, first after the arrival of Commodore Matthew C. Perry's U.S. black ships in 1853, Japan soon began to mimic the Western claim that imperialism was necessary to civilize "savages" by acquainting them with the spiritual and material benefits of modern technology and mechanisms of social control. This premise was actually discussed in Japanese political circles during the 1790's, including in the influential essay "A Secret Plan for Government," by Honda Toshiaki, which laid out Japan's four major imperative needs: to learn the effective use of gunpowder, to develop metallurgy, to increase trade, and to colonize nearby islands and more distant lands.

The shogunate's inability to deal with the influence of Westerners, coupled with rising domestic distress, led to the end of the regime, and in 1867, backed by a military coup, the emperor proclaimed the Meiji Restoration. With the return of power to the emperor for the first time in centuries, the young Meiji emperor set in motion rapid industrialization based on the Western model. Importing new military technology, industry, legal norms, and constitutional thought (along with a parliamentary system based on the German model) as well as new ideas in science, forms of dress, and food, the Meiji abolished status distinctions and centralized government.

The Japanese artist Hiroshige portrayed a U.S. warship in Tokyo Harbor—probably part of Commodore Perry's flotilla.

By constructing a new body politic around the notion of *kokutai*, which translates roughly as "national essence," Japan remade itself into a society focused on achieving the ultimate goal of becoming a major global player on the international scene. Though the actual end of the shogunate and the establishment of the imperial government following a Western model were handled entirely peacefully, through political petitions and the like, the years surrounding these events saw a revolution that was not entirely bloodless. The ensuing Satsuma Rebellion (1877), led by samurai Saigō Takamori, was the final attempt to

JAPAN, C. 1615

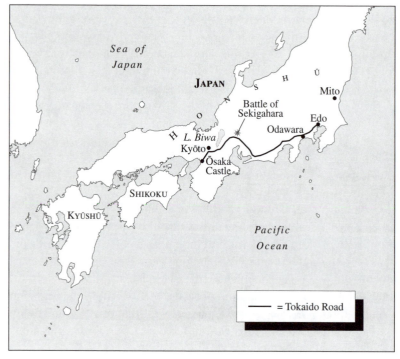

Sea of Japan

JAPAN

Battle of Sekigahara

Mito

Odawara

Edo

L. Biwa

Kyōto

Ōsaka Castle

SHIKOKU

KYŪSHŪ

Pacific Ocean

= Tokaido Road

Allied nation, with the acquisition of a colony on the Shandong Peninsula in China and membership in the League of Nations. However, Japan was continually left out of major discussions at the Paris Peace Conference of 1919.

By the 1920's, Japan became embroiled in the global Great Depression as overproduction and currency failures ravaged the world's economies. With threats from Russia and China in Manchuria, ultranationalist sentiments inside the Japanese military and outside the government accused the political parties of weakening Japan in their pursuit of self-interest. With a new emperor, Hirohito, on the throne by the late 1920's, critical voices within Japan appeared to be as dangerous to Japan's economic and national security as threats from abroad.

drag Japan back to an earlier period of feudal control, but it was quickly crushed.

By the end of the nineteenth century, Japan was transformed from a decentralized, largely agrarian land into a centralized, industrialized nation. The Japanese built trains, adopted Western-style facial hair and modes of dress, and allowed powerful business cartels called *zaibatsus* to control the flow of capital. They also came to understand that national defense would require expansion abroad. The Meiji government undertook two major campaigns in 1895 against the fledgling Qing government of China in the Sino-Japanese War and defeated the Russian fleet—becoming the first Asian country to defeat a Western power in combat—during the Russo-Japanese War (1904-1905). By entangling Japan in world affairs, the government attempted to balance contradictory impulses toward democracy and toward totalitarianism; at the same time, Japan was continually treated as a racially inferior power by most European countries. The results of World War I (1914-1918) saw Japan reap the benefits of its newfound status as an

MILITARY ACHIEVEMENT

Around 1600, the Japanese were focused first on defeating enemies militarily within their borders; by the nineteenth century, their focus was on challenging international rivals in several theaters in the Pacific Rim. The Tokugawa period was marked at first by a civil war that led to a struggle between members of the daimyo class as they fought to become the first unifier of Japan under the shogunate. After conquering his competitors at the Battle of Osaka Castle in 1615, Tokugawa Ieyasu inaugurated a long period of peace during which few outside invaders or internal struggles plagued the Japanese mainland.

It was really not until the nineteenth century, after the "opening" of Japan by the United States in 1853, that the Japanese began to be engaged in military conquest outside their national borders. After a treaty negotiation with the Chinese in 1871 that granted extraterritoriality, Japan expanded its influence by engaging in a five-month war with neighboring Taiwan over a dispute in the Ryukyu Islands that led to Japan's attaining control over the complete archipelago. The expanding empire next turned toward neighboring Korea, which was believed to be the "dagger" pointing at the heart of China. Diplomatic missions to Korea finally led to a complete breakdown in Japan's relationship with China in 1894, resulting in the Sino-Japanese War. During the nine months of this conflict, Japanese troops expelled the Chinese army from Korea, defeated the north Chinese navy, captured Port Arthur and the Liaodong Peninsula in south Manchuria, and seized a port on the Shandong Peninsula. The ensuing Treaty of Shimonoseki, signed in April of 1895, gave Japan Taiwan and the Pescadores, Port Arthur and the Liaodong Peninsula, an indemnity, and a promise by China to respect Korea's autonomy.

These military and diplomatic achievements did not last, however, as Russia, backed by other Western powers, forced Japan to cede all of its mainland acquisitions back to Russia. By 1900, Japan had begun the drive toward greater power status by signing an alliance with Britain and going to war against Russia in 1904-1905. Russia's holdings threatened Japanese interests in Korea, and when Russia refused to make concessions, Japan launched a surprise attack on Port Arthur. The Treaty of Portsmouth (1905), negotiated by the United States and President Theodore Roosevelt, gave Japan expanded power after the humiliating defeat of the Russian army and navy, which had sailed halfway around the world to engage the Japanese. Japan envisioned an empire that would bring prestige and power and would be a liberating force for what later ultranationalist Kita Ikki deemed a world of "Asia for Asians."

During World War I, Japan expanded both economically and diplomatically. By protecting sea lanes in the Pacific and mounting an offensive against the German-held Shandong Peninsula, Japan acquired a mandate over German-held islands in the region. Japan tried to impose its will on China through the Twenty-one Demands by the end of 1918, and many concessions were offered to Japan at the Versailles peace conference.

North Wind Picture Archives via AP Images

Japanese warships take Port Arthur during the bloodiest and most controversial battle of the Sino-Japanese War of 1894-1895.

Following World War I, Japan spent most of the 1920's expanding its military influence while at the same time playing an active role in the development of the world's economy. By 1930, the Japanese military had begun a full-scale plan to take over all of Manchuria, eventually setting up the Greater East Asia Co-Prosperity Sphere on the eve of World War II.

WEAPONS, UNIFORMS, AND ARMOR

Japanese military dress and weaponry in the pre-1868 period were highly personalized and unique for each of the individuals who served the shogun after 1614. Samurai were the knights of medieval Japan, and even during the Tokugawa period until the Satsuma Rebellion in the late nineteenth century, the samurai enjoyed a special place in Japanese society and military culture. The samurai's armor was strong

and elaborate in its ornamentation. Individual iron scales laced together were eventually replaced in the early seventeenth century by solid-plate technology. Dressing a samurai was an intricate ritual built into the code of bushidō; the process involved twenty-two steps. The signature piece of equipment was the ornate helmet, which consisted of an iron mask surrounded by decoration made of wood and papier-mâché. Proud samurai wore helmets of fantastic shapes that included buffalo horns, seashells, and catfish tails. In many cases, samurai armor was passed down from generation to generation.

Japanese weaponry of this period began with the *katana*, or samurai sword, forged to perfection and razor sharp within a resilient body. The katana was mainly a two-handed sword, and a samurai would normally carry a pair into combat, one short and the other long. The samurai also carried a *yumi*, or bow, made from a deciduous wood faced with bamboo,

F. R. Niglutsch

Young samurai rebels in training.

and an extremely lethal spear called a *yari*, which was an excellent weapon to use on horseback for stabbing opponents. As the samurai became less and less useful during the Great Peace, and their services dulled by lack of activity, masterless samurai, called *rōnin*, wandered from town to town looking for opportunity. Eventually, by the time of the Meiji Restoration, the emperor forbade the samurai to wear their weapons, thus altering a time-honored tradition that dated back to medieval Japan.

The era of reorganization under the Meiji brought a host of major changes to Japanese military tactics along with changes in armor and weaponry. With the adoption of the European style of raising citizen armies through conscription, traditional armor became obsolete. Adopting rifled muskets, cannon, and other forms of technology such as the machine gun, Japan set itself on the path toward military dominance in the Pacific. A new navy made up of steel ships purchased from Britain also altered the course of Japan's ability to dominate the region by allowing the nation to deploy troops with superior force.

After 1868, Japanese troops began wearing navy-blue uniforms similar to those worn by the French army and American troops during the U.S. Civil War era. This changed to a lighter shade of green after 1911, and the army added a summer khaki uniform based on the British style as well. Because Japanese army and navy officers were not issued uniforms by their branches of the service until the 1930's, commanding officers wore a wide variety of interpretations of military dress. High-ranking officials often wore sashes, called *senninbari*, that were fire red in color; these were believed to bring good luck and courage and to make the wearers immune to bullets. The Japanese military continued to incorporate elements of traditional warrior dress from the Tokugawa era until well after 1930.

MILITARY ORGANIZATION

The organization of Japanese armies from 1600 to 1930 evolved from an elite fighting corps of samurai armies commanded by individual daimyos to a modern imperial army after 1868 based on the European style of warfare. The size of a daimyo's army was determined by the assessed wealth of the daimyo's rice fields; thus the largest property owners could muster the largest armies. Troops were known as samurai—those who serve—a reflection of the hierarchical system of obligation, at the apex of which was the shogun. The *ashigaru* were low-level infantrymen drawn from the samurai ranks. Traditionally, the samurai were the only troops mounted on horseback. After the last great battle at Osaka Castle in 1615, samurai as a military class were given land and titles under Tokugawa rule.

The feudal system of retainers and landowners lasted until the Meiji Restoration of 1868, when the military was reorganized into the Japanese Imperial Army. Copying the Western style of military organization based on the German model of promotion through the ranks, the Japanese system was directly related to the political reorganization of the government. Army and general staffs reported directly to the emperor Meiji himself, and the military had virtually no oversight by the Japanese parliament, known as the Diet. The emperor surrounded himself with a small group of military advisers and had veto power over military spending. This system, based on the Prussian system designed after German unification in 1871, allowed an elite class of military advisers to expand their power throughout Japan's constitutional monarchy. Huge amounts of money were spent on military organization both before and after the Sino-Japanese War of 1894-1895, much of the funding going to the foremost general of the period, Yamagata Aritomo. Yamagata cast a long shadow over the Japanese military during the late nineteenth and early twentieth centuries. Along the way, Japan produced an efficient military schooling system, a well-organized active and reserve force, a professional officer corps that thought in terms of regional threat, and well-trained soldiers armed with the most advanced weapons of the day.

DOCTRINE, STRATEGY, AND TACTICS

In the period from 1600 to 1930, Japanese military strategy can be divided into two major eras. The first, from 1600 to 1868, mainly centered on the samurai warrior class, the members of which were controlled by the daimyos, or local territorial lords. These armies used cavalry tactics and close formations on horseback led by the samurai; daimyos led these divisions. Dismounted cavalry would be used in siege situations, along with ashigaru (foot soldiers). Castle towns provided defense to local townspeople and to daimyos' families; thus, during the struggle to inaugurate what became known as the Tokugawa era, Tokugawa Ieyasu needed to overrun Osaka Castle using artillery followed by a main assault using ground troops. Practicing ancient bushidō discipline and tactical approaches to combat, samurai armies after the Battle of Osaka Castle concentrated mainly on land development as their feudal responsibilities centered primarily on peace.

From 1868 to 1930, the Japanese military moved in a new direction in its uses of strategy and tactics. After the Meiji Restoration, Japanese modernizers traveled the globe and brought back to Japan the latest in military weapons and doctrine. The Choshu Five, a small coterie of Japanese, laid the groundwork for what has been called "technological plagiarism on a truly heroic scale." The Japanese government brought both French and German military advisers to Japan to set up military training posts and academies for the development of an officer corps. With the development and implementation of the Japanese Imperial Army, which served the newly restored emperor, Japan abolished all territorial land rights and installed mandatory military service in order to build a citizen army on the nineteenth century

Library of Congress

A woodcut depicting a rōnin (masterless samurai).

model. Using the German model of infantry tactics, the Japanese army grew quickly in both skill and maneuverability as it adopted new weapons such as the repeating rifle.

CONTEMPORARY SOURCES

All historical understanding of the Japanese samurai should begin with the seventeenth century text *Hagakure* (*Hagakure: The Book of the Samurai*, 1979). This history, written by a samurai who converted to Buddhism, chronicles the ethical path that all warriors must follow. The story of the 1615 Battle of Osaka Castle was reported by the first Japanese newspaper shortly after the battle, which also printed an image depicting the burning of the castle and the victory of Tokugawa Ieyasu. Probably the most significant document in regard to the Japanese military from the pre-Meiji era is political writer Honda Toshiaki's 1798 work, "A Secret Plan for Government," in which Honda lays out a program aimed at Japan's fulfilling four major needs: to learn the effective use of gunpowder, to develop metallurgy, to increase trade, and to colonize nearby islands and more distant lands. This program set the stage for Japan to embrace Western-style imperialism after 1868.

No understanding of the impact of the Meiji era would be complete without a reading from either Itō Hirobumi or Fukuzawa Yukichi. The former's influence on the Meiji Constitution (1889) is evident, and reading that document provides a glimpse into the source of the Japanese military's power. Fukuzawa urged Japan to embrace Westernization and to take a hard-line approach to foreign affairs. His work led to the publishing of an 1885 editorial titled "Escape from Asia," which became an anthem for the Japanese "national essence" after 1900. Finally, Lieutenant Tadayoshi Sakurai, a low-grade officer, wrote a fascinating account of a military engagement during the Russo-Japanese War titled "Attack upon Port Arthur, 1905"; this work gives the reader some understanding of the honor culture in the Japanese military during the imperial era.

BOOKS AND ARTICLES

Beasely, W. G. *Japanese Imperialism, 1894-1945*. New York: Oxford University Press, 1991.

Drea, Edward. *Japan's Imperial Army: Its Rise and Fall, 1853-1945*. Lawrence: University Press of Kansas, 2009.

Ebrey, Patricia Buckley, Anne Walthall, and James B. Palais. *East Asia: A Cultural, Social, and Political History*. Boston: Houghton Mifflin, 2006.

Gordon, Andrew. *A Modern History of Japan: From Tokugawa Times to the Present*. 2d ed. New York: Oxford University Press, 2008.

Jansen, Marius B. *The Making of Modern Japan*. Cambridge, Mass.: Harvard University Press, 2000.

Myers, Ramon, ed. *The Japanese Colonial Empire, 1895-1945*. Princeton, N.J.: Princeton University Press, 1987.

Paine, S. C. M. *The Sino-Japanese War of 1894-1895: Perceptions, Power, and Primacy*. New York: Cambridge University Press, 2005.

Turnbull, Stephen. *Osaka 1615: The Last Battle of the Samurai*. New York: Osprey, 2006.

FILMS AND OTHER MEDIA

Japan: Memoirs of a Secret Empire. Documentary. Public Broadcasting Service/Paramount, 2004.

The Last Samurai. Feature film. Warner Bros., 2003.

Letters from Iwo Jima. Feature film. Malpaso/Amblin, 2006.

Nova: Secrets of the Samurai Sword. Documentary. Public Broadcasting Service/WGBH, 2008.

The Seven Samurai. Feature film. Toho, 1954.

Shogun. Feature film. Paramount Pictures, 1980.

J. Nathan Campbell

CHINA
THE QING EMPIRE
Dates: 1644-1911

POLITICAL CONSIDERATIONS

The adoption of an isolationist policy by the Ming Dynasty (1368-1644) began a period of decline that ended in the downfall of the regime. This decline became evident by the beginning of the sixteenth century and was accelerated by the corruption of the bureaucratic infrastructure that destroyed the effectiveness of the central government. China's most significant domestic problem was the collapse of the empire's vast public works system. Widespread corruption led to misappropriation of funds meant for the construction and repair of the dikes and irrigation systems upon which China's agricultural life depended. This shortfall led to starvation and open rebellion and invasion by the Manchus from Mongolia. The Manchus captured Beijing in 1644, and by 1647 they had brought the rest of the nation under their control.

The new rulers of China established the Qing (Ch'ing) Dynasty (1644-1911), which would be the last dynasty in China's history. The new leadership retained much of the Ming's political structure, but it took a more activist role in the day-to-day operation of the government, placing Manchu officials in the most important positions. The Qing continued to use the Confucian examination system as the educational foundation of their governmental system. Despite the fact that the Qing maintained much of the traditional culture, many Chinese continued to consider them inferior and unfit to rule.

The early years of the Qing Dynasty were marked by a concerted effort to end the poverty of the rural population. The government passed reforms that lowered both the taxes and labor requirements of the peasants. The dynasty also allocated a considerable amount of money to the maintenance of the agricultural infrastructure. Regulations were also enacted to reduce the ability of the aristocracy to accumulate large amounts of agricultural land. These laws were the first modern attempt in China to enact meaningful land reform.

Most of these programs, however, were unsuccessful, and China's agricultural elite used the widespread hatred of the Manchus to reduce the authority of the Qing government. This allowed the aristocracy to violate new regulations and continue to amass large landholdings. The gulf between the rich and rural poor grew to dangerous proportions.

China's commercial sector also began to expand at an unprecedented rate. Much of this expansion was fueled by the new wealth of Western Europe and the silver from its mines in the Western Hemisphere. The Manchu government reacted to this new international economic reality by lifting the travel restrictions on Chinese merchants. This new freedom allowed the evolution of an extensive trade network that had far-reaching effects on Chinese society. The most important social impact of this trade was the creation of a powerful new class of merchants that controlled the majority of China's international commerce. This new class used its wealth and power to challenge Manchu authority, especially in southern China.

By the 1780's the Qing Dynasty was beginning to show signs of serious decline. The governmental bureaucracy was no longer the domain of the best and the brightest of Chinese society. The classical civil service examination system had been corrupted, and both cheating and favoritism had become commonplace. Wealthy landed aristocrats and merchants used their power to purchase influence within the government bureaucracy. Corrupt officials redirected money allocated for civil engineering projects into their own

CHINA UNDER THE QING DYNASTY, C. 1697

accounts. China's crumbling infrastructure set into motion a series of disasters that would greatly undermine the political and social stability of the nation. Most important, China now lacked the ability to feed its increasing population, and the empire was racked by peasant uprisings.

The nineteenth century was a political, social, and economic disaster for the Qing Dynasty. China was militarily humiliated by foreign powers, both European and Asian. Great Britain, in the Opium Wars (1839-1842), seized control of Hong Kong, and Japan, in the Sino-Japanese War (1894-1895), forced China to cede control of Korea. At the conclusion of each conflict, China was forced to sign a series of

CHINESE EXPANSION IN THE EIGHTEENTH CENTURY

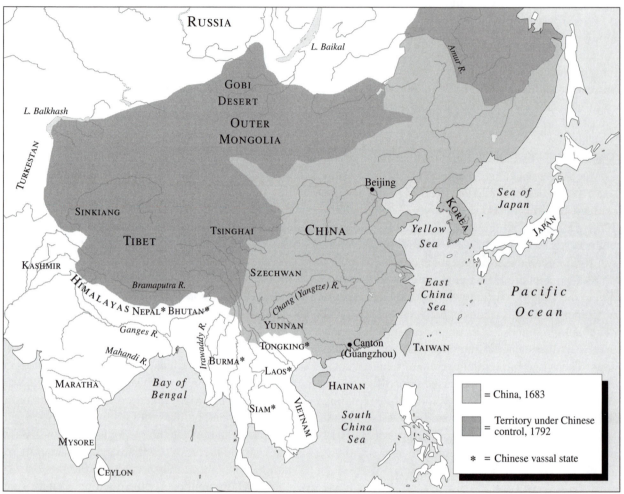

agreements that stripped the country of its national dignity.

In 1845 the British government forced China to sign a treaty that allowed the British to dictate economic policy and at the same time gave British nationals the power to operate free from the constraints of the Chinese legal system. This unrestricted power also enabled Christian missionaries to intensify their program to bring the Chinese population into the Christian sphere of influence. These policies undermined traditional Chinese culture and set the stage for China's most devastating nineteenth century civil conflict, the Taiping Rebellion (1850-1864).

The Taiping Rebellion lasted for more than a de-

cade and cost twenty million lives. An attempt to reform the social injustices inherent in the traditional Chinese social and political structure, it was motivated by the overwhelming feelings of disgrace and humiliation that had resulted from the Chinese defeat in the Opium Wars. A growing segment of Chinese society believed that history was passing China by, and if significant reforms were not made, the nation would be at the mercy of the growing power of the West. The social reforms, especially those concerning land redistribution and the rights of women, reflected the belief that the real power of the West rested in its mobile and egalitarian social structure.

The provincial gentry attempted a series of reforms to counter the incursion of Western influence. They sought to use the technology of the European powers to check imperial expansion. They wanted to modernize both the armed forces and China's infrastructure. This was done not to bring Chinese society into the modern world, but as a last-ditch attempt to preserve the traditional order. As these leaders became more powerful, the Manchus lost political control of the provinces.

The Qing Dynasty resisted all attempts at reform. The imperial government, allied with the traditional Confucian bureaucracy, worked steadfastly to preserve the old order. In the final years of the nineteenth century, the empress dowager Cixi (Tz'u-hsi; 1835-1908) attacked all attempts at reform, and her support of the Boxer Rebellion in 1900 would serve as a catalyst for the forces that opposed the dynasty.

As China entered the twentieth century, opposition to the Qing government permeated all segments of Chinese society. Alliances between the powerful merchant class and certain members of the scholar gentry set the stage for the overthrow of the Manchus. These two influential sectors of Chinese society envisioned a new China based upon the republican ideals of the West. In 1911 Sun Yat-sen (pinyin, Sun Yixian; 1866-1925) initiated a revolution that led to the downfall of the Qing Dynasty, and in 1912 the Chinese republic was established.

MILITARY ACHIEVEMENT

The last century of the Qing Dynasty was devoid of any significant military achievement and was witness to the collapse of China's defense establishment. This once-mighty nation was defeated by the armies of both Europe and Japan, which by the middle of the century had surpassed China's military in both tactical and technological skill. The military disasters suffered during this century not only threatened to make China into a colonial subject, but they also were at the heart of two bloody and disastrous civil uprisings.

The Opium Wars were the first of these great military failures and clearly exposed both the diplomatic and military weaknesses of China. By the beginning of the nineteenth century the British had created a very profitable system of international trade in English and South Asian textiles and Chinese tea. By the 1820's tea had become the most valued product in England and was consumed in large quantities throughout the British Empire. This demand resulted in a significant trade imbalance for the British, who attempted to correct the problem by increasing the opium trade with China. Initially, the Chinese government accepted the increase and even shared in the profits. Eventually, however, a number of prominent intellectuals began to speak out against the impact this narcotic was having on Chinese society. The most influential opponent of this trade was Lin Zexu (Lin Tse-hsu; 1785-1850), who held a powerful position within the Qing bureaucracy. When the British refused to stop dumping opium on the Chinese market, Lin Zexu ordered the European trading areas blockaded and had government officials destroy the warehouses that held the dangerous drug. The British military response initiated the Opium Wars.

The major problem facing the British was how to invade and defeat China without becoming bogged down in an extensive and potentially costly land war. The English military relied on their superior naval technology and built a series a small, highly maneuverable steamboats in their shipyards in South Asia. They armed the vessels with extremely accurate rotating cannons and transported them to the coast of China. These gunboats entered China's major river systems and engaged the Chinese navy at every opportunity. The old wooden ships of the Qing fleet were no match for these state-of-the-art vessels, and the British had an easy time gaining control of these inland waterways. This left China's great inland fortifications defenseless, and the Manchu government was forced to accept a British peace agreement.

As a result of its defeat in the Opium Wars, China was forced to sign the humiliating Treaty of Nanjing (1842), the first in a series of diplomatic agreements known as the "unequal treaties," which attacked China's basic sovereign rights. This devastating military defeat would have an important political, social, and cultural impact on the Manchu Dynasty.

Three decades before the onset of hostilities with Britain, most of Chinese society had already been introduced to the basic tenets of Western civilization. Christian missionaries had been extremely successful in converting a substantial number of Chinese to Christianity. Following the disastrous events of the Opium Wars, a large segment of Chinese society began to question the validity of many of its traditional beliefs. Many intellectuals believed it was time to set aside the Confucian worldview in favor of the Western model, which emphasized a blending of Christianity and the scientific method.

In conjunction with this cultural malaise, China's population was suffering from a series of domestic problems resulting from the corruption of the Qing bureaucracy. Rural China was in a state of complete collapse. There were widespread public health problems, and the government was no longer able to provide the services necessary to carry out the day-to-day operation of an orderly society. Revolutionary groups began to appear, claiming to have the answers to this social chaos.

This was the political climate that set in motion the events that would give rise to the Taiping Rebellion. This massive civil uprising was the most devastating event in nineteenth century world history. Between 1850 and 1865 twenty million Chinese would become casualties of the disease, famine, and destruction caused by this civil war.

The Bai Shangdi Hui (Pai Shang-ti Hui), or Society of Worshipers, was one of many secret, revolutionary organizations that grew out of the social and political discontent arising from the failure of the Qing Dynasty, and it played an important role in the rebellion. The majority of the society's members were rural poor who had lost confidence in the Manchu Dynasty. The central figure in the Taiping Rebellion was an emotionally unstable educator named Hong Xiuquan (Hung Hsiu-ch'üan; 1814-1864) who had suffered a nervous breakdown after failing to pass the required civil service examinations for a teaching position. During a particularly difficult emotional period he came to believe that he had been transported to Heaven, where he was informed that he was the second son of God and the younger brother of Jesus Christ. He believed that he was involved in defeating an uprising against God by a coalition of evil spirits, and that he had been directed by his heavenly father to return to earth and restore peace, justice, and harmony to his homeland by deposing the Qing Dynasty, which had lost its "mandate of Heaven."

The Taiping Rebellion was based upon the fundamental Christian belief in the

F. R. Niglutsch

British troops taking formal possession of Hong Kong at the conclusion of the First Opium War (1839-1842).

F. R. Niglutsch

Rebels gather during the Taiping uprising (1850-1864).

universal relationship and basic equality of all humankind in the eyes of God. The goal of the uprising was to create a society based upon social and economic equality. This new Western ideology challenged the traditional foundation of Chinese civilization, which was structured upon the Confucian model of the unchanging relationship between superior and subordinate. The rebellion's program of economic equality based upon the complete redistribution of land threatened China's landed aristocracy.

The Qing Dynasty was saved by a coalition of Chinese and international forces that eventually isolated and annihilated the rebel forces. Once again, however, the Chinese body politic was deeply frightened by these events, and the power and prestige of the Manchu Dynasty was degraded.

As the nineteenth century neared its conclusion, China faced a new threat from a traditional Asian competitor, Japan. These rivals had followed different courses in the nineteenth century. While China under the Qing Dynasty steadfastly fought to maintain its traditional structure and worldview, Japan openly and aggressively embraced Western science, technology, and educational models. After the arrival of Commander Matthew C. Perry (1794-1858), the Japanese realized that their future would be threatened if they ignored the technological superiority of the West. Unlike the Confucian traditionalists that fought to save the Qing Dynasty and its outdated and corrupt structure, Japanese intellectuals and political leaders undermined the feudal Tokugawa regime (1603-1867) and restored the emperor to a position of power. This period is known as the Meiji Restoration (1866-1868), and was a major turning point in the history of East Asia. Rather than limiting Japan's exposure to Western ideas, the new Japanese government sent the country's best and brightest to the most prestigious Western institutions of higher learning. Japan's goal was to learn as much as possible about these new scientific advancements so it would be able to prevent the West from making Japan into another China.

By the 1870's Japan was well into the process of industrialization, and by 1890 it had developed a new, highly technological and very powerful military force. Both the army and navy had utilized Western technology to increase their military effectiveness, and Japan could now declare itself a true international power. Japan's new political and military leadership were cognizant of the extent of European imperialism in Asia, and began to exercise its right to enter into this new international competition. Japan's new aggressive posture was supported by a highly developed sense of cultural superiority and a unique racial bias that supported the Japanese belief in the nation's right to dominate Asia.

The First Sino-Japanese War centered on the question of which country would control the Korean Peninsula. Because China had dominated the area for centuries, the Qing government believed that Korea remained within the Chinese sphere of influence. The Japanese challenged this perception in 1876 when they sent one of their new naval squadrons to forcibly open the peninsula to Japanese economic interests. All-out war was avoided when Japan and China signed the Treaty of Kanghwa (1876), which gave Japan trading privileges at two of Korea's ports. This was only a temporary solution, however; Japan fully expected eventually to dominate the area.

The Japanese military establishment continued to push for a military solution to the Korean question, and it was finally presented with an opportunity when the peninsula was the site of an anti-Japanese uprising in July, 1894. Units of Japan's new modernized army put down the rebellion, captured the Korean monarch, and forced him to remove all Chinese nationals from the country. Within two days, the Japanese navy had engaged the Chinese fleet stationed in the area and destroyed the *Kowshing*, a British steamer that was carrying Chinese reinforcements. Relations between the two nations continued to deteriorate, and war was declared on August 1, 1894.

The Chinese armed forces were decisively defeated on all fronts by the Japanese military. Chinese supply lines to their armies on the peninsula were severed when the Japanese navy destroyed the Chinese fleet in the Battle of Yalu River (1894). The bloodiest and most controversial battle was for control of Port Arthur (1894) on the Liaotung Peninsula in the Yellow Sea. Port Arthur's massive fortress was believed to be impenetrable. A Chinese army of 20,000 occupied Port Arthur, and during the campaign they enraged the Japanese by defiling the bodies of dead Japanese soldiers. The modernized forces of the Japanese army, using the latest assault tactics, breached the fortifications and destroyed the defending force. Emboldened by their overwhelming success, the Japanese military moved into Shantung Province and captured the important city of Weihaiwei (1895). Faced with total military collapse, China sued for peace and turned over a large section of Manchuria, along with Formosa (Taiwan) and the Pescadores Islands (P'eng-hu), to Japan. The Japanese victory in the Sino-Japanese War elevated Japan to a position of prominence in East Asia.

As the twentieth century began, China had lost the respect of most of the international community. In the span of five decades it had suffered two major military setbacks and had been torn apart by civil war. The United States, Japan, and the major nations of Western Europe had carved China into economic "spheres of influence," which allowed each nation to dominate the political and economic events of that region.

The systematic application of Western technology in China undermined an already weak and corrupt economic system. The construction of a modern infrastructure based upon rail transportation disrupted the lives of thousands of people. Railroads were both inexpensive and efficient, and drew business away from China's traditional transportation network. The most devastating example was the decline of the Grand Canal, the waterway that had been the backbone of China's domestic trade, linking the bureaucratic north with the agricultural south. Hundreds of families that had moved goods on the canal for generations were now among the growing numbers of unemployed, who crowded into China's urban areas. The decline in trade also affected the cities that had grown up along the route of the canal. Similar circumstances could be found in the rural provinces that depended upon cash crops for their economic success. Inexpensive high-quality cotton yarn produced in England's textile factories caused the collapse of the yarn industry in China.

China's traditional culture, based upon Confucian and Daoist principles, was also under attack. Christian missionaries were successful in converting thousands of Chinese. At the outbreak of the Boxer Rebellion in 1900, there were 3,000 Christian missionaries of various denominations operating throughout China. These missionaries tried to reform Chinese society based upon the social and religious principles of Christianity, focusing mainly upon human rights and concentrating their efforts toward increasing the status of women and children. These at-

tempted reforms clashed with the traditional values of Confucian society. The xenophobic Qings viewed the Christian missionaries as a substantial threat to the cultural heritage of China.

By the end of the nineteenth century, a group of conservative aristocrats had become a very powerful force in the Manchu government, with the primary goal of eradicating Western influence in China. These conservatives developed a plan of action that would take advantage of the large number of peasants and urban laborers who had lost their jobs to Western industrialization. A secret revolutionary organization known as the Yihequan (I-ho ch'üan), or Fists of Righteous Harmony, organized these unemployed men into an armed force and unleashed their anger upon the unsuspecting Westerners. The Boxers, as they would become known, linked China's overall decline to both Western economic interests

F. R. Niglutsch

Japanese forces enter China after crossing the Yalu River (1894).

and Christianity. Because most of the missionary stations were located in isolated rural areas, the Christian clergy were especially easy targets. The rebels took advantage of this situation and carried out a series of vicious attacks that included rape and mutilation.

The Western diplomatic community responded by creating a multinational strike force of more than 9,000 men to put down the uprising. The two most important engagements were at the cities of Tientsin (1900) and Beijing (1900), with especially brutal fighting at Tientsin. Most interesting to the historian of East Asian military history is the fact that the Japanese army played a crucial role in both battles. The success of the Japanese armed forces instilled considerable confidence within the military leadership and would be a significant factor in Japan's decision to engage Russia four years later. The Boxer Rebellion had disastrous effects on the Qing Dynasty. The victorious allies forced China to dismantle the majority of its armed forces and also fined it the equivalent of 333 million dollars.

WEAPONS, UNIFORMS, AND ARMOR

The history of weaponry during the Qing Dynasty reflects the cultural and intellectual conflicts found throughout Chinese society during this time period. Initially the Manchu armed forces modeled themselves after those of the Ming Dynasty, using the traditional weapons of the infantry and cavalry, including the sword, lance, and crossbow. After its humiliating defeat by the British in the Opium Wars, the Qing Dynasty sought to adopt the weaponry of the modern industrial nations, including not only the latest handguns and rifles but also new steam-powered ships and gunboats. A significant debate occurred within Chinese intellectual circles concerning the future of China's armed forces. This new military reality was widely discussed among an emerging class of intellectuals, who focused on the development of a new strategic doctrine. The failure of the Manchu government to employ these new theories would ultimately lead to the destruction of the Qing Dynasty.

The Ninth U.S. Infantry Gatling Gun Detachment in Beijing, protecting U.S. interests in China during the Boxer Rebellion (1900).

MILITARY ORGANIZATION

The organization of China's military went through two important changes during the nineteenth century. After the Opium Wars, China's military leaders blamed the poor performance of the armed forces on three major problems: poor training, lack of morale, and an absence of unit cohesion. These deficiencies would be corrected by the implementation of a model that would create a well-trained and highly motivated military fighting force. These reforms began with the officer corps, which would now be allowed to choose subordinates and create units that were based upon close working relationships between officers and soldiers. In the future, when recruits joined a unit, they would be obligated to obey only the orders of their commanding officer. The theory behind this military paradigm was that the average fighting man would perform much better in the heat of battle if he had absolute confidence in his superiors. These reforms were the foundation of China's military organization until its humiliation in the First Sino-Japanese War.

In 1895, after the First Sino-Japanese War, the Chinese military initiated sweeping changes in the organizational structure of its armed forces. These changes were based upon the regulations used by the armies of the industrial nations and were the result of the latest research conducted in the most prestigious military academies in the world. The foundation of this new organizational structure was the creation of a large permanent professional army. This new force would consist of two divisions, each having two infantry brigades and one cavalry and artillery unit. The enlisted personnel would serve four years of full-time duty and would then be placed on First Reserve unit duty. As First Reserves, they would be classified as civilians but would be required to report for training one month per year. During this time enlisted personnel would receive 50 percent of their regular army pay. At the end of three years, the soldiers would then be transferred to Second Reserve units, where they would serve for another four years, after which they would be released from military service. The theory behind this force structure was that China would always have a large supply of trained military personnel to draw upon in a time of crisis.

DOCTRINE, STRATEGY, AND TACTICS

The most dynamic area of Chinese military policy during this time period dealt with the development of philosophy and doctrine. During the nineteenth century, many of China's best intellectuals focused upon the creation of a sound philosophical military model that would provide China with the organization it so desperately needed.

The first significant work in this area was carried out in the years following the Opium Wars by the Qing historian and geographer Wei Yuan (Wei Yüan; 1794-1854), who published a book on the planning of coastal defenses, in which he made two important observations about the future of Chinese security. First and foremost was that the Qing government needed to accept that European ships and guns were superior to those of China. Wei Yuan suggested that the emperor should allocate funding for both the purchase of these weapons and the creation of a military industrial complex that would enable China to manufacture similarly high-quality armaments.

Wei Yuan also argued that the success of Western armies was based upon the quality of their military personnel. Every Western army paid both high wages and good benefits, a requirement in the modern world of training, discipline, and action under fire. Wei Yuan advocated China's development of a military pay structure that would attract strong, intelligent, and loyal recruits.

Wei Yuan noted that once the nation made these basic changes, it must then develop the correct plan of implementation utilizing both military and diplomatic strategies. He believed that China needed to realize that it did not possess the military power to actively engage potential adversaries either in the South China Sea or along its coastline and instead should concentrate on protecting its inland waterways where it could use its vast territory and large population to its best advantage. Many military historians believe that Wei Yuan was the first to conceive of the strategy of a "retrograde defense," based upon drawing a potential enemy deep into one's own interior, isolating and then destroying it.

Like most intellectuals of his day, Wei Yuan believed that the use of the military must never be the first choice, but should be considered only when all other diplomatic alternatives have been exhausted. It was thought that a great leader should always use a combination of military alliances and international trade as the foundation of foreign policy. The ancient tradition of using one "barbarian" to control another was still relevant, and an extensive knowledge of current events was a necessary tool in advancing this strategy. Positioning one's nation to take advantage of the current imperialist competition among the industrial nations could one day produce fruitful results. Wei Yuan also adhered to the concept that trading partners rarely entered into military conflict with one another, and he lobbied extensively for China to open its doors to foreign trade.

The second great strategist of the post-Opium War period was Feng Guifen (Feng Kuei-fen; 1809-1874). Like Wei Yuan, he believed that China should adopt Western weaponry, but that it should also master the new scientific and technological knowledge that formed the theoretical foundation of this new world order. He believed that China's military security was linked to the reform of its educational system. In the future, Chinese schools would have to offer courses in modern mathematics, chemistry, physics, and astronomy. Feng Guifen advocated these reforms as part of a Self-Strengthening Movement (1861-1895) that would propel China into the twentieth century.

The late nineteenth century witnessed the rise of a group of military philosophers who based their work on the teachings of Confucius (551-479 B.C.E.). They referred to themselves as Confucian rationalists, and believed that China's future was to be found in a combination of Western science and Confucian ethics.

The first of these Confucian military theorists was Zeng Guofan (Tseng Kuo-fan; 1811-1872), who occupied a position of authority within the Qing bureaucracy. He had received his military training under battlefield conditions when he was directed to organize the central Chinese militia during the Taiping Rebellion. As a result of this experience, he developed a military philosophy that in fact utilized both Western technology and Confucian philosophy. Tactically, he concluded that a commander should always follow the doctrine of the concentration of force. If one divides one's unit it will necessarily become weaker and give one's opponent the advantage. In conjunction with this fundamental reality, he created the overriding concept of the "master-guest" theory of the battlefield, arguing that the successful commander will always choose to be on the defensive, because the true position of strength is found in knowing both the adversary's objectives and tactics.

A commander who initiates an engagement will be acting on insufficient information and will become the "guest" on the battlefield. In turn, a commander who waits until the enemy moves will have the necessary information to defeat the opposing force, thus becoming "master" of the battlefield. This strategy of battlefield defense employed two fundamental Confucian beliefs. The military philosophy of Confucius was based upon the ethical premise that aggressive offensive warfare was immoral. The only reason to use military force, according to Confucius, was in defense of the nation, and thus all military philosophy should focus on the development of defensive strategies. In addition, the Confucian system focused upon the development of a personal moral code, the concept Zeng Guofan adapted to his military theory. He believed that the most important element in any military doctrine was the human factor. An army consisting of an officer corps soundly grounded in Confucian philosophy could always be counted on to make the correct battlefield decisions. Zeng Guofan believed that most military failures were caused by hasty, ill-conceived actions made by officers who were driven by their own arrogance. He maintained that the unphilosophical soul was more concerned with personal glory, which would cloud one's judgment and lead to catastrophe. These two Confucian principles were the basis of Zeng Guofan's defensive strategy.

The second great Confucian strategist was Li Hongzhang (Li Hung-chang; 1823-1901), who as a young man scored at the highest level in the Confucian examination system. Like most of his predecessors, he believed that China had to develop the capacity to produce modern weapons. He was the first modern Chinese military philosopher to develop a combined-arms doctrine that employed both ground and naval forces in a strategic defense. Li Hongzhang believed that a modernized navy would still be unable to defend China's extensive coastline, and he recommended that the army be utilized to defend China's most important harbors and that the Navy be held in reserve and used against an invading force after the axis of attack had been established.

The Confucian worldview, especially in its focus on the importance of good education, played a prominent role in the development of Li Hongzhang's doctrine. Li Hongzhang advised the Qing government to change the examination system that was used to recruit members of the officer corps to reflect the technical expertise necessary to successful operation on the modern battlefield. He wanted to develop a truly integrated curriculum that emphasized both traditional ethics and modern technology.

The Qing government, however, placed too much emphasis upon modern weaponry and not enough on the creation of a system that would attract and keep officers of the highest quality. When China engaged Japan in the First Sino-Japanese War, this weakness undermined the effectiveness of the Chinese army and resulted in a humiliating defeat.

CONTEMPORARY SOURCES

Most of the ideas of the nineteenth century Chinese military theorists can be found in publications of their collected works. The most respected publication of the period was written by Wei Yuan. In *Haiguotuji* (1844; also known as *Hai-kuo t'u chih*, an illustrated handbook of maritime countries), Wei formulated the basic principles of nineteenth century Chinese military thought.

BOOKS AND ARTICLES

Edgerton, Robert. *Warriors of the Rising Sun: A History of the Japanese Military*. Boulder, Colo.: Westview Press, 1997.

Gelber, Harry Gregor. *Opium, Soldiers, and Evangelicals: Britain's 1840-42 War with China, and Its Aftermath*. New York: Palgrave Macmillan, 2004.

Hsin-pao, Chang. *Commissioner Lin and the Opium War*. New York: W. W. Norton, 1970.

Lorge, Peter. "War and Warfare in China, 1450-1815." In *War in the Early Modern World*, edited by Jeremy Black. Boulder, Colo.: Westview Press, 1999.

_____. *War, Politics, and Society in Early Modern China, 900-1795*. New York: Routledge, 2005.

Mackenzie, S. P. "The Armies of the Heavenly Kingdom and the Taiping Rebellion in China, 1850-68." In *Revolutionary Armies in the Modern Era: A Revisionist Approach*. New York: Routledge, 1997.

Perdue, Peter C. *China Marches West: The Qing Conquest of Central Eurasia*. Cambridge, Mass.: Belknap Press of Harvard University Press, 2005.

Spence, Jonathan D. *God's Chinese Son: The Taiping Heavenly Kingdom of Hong Xiuquan*. New York: W. W. Norton, 1996.

Swope, Kenneth, ed. *Warfare in China Since 1600*. Burlington, Vt.: Ashgate, 2005.

Waley-Cohen, Joanna. *The Culture of War in China: Empire and the Military Under the Qing Dynasty*. New York: I. B. Tauris, 2006.

Worthing, Peter. *A Military History of Modern China: From the Manchu Conquest to Tian'anmen Square*. Westport, Conn.: Praeger Security International, 2007.

FILMS AND OTHER MEDIA

Eternal Emperor: Emperor Kangxi in Qing Dynasty, 1654-1722. Documentary. Peninsula Audiovisual Press, 2007.

Eternal Emperor: Emperor Qianlong in Qing Dynasty, 1711-1799. Documentary. Peninsula Audiovisual Press, 2007.

The Opium War. Feature film. Golden Harvest, 1997.

Richard D. Fitzgerald

IMPERIAL WARFARE

Dates: 1857-1945

POLITICAL CONSIDERATIONS

The one hundred years between 1850 and 1950 constituted one of the most violent and troubled periods in all of recorded history. It witnessed the growing reliance of governments on military power to resolve European and colonial disputes, the competition for dominance among ideologically opposing camps, and the loss of millions of lives in wars. Yet, at the same time, this age experienced increased prosperity, enhanced longevity, and the ascendancy of liberal ideals that were focused on eliminating the causes for the distress. In 1857 Britain experienced the Sepoy Rebellion in India, when Muslim soldiers refused to bite pork-greased cartridges that were required for a new rifle. Although Britain suppressed the revolt and established direct control over India, the Sepoy Rebellion exemplified the cultural divide between the European powers and their non-Western colonies. The revolt was more than a resistance to the British affront to Muslims; it was a reaction to Britain's foreign presence and power.

Between 1870 and the outbreak of World War I in 1914, European nations frequently were involved in colonial disputes and wars while peace was sustained on the European Continent itself. The most active imperial powers were Britain, France, Italy, and, after 1885, Germany, the United States, and Russia. Imperialism gained support in the 1870's under the leadership of British prime minister Benjamin Disraeli (1804-1881), the new leaders of the French Third Republic, and the government of Kaiser Wilhelm (William) II (1859-1941) of Germany. They believed that imperialism reflected the natural state of affairs, demonstrated national power, and provided sources of raw materials and markets for manufactured products. Within increasingly democratic societies anti-imperialists, such as William Ewart Gladstone (1809-1898), developed support and, on occasion, gained power.

The principal colonial rivalries prior to 1900 focused on Britain, the preeminent imperial power. The French opposed Britain in the Middle East, constructing the Suez Canal, but they lost the canal and their influence in the region when Disraeli managed to acquire for Britain a controlling interest in the canal in 1876. Later, France and Britain were almost brought to the point of war during the Fashoda Incident (1898-1899), which involved control of the Upper Nile and hegemony in East Africa.

The British were also colonial rivals of the Russians. In 1878 Disraeli thwarted the Russian military successes against the Ottoman Turks (1877-1878); as a result of the Treaty of Berlin (1878), Britain obtained Cyprus, and Russia only partially achieved its objectives. Britain and Russia opposed each other in the Anglo-Afghan Wars (1839-1842; 1878-1880) and were competitors in Persia and China. In 1891 France and Russia entered into an alliance directed at a defensive war with Germany. The Germans allied themselves with Austria-Hungary and Italy. In 1898 Britain began a move away from political and diplomatic isolation. Although the initial preference was for an agreement with Germany, Britain was rebuffed and sought to resolve its colonial disputes.

In 1902 the Anglo-Japanese Alliance was formalized; it required the signatories to adopt a position of benevolent neutrality in the event that one of them was attacked by a third party. In 1904 the Anglo-French Entente, or the Entente Cordiale, resolved the colonial dispute between France and Britain over Africa. Britain agreed to recognize Northwest Africa as a French sphere of influence, and France recognized Northeast Africa as a British sphere of influence. Despite British support for Japan in the Russo-Japanese War (1904-1905), the colonial disputes between Russia and Britain were addressed in the Anglo-Russian Entente of 1907. Britain received Afghanistan and the southern third of Persia as spheres of influence;

IMPERIAL HOLDINGS IN AFRICA AS OF 1914

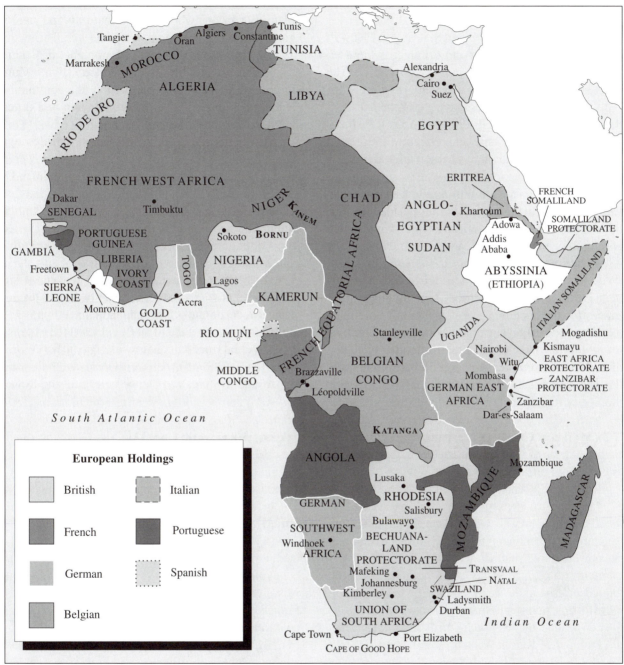

Russia obtained the northern third of Persia and shared with Britain the opportunity to economically exploit central Persia. Both parties recognized Tibet as part of China. Relations between the German Em- pire and the Anglo-French-Russian alliance were strained over German involvement in Morocco, East Africa, and the Far East. During this period the United States emerged as an imperial power, with participation in the Spanish-American War (1898) and expansion in the Pacific. As a result of the war with Spain, the United States acquired Puerto Rico and the Philippines. The United States seized Hawaii from a native government and occupied several islands, including Pago Pago, in the South Pacific. The United States and many European states were involved in the internal economic life of the decadent Qing Dynasty in China. In 1900 the Boxer Rebellion, motivated by the Manchus and reflecting antiforeign sentiment, was put down by an international military force.

With the outbreak of World War I in 1914, the contending parties extended the conflict to their colonies. German positions in Africa and China were vulnerable, and the British and French defeated the German forces. In January, 1918, U.S. president Woodrow Wilson (1856-1924) advanced his Fourteen Points as a basis for a peace settlement. Incorporated into the document was a clear anti-imperialist sentiment; Wilson wanted a world without empires, in which the independence and interests of native populations were respected. Although the Paris Peace Conference (1919) paid token attention to this

view, it was ignored in the text of the treaty. Nonetheless, Wilson's anti-imperialism had the support of many Europeans who believed that imperial rivalry had contributed to the outbreak of the war. During the 1920's anti-imperialism gained momentum. Britain moved toward granting independence to India. More important, in the new Soviet Union, the communist leaders denounced Western imperialism and urged all native peoples to revolt.

Also during the 1920's a new totalitarian ideology called fascism grew in influence, coming to power in Italy in 1922, in Germany in 1933, in Spain in 1939, and in Japan in 1940, although the turn toward fascism in Japan had begun during the 1920's. Unlike the liberal democracies, the fascist states supported the continuation and expansion of their empires. They challenged the progressive view of society in which liberty and individual values were valued. Authoritarian and antidemocratic, the fascist states advanced a corporate political agenda that emphasized collective or national and racist values at the expense of individual freedoms. The resulting conflict, World War II (1939-1945), between Germany, Italy, and Japan and the Western democracies and the Soviet

CARIBBEAN THEATER OF THE SPANISH-AMERICAN WAR

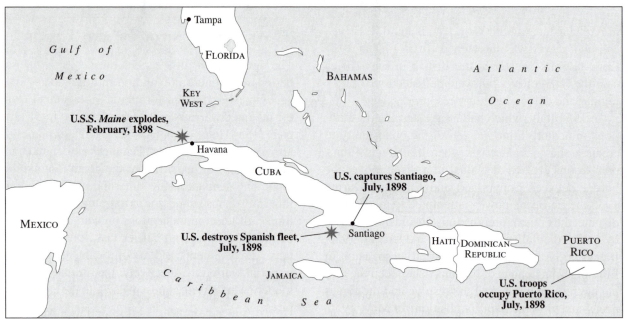

Union, was the deadliest and most gruesome conflict in history. The victors came to recognize not only the folly of imperialism but also its drain on national economies. Regrettably, the Cold War (1945-1991) between the Soviet Union and its allies and the Western democracies resulted in extending variations of imperialism as the two camps competed for global support.

MILITARY ACHIEVEMENT

The significant military achievements of the imperial era were the successful defense and extension of the British Empire during the Zulu War (1879), the Anglo-Afghan Wars, and World Wars I and II; the notorious defeat of Ethiopia by Italians; and the American reacquisition of the Philippines from Japan. In 1879 the Zulu King Cetshwayo (c. 1832-1884) defeated the British in the Battle of Isandhlwana on January 22, 1879, and threatened the British position in South Africa. Britain responded, defeating the Zulus in the Battle of Ulundi on July 4, 1879, and neutralizing the Zulu threat.

British wars against Afghanistan in the 1870's and 1880's were directed at local chieftains and the Russians who could threaten the northern gateway to India. In both instances British influence prevailed and, in 1907, Russia recognized the British influence in Afghanistan. In both World Wars I and II, British colonial power was threatened. In 1914 and 1915 German units threatened the British in East Africa near the Bandu River but were defeated by Britain's regular and colonial military resources.

In 1934 Italy, which had long entertained aspirations to acquire Ethiopia, seized the opportunity to create a war-in-sight crisis when Italian and Ethiopian troops clashed at Ualual in a dispute over the border between Somaliland and Ethiopia. During 1935 the European powers attempted to mediate the dispute; the French foreign minister sold out Ethiopia by giving the Italians a free hand. In October, 1935, Italian army and naval units started an invasion of Ethiopia. The League of Nations denounced the Italian aggression but lacked the resolve and the forces necessary to implement its position. In May, 1936,

Italian forces occupied Addis Ababa after a spirited resistance by the Ethiopians and, in the same month, they announced the annexation of Ethiopia. The Italian military action involved mechanized forces including planes and tanks; they were opposed by poorly equipped Ethiopians who could not mount a defense against such power.

After the Spanish-American War the United States acquired the Philippine Islands. A politically reluctant imperial power, the United States was moving the Philippines toward self-government in the 1930's. Shortly after the Japanese attack on Pearl Harbor on December 7, 1941, the Philippines were attacked and an invasion was initiated. By May 6, 1942, the last American outpost, the island fortress at Corregidor, had fallen to the Japanese. The United States, confronted with a global struggle, never lost sight of its defeat in the Philippines. On October 19, 1944, the United States launched a successful amphibious invasion of the Philippines under the leadership of General Douglas MacArthur (1880-1964); the Japanese forces were removed in 1945. In the struggle for the Philippines, the United States relied on active support from native resistance forces and on the general sympathy of the populace. Shortly after the war was won, the Philippines were granted full independence in 1947.

WEAPONS, UNIFORMS, AND ARMOR

The development of weapons during this imperial period constituted a revolution in armaments. This age witnessed the transformation in personnel from the mounted warriors of the Charge of the Light Brigade (1854) to pilots of German jet fighter planes. It also experienced the radical changes associated with modern gunnery and artillery, the invention of automatic and semiautomatic firearms, mechanized armor (tanks), the submarine as a strategic weapon, the impact of telecommunications on war, and the birth of the modern aircraft carrier task force. Many of these developments had a significant impact upon imperial warfare. Collectively, the dramatic cost of modern warfare led, almost in itself, to the end of empires.

In 1857, Muslim soldiers in India refused to bite pork-greased cartridges that were required for a new rifle. Although the British executed such rebels and established direct control over India, the Sepoy Rebellion exemplified the cultural divide between the European powers and their non-Western colonies.

By the end of the nineteenth century smokeless powder and bolt-action and magazine-repeating mechanisms had been developed and adopted by most major armies. The machine gun, capable of firing hundreds of rounds per minute, had been perfected. The French Hotchkiss, Austrian Schwarzlose, British Lewis, and American Browning guns were among the more advanced machine-gun models produced. The impact of these weapons in colonial wars against poorly defended or undefended native peoples was devastating. The imperial powers viewed these technical innovations as important because they were cost-effective and reduced the number of regular troops that had to be assigned to the colonies.

New cannons and artillery pieces advanced the effectiveness of the earlier Armstrong guns that had been deployed effectively against the Maoris in New

Zealand and in China during the Opium Wars (1839-1842) that secured for Britain the control of Hong Kong. With grenades, grenade launchers, and rocket-propelled weapons, the European and American governments continued to develop a dazzling array of lethal weapons that were designed for defense from one another but which also could be used to suppress native populations. The new weapons technology, with planned obsolescence, established a built-in arms race that became an important component in global culture. By 1940 the U.S. Army was equipped with the very efficient, gas-chamber-powered, semi-automatic M1 rifle.

Combat uniforms evolved during this period from the brightly colored and decorated uniforms of the past into more practical uniforms that concealed the troops from the enemy. Combat in imperial wars resulted in the adaptation of standard uniforms in accord with the local conditions; uniforms were made of varying weights to provide comfort in diverse climates.

The advent of steel and the need for mobility in the field resulted in less and lighter armor for the individual soldier. The most important component was the helmet, which protected the soldier's head from rifle fire as well as from shrapnel from artillery, grenades, and mortar fire. Reinforced steel also protected heavy gun emplacements, fortified riverboats, fortified trains and transports, and other military devices that were used in imperial wars.

MILITARY ORGANIZATION

Military organization during the era of imperial warfare reflected the movement toward a trained professional officer corps, the importance of strategic and tactical planning, the need for continuous preparedness training, and the value of utilizing science and technology in advancing weaponry. The model of the German General Staff was replicated throughout Europe with varying success. Although the European nations developed plans for the deployment of multidivision forces in the event of hostilities at home, their approach to military organization at the imperial level was much more limited.

Because of costs, all of the imperial powers attempted to develop reliable local forces that included natives at the soldier and noncommissioned officer levels; they were led by European officers. Further, in most instances, the organization of the defense of imperial colonies was predicated upon sustaining a supply line to the mother country through which reinforcements could be sent if necessary; a reliable navy was required to support a global empire. Without doubt Britain had the most sophisticated imperial military organization. Not only did Britain have the means to support its dominions and crown colonies in the event of attack, but it also developed plans for the colonies to support Britain in the event of a European or global conflict. This imperial military organization was effective during periods of peace or occasional local conflict, but, with the exception of Britain, for most nations it proved ineffective because of inadequate forces and the precarious nature of the lines of supply.

DOCTRINE, STRATEGY, AND TACTICS

Central to an understanding of the doctrines, strategy, and tactics employed in imperial warfare is the recognition of four major points. First, colonial wars between European industrialized nations were frequently fought using the same concepts and practices that would have been used in Europe. In most instances, the number of troops was considerably fewer and there were adaptations to the locale and conditions. Nonetheless, colonial encounters such as those at Fashoda were approached using the same conceptual framework.

Second, in situations where native forces or populations were involved, innovations were mandated; guerrilla warfare had to be met with a nontraditional response. In most instances, Europeans and Americans relied increasingly on technological innovations in weaponry to defeat colonial opposition. For example, the use of advanced naval and airpower assets had some limited success in defeating native forces. However, as national identity or ideologically driven revolts increased, Europeans and Americans recognized that control of the land could not be achieved by technology alone.

Third, it is important to recognize that the political support for imperialism within European and American societies varied greatly during the century from 1850 and 1950. Indeed, as indicated previously, most European and American generations included an active component opposed to imperialism and imperial wars. European and American leaders found themselves condemning the imperialism of Nazi Germany and Fascist Italy and Spain but defending their own imperial policies; the legitimacy of imperialism was undermined by values and beliefs inherent in democratic liberalism.

Finally, it is important to recognize that all twentieth century wars have been viewed as national struggles. Although the level of commitment may vary, a general political will to fight is considered a requirement. Thus, in the postimperialist era of the 1960's, with the absence of such a will, there was an abandonment of colonial struggles that were not defensible on the grounds of national defense.

The most significant factor that altered military doctrine, strategy, and tactics was the revolution in industry, technology, and communications that began in the mid-nineteenth century. Military strategists had to consider the rapid deployment of troops and the delivery of firepower through new weaponry. The advantage provided by new weapons was short-lived; enemies quickly adjusted and developed effective countermeasures. Ongoing weapons development became essential. The combination of modern military technology with successful strategies and tactics allowed for the deaths of millions of people. The resulting carnage led to a consensus against the continuing cycle of warfare, manifested in the twentieth century establishment of the League of Nations, the United Nations, and the European Union.

CONTEMPORARY SOURCES

Strategic military theory and practices were elevated to a professional level with the emergence of general staffs and the educational support services that emerged in the post-Napoleonic period. Throughout the period of imperial warfare strategists and tacticians considered Napoleon Bonaparte's military planning and successes. Likewise European military thinkers studied the relevant memoirs and works on strategy and tactics that became available in great numbers following the American Civil War.

National military colleges and schools, such as the United States Military Academy at West Point, New York, trained generations of officers in strategic military theory and practices. One of the most renowned contemporary sources of this era was Alfred Thayer Mahan (1840-1914), who wrote *The Influence of Sea Power on History, 1660-1783* (1890) and *Naval Strategy Compared and Contrasted with the Principles and Practices of Military Operations on Land* (1911). Another was General Alfred von Schlieffen (1833-1933), author of the famous Schlieffen Plan (1905), a German war strategy that became operational in August, 1914, with the outbreak of World War I. The primary military theorist of the late 1930's was Field Marshal Erich von Manstein (1887-1973), whose Blitzkrieg tactics were successful during the early years of World War II.

Other influential contemporary sources were Helmuth von Moltke the Elder (1800-1891), the military architect in the unification of Germany and the author of *Moltke's Militärische Korrespondenz aus den Dientschriften des Krieges* (1866; *Moltke's Projects for the Campaign of 1866*, 1907) and the Russians Vladimir Ilich Lenin (1870-1924) and Leon Trotsky (1879-1940), the architects of the 1917 Russian Revolution. Advocates of mechanized forces included Heinz Guderian (1888-1954), Basil Liddell Hart (1895-1970), and J. F. C. Fuller (1878-1966). Giulio Douhet (1869-1930) and William "Billy" Mitchell (1879-1936) recognized the importance of airpower and its impact on all aspects of warfare. Warfare in the colonies was considered by T. E. Lawrence (1888-1935), Mao Zedong (1893-1976), and Joseph-Simon Gallieni (1849-1916).

BOOKS AND ARTICLES

Barthorp, Michael. *The Zulu War: Isandhlwana to Ulundi*. London: Cassell, 2002.

Bayly, Christopher Alan. *Imperial Meridian: The British Empire and the World*. New York: Longman, 1989.

Black, Jeremy. "1783-1914: Wars of Imperialism." In *Why Wars Happen*. New York: New York University Press, 1998.

Chaliand, Gérard. *Art of War in World History: From Antiquity to the Nuclear Age*. Berkeley: University of California Press, 1994.

Creveld, Martin van. *Technology and War: From 2000 B.C. to the Present*. New York: Free Press, 1989.

David, Saul. *Victoria's Wars: The Rise of Empire*. New York: Viking, 2006.

De Quesada, Alejandro. *The Spanish-American War and Philippine Insurrection, 1898-1902*. Illustrated by Stephen Walsh. Botley, Oxford, England: Osprey, 2007.

Dupuy, Trevor N. *Evolution of Weapons and Warfare*. New York: Da Capo Press, 1990.

English, Allan D., ed. *Changing Face of War: Learning from History*. Montreal: McGill-Queen's University Press, 1998.

Fremont-Barnes, Gregory. *The Indian Mutiny, 1857-58*. Botley, Oxford, England: Osprey, 2007.

Keegan, John. *History of Warfare*. New York: Alfred A. Knopf, 1993.

Killingray, David, and David Omissi, eds. *Guardians of Empire: The Armed Forces of the Colonial Powers, c. 1700-1964*. Manchester, England: Manchester University Press, 1999.

MacKay, Kenneth. *Technology in War: The Impact of Science on Weapons Development and Modern Battle*. Englewood Cliffs, N.J.: Prentice-Hall, 1984.

McNeill, William H. *The Pursuit of Power: Technology, Armed Force, and Society Since A.D. 1000*. Chicago: University of Chicago Press, 1982.

Porch, David. *History of Warfare: Wars of Empire*. New York: Cassell Academic, 2000.

————. "Imperial Wars: From the Seven Years' War to the First World War." In *The Oxford History of Modern War*, edited by Charles Townshend. New York: Oxford University Press, 2005.

Preston, Diana. *A Brief History of the Boxer Rebellion: China's War on Foreigners*. London: Robinson, 2002.

Silbey, David J. *A War of Frontier and Empire: The Philippine-American War, 1899-1902*. New York: Hill and Wang, 2007.

FILMS AND OTHER MEDIA

The British Empire in Color. Documentary. History Channel, 2008.

The Century of Warfare. Documentary. Time-Life Video, 1994.

Congo: White King, Red Rubber, Black Death. Documentary. Périscope Productions, 2003.

William T. Walker

WARFARE
IN THE
INDUSTRIAL
AGE

THE AGE OF BISMARCK

Dates: 1863-1890

POLITICAL CONSIDERATIONS

The Congress of Vienna, held to settle European affairs after the Napoleonic Wars (1793-1815), completed its work in 1815 after deciding not to unite the German states, creating instead the German Confederation of thirty-nine principalities that replaced the Holy Roman Empire. Austria, the leading German state, was ruled from Vienna by Germans but also included a dozen other nationalities. The strongest of the remaining German states, Prussia, stretched across north-central Europe, its western end separated from its eastern, its pride drawing it to claim leadership of the non-Austrian Germans, and its power unequal to the project.

When Austria was weakened in 1848 by a liberal revolution in the capital and indifferent performance in putting down an uprising in its Italian provinces, Prussia dared support the Frankfurt Parliament's proposal of a league of the northern German states. The Austrians mobilized for war and Prussia had to endure a humiliating loss of face. In 1862 the ultra-royalist diplomat Otto von Bismarck (1815-1898) became Prussian foreign minister and president of the cabinet. He immediately took up the project of unifying the northern Germans. When the king of Denmark, a former Austrian ally, died in 1863, Bismarck perceived Austria's isolation. Austria could expect aid neither from Russia, with which it was at odds over the Balkans, nor from France, which supported the Italian struggle to drive the Austrians back beyond the Alps. Bismarck created a diplomatic crisis that united Austria and Prussia in a successful war against the Danes in 1864, then saw to it that serious friction arose between the victorious allies. The resulting Austro-Prussian War (1866) defeated Austria in only seven weeks and gave Prussia unquestioned leadership of the northern Germans. When Bismarck provoked the French emperor Napoleon III (1808-1873) into a rash declaration of war in 1870, France was isolated because both Italy and Austria feared the speed of German mobilization. France fell in six weeks, though the mopping up took several more months. The German Empire, a union of all the Germans outside Austria, was proclaimed at the Hall of Mirrors in the Palace of Versailles in 1871.

MILITARY ACHIEVEMENT

In 1864 Prussia took advantage of a diplomatic contretemps to join with Austria in wresting the provinces of Schleswig and Holstein from Denmark. The best way to force the issue was to overrun the provinces, which the Prussians and Austrians were able to

Otto von Bismarck, Prussian statesman and engineer of German unification.

do because of the speed of Prussian mobilization, the élan of the Austrian troops, and the effectiveness of Prussian fire tactics. When Prussia made war on Austria in 1866, its aim was to advance three armies as quickly as possible into northern Austria to forestall an Austrian invasion of Prussia and to create the opportunity for an encirclement of Austria's main force. The Austrians, forced to fight against both the Prussians in the north and the Italians in the south, mobilized in a leisurely fashion, preferring to fight a defensive battle anchored on one of its fortresses, thus missing the opportunity to deal with the Prussian armies individually. Although its northern army escaped encirclement at the Battle of Königgrätz

(1866), Austria lost 44,000 men to 9,000 Prussians and had to sue for peace.

Because of its 1866 victory, Prussia was able to persuade many German states to join effectively in league with Prussia and create a far larger army, the Army of the North German Confederation. During the 1870 diplomatic crisis with France, this force was able to appear on France's eastern frontiers with incredible speed and to force its will upon the French army. By contrast, French mobilization was slow and confused—the strategic plan little more than a pious wish to march to Berlin via the Palatinate—and coordination between its armies was almost nonexistent. Using superior artillery to great advantage, the Prus-

UNIFICATION OF GERMANY, 1863-1871

Prussia

Added in 1864

Added in formation of the North German Confederation, 1867

Added to form the German Reich in 1871

sians pinned one French army in Metz and forced the other to surrender along with Emperor Napoleon III, then proceeded to besiege Paris and dictate their terms of peace.

WEAPONS, UNIFORMS, AND ARMOR

One of the decisive events in weapons technology during the era of Bismarck was the invention of the Dreyse needle gun, which the Prussian army adopted in 1848. A breech-loading rifle, Dreyse's weapon used a needle-shaped firing pin to strike a percussion cap of fulminate of mercury in the middle of the powder charge. This mechanism made possible a rate of fire five to seven times faster than that of troops using muzzle-loaders. The Dreyse's firing pin eroded quickly, its breech was so badly sealed as to endanger the user and dissipate velocity, and the stiffness of its bolt action was such that troops in battle sometimes had to hammer it open or closed with a rock. The weapon was sighted to 400 yards. The chief objection made to its use was that it would lead to huge wastage of ammunition, leaving its users defenseless as a battle progressed. Helmuth von Moltke the Elder (1800-1891), the military architect of the unification of Germany, insisted that training would develop fire discipline and forced the Prussian army to rely on fire tactics. The Austrians were going in the other direction. In their 1859 war with Piedmont and France, the Austrian troops were armed with the Lorenz, an excellent muzzle-loading rifle that was sighted to 600 yards. Because of their unfamiliarity with the new weapon, which had a slow loading sequence, the Austrian troops could not use it correctly and were mowed down by the bayonets of the French, who attacked in shock columns. After the war, Austria decided to use the column rather than the line as their battle formation and came to regard the Lorenz rifle as merely a good mounting for a bayonet.

Sobered by the way in which the needle gun had cut huge swaths in the Austrian army at the Battle of Königgrätz in 1866, the French army adopted the breech-loading rifle invented by Antoine-Alphonse Chassepot (1833-1905), a vastly improved needle gun. Because the percussion cap was at the rear of the

Helmuth von Moltke the Elder, chief of the Prussian General Staff and the military architect of the unification of Germany.

cartridge, the needle was shorter and eroded less; a superior breech seal made the weapon safer and effective at 1,600 yards.

Rapid improvements in artillery also changed the battlefield. Using a mixture of bronze muzzle-loaded smoothbore cannon and unreliable breechloaders that tended to explode and butcher their crews, Prussia's artillery was inferior to that of Austria during the Austro-Prussian War. Moreover, the Prussian gunners were inferior in both training and ability, giving the Austrians a fire capability one-third greater than that of their foes. In the next few years, however, the Prussians rearmed with the steel cannon whose rifling and superior breech mechanism deepened the battlefield to 7,000 yards. In 1870 the French were still using inferior bronze muzzle-loaders and had weakened their artillery with the addition of the *mitrailleuse*. An early Gatling-type machine gun with twenty-five crank-turned barrels, the mitrailleuse could deliver 150 shots per minute. The French army, however, did not site and use the mitrailleuse as it did later machine guns. Instead it placed them with the artillery, dividing its batteries in thirds, with two six-cannon batteries and a battery of ten mitrailleuses. Because cannons had far greater ranges, the mitrailleuses were easily destroyed by Prussian fire, and the system was an overall weakening of the French artillery capability.

MILITARY ORGANIZATION

The sizes of armies increased remarkably in the nineteenth century, and their control became possible only through their organization into two or more corps, each the size of an eighteenth century army. Each corps was then organized into two or more divisions to facilitate command and control. Professional general staffs became increasingly necessary to plan and support mobilization, logistics, and operations. However, not all nations adopted the general staff system. Those that did develop such staffs often employed them merely as clerks to field commanders.

Helmuth von Moltke became chief of the Prussian General Staff in 1858 and strengthened it by selecting only the most outstanding graduates of the military academy to undergo staff training. Some of these officers then moved into field commands. Those who remained with the staff were rotated periodically into field armies. In this way, the barriers between staff and field personnel were gradually erased, and each better understood and relied on the other. Moltke realized that the advent of mass armies meant that a general headquarters could deploy armies wisely only for strategic purposes and must leave tactical responsibilities to field commanders. Between 1858 and 1866, he and the Prussian minister of war, Count Albrecht von Roon (1803-1879), increased the Prussian army from 100,000 to 300,000 men. They bound the Landwehr, a citizen militia, more tightly to the regular army by requiring that Landwehr recruits come from the ranks of ex-regulars and by giving command of the Landwehr recruits to officers from the regular army. After the Prussian victory over Austria, Prussia was able to create the Army of the North German Confederation, using armies of the other German states organized into corps and subordinated to Prussian control. This army was able to put 983,000 men into action against France in 1870.

The lightness with which the Austrians took the institution of general staff is evident from the fact that in 1860 they made Ludwig von Benedek (1804-1881) both Chief of Imperial General Staff and Commander of the Army of Italy based in Verona. Four years later, Benedek arranged that the staff job go to his friend, Baron Alfred Henikstein, who promptly recommended that the position be abolished. When Benedek took over command of the Northern Army upon its mobilization in 1866, Henikstein went with him into the field while remaining as staff chief. Soldiers were recruited from all of the empire's nationalities for a seven-year hitch. Nine different languages were used in training, but only German was used for giving commands in battle. On the eve of war in 1866, Austria could put 528,000 men in the field: 175,000 in the north, 75,000 in Italy, the rest on fortress duty. An additional 150,000 were expected from Austria's allies among the other German states.

The French army suffered from inadequate military schools, lack of expertise in its officer corps, and a woeful lack of ability to plan, organize, and supply on any large-scale level. Its recruits were selected annually by lottery, one portion to serve for seven years and provide the nucleus of a long-service professional army, and the other to receive minimal training as a reserve. Impressed by the Prussian victory over Austria, the French in 1868 attempted to increase the size of their army by having the long-term recruits serve for five years as regulars and four years as reservists, while the short-term recruits were trained for five months as a reserve. Those who escaped the lottery had to enter a national guard in which they had two weeks of training per year for five years. This system meant that the regulars and reserves would number nearly 500,000 in 1870, 300,000 of whom could be mobilized in three weeks, while the national guard would number over 417,000, with about 120,000 available for service.

DOCTRINE, STRATEGY, AND TACTICS

From the beginning of the nineteenth century, fortresses became increasingly obsolete as the ever-

F. R. Niglutsch

Otto von Bismarck (left), with French ministers Adolphe Thiers (center) and Jules Favre, negotiating peace terms at the conclusion of the Franco-Prussian War in 1871.

larger armies masked them with troops to prevent sallies and simply maneuvered around them. The Prussians gradually came to view the aim of war as being to crush the enemy's army and to destroy his will and ability to resist. The Austrians, however, continued to expend huge amounts of money on fortress systems such as the Quadrilateral, a system of four mutually supportive fortresses in northern Italy, the northernmost of which guarded Bohemia, and a series of fortified areas on the French frontier.

The French first utilized the potential of railways for quickly mobilizing armies and used this ability to call a Prussian bluff in 1859. Spurred both by this episode and by the realization that Prussia was extremely vulnerable because of its level plains and geographical configuration, Moltke decided that

Prussia needed war plans that emphasized extremely quick mobilization, rapid deployment, and a forward strategy that forced the enemy to fight on its own soil. He and Roon improved railways, adapting their trackage and the interior of their wagons for army use, and stringing telegraph lines along them for instant communication. In the war against Denmark, Moltke realized that railroads could be used for maneuvers as well as for mobilization and logistics. This insight, in combination with the needle rifle, led him to rely more on fire tactics than shock tactics.

The standard battle plan of the era emphasized shock tactics. The enemy's line would be disrupted first by cannonade, then by sharpshooting skirmishers and dragoons. The regular regiments would then surge forward in a massive assault to break the enemy line and unleash a cavalry pursuit of the disorganized survivors. Moltke envisioned using rifle companies such as skirmishers to disrupt the enemy line and carry out a tactical envelopment. In this way, small units trained in riflery and moving and shooting from cover could destroy far larger enemy formations. These small-unit tactics were the mirror image of the movement of armies, for Moltke envisioned spreading his forces into a wide net to envelop the enemy's army. Railroads enabled him to bring armies from different parts of Prussia and concentrate them at the point of battle. When this method of making war worked brilliantly against the Austrians, the French began to reevaluate their reliance on columnar shock tactics and to seek a doctrine built around finding and holding superior positions. Given their long emphasis on the role of morale in shock tactics and the offensive character of their war plan against Germany, the French had not resolved the problem by the start of hostilities in 1870.

CONTEMPORARY SOURCES

Invaluable contemporary accounts of the weaponry, strategy, tactics, and operations of Bismarck's wars are to be found in Prusso-German official histories, *The Campaign of 1866 in Germany* (1872), compiled by the Department of Military History of the Prussian Staff, and the five-volume *The Franco-German War, 1870-1871* (1874-1884), by the English War Office. The Austrian official history of the Danish war, *Der Krieg in Schleswig und Jütland in Jahre 1864* (1870; the war in Schleswig and Jütland in 1864) is by Friedrich von Fischer (1826-1907). The five-volume official French history of the Franco-Prussian War, *La Guerre de 1870/71* (1901-1912; the war of 1870-71) is more cold-eyed and rigorous for having appeared so long after the fact. Moltke's military writings are voluminous. The most useful for the period in question are *Moltke's militarische Korrespondenz aus den Dienstschriften des Krieges 1866* (1896; *Moltke's Projects for the Campaign Against Austria*, 1907) and *Geschichte des deutschfranzösischen Krieges von 1870-71* (1891; *The Franco-German War of 1870-71*, 1891). A good selection is available in Daniel J. Hughes's edited volume *Moltke on the Art of War: Selected Writings* (1993).

An analysis of the military lessons of Austria's war against Piedmont and France in 1859 that was important for the formation of Austrian tactics in the Seven Weeks' War is Anton von Mollinary's *Studien über die Operationen und Tactique* (1864; studies on the operations and tactics). A thoughtful and influential eyewitness account on the first of Bismarck's wars is Antonio Gallenga's *The Invasion of Denmark in 1864* (1864). Louis Jules Trochu's *L'Armée français en 1867* (1867; the French army in 1867) provides a description of the French army. The key and crucial role of artillery is thoroughly explored in Carl Edouard von Hoffbauer's *Die deutsche Artillerie in dem Schlachten und Treffen des deutsche-französischen Krieges, 1870-1871* (1876; German artillery in the Franco-Prussian War), and the military use of railroads is analyzed in Alfred Ernouf's *Histoire des chemins de fer français pendant la guerre franco-prussienne* (1874; the history of the French railroad during the Franco-Prussian War). F. F. Steenacker's *Les Télégraphes et les postes pendant la guerre de 1870-1871* (1883) discusses military telegraphy.

BOOKS AND ARTICLES

Badsey, Stephen. *The Franco-Prussian War, 1870-1871*. Botley, Oxford, England: Osprey, 2003.

Bucholz, Arden. *Moltke and the German Wars, 1864-1871*. New York: Palgrave, 2001.

_____. *Moltke, Schlieffen, and Prussian War Planning*. New York: Berg, 1991.

Carr, William. *The Origins of the German Wars of Unification*. New York: Longman, 1991.

Citino, Robert M. "Moltke's Art of War: Innovation and Tradition." In *The German Way of War: From the Thirty Years' War to the Third Reich*. Lawrence: University Press of Kansas, 2005.

Embree, Michael. *Bismarck's First War: The Campaign of Schleswig and Jutland, 1864*. Solihull, West Midlands, England: Helion, 2006.

Gates, David. "The Franco-Prussian War." In *Warfare in the Nineteenth Century*. New York: Palgrave, 2001.

Howard, Michael. 1992. Reprint. *The Franco-Prussian War*. New York: Routledge, 2001.

Shann, Stephen, and L. Delperier. *The French Army of the Franco-Prussian War*. Botley, Oxford, England: Osprey, 1991.

Showalter, Dennis F. *Railroads and Rifles: Soldiers, Technology, and the Unification of Germany*. Westport, Conn.: Greenwood Press, 1975.

Solka, Michael. *German Armies, 1870-71: Prussia*. Illustrated by Darko Pavlovic. Botley, Oxford, England: Osprey, 2004.

———. *German Armies, 1870-71: Prussia's Allies*. Illustrated by Darko Pavlovic. Botley, Oxford, England: Osprey, 2005.

Wawro, Geoffrey. *The Austro-Prussian War: Austria's War with Prussia and Italy in 1866*. Cambridge, England: Cambridge University Press, 1996.

———. *The Franco-Prussian War: The German Conquest of France in 1870-1871*. New York: Cambridge University Press, 2003.

———. *War and Society in Europe, 1792-1914*. New York: Routledge, Chapman and Hall, 2000.

FILMS AND OTHER MEDIA

Battles That Changed the World: The Franco-Prussian War. Documentary. Madacy Records, 1997.

Bismarck: Germany from Blood and Iron. Docudrama. Phoenix Learning Group, 2008.

Field of Honor. Thierry Brissaud, 1987.

The History of Warfare: The Franco-Prussian War, 1870-71. Documentary. Cromwell Productions, 2007.

Joseph M. McCarthy

THE "GREAT" WAR
WORLD WAR I
Dates: 1914-1918

POLITICAL CONSIDERATIONS

Beginning in 1871, with the unification of Kaiser Wilhelm (William) I's (1797-1888) German Reich through the diplomacy of Chancellor Otto von Bismarck (1815-1898) and the efficiency of the Prussian Army, the balance of power in Europe began to change. The swift German defeats of Denmark in 1864, Austria in 1866, and France in 1870-1871 had created a central European state that alarmed all nine of its neighbors. France, clearly seeking revenge for its defeat and for the loss of Alsace-Lorraine, was ready to join other states in a coalition against Germany. Bismarck maintained friendly agreements with Russia and Austria, thus isolating France. By 1882 this agreement had culminated in a Triple Alliance of Germany, Austria-Hungary, and Italy, as well as a nonaggression understanding with Russia.

The Bismarck system was weakened by the 1887 refusal of German banks to extend new loans to Russia, causing the czar to turn to French bankers. After Bismarck's 1890 dismissal by Kaiser Wilhelm (William) II (1859-1941), the German treaty with Russia lapsed, and a Franco-Russian defensive military alliance followed in 1894. Britain's search for allies after the Second Boer War (1899-1902) led to an alliance with Japan, a 1904 colonial "entente" with France, and a similar understanding with Russia in 1907. Although Britain was not bound under the agreement to support France and Russia, and Italy had expressed reservations on its obligations to the alliance, the average European citizen saw the powers as rival camps—Triple Alliance versus Triple Entente. In 1914 neither the people nor the leaders of the larger European powers were planning for or seeking war, although they all sought military security and considered their windows of opportunity for military success. After the war broke out, the forces aligned with the Triple Alliance became known as the Axis, or Central, Powers. The forces aligned with the Triple Entente became known as the Allied Powers.

Whereas Russia had the manpower and Britain the sea power for a long war, Germany's chances seemed better in a short conflict. General Alfred von Schlieffen (1833-1913), the German chief of staff from 1891 to 1905, devised a plan for a quick march through central Belgium aimed at enveloping Paris within six weeks, so that some German troops could be entrained back to Berlin to save it from the slower advance of the Russians. This meant, however, that Germany would have to invade Belgium within a few days of any Russian mobilization. In the 1914 crisis following the assassination of the Austrian crown prince Francis Ferdinand (1863-1914) and his wife by pro-Serb extremists on June 28, 1914, Germany gambled that Russia would stay neutral while Austria defeated the Serbs. When the czar ordered mobilization on July 30, Germany's Kaiser Wilhelm II, Chancellor Theobald von Bethmann-Hollweg, and Chief of Staff General Helmuth von Moltke (1848-1916) all felt compelled to put the Schlieffen Plan into action, declaring war on Russia and mobilizing on August 1 to attack France through Belgium. In all the belligerent states of 1914, the leaders, press, and public felt sure that they had no choice but to fight, that their enemies had forced them to defend themselves.

Nationalism and moral righteousness fanned by newspaper jingoism excited overwhelming support for a war that was expected to be brief, with winners and losers determined by a few battles. Many young men were ready to volunteer for a bit of excitement before settling down. As Winston Churchill put it, "they sought adventure but found death."

The invasion of Belgium became a serious moral handicap for Germany. Allied propaganda built on this violation of neutrality and treaties with stories of atrocities in occupied Belgium that depicted the Germans as bestial criminals. Further, the German advance on Paris bogged down in stalemated trench warfare, and the German defeat of the Russians at Tannenberg in August, 1914, and at the Masurian Lakes in September, 1914, was not decisive, partly due to Austria's poor showing on the eastern front. Although a negotiated peace might have been possible at the end of 1914, public opinion was not prepared for it, and it would not have met the demand for future security against aggression. The German armies were successful enough in 1914 to overrun most of France's northern industrial zone. As they held off the Russians, the Ottoman Empire joined the Central Powers, the former Triple Alliance, in October, 1914, hoping to pay off old scores against Russia, Britain, and France. Japan also joined with Germany in August, occupying Germany's Far Eastern bases, especially that of Qingdao, in China's Shandong province.

In 1915 French marshal Joseph-Jacques Césaire Joffre (1852-1931) mounted offensives that he termed as "nibbling" against the German troops, now commanded by General Erich von Falkenhayn (1861-1922). On the eastern front, the failure of Russia's offensive encouraged Bulgaria to join the Central Powers, combining with Austria to drive the Serb army out of Serbia. An August 6, 1915, Anglo-French naval attempt to open the Dardanelles, a narrow strait between Turkey and Europe, as a supply route to Russia failed. These debacles brought about a coalition cabinet in Britain, and Winston Churchill was dropped from the Admiralty. The British also committed an expedition to occupy Basra, a southeastern Iraqi port, and to move up the Tigris River toward Baghdad in Turkish Mesopotamia. Italy joined the Axis Powers, with the promise of land in the Trentino, the Tyrol, and the Dalmatian coast as well as extra-European colonies. In a further Eastern diversion, Axis troops occupied Salonika as a check to Bulgaria. Germany fell into a quarrel with the United States over American lives lost in the May 7, 1915, torpedoing of the British liner *Lusitania*. When U.S. president Woodrow Wilson (1856-1924) threatened war, the Germans promised in May of 1916 to restrict their submarine tactics to the nearly prohibitive terms demanded by the United States.

It was widely expected that 1916 would be a year of decisive battles. The Allied plan for simultaneous convergence on Germany was anticipated when Falkenhayn launched a major assault on French fortifications at Verdun in February. Russia's June attack on Austria, the Brusilov Offensive, encouraged Romania to join the Allies, while the British Expeditionary Force under Sir Douglas Haig (1861-1928) made a major attack on the Germans in the Battle of the Somme (1916). The Germans did not take Verdun, but they rescued the Austrians and overran nearly all of Romania. This success did not quite make up for a potato blight in Germany and a subsequent "turnip winter" for the civilians. In Mesopotamia the British advance army of 10,000 was defeated

TURNING POINTS

Aug., 1914	German planes bomb Paris.
Sept., 1914	German U-9 submarines torpedo Allied ships.
Apr., 1915	First aerial "dogfight" takes place.
May, 1915	German zeppelins bomb London.
May, 1915	German submarine torpedoes the *Lusitania*, enraging the American public.
Aug.-Dec., 1915	Anglo-French attack on the Gallipoli Peninsula fails to exploit the "soft underbelly" of the Central Powers.
May, 1916	Battle of Jutland effectively ends German naval threat.
June, 1916	Limitations of heavy artillery bombardment exposed in the Battle of the Somme.
Apr., 1917	United States enters the war on the side of the Allies.
May, 1917	Allies establish Atlantic convoy system.
Nov. 20, 1917	British make a successful tank attack at Cambrai.
Mar., 1918	Following the Bolshevik Revolution of November, 1917, Russia leaves the war.

WORLD WAR I: WESTERN FRONT, 1915-1917

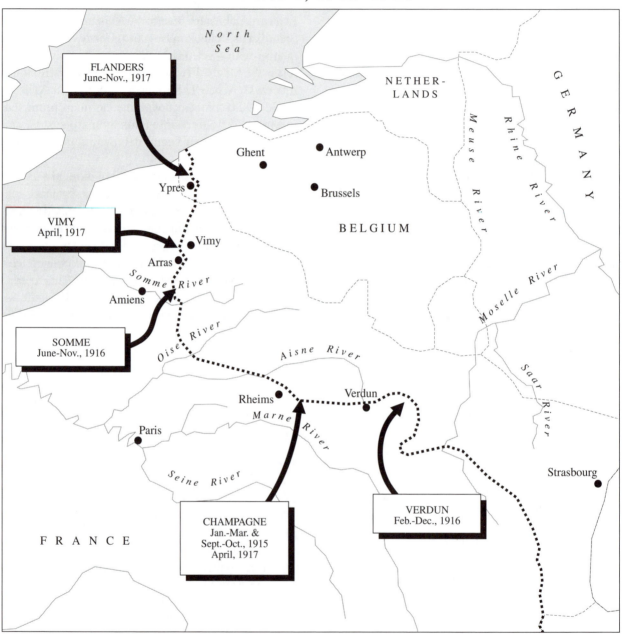

and surrendered. The May, 1916, naval Battle of Jutland proved a tactical success for Germany but a strategic success for the continuing British blockade. The British losses on the Somme were heavy, and the Easter Rebellion in Ireland rounded out another grim year. In the United States, 1916 was a year of pre-

paredness rallies and appropriations. After his re-election, President Wilson asked both the Allied and the Axis Powers to state their specific war aims, but each side replied in vague terms. The restriction of territorial annexations gained support among those tired of the war, but there was no agreement on the possession of the Alsace-Lorraine region on the French-German border.

By March of 1917, street demonstrations in the Russian cities of St. Petersburg and Moscow had become uncontrollable. Czar Nicholas II abdicated, and a government of moderates was formed, headed by Prince Georgy Lvov (1861-1925) and dominated by Aleksandr Kerensky (1881-1970). Attempts to continue the war were unsuccessful. Peace, bread, and land were the popular demands, and on that program, Vladimir Ilich Lenin (1870-1924) and the Bolsheviks took power in November, signed an armistice on December 15, and accepted a treaty at Brest Litovsk on March 3, 1918.

The German General Staff, headed since 1916 by Paul von Hindenburg (1847-1934), with Erich Ludendorff (1865-1937) as his strategic guide, viewed the Russian collapse as Germany's chance for total victory. The Germans calculated that an all-out submarine campaign would defeat Britain by 1918, that America would never risk sending troops across a submarine-dominated Atlantic, and that German soldiers from the eastern front would give the Reich the manpower it needed to crush France in 1918. Diplomatic alternatives were not explored. The resumption of unrestricted submarine warfare in February, 1917, was an open challenge to Wilson's policy. The so-called Zimmermann note, an intercepted German telegram made public proposing an alliance of Germany, Mexico, and Japan in war against the United States, was clearly a hostile act that Americans treated as such. The United States declared war on Germany on April 6, 1917. The United States chose to fight as an "Associated Power," against war and autocracy and for peace, humanity, and justice, without seeking territory as the spoils of victory.

After the failure of a French offensive in April, 1917, was followed by a mutinous "sit-down" in several French army divisions, General Henri-Philippe Pétain (1856-1951) became French commander in chief, restoring confidence with a strategic choice to "wait for the tanks and the Americans." The Italians were outgeneraled in the autumn Battle of Caporetto (1917), losing heavily in prisoners as they were driven from the Isonzo River back to the Piave River. These German successes, however great, could not make up for the facts that Britain had been saved by the transatlantic convoy system and that U.S. troops had begun arriving in France in June of 1917.

The Russian (Bolshevik) Revolution, which had also begun in 1917, and the American entrance into the war had, by 1918, given the war an increasingly ideological meaning. After the Bolsheviks published the Axis Powers' secret treaties, *The New York Times* editorialized that Russian revolutionary leader Leon Trotsky was "not a gentleman," but, in fact, the treaties' evidence of haggling over territorial loot insulted the sacrifice of millions of lives. The promise of self-determination, democracy, and justice espoused in both Wilson's program for a just settlement of the war, known as the Fourteen Points, and Lenin's propaganda encouraged separatism in

Popperfoto/Getty Images

Hunched British soldiers advance during the trench warfare of the Battle of the Somme (1916).

Austria-Hungary and the Ottoman Empire, as well as in Ireland and Asia. Ludendorff ignored the political trends and the possibilities of defensive strategy and gambled that he could find military victory in France with a well-planned attack and revised infantry tactics. His offensive broke the front and gained ground, but again the troops outran their reinforcements and supplies. When the Allies, finally united under the command of French marshal Ferdinand Foch (1851-1929), struck back in mid-June with the advantage of tanks and air support, the overextended German lines could no longer halt the Allied attacks. In September, Ludendorff declared victory out of reach, and in October the German chancellor asked Wilson for armistice terms based on the Fourteen Points. Negotiations proceeded as Bulgaria made terms on September 29, Turkey on October 31, and Austria on November 4. Part of the German navy mutinied on October 29, and an armistice delegation left Berlin for France on November 7. Demonstrations in Berlin led Kaiser Wilhelm to abdicate on November 9 and flee to Holland the following day. The German delegates, now representing a new government, signed an Armistice at Compiègne on November 11. President Wilson arrived in Europe on December 13, 1918, hailed as a powerful idealist bringing peace, democracy, justice, and security at the end of the "Great War."

A midget submarine pulls up beside a German U-boat in 1917.

Military Achievement

Germany's goal in the major theater of World War I was to defeat France by taking Paris within six weeks and then shifting troops eastward to stop the invading Russians. The drive for Paris failed. The Germans were stymied by problems with supplies and reinforcements that were multiplied with the distance from the German railheads, whereas the French used their own transport network, centered on Paris, for rapid countermoves.

Falkenhayn's 1916 attrition strategy in the attack of Verdun killed almost as many Germans as Allies and was basically unsound, given the Allied predominance in manpower. Colonel Max Hoffman's (1869-1927) 1917 campaign on the eastern front took advantage of the Russian Revolution to drive the Russians to accept German peace terms and created an opportunity for a negotiated peace that was acceptable to Germany. Ludendorff, in the west, preferred to gamble on submarines and a 1918 capture of Paris before American intervention could be effective. A better German foreign policy might have been the avoidance of a two-front war or the negotiation of an acceptable peace plan in late 1916 or early 1917. Germany's wartime aims for territory or dominance in Europe, Africa, and the Middle East were militarily impractical.

The French offensive aims never achieved their ostensible goals until the Ludendorff Offensive of 1918 depleted German manpower. Only then could the French achieve the obvious goal of gaining Alsace-Lorraine plus security. France's Plan 17 in 1914 was geographically unsound and misjudged the location of the German attack, but it drew the German battle eastward and away from Paris. Joffre's 1915 "nibbling" with bombardments was ineffective, and General Robert-Georges Nivelle's (1856-1924) "surprise breakthrough" in 1917 had been too widely advertised to surprise anyone. Pétain's defensive strategy gave the French army a chance to recover, a sensible goal after the French army mutinies of 1917. The French general staff was generally less effective than its German counterpart but made fewer costly mistakes.

The Russian goals of taking Berlin, threatening Vienna, and dominating Constantinople at least had the advantage of a numerous, courageous, and usually uncomplaining infantry. Against Austrian and Turkish forces, the Russians had many successes, limited only by inadequate transportation. Against the Germans, however, the Russian army officers seemed to be too preoccupied by the probability of defeat to act on the possibility of success. With a shortage of both experienced noncommissioned ranks and competent officers, the quality of Russian army leadership was so bad that the troops were losing faith in the army leaders, even as the home front was losing faith in the government and the czar.

Britain achieved some limited and peripheral goals: It prevailed narrowly in the Battle of Jutland; it maintained a blockade of the Central Powers; it brought world, and especially U.S., resources to the western front despite German submarines; it helped to finance the Allies; it did most of the fighting in Germany's African colonies, in the Middle East, and at the Dardanelles and Gallipoli; and it committed a sizable army to the western front. These were significant goals and achievements. Without victory over the submarines, there might well have been no Allied victory in the European theater. On the other hand, Germany's chief threat to Britain was economic, and on that score, the liquidation of Britain's overseas investments to finance the war benefited the United States more than it hurt Germany and was certainly an important step in Britain's later decline as a world power.

Austria did occupy Serbia in 1915, thereby more or less achieving Austria-Hungary's goal to eliminate Serbia as a factor in Balkan politics. It also held off the Italians until the collapse of 1918, but its campaigns against Russia lacked direction, and of course the 1918 wave of "self-determination" simply dissolved the polyglot Habsburg Empire. The Treaty of Versailles that ended the war in 1919 drew very restricted boundaries for Hungary and forbade the Austrian remnant from making any political or commercial union with Germany.

The Allied Powers had made generous territorial promises to Italy for joining them in 1915, and the Italian Army's military goal from 1915 to 1918 was to take the Austrian capital of Vienna. Adverse geography and an army that was both poorly equipped and poorly trained stalled the Italians on the Isonzo River, until their defeat at Caporetto forced them to develop assault squads that finally won the Battle of Vittorio Veneto (1918) as Austria-Hungary collapsed. Even though Italy did gain the Trentino, Tyrol, and, later, Fiume, in the Treaty of Versailles, it still felt short-changed. The Ottoman Empire wished to gain territory, such as the Suez Canal, from the British, and land in the Caucasus from Russia, but was more successful in defensive campaigns, such as Gallipoli (1915-1916). In the Balkans, the Serbian army had been forced out of Serbia into Salonika, a French territory, but in the Treaty of Versailles, the Serbian premier gained leadership over the kingdom of Serbs, Croats, and Slovenes. Bulgaria had joined the Central Powers to invade Serbia but lost border enclaves in the Treaty of Versailles. Romania's goal had been to gain Transylvania, and despite a complete military defeat, did so at Paris; it had also regained Bessarabia from Russia under the earlier Treaty of Brest Litovsk. Greece had the distinction of being forced into the war by the British and French for modest territorial gains. Belgium had wanted Luxembourg but had no means of armed occupation. Japan's goal had been to acquire German bases and islands in the Far East, and its army and navy enforced these claims. Japan's military presence in Shandong and Siberia and its naval construction program aroused U.S. hostility.

The United States entered the war on April 6, 1917, participating in the battles of 1918 as an "Associated Power" on the Allied side. The American political goals were to defeat Germany, "making the world safe for democracy" and ending war by means of a League of Nations based on self-determination and justice. The U.S. military goal was German surrender.

WEAPONS, UNIFORMS, AND ARMOR

In 1914, as oversized armies met in the European theater, increased firepower made battlefields impassable for conventional infantry assaults. The previously ineffective *mitrailleuse* came into its own: Situated to cover enemy troop concentrations and used in short bursts to avoid overheating and jamming, these machine guns, whether water-cooled Maxims or air-cooled Hotchkiss types, fired 400 to 600 rounds per minute. Also, bolt-action repeating rifles, such as the German Mauser Gewehr 98, the British Lee-Metford, the Austrian Mannlicher Model 1895, the Italian Mannlicher-Carcano, the French Lebel M-1e 1886/93, the Russian Nagant, and later, the American Springfield, achieved a range, accuracy, and rate of fire unprecedented in European warfare. Battles of encounter became a story of heavy losses, entrenchment, barbed wire, and stalemate.

Light field artillery was used to attack the trenches, ranging from the 75-millimeter gun (known in French as the *soixante-quinze*) to the 105-millimeter howitzer. The Germans used 30.5-centimeter Skodas and 42-centimeter Krupps Big Berthas for howitzer shelling of the forts at Liège and Namur. Larger artillery, such as the "Paris gun," used by the Germans to shell Paris in 1918, had to be moved by rail. Antitrench bombardments, however, so cratered the terrain as to slow down the assault troops, a self-defeating result.

The mining of enemy trenches, as by the British at Messines Ridge in June, 1917, was effective but caused massive terrain dislocation and took a great deal of time for a limited gain. Flamethrowers were tried with good results at close quarters but without achieving major breakthroughs. Poison gas, under the right conditions, could break down a line of defense, but advancing in gas masks was slow work and some gases persisted for days. Repeatedly, attacking armies were hampered in moving men and supplies across ravaged battlefields while retreating armies drew on rapid support from the rail center it was defending. For most of World War I defense was a stronger position than offense in terms of reinforcement and supply.

Another defensive form, the blockade, dominated the war at sea, but undersea and aerial weapons threatened the traditional line of battle style of naval warfare. Submerged mines kept the British from entering the Dardanelles in 1915 and effectively kept them out of the Baltic Sea. Aerial reconnaissance at sea by dirigibles, blimps, and airplanes became a new factor, and German diesel-electric submarines did

U.S. infantry soldiers fire a 37MM machine gun at Germans during a battle in the Argonne Forest in 1918.

much more damage to Allied warships and world commercial shipping than did any of its surface warships. These submarines were also a major factor in the 1917 entry of the United States into the war, which ensured Germany's defeat.

Aerial warfare captured the imagination of the public, but the comparative airpower of the European states in 1914 is difficult to put in quantitative terms, because too many variables are involved. France apparently had from 200 to 250 serviceable airplanes. Germany had a few more, as well as zeppelins. Britain claimed only 35 planes but could be compared at 135. Austria-Hungary had 36, and Belgium 24. Russia purchased 250 foreign planes in 1913 to add to

those of its own production but listed only about 100 total pilots. Wartime production greatly increased these numbers.

The first aerial reconnaissance and bombing began in 1914, when machine guns were mounted on airplanes. American aircraft designer Anthony H. G. Fokker (1890-1939) equipped his 1915 German planes with interrupter gears for forward firing through the propeller. Germany's zeppelins were useful only in long-range bombing, and its airplane production was limited by an inadequate supply of engines. During the war airplanes improved greatly in both general reliability and strength of construction. Pilots were not usually issued parachutes, giving them an incentive to land their planes safely if hit. Survivors could not remember any "dogfights" quite as crowded as those depicted in later Hollywood films.

Armored trains and armored cars were not new, but they could not cross trenches. In 1916, British Colonel Ernest Swinton (1868-1951) developed a "land warship," code-named "tank," with a caterpillar tractor-type continuous tread stretched over a long and rigid track. This tread gave the 30-ton vehicle the ability to cross trenches while carrying 6-pound guns or machine guns in side-mounted gun platforms as it advanced through the German defenses. In 1918 Britain produced a 14-ton Whippet model tank with a machine gun, and France introduced the 6.5-ton Renault Char-Mitrailleuse with a 360-degree turret. The British used a few tanks on the Somme in 1916 and successfully at Cambrai in 1917. Germany produced a few 30-ton tanks and only prototypes for a lighter machine. Germany's western offensive in 1918 depended chiefly on the use of captured Allied tanks. Despite their persistent tendencies to ditch or break down, tanks were the Allies' best new weapon in 1918. Although the tank became a tactical breakthrough weapon in World War I, it was not yet capable of leading a sustained offensive.

Several elements of civilian life came to have military significance. Trucks became necessary links between railheads and battlefields, although horses still pulled field artillery. Telephones and wireless telegraphy became variably useful. Voice radio would have been very useful for conveying reports and orders over large combat areas, but the transmitting and receiving equipment had a limited range.

By 1914 armor at sea had been maximized. Waterline "blisters" were added to battleships for protection against mines and torpedoes, but the addition of any more deck armor to protect against aerial bombs or the plunging fire of long-range shooting would have made ships top-heavy and ready to capsize. German compartmentalization and wider dry docks gave the Germans stronger ships at Jutland.

Armor on land principally concerned tanks. Although World War I tanks had enough armor to stop ordinary rifle or machine-gun bullets, .50-caliber or larger high-velocity bullets would penetrate them. The size of tank needed to cross trenches meant a large vehicle that was only thinly covered. Basically, tanks needed more horsepower, which ideally came from diesel engines.

European uniforms became discreetly drab after the Russo-Japanese War (1904-1905) showed the advantage of camouflage. Khaki or gray-green colors prevailed. Shoulder and collar patches identified different units and rank. Headgear, such as a forage cap, tin hat, turban, or fez, was distinctive. In 1914 the exceptions in uniform uniformity were the French, whose press and politicians had insisted on the troops' traditional blue coat and red trousers, and the Scots, whose kilts were covered by khaki aprons for the field.

MILITARY ORGANIZATION

The belligerents of World War I originally organized their military forces along the same general lines developed during the French Revolution (1789-1799). The head of the government or the war cabinet determined war policies for the army and navy. The service chiefs developed and executed the military war plans. This latter group was described as General Headquarters (GHQ) in Britain and the United States, as Grand Quartier Géneral (GQG) in France, as Stavka in Russia, and Oberste Heeresleitung (OHL) in Germany.

The land forces were divided into army groups of field armies composed of corps. The corps was an all-arms group including two infantry divisions, a cavalry brigade or division, an artillery brigade, and several support groups. The division continued to be a basic all-arms unit capable of independent action if ordered and composed of brigades, regiments, battalions, companies, platoons, and squads in diminishing order of size. A typical infantry division included headquarters personnel, two or three brigades of infantry, one or two regiments of field artillery, a squadron or up to a regiment of cavalry, a battalion or regiment of engineers, one or more signal companies (in the United States, this included airplanes as well as telegraph and radio), ambulance companies, field hospitals, a base hospital, ammunition and supply services, and food services. European divisions might number 10,00 to 15,000, and U.S. divisions in Europe 25,000 to 30,000. Cavalry divisions were much less numerous in personnel. Some divisions were specialized, such as investment divisions for sieges or mountain (Alpine) divisions.

This multiplicity of functions meant that while battlefield firepower increased, the number of riflemen decreased in favor of the new special services. In military jargon, there was "less teeth and more tail," especially in the United States' overseas divisions. Indeed, some servicemen might find that apart from boredom, mud, and the danger of being killed or wounded, they were better fed and cared for than they had been in civilian life.

The development during World War I of infiltration squads and supporting assault battalions meant special selection, training, and organization for these shock troops, or combat teams, as they would later be called. At the time this separation of an elite infantry force was controversial for being potentially harmful to general army morale. Is is considered in some accounts as a factor in Germany's 1918 military defeat.

The new weapons of World War I were sometimes seen as a threat to senior army ranks. Young officers ambitious for promotion might be drawn to a new technical field, to which older officers found it difficult to adjust, and claim the need for an independent organization with its own system of funding, control, and promotion. Submarines were safely under navy control, and aircraft carriers could be limited, but a separate Royal Air Force, such as the British established in 1918, was an unwelcome competitor for shrinking postwar military budgets. There was widespread agreement that tanks should be nothing more than ancillary to infantry operations.

The general staff system of army administration, planning, and command, used with great success by Germany in the nineteenth century, was widely copied but with very mixed results in World War I. The German staff was efficient in the military field but calamitous in trying to shape general strategy and foreign policy. The French staff managed its generals fairly well but did not do much for the front-line sol-diers. Otherwise, general staffs tended to defer to the commanding general without giving him needed information. Britain's imperial general staff suffered from the fact that the British had little regard for military desk jobs and opted instead for field commands. Although the United States had capable staff chiefs, it still seemed that General John Pershing did too much of his own staff work. On the whole, most countries felt that their own general staff needed improvement and that the German staff should be abolished. The abolition turned out to be only a matter of form.

DOCTRINE, STRATEGY, AND TACTICS

Nineteenth century military theory, attempting to borrow its principles of war from the French Revolutionary Wars (1792-1802), concluded that mass citizen armies had outmoded the older professional armies of the eighteenth century and that the offensive campaigns of French emperor Napoleon Bonaparte (1769-1821) showed how these mass armies should be used to win wars. The doctrine of the offensive became established at military academies. In the Crimean War (1853-1856), the American Civil War (1861-1865), the Wars of German Unification (1864, 1866, 1870-1871), and the Russo-Japanese War (1904-1905), victory went to invaders pursuing the offensive, although the cost to the attacking infantry increased. Breech-loading cannon and repeating rifles with longer effective ranges made frontal assaults increasingly costly, and railways gave defenders a quick deployment against any strategic flank attack. Although it took little training to fire a rifle from a defensive position, the half-trained recruits of mass armies might not be as willing and able to press home a successful bayonet attack.

In France the doctrine of the offensive became even more imperative as military leaders appreciated that the predictable speed of a German offensive aimed at Paris would need to be matched by a fast-moving Franco-Russian offensive converging on Berlin. According to the French high command, the French infantry would need to have the spirit, discipline, and courage to attack and win by the bayonet against ever-increasing odds. The Germans held a similar philosophy.

The western front battles of 1914 began as open-field encounters of deadly firepower that drove the troops into hasty trenches. The short lesson was "bullets kill men, and earth stops bullets." The dominant tactic from 1915 to 1917 was bombardment by more and bigger howitzers. This offensive was undeniably more wracking for the target infantry, and fatal for some outposts, but it destroyed the element of surprise and left a scarred no-man's-land of a battlefield that was too chewed up for an offensive advance. Extensive mining could destroy an entire enemy entrenchment, but again, the zone of destruction was difficult for the attackers to cross. This method was effective, but time-consuming and expensive. Attacks with poisonous gases were frequently surprising and damaging to the defenders but also caused problems for the attackers. Tank attacks were promising but not very effective in 1916 and 1917.

French general Nivelle promised a new kind of offensive when he replaced Marshal Joffre in 1917. On paper his plan did seem to incorporate some of the flexible infiltration ideas advocated by earlier theo-

rists, but when the plan was fully explained to the politicians, and through the press to the public, including the Germans, its failure became inevitable.

"Vertical infiltration" was more successfully developed by the Germans for their breakthrough against the Russians at Riga (1917). The same methods accounted for some of the Austro-German success against Italy at Caporetto. The surprising strength of the Ludendorff Offensive in 1918 again showed the effectiveness of these methods. The Allies followed somewhat similar offensive methods later in 1918, but these tended to be tank-led breakthrough and penetration tactics against German troops who were increasingly willing to surrender.

Vertical infiltration, as developed by the Germans during World War I, was basically an infantry attack involving several new tactics. The spear point was to be a squad of fourteen to eighteen storm troopers, or (in German) *Sturmtruppen*, attacking on several principles. The first was the use of reconnaissance to find weak spots, infiltrating in surprise night penetrations, deceptive preparations, and short bombardments, moving forward, and bypassing strong points. After this initial infiltration, platoons, companies,

WORLD WAR I: OFFENSIVES ON THE WESTERN FRONT, 1918

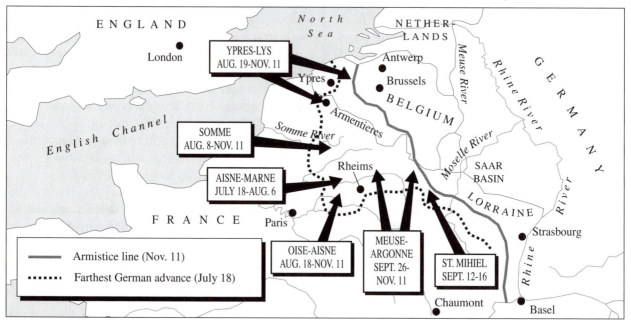

and larger units would also move forward and widen the breakthrough. The infiltration squad would use light machine guns or portable submachine guns such as the Madsen, Bergmann, or Parabellum, as well as grenades and grenade launchers, light trench mortars, gas shells, and sometimes flamethrowers. Batallion support followed with machine gun companies, light artillery companies, and heavier, individually placed guns. Ideally aerial bombing and strafing would find targets of opportunity. The principle of momentum held that the assault and support units should always keep moving. The assault team included engineers to ensure that reinforcements, replacements, and supplies could be moved directly from the rear to the front.

Clearly, these were ideal principles. In practice, the logistical problems of moving equipment from the railhead to the forward storm troopers could not keep an advance going indefinitely. Also, many generals rejected the idea of elite storm troopers as bad for general army morale. However, the resemblance of these early troops to World War II German Panzer divisions and to later U.S. assault team formations is clear enough to show the eventual significance of these tactics for future offensives.

In Britain and France the lessons that generals learned in 1918 mattered less to the public, press, and political leaders than did the preceding four-year western front stalemate and slaughter. The doctrine of the offensive and the strategy of attrition were discredited among the postwar disillusioned, or "lost," generation. Without American or Soviet support, the remaining Allies adopted a defensive doctrine, believing that the Maginot line, a line of fortifications along the French-German border, and a British naval blockade would be enough to defeat Germany economically. This strategy was crushed by the German Blitzkrieg of 1940.

CONTEMPORARY SOURCES

The best prewar analysis of World War I fighting was that of Ivan Bloch (1836-1902), a Russo-Polish financier. His *The Future of War in Its Technical, Economic, and Political Relations: Is War Now Impossible?* (1899), a one-volume English-language summary of his work, displays outstanding military and logistical insight as well as a curiously poor grasp of wartime government finance. General Friedrich von Bernhardi's (1849-1930) *The War of the Future in the Light of the Lessons of the World War* (1920) was notable for its author's distrust of the Schlieffen Plan.

Once the shooting started, morale-boosting propaganda replaced news in press reports. German reporting was censored, and British, French, and Russian correspondents were not permitted in the war zones. "Official sources," meaning either an "information office" or a military service department, issued statements, which correspondents duly reported. Philip Gibbs (1877-1962), a popular British correspondent, collected his reports in wartime books such as *The Soul of the War* (1915).

Letters from soldiers at the front were a better source of information, and in 1914 some British provincial weeklies published these generally optimistic reports from local soldiers. Government censorship halted this practice by 1915, only allowing publication of handouts by government agencies.

U.S. publications from 1914 to 1917 generally followed the lead of British and French accounts but also included reports from the Central Powers. The Germans conducted journalists such as Irvin S. Cobb (1876-1944) on guided tours to verify their claims of success, reflected in Cobb's *Paths of Glory: Impression of War Written at or Near the Front* (1915). The British and French followed the Germans' example in 1915. U.S. newspapers and magazines were at least more balanced than those of the belligerents and somewhat more realistic in estimating the hardships of the war.

The Russian Revolution of 1917 was reported somewhat confusedly in the Western press. The Communist takeover was reported with reasonable accuracy by some British reporters, as well as the American John Reed (1887-1920) of *The Masses*, but much of the press was misled into following inaccurate reports in *The Times* of London and *The New York Times*, both of which pursued an anti-Bolshevik crusade as the war ended.

Many of the war's major participants, including Joffre, Foch, Pétain, Pershing, Ludendorff, Falkenhayn, Hindenburg, and Liman von Sanders, released postwar memoirs. Viscount Edward Grey's (1862-1933) *Twenty-five Years, 1892-1916* (1925) discounted his own influence on events. Georges Clemenceau (1841-1929) delivered a mordant verdict on human nature in *Grandeur and Misery of Victory* (1930). David Lloyd George's (1863-1945) war memoirs and memoirs of the Paris Peace Conference were somewhat feline about his late associates, especially Field Marshal Douglas Haig. Haig's letters and papers were finally published in 1952, revealing a surprisingly extravagant concern for petty grievances.

Diplomatic histories used government documents and memoirs, and American "revisionists" blamed either Russia and France or civilization at large for the war. Luigi Albertini (1871-1941) published an extensively researched three-volume history entitled *The Origins of the War of 1914* (1952-1957), which seems definitive. German historian Fritz Fischer has taken a highly critical and controversial view of his own country's responsibility for World War I.

Disillusionment with war's ideals and conduct was prevalent throughout the 1920's and 1930's. Gibbs's *Now It Can Be Told* (1920) revised the tone of his earlier reporting to accommodate the prevailing public sentiment. Arthur Ponsonby's (1871-1946) *Falsehood in Wartime: Propaganda Lies of the First World War* (1991) exposed Allied propaganda. America's chief propagandist, George Creel (1876-1953), explained how he had misled the gullible in *How We Advertised America* (1920). A legion of poets portrayed the slaughter of the war in emotionally horrific language, although Robert Graves (1895-1985) in *Goodbye to All That: An Autobiography* (1929) showed a nostalgic view of the bad old times. One literary critic cynically suggested that in the next war, poets should not be allowed in the trenches.

Most novelists took a jaundiced view of the war. *Tell England: A Study in a Generation* (1922), by Ernest Raymond (born 1888); *Education Before Verdun* (1936), by Arnold Zweig (1887-1968); *A Farewell to Arms* (1929), by Ernest Hemingway (1899-1961); *The General* (1936), by C. S. Forester (1899-1966); and the highly readable *Im Westen nichts Neues* (1929, 1968; *All Quiet on the Western Front*, 1929, 1969) by Erich Maria Remarque (1898-1970) all depicted the war in somber tones. Perhaps significantly, Fritz von Unruh's (born 1885) *The Way of Sacrifice* (1928) implied that the killing was justifiable, and Ernst Junger's (born 1895) *Storm of Steel: From the Diary of a German Storm-troop Officer on the Western Front* (1929) presented the war as at once terrible and glorious.

Letters and diaries from the trenches have remained as the best source on what the war was like for the average soldier. Among the many examples, J. C. Dunn's (1871-1955) *The War the Infantry Knew, 1914-1918* (1938), James Lockhead Jack's (1880-1962) *General Jack's Diary* (1964), and *Voices from the Great War* (1981), compiled by Peter Vansittart, are useful examples, although predominantly from the officer's viewpoint. Denis Winter's *Death's Men: Soldiers of the Great War* (1978) and Lyn Macdonald's *Somme* (1983) are perhaps the most successful articulations of the voice of enlisted men in World War I.

BOOKS AND ARTICLES

Asprey, Robert B. *The German High Command at War*. New York: William Morrow, 1991.

Barton, Peter, Peter Doyle, and Johan Vandewalle. *Beneath Flanders Fields: The Tunnellers' War, 1914-1918*. Staplehurst, England: Spellmount, 2005.

De Groot, Gerard J. *The First World War*. New York: Palgrave, 2001.

Downes, Alexander B. "The Starvation Blockades of World War I: Britain and Germany." In *Targeting Civilians in War*. Ithaca, N.Y.: Cornell University Press, 2008.

Goldstein, Donald M., and Harry J. Maihafer. *America in World War I: The Story and Photographs*. Washington, D.C.: Brassey's, 2004.

Griffith, Paddy. *Battle Tactics of the Western Front*. New Haven, Conn.: Yale University Press, 1994.

Halpern, Paul G. *A Naval History of World War I*. Annapolis, Md.: Naval Institute Press, 1994.

Jukes, Geoffrey, Peter Simkins, and Michael Hickey. *The First World War*. 4 vols. Botley, Oxford, England: Osprey, 2002.

Kitchen, Martin. *The German Offensives of 1918*. Stroud, Gloucestershire, England: Tempus, 2005.

Morrow, John H., Jr. *The Great War in the Air: Military Aviation from 1909 to 1921*. Washington, D.C.: Smithsonian Institution Press, 1993. Reprint. Tuscaloosa: University of Alabama Press, 2009.

Neiberg, Michael S., ed. *The World War I Reader: Primary and Secondary Sources*. New York: New York University Press, 2007.

Palazzo, Albert. *Seeking Victory on the Western Front: The British Army and Chemical Warfare in World War I*. Lincoln: University of Nebraska Press, 2000.

Robbins, Simon. *British Generalship on the Western Front, 1914-18: Defeat into Victory*. New York: F. Cass, 2005.

Samuels, Martin. *Doctrine and Dogma: German and British Infantry Tactics in the First World War*. New York: Greenwood Press, 1992.

Saunders, Anthony. *Dominating the Enemy: War in the Trenches, 1914-1918*. Stroud, Gloucestershire, England: Sutton, 2000.

Sheffield, Gary, ed. *War on the Western Front*. Botley, Oxford, England: Osprey, 2007.

Smith, Leonard V. *Between Mutiny and Obedience: The Case of the French Fifth Infantry Division During World War I*. Princeton, N.J.: Princeton University Press, 1994.

Tucker, Jonathan B. *War of Nerves: Chemical Warfare from World War I to Al-Qaeda*. New York: Pantheon Books, 2006.

FILMS AND OTHER MEDIA

All Quiet on the Western Front. Feature film. Universal Pictures, 1930.

The Dawn Patrol. Feature film. Warner Bros., 1938.

Deathwatch. Feature film. Lions Gate Entertainment, 2002.

A Farewell to Arms. Feature film. The Selznick Studio, 1957.

The First World War. Documentary series. Wark Clements, 2003.

Flyboys. Feature film. MGM, 2006.

Fräulein Doktor. Dino De Laurentiis, 1969.

Gallipoli. Documentary. Cinema Epoch, 2005.

Gallipoli. Feature film. Australian Film Commission, 1981.

Grand Illusion. Feature film. R.A.C., 1937.

The Guns of August. Documentary. MCA Universal, 1964.

In Love and War. Feature film. Warner Bros., 1996.

Lawrence of Arabia. Feature film. Horizon, 1962.

The Lighthorsemen. Feature film. Columbia TriStar, 1987.

The Lost Battalion. Television film. A&E, 2001.

Passchendaele. Feature film. Alliance Films, 2008.

Paths of Glory. Feature film. Bryna, 1957.

Regeneration. Feature film. Artificial Eye, 1997.

The Trench. Feature film. Arts Council of England, 1999.

A Very Long Engagement. Warner Independent, 2004.

World War I. Documentary. Encyclopedia Britannica Educational Corporation, 1957.

World War I: The Great War. Documentary. History Channel, 2009.

K. Fred Gillum

THE SPANISH CIVIL WAR

Dates: 1936-1939

POLITICAL CONSIDERATIONS

In July of 1936, the government of Spain's five-year-old Second Republic, an unstable popular front composed of liberal democrats, socialists, and communists, came under fire from the political right. After failing to gain control in either February's election or the ensuing wave of assassinations, the National Front, an alliance of conservative democrats, monarchists, and fascist parties, including the militant Falange Española, now followed a clique of disloyal army officers in open revolt. The Spanish Roman Catholic Church sided with the revolutionaries.

Like these civilian political factions, Spain's armed services were divided. Ninety percent of the army's officers and fifty percent of its enlisted men chose to follow their rebellious generals. In the navy, however, the crews of all but three ships mutinied against rebel officers, and more than half of the air force remained loyal. Further confounding the Nationalist bid for an early victory were numerous unity of command problems. The Nationalist general Francisco Franco (1892-1975), who had opposed an earlier coup, emerged as the sole leader of the rebellion only after one potential rival had fallen to a Republican firing squad and another had died in a plane crash while attempting to return from exile. During the early campaigns, Falangist militiamen often mobilized and operated beyond the pale of Franco's authority. Carlists, who longed for the ultimate return of the monarchy, acted similarly. Although both Nazi Germany and Fascist Italy provided military aid, foreign intervention did not decide the war's outcome.

Whereas the socially disparate Nationalists gave vent to their hatred of the "Red Republic" by eventually conceding all command authority to Franco, Loyalist hatred for fascism occasioned no parallel sacrifice. Although fighting on the side of the Republican Popular Army, Basque and Catalán separatists continued to resist central authority, as did Spain's two most powerful trade unions and its anarchists. Like the Falangists and Carlists, these groups mobilized their own militias and frequently fought independently of the army they should have been assisting. Some Republican dissidents also fought against the Popular Army and the government it represented. This resistance was often provoked by members of Soviet military- and political-aid missions who reserved Soviet tank, artillery, and air support for communist formations. Soviet operatives assassinated some noncommunist Popular Front members as well. Tyrannical acts such as these eventually damaged Republican morale beyond repair.

MILITARY ACHIEVEMENT

More unified in spirit than their enemies, the Nationalists were ultimately successful in their bid to overthrow the Republic. Nevertheless, several factors limited their efforts. First, because trade unionists sided with the Republic, the rebels had to take Spain's industrial centers by force; the two largest cities, Madrid and Barcelona, remained under government control until the war's final weeks. Second, Nationalist objectives, like Republican ones, were often chosen for political rather than military reasons. Third, because Franco often differed with his German and Italian advisers on tactics, troop dispositions, and objectives, some of the advantage that otherwise would have accrued from foreign military assistance was negated.

During the war's first phase, from July, 1936, to March, 1937, four Nationalist columns converged on the capital at Madrid but failed to break in, partly because of fanatical Republican resistance at University City, on the Jarama River, and at Guadalajara, and partly because Nationalist general Emilio Mola's (1887-1937) estimate that a "Fifth Column" of sym-

DIVISION OF SPAIN, 1936

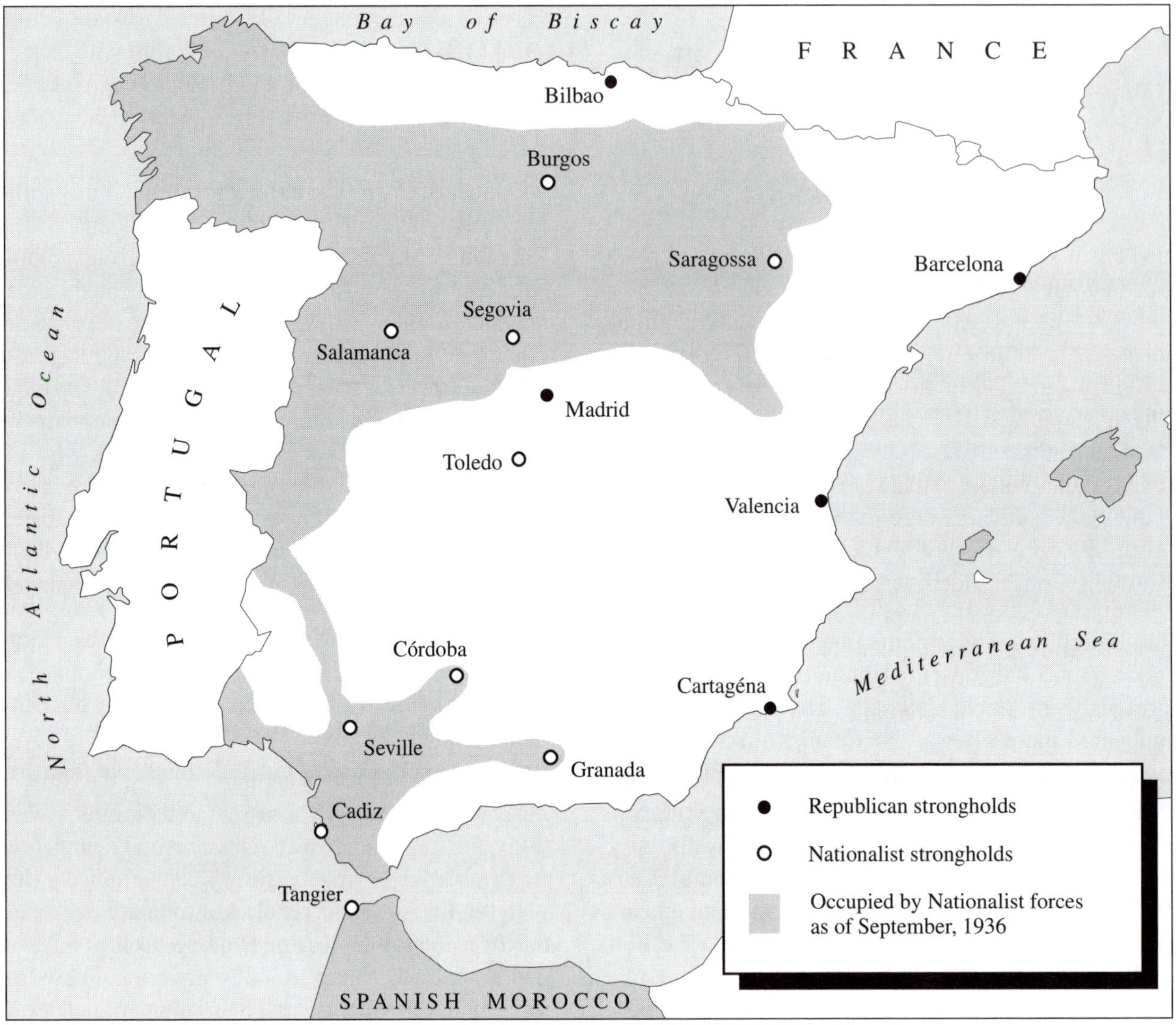

Bay of Biscay

F R A N C E

● Bilbao

○ Burgos

○ Saragossa

● Barcelona

Segovia ○

○ Salamanca

● Madrid

Toledo ○

Valencia ●

North Atlantic Ocean

P O R T U G A L

Mediterranean Sea

Córdoba ○

Cartagéna ●

○ Seville

○ Granada

Cadiz ○

Tangier ○

SPANISH   MOROCCO

● Republican strongholds

○ Nationalist strongholds

Occupied by Nationalist forces as of September, 1936

pathizers would disrupt the defenses from within had proven unduly optimistic. Stalemated around Madrid, both Franco and his Republican counterpart, José Miaja (1879-1958), looked elsewhere for advantages during the war's second phase, from April, 1937, to February, 1938. Franco reinforced Mola's Army of the North and took the ports and industrial centers along the Bay of Biscay, whereas the next Republican offensives focused on Aragon, where in the spring of 1937, a handful of Nationalist troops were holding a 200-mile front. The Republic's Army of

the East was slow to attack, and the Nationalists reacted, saving Saragossa (1937) and retaking Teruel (1937-1938). The Republic's loss of Teruel proved especially costly in terms of men, equipment, and the consequent loss of Soviet aid. During the war's final phase, the Republic was in a state of collapse, and only the rebels were capable of strategic offensives. Franco drove eastward to the Mediterranean in March and April of 1938 and isolated Catalonia from the remainder of Republican territory. In January, 1939, he took its key city, Barcelona. The defenses of

Madrid finally collapsed on March 27, 1939, ending a war that had cost more than 600,000 Spanish lives.

WEAPONS, UNIFORMS, AND ARMOR

Despite some small-scale experimentation with tactical aviation and armor, the opposing armies were composed mainly of nonmechanized infantry. Often poorly supported and partially equipped with leftovers from World War I, the Riff War (1919-1926), and the Russian Civil War (1918-1921), both armies also used captured weapons extensively. Because the prewar Republic's standard-issue service rifle, the bolt-action, 7.65-millimeter Model 1893 Mauser, was in short supply, a number of substitutes appeared, including the Italian 6.5-millimeter Carcano and the Russian 7.62-millimeter Mosin-Nagant. Far less common were submachine guns, which included the Italian Beretta MP-28, the Soviet PPD-34, and the Spanish-built Lanchester. French military aid to the Republic included some World War I surplus air-cooled machine guns: the Hotchkiss Mk1 and the notoriously unreliable Chauchat. The Italian Breda 30 appeared more often in Nationalist ranks. Belt-fed, water-cooled machine guns of the Maxim-Vickers type were more common on both sides, but their heavier weight rendered them less suitable for highly mobile operations. The proliferation of rifle and machine gun calibers and types produced logistical nightmares for Nationalists and Republicans alike.

All but a few pieces of artillery on both sides were towed, and these guns, like the infantrymen they supported, were far more thinly scattered than they had been on the western front from 1914 to 1918. The road and rail networks of Spain could not have supported massive World War I-style artillery barrages or supplied World War-sized armies.

The numerous irregular units, foreign volunteers, and shortages of supplies during the Spanish Civil War gave rise to a multitude of uniform types, but there were a few frequently recurring features. The prewar Spanish Peninsular Army-issue khaki pants, khaki shirt with pleated patch breast pockets, and thigh-length *guerra* tunics were numerous on both sides. Civilian items were especially common in Republican ranks. These included corduroy pants and jacket, usually brown, the leather or cloth *cazadora* windbreaker, and the *mono*, a lightweight brown corduroy coverall. Although both sides used the Spanish M-1926 helmet, augmented by the Republic with French Adrian M-1916's and M-1926's, prewar-issue *isabellinos*, or forage caps, were more common in the two armies. Black, brown, and olive drab berets were especially common on the Republican side, but these colors rarely reflected the wearer's arm of service, as in other armies. The red beret was more frequently seen on Carlist monarchists fighting for Franco than on communist Republicans. Woolen field caps, such as the peaked *pasa montana*, were more popular with both sides in winter. Footwear was similarly nonstandard. In the summer, prewar-issue boots often gave way to lower-cut brogans or the cooler but flimsier *alpargato* sandals.

Among these two opposing armies, the interven-

TURNING POINTS

Oct., 1936	First tank-versus-cavalry and tank-versus-tank engagements of the Spanish Civil War, near Esquivias, south of Madrid.
Mar., 1937	Destruction of a poorly supported Italian armored column by conventional Republican arms near Trijeque, northeast of Guadalajara.
Apr., 1937	The Condor Legion's air arm bombs Guernica, killing approximately 2,100 of the town's 8,000 inhabitants in arguably the first premeditated use of terror bombing.
Oct., 1937	Republican armored assault at Fuentes de Ebro fails because of poor coordination with infantry, artillery, and air support, contributing to the dismantling of the Soviet Army's independent armored formations on the eve of World War II.
Feb., 1938	In the first significant combat test of the tactic of dive-bombing, the Condor Legion's air arm attacks Republican positions near Teruel.

ing powers placed small numbers of up-to-date weapons and advisory groups to train Spanish clients in their use. Several hundred German 5.8-ton Pzkw I light tanks (but never more than 180 at a time) served on the Nationalist side, as did a similar number of the Italian 4.6-ton CV-33 tankettes. Both were thinly armored—the CV-33 had no turret or roof armor—and equipped with machine guns only. In crew protection and gun power the Soviet-supplied Republican tanks, the 9-ton T-26B and 11-ton BT-5, were far superior; both mounted 45-millimeter cannons. Low-wing fighter aircraft with retractable landing gear made their debut in Spain, but here the Soviet Polikarpov 1-16 was quickly outclassed by the German Messerschmitt Bf-109. Later variants of the Bf-109 and the Junkers Ju-87 Stuka dive-bomber would play prominent roles in Germany's early victories of World War II (1939-1945), as would the twin-engined Dornier Do-17 and Heinkel He-111 bombers, also introduced in Spain. However, these modern aircraft served side by side with more numerous biplanes of the previous generation and, like the tanks, in numbers too small to tip the strategic balance. Among the German antiaircraft contingent were four batteries of 88-millimeter guns, which proved equally effective in the direct-fire role against ground targets at Brunete (1937) and after. Unlike other weapons tested in Spain, the dual-purpose "88" neither became obsolete nor required significant improvement during World War II.

MILITARY ORGANIZATION

Both opponents in the Spanish Civil War were undersupplied and employed semi-independent militias, and neither had an effective centralized replacement system. For these reasons, standardized tables of organization and equipment were slow to take hold. During the first year of the war, for example, the all-communist Fifth Regiment grew into the Popular Army's V Corps. Other Republican units, notably the component battalions of the five International Brigades, shrank and consolidated as they sustained severe losses. Nationalist formations consolidated as well but more often retained prewar schemes of orga-

nization, which varied from Spain's Army of Africa to its Peninsular Army.

By 1938, the infantry division commanded by a coronel had become the basic building block of both armies, its strength fluctuating between 6,000 and 10,000 men. The Republican division usually comprised three Soviet-style mixed brigades, each of which was authorized as four battalions, but usually assigned three; a *grupo* of four artillery batteries; and an antitank battery. In some Nationalist divisions, the less standardized *agrupación* supplanted the brigade, and a single agrupación might include both African and Peninsular formations. Army of Africa formations included the *tabor*, a company-sized unit, and the *bandera*, two tabores supported by a heavy-weapons company. These sometimes served in the same divisions as Peninsular Army battalions. In both armies, a corps generally comprised three divisions, and an army, two or more corps.

DOCTRINE, STRATEGY, AND TACTICS

Historians who wrote during and immediately after World War II often regarded the Spanish Civil War as an ideal laboratory in which the Condor Legions, the military aid sent by Germany, could test the technologies and tactics of what later became known as Blitzkrieg, or "lightning war." Such a view supported contemporary efforts to explain the Allied failures from 1939 to 1941 and stemmed from a germ of truth: German advisers had indeed preferred to coordinate the movement of tanks with that of the other arms and, sometimes, to mass the mechanized elements in tactically independent formations. However, more recent scholarship indicates that, although often frustrated in their efforts, many Soviet advisers to the Popular Army had favored similar improvements.

Although Spain often proved a viable testing ground for prototypes of weapons later variants of which would see action in World War II, those prototypes were too few for reliable assessments of doctrine. Other factors compounded this deficiency. First, few Spanish commanders assigned doctrinal reform a high priority. Second, foreign luminaries who did, such as Germany's Heinz Guderian (1888-

Three tanks in battle during the Spanish Civil War, which proved a testing ground for the European forces that later fought World War II.

1954) and the Soviet Union's Mikhayl Nikolayevich Tukhachevsky (1893-1937), saw their nations' respective Spanish commitments as politically imposed burdens to be dealt with by subordinates. They preferred to conduct tactical experiments at home, away from prying eyes.

Guderian, the principal designer of Germany's tank forces, believed that tanks should attack in large, dense concentrations against narrow segments of the enemy's line. Unlike the Allied tank attacks of World War I, Guderian's attacks were to be accompanied by mechanized infantry and engineers and supported by dive-bombers rather than conventional towed artillery, which could not be expected to keep up. Once through the thick crust of forward defenses, the ground arms were to avoid dense concentrations of enemy troops where possible and spread out, making counterattack difficult. These densely packed Panzer spearheads were necessary not only to overcome en-

emy resistance but also to maintain the momentum of the advance even when some of the tanks suffered mechanical failure.

Wilhelm Ritter von Thoma (1891-1948), Guderian's proxy in Spain, faced not only prohibitive shortages of tanks and crews but also difficulty in training the Spanish. They were, in his words, "quick to learn but also quick to forget." Thoma also came to doubt that a battalion of tanks could be controlled by radios during the attack, and he urged Guderian, unsuccessfully, to have them removed. In the latter phases of the Ebro Counteroffensive (1938), Nationalist tank operations began to resemble Guderian's ideal, but previous Republican losses were largely to blame for that.

The Italians also experimented with mechanized forces, but the Italian *guerra celere*, "fast war," suffered even more from lack of training, leadership, and resources. At Guadalajara in March, 1937, a battalion of CV-33's was destroyed when it outran supporting infantry and air cover. The subsequent Republican counterattack regained almost all of the lost territory, and all but a few Western observers interpreted the Italian failure as an indictment of all independent mechanized operations. Later Italian success in the Catalonia Offensive (1938-1939) drew far less commentary, as the Popular Army was then in its final stages of collapse.

The senior Soviet tank officer in Spain, Dmitri Pavlov (1897-1941), interpreted similar Republican failures as proof that the independent mechanized formations designed by Tukhachevsky in 1932 should be cannibalized and tied piecemeal to nonmechanized infantry. Tukhachevsky, like Guderian, believed that only tactically independent mechanized penetration could win land wars and, during 1936 and 1937, some of Pavlov's subordinates agreed. Two events settled the debate. The first was Tukhachevsky's trial and execution during the Purge of 1937, which rendered "Deep Battle" tank doctrine politically incorrect. The second was the failure of two Republican tank battalions to break through Nationalist defenses at Fuentes de Ebro on October 13, 1937. Although this defeat had been foreordained by poor planning and training, it nevertheless provided the ambitious Pavlov with more ammunition to use against a rival philosophy. His victory, and the consequent dismantling of Tukhachevsky's large formations, contributed to the Soviet defeat in 1941.

The relationship between Spanish Civil War air operations and doctrinal progress was also inconsistent. The most strategically significant use of aircraft—the airlifting of Nationalist forces from Spanish Morocco—made little impression on the Germans, for whom airlift capacity was to remain a third priority during World War II. Dive-bombing was indeed a higher priority, but the Germans had already committed to it by 1936, and only one Stuka ever appeared over Spain before January, 1938. Condor Legion fighter pilots, led by Werner Mölders (1913-1941), developed the "finger four" formation that they would use so effectively during World War II, whereas the bombers they escorted sometimes flew against civilian targets, as at Guernica (1937). Even so, the Luftwaffe never developed strategic bombardment or long range escort capabilities.

If Nationalist and Republican commanders had been more receptive to tactical innovation, a thoroughgoing doctrinal revolution would have been difficult anyway. Unlike the European battlefields of World War II, much of Spain was too mountainous for mechanized operations, and its road and rail networks were poor. Foreign instructors were few, and conducting hands-on training through translators was exceedingly difficult. On the Republican side, this lack of communication was especially problematic: In the first Soviet tank training detachment to arrive in October, 1936, only one man spoke Spanish.

CONTEMPORARY SOURCES

Ferdinand Miksche's *Attack: A Study of Blitzkrieg Tactics* (1942) argues that Spain was the perfect tactical laboratory for the intervening powers who would later fight World War II, and that the Allies failed to conduct the proper experiments or draw the correct conclusions when the Condor Legion did. More general accounts from the International Brigades are plentiful, but most mix political ideology with more strictly military matters. Arnold Vieth von Golssenau's *Der spanische Krieg* (1955; the Spanish War), written under the pseudonym Ludwig Renn, is among the best. English-language sources concentrate mainly on the Fifteenth Brigade, in which most of the American, British, and Canadian volunteers served. These include *Our Fight: Writings by Veterans of the Abraham Lincoln Brigade, Spain, 1936-1939* (1969), edited by Alvah Bessie and Albert Prago, and *English Captain* (1939) by Tom Wintringham. Spanish Republican accounts, even when useful, often mix polemics and tactics, as in the memoirs of rival communist commanders Juan Modesto, *Soy del Quinto Regimiento* (1969; I am of the Fifth Regiment) and Enrique Líster, *Nuestra Guerra* (1966; our war). Ramón Sender includes a revealing account of the first Republican tank operation in *Counter-attack in Spain* (1937), whereas Jose Miaja's chief of staff Vicente Rojo provides a view from Popular Army headquarters in *España heroica* (1942).

Fewer Nationalist sources have made it into English, but no study of the tank attack at Fuentes de Ebro can be complete without the interview related by Henry J. Reilly in the article "Tank Attack in Spain," published in the July/August, 1939, issue of *Cavalry Journal*. German frustrations in the area of doctrinal development are recounted by Gustav Diniker in his article "Betrachtungen über die Bewertung von Erfahrungen mit Kriegsmaterial in Spanien," in the June, 1937, issue of *Wissen und Wehr*.

Books and Articles

Baxell, Richard. *British Volunteers in the Spanish Civil War: The British Batallion in the International Brigades, 1936-1939*. New York: Routledge, 2004.

Beevor, Antony. *The Battle for Spain: The Spanish Civil War, 1936-1939*. Rev. ed. New York: Penguin Books, 2006.

Bolloten, Burnett. *The Spanish Civil War: Revolution and Counterrevolution*. Chapel Hill: University of North Carolina Press, 1991.

Carver, John. *Airmen Without Portfolio: U.S. Mercenaries in Civil War Spain*. Westport, Conn.: Praeger, 1997.

Coverdale, John F. *Italian Intervention in the Spanish Civil War*. Princeton, N.J.: Princeton University Press, 1975.

Eby, Cecil D. *Comrades and Commissars: The Lincoln Battalion in the Spanish Civil War*. University Park: Pennsylvania State University Press, 2007.

Elstob, Peter. *The Condor Legion*. New York: Ballantine, 1973.

Henry, Chris. *The Ebro, 1938: Death Knell of the Republic*. Botley, Oxford, England: Osprey, 1999. Reprint. Westport, Conn.: Praeger, 2004.

Howson, Gerald. *Arms for Spain: The Untold Story of the Spanish Civil War*. New York: St. Martin's Press, 1998.

Jensen, Geoffrey. *Franco: Soldier, Commander, Dictator*. Washington, D.C.: Potomac Books, 2005.

Keene, Judith. *Fighting for Franco: International Volunteers in Nationalist Spain During the Spanish Civil War, 1936-1939*. New York: Leicester University Press, 2001.

Landis, Arthur. *Death in the Olive Groves: American Volunteers and the Spanish Civil War, 1936-1939*. New York: Paragon House, 1989.

Lannon, Frances. *The Spanish Civil War, 1936-1939*. Botley, Oxford, England: Osprey, 2002.

Proctor, Raymond. *Hitler's Luftwaffe in the Spanish Civil War*. Westport, Conn.: Greenwood Press, 1983.

Wyden, Peter. *The Passionate War*. New York: Simon and Schuster, 1983.

Films and Other Media

For Whom the Bell Tolls. Feature film. Paramount, 1943.

Land and Freedom. Feature film. Kino Film Company, 1995.

Libertarias. Feature film. Warner Home Video, 1996.

Pan's Labyrinth. Feature film. Warner Bros., 2006.

The Spanish Civil War. Documentary. MPI Home Video, 1987.

The Spanish Earth. Docudrama. Prometheus Pictures, 1937.

John Daley

WORLD WAR II
UNITED STATES, BRITAIN, AND FRANCE
Dates: 1939-1945

POLITICAL CONSIDERATIONS

At the end of World War I (1914-1918), there was no longer a balance of power in Europe. Britain and France had been physically devastated and were close to financial bankruptcy; Germany had been defeated and disarmed; Russia, by then the Soviet Union, had been excluded as a result of the Russian Revolution (1917-1921) and the spread of Communism. The United States had withdrawn from European affairs, devoting its attention to the Western Hemisphere and the Pacific and leaving Britain and France as the only real powers in an unstable political and military system. France decided to strengthen its border defenses, known as the Maginot line, using the Treaty of Versailles (1919) to prevent the rearmament of Germany and entering into a series of security alliances. Great Britain, perceiving no serious threat, returned to the advancement of its imperial interests, relying upon its navy for defense. Although both Britain and France belonged to the League of Nations created at the end of World War I, neither saw this organization as a credible deterrent to war.

With the exception of the persistent threat of Communism, the 1920's witnessed a lessening of international tensions, with the drafting of the Locarno Pact (1925), establishing Germany's western borders; the Kellogg-Briand Pact (1928), renouncing the use of war in settling international disputes; and the entrance of Germany into the League of Nations (1926).

Everything changed, however, after the U.S. stock market collapsed in 1929. Financial and economic crisis brought political instability and a renewal of international tensions. On January 30, 1933, Adolf Hitler (1889-1945) came to power in Germany. Italy began to assert its authority under Fascist dictator Benito Mussolini (1883-1945), and Fascism spread into Romania and Hungary, as the rest of Eastern Europe began to disintegrate. At the same time, Communist activities directed by Communist International (Comintern), the Communist organization founded by Vladimir Ilich Lenin (1870-1924), under the control of the Soviet Union increased. Governments were forced to direct all available resources to provide social services for the large numbers of unemployed and destitute.

International tensions escalated after Hitler began to rebuild German military power. In 1933, after the League of Nations refused to weaken the restrictions on German rearmament, Hitler's Germany left the organization. In 1935 the Saar was returned to Germany in response to a wave of Nationalist propaganda, and Hitler then attempted to take over Austria. Britain and France were able to thwart Hitler but only with the support of Mussolini, who allied with Hitler two years later when Britain and France refused to support his conquest of Ethiopia. In 1936 Hitler and Mussolini also sent aid to Nationalist general Francisco Franco (1892-1975) in Spain at the beginning of the Spanish Civil War, whereas the West relied on sanctions and weak protests. By 1936 Germany under Hitler and his National Socialist Party (Nazis) had begun to rearm at a frantic pace, whereas Britain, France, and the United States used almost all of their resources to bolster their economies. However, it should be noted that a considerable amount of the Works Progress Administration (WPA) spending in the United States was devoted to military purposes, including the building of two aircraft carriers and several military posts. Britain, in the meantime, had devoted a large portion of its 1936, 1937, and 1938 defense budgets to the building of radar stations and the infrastructure of an early warning system.

In 1936 military-age Germans outnumbered their French counterparts two to one. France, the key to Allied defense against Nazi aggression, realized that it would be unable to match either German manpower or German industrial production. For a short time, the French government actively sought an alliance with the Soviet Union, but this alliance never materialized, due to the purges of Joseph Stalin (1879-1953) in the late 1930's. Increasingly forced to rely on a defensive strategy, France became more obviously weak, taking no action when Hitler remilitarized the Rhineland in 1937.

Meanwhile, Britain had decided that some kind of accommodation or appeasement could be reached with Hitler, offering only perfunctory protests when Hitler remilitarized the Rhineland and carried out his Anschluss, or annexation, of Austria in early 1938. When Hitler demanded that something be done about Czechoslovakia, the British, with French acquiescence, decided to appease Nazi Germany rather than risk a war they were not prepared to fight. In September, 1938, the British and French leaders, Neville Chamberlain (1869-1940) and Édouard Daladier (1884-1970), allowed Hitler to seize the Sudetenland, which included most of Czechoslovakia's defenses and armament industries, in return for Hitler's promise that he would meet with them to negotiate future problems. In March, 1939, Hitler violated the agreement and seized the rest of Czechoslovakia.

Neither France nor Britain had begun to rearm seriously until the crisis over the Sudetenland, and they thus negotiated from a position of weakness. For example, all of the aircraft used by Britain to fight the Battle of Britain (1940) were manufactured after the Czech crisis. Although both France and Britain had begun to rebuild their military forces in early 1939, their action was too little, too late. When the Polish crisis escalated into war with the Nazi invasion of Poland on September 1, 1939, neither France nor Britain was prepared to fight. In actuality, the military weakness of Britain and France encouraged Nazi aggression and added to the crises that led to World War II.

The United States was even further behind its European allies in military development. Preoccupied with the efforts to deal with the Great Depression and perceiving no immediate external threat to national security, the U.S. Army was less prepared to wage war than it had been in any time since the American Civil War (1861-1865). Ranked equally with Britain and Japan in naval power, in 1939 the United States was ranked seventeenth in overall military strength, behind both Spain and Romania. The U.S. armed forces had no tanks, few first-line fighter aircraft, and barely enough rifles for its army.

It should be remembered that the United States, disillusioned by the outcome of World War I, was determined to stay out of World War II. However, as British and French power in the Pacific diminished as

TURNING POINTS

Sept. 1, 1939	Germany invades Poland, leading to British declaration of war.
Mar., 1940	Lend-Lease Act in the United States establishes the principle of providing military aid to Great Britain.
Aug., 1940	Germans begin the Battle of Britain, a series of air raids over Britain aimed at destroying British infrastructure and morale.
Dec., 1941	The United States enters World War II after the Japanese bombing of the U.S. Navy fleet at Pearl Harbor, Hawaii.
Nov., 1942	Anglo-American force invades French North Africa.
June 6, 1944	Allies begin invasion of Normandy, France, on "D day," marking the largest amphibious operation in history and the beginning of Allied victory in Europe.
Aug. 6, 1945	The first atomic bomb to be used against a civilian population is dropped by the United States on the Japanese city of Hiroshima, killing more than 70,000 people and hastening the end of the war.

Smoke looms on the horizon after the first mass air raid on London during World War II.

a result of the fighting in Europe, the Japanese began to seize the opportunity to expand their influence in the region. Although the U.S. armed forces were in a weakened state, U.S. interests in the Pacific, mainly in China and the Philippines, had to be protected. A series of crises, misunderstandings, and miscalculations on both sides resulted in the Japanese decision to attack the United States Pacific Fleet at Pearl Harbor, Hawaii, on December 7, 1941. Unprepared, the United States suddenly found itself involved in World War II.

MILITARY ACHIEVEMENT

The military role of France during World War II was limited by its early defeat and surrender in 1940. Hampered both by its reliance on the fixed fortifica-

tions of the Maginot line and by its refusal to create a modern armored force, the French army was neither doctrinally nor technically capable of defeating the Germans. Later in the war, however, the First French Army, equipped and supplied by the United States and commanded by General Jean-Marie-Gabriel de Lattre de Tassigny (1889-1952), performed well and helped to liberate France.

The British army did no better than the French. Defeated on the frontier of France in 1940, it was forced to retreat to Dunkirk and had to be evacuated, leaving behind all of its heavy equipment. Only in the initial battles against the Italians in North Africa did the British army emerge victorious. The Royal Air Force did perform better: With their Spitfire and Hurricane fighters, both guided by sophisticated early-warning radar systems, they were able to defeat the German air force, or Luftwaffe, and prevent the invasion of Britain. At the same time the heavy bomber force under British air marshal Arthur T. Harris (1892-1984), after concluding that daylight bombing would be too costly, began the successful development of night bombing operations. Harris developed the concept of "saturation bombing"; in May, 1942, he attacked Cologne with 1,000 planes and destroyed 600 acres of the city. However, high losses of 970 bombers between May and November, 1942, hampered his efforts.

British military performance, even when supported by a large infusion of U.S. aid, improved little in the desert battles against German commander Erwin Rommel's (1891-1944) Afrika Korps. Problems with command and control, armor, and leadership led to numerous British defeats. At the same time, the British army in the Far East was outfought and outmaneuvered by the Japanese, resulting in one of the worst defeats in British history, at Singapore (1941-1942). The situation did begin to improve when British generals Harold Alexander (1891-1969) and Bernard Law Montgomery (1887-1976) reorganized the British Eighth Army and won the Battle of El Alamein (1942). At the same time the British army came increasingly under U.S. control, both logistically and tactically.

Although the United States had not been prepared to fight a war when the Japanese attacked Pearl Harbor, the nation quickly mobilized its vast resources and was able to launch offenses in both North Africa and the South Pacific within less than a year. Although its initial performance was unimpressive, the U.S. Army was victorious at the Battles of the Kasserine Pass (1943) and New Guinea (1943). Three factors played a major role in early U.S. victories: material superiority, command of the air, and adaptability to changing circumstances.

Due in large measure to the training provided by the government and armed forces service schools, senior officers were intellectually prepared for a global war. The logistical accomplishments of the army and navy were formidable. Despite initial problems and some brief shortages of critical supplies, the U.S. servicemen and their allies were amply supplied with everything they needed to fight the war. Another area of exceptional performance was the U.S. artillery, which used forward observers and new operational techniques. The U.S. artillery proved to be the most successful arm of the service, a fact repeatedly remarked upon by captured German soldiers.

The U.S. Army excelled in two other aspects of warfare: air and amphibious operations. In the air, using heavy bombers such as B-17's and B-24's, the U.S. Army Air Corps was able to destroy much of Nazi Germany's infrastructure, making it very difficult to maintain production. In the Pacific the B-29's were even more successful in destroying Japanese industrial production. Although strategic bombing did not win the war, as some prewar theorists had predicted, it did play a significant role in the defeat of the Axis Powers. Amphibious operations were very difficult, and much of the necessary equipment had to be developed during the war. Thanks to U.S. engineer-

NARA

An F6F-3 Hellcat crash-lands onto the USS Enterprise *in November, 1943. Lieutenant Walter L. Chewning, Jr., climbed up the aircraft to assist the pilot to a successful escape.*

ing and production genius, the United States was able to carry out successful landings on hostile beaches in both the European and Pacific theaters of operation. The most important amphibious operations were the landings during Operation Overlord on Normandy beaches launched on June 6, 1944 (D day), which marked the start of the final campaign of World War II.

British and American intelligence was able to break the German and Japanese codes during the war, thereby gaining advanced warning of enemy intentions. At Bletchley Park, 50 miles north of London, Britain assembled a large group of cryptologists, who successfully decrypted the German codes throughout the war, providing real-time intelligence to the commanders in the field. The Allied intelligence system was code-named Ultra, and its existence was not revealed until almost twenty years after the war ended. At the same time, U.S. cryptologists broke the Japanese codes. Despite this success, however, the United States was surprised by the Japanese attack on Pearl Harbor, and reliance upon the Ultra codes contributed to the failure of U.S. intelligence to realize the seriousness of the German attack in December, 1944, that resulted in the Battle of the Bulge (1944-1945).

Perhaps the greatest military achievement during World War II was the development and use of the atomic bomb by the United States. Rarely has a single weapon so changed the nature of warfare and the

NORMANDY INVASION, 1944

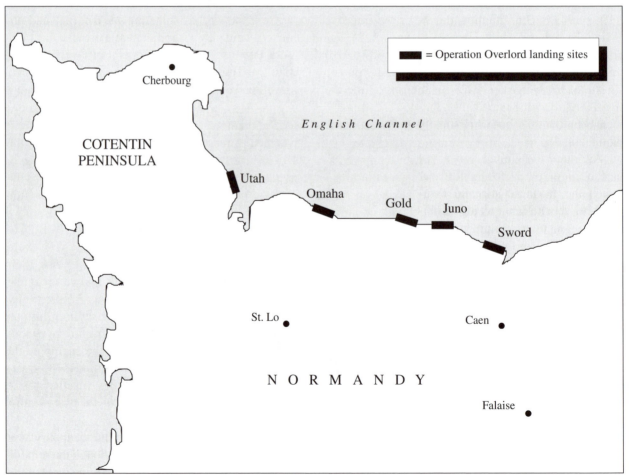

global balance of power. The decision to drop the atomic bomb, though controversial, hastened the end of the war.

WEAPONS, UNIFORMS, AND ARMOR

World War II witnessed the development and deployment of a large number of weapons ranging from the M1 Garand rifle to the atomic bomb. Science and technology played a greater role in the operational aspects of World War II than in those of any other war in history. In fact, a whole new area of military operations, called operational analysis, developed from the application of science to military problems. Operational analysis dealt with everything from the best depth at which to set depth charges to the most efficient force structure for combat divisions.

General Dwight D. Eisenhower briefs paratroopers in preparation for the D-day invasion.

During the 1920's and 1930's the British experimented with a wide variety of armored vehicles, as well as other weapons systems. However, due to a lack of funding and a perceived lack of a serious military threat, these experiments were carried no further. The British went to war in 1939 with an army that was essentially equipped with slightly upgraded World War I weapons, except for the Spitfire and Hurricane fighters and some heavy bombers, which were developed late in the war. This failure in military modernization resulted in an increasing reliance throughout the war upon U.S. weapons, especially tanks and armored vehicles. After its defeat in 1940, the reconstituted French army that fought alongside the Allies in 1944 and 1945 relied almost entirely upon American weapons.

Within a year after the United States' entry into the war, the country had become the "Arsenal of Democracy," providing weaponry and supplies for all of the Allies, including the Soviet Union. At the same time, it equipped the ninety-division U.S. Army with

excellent weapons. The standard infantry weapon was the M1 Garand, which was a gas-operated, clip-fed, semiautomatic rifle that fired eight shots and weighed 9.5 pounds. The artillery, especially the 105-millimeter howitzer and the 155-millimeter gun, used the fire-control system developed early in the war and proved to be the most effective arm of the army.

In the air, the U.S. heavy bombers (B-17's, B-24's, and B-29's) and fighters (P-47's and P-51's) were dependable and proved capable of defeating their adversaries. One of the less well known technical triumphs of American ingenuity was the proximity (V.T.) fuse. Actually a small radar set built into an explosive shell, it was so effective that no one was allowed to fire it over land, for fear the enemy might get their hands on one that did not explode. The greatest success of American technology was the atomic bomb, which hastened the end of the war against Japan and revolutionized warfare.

The greatest failure of American weaponry was the M4 Sherman medium tank. Although the reliable Sherman tank was capable of performing most of the tasks assigned to it, it had not been designed to be an antitank weapon and failed when called upon to engage the German medium or heavy tanks known as Panthers and Tigers. Produced in large numbers, more than 40,000, it provided armor not only for the U.S. Army but also for the British, French, and Polish forces in Europe. The M26 Pershing, which was designed to fight other tanks, was introduced at the end of the war but arrived too late to have any real effect. Only 700 Pershings were shipped to Europe.

MILITARY ORGANIZATION

At the beginning of World War II, the British Expeditionary Force (BEF) was dispatched to France. While retaining its independence, it served under the French commander General Maurice-Gustave Gamelin (1872-1958) and later General Maxime Weygand (1867-1965). Organized into two army groups, the French concentrated the bulk of their mobile forces in the north with the BEF. After the defeat of France and the evacuation of the BEF from Dunkirk, most of the French army became a home-defense force. The remainder, along with Commonwealth forces, were sent to North Africa, whereas the British army stationed in India under separate command was used to reinforce the defenses in the Near East and Asia.

After the United States entered the war, the British army, although more experienced, came under U.S. field command. At the highest levels, the military command structure was the Combined Chiefs of Staff, consisting of the U.S. Joint Chiefs of Staff and the British Imperial General Staff. Although the Combined Chiefs of Staff operated on the principle of unanimity, the United States was decidedly the dominant partner. The staffs of both countries became more elaborate as the war progressed. The U.S. Joint Chiefs of Staff became increasingly involved in the formulation of U.S. foreign policy during the war. When the North African campaign began, the Free French were brought in as a junior partner. However, this relationship remained tenuous throughout the war because of President Franklin D. Roosevelt's (1882-1945) personal distrust of the French leader, General Charles de Gaulle (1890-

1970). Although the Soviet Union was an ally, it was seldom involved in military decisions at the strategic or tactical level.

The war was fought by the Allies—mainly the United States, Britain, and France—in four theaters of operation. The European theater was commanded by U.S. general Dwight D. Eisenhower (1890-1969), who had taken direct control over the cross-Channel invasion, prompting Field Marshal Alexander to take control of the Italian campaign. In the Pacific theater, the Southeast Pacific was commanded by General Douglas MacArthur (1880-1964), the Central Pacific by Admiral Chester W. Nimitz (1885-1966), and the China-Burma-India theater by Admiral Louis Mountbatten (1900-1979). For a brief period during the Guadalcanal campaign in the Solomon Islands, there was a further division called the South Pacific theater, commanded by Admiral William F. Halsey (1882-1959). In all of these commands there were joint staffs of U.S., British, and other Allied officers. The Americans were in command and provided most of the forces who fought in all theaters, except the China-Burma-India theater. One major difference in operations should be noted: in the European theater of operation, Commonwealth—mainly Canadian—troops remained as part of the British command, whereas in the Southwest theater of operations, the Australian army served directly under MacArthur.

The reconstituted French army served not as a separate force but rather as one of the armies under U.S. command. One of the primary reasons for this arrangement was U.S. responsibility for logistical support. At the end of the war, the First French Army was separated and given its own sector of Germany to occupy.

Cooperation between the Western Allies and the Soviet Union was difficult at best. At the beginning of the war, due to British resistance to an early cross-Channel invasion, U.S. staff officers had been more favorable to the Soviet Union. However, as the war progressed and Soviet intentions in Eastern Europe became apparent, the U.S. Joint Chiefs of Staff became increasingly hostile to the Soviets. The resulting mutual suspicion contributed to the beginning of the Cold War.

DOCTRINE, STRATEGY, AND TACTICS

A nation's military doctrine generally determines the nature of its weapons development, strategy, and tactics. During the years immediately following World War I, all of the major powers reevaluated their military in light of the lessons learned in that war. The French came to the conclusion that defensive fortifications such as Verdun were their best option along with an infantry force supported by artillery and some armor. They believed that such a force would be able to take the offensive only in a limited way, using armor basically as mobile artillery to support the infantry rather than as an independent force capable of disrupting the enemy's lines.

Britain experimented with a variety of armor operations during the interwar years. For example, General Sir Percy Hobart conducted deep penetration armor maneuvers in 1935. However, the lack of adequate funding and the absence of a clear threat limited any deployment to small units more suitable for use as an empire constabulary rather than a continental army.

American planners such as Colonel George S. Patton did conceive of the use of large armored formations but the absence of any real threat, the financial restraints created by the Great Depression and the conviction that the United States would not be involved in a European war in the future resulted in inadequately trained and equipped forces. The army

Naval Historical Center/USCG Collection

Omaha Beach, June, 1944, in the early days of Operation Overlord following the D-day invasion.

and many planning staff did develop very extensive plans (the Rainbow Plans) and realized many of the possible difficulties that were found later in the war. For example, under the leadership of Major Earl H. Ellis (USMC), doctrine and planning for amphibious warfare were developed prior to the war.

By not entering the war until December of 1941, American planners were able to take advantage of the experience of both the Allies and the Germans. The decision to create only a ninety-division army hampered some operations, especially the large-scale armor attacks favored by the Germans and the Russians. Much of American doctrinal development during the war centered on the use of the vast material advantage that the United States possessed, especially in artillery and airpower.

In the area of airborne operations, the U.S. Army developed the doctrine, organization, equipment, and tactics during the early part of the war. After basing much of their development on reports of German successes in 1939 and 1940, the U.S. airborne units and their British counterparts proved to be some of the most effective fighting forces in the European theater of operations, despite their limited use. The 82nd and 101st Airborne Divisions were considered two of the best.

From the beginning of U.S. involvement in the war, the Allied strategy was "Europe first." Although unable to launch a cross-Channel invasion in 1942, the Allies attacked Germany first in North Africa (Operation Torch) and then in Sicily (Operation Huskey). At the same time priority was given to the heavy bomber offensive against Germany.

After the successful landings at Normandy, Allied strategy in Europe was a broad-front strategy. Rather than concentrate on one or two major thrusts, as the British commander Field Marshal Montgomery advocated, Eisenhower opted to attack along the entire front, forcing the German army to retreat back into Germany and ultimately destroying its ability to fight. Probably the greatest failure of American strategy was Eisenhower's decision to stop his advance at the Elbe River, allowing the Soviets to take Berlin and consequently to occupy all of Eastern Europe.

In the Pacific, General MacArthur directed an island-hopping strategy that avoided Japanese strong points. At the same time the Japanese were further stretched by the U.S. decision to shift the axis of their attacks along two fronts: the Southwest Pacific from New Guinea through the Philippines and the Central Pacific. The Japanese surrendered before they were actually invaded.

CONTEMPORARY SOURCES

Discussion of the role of armor and airpower dominated writing about military theory both before and during World War II. French military thinking was dominated by the French World War I experience, as seen in the *Provisional Instructions Concerning the Tactical Utilization of Larger Units* drawn up in 1921 and revised in 1936, which stressed firepower, the power of fortifications, and the need to increase the offensive power of the infantry. Colonel Charles de Gaulle was one of the few officers who disagreed. In his books *Vers l'armée de métier* (1934; *The Army of the Future*, 1940) and *Fil de l'épée* (1932; *The Edge of the Sword*, 1960), he described many of the elements of the modern armored division and suggested that France organize a large armored force to protect its northern front.

Two British theorists also were important in the development of armor doctrine: Major General J. F. C. Fuller (1878-1966) and Captain Basil Liddell Hart (1895-1970). In his books *The Foundations of the Science of War* (1926), *On Future Warfare* (1928), and *The Army in My Time* (1935), Fuller criticized British military doctrine and advocated a force structure that relied heavily on armor and airpower. Liddell Hart's works *The British Way in Warfare* (1932) and *Thoughts on War* (1944) provided the most insightful and influential studies on military doctrine of the period. Liddell Hart probably had a greater impact on German than British military history. Although George S. Patton (1885-1945) and other American officers had written numerous articles in service journals about the future of armor, they had little impact until the war.

No one made greater claims than the air theorists. Air marshalls Hugh Trenchard (1873-1956) and Arthur T. Harris believed that strategic bombing could defeat the enemy and win the war without the huge loss of life that would result from a land campaign. Although they did not write any books, their views were widely known through interviews and news articles. The most influential books written during the period included those of Sir John Slessor (born 1897), *Air Power and Armies* (1936), and J. M. Spaight (born 1877), *Air Power and the Cities* (1930), *Air Power in the Next War* (1938), and *Bombing Vindicated* (1944). Liddell Hart was more balanced in his view of the importance of airpower in his book, *When Britain Goes to War* (1935). Two American officers, Lieutenant General Henry Harley "Hap" Arnold (1886-1950) and Brigadier General Ira C. Eaker (1896-1987) wrote three books dealing with airpower, which were designed to encourage public support for the expansion of the air force: *This Flying Game* (1936), *Winged Warfare* (1941), and *Army Flyer* (1942).

BOOKS AND ARTICLES

Bull, Stephen, and Gordon L. Rottman. *Infantry Tactics of the Second World War*. Botley, Oxford, England: Osprey, 2008.

Chamberlain, Peter, and Charles Ellis. *British and American Tanks of World War II: The Complete Illustrated History of British, American, and Commonwealth Tanks, 1939-1945*. New York: Arco, 1969.

Davies, Norman. *No Simple Victory: World War II in Europe, 1939-1945*. New York: Viking, 2007.

Doubler, Michael D. *Closing with the Enemy: How GIs Fought the War in Europe, 1944-1945*. Lawrence: University Press of Kansas, 1994.

Ellis, John. *Brute Force: Allied Strategy and Tactics in the Second World War*. New York: Viking, 1990.

Hart, Stephen A. *Montgomery and Colossal Cracks: The Twenty-first Army Group in Northwest Europe, 1944-1945*. New York: Praeger, 2000.

Mansoor, Peter R. *The GI Offensive in Europe: The Triumph of American Infantry Divisions, 1941-1945*. Lawrence: University Press of Kansas, 1999.

Marston, Daniel, ed. *The Pacific War Companion: From Pearl Harbor to Hiroshima*. Botley, Oxford, England: Osprey, 2007.

Meyers, Bruce F. *Swift, Silent, and Deadly: Marine Amphibious Reconnaissance in the Pacific, 1942-1945*. Annapolis, Md.: Naval Institute Press, 2004.

Murray, Williamson, and Allan Millett. *To Win the War: Fighting the Second World War*. Cambridge, Mass.: Harvard University Press, 2000.

_____. *World War II*. Vol. 3 in *Military Effectiveness*. London: Allen and Unwin, 1988.

Overy, Richard. *Why the Allies Won*. New York: W. W. Norton, 1995.

Rottman, Gordon L., and Derrick Wright. *Hell in the Pacific: The Battle for Iwo Jima*. Botley, Oxford, England: Osprey, 2008.

Schaffer, Ronald. "The Bombing Campaigns in World War II: The European Theater." In *Bombing Civilians: A Twentieth-Century History*, edited by Yuki Tanaka and Marilyn B. Young. New York: New Press, 2009.

Van Creveld, Martin. *Fighting Power: German and U.S. Army Performance, 1939-1995*. Westport, Conn.: Greenwood Press, 1982.

Watt, Donald Cameron. *Too Serious a Business: European Armored Forces and the Approach to the Second World War*. New York: W. W. Norton, 1975.

Weigley, Russell F. *Eisenhower's Lieutenants: The Campaign of France and Germany, 1944-45.* Bloomington: Indiana University Press, 1981.

Willmott, H. P. *The Great Crusade: A New Complete History of the Second World War.* Rev. ed. Washington, D.C.: Potomac Books, 2008.

FILMS AND OTHER MEDIA

Band of Brothers. Television miniseries. Home Box Office, 2001.

The Bridge on the River Kwai. Feature film. Columbia, 1957.

A Bridge Too Far. Feature film. United Artists, 1977.

Casablanca. Feature film. Warner Bros., 1942.

D-Day: The Total Story. Documentary. History Channel, 1994.

Enigma. Feature film. Miramax Films, 2001.

Enola Gay and the Bombing of Japan. Documentary. Brookside Media, 1995.

Letters from Iwo Jima. Feature film. Malpaso/Amblin, 2006.

Pearl Harbor: Two Hours That Changed the World. Documentary. ABC, 1991.

Tora! Tora! Tora! Feature film. Twentieth Century-Fox, 1970.

The War. Documentary series. Public Broadcasting Service, 2007.

The World at War. Television miniseries. British Broadcasting Company, 1974.

Jachin W. Thacker

WORLD WAR II
THE SOVIET UNION
Dates: 1939-1945

POLITICAL CONSIDERATIONS

When the Germans invaded the Soviet Union on June 22, 1941, they turned what had been a relatively localized readjustment of the balance of power in Europe into a continent-wide total war. Despite the mythology that surrounds events such as the fall of France in May and June, 1940, and the landings at Normandy on June 6, 1944 (D day), the European theater in which World War II was fought and won (by the Allies) was on the eastern front. The majority of Germany's resources—men, tanks, airplanes, and other weapons—were committed there; the great preponderance of the casualties were suffered there; and it was there that the Soviet Union first retreated, then held, and then finally pushed back the German advance. The Soviets ultimately succeeded through a combination of sheer numbers, implacable stubbornness, and a series of war-winning weapons and strategies that the Germans could match only belatedly and incompletely.

The Soviet experience had, in essence, two overall phases. In the first, the Soviets desperately tried to overhaul and re-create the organization, equipment, and doctrine of their military, while at the same time attempting to prevent an utter rout by the Germans. The second came as the Soviets succeeded at that gargantuan task and created a military with the soldiers, training, and ability to defeat the Germans. That accomplishment, possibly more than any other, ensured Germany's defeat in World War II.

The political context of the Soviet Union during World War II centered on the regime of Communist dictator Joseph Stalin (1879-1953). Stalin had decimated the officer corps of the Red Army before the war, seeking to eliminate threats to his control. Because of Stalin's purges, the army that fought the Germans was led to a large extent by officers who were learning on the job. Stalin's usually paranoid nature deserted him in 1941, when he refused to believe numerous internal and external warnings of the impending German attack. As a result, on June 22, Operation Barbarossa, the German attack on the Soviet Union, achieved strategic surprise. The initial attacks quickly cut through and rapidly encircled Soviet forces that had been deployed on orders from Stalin, on the Soviet frontiers. The result was disastrous. Within two months, hundreds of thousands of Soviet soldiers were captured, and the Soviet military was decimated. It would not recover the initiative until 1943.

Stalin did not deal well with the outbreak of war. The invasion itself threw him into a state of shock. He did not make a radio broadcast to the nation until July 3, 1941, and remained largely out of sight after that. As the Germans advanced steadily into the Soviet Union, he grew more and more frantic, worrying as much about his loss of power as the loss of Soviet land. When the Germans reached the outskirts of Moscow, Stalin was close to a nervous breakdown.

Stalin's anxiety created a temporary and partial vacuum at the top of the Soviet hierarchy, but it also had two beneficial effects. First, it allowed senior army officers, such as Marshal Semyon Konstantinovich Timoshenko (1895-1970) and Marshal Georgy Konstantinovich Zhukov (1896-1974), to put their stamp on a reorganization and revitalization of the Soviet army. Second, it forced Stalin and his commissars to turn from the Communist Party toward Russian nationalism as the center of Russian loyalty. Within weeks after the German invasion, messages from the Kremlin began to emphasize the Russian motherland rather than the Communist Party. This appeal to nationalism revitalized the Russian popula-

TURNING POINTS

Aug. 31, 1939	The Soviet Union and Germany sign a mutual nonaggression pact.
June, 1941	The Germans begin Operation Barbarossa, their invasion of Russia.
Aug., 1942-Jan., 1943	The Russians withstand the German Siege of Stalingrad, marking the ultimate German failure on the Russian front.
July, 1943	The Russians defeat the Germans at the Battle of Kursk, one of the largest tank battles in history.
Apr.-May, 1945	The Russians wage air, artillery, and tank attacks in the Battle for Berlin, at which the Germans ultimately surrender, ending the war.

tion in a way that an appeal to the Communist Party, stained by years of purges and violence, probably never could have.

Stalin recovered his nerve after winter brought the German offensive to a halt. For the next two years, however, he was politically pinned by the success of the Germans. He had to allow his generals their lead, in the hope that they would be able to prevent the conquest of the Soviet Union. This openness could be seen most clearly in early 1943, when Stalin reluctantly accepted the recommendation of his generals to stay on the strategic defensive until late in the summer.

The political atmosphere changed significantly in late 1943 and early 1944. When it became clear that the Soviets would be able to push the Germans out of Russia, Stalin began reasserting his authority over the Soviet system. He took direct control of the final Soviet offensive into Poland and Germany in January, 1945, effectively undercutting the power of Zhukov, his most successful general.

In addition, Stalin began thinking about the shape of the postwar world. His primary goal was to ensure that the Soviet Union had a military buffer around it of states controlled or influenced by the Kremlin. This strategy had military effects most obviously in Poland, where from August through October, 1944, Stalin halted the forward advance of the Soviet army to allow the Germans time to deal with an uprising of the

Polish resistance in Warsaw. He had his own Polish government ready in Moscow and eagerly took the chance to eliminate any rivals to it.

By the end of the war, Stalin's paranoia had again reached epidemic proportions. He saw, in everything, a threat to his rule. Perhaps the two most endangered groups at this point were returning prisoners of war, who were likely to be executed or shipped to Siberia because of their supposed contamination by Nazi ideals, and successful generals, whom Stalin believed posed a political threat to him. Stalin's personal paranoia echoed a national paranoia that feared another invasion. Both of these paranoias contributed strongly to the start of the Cold War.

MILITARY ACHIEVEMENT

The Soviet military achievement was simple. The Soviet army absorbed the greatest weight of the German assault and turned it back. This was more than simply a victory over a particular nation. It was also a victory over a particular kind of warfare. The German Blitzkrieg, or "lightning war," methods had seemed unbeatable, first in Poland in September and October, 1939, and then in France in May and June, 1940. In both cases, the German Panzer armies had swept past and through their opponents, destroying them within weeks at relatively minimal cost.

German invincibility had seemed to continue in the first six months of the invasion of Russia. The Russians managed, through their doctrinal reorganizations, their employment of land and space, and their studied use of the winter conditions, to shatter the spearheads of the German offensives and turn them back.

The prime example of this achievement was at Kursk in 1943, when the Germans attacked a salient, or defensive fortification, in the middle of the Russian lines. Because the Germans' choice of target was obvious, the Soviets had time to build up an enormous set of fortified defensive lines backed by mobile armored forces. The defensive lines absorbed and bled the German armored spearheads, and the armored forces mounted a series of punishing counterassaults. The result, as it would be for the last two years of the war, was a decisive victory for the Russians and a costly loss for the Germans.

WEAPONS, UNIFORMS, AND ARMOR

Soviet weapons tended to be simple but also reliable. They had to be easily manufactured in relatively primitive factories by workers with minimal skills. They had to function in conditions that ranged from the appalling heat of the southern summer to the bitter cold of the northern winter. The results were, for the most part, ruggedly designed and built weapons that could absorb an enormous amount of punishment, both military and environmental, and keep on going. This held true for weapons ranging from the smallest to the largest. Soviet infantry weapons, such as the crude but effective PPSh41 submachine gun, were hard-wearing and reliable. The 11-2 Sturmovik ground-attack plane could take enormous punishment and return to base.

Oddly, the Soviets nonetheless managed to produce some weapons that not only were reliable and hard-wearing, but also surpassed those of the Germans in technological and military effectiveness. The T-34 tank is the classic example. Its sloped armor shrugged off German shells; its high-velocity 76-millimeter (later 85-millimeter) gun could easily destroy any of the then-operational German tanks; and its wide treads allowed it to drive easily over most mud and snow. With its powerful but reliable diesel engine, the T-34 outclassed anything the Germans put in the field in 1941 and 1942. The later German supertanks—the Panther and the Tiger—were, for the most part, desperate reactions to the T-34.

MILITARY ORGANIZATION

In the initial stages of World War II, Soviet military organization was both ineffective and confused. The largest unit in the army was the corps, consisting of nearly 40,000 men and, supposedly, nearly 1,000 tanks. Few of these corps were up to strength, and their units tended to be dispersed widely and, worse, to answer to different regional headquarters. The Soviets thus had neither the large-scale forces needed for a war of maneuver nor the central organization to use the forces they had effectively.

The near-destruction of the military in the initial months of the war led to its drastic and fundamental reorganization, done on the fly and even as Soviet forces were being forced back to Moscow. The military was commanded from the top by the Stavka, a group that encompassed both the Supreme High Command, led by Stalin, and the General Staff of officers, who advised the Command.

At first, there were three Main Commands, each of which controlled several fronts, responsible to the Stavka. Stalin and his generals made such a habit of bypassing the Main Command commanders that this tier was soon abolished, and the front commanders became the next organizational level for the rest of the war. These fronts were centered on geographic areas, such as Leningrad, the trans-Caucasus, or Moscow. Each front headquarters controlled all the military forces within that area, armored, air, or infantry. Such headquarters often found themselves barely able to control such an enormous responsibility, and as the war continued, the Soviets increased the number of fronts.

Very quickly, the Stavka abolished the corps and replaced it with a smaller field army. It did so because of both the shortage of equipment, especially tanks, and the lack of experienced midlevel officers.

Along with this reorganization came renewed power for the political commissars who controlled the army on behalf of the Communist Party. Commissars were present at every level of command. It was not until late 1942 that the commissars lost much of their power, as Stalin reined them in to reduce any threat to his personal power.

Below the front level, Soviet organization in the first months was chaotic, broken up by the rapid retreat. Beginning in 1942, however, the Stavka began to build up mobile mechanized units, in somewhat of a return to the prewar deep-penetration ideas.

WORLD WAR II: THE EUROPEAN THEATER

The first units were tank corps, which had about 8,000 men and 100 to 200 tanks. Larger units were soon created, which eventually became tank armies in 1943. These were made up of several tank corps and supporting units. The purpose of these highly mobile tank armies was to exploit gaps in the German defenses created by rifle infantry units. The tank armies proved highly successful and fought their way to the gates of Berlin.

DOCTRINE, STRATEGY, AND TACTICS

Soviet grand strategy shifted as the war went on. Prior to the war, the official Soviet doctrine, as laid out by people such as Marshal Mikhayl Nikolayevich Tukhachevsky (1893-1937) in the 1920's and 1930's, emphasized the idea of offensive deep penetrations led by mechanized units, aimed at breaking through the World War I static defenses and exploiting the gaps before the enemy gathered itself. The strategy was similar to German conceptions and was driven by geography as well as technology. The immense distances and relatively flat terrain of western Russia meant that campaigns rarely remained static. Such strategy relied, however, on an experienced and able senior officer corps, the very group that had suffered calamitously in Stalin's purges.

Thus in the early months of World War II, the prewar doctrine was essentially thrown out the window, and grand strategy centered on the defensive, as the country struggled to survive. The Soviets remade their doctrine on the fly, bowing to the dictates of necessity. In the first year of the war, the holding of critical centers such as Leningrad and Stalingrad was the key.

As the tide shifted, the Soviet leadership began to look to a series of massive counteroffensives that built upon one another to sweep them back through their lost territory and into Germany. The 1942 fall offensives, which included a pincer movement on the German forces at Stalingrad and a major assault on the German army group facing Moscow, were perceived as the foundation for a wave of attacks that would end the war.

Although the Stalingrad Offensive (1942-1943) was an enormous success, the German defenses tightened afterward, and the exhausted and worn-down Soviet forces needed time to rebuild. Stalin and the Stavka had to accept reluctantly that the war could not be won quickly. They thus turned to the idea of local attacks, which would both push back and bleed the German forces, interspersed with periods during which both sides rebuilt their forces.

This was the pattern the Soviets followed after their victory at Kursk. Thus, from December, 1943, through April, 1944, Soviet armies in the south pushed back the German forces in the Ukraine, while attacks in the north finally freed Leningrad after three years of encircle-

ment. Once those offensives had met with success, the Soviets paused and built their forces up in the center, eventually attacking the Germans in front of Minsk in June, 1944. The near-continuous assaults and the shifting of theaters wrong-footed and wore down the German defenders. It allowed the Soviets to pick their targets and build up forces as required.

Soviet operational strategy was based on gathering overwhelming numbers and firepower at the point of decision, whether in attack or defense, and using it to overcome the Germans. Once the infantry and artillery had created a break, mobile mechanized forces came up to exploit the gap, surge far into the German rear, and cut off the Wehrmacht forces. That was the theory, anyway. In execution, Soviet commanders often committed their mobile reserves too early and allowed them to be destroyed by the German defenders. This occurred as late as April and May, 1945, when Zhukov put in his armored forces too early during the Battle of Berlin, causing them to be entangled not only by the German defenders but also by the logistical tails of their own infantry. For the greater part, however, the Soviets found immense success with this strategy, successfully cutting off the German army led by Friedrich Paulus (1890-1957) outside Stalingrad in the winter of 1943, and then, in

Hulton Archive/Getty Images

Russians race to take up a new position near Stalingrad.

June through August, 1944, sending the German Army Group Center on a retreat from the Ukraine and killing or capturing more than 400,000 Wehrmacht soldiers in the process.

Two external factors aided the Russian strategy. The first was Adolf Hitler's obsessive refusal to allow his commanders to retreat to more defensible positions. His "stand-fast" orders, as at Stalingrad, played right into the Soviet strategy by setting Wehrmacht units up to be encircled. Second, Dodge trucks provided through the U.S. Lend-Lease program formed the Soviet logistical spine and kept the armored spearheads resupplied and refueled.

Soviet tactics relied on infantry-armor combinations, backed up by overwhelming fire support from both artillery and ground attack aircraft. A typical assault in 1944 or 1945 began with reconnaissance battalions infiltrating the German defensive lines to seize key points. As this was occurring, artillery and air units would pound the Germans to soften them up for the assault. After the initial phase, the bombardment would shift to targets in the rear, allowing an assault on the German lines by infantry, heavy armor, and combat engineers. Finally, combined-arms groups would follow up and take advantage of newly made gaps to begin encircling the German forces.

The cost of this strategy was enormous. Estimates of Soviet military casualties ranged from twenty to forty million soldiers. Civilian casualties may have been higher. Overall it was estimated that the Soviet Union lost up to twenty eight million dead. In addition to the human cost, the western half of the Soviet Union was dealt an enormous economic and social blow. Millions of people were made refugees, and the industrial infrastructure was either destroyed, captured, or uprooted. For the second time in the century, European Russia had borne the brunt of total war. It was an experience the Russians wished never to repeat, and, more than anything, this desire would inform their postwar behavior.

When the Soviet army rolled into Berlin in May, 1945, it was perhaps the most powerful army the world had ever seen. It had successfully learned from the disasters of 1941 and 1942 and applied the harsh lessons of total war to its doctrine, organization, and technology. It had rebuilt itself, even while fending off the Wehrmacht deep in the Russian steppes. It had done so at immense cost in the lives of both soldiers and civilians, but it had done so victoriously. Perhaps the only military to undergo a similarly triumphant transformation was the United States Navy during the Pacific war against Japan from 1941 to 1945. In essence, the Soviet military, supported by the iron will of the Russian people, had ended the Nazi threat. Rightly, their performance in the "Great Patriotic War" was viewed with pride.

CONTEMPORARY SOURCES

A vast array of material has been published in Russia on World War II, but little of it has been translated into English, the major exceptions being Vasili I. Chuikov's *The End of the Third Reich* (1967) and *The Memoirs of Marshal Zhukov* (1971). As a result, most of the available sources for the eastern front in World War II have tended to lean heavily toward the German point of view. During the Cold War, access to Soviet documents was limited, but that changed in the 1990's. The collapse of the Soviet Union made thousands of pages of documents and other contemporary sources available. Although this access has remained restricted and the Russian Federation's "processing" has often affected the content of available material, the change in attitude has been remarkable. The new sources have allowed a flowering in studies of the Soviet experience during World War II, led by such scholars as David Glantz. Harold Orenstein's *The Evolution of Soviet Operational Art, 1927-1991: The Documentary Basis* (1995) is probably the best English-language account of the important Soviet documents. Simon Sebag-Montefiore's *Stalin: The Court of the Red Tsar* (2003), was based on hitherto unprecedented access to Stalin's own records. There have also been many accounts, previously available only in Russian, that have been translated into English or German, such as D. F.

Loza's *Commanding the Red Army's Sherman Tanks* (1996) and his *Fighting for the Soviet Motherland* (1998) as well as Gabriel Temkin's *My Just War: The Memoir of a Jewish Red Army Soldier in World War II* (1998).

Books and Articles

Dunn, Walter S. *Hitler's Nemesis: The Red Army, 1930-1945*. Westport, Conn.: Praeger, 1994.

Erickson, John. *The Road to Berlin: Continuing the History of Stalin's War with Germany*. Boulder, Colo.: Westview Press, 1983.

_____. *The Road to Stalingrad*. New York: Harper and Row, 1975.

Forczyk, Robert. *Leningrad, 1941-44*. New York: Osprey, 2009.

Glantz, David M. *Stumbling Colossus: The Red Army on the Eve of World War*. Lawrence: University Press of Kansas, 1998.

Glantz, David M., and Jonathan House. *When Titans Clashed: How the Red Army Stopped Hitler*. Lawrence: University Press of Kansas, 1995.

Jukes, Geoffrey, *The Second World War (5): The Eastern Front, 1941-1945*. New York: Osprey, 2002.

Morgan, Hugh. *Soviet Aces of World War 2*. New York: Osprey, 1997.

Rottman, Gordon L. *Soviet Field Fortifications, 1941-45*. New York: Osprey, 2007.

_____. *Soviet Rifleman, 1941-45*. New York: Osprey, 2007.

Sakaida, Henry. *Heroes of the Soviet Union, 1941-45*. New York: Osprey, 2004.

Shukman, Harold, ed. *Stalin's Generals*. New York: Grove Press, 1993.

Smith, Myron J. *The Soviet Army, 1939-1980: A Guide to Sources in English*. Santa Barbara, Calif.: ABC-CLIO, 1982.

Stolfi, R. H. S. *Hitler's Panzers East: World War II Reconsidered*. Norman: University of Oklahoma Press, 1991.

Zaloga, Steven J. *The Red Army of the Great Patriotic War, 1941-45*. New York: Osprey, 1989.

Films and Other Media

Army Group North: The Werhmacht in Russia. Documentary. Cromwell Productions, 1999.

Ballad of a Solider. Film. Mosfilm, 1959.

The Battle of Russia. Documentary. Hughes Leisure Group, 1991.

Defiance. Film. Paramount Vantage, 2008.

Enemy at the Gates. Film. Paramount Pictures, 2001.

The World at War. Documentary. Thames Television, 1973.

David Silbey

WORLD WAR II
GERMANY AND ITALY
Dates: 1933-1945

POLITICAL CONSIDERATIONS

In the years between 1918 and 1933, German armed forces assumed a political posture fundamentally hostile to the young Weimar Republic created at the end of World War I, blaming that state for Germany's humiliating defeat in the war, for its enduring political turmoil and economic problems, and for the perceived fraying of its social fabric. For more than a decade after the end of World War I, the German military tried to circumvent the constraints imposed upon it by the Treaty of Versailles (1919). With that treaty, the victorious Allies had abolished German conscription, limited the size of the German army to 100,000 men (including 5,000 officers) obligated to 12-year terms of service, reduced the German navy to 15,000 men without capital ships or submarines, and forbidden Germany to create and maintain a separate air force. Furthermore, Germany was not allowed to maintain any armor, heavy artillery, or chemical weapons. The Allies, especially France, clearly intended to limit the role of the German army largely to constabulary duties, thereby preventing the reemergence of any substantial military threat.

The Versailles treaty elicited virtually universal disapproval across the political spectrum in Germany; the armed forces themselves took steps to rearm covertly both within and outside the Reich. The General Staff, forbidden by the Allies, emerged in embryonic form in one of the administrative offices of the army. Men who were trained in the numerous flying clubs that emerged in Germany entered the army to form the core of a future air force. During the 1920's officers tested armored warfare doctrine and practiced chemical warfare in the Soviet Union, another nation that regarded itself as a pariah in the Ver-

sailles settlement. "Police units" began to arm and train secretly, forming what was called the "black Reichswehr," or "black defense force."

Any examination of the German military between 1933 and 1945 must address the central role of Adolf Hitler (1889-1945), who combined the function of chief executive of the Nazi state with that of supreme commander of the armed forces. Consequently, the rise to power of the National Socialist German Workers' (Nazi) Party had profound implications for the armed forces. Hitler, appointed chancellor in January, 1933, had repeatedly and explicitly called for the abolition of the Treaty of Versailles and for the rearmament of Germany. The Nazis espoused a worldview predicated on a virulently racist and anti-Semitic social Darwinist conception of struggle among nations and individuals for resources and power. A perceived racial hierarchy of peoples placed the "Aryan" Germans at the top, the Germanic and Latin peoples of Europe in the middle, non-Europeans and Slavs near the bottom, and Jews in the lowest category. Hitler fervently believed the Jewish people to be the source of capitalism, Socialism, and Marxism, and he felt that the sole intention of the Jews was to corrupt and ultimately destroy the so-called Aryan race. Consequently, he believed, the Aryans had to eliminate the Jews and expand Aryan territory into the Soviet Union in order to survive and flourish. Germany would acquire this "living space" in Eastern Europe only through military conquest, which, in turn, hinged on rapid rearmament and expansion.

Following the death of President Paul von Hindenburg (1847-1934) on August 2, 1934, Hitler combined the offices of chancellor and president and required civil servants and members of the armed forces to swear a personal oath of loyalty to him. Between 1935 and 1939, Germany openly rearmed and expanded its territorial boundaries. In March of 1935, Hitler announced the reintroduction of conscription and the existence of a German air force, or Luftwaffe, thereby abandoning any pretense of honoring the Treaty of Versailles. Initial British and French indifference to growing German assertiveness can be explained by fear of a military conflict potentially costlier than World War I, preoccupation with domestic political and economic issues, latent guilt about the perceived severity of the Versailles treaty, and Hitler's adroit invocation of the right to national self-determination.

The German armed forces generally distinguished themselves during both this time period and the war years through their willingness to support Hitler's long-term goals of territorial conquest. Hitler drew on old German traditions of loyalty, duty, and honor, citing the personal oath that each member of the military took upon induction and general agreement with the political goals of the regime, to turn the German military into a willing and able instrument of his will. He also ensured the cooperation of senior commanders with enormous bribes. The government created a separate, fourth armed service, the armed Schutzstaffel, or SS, parallel to but separate from the regular army, navy, and air force. This force provided the regime with its own Praetorian Guard, which literally served as Hitler's bodyguard and army. In this way, Hitler developed a counterweight to the regular military, which he did not completely trust.

It is important to note that the armed forces generally agreed with the regime's policies. When disagreement arose, it usually centered on details and not on the general intent of policy. For example, Hitler believed that time would only serve the interests of Germany's enemies. Consequently, he informed the armed forces at a secret conference in November, 1937, of his intention to wage war and defeat Austria, Czechoslovakia, France, and Great Britain by 1943 at the latest.

After that time, he believed, the major European powers would have enhanced their military capabilities sufficiently to defeat Germany. Many generals questioned the timetable but not the substance of Hitler's intentions. Most senior commanders, then, did not oppose wars of aggression as long as Germany could wage them when and where it wanted. Although some officers contemplated staging a coup in 1938, and others would mount unsuccessful assassination attempts against Hitler, the majority of Hitler's soldiers, sailors, and airmen readily did his bidding. Indoctrination with Nazi ideals, fear, corruption, and careerism all played a role in the acquiescence of Germany's military to Hitler's will.

Although Italy had been on the victorious side at the end of World War I, many Italians were angered by the Treaty of Versailles, which barely rewarded Italy for its efforts. What particularly angered Italy was the refusal to hand the city of Fiume to the Italians, who took it and briefly held it. With the country having the potential of degenerating into chaos, in 1922 Benito Mussolini came to power and started to rebuild Italian pride, albeit at the cost of democracy—his Blackshirts attacked communists and democrats alike.

The new Italian army that emerged under the Fascist rule of Mussolini was essentially—with the royal

German chancellor Adolf Hitler and Italian dictator Benito Mussolini in Munich, Germany, in 1934.

TURNING POINTS

1919	The restrictions imposed on the German military by the Treaty of Versailles at the end of World War I meet almost universal disapproval across the political spectrum in Germany.
1933	Adolf Hitler, leader of the National Socialist German Workers' (Nazi) Party, is appointed chancellor of Germany and calls for the abolition of the Treaty of Versailles and the rearmament of Germany.
1939	Hitler uses combined arms forces to invade Poland, which is then partitioned between Germany and the Soviet Union.
1941	Germany invades the Soviet Union, advancing as far as Moscow and Leningrad.
Jan. 20, 1942	Wannsee Conference finalizes plans for extermination of the Jews.
1942-1943	The Russian defeat of the Germans at the Siege of Stalingrad marks the ultimate German failure on the Russian front.
July, 1943	The Germans are defeated by the Russians at the Battle of Kursk, one of the largest tank battles in history.
1945	The German city of Berlin is besieged by Russian air, artillery, and tank attacks that ultimately bring about German surrender.

army, navy, and air force—continuing the traditions prior to 1922. These remained nominally under the command of the king of Italy. However, there was also the Milizi Volontaria per Sicurezza Nazionale (MSVN), which was the military arm of the Fascist Party and under Mussolini's direct control. These forces were involved in fighting in foreign wars, as well as when Italy itself was invaded by the Allies in 1943.

MILITARY ACHIEVEMENT

The German military registered some of the most impressive accomplishments in the annals of warfare before sustaining one of the costliest defeats in recorded history. The conquest of Poland in September 1939 was their first victory, but achieved at a cost. However it was followed by lightning campaigns in Denmark and Norway in April, 1940, before its greatest victory in May and June of 1940, when the Germans, skillfully combining armor, infantry, and aircraft, conquered territory in the Benelux countries and France, over which they and the Allies had fought for months and years during World War I. The conquest of Belgium witnessed the first large-scale use of air-dropped paratroopers in history. In April of 1941 the Germans rapidly conquered Greece and Yugoslavia. Concurrently they waged a protracted war in North Africa, where they had initially intervened to assist Italy in its failed attempt to conquer Egypt. There, German forces would continue to engage the Allies until May of 1943. In 1941 and 1942 Germans advanced in the Caucasus to the border of Asia and in Egypt toward the Nile Valley and sank numerous American ships within sight of the eastern seaboard of the United States.

In the East, Germany mounted the largest invasion in world history on June 22, 1941, with its attack on the Soviet Union. That summer and fall, German forces captured more than 3 million Soviet prisoners and killed and wounded countless numbers of Red Army troops. German units advanced to the outskirts of Moscow before a Soviet counteroffensive, attenuated supply lines, and the harsh Russian winter blunted and then repulsed the German offensive. Despite this setback, the Germans would continue to mount offensives in the Soviet Union, until they suffered a major defeat at the hands of the Red Army during the massive armored offensive at Kursk in July, 1943. In the context of the savage ideological conflict against their dual enemies, Judaism and Bolshevism, what the Nazi regime called "Judeo-Bolshevism," the Germans inflicted casualties amounting to some twenty-five or twenty-six million dead Soviet civilians and military personnel.

At roughly the same time, in the summer of 1943,

losses in German submarines began to exceed replacements in the bitter and protracted Battle of the Atlantic, and the Combined Bomber Offensive mounted by the strategic bomber forces of Great Britain and the United States against strategic targets in Germany began to wear down the German air force over the Reich itself. Historians, therefore, generally consider 1943 the year in which World War II began to turn irrevocably against Germany. Nevertheless, despite the growing material strength, proficiency, and determination of the Allies, German troops conducted skillful fighting withdrawals from Italy, northwestern Europe, and the Soviet Union, exacting heavy casualties even as they retreated. German troops distinguished themselves through tactical

virtuosity, resilience, and determination. German scientists developed and the Reich launched the V-1 and V-2 rockets, the first cruise missiles and ballistic missiles, respectively, at targets in Great Britain, Belgium, and the Netherlands. Germany had thereby in some respects advanced to the frontier of aerospace research and technology.

The Italian army fought over a longer period than the Germans, but with far less success. Although the Italians were involved in the attack of Corfu in 1923, their first major military action was with the invasion of Abyssinia in 1935-1936. Although well organized, the Italians were more prepared for a European war, and that invasion had not allowed for the poor conditions of roads and the bitterness of the guerrilla

Parisians flee the city as German troops approach in 1940.

warfare waged by the Abyssinians, which hindered the Italian advance considerably. Although the Italians achieved a victory, it was not an easy one. Italian soldiers also fought in the Spanish Civil War, though technically as volunteers. Subsequently, in April of 1939, the Italians invaded Albania in what proved to be their easiest military action. That against France in June of 1940 was badly managed and again did not allow for the ground conditions. In October, 1940, the Italian invasion of Greece and its subsequent actions in Yugoslavia also went badly. Italians fought the Allies in North Africa and from 1941 in the Soviet Union. However, it was during the Allied invasion of Italy in 1943 when the Italian army fought most tenaciously, although by that time some were supporting the Allies and others, with German support, were holding back the Allied advances in southern Italy.

In July, 1943, a U.S. soldier looks out over the city of Gela, Sicily, at explosions off the coast.

WEAPONS, UNIFORMS, AND ARMOR

Most of the German army during the war carried a version of the Mauser Gewehr 98, a 7.92-millimeter, bolt-action rifle with a five-shot magazine. The weapon weighed approximately 4 kilograms and had a range of 800 meters. Submachine guns issued to German troops included the MP38 and MP40, which differed only in external appearance. The MP38 had a smooth case, whereas the MP40 had a ridged one. This weapon carried thirty-two rounds of 9-millimeter ammunition in its magazine and weighed slightly more than 4 kilograms. It had a rate of fire of 500 rounds per minute and a range of approximately 100 meters. The standard machine gun was the MG34, which remained in service until it was phased out by the MG42. That weapon, in turn, was superseded by the MG45. All three machine guns could be fired as either a light, with a bipod, or a heavy machine gun, with a tripod. The MG34 and MG42 used 7.92-millimeter ammunition, whereas the MG45 fired 7.62-millimeter rounds. The rate of fire was 900 rounds per minute in the light machine gun configuration and 300 rounds per minute in the heavy machine gun configuration.

Field artillery consisted of guns and howitzers ranging from 7.5 to 10.5 centimeters in caliber. Heavy field artillery guns ranged in caliber from 15 centimeters upward. The Germans also used a 28-centimeter rail gun that weighed 218 tons and fired a 255.5-kilogram shell. Another very famous artillery piece was the 8.8-centimeter antiaircraft gun, which fired a hypervelocity round and proved especially effective as an antitank weapon.

The best-known piece of German apparel was perhaps the jackboot, made of black leather and worn by all units except mounted troops. The "marching boot" extended up the leg to just below the knee; the sole was heavily studded, and the tip steel-tipped. The infantryman's trousers were gray, straight-legged, and unpiped except for those that formed part of parade dress. The single-breasted tunic was fastened down the front by five dull metal buttons. The turned-down collar consisted of a dark green cloth, and a patch indicating the arm of service adorned each side of the collar join. Eyelet holes in the tunic waist could hold support hooks for the leather waist belt and the equipment that fitted onto it.

The standard greatcoat was double-breasted, field gray in color, with a green collar. It was worn by all ranks, up to that of general, and by all arms of service. Helmets appeared in five basic sizes and weighed between .82 and 1.2 kilograms. Two holes provided ventilation, and a lining of thin leather cushioned the crown of the wearer's head. Soldiers of all ranks wore a peaked cap with a field gray top, a dark-green cap band, and a shiny ridged peak.

The Germans designed some formidable tanks during the war. Especially notable were the Mark V, or Panther, sometimes described as the best tank of the war. It weighed approximately 53 tons and was powered by a 700-horsepower engine with a capacity of 23 liters. Its 7.5-centimeter gun offered good penetration of enemy armor, and its steeply sloped superstructure made it more difficult for enemy gunners to score direct hits on the turret. With a weight of nearly 70 tons, the Mark VI, or Tiger, was the heaviest operational tank of any combatant nation during the war. It carried an 8.8-centimeter gun and was heavily armored, with its turret front 10 centimeters thick. This bulk and heavy armor might well have reflected the defensive nature of warfare conducted by Germany during the last two years of the war. Germany also developed and deployed a tank-destroyer version of the Panther tank. This vehicle used the same basic chassis as the Panther and carried an 8.8-centimeter antitank gun in an enclosed, turretless superstructure.

Mussolini, the Italian dictator, boasted that he could raise some 8 million bayonets. However, at full strength there were only slightly more than 2.5 million under arms. The Italians' equipment varied considerably with the location of the fighting, with the elite Alpini, who defended Italy's northern frontier, being well armed, but with many others in the Italian forces being armed with the single bolt-action Mannlicher-Carcano Model 1891. As with weapons, the Italian army had a range of uniforms. These varied because of the climate in the areas where they were fighting. In Abyssinia and later in North Africa, the Italians wore khakis, either large, baggy trousers or shorts. In Europe, their armies wore gray woolen clothes.

MILITARY ORGANIZATION

Hitler, in his capacity as führer (leader), retained overall direction of the German armed forces, collectively called the Defense Force, or Wehrmacht. A war minister had exercised high command until the dissolution of the war ministry in 1938. Hitler then established a high command of armed forces (OKW) as the body through which he would direct the war. He appointed Wilhelm Keitel (1882-1946), who distinguished himself through particular obsequiousness, as chief of staff and Alfred Jodl (1890-1946) as head of operations.

Hitler exercised tight control over Germany's conduct during World War II for several reasons. First, each member of the armed forces was bound to him by the oath of loyalty. Second, the Prussian army officer code had fostered introspection and emphasis on the purely technical aspects of the conduct of war. Consequently the German officers excelled at the tactical level, performed well at the operational level, and proved deficient at the strategic level. Hitler, however, believed that he possessed an infallible grasp of strategy and in the course of the war began to involve himself increasingly in the details of military operations. He did so both because of his growing confidence in himself, especially after Germany's stunning victories in 1940, and because of his growing distrust of his senior commanders. Hitler had, after all, advocated the attack on Poland and the Benelux countries against the advice of most of his senior commanders, who feared that Germany was insufficiently prepared for full-scale war at the time. The rapid victories had vindicated Hitler in his own eyes and, it should be noted, in the perception of many others as well.

The armed forces lacked a single voice, and this allowed Hitler to exercise his tight control over them. The service chiefs all had direct access to him, but usually they acted as partisans of their own branches and not in tandem with the other armed forces. Hitler also actively encouraged his subordinates in the military as well as the civilian branches of government to compete among themselves. He thereby preserved for himself the role as final arbiter in any dispute and prevented any power block from forming against him. Unfortunately for Germany, this approach also largely prevented effective coordination of the armed forces into an instrument of coherent strategy.

Mussolini directly controlled the MSVN, the militia, which remained loyal to him. The royal army, navy, and air force were technically under the command of the King of Italy, and thus when Mussolini was deposed in 1943, some supported the new pro-Allied Fascist government, while others remained loyal to Mussolini.

DOCTRINE, STRATEGY, AND TACTICS

Any discussion of tactics and strategy should begin with definitions. One working definition of tactics is the application of doctrine, or techniques involving the deployment of personnel and weapons, to the winning of individual military engagements. The lieutenant commanding a platoon of perhaps thirty to fifty infantrymen would apply doctrine learned in training and through battlefield experience to defeat an enemy platoon by deploying his machine guns in one location, his mortar team in another, and so forth. On the next level, scholars point to operations as a subset of military affairs. Operational warfare involves the application of doctrine to win campaigns, such as the German conquest of France in 1940. In the spring of 1940, then, German commanders used resources at their disposal to defeat an enemy in a series of military engagements of regional geographic expanse and relatively brief duration. Strategy occupies the highest level of military affairs and consists

of the harnessing of economic, military, and political resources to secure a political victory in a military conflict. One could sum up Germany's performance during World War II by noting that the Germans excelled tactically, performed well operationally, and ultimately proved woefully deficient strategically. Good tactics will allow a combatant nation to win battles, whereas good strategy will allow it to win wars.

Several factors explain this phenomenon. The Germans emphasized rigorous and realistic training and initiative. Convalescing veterans would train new units of soldiers and thereby impart, at least theoretically, valuable experience to recruits. The army also exercised great care in selecting soldiers from the same geographic areas to serve in the same units, thereby strengthening unit cohesion. As casualties mounted, however, this practice became ever more difficult to implement. Soldiers were encouraged to think two levels above their rank. Consequently, if their immediate superiors were killed or disabled in combat, subordinates could assume control. The German military distinguished itself through its use of mission-oriented orders. A commander would order his subordinate to complete a certain task at a specific location during a specified time period, such as the holding of a ridge against advancing American tanks. The way in which a subordinate subsequently executed the order, however, was usually his own responsibility. Such an approach lent itself to a flexible response to combat, which by its very nature is fluid. Good tactics, in turn, allowed the armed forces to execute successful campaigns between 1939 and 1941.

Germany's deficiencies manifested themselves most vividly at the strategic level and explain the Reich's ultimate defeat at the hands of the Allies. Hitler's control of the armed forces meant that his background and views affected the conduct of the German military significantly. He was determined to avoid the stalemate that had characterized the western front during World War I. He also believed that the collapse of the home front had caused Germany's defeat during that war. Consequently, the Germans could avoid defeat by mounting swift attacks using combined arms. German infantry, armor, and aircraft would mount coordinated strikes against the en-

The rubble of bombed-out buildings in Hamburg, Germany, in July, 1945.

emy's weak points and then punch through the front line. The regular infantry, marching on foot as it had from 1914 to 1918, would subsequently encircle and either destroy or capture enemy troops. Hitler believed that this "mailed fist" would ensure swift victory, which in turn would mean that the Reich could eschew full-scale mobilization and the ensuing sacrifices that would be required of the civilian population, such as rationing and the mobilization of male and female civilians in war-related industries.

The Germans proved singularly unable to organize their economy efficiently, due to competing loci of power within the Nazi Party and government and to the sheer ineptitude of those tasked to run the country during wartime. The Germans, unlike the Allies, also had never waged real coalition warfare. There was, for example, no Combined Chiefs of Staff link-

ing the highest-ranking German, Italian, and Japanese commanders. Germany's fate was sealed by Hitler's fervent belief in both his own infallibility and the ascendancy of willpower over material preponderance, by his overestimation of German capabilities and concurrent underestimation of Allied capabilities, and by the subservience of the German armed forces. Germany's enemies, in contrast, all learned from their mistakes, improved their own initially inadequate tactics, and mobilized their economies for full-scale war much earlier and more efficiently.

Unlike the German army, the Italians were not nearly so well mechanized, and they continued to make heavy use of horses, which in Abyssinia and Albania proved effective given the poor roads. However, this reliance proved to be a weakness elsewhere, especially during the Allied invasion of Italy. The Italians' tactics prior to that invasion had been to try to extend Italy's colonial power, whether over Abyssinia, Albania, North Africa, Yugoslavia, or the Ionian Islands. Italy was also providing troops for the German war effort in the Soviet Union. Later Italy's objective was to prevent an invasion on its own soil. After the 1943 invasion, the Italians fragmented, with some supporting the Allies and others remaining loyal to Mussolini.

CONTEMPORARY SOURCES

Two very important contemporaneous sources are *The German Army* (1939), by Herbert Rosinski (1903-1962), and *The Handbook of German Military Forces* (1945), by the U.S. War Department. Rosinski assessed the performance and thinking of the Germans and discussed at length the changes that had transpired in the mindset of German commanders. The breadth of vision that had characterized the nineteenth century reformers Gerhard Johann David von Scharnhorst (1755-1813) and August von Gneisenau (1760-1831), Rosinski argued, had yielded to a narrowly technocratic approach to war that emphasized tactical and operational proficiency at the expense of the vital, and ultimately decisive, element in military affairs: strategy. The handbook provides the reader with a plethora of valuable technical information about the organization, weapons, and equipment of the German armed forces and likely provided the U.S. Army with a most useful tool as it fought Germany in the waning days of World War II. An invaluable translation entitled *Hitler's War Directives, 1939-1945*, edited by H. R. Trevor-Roper, appeared in several editions (London: Pan, 1966). Hitler's own *Mein Kampf* (1925-1927; my struggle) is available in English translation by Ralph Manheim (1939; reprint, Boston: Houghton Mifflin, 1999), and the 1935 diary of his lover Eva Braun can be read in a 2000 edition from Spectrum International, *The Diary of Eva Braun*.

Although Mussolini tried to encourage the martial spirit in Italy, compared to the information on the German army there are far fewer works on the Italians available in English. Some of these include Primo Levi's *Se questo è un uomo* (1947; *If This Is a Man*, 1956; revised as *Survival in Auschwitz: The Nazi Assault on Humanity*, 1961); Eugenio Corti's *Few Returned: Twenty-eight Days on the Russian Front, Winter 1942-1943* (1997); and Donna M. Budani's *Italian Women's Narratives of Their Experiences During World War II* (2003).

BOOKS AND ARTICLES

Bartov, Omer. *Hitler's Army: Soldiers, Nazis, and War in the Third Reich*. New York: Oxford University Press, 1991.

Beevor, Antony. *Stalingrad*. New York: W. W. Norton, 1998.

Bennett, Ralph. *Intelligence Investigations: Collected Papers of Ralph Bennett*. London: F. Cass, 1996.

Corum, James. *The Roots of Blitzkrieg*. Lawrence: University Press of Kansas, 1992.

Doughty, Robert. *The Breaking Point: Sedan and the Fall of France, 1940*. Hamden, Conn.: Archon, 1990.

Halder, Franz. *The Halder War Diary, 1939-1942*. Novato, Calif.: Presidio Press, 1988.

Hayward, Joel. *Stopped at Stalingrad: The Luftwaffe and Hitler's Defeat in the East, 1942-1943*. Lawrence: University Press of Kansas, 1998.

Jowett, Philip S. *The Italian Army, 1940-45: Africa, 1940-43*. New York: Osprey, 2001.

_____. *The Italian Army, 1940-45: Europe, 1940-43*. New York: Osprey, 2000.

_____. *The Italian Army, 1940-45: Italy, 1943-45*. New York: Osprey, 2001.

Millett, Allan, and Murray Williamson. *A War to Be Won: Fighting the Second World War.* Cambridge, England: Belknap Press, 2000.

Nicoll, David. *The Italian Invasion of Abyssinia, 1935-36*. New York: Osprey, 1997.

Thomas, Nigel. *German Army in World War II*. New York: Osprey, 2002.

_____. *The German Army, 1939-45*. 5 vols. New York: Osprey, 1997-2000.

Weinberg, Gerhard. *Hitler, Germany, and World War II*. New York: Cambridge University Press, 1995.

_____. *A World at Arms*. New York: Cambridge University Press, 1994.

FILMS AND OTHER MEDIA

Das Boot. Feature film. Columbia Pictures/Bavaria Film, 1981.

Massacre in Rome. Feature film. Carlo Ponti, 1973.

Mussolini and I. Television miniseries. HBO, 1985.

The Pianist. Feature film. Focus Features, 2002.

Schindler's List. Feature film. Amblin Entertainment, 1993.

The Sorrow and the Pity: Chronicle of a French City Under the Occupation. Documentary. Milestone Film & Video, 2001.

Tea with Mussolini. Feature film. Metro-Goldwyn-Mayer, 1999.

Triumph of the Will. Propaganda film. Reichsparteitag-film, 1935.

The World at War. Documentary. Thames Television, 1973.

Oliver Griffin

WORLD WAR II
JAPAN
Dates: 1931-1945

POLITICAL CONSIDERATIONS

The core of Japan's military institution, the Imperial Japanese Army, began its ascendancy to political dominance in the 1930's. Through the intimidation and, often, the assassination of its political opponents, the military succeeded in controlling the inner circle of advisers to the Japanese emperor, Hirohito (1901-1989). The army, citing its loyalty to the emperor, subscribed to a theory of preparation for total war and devised a master plan that sought to make Japan the primary political power in Asia and the Pacific.

The Japanese Kwantung Army, which, following World War I, had occupied bases in Manchuria by treaty with the Chinese, provoked a confrontation with local Chinese authorities there and launched a series of military strikes that ended with the occupation of Manchuria in 1931. Six years later, in the vicinity of the Marco Polo Bridge near Beijing, the Japanese alleged an attack by elements of the Chinese Nationalist Army and launched a campaign of full-scale warfare against China in an attempt to dominate, control, and occupy much of the country.

The U.S. government, together with a number of Western European nations, sought to oppose the Japanese expansion. These nations launched an economic embargo seeking to limit the growth of Japanese military and naval power. Because Japan lacked many of the natural resources needed to produce the supplies and equipment required to fuel a powerful military machine, these restrictions prompted the more aggressive elements in the Japanese army to press for an all-out war against the United States and its European supporters, mainly the British, Dutch, and French, all of whom had colonies on both the South Asian continent and the islands situated off it.

In September, 1939, the Japanese, seeking to counteract the power of the Allied nations, signed the Tripartite Pact with Germany and Italy, allying itself with those two Fascist nations in their confrontation with France and England.

In 1940 Japan had established bases in French Indochina—the present-day countries of Vietnam, Laos, and Cambodia. On December 7, 1941, the Japanese launched a surprise attack on the American naval base at Pearl Harbor, in Hawaii, while at the same time invading the Philippines and the Malay Peninsula. The Japanese forces then attacked the Dutch East Indies, which they seized for its critical oil fields.

MILITARY ACHIEVEMENT

The initial attacks by Japan's armies and navy proved to be spectacularly successful. The task force that attacked Pearl Harbor consisted of six aircraft carriers with 183 planes aboard and supporting vessels. This force wreaked havoc on the unprepared American fleet tied up at the base. The Americans lost or suffered severe damage to eighteen warships. Some 2,335 sailors were killed, and an additional 1,178 were wounded. The Japanese lost only twenty-nine aircraft and fifty-five flyers in the attack. The Imperial fleet returned to home base with no loss to its surface units.

The isolated Central Pacific U.S. bases at Guam and Wake Island fell quickly to the Japanese, who also occupied both Kiska and Attu, in Alaska's Aleutian Island chain, forestalling any move by the United States to use the Aleutians as a base in a retaliatory attack.

The Imperial Japanese Army also enjoyed a series of quick successes in its campaigns in the Philippine

Islands, the Malay Peninsula, and the Dutch East Indies. Although the Americans put up spirited defenses on Luzon's Bataan Peninsula and Corregidor, by April 9, 1942, the Japanese had secured control of the Philippines. General Douglas MacArthur (1880-1964), commanding the combined American and Filipino forces, had received his orders to leave for Australia before the actual fall of the Philippines. President Franklin D. Roosevelt (1882-1945) and the Allies needed him to prepare that continent against attack in the event that the Japanese moved in that direction.

The British defense of Malaya and Singapore proved to be even more disastrous. Despite numerical superiority, the British were no match for the Japanese infantry, whose units included the best of the Imperial Japanese Army. By February 15, 1942, Japan had captured Singapore, gaining control of the entire Malay Peninsula.

The Japanese had advanced into both Burma and the Dutch East Indies as well, ensuring the island empire's supply of both rice and oil. In fewer than one hundred days, the Japanese military had accomplished all of the goals originally established by Imperial General Staff.

The euphoria of these early Japanese victories had disappeared by mid-1942. Their advance in the Pacific islands was far less successful. In April of that year, U.S. B-25 bombers flew off a carrier to conduct a raid on the cities of Tokyo, Yokohama, Kobe, and Nagoya. Moreover, the Americans turned back Japanese invasion fleets intent on taking all of New Guinea to the south and Midway, formerly Brooks Islands, to the east. In the latter battle, a turning point in the war, the Japanese lost four virtually irreplaceable aircraft carriers and some of their best naval aviators. General MacArthur then began a campaign to recover all of New Guinea and to take back the Philippines. This action by the Americans ended the threat of Japanese invasion of Australia.

Simultaneously, the U.S. Navy began a series of attacks on Japanese island bases in the mid-Pacific: the Gilbert Islands, the Marshall Islands, the Mariana Islands, and the Caroline Islands. One by one, these critical outposts fell to the U.S. Navy and U.S. Marines, leaving Japan open to both direct air attack and the threat of the ultimate invasion of the home islands themselves.

By August, 1945, U.S. military forces had succeeded in reconquering all of the Pacific bases previously seized by the Japanese. They had even captured the island of Okinawa, the key Japanese base in the Ryukyu Island chain, only 380 miles south of Kyūshū, one of the Japanese home islands. The U.S. forces had also severed Japan's supply lines to the south, depriving the Japanese of raw materials, such as oil, that were critical to their ability to continue the war. The ultimate weapons in the U.S. attack proved to be the two atomic bombings of the cities of Hiroshima and Nagasaki, which forced Hirohito to surrender.

WEAPONS, UNIFORMS, AND ARMOR

During the late 1930's, the Japanese government built a powerful military and naval machine. Its infantry, artillery, and air forces acquired extensive ex-

TURNING POINTS

July, 1937	Japan invades China.
Dec. 7, 1941	The Japanese attack on the U.S. fleet at Pearl Harbor, Hawaii, brings the United States into World War II.
June 4-7, 1942	Japanese loss of aircraft carriers at the Battle of Midway undermines the possibility of holding earlier gains in the Pacific.
1944	The Japanese begin kamikaze attacks on Allied ships in the Pacific.
Apr., 1945	In the last major amphibious offensive of World War II, U.S. forces invade Okinawa and, after meeting fierce resistance, seize the island from Japan.
Aug. 5, 1945	The United States drops an atomic bomb on the Japanese city of Hiroshima, killing more than 70,000 people.
Aug. 15, 1945	Emperor Hirohito announces Japan's surrender.

World War II: Japan and the Pacific Theater

perience in Manchuria and in their invasion of China. The Imperial Japanese Army relied heavily upon a well-trained, mobile, and aggressive infantry that was trained and skilled in hand-to-hand combat. During the Malayan Campaign, for example, the British forces with their motorized equipment were handicapped by narrow roads through the heavy jungle. The Japanese infantry mounted bicycles to navigate the landscape, riding on the wheel rims when they blew tires and shouldering their bicycles to ford rivers.

The enlisted man in the Japanese army was dressed poorly. He seldom shaved and wore a patched uniform with unpolished boots and insignia. He was poorly armed, with only a rifle and a bayonet. He walked rather than marched. Extremely fit, he covered surprising distances.

The quality of the machine guns available to the Japanese infantry remained marginal, especially since infantry tactics counted on heavy machine-gun support. Japanese tank and artillery support fell far below the level of that of their enemies. Tanks operated more in the capacity of armored personnel carriers than of powerful mobile heavy weapons. Artillery had proven unnecessary in the Chinese campaign, mainly because the Chinese themselves lacked formidable artillery support. The situation changed radically when the Japanese forces had to fight against heavily armed U.S. land and sea forces.

The Japanese air forces depended primarily on their speedy, highly maneuverable Mitsubishi A6M2 Zero fighters. Early in the war these aircraft dominated the skies over China, the Dutch East Indies, and the Philippines. Opposing pilots could not match the Zero's speed. The Zero fighters, flown by skilled and highly trained pilots, dominated the opposition. Although the plane proved to be mechanically superior to those of Japan's opponents, it was never modified in any meaningful way from its initial model. As the war progressed, the U.S. aircraft industry began to turn out planes that were both faster and better equipped than the Zero. The Japanese plane's lack of armor also resulted in a higher mortality rate among its corps of pilots. Another, often fatal, flaw lay in the plane's lack of self-sealing fuel tanks. The Japanese bomber fleet suffered even more from a lack of sufficient armor. The bombers, handicapped by slow speed as well as the vulnerable fuel tanks, found themselves easy targets for Allied pursuit aircraft.

The Japanese navy built a formidable naval force centered around several super-battleships of the Yamato class, the largest vessels of that category ever built. However, these capital ships played no meaningful role in the naval battles that occurred after the American navy recovered from the Pearl Harbor attack. Most naval authorities suggest that Japan might have been more successful had it instead built more aircraft carriers, because these ships proved to play a critical role in the naval warfare of World War II. The Imperial Japanese Navy lost many of its carriers early in the war, in May, 1942, at the Battle of the Coral Sea, but more important at the Battle of Midway from June 3-6. Japanese industry was unable to build replacements quickly enough to keep up with its opposition. The Japanese also lacked a sufficient number of support vessels, especially for the transport of critical supplies, such as oil from the Dutch East Indies.

The Japanese submarine fleet did not conduct long-range raiding campaigns on U.S. shipping, as did the German fleet in the Atlantic Ocean. More often it operated either as part of larger fleet units or as supply ships for the army's increasingly isolated Pacific island bases. U.S. submarines, in contrast, preyed constantly upon the limited number of Japanese merchant ships and the extended supply lines on which Japan depended to move materials to its home islands.

MILITARY ORGANIZATION

Japan had, by 1940, become a totalitarian nation. The military, utilizing Hirohito as a symbol, had organized Japanese society into a cohesive body dedicated to the worship of the emperor and total obedience to a government dominated by the leaders of the Japanese Imperial Army and Navy. Civilian diplomats, including the country's prime minister, served only to cover the aggressive planning of the military factions. Japanese industry no longer operated as a competitive economic entity in the world market, as manufacturers subordinated themselves to government control and dedicated themselves to meeting the needs of the armed forces.

The war in China had, however, decimated both Japan's manpower and its resources. By mid-1941 Japan had already lost 185,000 soldiers, and peace in China remained elusive to Japanese planners. The Japanese High Command, however, insisted on the empire's expansion to provide the raw material necessary for the growth of Japan as a major global power.

One critical factor continued to plague the military hierarchy throughout the 1930's and 1940's: An intense rivalry existed between the army and navy factions. Each force had its own assessment of the direction the armed forces should take, and they quarreled constantly over the country's military priorities.

The Japanese army saw Japan's major long-term enemy to be the Soviet Union and its implied threat of a communist world revolution and sought to concentrate the empire's resources on a continuing buildup of its ground forces and support troops on the Asian mainland itself. The army saw the European colonies on the continent's southern boundaries as the solution to its needs for basic commodities to strengthen its military capabilities. It was prepared to go to war with the United States only if that country denied Japan the raw materials necessary to create and maintain a self-sufficient empire.

The Japanese navy saw the United States as Japan's primary threat. It recognized the potential of the powerful American fleet, with its capabilities for a wide range of operations throughout the Pacific, its virtually unlimited supply of fuel, and its shipyard construction capacity. The navy sought to increase substantially its number of capital ships in order to confront the American navy on an equal basis. It preferred to postpone any conflict with the United States until Japan was strong enough to meet the U.S. fleet on equal terms.

Admiral Isoroku Yamamoto (1884-1943), commander in chief of the Imperial Navy's combined fleet at the time of the attack on Pearl Harbor, was not carried away by the success of the raid. He believed that his country would have to force the United States to sue for peace within six months of the attack or the opportunity for a successful outcome of the conflict would be lost. Subsequent events proved him correct: After suffering initial reverses, the United States rebounded to seize control and, ultimately, to win the conflict.

NARA

On May 11, 1945, in the Pacific theater, two Japanese kamikaze pilots directed their aircraft into the USS Bunker Hill *off Kyushu.*

Both arms of the Japanese military maintained their own separate air forces, as did those of the United States. However, the U.S. Army and Navy generally cooperated, with joint strategies. The Japanese army and navy did not; the two arms operated individually, often without effective communication. For example, in December, 1941, during the first naval attack on Clark Field in the Philippines, Japanese army bombers flew into the path of the incoming naval aircraft conducting an assault of the field.

On occasion the two separate air arms deliberately withheld critical information from each other. At Nagoya's Mitsubishi factory, workers strung a curtain between projects separately assigned to the site by the army and navy, thus preventing an interchange of ideas between the two groups. Throughout the war the army and navy took turns condemning the other for operational failures.

U.S. Navy

The tail section of a Japanese Suisei aircraft on the deck of the USS Kitkun Bay *after exploding over the ship.*

DOCTRINE, STRATEGY, AND TACTICS

Both the Japanese army and navy adopted the warrior code of bushidō as a way of life. This philosophy came to be defined as one of absolute loyalty to the emperor and of bravery, frugality, simplicity, and unhesitating sacrifice. The military government sought to indoctrinate the people of Japan with the same spirit of self-sacrifice. The island nation's enemies came to realize that Japanese soldiers, sailors, and even civilians would fight to the death and would rather die than surrender. In battle after battle, despite overwhelming evidence that further conflict was useless, Japanese soldiers fought until killed by the enemy. Only at the very end of the war, on Okinawa, did numerous members of the Imperial Japanese Army surrender.

The officer caste demonstrated an even greater degree of commitment to bushidō. When faced with certain defeat, many officers chose to commit seppuku, or ritual suicide, by disemboweling themselves, a practice also known as hara-kiri. If time did not permit, they ordered their aides to dispatch them with a pistol shot to the head.

In late 1944 in the Philippines, and later during the Battle of Okinawa, the Japanese army and navy air forces began to organize a special attack corps called the Kamikaze, (*kamikaze* means "divine wind"). The name recalled a typhoon that struck the Japanese home islands in 1281, destroying a Mongol fleet invading from the Asian mainland and saving the island nation. The flyers of the Kamikaze Special Attack Corps deliberately rammed their aircraft into Allied naval vessels, at formidable cost to the ships and men serving aboard them.

Japanese officer candidates began at the age of fourteen as recruits in military prep schools. At seventeen, promising aspirants transferred to a more advanced preparatory school in Tokyo, where their real training began. Future officers completed their schooling at the military academy in Ichigaya. Subjected to constant heavy indoctrination, they adopted the concept of "a will which knows no defeat." Their mentors emphasized physical conditioning and discouraged independent thinking. Future officers were expected to subscribe fully to the bushidō code. They, in turn, demanded the same obedience to orders from the enlisted personnel under them.

Throughout the many battles for the islands of the Pacific, the sites were secured by invading U.S. soldiers only after every last Japanese fighter was killed. On Saipan and Okinawa, Japanese civilians, both men and women, joined the doomed soldiers in the final conflict. In the case of Okinawa, 150,000 civilians, one-third of the island's population, died following the U.S. invasion, often accompanying and aiding soldiers and sailors of the Imperial Army and Navy.

The bushidō code had its dark side. By Western standards Japanese army and navy units engaged in substantial violations of human rights in their contact with civilian populations in conquered lands and with captured military prisoners. After seizing the city of Nanjing from Chinese forces in 1937, the Imperial Japanese Army ran amok, slaughtering an estimated 250,000 of the city's civilian population. Tens of thousands of Chinese civilians were also massacred in Singapore soon after the Japanese capture of the city.

In another example of contempt for those who chose to surrender, during the so-called Bataan Death March (1942) Japanese soldiers killed thousands of captured American and Filipino troops suffering from illness and exhaustion. After their surrender some of the weakened and starving prisoners had failed to keep pace with the march to prison camps ordered by their conquerors. Those who fell behind were summarily shot or beaten to death. A similar series of atrocities took place on the Burma-Siam Railroad, and in the Sandakan Death March. In these cases and in many others, the Japanese failed to recognize the precepts of the Geneva Conventions as they applied to the humane treatment of prisoners of war.

The overall strategy of the Japanese military counted on the capture of critical Southeast Asian areas that were rich in resources. Once secured, the army was prepared to hold these bases tenaciously, while the navy protected the seas around them. The Japanese High Command expected the troops in the field to resist to the last man any forces seeking to dislodge them. Unfortunately for the Japanese strategists, Japan lost both air and sea supremacy as the war continued. The island bastions fell one by one. Finally, U.S. forces dropped atom bombs on cities in the home islands, which the Japanese could no longer successfully defend.

Tactically the Japanese military depended on the tenacity of its infantry, termed by the military propaganda as "men of spirit." Adopting this concept, the infantry followed a pattern of aggressive offensive tactics. Convinced of his superior physical conditioning, the Japanese soldier sought to close with the enemy and engage in hand-to-hand combat, often in nighttime sneak attacks. The military planners designed this approach to terrify their opponents.

With the use of Kamikaze air and sea formations, the Japanese High Command believed it could exact such fearful losses on U.S. naval and civilian shipping that the United States would refrain from trying to invade the Japanese home islands. Even after the Japanese armed forces lost their ability to stop the advancing Allied armies, they prepared to give up their lives rather than surrender. This Japanese commitment to self-destruction, as well as the potential loss of both American and Japanese civilian lives, motivated U.S. president Harry S. Truman (1884-1972) to use atomic bombs on Hiroshima and Nagasaki in order to convince Japanese emperor Hirohito to surrender his nation.

CONTEMPORARY SOURCES

English translations of Japanese texts actually written during World War II are rare. Some insight into the Japanese thinking at the time can be found in Paul S. Sakamaki's *I Attacked*

Pearl Harbor (1949) and in Nyozekan Hasegawa's *The Japanese Character* (1966), which contains a collection of essays written between 1935 and 1938. There were also a few other autobiographical works, such as Ashihei Hino's *War and Soldier* (1940) and R. Nagatsuka's *I Was a Kamikaze* (1973). Masanobu Tsuji's *Singapore: The Japanese Version* (1960) remains one of the few accounts in English by an officer involved in planning the Pacific war. During the 1930's, the Japanese published a large number of propaganda magazines, such as *Contemporary Japan*, that include details on the military but that tried to portray Japan as suffering from the depredations of other countries.

The best contemporary American source of information on Japanese thinking and action can be found in Ruth Benedict's *The Chrysanthemum and the Sword* (1946). A cultural anthropologist, Benedict presented a graphic analysis of Japanese thinking and customs at the time of World War II. One chapter of her book contains a specific analysis of the thinking of the Japanese military.

The writings of American military personnel found in government reports and military journals also furnish a Western analysis of Japanese military activity. Among these are *The Japanese Story of the Battle of Midway* (1947), compiled by the U.S. Office of Naval Intelligence and published by the U.S. Government Printing Office. There are also official histories by the British, such as S. Woodburn Kirby's *The War Against Japan* (5 volumes, from 1957), and by the Australians, starting with Lionel Wigmore's *The Japanese Thrust* (1957).

BOOKS AND ARTICLES

Agawa, Hiroyuki. *The Reluctant Admiral: Yamamoto and the Imperial Navy*. Tokyo: Kodansha International, 1979.

Allen, Thomas B., and Norman Polmar. *Code-Name Downfall: The Secret Plan to Invade Japan and Why Truman Dropped the Bomb*. New York: Simon and Schuster, 1995.

Astor, Gerald. *Operation Iceberg: The Invasion and Conquest of Okinawa in World War II*. New York: Dell, 1995.

Goldstein, David M., and Katherine V. Dillon, eds. *Fading Victory: The Diary of Admiral Matome Ugaki, 1941-1945*. Pittsburgh, Pa.: University of Pittsburgh Press, 1991.

Harries, Meirion, and Susie Harries. *Soldiers of the Sun: The Rise and Fall of the Imperial Japanese Army*. New York: Random House, 1991.

Jones, Don. *Oba, the Last Samurai: Saipan, 1944-1945*. Novato, Calif.: Presidio Press, 1986.

Jowett, Philip. *The Japanese Army, 1933-45: 1931-42*. New York: Osprey, 2002.

_____. *The Japanese Army, 1933-45: 1942-45*. New York: Osprey, 2002.

Rottman, Gordon L. *Japanese Army in World War II: Conquest of the Pacific, 1941-42*. New York: Osprey, 2005.

_____. *Japanese Army in World War II: The South Pacific and New Guinea, 1942-43*. New York: Osprey, 2005.

Sakai, Saburo. *Samurai!* New York: Pocket Books, 1996.

Sakaida, Henry. *Imperial Japanese Navy Aces, 1937-45*. New York: Osprey, 1998.

_____. *Japanese Army Air Force Aces, 1937-45*. New York: Osprey, 1997.

Taaffe, Stephen R. *MacArthur's Jungle War: The 1944 New Guinea Campaign*. Lawrence: University Press of Kansas, 1998.

Yahara, Hiromichi. *The Battle for Okinawa*. New York: John Wiley and Sons, 1995.

FILMS AND OTHER MEDIA

Enola Gay and the Bombing of Japan. Documentary. Brookside Media, 1995.
Kamikaze: Death from the Sky. Documentary. MPI Home Video, 1989.
Letters from Iwo Jima. Feature film. Malpaso/Amblin, 2006.
Okinawa: The Final Battle. Documentary. History Channel, 1996.
Pearl Harbor: Two Hours That Changed the World. Documentary. ABC, 1991.
Survivors. Documentary. Steven Okazaki, 1982.
The World at War. Documentary. Thames Television, 1973.

Carl Henry Marcoux

WARFARE IN THE POLITICAL AGE

CHINA
MODERN WARFARE
Dates: Since 1912

POLITICAL CONSIDERATIONS

Late nineteenth century China was ruled by the imperial government of the Qing (Ch'ing) Dynasty, which had its capital at Beijing (Peking). Although the royal family and most senior officials were Manchus, an ethnically and linguistically distinct Northeast Asian people who had overthrown the native Chinese Ming Dynasty in 1644, ethnic Chinese elites retained control over local affairs. China's military apparatus atrophied, and clashes with expanding European powers led to stunning military defeats. Meanwhile, China's economy failed to sustain industrial development, and widespread peasant rebellions compounded economic instability and further eroded the Manchus' political authority.

The imperial government authorized a military modernization program designed by scholar and military strategist Li Hongzhang (Li Hung-chang, 1823-1901). Li oversaw the construction of weapons factories and shipyards, but financial and political difficulties stunted his efforts. After Li's forces were defeated by Japan during the First Sino-Japanese War (1894-1895), Japan took control of the island of Taiwan, humiliating the Qing court and sparking an expansion of Li's military modernization program. Li's reforms elevated a new generation of Chinese military commanders, who soon threatened the weakened Manchus. The Boxer Rebellion (1900), an antiforeign uprising by secret societies, further demonstrated Qing vulnerability, with the court initially hoping that they could use the uprising to achieve their objectives without having to commit their army, although they eventually did so with disastrous results. The court's decision to form a national assembly in 1910 failed, and the imperial government collapsed in 1911.

Attempts to restore the Qing Dynasty continued until 1919. Meanwhile, competition had developed between isolationist military officers led by General Yuan Shikai (Yuan Shi-k'ai, 1859-1916), based in northeastern China, and the pro-Western Nationalist Party, or Guomindang (Kuomintang), led by Sun Yat-sen (Pinyin, Sun Yixian, 1866-1925), based in southern China. Sun's meager armed forces were crushed by Yuan's allies in 1913, and the introduction of democratic elections was cut short. Yuan's associates arranged for him to be named emperor, but his death in 1916 ended their cooperation. Instead, their armies clashed with each other during China's Warlord Period (1916-1928).

Sun Yat-sen sought democratic government in China, but he recognized that military unification must precede political modernization. Sun's small force was defeated in 1922 by the warlords of central China. Nonetheless, Sun's Nationalist Party opened the Huangpu (Whampoa) Academy to train officers loyal to Sun and the academy's president, General Chiang Kai-shek (Pinyin, Jiang Jieshi, 1887-1975). Before Sun's death in 1925, the Nationalist Party formed an alliance with the small Chinese Communist Party, which drew its support chiefly from China's tiny urban working class. Communist leader Zhou Enlai (Chou En-lai, 1898-1976) was the chief political instructor at Huangpu, and soon both Nationalists and Communists were recruiting officer trainees there.

This period of alliance, known as the First United Front, ended when Chiang's forces attacked Communist networks in August, 1927. The Communists fought back but were scattered. A splinter group, led by Mao Zedong (Mao Tse-tung, 1893-1976) retreated into a mountainous hinterland and began recruiting peasants to party membership. Meanwhile,

Chiang unified most warlord armies under his command. During the early 1930's, he attacked Mao's base areas, and the Communists' peasant army was forced to retreat to more remote rural areas in China's interior on a 6,000-mile trek known as the Long March.

Meanwhile, Japan's encroachment into China's northern provinces expanded in the mid-1930's to include central China. In 1936 a new alliance, known as the Second United Front, was forged between the Nationalists and Communists, who pledged to cooperate against Japan. Mao used the respite from Nationalist attacks to expand the Communist Party. As the 1940's began, Japan advanced into southern China and most of Southeast Asia, while the Nationalist armies quietly awaited Allied victories over Japan in the Pacific. The Communists, meanwhile, achieved wide popularity by harassing Japanese troops and installations and by implementing land reforms and building Party networks behind Japanese lines.

After Japan surrendered in 1945, units of the Communist-led People's Liberation Army (PLA) occupied the rural areas of most northeastern provinces, while Nationalist forces were airlifted to the major cities. Military clashes soon escalated into a full-scale civil war. With widespread popular support, Communist forces swept through northern and central China. Hundreds of thousands of Nationalist troops fled or defected. Finally, in late 1949, the remaining Nationalist troops gathered on the island of Taiwan, where Chiang established a government-in-exile. The Communist Party under Mao founded its national government in Beijing in October, 1949.

In 1950, acting as the Chinese People's Volunteers, PLA troops entered Korea in aid of the Korean communists' quest to unify the peninsula. Chinese Communist troops also reinforced the coast nearest Taiwan, pursued remnant Nationalist units along the border with Indochina and Burma, and moved to establish Communist Party authority in Tibet. In Korea, however, the PLA faced U.N. forces led by the United States until a ceasefire agreement was concluded in 1953. There was also a war with India from June until November 1962.

During the late 1950's political tensions between Beijing and Moscow caused cancellations of Soviet aid programs. Small clashes between Chinese and Soviet border guards began in 1962 and continued until 1969, when main force units fought at the Ussuri River. Meanwhile, China inaugurated a nuclear weapons program in the early 1960's. By 1967, after testing both fission and hydrogen weapons, China had become a full-fledged nuclear power. China also provided military aid to the Communist regime in northern Vietnam, then involved in a protracted war involving U.S. forces.

Despite upheavals during the Cultural Revolution (1966-1976), China's military was safeguarded. However, the troops' military effectiveness suffered when they were assigned to construction, agricultural, and other civilian tasks. In a short-lived operation against Vietnamese Communists in 1979, PLA units were defeated, but not before inflicting some damage on their opponents. Communist leader Deng Xiaoping (Teng Hsiao-p'ing, 1904-1997) introduced free enterprise and relaxed political controls, unleashing protests in 1986 and 1987. Responding to a student-led free speech movement, the PLA suppressed protests in Beijing's Tiananmen Square in 1989. The resulting deaths of students and civilians provoked international condemnation of the Communist government. During the 1990's propaganda reinforced the PLA's allegiance to the Communist Party, while its manufacturing and other economic enterprises were privatized.

Also during the 1990's there was an overhaul of Chinese military tactics and weaponry. Both were modernized with two major objectives. The first was the maintenance of Communist Party control within China itself. After the events in Tiananmen Square in 1989, there were few major protests in most of China, but there were many in Tibet and among the Uighurs of northwest China. The Chinese government undertook to allow freedom of speech in Hong Kong after 1997, and they have done so. When, in 1996, it looked as though Taiwan might declare independence rather than maintaining itself as the Republic of China, the political leadership and military of the People's Republic flexed their muscles by firing missiles over Taiwan. Later they changed their approach to be far more conciliatory.

However, the more important developments within the military were to face possible confrontations from outside. The controversy over the U.S. spy plane incident (the Hainan Island incident in April, 2001) demonstrated to the Chinese that there was still a worry about U.S. incursions. With the Chinese continuing to invest heavily in their air force, there was also uncertainty over events in North Korea and the possibility of the Chinese intervening to support the North Korean government should it face an external invasion.

MILITARY ACHIEVEMENT

China's defeat in 1895 bolstered the position of Manchu reformers who endorsed military modernization. Their great accomplishment was the creation of the "New Armies," in which Chinese soldiers were uniformly organized under professional officers and armed with modern weapons. These brigades were trained in European tactics, organized into specialist battalions that included artillery and engineers, and armed with imported European weaponry.

In the 1920's warlord armies undermined domestic order and caused economic havoc. The unification of most warlords under the Nationalist Party of Generalissimo Chiang Kai-shek reestablished Chinese political unity and laid the foundation for the reemergence of a united Chinese state.

From 1934 to 1935 the Communist Party leadership under Mao Zedong was able to preserve an experienced corps of military leaders by undertaking the "strategic retreat" known as the Long March. By withdrawing rather than confronting superior Nationalist troops, the Communists retained an autonomous and politically reliable military force. This

TURNING POINTS

1928	Chiang Kai-shek captures Beijing and, as leader of Nationalist Party, heads China's first modern government.
1934-1935	Mao Zedong leads his Communist forces on 6,000-mile strategic retreat known as the Long March.
1937	Japan invades China, initiating Second Sino-Japanese War (1937-1945).
1946-1949	Civil war rages between Nationalist and Communist Party forces, resulting in the triumph of Communism and in Chiang Kai-shek's flight to Taiwan.
Oct., 1950	Chinese troops intervene in the Korean War.
Nov. 10, 1950	China invades and conquers Tibet.
Jan.-Feb., 1955	People's Republic of China and the Republic of China (Taiwan) battle over islands in the Taiwan Straits.
Mar.-Apr., 1959	Tibetan insurrection is quashed.
Oct.-Nov., 1962	China fights a border war with India.
1964	The People's Republic of China conducts its first successful nuclear weapons test.
1966	Mao Zedong initiates a decade-long Cultural Revolution to purge his opponents from the Communist Party and renew the people's revolutionary spirit.
Feb.-Mar., 1979	Border war with Vietnam.
Apr.-June, 1989	Chinese government monitors and militarily disperses Tiananmen Square democracy protests.
1993	"Revolution in Military Affairs" leads to the reorganization of the army along modern lines.
July, 2009	Urumqi riots are quashed.

People's Liberation Army engaged both U.S. and U.N. forces during the Korean War (1950-1953). The PLA achieved virtually complete surprise in moving some 400,000 troops into North Korea to stop the Allied advance toward the China-Korea border in October, 1950. Chinese manpower, aided by Soviet air and technical support, scored major victories against Allied forces, eventually culminating in cease-fire negotiations and a stable division of the Korean peninsula.

Despite international isolation and domestic upheavals in the late 1950's and 1960's, Communist Party officials, military leaders, and engineers developed China's nuclear weapons program. After the

CHINESE CIVIL WAR, 1926-1949

first successful test shot in 1964, China's military establishment also undertook development of missile-based weapons delivery systems.

The PLA, which managed manufacturing, agricultural, and transportation systems during the 1970's and 1980's, shed its auxiliary enterprises during the 1990's. Free market companies assumed some functions; others were eliminated completely. At the same time, through joint ventures with foreign companies, the PLA acquired advanced military technologies, especially in the aerospace sector.

In 2003, China managed to launch its first man into space, an event that heralded a major space program with undoubted military objectives. The Chinese have also managed to keep up a modernization of their air force and missile technology.

WEAPONS, UNIFORMS, AND ARMOR

China's imperial army was equipped chiefly with simple metal weaponry, particularly swords, shields, and spear-tipped poles. The bow and arrow were standard equipment as late as 1910. "Bannermen," the Qing Dynasty's regular troops, included some units selected for "modernization." These troops were issued flintlock muskets, outdated by European standards. Each soldier carried his gunpowder ration in a vulnerable bamboo case.

In the early 1900's the "New Armies," composed of native Chinese, planned for artillery units to be attached to each division; in reality, however, the use of artillery pieces and ordnance was rare. Infantry firearms varied in design and caliber and included weapons of Japanese, German, and French manufacture, as well as locally produced copies. Ammunition was frequently unavailable. Both artillery and muskets were manufactured using British designs at the Jiangnan (Chiangnan) Arsenal near Shanghai. The modernized Beiyang (Peiyang) Fleet was commanded by military reformer Li Hongzhang and included China's earliest armored elements, metal-plated gunwales and armored steamships from the Fuzhou (Fuchou) Arsenal.

From 1911 China's armies adopted European-style uniforms of cotton tunic coats with standing collars, trousers, and peaked caps. Winter outfits included quilted jackets and leather boots. Rank insignia were adopted and affixed to cuffs and caps, with colored shoulder straps and cap bands indicating branch of service. Labor units assisting the Allies during World War I wore tunic and trouser outfits without insignia, and cloth shoes.

During the Warlord Period, the number of men under arms in China grew rapidly. Primarily landless laborers, warlord soldiers enlisted for three-year to five-year tours of duty. Weaponry symbolized status, and functioning weapons quickly passed on to new owners from dead or wounded soldiers. Machine guns and artillery were scarce, as were spare parts. In the northern provinces cavalry units were common, but southern unfamiliarity with horses stunted cavalry development there. Chiang Kai-shek contracted with U.S., Soviet, and British arms dealers to supply his Nationalist troops, who received huge quantities of weapons, ammunition, and supplies from the U.S. government during the Chinese Civil War (1926-1949).

After World War II (1939-1945), Communist forces seized Japanese weapons and supplies, including winter uniforms of leather boots, lined caps, and quilted jackets. During the Civil War, Nationalist troops also lost large stockpiles of U.S. military equipment, including heavy artillery, machine guns, and explosives, to the Communists, who later used it against U.S. troops in Korea. At the same time Chinese troops were sent to Korea with inadequate clothing, including lightweight summer uniforms, shoes made of rubber and canvas, and few hats or gloves.

The PLA in the early 1950's had few trucks, aircraft, or ships and lacked modern logistical systems. The Soviet Union provided some vehicles and ships and supervised development of specialized systems such as quartermaster, field communications, and antiaircraft batteries. Soviet advisers also oversaw the introduction of rank insignia on PLA uniforms, a step that Chinese leaders had opposed as elitist.

After Soviet aid was withdrawn in 1959 and 1960, Chinese research and development efforts accelerated. The PLA Navy produced antiship missiles, underwater ordnance, submarine weapons systems, and electronic countermeasures technology. A first generation of Chinese destroyers, submarines, deep-water survey vessels, and frigates was introduced during the 1960's. Antisubmarine destroyers became a production priority in the 1970's, as did mine sweepers and acoustic guidance systems for submarine missiles. During the 1980's development of nuclear-powered submarines became a premier national goal. In 1985 China's leaders endorsed a plan to prepare for "local war under high-tech conditions," and ordered the military integration of computer technology. In 1999 a ten-year plan was adopted for investments in highly advanced weaponry, including submarine-launched ballistic missiles and missile defense systems.

After China's nuclear weapons capability was demonstrated in 1964, the development of more advanced delivery systems became a priority. In 1965 research began on intercontinental ballistic missiles capable of delivering nuclear warheads to the continental United States, a goal achieved in the mid-1980's. In 1957 PLA soldiers began to be outfitted with increasingly sophisticated radiation protection equipment, including face masks, disposable clothing, and special rubber boots and gloves. This would increase in later decades, especially after the war with Vietnam in 1979. The lack of success in that conflict saw an overhaul of the supply systems for soldiers.

The launching, in 2003, of the first Chinese Taikonaut (astronaut) into space was greeted with great pride by the Chinese and represented a major move for the Chinese military into space technology on top of an extensive series of satellites.

MILITARY ORGANIZATION

During the late Qing period, the imperial Manchu and native Chinese bureaucracies each maintained distinct military organizations. Manchu forces known as "bannermen" were responsible for national defense, whereas Chinese armies and militia managed civil administration, revenue collection, and local security. Economic dislocations cut the number of bannermen supported by the imperial government from 250,000 in 1840 to about 170,000 in 1900. Bannermen were compulsorily enrolled from Manchu clans and organized into a series of "banners," sociomilitary groups based on kinship among the clans. Manchu soldiers were traditionally skilled horsemen, but cavalry units had disappeared by 1895, and in many imperial garrisons bannermen were primarily bureaucrats.

After China's defeat by Japan in 1895, officer training academies were opened with Japanese instructors, most of them influenced by the German principles of military conscription, centralized command, and standardized troop organization. In 1904 an imperial commission approved plans for a new national army of native Chinese, composed of thirty-six divisions manned at half strength during peacetime. European systems of officer ranks and reserves were introduced, with supplies and logistics managed at the divisional level. The divisions raised were poorly armed, and junior officers developed personal loyalties to their commanders rather than to the government. Yuan Shikai emerged as a leader from among these commanders, and between 1908 and 1911 con-

servative Manchu officials tried unsuccessfully to remove troops from his control. After the collapse of the Qing Dynasty, Yuan utilized his personal networks to consolidate his power.

During the Warlord Period following Yuan's death in 1916, his allies raised larger armies with less stringent organizational schedules. Personal loyalties meant that officers of like rank were not interchangeable, and the lack of weapons and training inhibited the development of specialized units such as artillery and engineers. In 1937 Nationalist general Chiang Kai-shek reorganized the Nationalist Army to promote his political allies. A system of regional war theaters was devised under which Chiang's trusted lieutenants were concentrated in northern and central China near Communist base areas. Less reliable warlord armies lately merged with Nationalist forces were deployed against the Japanese in the coastal provinces.

The internal characteristics of the Communist People's Liberation Army (PLA) reflected its rural origins. Many of its early officers had no formal command training and relied heavily upon personal connections to consolidate their authority. Regional field armies, each with a particular mix of peasants and professionals, emerged during the 1930's. The PLA also developed large labor corps recruited from the peasantry for transportation and construction projects. Their recruitment relied upon propaganda and coercion rather than forced conscription. Soldiers and laborers were induced to "volunteer" to help their villages meet manpower targets. Terms of service were unlimited, and no leave was permitted.

During the 1930's the communist military organization gained a commissariat, a system of Communist Party operatives whose structure paralleled that of the army. The commissars' function was to assure the allegiance of the military forces to the Party. Political surveillance was conducted from the squad level up using the "three by three" method, in which each soldier was observed by two others whose reports influenced both his and their advancement. The commissariat was governed by the General Political Department of the Communist Party, and the PLA was controlled by the Central Military Commission under the Party's Central Committee.

By 1944 Communist troops numbered 500,000 soldiers and 2.1 million militia, distributed among ten base areas in northern and central China. During the Civil War the PLA expanded both by recruiting peasants and by absorbing Nationalist defectors. In mid-1946 there were 1.3 million PLA regulars, in 1947 there were 2 million, in 1948 there were 2.8 million, and in early 1949 there were 4 million. Because PLA commanders anticipated huge losses during the Korean War, most of the main force units deployed were politically suspect former Nationalists. Ultimately fifty-five divisions, almost one-half the PLA's effective strength, were committed. Each division had three infantry regiments, an artillery battalion, and multiple auxiliary units. Transport, signal, and supply corps were attached to each regiment, and total division strength was around 10,000 men.

The Korean experience and Soviet advisers influenced the modernization of the PLA, equipping it for conventional rather than guerrilla conflict. In the mid-1950's the PLA's "field army" designation was abandoned, and troops were instead organized into thirteen military districts. In 1955 a massive demobilization discharged 4.5 million men, and conscription was instituted to maintain PLA strength at 3 million; demobilized veterans manned militia units. In 1948 PLA forces in coastal areas developed specialized marine units, and a separate naval command was created in 1950. By the mid-1960's the PLA Navy comprised three fleets with administrative and operational bases at Qingdao (Tsingtao), Shanghai, and Guangzhou (Canton). The PLA's air wing was organized in the early 1950's with Soviet aircraft and training. In the 1960's China began manufacturing military aircraft based on Eastern European and Soviet designs, and PLA air defense units assumed responsibility for radar, early warning, and antiaircraft

installations. By the mid-1980's the PLA Air Force was the third largest in the world, comprising sixty-one hundred total aircraft including fighters, bombers, helicopters, transports, and reconnaissance airplanes.

A special PLA unit, the Second Artillery, was created in 1959 to exercise control of nuclear weapons, but its structure remains secret. A special weapons production and testing force was also established. Selected air squadrons trained for airborne nuclear weapons deployment, and the military oversaw development of a ballistic missile-based warhead delivery system in the 1960's and 1970's. Specially trained units were made responsible for the security of fissionable materials and nuclear devices.

In the 1980's and 1990's these and other units trained in high-technology fields, including air de-

Hulton Archive/Getty Images

Mao Zedong in the 1930's, speaking before the Kangdah Cave University, calls for resistance against the Japanese.

fense, submarine warfare, and intelligence were en-larged. The proliferation of specialist arms of the PLA demonstrated the Chinese military's doctrinal shift from popular participation in a "people's war" to the articulation of main force operational plans appropriate to a technically advanced battlefield environment.

During the 1990's, the Chinese were involved in continuing to develop their missile program and their nuclear arsenal. In 1996 missiles were fired over Taiwan as a warning as the people there voted and it looked as though they might seek independence ending the Republic of China. The Chinese government has built up its navy, which was involved in disputes over the Spratly Islands and some other islands in the South China Sea. With the increasing wealth of China, many Chinese military officers began to travel overseas far more than ever before, and this led to far greater engagement between the Chinese military and other countries than ever before.

DOCTRINE, STRATEGY, AND TACTICS

In the late 1800's Qing military administrators relied upon long-standing convictions about China's invulnerability to attack, based on both its geography and traditional assumptions about the superiority of Chinese civilization. Deployment of the Manchu bannermen followed a garrison strategy in which permanent encampments were placed near key cities and transportation routes. This strategy left troops isolated from local economic and political activity. Stagnant social climates resulted, as the bannermen's family compounds rather than their military units became the focus of garrison activity.

Although Chinese troops had virtually no role in World War I (1914-1918), warlord officers were influenced by European battlefield experiences. With modern weapons in short supply, warlord armies regularly used close-order infantry tactics. The general scarcity of heavy weaponry benefited any force capable of fielding even a single piece of artillery. Fortresses and cities protected for generations by mud brick walls were suddenly vulnerable to damaging artillery attacks.

Communist theoretician Mao Zedong began developing his base area strategy in the late 1920's. He combined policies such as land reform, popular with China's huge population of poor peasants, with political propaganda and recruitment to military organizations. These forces, using primarily small-unit guerrilla tactics, could protect the economic and political activities inside the zone, while political operatives expanded the area under Communist control. According to Mao, eventually the politicized rural areas would engulf urban areas and the Communist Party would seize power on a national scale. Mao also proposed the general doctrine of "people's war," in which all classes and segments of Chinese society would unite to preserve China's national integrity in the face of external aggression. When Nationalist forces overwhelmed the Communists in the early 1930's, Mao espoused the tactic of "strategic retreat," surrendering territory and conserving his forces rather than defending specific territories. When Japanese expansion and Nationalist attacks imperiled the Communist organization, Mao endorsed the "united front" approach, cooperating with the Nationalists against Japan.

Meanwhile, Nationalist troops in the coastal provinces conducted "fighting withdrawal" operations in the face of Japanese offensives, denying the Japanese important assets by destroying rail lines, rolling stock, and telegraph lines. In 1938 Chiang Kai-shek's "scorched-earth" tactics extended to destruction of earthen retaining walls on the Huang, or Yellow, River, flooding huge tracts and causing millions of deaths. After 1945 Nationalist troops concentrated in cities and guarded rail lines. In 1947 the PLA adopted a battle-intensive strategy aimed at destroying Nationalist troops in Manchuria rather than capturing and holding territory. Using frontal assault tactics and attacking rail lines, the PLA under General Lin Biao (Lin Piao, 1907-1971) crushed Nationalist garrisons and captured weapons and supplies. Tens of thousands of demoralized Nationalist soldiers defected, while PLA encircling operations scored victories throughout northern and central China.

Mao's doctrine of warfare posited that China's huge population provided it with special military advantages, including a unique ability to sustain huge manpower losses. This doctrine informed the decisions of Chinese commanders in Korea, who compensated for inferior weapons with "human wave" tactics, committing large forces to successive assaults on a target despite high casualty rates. Mao's doctrine also applied to nuclear strategy. He scoffed at American nuclear superiority, declaring that only a "few million" Chinese could be eliminated in a nuclear attack, while hundreds of millions would remain capable of defending the country. Under Mao,

PLA commanders emphasized development of a "second strike" capability that would enable China to deliver warheads to targets even after being attacked with nuclear weapons.

After Mao's death these doctrines were replaced by a new emphasis on military modernization. In the event of external attack Chinese commanders would deploy professional troops with sophisticated equipment and use positional warfare tactics, rather than rely on guerrilla tactics and mass resistance by the Chinese people.

CONTEMPORARY SOURCES

Mao's development of a rural-based, politico-military strategy was the most significant and influential strategic doctrine originating in twentieth century China. Its first detailed explication appeared in 1927 in "Report on an Investigation of the Peasant Movement in Hunan," in which Mao defined a Communist-led revolution originating among rural agricultural peasants rather than urban industrial workers, as Soviet orthodoxy dictated. In "The Struggle in the Chinkiang Mountains" (1928) Mao described the breadth of the peasantry's support for the Communist military apparatus and emphasized the importance of concentrating forces on specific targets. In "Problems of Strategy in China's Revolutionary War" (1936) Mao argued that despite its shortcomings, the Communist-led military could prevail over larger and better-equipped forces by utilizing guerrilla and mobile main force operations. He accepted the need for a protracted struggle and for a "strategic defense" that would conserve military strength and exploit tactical opportunities. Mao's "Problems of Strategy in Guerrilla War Against Japan" (1938) outlined procedures for recruiting peasants and explained his famous revolutionary formula on rural areas engulfing the cities. Finally Mao explained the combination of main force military units with a mobilized peasantry to achieve a revolutionary victory in "The Present Situation and Our Tasks" (1947).

During the 1960's and 1970's, the Foreign Languages Press in Beijing published reminiscences of many generals, officers, and ordinary soldiers, but these rarely contained much more than anecdotes about famous incidents or battles. More detailed biographical and autobiographical works have been published in Chinese, although few have been translated into English, and of these generally only extracts have been published.

BOOKS AND ARTICLES

Beckett, Ian, ed. *Communist Military Machine*. London: Bison, 1985.

Benton, Gregor. *Mountain Fires: The Red Army's Three-Year War in South China, 1934-1938*. Berkeley: University of California Press, 1992.

Bodin, Lynn. *The Boxer Rebellion*. New York: Osprey, 1979.

Chen, Jian. *China's Road to the Korean War: The Making of Sino-American Confrontation*. New York: Columbia University Press, 1994.

Cheung, Tai Ming. *Fortifying China: The Struggle to Build a Modern Defense Economy*. Ithaca, N.Y.: Cornell University Press, 2009.

Corfield, Justin J. *The Australian Illustrated Encyclopedia of the Boxer Uprising, 1899-1901*. McCrae, Vic.: Slouch Hat Books, 2001.

Crossley, Pamela K. *Orphan Warriors: Three Manchu Generations and the End of the Qing World*. Princeton, N.J.: Princeton University Press, 1990.

Dorman, James E., Jr., and Nigel de Lee. *The Chinese War Machine*. London: Salamander, 1979.

Dreyer, Edward L. *China at War, 1901-1949*. London: Longman, 1995.

Fathers, Michael, and Andrew Higgins. *Tiananmen: The Rape of Peking*. London: Independent, 1989.

Harrington, Peter. *Peking, 1900: The Boxer Rebellion*. New York: Osprey, 2001.

Joffe, Ellis. *The Chinese Army After Mao*. London: Weidenfeld and Nicolson, 1987.

Jowett, Philip. *The Chinese Army, 1937-49: World War II and Civil War*. New York: Osprey, 2005.

————. *Chinese Civil War Armies, 1911-49*. New York: Osprey, 1997.

Kane, Thomas M. *Ancient China on Postmodern War: Enduring Ideas from the Chinese Strategic Tradition*. New York: Routledge, 2007.

Lampton, David M. *The Three Faces of Chinese Power: Might, Money, and Minds*. Berkeley: University of California Press, 2008.

Lewis, John Wilson, and Xue Litai. *China Builds the Bomb*. Stanford, Calif.: Stanford University Press, 1988.

Li Xiaobing. *A History of the Modern Chinese Army*. Lexington: University Press of Kentucky, 2007.

Lilley, James R., and David Shambaugh, eds. *China's Military Faces the Future*. Washington, D.C.: American Enterprise Institute/M. E. Sharpe, 1999.

Maxwell, Neville. *India China War*. New York: Pantheon Books, 1971.

Roe, Patrick C. *The Dragon Strikes: China and the Korean War, June-December, 1950*. Novato, Calif.: Presidio Press, 2000.

U.S. Department of Defense. Office of the Secretary. *The Military Power of the People's Republic of China: Annual Report to Congress, 2009*. Washington, D.C.: Author, 2009.

Wasserstein, Bernard. *Secret War in Shanghai*. Boston: Houghton Mifflin, 1998.

FILMS AND OTHER MEDIA

Assembly. Huayi Brothers, 2007.

China Rising: The Epic History of Twentieth Century China. Documentary. Granite Productions for Yorkshire Television, 1992.

The Sand Pebbles. Feature film. Argyle/Solar, 1966.

The World at War. Documentary. Thames Television, 1973.

Laura M. Calkins

THE COLD WAR
THE UNITED STATES, NATO, AND THE RIGHT
Dates: 1945-1991

POLITICAL CONSIDERATIONS

The World War II (1939-1945) alliance of the United States, Great Britain, France, China, and the Soviet Union against the Fascist regimes in Germany, Italy, and Japan masked fundamental ideological differences among the Allies, which became apparent as the victorious powers attempted to reorder international relationships. The United States, as leader of the democratic, capitalistic nations, promoted free elections, collective security through the United Nations, and freedom of trade. The Soviet Union, still stinging from the loss of twenty million dead during the war and fearful of American nuclear capability, was intent on securing its borders and surrounding itself with subservient, communist governments. As a result of these differing goals, the United States and the Soviet Union clashed over occupation of Japan, the Soviet withdrawal from Persia, the selection of postwar governments throughout Eastern Europe, the development of nuclear weapons, and the eventual fate of Germany and Berlin, which had been divided among the European victors at the end of the war. On February 9, 1946, Soviet leader Joseph Stalin (1879-1953) followed an ideological line in blaming capitalism for World War II, thus justifying an aggressive five-year plan of rearmament.

In reaction to Soviet exploitation of postwar economic instability in Europe, particularly in Greece and Turkey, American leaders implemented two programs designed to forestall Soviet influence. The Truman Doctrine (March, 1947) called for a policy of global containment of communism and offered American support for free peoples resisting foreign domination. Its economic counterpart was a European recovery program proposed by Secretary of State George C. Marshall (1880-1959) in June, 1947,

with the rebuilding of the German economy at its heart. The Marshall Plan and related programs had by 1954 funneled $41 billion worth of economic and military assistance to Germany, Japan, and the countries of Western Europe, helping centrist and conservative governments to consolidate their political positions.

The United States also restructured its foreign policy institutions. The National Security Act (1947) and subsequent reforms reorganized all the military service branches under the Department of Defense, established a National Security Council to advise the president, and created the Central Intelligence Agency (CIA) to gather intelligence and conduct covert operations. Fear of revived German aggression and continued Soviet expansion led to the development in April, 1949, of the North Atlantic Treaty Organization (NATO), which provided for a unified military command structure in common defense of Western Europe. Original members included the United States, Canada, Belgium, Denmark, Great Britain, Iceland, Italy, Luxembourg, the Netherlands, Norway, and Portugal. Greece and Turkey joined in 1952, Spain in 1982. France withdrew from the military command structure in 1966, though continued diplomatic support. When West Germany was brought into NATO as a full partner in 1955, the Soviet Union responded by drawing its East European satellites—East Germany, Poland, Czechoslovakia, Hungary, Romania, Albania, and Bulgaria—into the comparable Warsaw Pact.

Fearing that American influence would follow Marshall Plan aid, the Soviet Union prohibited the governments of East European countries—East Germany, Poland, Czechoslovakia, Hungary, Bulgaria—from participating. Creation of the Communist Information Bureau (Cominform) brought communist parties more tightly under Soviet control. Two events in 1949 raised the international diplomatic position of the Soviet Union to one of near equality with the United States, creating the superpower rivalry that lasted until 1991. After four years of civil war in China, the Russian-backed Communists under Mao Zedong (Mao Tse-tung; 1893-1976) defeated the pro-Western Nationalist Party of Chiang Kai-shek (Jiang Jieshi; 1887-1975), driving him to the island of Taiwan. In the same year, Russian scientists successfully exploded their first atomic bomb.

By 1950 the world had become clearly polarized in an ideological struggle known as the Cold War. For more than four decades, almost every facet of international relations was a battleground between the United States and its democratically oriented allies on one hand and the Soviet Union and other communist countries on the other. Both superpowers vied for supremacy in weapons, space, economics, security, and influence in the undeveloped ("Third World") nations. Ironically, with two superpowers possessing nuclear weapons by 1949, direct confrontation be-

came so dangerous that the United States and the Soviet Union never engaged in direct warfare, instead choosing to compete through surrogates and to protect themselves by developing increasingly sophisticated technologies that made traditional warfare untenable.

Cold War tensions peaked in times of crisis, such as the Korean War (1950-1953), the Cuban Missile Crisis (1962), the Vietnam War (1961-1975), and the Soviet-Afghan War (1979-1989), with intermittent periods of cautious negotiation. When ideological and territorial disputes between Russia and China became public in the late 1950's, the democratic world was cautiously optimistic, but authentic information was hard to obtain, and it would be many years before people appreciated the extent of the rift. The most promising period of détente came in the wake of President Richard Nixon's (1913-1994) 1969 Vietnamization policy in Southeast Asia, in which the basis of U.S. policy in Vietnam was shifted from international ideological struggle to local civil war. Strategic Arms Limitation Talks (SALT) began in

National Archives

President John F. Kennedy meets with U.S. Air Force staff to discuss surveillance flights over Cuba in October, 1962.

TURNING POINTS

July 16, 1945	First successful test of the atomic bomb is made at Alamogordo, New Mexico.
Feb. 22, 1946	George F. Kennan's "Long Telegram" articulates the rationale behind Soviet aggression and advocates a firm U.S. response, with force if necessary.
Mar. 12, 1947	President Harry S. Truman introduces the "Truman Doctrine," committing the United States to responsibility for defending global democracy, a clear signal of U.S. intention to check Soviet expansion and influence.
Oct. 4, 1957	The Soviet Union launches the world s first artificial earth satellite, inaugurating the space race, sparking a reassessment of U.S. military and technologic capabilities, and providing impetus for the development of both a space program and more sophisticated weapons-delivery systems.
Oct. 14, 1962	A U.S. pilot takes pictures indicating that Soviets are placing missiles on Cuba, and the ensuing crisis takes the world to the nuclear brink before ending on October 26.
1965	The United States pursues a policy of escalated military involvement in Vietnam.
1970-1979	The United States engages in a policy of détente, seeking to establish more stable relations between it and NATO and the Soviet Union, China, and their respective allies.
Jan. 23, 1980	After an Iranian mob takes over the U.S. embassy in November, 1979, and the Soviet Union invades Afghanistan in December, 1979, the United States vows that it will consider threats to the Persian Gulf region as threats to its vital interests.
Mar. 11, 1985	Mikhail Gorbachev is chosen as the new General Secretary of the Soviet Union, and his reforms initiate a thaw in relations between the United States and the Soviet Union.
Dec. 8, 1987	U.S. president Ronald Reagan and Soviet general secretary Gorbachev sign the INF Treaty governing intermediate nuclear forces (INF) and calling for the destruction of U.S. and Soviet missiles and nuclear weapons.
1989	The dismantling of Germany's Berlin Wall signifies the end of the Cold War, as U.S president George H. W. Bush promises economic aid to the Soviet Union.

November, 1969, concluding with the SALT I agreement (May 26, 1972), which prohibited nationwide deployment of antiballistic missile systems and declared a five-year moratorium on strategic rocket launch systems. In the same year, Nixon made a historic trip to Beijing, leading to marginally better relations with the Chinese.

After decades of massive military spending, the Soviet Union had achieved a rough technological parity with the United States by the 1980's. Beginning in 1985 Soviet president Mikhail Gorbachev (born 1931) attempted to modernize Soviet political and economic institutions by restructuring the government and allowing greater freedom of expression. In March, 1988, he declared a policy of nonintervention in Eastern Europe, which rapidly led to the ouster of communist officials (1989). In December, 1989, Lithuania became the first Soviet republic to abolish the communist monopoly of political power,

with other republics following suit. In 1990, the Soviet government cut back aid to communist regimes. After prolonged strikes, negotiations, and threats, the Warsaw Pact was disbanded in 1991, and the Soviet Union finally ceased to exist on December 25, 1991, leaving the United States as the only world superpower.

MILITARY ACHIEVEMENT

The principal goal of United States and NATO troops during the Cold War was to contain communism within borders established during and shortly after World War II. A major NATO action in Korea, dominated by American troops, successfully stopped North Korean communist expansion south of the thirty-eighth parallel. From the 1950's, Western ideological commitment to democratic governments was complicated by two important prewar rivalries. First, indigenous nationalistic movements in Africa and Asia, seeking to free themselves from American influence or European colonial domination, were attracted by the communist model of anticapitalist, state-controlled economies, and by the offer of economic and military assistance from the Soviet Union. Second, and closely related to emergent nationalism, was the conflict between Jews and Arabs, which had been simmering since the advent of the Zionist movement in the 1880's, and which broke out into open conflict with the creation in 1948 of the state of Israel. Although Germany and the United States played a major role in building up the Israeli military, and the Soviet Union contributed heavily to the modernization of armed forces in Egypt, Syria, and Iraq, both superpowers stood aside from combat during the Israeli Wars (1948-1949, 1956, 1967, 1973, 1982).

Important developing nations such as Egypt, India, and Indonesia declared themselves neutral in the Cold War in 1955, but many undeveloped countries found it difficult to resist superpower pressure and enticement. Fidel Castro (born 1926 or 1927) led Cuban rebels in overthrowing the pro-American Batista regime in 1959, then joined the communist bloc in 1960. The threat posed by a socialist government in the Western Hemisphere led the United States to support the disastrous Bay of Pigs invasion (April 17, 1961). Increasing Russian support of Cuba, including the installation of silos that could house missiles capable of supporting a nuclear attack on the United States, led to the Cuban Missile Crisis of 1962. An American blockade and intense negotiations forestalled direct conflict, as the Soviets agreed not to deploy offensive weapons, though limited numbers of Russian troops remained in Cuba until 1991. Fearing further communist expansion in the Caribbean, the United States sent troops to the Dominican Republic (1965-1966) and Grenada (1983) to support pro-Western regimes.

In the wake of the French defeat in Indochina (1954), the United States in 1961 pledged to support South Vietnam in combating communist guerrillas known as Viet Cong. Despite the commitment of more than 500,000 troops at the height of the war (1964-1973) in Vietnam, the United States was un-

successful in halting infiltration by the Viet Cong and North Vietnamese troops, supported independently by the Soviet Union and the People's Republic of China. In 1975 Communist governments were established in Vietnam, Laos, and Cambodia. Throughout Africa, the Middle East, Asia, and Latin America, the U.S. government secretly worked to undermine communist expansion. Communist or procommunist movements were successful in Ethiopia (1974), Guinea-Bissau (1974), Mozambique (1975), Angola (1976), and Nicaragua (1979) but were defeated in the Philippines (1945-1954), Burma (1948-1950), Malaya (1948-1960), Guatemala (1954), Indonesia (1965-1966), Chile (1973), Afghanistan (1978-1988), and El Salvador (1980-1992).

WEAPONS, UNIFORMS, AND ARMOR

Early Cold War battlefield weapons and uniforms were little changed from those of World War II. All NATO military organizations employed some form of khaki in varying shades of tan, green, or camouflage, depending on conditions of deployment, with other colors generally reserved for dress purposes. Battle uniforms were generally olive drab, with camouflaged U.S. M-1 helmets. The beret was the most common nonbattle headgear for NATO armies.

The M-1 .30-06 rifle remained standard issue for U.S. troops throughout the Korean War, though early prototypes of the M-14 rifle were being tested. Debates over standardization of ammunition among NATO countries led to adoption of the 7.62-millimeter round in 1953. The M-14 was finally adopted by the U.S. Army in 1957. It was replaced in 1966 as standard issue by the M-16 5.56-millimeter assault rifle, which was lighter, faster, and cheaper to manufacture. By 1969, almost all U.S. Army and Marine units were equipped with M-16's. At least a dozen countries used some version of the M-16 throughout the Cold War.

The M47 and M48 were the main battle tanks (MBTs) most commonly used by the United States and its allies during the 1950's. Though highly adaptable and still in service in the 1980's, they were increasingly replaced from 1966 by the M-551 Sheridan light tank, from 1979 by the M-60 MBT, and from 1985 by the German Leopard 2. The most effective versions were fitted with British-designed 105-millimeter L7A1 rifled guns. The most advanced MBT of the Cold War was the U.S.-designed M-1 Abrams, developed during the 1970's and increasingly deployed in the 1980's.

In the air, NATO forces were outnumbered, generally about three to two, by those of Warsaw Pact nations. With better pilot training and superior equipment, however, NATO was able to maintain tactical superiority. The B-52, in several versions, remained the primary strategic bomber from the time it was introduced in 1955 until the end of the Cold War. The F-86 Sabre was the backbone of the American fighter force in the 1950's. The F-111 was the principal attack aircraft from 1967 until the introduction of the F-14 Tomcat, which was put into service in 1972 and remained the principal interceptor. During the 1980's, the NATO aircraft inventory included large numbers of American F-111's, F-15's (the primary air-superiority fighter), F-16's, F-104's, British/German/Italian Tornados, Anglo-French Jaguars, and several versions of the French Mirage. The first B-1B Lancer, designed to replace the B-52, was put into service in 1986.

The proliferation of nuclear weapons was at the heart of the Cold War arms race. In 1949, the United States possessed between fifty and one hundred nuclear weapons. During the Korean War it added more than one hundred each year and in 1952 developed the hydrogen bomb. During the Eisenhower administration, the U.S. nuclear arsenal grew from 1,000 to 18,000 warheads. Just as important as the weapons

U.S. Department of Defense

The USS Vincennes, *a guided missile cruiser, firing an antisubmarine rocket during trials in 1985.*

themselves were the means of delivering them. In 1950 the United States possessed 38 B36's, which provided the first true intercontinental delivery capability. In 1957 the Soviet Union successfully launched the first satellite, Sputnik, and the first intercontinental ballistic missile (ICBM), leading to an intensification of American research and development of similar capabilities. In early 1962, the United States enjoyed a significant lead in both heavy bombers, with 639 B-52's alone to 100 Russian bombers, and ICBMs, with 280 U.S. to 35 Russian missiles. By the early 1970's, however, the Soviet Union had surpassed the United States in the production of both, though each country had many times the number of nuclear weapons necessary for annihilating both its adversary and the earth itself.

After the peak period in Vietnam, the U.S. military reached its low point in numbers (420,000) in 1972 and remained relatively weak in troop strength, quality, and morale throughout the 1970's. At the same time, the Soviet Union made massive strides in improving the quality of its air force, navy, and missile delivery systems, leading to much debate in NATO countries about basic defense doctrines. With the growing strength of the Soviet Union and increased U.S. responsibilities in the wake of the Iranian Revolution of 1979, President Jimmy Carter issued Presidential Directive 59 (July, 1980), which ordered significant development of new forces designed to win a limited nuclear war. This was followed by the aggressive administration of President Ronald Reagan (1981-1989), which spent more than $2 trillion in building up both conventional and nuclear weapons, including the controversial space-based Strategic Defense Initiative (SDI), commonly called Star Wars, in 1983. As the Cold War drew to a close, NATO forces included about 1.1 million troops; 20,000 main battle tanks; 3,250 combat aircraft; and 650 attack helicopters, all excluding potential French contributions.

MILITARY ORGANIZATION

Throughout the Cold War, mobile army infantry units were central to the projection of American power. The U.S. Army was organized into sixteen regular divisions for fighting. Ordinarily ten of these were divided among five continental U.S. armies, and one was assigned to Hawaii. The remaining five divisions comprised two field or tactical armies, four being part of the Seventh Army in Germany, and one, along with the entire army of the Republic of Korea, comprising the Eighth Army. Of these, four were Armored Divisions, five were Mechanized Infantry Divisions, five were Infantry Divisions, one was an Air Assault Division, and one was an Airborne Division. Each division had its own supporting artillery.

In the event of war in Eastern Europe, which was the most likely scenario early in the Cold War, the U.S. Army Europe (USAREUR) would have become part of NATO's Central Army Group, which would have been responsible for the ground war from the North Sea to the Bavarian Alps. Under ideal conditions, the U.S. Seventh Army would have been joined by two British divisions, eight to twelve German divisions, one Belgian division, and two Dutch divisions. The exact French contribution in the event of a Soviet attack was unknown, but it was estimated that it would be a force of sixteen divisions.

The governing body of NATO was the North Atlantic Council, comprising ambassadors of member states. Headquartered in Brussels, the Council was headed by a European secretary general. A multinational Defense Planning Committee developed strategic policy. NATO military commands were supervised by a Military Committee of permanent military representatives from each state, with the exception of Iceland. Territorial commands were divided into those of the Supreme Headquarters, Allied Powers in Europe (SHAPE), deployed on the continent and commanded by an American general; the Allied Command, Atlantic (ACLANT), responsible for the North Atlantic region and commanded by an American admiral; and the Allied Command, Channel (ACCHAN), responsible for the English Channel and North Sea regions and usually commanded by a British admiral. A Nuclear Defense Affairs Committee (NDAC) made up of defense ministers established general policy for use of nuclear weapons.

In non-European conflicts, the United States depended first upon the Rapid Deployment Joint Task

Force (RDJTF), which included Army airborne, air assault, infantry, and mechanized divisions; armored and air cavalry brigades; two Ranger battalions; a Marine Amphibious Force; twelve tactical fighter and two tactical reconnaissance squadrons; two tactical airlift wings; one surface action group; and three carrier battle groups; along with five aerial patrol squadrons. Once deployed in an ongoing conflict such as Vietnam, the military force was restructured to meet existing circumstances. With the breakup of the Soviet Union in 1991, France wished for the European Community (EC) to take over many of the responsibilities of NATO, though Great Britain and other countries opposed any actions that might undermine defense ties with North America. The major questions facing NATO as the Cold War drew to an end involved relationships with nations of the old Warsaw Pact, which had been disbanded in 1991, and the fate of some 27,000 nuclear weapons scattered in the former Soviet republics of Russia, Ukraine, Belarus, and Kazakhstan.

DOCTRINE, STRATEGY, AND TACTICS

Fearing an increasing and overwhelming Soviet influence in world affairs, the United States based its military doctrine upon the belief that the Soviet Union was ideologically committed to relentless expansion, which in turn required a "rapid buildup of the political, economic, and military strength" of countries committed to political freedom. The countries of NATO, however, were never willing to maintain an army large enough to counter a conventional invasion by the Soviet Union. NATO therefore embraced a policy of massive retaliation, including U.S. use of strategic nuclear weapons, to fend off Russian invasion. Almost from the beginning of the Cold War, the nuclear strategy of both nations was one of deterrence, based upon the perception by both sides

of the suicidal nature of any nuclear attack. In order for deterrence to work, however, it was necessary to convince the Soviet Union that nuclear weapons might be used if necessary and that any initial Soviet attack would be unsuccessful in removing the U.S. threat. In 1967, after the Soviets acquired intercontinental nuclear capability, NATO shifted to a doctrine of flexible response, suggesting that lower levels of force might be used. In terms of conventional warfare, U.S.-NATO doctrine stressed defense and technological superiority, with an emphasis on the importance of winning the first battle of a future war. The threat of tactical nuclear attack remained integral to the defense of Europe, as Warsaw Pact countries could within weeks have mobilized vastly superior conventional forces. In the early 1980's, for instance, NATO forces were outnumbered five to one in men, seven to one in armored vehicles, five to one in artillery, and between two and three to one in aircraft.

Outside Europe, the United States lacked a clear doctrine of intervention. Trained through World War II to fight total wars of annihilation, they responded uneasily to the limited objectives of warfare enjoined by potential nuclear destruction. This led to a confusion of U.S. purpose in Korea, Vietnam, Lebanon, and Nicaragua, and highly publicized conflicts, which saw General Douglas MacArthur (1880-1964) relieved of command in Korea in 1951, massive antiwar demonstrations from 1966 to 1973, and the public conviction of Colonel Oliver North (born 1943) in 1989. After the Soviet invasion of Afghanistan (1979) ended the last remnants of détente, the election of Ronald Reagan (born 1911) as president in 1981 led to a simplistic but clear doctrine that appealed to Americans after the malaise and military decline of the 1970's. The Reagan Doctrine (1985) was designed "to nourish and defend freedom and democracy" from "Soviet-supported aggression," and led to active involvement in affairs in Grenada, Nicaragua, and Afghanistan.

CONTEMPORARY SOURCES

In an age of easy access to both battlefields and print, the number of contemporary sources is immense. The amount of documentation is further augmented by memoirs of government officials, which in an age of limited political warfare become as important as those of field commanders. Important accounts by general officers include those by Matthew B. Ridgway, *Soldier: The Memoirs of Matthew B. Ridgway, as Told to Harold H. Martin* (1956); Douglas MacArthur, *Reminiscences* (1964); Paul Ely, *L'Indochine dans la tourmente* (1964; *Indochina in Turmoil*, 1964); Henri Navarre, *Agonie de l'Indochine, 1953-1954* (1956; *Agony of Indochina*, 1956); William Westmoreland, *Report on the War in Vietnam, as of 30 June, 1968* (1969) and *A Soldier Reports* (1976); and Alexander Haig, *Caveat: Realism, Reagan, and Foreign Policy* (1984). Among hundreds of personal accounts by soldiers are those of Martin Russ, *The Last Parallel: A Marine's War Journal* (1957); Frederick Downs, *The Killing Zone: My Life in the Vietnam War* (1978); Francis J. West, *Small Unit Action in Vietnam: Summer, 1966* (1967); Philip Caputo, *A Rumor of War* (1977); Al Santoli, *Everything We Had: An Oral History of the Vietnam War* (1981); Wallace Terry, *Bloods: An Oral History of the War by Black Veterans* (1984).

Presidential positions can be followed in the ongoing publication *Public Papers of the Presidents*. The early years of the Cold War are described in the works of Harry S. Truman, *Memoirs* (1955, 1956); Dean Acheson, *The Pattern of Responsibility* (1952); Henry Stimson and McGeorge Bundy, *On Active Service in Peace and War* (1948); James Forrestal, *The Forrestal Diaries* (1951); Dean Acheson, *Present at the Creation: My Years in the State Department* (1969); George F. Kennan, *Memoirs, 1925-1950* (1967);

The Eisenhower years can be followed in Dwight D. Eisenhower's *Mandate for Change, 1953-1956: The White House Years* (1963); Anthony Eden's *Full Circle: The Memoirs of Anthony Eden* (1960); Adlai Stevenson's *The New America* (1957); Peter G. Boyle (editor), *The Churchill-Eisenhower Correspondence, 1953-1955* (1990); and Charles Bohlen's *Witness to History, 1929-1969* (1973). The Kennedy and Johnson years are covered in John Kenneth Galbraith's *Ambassador's Journal: A Personal Account of the Kennedy Years* (1969); Henry Cabot Lodge's *The Storm Has Many Eyes: A Personal Narrative* (1973); Arthur M. Schlesinger, Jr.'s *A Thousand Days: John F. Kennedy in the White House* (1965); Lyndon Johnson's *The Vantage Point: Perspectives of the Presidency, 1963-1969* (1971); Dean Rusk's *As I Saw It* (1990); George Ball's *The Past Has Another Pattern* (1982); and Clark Clifford's *Counsel to the President: A Memoir* (1991).

The latter stages of Vietnam and the 1970's are covered in *RN: The Memoirs of Richard Nixon* (1978); Henry Kissinger's *White House Years* (1979); *The Pentagon Papers, as Published by the New York Times* (1971); Jimmy Carter's *Keeping Faith* (1982); and Zbigniew Brzezinski's *Power and Principle* (1982) and *The Grand Failure* (1989). The final years of the Cold War are dealt with in Ronald Reagan's *An American Life* (1990); Caspar Weinberger's *Fighting for Peace* (1990); Margaret Thatcher's *The Downing Street Years* (1993); and Oliver North's *Under Fire* (1991).

BOOKS AND ARTICLES

Black, Jeremy. *War Since 1945*. London: Reaktion, 2004.

Collins, John M. *U.S.-Soviet Military Balance: Concepts and Capabilities, 1960-1980*. New York: McGraw-Hill, 1980.

Cowley, Robert, ed. *The Cold War: A Military History*. New York: Random House, 2005.

Freedman, Lawrence. *The Cold War: A Military History*. London: Cassell, 2001.

Gabriel, Richard A. *Fighting Armies: NATO and the Warsaw Pact—A Combat Assessment*. Westport, Conn.: Greenwood Press, 1983.

Glynn, Patrick. *Closing Pandora's Box: Arms Races, Arms Control, and the History of the Cold War*. New York: Basic, 1992.

Graebner, Norman A., Richard Dean Burns, and Joseph M. Siracusa. *Reagan, Bush, Gorbachev: Revisiting the End of the Cold War*. Westport, Conn.: Praeger Security International, 2008.

Jordan, Robert S. *Norstad: Cold War NATO Supreme Commander*. New York: Palgrave, 2000.

LaFeber, Walter. *America, Russia, and the Cold War, 1945-2006*. 10th ed. Boston: McGraw-Hill, 2008.

Mayers, David. *The Ambassadors and America's Soviet Policy*. New York: Oxford University Press, 1995.

Miller, D. M. O., et al. *The Balance of Military Power*. New York: St. Martin's Press, 1981.

Oberdorfer, Don. *The Turn: From the Cold War to a New Era*. New York: Poseidon Press, 1991.

Schmidt, Gustav, ed. *A History of NATO: The First Fifty Years*. 3 vols. New York: Palgrave, 2001.

Stone, David. *Wars of the Cold War: Campaigns and Conflicts, 1945-1990*. London: Brassey's, 2004.

Thomas, Nigel. *NATO Armies, 1949-87*. Botley, Oxford, England: Osprey, 1987.

Tsouras, Peter G., ed. *Cold War Hot: Alternate Decisions of the Cold War*. Mechanicsburg, Pa.: Stackpole Books, 2003.

Von Mellenthin, F. W., and R. H. S. Stolfi. *NATO Under Attack: Why the Western Alliance Can Fight Outnumbered and Win in Central Europe Without Nuclear Weapons*. Durham, N.C.: Duke University Press, 1984.

Wenger, Andreas, Christian Nuenlist, and Anna Locher, eds. *Transforming NATO in the Cold War: Challenges Beyond Deterrence in the 1960's*. New York: Routledge, 2007.

FILMS AND OTHER MEDIA

The Cold War. Documentary. Cable News Network, 1999.

Dr. Strangelove: Or, How I Learned to Stop Worrying and Love the Bomb. Feature film. Columbia Pictures, 1964.

Fail-Safe. Feature film. Columbia Pictures, 1964.

The Falcon and the Snowman. Feature film. Metro-Goldwyn Mayer, 1985.

Spy in the Sky. Documentary. Public Broadcasting Service, 1996.

The Spy Who Came in from the Cold. Feature film. Salem, 1965.

John Powell

THE COLD WAR
THE SOVIET UNION, THE WARSAW PACT, AND THE LEFT
Dates: 1945-1991

POLITICAL CONSIDERATIONS

In the initial years after World War II (1939-1945), there remained hope for a continuation of the Soviet-American wartime alliance, but suspicions on both sides opened a rift between the two superpowers. The new phenomenon of nuclear and thermonuclear weapons, combined with the introduction of intercontinental missiles in the late 1950's, had made a third world war "unthinkable," giving the "war" its name. Still, over the four decades of the Cold War confrontation, a number of crises defined the U.S.-Soviet relationship and affected the nations' military preparation.

In 1948 the Soviet Union cut off access to the western sectors of Berlin, located in Soviet-controlled East Germany. The United States and its allies defeated this strategy without resorting to war by using massive airlifts to support civilians. In 1949 the Soviet Union detonated its first atomic device, and in 1954, a year after the United States had done so, it developed a hydrogen bomb. After the West formed a military alliance, the North Atlantic Treaty Organization (NATO) in 1949, the Soviet bloc countered with the Warsaw Pact in 1955. The original countries of the pact were Albania, Bulgaria, Czechoslovakia, East Germany, Hungary, Poland, Romania, and the Soviet Union. Albania withdrew in 1968, seven years after it had severed relations with the Soviet Union. Romania refused to join the other pact members in the 1968 invasion of Czechoslovakia. In 1956 the Hungarian Uprising and subsequent Soviet invasion did not bring a Western military response, leading Moscow to understand that the United States would tacitly recognize Soviet mastery over their satellites.

After the death of Soviet dictator Joseph Stalin in 1953, the new Soviet leader, Nikita Khrushchev (1894-1971), followed a policy of "peaceful coexistence" with the West. He made several trips to the United States both to participate in the United Nations proceedings and as a guest of President Dwight D. Eisenhower (1890-1969). The Soviets made new strides toward international prestige in 1957 when they launched the first human-made Earth-orbiting satellite, Sputnik, and in 1961 when they were the first to put a man in space.

In 1960 the improving relations between the superpowers suffered a setback—the U-2 incident following the shooting down of a U.S. spy plane while on a reconnaissance mission over the Soviet Union. This incident brought to public attention the reality of intercontinental missiles, rockets that could be launched from the territory of one adversary to that of the other.

In the early 1960's a number of Cold War crises further disturbed the efforts at political relaxation. In 1961 East Germany erected the Berlin Wall to stop "illegal" emigration to West Berlin. However, undoubtedly the greatest danger of the whole Cold War was the Cuban Missile Crisis of 1962, during which the United States demanded that the Soviets remove weapons from Cuba. There was during this crisis a greater possibility of escalation to nuclear warfare than at any other time during the entire Cold War period. However, the issue was resolved without war breaking out. The missiles were removed and the U.S. government agreed not to try to overthrow the pro-Soviet regime of Fidel Castro (born 1926 or 1927).

After the Cuban Missile Crisis, the Soviet Union

and the United States began measures to ease military tensions in an era of détente. The two nations installed a hotline connection between Moscow and Washington, D.C., to prevent accidental disasters. The powers engaged in the Strategic Arms Limitation Talks (SALT) in 1972 and 1974 and the Strategic Arms Reduction Talks (START) in 1986 and also agreed to nuclear test ban treaties and conventional arms reduction talks. Nevertheless the arms race between the two superpowers continued, especially in the increase of nuclear arms and missiles of various types. Both sides developed the capacity to destroy the world many times over. Although both nations also developed sophisticated chemical and biological weapons, talks limiting these were more successful than those concerning nuclear bombs.

After a period of economic setbacks and political difficulties, Khrushchev was dramatically and suddenly replaced by Leonid Brezhnev (1906-1982) in October, 1964. Although Moscow continued to seek détente with the United States, Cold War crises continued. The rift between the Soviet Union and China that had begun under Khrushchev widened, at times breaking out in actual armed conflict on the borders. The Soviet Union also became involved in a long war in Afghanistan (1979-1989).

During the 1980's the Soviet Union softened its confrontational stance, especially after Mikhail Gorbachev (born 1931) became the country's leader in 1985 and a nuclear disaster occurred at Chernobyl in 1986. Although both the Soviet Union and the United States signed new agreements, both nations also considered employing satellite-based Strategic Defense Initiative (SDI) programs, known as Star Wars. In

National Archives

Soviet Cold War leader Nikita Khrushchev speaks at the Fourth Convocation of the Fourth Session of the Supreme Soviet in January, 1956.

1991, after a failed attempt by hardliners to overthrow Gorbachev, the Soviet Union dissolved, the Communist Party lost power in Russia, and the Cold War ended.

MILITARY ACHIEVEMENT

The Soviet Union prepared for any eventual confrontation while hoping to deter the United States. Moscow continued to develop offensive and defensive weapons systems and strategies, despite mutual attempts at limitation. Like the United States, the Soviet Union came to depend on military complexes that greatly affected the economy, politics, and social structures. The military's prestige, which had fallen substantially during the Stalinist purges of the 1930's, increased in great measure. After World War II the Soviet Union established its dominance over Eastern Europe. In one sense Moscow saw this dominance as its "right," a part of the spoils of war. However, much of the territory was land that Russian imperialists had coveted since the time of the czars; some of it had actually been part of the old empire. However, Moscow did not incorporate these countries of Eastern Europe into the Soviet Union, as it had done with the Baltic states and parts of Finland and Romania that it had taken over in 1940 and 1941. Instead, the Kremlin established these Communist-led states as "people's republics." Over the course of the Cold War the Eastern European governments declared that they had evolved into the Marxist stage of socialism and changed to "socialist republics."

A major factor in the Soviet control of Eastern Europe was fear of another massive land attack and invasion of its territory across the northern tier of states, as France had done in 1812 and Germany had done in 1941. Thus tighter military control was maintained over Poland, Hungary, Czechoslovakia, and East Germany than over Romania, Bulgaria, Yugoslavia, and Albania, the southern states, which had more leeway for independent action. Stalin expelled Yugoslavia from the Communist Information Bureau (Cominform), Moscow's association of Communist states, in 1948. Albania severed relations with Moscow in 1961. Romania often opposed the

TURNING POINTS

1949	The Soviet Union tests its first atomic bomb.
1953	The Soviet Union tests a hydrogen bomb.
1957	The Soviet Union successfully tests an intercontinental ballistic missile.
May 1, 1960	U.S. U-2 spy plane is shot down over the Soviet Union.
1962	The Cuban Missile Crisis brings the United States and the Soviet Union closer than ever before to the brink of nuclear war.
1968	The Soviet Union invades Czechoslovakia, establishing the Brezhnev Doctrine of Soviet military domination over Warsaw Pact states.
1970-1979	During an era of détente, more stable relations prevail between the Soviet Union and the United States and their respective allies.
1985	Mikhail Gorbachev is chosen as the new general secretary of the Soveit Communist Party, and his reforms initiate a thaw in relations between the Soviet Union and the United States.
1987	U.S. president Ronald Reagan and Soviet general secretary Gorbachev sign the INF Treaty governing intermediate nuclear forces (INF) and calling for the destruction of U.S. and Soviet missiles and nuclear weapons.
1989	Gorbachev is elected state president in the first pluralist elections since 1917, and by the end of the year all Warsaw Pact nations had overthrown their communist leadership.
1991	After the Baltic States of Estonia, Latvia, and Lithuania are granted independence and other former soviets join the Commonwealth of Independent States, Gorbachev resigns as president and the Soviet Union is officially dissolved.

A U.S. Air Force C-54 landing at Berlin's Templehoff Air Base during the Berlin Airlift in 1948.

Soviet Union and sometimes sided with the West. Only Bulgaria remained steadfastly loyal to the Soviet bloc.

Soviet armed forces were stationed in force in the northern tier. During the mid-1980's there were 194 active divisions including tank, motorized rifleman, and airborne. Sixty-five of these were stationed in the western Soviet Union, and thirty in Eastern Europe.

The six Warsaw Pact allies had an additional fifty-five divisions. After Hungary attempted to break away from the Soviet orbit in 1956, Khrushchev sent in the army and restored the Kremlin's military control over the state. Brezhnev repeated this action in Czechoslovakia in 1968, after the liberalizing Prague Spring reforms of Alexander Dubček (1921-1992). The Brezhnev Doctrine confirmed Soviet domination of Warsaw Pact states, and, with the exception of Romania, the remaining Warsaw Pact states joined the Soviet forces in the invasion.

Outside the territory of the Soviet Union and East-ern Europe, during the Cold War, Soviet military advisers were active in a number of countries, and Soviet soldiers were occasionally employed in an advisory capacity. Certainly the Soviet Union was keen to test its weaponry, and Soviet planes were used in the Korean War, albeit disguised. The Soviet Union tested its air defense systems in Hanoi during the U.S. bombing of the city during the Vietnam War.

Apart from Afghanistan, where the Soviet Union deployed large numbers of soldiers from 1979, the Soviet Army advisers were active in many other countries. In Latin America, there were Soviet advisers in Cuba after the rise to power of Fidel Castro, and later in Grenada, sparking the U.S. invasion in 1983. In Africa, Soviet advisers were present in Egypt, and in the wars in Angola and Mozambique, as well as in Libya and Ethiopia. All six countries made heavy use of Soviet weaponry.

Actively engaged in the Middle East, the Soviet

Union had close military ties with Syria, and with Iraq. Its advisers were in Baghdad during the Iran-Iraq War, and when Iraq invaded Kuwait in 1990. Indeed, a large part of Saddam Hussein's army was equipped with Soviet weaponry. India also was a Soviet ally and purchaser of Soviet weaponry, as has been North Korea and Vietnam. The Soviet Union was also in contact with many of the communist parties in Asia and elsewhere in the world.

WEAPONS, UNIFORMS, AND ARMOR

The Soviet weapons of the Cold War were planes, missiles, nuclear weapons, submarines, and tanks. The country also kept and employed conventional armies and weapons. Moscow carried out military invasions against Warsaw Pact allies Hungary and Czechoslovakia, engaged in a border skirmish with China (1969), and waged war in Afghanistan. Like the United States, the Soviet Union maintained large stockpiles of thermonuclear weapons.

The Soviets had surface-to-surface, surface-to-air, and air-to-air missiles. The latter two were used against aircraft by heat- and electronics-seeking guidance systems. Intercontinental ballistic missiles (ICBMs) and intermediate-range ballistic missiles (IRBMs) were usually armed with nuclear warheads, whereas short-range missiles employed high explosives. Surface-to-surface missiles also could be launched from ships. Cruise missiles, placed in use in the 1970's, are continuously powered and more able to evade defenses. They fly at low altitudes and are accurate and inexpensive weapons.

By 1989 the Soviets had upgraded their ICBMs to the SS18-MOD5, SS-25 for road-mobile units, and SS-24 for rail-mobile and silo-launched missiles, replacing earlier missiles that had included the SS11, SS17, SS18-Satan, and SS19-Stiletto.

Soviet submarines of the Typhoon class were armed with SS-N-20 missiles, and Delta IV-class submarines were armed with SS-N-23 missiles. Yankee-class submarines had intermediate cruise missiles. Soviet Black Jack and Bear-H strategic aircraft also were armed with cruise missiles. The Soviets also employed AS-15 long-range cruise missiles.

The older Midas and Bison planes were used for in-flight refueling of the Bear-H. The SS-N-21 was a land-based cruise missile.

Intermediate-range missiles included the mobile SS-4 Sandal MRBM and SS-20 IRBM. SS-12's, SS-23's, and SS1-Scuds were short-range missiles. Soviet strategic surface-to-air missiles (SAMs) included the SA-2, SA-3, SA-5, SA-10, SA-12A/Gladiator, and the SA-X-12B/Giant. Other Soviet aircraft were the Fulcrums, MiG-31 Foxhounds, and SU-27 Flankers. The long-range Gazelle and Galosh antiballistic missiles were designed for antimissile defense. The Soviets had a space-based defense system, the Global Navigation Satellite System (GLONASS), and antisatellite missiles such as the SL-11. During the 1980's the Soviet Union introduced missiles with multiple nuclear warheads, multiple independently targetable reentry vehicles (MIRVs), on intercontinental missiles.

Tanks had always been a major part of the Soviet Red Army. In the 1960's the Soviets began use of the T-64, the first real improvement since World War II. The improved T-64A and T-72 followed. In the 1980's the standard was the T-80 model with nuclear, biological, and chemical protection and enhanced firepower. More than 1,400 T-80's were stationed in Eastern Europe, in addition to a greater number of the older models. During this period the Soviets also replaced their old artillery with mobile and self-propelled 152-millimeter guns with nuclear capability, 240-millimeter mortars, 203-millimeter self-propelled guns, and a 220-millimeter multiple rocket launcher capable of firing chemical and high-explosive munitions.

In Afghanistan the Soviet forces relied on search-and-destroy tactics, especially in aerial attacks. MI-6 Hip, MI-8 Hook, and the most modern MI-24 Hind helicopters sought out guerrilla strongholds while fixed-wing aircraft carried out carpet bombing attacks. However, the Afghan guerrillas' heavy machine guns forced the helicopters to fly higher and lessened their effectiveness. In the first years of the war in Afghanistan, the Soviets used tank columns supported by helicopters to attack villages suspected of hiding insurgents. Although many villages were destroyed, this tactic was ineffective against the guerrillas. In order to keep their casualties low, Soviet infantry rarely engaged in open battle.

Soviet airborne brigades were sent into Afghanistan by helicopter. The Soviets would also encircle Afghan villages and then move in from different directions. After 1982 they began to use smaller, more flexible units, but their reliance on helicopters led to the United States arming the Afghan resistance with surface-to-air missiles, which changed the nature of the war considerably.

By 1984 Soviet equipment losses included 546 aircraft, 304 tanks, 436 armored personnel carriers, and more than 2,700 other vehicles. Soviet forces in Afghanistan were attached to the Fortieth Army in Soviet Central Asia. Initially they sent five airborne and four motorized rifleman divisions. Elements of six other rifleman divisions and smaller units were added. Weapons included T-72 tanks and 152 self-propelled howitzers. The Soviets also employed MI-24 gunships and Sukhoi Su-25 frogfoot fighter-bombers and MiG fighters. New weapons included the AGS-17 automatic grenade launcher and the Kalashnikov AK-47 rifle. Although Western sources accused the Soviets of using chemical warfare and antipersonnel butterfly mines in the war, Moscow denied such claims. In 1988 the Soviets introduced Scud missiles and continued to launch them into Afghanistan until 1991, even after the war was officially over.

National Archives

Shortly after Germany's partition, signs appeared in West Berlin warning residents about the new international boundaries; this one says, "Pay attention—only ten meters [away]."

MILITARY ORGANIZATION

The highest Soviet command structure consisted of three parts: the Council of Defense, led by the General Secretary of the Communist Party and including the highest political and military leaders; the Chief Military Council, the chief officials of the ministry of defense; and the General Staff, known as the Stavka. Although the first two units were political bodies, the Stavka was the actual military command. It included the Assistant for Naval Affairs, the Political Section, the Scientific Technological Committee, and ten directorates: Operations, Intelligence, Organization-Mobilization, Military Science, Communications, Topography, Arrangements, Cryptography, Military Assistance, and Warsaw Pact.

The Stavka also stood in command above the various armed services: Army, Navy, Air Force, Strategic Rocket Forces, and the National Air Defense. Special troops such as the chemical, engineering, signal, and civil defense corps were directly under the ministry of defense.

Each of the five services had a commander in

chief, one or more first deputy commanders in chief, and a chief of political administration equal in level to the first deputies. There were in addition several deputy commanders. The army and air force were deployed in sixteen military districts within the Soviet Union. The navy was deployed in four fleets. The countries of the Soviet allies were integrated into Moscow's command structure through the Warsaw Pact.

Within the Warsaw Pact, there was a Combined Supreme Command, established in 1956 with its headquarters in Moscow. This controlled all the armed forces of the members of the Warsaw Pact, the Soviet army being divided into those based in Germany and those under the three commands: the Baltic, Belorussian, and Carpathian military districts.

Within the Red Army itself, apart from the regional divisions, the army, at its height in the 1980's, included some 210 divisions within the ground forces. These all included soldiers who were ready for immediate action as well as those required to be called up, including reservists. National service existed throughout the Soviet Union, and this ensured that all adult males within the country had some degree of military training and were able to be called up to serve alongside regular soldiers. However NATO

analysts believed relatively few were able to be called up straightway, considerably reducing the actual fighting strength for a sudden conflict.

DOCTRINE, STRATEGY, AND TACTICS

Soviet military doctrine had two aspects: political and technological. The political aspect was linked to the principles of Marxism-Leninism and, in theory, placed Soviet arms in the service of maintaining the safety of the Soviet Union and other socialist states and in the service of international socialism. The more practical technological aspect called for the maintenance of a modern military, with nuclear arms, missiles, and other weaponry capable of matching that of the forces of their potential enemies: those of NATO and, in later years, China. Soviet doctrine sought to prevent a nuclear attack, and the nation's great stockpile of nuclear weapons and delivery systems supposedly served as a deterrent.

Although publicly denying it, Moscow did not rule out the use of a preemptive strike. The Soviets kept their nuclear arsenals ready to be deployed at a moment's notice. The Stavka developed massive retaliation, second-strike, and flexible response strategies. The country's arsenal included tactical nuclear weapons.

In 1968, as Alexander Dubček carried out liberalizing reforms in Czechoslovakia, Soviet forces invaded and returned the country to Moscow's hardline socialism. Although this action was part of the Soviet policy of keeping the northern tier of Eastern Europe under control, it also established the Brezhnev Doctrine, that Soviet military force would ensure that no socialist country would shed Soviet ideological principles.

The Soviet Union's most serious "hot" war of the Cold War era was in Afghanistan. On December 27, 1979, the Soviet army invaded Afghanistan after a factional dis-

National Archives

West Berliners look across the wall at East Berlin in 1961.

pute among the Afghan leaders threatened the pro-Moscow government there. The Soviet forces, initially 80,000, had increased to 120,000 by the end of the war in 1988. In addition Moscow sent about 10,000 military and civilian advisers. The Afghan army fighting under Soviet command had an additional 40,000 troops. The government and Soviet forces were engaged in a guerrilla war by a broad coalition of opponents with over 150 small units supplied with American and other foreign arms and operating out of neighboring Pakistan. The Soviet military doctrine, geared toward tank and infantry battles in flat areas, was unprepared for mountainous insurgency warfare, and their forces suffered from inappropriate training, deficient equipment, and low morale. With Mikhail Gorbachev's coming to power in 1986, Soviet efforts evolved away from winning the war and propping up the regime toward finding a way to withdraw. The war in Afghanistan was a major cause of the downfall of the Soviet Union and the end of the Cold War. The official Soviet casualties were 13,310 dead, 35,478 wounded, and 311 missing.

The invasion of Afghanistan extended the Brezhnev Doctrine beyond Eastern Europe. However, unlike Czech leaders in 1968, the Afghani leaders were not moving away from Marxism. Their factional fighting caused instability and opened the door for counterrevolution. The invasion took place during the American-Iranian hostage crisis, and the Soviet Union feared the spread of the fundamental Islamic movement into the Muslim republics of the Soviet Union.

CONTEMPORARY SOURCES

Among the most important contemporary sources on the Cold War are the various Jane's Information Group's military series, especially *All the World's Aircraft*, published annually, and *Jane's Missiles and Rockets*. The Defense Intelligence Agency published a series entitled *Soviet Military Power* (1979). There are a number of collections of documents including Edward H. Judge and John W. Langdon's *The Cold War: A History Through Documents* (1999). Memoirs of Soviet leaders include those of Nikita Khrushchev, *Vospominananiia* (1970; *Khrushchev Remembers*, 1970), and Leonid Brezhnev, *Vospominananiia* (1982; *Memoirs*, 1982). Within the Soviet Union, and now the former Soviet Union, a large number of memoirs were published in Russian, and some have been translated into English. These include accounts of the war in Afghanistan such as Gennady Bocharov's *Russian Roulette: Afghanistan Through Russian Eyes* (1990) and Svetlana Alexievich's *Zinky Boys: Soviet Voices from a Forgotten War* (1992).

BOOKS AND ARTICLES

Carbonnell, Nestor. *And the Russians Stayed: The Sovietization of Cuba a Personal Portrait.* New York: Morrow, 1989.

Gabriel, Richard A. *The Mind of the Soviet Fighting Man: A Quantitative Survey of Soviet Soldiers, Sailors, and Airmen.* Westport, Conn.: Greenwood Press, 1984.

Koch, Fred. *Russian Tanks and Armored Vehicles, 1946 to the Present: An Illustrated Reference.* Atglen, Pa.: Schiffer, 1999.

Mathers, Jennifer G. *The Russian Nuclear Shield from Stalin to Yeltsin.* New York: Oxford University Press, 2000.

Reese, Roger R. *The Soviet Military Experience: A History of the Soviet Army from 1917-1991.* London: Routledge and Kegan Paul, 2000.

Rottman, Gordon L. *The Berlin Wall and the Intra-German Border, 1961-89.* New York: Osprey, 2008.

————. *Warsaw Pact Ground Forces.* New York: Osprey, 1987.

Schwartz, Richard Alan. *The Cold War Reference Guide: A General History and Annotated Chronology, with Selected Biographies.* Jefferson, N.C.: McFarland, 1997.

Ward, Robin, and Geoffrey Jukes. *Soviet General's Database.* Canberra: Australian National University, 1999.

Zaloga, Steven J., and James Loop. *Soviet Bloc Elite Forces.* New York: Osprey, 1985.

FILMS AND OTHER MEDIA

Afghan Breakdown. Feature film. Lenfilm, 1990.

Cold War. Documentary. Warner Home Video, 1998.

Frederick B. Chary

ISRAELI WARFARE
Dates: Since 1948

POLITICAL CONSIDERATIONS

Israel is a state measuring 27,000 square kilometers (including the West Bank and Gaza), with about 20,000 square kilometers within the Green Line, Israel's pre-1967 border. It has a population of about 6 million. It is a country where there is no distinction between foreign and defense policy and where the prime minister traditionally holds the defense portfolio. Israel has concluded peace agreements with Egypt and Jordan but is still technically in a state of war with all its remaining neighboring countries.

MILITARY ACHIEVEMENT

The formation of the Israeli army goes back to the 1920's and 1930's, when Jewish settlements needed protection against attacks by local Arab forces and the British mandate government. As the numbers of Jewish immigrants to Palestine, both legal and illegal, increased, a military force known as the Haganah (Hebrew for "defense") was founded. After statehood in 1948, the Haganah became the core of the Israel Defense Forces (IDF). The IDF initially functioned as a militia of volunteers, lacking any ranks or uniforms. It also had an elite unit as a special strike force known as the Palmach. This unit was based on the *kibbutzim*, or cooperative settlements, which served as frontline fortresses during the 1948 Arab-Israeli War. The youth of these settlements were organized as agriculturalists and military reservists, receiving training as members of a special organization known as Nahal. Other assault strike forces were founded by various factions of the Jewish underground, such as the Irgun Zvai Leumi, headed by Menachem Begin; the Stern, led by Yitzhak Shamir; and Lohamei Herut Yisrael. These were later merged with the Haganah, which became the IDF. From

these beginnings and due to the revolutionary origins of these forces, the lines between the civilian and military organizations were blurred. The Israeli Air Force (IAF) dates to 1947, when the Air Service, or Sherut-Avir, was created from eleven single-engine light aircraft. Several old aircraft were purchased from the British army, to be renovated and flown by pilots with prior experience in the British Royal Air Force.

The country's response to border attacks by guerrilla groups in the past has been described as a form of massive retaliation. Following the American campaign in Iraq, however, the Israelis resorted to short military operations of the shock-and-awe type (the military technique of overwhelming the enemy with "rapid dominance" by means of extreme speed and force), which they amply utilized in Operation Cast Lead (2006) against Gaza. Despite the apparent success of its offensive doctrine, Israel found itself continuously embroiled in wars. Its persistent occupation of the West Bank, for instance, has reserved policy initiatives for the Arab side, leading to two uprisings (intifadas) and continuous internal and sporadic attacks by Palestinian militants.

Israel's clear qualitative edge and regional monopoly over nuclear weapons failed to create a state of total security as a result of several factors. One of these is the potential failure of advance warning by military intelligence, as in the 1973 October War (Yom Kippur War). Another factor that developed during that same war was the coming together and coordinated military attacks by two neighboring Arab states, namely Egypt and Syria. Israel's Military Intelligence Directorate (MID) plays a large role in provoking or instigating military attacks by providing early warning to the government about suspicious enemy troop movements or similar activity along the country's borders. The MID is a standing corps, just like the air force, which is charged with responding to surprise attacks until the reservists are fully mobilized. More important, the ability of the air force to mount a preemptive attack and render quick support for ground troops has lost its deterrent effect, largely because of the emergence of Arab guerrilla forces, which challenge Israel's seemingly limitless ability to deliver painful blows to its enemies. The lessons of the failed 1982 invasion of Lebanon, which saw Israeli troops hold the Lebanese capital under siege, are implicated in the Sabra and Shatila massacres of civilian Palestinians in September, 1982 (witness the abortive failure of the Israeli-Lebanese treaty and eventual retreat back to Israel's northern region). These failures have severely lowered Israeli faith in the effectiveness of their own superior air power and ground troops.

The Israeli attack on the Lebanese guerrilla force Hezbollah in December, 2006, was also thwarted by the unexpected show of force on the part of Lebanese irregular troops. Additionally, the U.S.-Israel alliance came under scrutiny when the 1990-1991 Gulf War forced the United States to exclude Israel from participation, even after Israel suffered from Scud missile attacks launched by the Iraqi government of Saddam Hussein. Maintaining an American-Arab military alliance during the liberation of Kuwait demonstrated Israel's limited usefulness as the United States' great strategic ally in the region. This same alliance also suffered when the Cold War ended, leaving in its wake any threat of an imminent Soviet attack on the Middle East.

WEAPONS, UNIFORMS, AND ARMOR

Early weapons of the IDF were acquired from the United States and Czechoslovakia during and just before the 1948 Arab-Israeli War. Many volunteer pilots and military personnel arrived from several countries and with varied military experience acquired during World War II. By the end of 1948, the air force had swelled to more than one hundred planes and 660 volunteer pilots and skilled mechanics.

Popperfoto/Getty Images

Jewish soldiers training in Palestine in 1948.

Israeli ground forces developed into an impressive machine, so that by the 1980's they ranked third in the world after the United States and the Soviet Union. By the 1980's, regular ground troops numbered around 450,000, divided among ten mechanical brigades, thirty-three armored brigades, twelve territorial/border infantry brigades, and fifteen artillery brigades. With the rise of the Chinese and Indian militaries, the Israeli military fell back to fifth rank in terms of effectiveness, mobility, and offensive capability. By 1994, ground forces had reached 558,112, divided into forty-two armored brigades, twenty-one infantry brigades, and six territorial brigades. Normally, ground forces would be mobilized within forty-eight hours, although this has been relaxed in recent years. Today, only 30 percent of the ground forces constitute a standing army, while the rest are maintained as reserves, who wear a uniform only one month out of the year.

The IAF increased in 1983 to 830 aircraft, and in 1993 to 1,052 aircraft, its personnel swelling from 37,000 to 45,889. The effectiveness of Israel's air power is due to keeping technical and administrative personnel per combat aircraft to a minimum. The IAF relies heavily on ground troops, maintaining only 25 percent of its air force pilots and personnel as reserves. The IAF pilot-training program was always unusually rigorous. Students aspiring to serving with the air force are required to go through a demanding set of initial tests and psychological profiling. Unlike other countries, where pilot candidates are expected to receive a college degree first, Israel enrolls successful candidates immediately after they complete high school. Students' training usually lasts about twenty months before they learn how to operate some aircraft. Students are then immersed in a regimen of applied mathematics, physics, and other scientific subjects, and are put through rigorous infantry training.

Israel is known to have acquired a significant nuclear capability, amounting to three hundred nuclear warheads by the beginning of the twenty-first century. Israel has the capacity to deliver these warheads but managed to avoid signing the United Nations' Nuclear Non-Proliferation Treaty. It is believed that Israel built two nuclear reactors, one at Nahal Soreq and one at Dimona in the Negev. The former was provided by the United States and devoted mostly to research and the training of scientists; the other was based on French technology and built in the late 1960's. Uranium was always acquired surreptitiously from a variety of European and African sources. The United States attempted to subject the Dimona reactor to inspection during the Kennedy administration but was deliberately misled about its true purposes. Israel's means of delivery of atomic payload is based on a ballistic missile code-named Jericho. It was developed in the mid-1980's based on a French design by the firm of Marcel Dassault. According to some reports, Israel maintains nuclear bases at various locations in the Galilee region. Israel is also suspected of developing chemical and biological weapons at its Nes Ziona plant south of Tel Aviv. Prime Minister Menachem Begin (1913-1992) resisted U.S. pressure during the Camp David negotiations in the 1970's to halt his country's nuclear program as a price for peace with Egypt. He also initiated the Begin Doctrine, which stated that no state in the region would be allowed to develop a nuclear capability threatening to Israel. This policy led to Israel's raid on the Osirak nuclear plant near Baghdad in 1981, the first such an attack on a nuclear facility in modern times.

Israel's defense industries had a modest start when Bedek Aircraft, Ltd., was formed by the late 1940's, in order to provide maintenance services for the country's fledgling air force. Later, this company developed into Israel Aircraft Industries (IAI), which began to produce its own line of combat aircraft, transport jets, and other vehicles. Spurred by frequent arms embargoes due to the desire of the United States and other countries to curtail Israel's frequent initiation of wars, and fearful of Egypt's acquisition of immense arms supplies from Czechoslovakia in the mid-1950's, Israel began to manufacture most of its own weapons. This effort was greatly aided by its own scientifically trained population, U.S. funds for research, and the early availability of markets for its weapons in Central and South America, Africa, and East Asia. Israel's main weapons industries have always been state-owned. They include Israel Military Industries, the Raphael Armament Development Authority, and the Haifa Shipyards. These produce a variety of weapons often based on U.S. technology, such as the Kfir, its fighter plane; the Merkava, a highly rated battle tank; missile-carrying boats; a large selection of artillery pieces; and a variety of missiles. In addition, Israel produces radar, computers, and much electronic equipment, provided by the IAI's subsidiary Elta Electronic Industries. The Haifa-based Soltam Company produces guns and howitzers.

The Israeli arms industry is the country's main economic endeavor, employing an estimated one-third of the Israeli labor force and generating more than a billion dollars in annual arms sales abroad. Israel ranks in the top ten exporters of arms worldwide. Israel's arms sales are often in direct competition with the American arms industry, even though it is highly dependent on U.S. fiscal and technological assistance. One example of this relationship was the Lavi project, which sought to build a fighter plane, supported by U.S. credits that Congress approved in 1983. The Lavi project, which employed four thousand skilled workers, was canceled by the Israeli cabinet in 1986 because of its excessive cost to the United States (in the amount $2 billion). U.S. strategic cooperation with Israel and the sharing of advanced military technology were always justified by access to battlefield testing of weapons in Israel's various wars. The United States also frequently overlooked its own legislation prohibiting the use of American-supplied arms in aggressive wars, such as the Foreign Assistance Act of 1961 and the Foreign Sales Act of 1968.

MILITARY ORGANIZATION

The least important branch of IDF is the navy, although this is also changing. The navy is the smallest of the three branches because of the country's limited coastline of about 225 kilometers, which includes Gaza. After the Israeli destroyer *Eilat* was sunk by Egyptian missiles in the June war of 1967 (the so-called Six-Day War), Israel began to acquire small but fast-track boats designed by the West German firm Lürssen Werft, which were actually produced by a French company. These were fitted with Israeli

Gabriel surface-to-surface missiles. Eventually, Israel developed an advanced type of this design in its own Haifa shipyards. By 1993, the navy was estimated to have 12,402 units, including submarines. By 2004, Israel had guaranteed the regional superiority of its navy by acquiring German submarines of the Dolphin type, equipped with nuclear cruise missiles.

Thus, while the Israeli IDF suffer from a dramatic negative quantitative comparison with the standing armies of the surrounding Arab countries, even when all the reserve units are mobilized, Israel continues to enjoy a decisive qualitative edge when it comes to the total effectiveness of its units. Israel's limited territorial depth made it vulnerable prior to the acquisition of Sinai, the Golan Heights, and the West Bank in the 1967 war. Although much ameliorated, this vulnerability continues to be addressed through a strong and extensive early-warning system. Israel's dependence on a vast army of reservists and its frequent lengthy mobilization of manpower and civilian transport vehicles often resulted in severe economic disruption. This was the case prior to the 1967 war, when a month-long period of mobilization along all fronts aggravated the political crisis, leading to a preemptive attack against all surrounding Arab air bases.

DOCTRINE, STRATEGY, AND TACTICS

Israel's military doctrine has changed over the years but has remained based on the principle of military and psychological deterrence. This doctrine was intended to discourage attacks on Israel's population centers or on its vital strategic assets, such as its nuclear reactors. Because of its lack of strategic depth prior to 1967, Israel always felt justified in launching preemptive attacks. Known as the "operational plan," this doctrine called for delivering simultaneous offensive attacks against all of its neighboring Arab airfields. These strikes depended greatly on reports by military intelligence and its policy recommendations, as well as on a variety of intelligence sources and on coordinating with all branches of the military services. Because of the IDF's numerical inferiority when compared to the total strength of surrounding Arab armies, they enjoy a qualitative edge in terms of air power and the speed with which they can carry out a mission. Israel relies heavily on an early-warning system based on the work of military intelligence.

Israel's faith in its own strategic doctrine changed as a result of its 1967 occupation of the West Bank and Gaza, home to large Palestinian populations who therefore became subject to Israeli control. Since Israel's armed forces are made up largely of ordinary citizens serving as reservists, they easily became highly sensitive to psychological pressures resulting from a permanent military occupation of a densely populated territory. More and more Israelis expressed a reluctance to function as an occupation army charged

Israeli paratroopers stand ready to shoot Hamas militants in the Gaza Strip in January, 2009.

with containing a civilian population. The reputation of the military institution was tarnished as a result of its failure to deliver a decisive blow to Hezbollah's forces in southern Lebanon. Israel's previous vocalization of potentially targeting the Jordanian territory in case of an imminent attack from the east was relinquished after the signing of the Israeli-Jordanian peace agreement in 1994. The same strategic shift occurred as a result of relinquishing control over Sinai in the Camp David Accords (1978). By 2010, Israel found itself on the horns of a dilemma, being forced to develop a new strategic doctrine while a solution for the Palestinian issue remained as elusive as ever.

A new challenge to Israel's nuclear hegemony in the Middle East materialized when Iran began developing its own nuclear capability. When Egypt and the United States attempted to persuade Israel to give up its nuclear weapons as an attempt to solidify the Camp David peace treaty, Israel refused to do so until every Arab state in the area signed a similar treaty with Israel. By the late 1970's, Israel had finalized the so-called Begin Doctrine, which reflected the views of Prime Minister Begin and his stance during these negotiations. It was there that he announced Israel's determination to resist any effort to develop a

rival nuclear power in the region. Any such nuclear state would be considered a threat to Israel's security and must be forced to dismantle such weapons. Israel's 1981 attack on the Osirak reactor in Iraq was the first response to such a threat, an attack that was severely criticized by the U.N. Security Council. How far Israel would go in order to replicate its attack on the Iraqi reactor vis-à-vis Iran remained unclear, but it was clear that Israel had decided to enforce a wide territorial doctrine when it came to this type of weapon. Such a situation was averted during Prime Minister David Ben-Gurion's years in office (1955-1963), when he sought to cultivate close relationships with countries, such as Turkey and Iran, lying within Israel's outer rim.

The removal of the shah of Iran, Mohammad Reza Shah Pahlavi, from office in 1979 and his replacement with a radical Islamic regime at odds with Israel's claims of nuclear monopoly in the Middle East posed new threats to the entire region. The danger of instigating a nuclear duel between Israel and its challengers became real. In 2008, it was revealed that Israel's air force had been practicing to mount a strike on the Iranian reactor and Iran had test-fired a new missile capable of reaching Israel. These Israeli maneuvers were reminiscent of the building of a model of the Osirak reactor in Israel in order to practice mounting a strike against it. Any such attack on Iran's nuclear reactor was expected to come in the form of serial bombings, which would provide ample opportunity for Iranian retaliation.

Even though a nuclear attack against Egypt's most vulnerable strategic asset, the Aswan Dam, was averted by the signing of the Camp David agreement and these two countries' adherence to their international obligations, by 2010 it seemed that Israel had used uranium-based weapons in some of its recent wars. It is known that Israel has used weapons (such as American "buster bombs," which were dropped on Hezbollah's offices in Beirut in the 2006 cam-paign) proscribed by the third protocol of the Geneva Conventions. Both the United States and Israel have declined to sign these conventions. Cluster bombs and phosphorus bombs were used in the 2008 attack on Gaza. The British scientific secretary of the European Committee on Radiation Risk, Christopher Busby, concluded upon testing soil samples that Israel during the 2006 Lebanese campaign must have used a new weapon with a nuclear fission device or a bunker-busting uranium penetrator weapon. The latter may have used enriched uranium, rather than depleted uranium. The Israelis continued to argue, however, that the Geneva Conventions did not cover many of these nuclear waste weapons.

CONTEMPORARY SOURCES

As the field is a relatively current one, there is much in the way of archival, firsthand material on the history of the Israeli military. Much information on the early wars surrounding the founding of the state of Israel is available in the David Ben-Gurion Archive, held at the Ben-Gurion University of the Negev's Sede Boker campus. The archive contains not only Ben-Gurion's personal papers and speeches, but also the minutes of meetings and other documents produced by Israel's first prime minister. In addition, the Israel State Archives in Jerusalem holds its record groups 72 and 153, which contain the private papers of many prominent Israeli politicians and government officials.

BOOKS AND ARTICLES

Bar-On, Mordechai. *Never-Ending Conflict: Israeli Military History*. Mechanicsburg, Pa.: Stackpole Books, 2006.

Dunstan, Simon. *The Yom Kippur War: The Arab-Israeli War of 1973*. New York: Osprey, 2007.

Karsh, Efraim. *The Arab-Israeli Conflict: The Palestine War 1948*. New York: Osprey, 2002.

Maman, Daniel, Eyal Ben-Ari, and Zeev Rosenhek, eds. *Military, State, and Society in Israel: Theoretical and Comparative Perspectives*. Piscataway, N.J.: Transaction, 2001.

Varble, Derek. *The Suez Crisis 1956*. New York: Osprey, 2003.

FILMS AND OTHER MEDIA

Beaufort. Feature film. Keshet Broadcasting, 2007.

Cast a Giant Shadow. Feature film. Batjac Productions, 1966

Clear Skies: The Story of the Israeli Air Force. Documentary. TES Video, 1990.

The Fifty Years' War: Israel and the Arabs. Documentary. Public Broadcasting Service, 2000.

Operation Thunderbolt. Feature film. Warner Bros., 1978.

Six Days in June: The War That Redefined the Middle East. Documentary. WGBH Boston, 2007.

Ghada Talhami

THE COLD WAR
THE NONALIGNED STATES
Dates: Since 1955

POLITICAL CONSIDERATIONS

The term "nonaligned states" refers to those nations that attempted to stake out independent positions between the American- and Soviet-led power blocs in the international politics of the Cold War. A seminal event in the collective history of these states was the Asian-African Conference held in Bandung, Indonesia, in April, 1955; the nations attending this conference adopted a declaration promoting world peace and cooperation and expressing their desire not to become involved in the Cold War.

The ideals of peace, cooperation, and independence in international affairs became the founding principles of the Non-Aligned Movement (NAM), which was established in Belgrade, Yugoslavia, in 1961. This organization was largely the brainchild of Egyptian president Gamal Abdel Nasser (1918-1970), Indian prime minister Jawaharlal Nehru (1889-1964), and Yugoslavian president Tito (Josip Broz, 1892-1980). NAM was intended to form the basis of an alliance as close as that of the North Atlantic Treaty Organization (NATO) or the Warsaw Pact, but it demonstrated little of the same cohesion. Some member states became involved in armed conflicts with other members during the Cold War period, most notably India and Pakistan (1965 and 1971).

Despite the stated aims of noninvolvement in the geopolitics of the Cold War, regional or global tensions, such as conflicts with neighboring states, have ultimately compelled many member states to demonstrate close ties to one or the other of the two superpowers throughout this period. Since the end of the Cold War in 1991, NAM has struggled to find international relevance. While Egypt and India remain member states, the states of the former Yugoslavia have expressed little interest in membership, electing instead to hold observer status in the organization.

MILITARY ACHIEVEMENT

Throughout the period of the Cold War, the conflicts waged by the nonaligned states tended to evolve from border disputes or displays of nationalism. Because the states involved in these conflicts found they could gain military advantage over their regional opponents through closer relations with one or the other of the two superpowers, these localized wars often threatened to spiral out of control and lead to much wider and deadlier conflicts.

In 1956, Nasser oversaw Egypt's nationalization of the Suez Canal, sparking an invasion by a joint Israeli, British, and French task force to compel the Egyptian government to relinquish control of the canal. Ten years later, he hatched a plot with neighboring Arab states to overrun Israel, resulting in the disastrous Six-Day War of June, 1967, and the Israeli occupation of Egypt's Sinai Peninsula. Finally, in October, 1973, Nasser's successor as Egyptian president, Anwar el-Sadat (1918-1981), launched a surprise attack against Israel to regain the Sinai Peninsula (the conflict camed to be called the October War or the Yom Kippur War). In 1956 and 1967, Nasser had been emboldened to act by his close ties with the Soviet Union, which had been arming and training Egypt's soldiers. In 1956, the U.S. government forced a cease-fire on the belligerents before the situation escalated and led to a confrontation between the Soviet Union and the Western powers that opposed Nasser. In 1973, the American and Soviet govern-

Pakistani protesters burn effigies and flags outside the Indian embassy in Islamabad in January, 1997. The two countries' long-standing conflict was supported during the Cold War by the opposing superpowers.

ments both intervened to bring hostilities to an end and restore the regional balance of power.

In 1965, India went to war with neighboring Pakistan over the territory of Kashmir. The dispute dated back to 1947, when India won independence from Britain, at which time the partitioning of British India into the independent nations of India and Pakistan left the status of Kashmir unresolved. Hostilities opened on September 1, 1965. After the Indian army had made significant headway into Pakistan the war appeared headed for a stalemate, prompting the Soviet Union and the United States to intervene as peace brokers for India and Pakistan, respectively. Following the war, India developed close ties with the Soviet Union, culminating in the Indo-Soviet Treaty of Cooperation and Friendship to balance Pakistan's increased support from the United States.

The two countries were at war again in 1971 over Pakistan's repression of members of the Bengali independence movement in East Pakistan. This time India won a decisive victory, resulting in the secession of East Pakistan, now Bangladesh, from Pakistan.

WEAPONS, UNIFORMS, AND ARMOR

Egypt, Yugoslavia, and India all came to rely heavily, although not exclusively, on the Soviet Union for their armaments during the Cold War. Much of the Egyptian military was equipped by the Soviet Union and Czechoslovakia until the 1980's. In 1955, the Egyptian air force consisted of MiG fighters, Ilyushin Il-28 bombers and Il-14 transports, and Yak-11 trainers accompanied by Czechoslovakian instructors. In the 1960's the Egyptian government introduced the Soviet-made MiG-21 into the Egyptian air force. The MiG-21 is a short-range interceptor with mach 2 capability. It has a delta-wing design, which allows for fast climbing but results in a rapid loss of speed on turning. During the Six-Day War, Egyptian ground forces included approximately ninety World War II-era Soviet T-34 tanks with 85-millimeter guns.

Throughout the 1960's the Yugoslav People's Army operated about one thousand Soviet T-54 and T-55 tanks. In the late 1970's, Yugoslavia obtained an additional seventy Soviet T-72's, followed by more than four hundred Yugoslav M-84's. The M-84 battle tank is a domestically manufactured and improved version of the T-72; improvements over the T-72 include a domestic fire control system, improved composite armor, and a 1,000-horsepower engine. The M-84 has a crew of three and is armed with a 2A46 125-millimeter smooth-bore cannon.

The principal fighter jets of the Yugoslav air force were also MiG-21 Interceptors. In addition, Yugoslavia relied on SOKO G-2 Galeb trainers, which were the first Yugoslav-made jet aircraft. The Galeb, a straight-wing aircraft powered by a Rolls-Royce Viper Mk 22-6 turbojet, was used primarily for combat training of Yugoslav military air force academy cadets.

During the 1960's, the bulk of India's tank complement consisted of older American-made M4 Sherman tanks and the British-made Centurion Mk7's. The Centurions, with their 105-millimeter guns, were particularly useful during the 1965 war between India and Pakistan. India's ground forces at that time also included French-made AMX-13's, Soviet-made PT-76's, and American-made M3 light tanks.

In 1974, India conducted an underground nuclear test, making it the first nonaligned nation to possess nuclear weapons. Despite criticism and international sanctions, India had refused to sign the Nuclear Non-Proliferation Treaty of 1968, arguing that the treaty was discrimi-

natory because it allowed those countries that had acquired nuclear weapons prior to the agreement—the United States, the Soviet Union, Great Britain, France, and China—to retain their arsenals.

MILITARY ORGANIZATION

Prior to the dissolution of the nation of Yugoslavia in late 1991, the Yugoslavian military was the fourth strongest in Europe. The Yugoslav People's Army, which had its origins in the partisan movement of the Yugoslav People's Liberation War against the Nazi occupiers during World War II and was the principal military organization of the Socialist Federal Republic of Yugoslavia (1943-1992), comprised an army, navy, and air force. These three services were organized into four military regions: Belgrade, Zagreb, Skopje, and the Split naval region. The ground forces of the Yugoslav People's Army made up the bulk of the country's military forces and consisted of infantry, armor, artillery, and air defense as well as signal, engineering, and chemical defense corps. The Yugoslav air force was responsible for transport, reconnaissance, and the country's national air defense system. The backbone of the Yugoslav navy was the Adriatic Fleet, which was headquartered at Split. In 1992 the Yugoslav People's Army was dissolved along with the Socialist Federal Republic of Yugoslavia, as the newly independent republics adopted their own militaries.

The Indian armed forces consist of the three branches of army, navy and air force. The Indian army was formed soon after India achieved indepen-

TURNING POINTS

June 5, 1967	Israel launches surprise attack on Arab air forces, beginning the Six-Day War.
Oct. 21, 1967	Egypt sinks Israeli destroyer *Eilat* with a Soviet Styx cruise missile.
Oct. 6, 1973	Egypt launches air strike against Israel, beginning Arab-Israeli October War.
1979	The Iranian Revolution ends Iran's close military ties with the United States.

dence and retained most of the regiments of the British Indian army. Throughout the conflicts that India fought during the first half of the Cold War, coordination between the Indian air force and the Indian army was quite poor. For example, during the war between India and Pakistan in 1965, the Indian air force was used extensively, but it acted independently of the army, conducting raids deep into Pakistani territory in obsolete World War II-era aircraft that ultimately surrendered air superiority over the combat zones to the Pakistani air force. The primary mission of the Indian navy during that period was to patrol India's coast, but during the 1971 war with Pakistan the navy played a significant role in the bombing of the Karachi harbor.

The Egyptian military originally consisted of three branches: army, navy, and air force. Following the disastrous events of the Six-Day War, however, during which a surprise attack by the Israeli air force destroyed most of Egypt's planes on the ground, Egypt added a fourth service branch: the Egyptian Air Defense Command. It was patterned on the Soviet Union's antiaircraft defense branch and integrated all of Egypt's air defense capabilities, including antiaircraft guns, missile units, interceptor planes, and radar and warning installations.

DOCTRINE, STRATEGY, AND TACTICS

Since the Bandung Conference, the nonaligned states have articulated a commitment to world peace and stability, placing particular emphasis on disarmament. NAM has promoted international cooperation to ensure the collective security of all nations. Regional disputes and tensions between aligned and nonaligned states have sometimes jeopardized this multilateral approach to international relations. Therefore, throughout the Cold War the nonaligned states adopted more unilateral tactics to preserve their national security.

Throughout its postindependence existence, the Indian army has had the primary responsibilities of defending India from external aggression, maintaining peace and security within India, and patrolling the nation's borders. This translated into an aggressive forward policy adopted in 1959 regarding disputed border areas with China. According to this tactic, Indian border-patrol units continuously pushed their posts deeper into Chinese territory. When it was apparent that China was pursuing a similar tactic in India, the situation rapidly deteriorated until the two sides were at war in 1962. India's nuclear strategy, on the other hand, has been one of deterrence. It is governed by a doctrine of "no first use" against any other nuclear power and "no use" against any nonnuclear state.

Given Egypt's close connection to the Soviet Union, many of its military tactics were based on Soviet doctrine. For example, during the 1967 Six-Day War, the deployment of Egyptian ground forces in the Sinai reflected a Soviet defensive posture, where mobile armor units were placed at a strategic depth behind the infantry to provide a dynamic defense while the infantry units engaged in defensive battles. Following its defeat in that war, Egypt carried out a prolonged strategy of attrition against the Israeli air force. Two Egyptian aircraft would penetrate Israeli airspace to bait an Israeli response. When Israeli interceptors (usually four to eight) arrived to engage the Egyptian planes, they would be attacked from behind by an additional dozen Egyptian fighters that had been lying in wait well below Israeli radar.

The Yugoslav People's Army had an operational military doctrine based on a concept of total war called "total national defense." According to this doctrine, the People's Army assumed the role of defending the borders from any invaders long enough for the territorial defense forces to engage the enemy forces and begin wearing them down through partisan tactics. Under this concept the entire population was to participate in the war effort, including through armed resistance, armament production, and civil defense.

CONTEMPORARY SOURCES

Two important contemporary works provide valuable information on the nonaligned states as a whole. The first is George McTurnan Kahin's *The Asian-African Conference, Bandung, Indonesia, April 1955* (1956). This is a very accessible work that details the events that occurred during the 1955 Bandung Conference. The first half of the volume presents the author's account of the conference based on his own experiences as an observer at the open sessions, and the second half provides transcripts of the speeches delivered by key attendees as well as the conference's final communiqué. The second collection, *The Conference of Heads of State or Government of Non-aligned Countries* (1961), edited by Slobodan Vujović, contains speeches from the 1961 summit of nonaligned nations held in Belgrade, where NAM was established.

English versions of contemporary sources of the military affairs of the nonaligned states during the Cold War do not appear to be extensive. The Indian Ministry of External Affairs and the United Nations published a four-volume collection of some of the U.N. Security Council proceedings on the 1965 India-Pakistan conflict: *India-Pakistan Security Council Documents, September-December, 1965*. On the 1971 India-Pakistan conflict, a document collection titled *The Fourteen Day War* was published in 1972. Additionally, the heads of state of Yugoslavia, Egypt, and India left partial records of their respective nations' foreign policies during the Cold War. Regarding Yugoslavia, two works have been published that deal specifically with nonalignment: *Tito o nesvrstanosti* (1976; *Tito on Non-Alignment*, 1976) and *Govori Predsednika SFRJ Josipa Broza Tita na konferencijama nesvrstanih zemalja* (1979; *Tito and Non-Alignment: President Tito's Addresses at Conferences of Non-aligned Countries*, 1979). Nasser similarly documented his position in *President Gamal Abdel Nasser on Non-Alignment* (1964).

Nehru left several collections that outline India's diplomacy during the period of his leadership. These include a volume of speeches titled *India's Foreign Policy: Selected Speeches, September 1946-April 1961* (1961) along with two volumes that deal with his thoughts on India's relations with China in the lead up to and during the 1962 border war: *The Prime Minister on Sino-Indian Relations* (1961) and *Chinese Aggression in War and Peace: Letters of the Prime Minister of India* (1962). Finally, Nehru's daughter, Indira Gandhi, who was prime minister of India during the 1971 India-Pakistan conflict, published *Selected Speeches and Writings of Indira Gandhi: The Years of Endeavour, August 1969-August 1972* (1975).

BOOKS AND ARTICLES

Aloni, Shlomo. *Arab-Israeli Air Wars, 1947-82*. New York: Osprey, 2002.

Laffin, John. *Arab Armies of the Middle East Wars, 1948-73*. New York: Osprey, 1982.

Marston, Daniel P., and Chandar S. Sundaram, eds. *A Military History of India and South Asia: From the East India Company to the Nuclear Era*. Westport, Conn.: Praeger Security International, 2007.

Meital, Yoram. *Egypt's Struggle for Peace: Continuity and Change, 1967-1977*. Gainesville: University Press of Florida, 1997.

Milivojević, Marko, John B. Allcock, and Pierre Maurer, eds. *Yugoslavia's Security Dilemmas: Armed Forces, National Defence, and Foreign Policy*. New York: St. Martin's Press, 1988.

Pollack, Kenneth M. *Arabs at War: Military Effectiveness, 1948-1991*. Lincoln: University of Nebraska Press, 2002.

Rajan, M. S. *Nonalignment and Nonaligned Movement: Retrospect and Prospect*. New Delhi: Vikas, 1990.

Roberts, Adam. *Nations in Arms: The Theory and Practice of Territorial Defence*. 2d rev. ed. London: Macmillan, 1986.

Westad, Odd Arne. *The Global Cold War: Third World Interventions and the Making of Our Times*. New York: Cambridge University Press, 2005.

Wirsing, Robert G. *India, Pakistan, and the Kashmir Dispute: On Regional Conflict and Its Resolution*. New York: St. Martin's Press, 1994.

FILMS AND OTHER MEDIA

Border. Feature film. J. P. Dutta, 1997.

India and Pakistan at Sixty. Documentary. British Broadcasting Corporation, 2007.

The Six-Day War: Then and Now. Documentary. Cable News Network, 2007.

The Suez Crisis. Documentary. 3BM Television, 1997.

Tito. Documentary. Bindweed Soundvision, 2001.

Turning Points in History: Showdown at Suez. Documentary. Foxtel, 2007.

Geoff Stewart

Colonial Wars of Independence
Dates: 1935-1991

Political Considerations

In the late nineteenth century a combination of increasing European industrialization, expanding trade and finance from growth centers in North America and Western Europe, and developing technological advances in transportation and communications fostered a global expansion of the imperial powers' political and military domination. In Asia, China's military and industrial underdevelopment allowed Britain, France, the United States, and Japan to assert colonial control over such former Chinese tributary states as Burma (1824-1885), Indochina (1862-1895), and Taiwan (1895), while also creating neocolonial spheres of influence in Thailand (1896) and in China itself (1839-1945). The vast interior of Africa, meanwhile, was visited by semiofficial European explorers and missionaries and was conquered by European troops operating from coastal bases beginning in 1880. Earlier European coastal encroachments that facilitated the slave trade, such as those of Portugal, were expanded.

A European-based alliance system preserved international balances of power in Europe, Asia, and Africa until the start of World War I (1914-1918). After the war the victorious Allies awarded themselves control over former German and Ottoman possessions in Africa, Asia, and the Middle East. The anomalous position of the former German colony of South-West Africa, seized by South Africa during World War I, was resolved when, in 1920, the League of Nations made it a mandate territory of South Africa, to eventually be known as Namibia.

Although colonial powers had various purposes for waging colonial wars, they generally sought to extend or preserve a global presence unfettered by the geographic limitations of their metropolitan homelands. In the late twentieth century this impulse came into conflict both with evidence of the military vulnerability of the European powers, many of which suffered defeat during World War II (1939-1945), and with increasing demands for self-determination from colonized peoples. Against these currents Italy had tried reinventing itself as a great power by invading Ethiopia in 1935, hoping not only to create a new colony but also to redress an earlier embarrassing military defeat it had suffered in 1896. Japan's occupation of Chinese territory from 1931 to 1945 and of European colonies in the Southeast and Southwest Pacific from 1940 to 1945 during World War II exchanged one occupying power for another, fueling nationalist resolve and greatly complicating the efforts of British, French, and Dutch troops to reassert their colonial authority after Japan's defeat. In the postwar economy European powers needed the natural resources provided by the colonies, but they also struggled to recover their international prestige after the damage of World War II. The same factors, resources and prestige, were interpreted differently by other colonial powers. The United States rapidly agreed to Philippine independence, linking it to the American ideal of freedom by selecting July 4 as Philippine Independence Day in 1946. Between 1956 and 1975 Spain withdrew from virtually all its colonial territories without armed confrontation: Morocco in 1956; the Republic of Equatorial Guinea in 1968; and the Spanish Sahara in 1976. Belgium also relinquished direct political authority in the Congo (1960) and Rwanda (1962), but did so without assuring the emplacement of stable successor governments.

As time passed, the motives of colonial powers changed. In the 1950's Britain and France deployed troops to certain colonies to protect expatriates from violence launched by local nationalists and to preserve sufficient order to allow a smooth transition of authority to local elites sympathetic to the West. Portugal's calculus was different. It made its overseas colonies provinces of the motherland and tenaciously defended its colonial system, particularly after the embarrassment caused by India's easy seizure of Portuguese Goa in 1961. Throughout the 1960's and 1970's Portugal used force to suppress independence movements in Guinea-Bissau, Mozambique, and Angola, with disastrous results.

Networks of anticolonial nationalists readily evolved, including the Pan-African Congress movement of the 1920's and 1930's, the Communist International movement of the 1930's and 1940's, and the Nonaligned Movement of the 1950's and 1960's. Through these and other initiatives, anticolonial insurgents gained international recognition and built political alliances. Meanwhile, nationalist leaders, who endorsed social changes such as land reform in addition to anticolonial causes, often conceived of their movements as "national liberation struggles." Of these, many included well-organized local Communist parties whose leaders studied the strategies developed and employed by Mao Zedong (Mao Tsetung; 1893-1976) in the Chinese Civil War (1926-1949). Material and political support from the Soviet Union and China bolstered anticolonial forces in several colonies. These facts greatly complicated the international context of many colonial wars, as East-West tensions became integrated with local colonial politics. Once local nationalists embarked upon an armed struggle, whatever its external orientation, colonial powers were loath to withdraw without first quashing the armed rebellion. Typically each side in the ensuing conflict interpreted the military activities of the other as an escalation of the conflict, and partisan support galvanized on each side as casualties and costs mounted.

For their part, local nationalists could not organize cohesive political, let alone military, opposition where some form of genuine antipathy to imperial rule did not already exist. Leaders sought to transform local dissatisfactions into an organized resistance movement through propaganda, recruitment, and political instruction. Leaders also carefully monitored East-West tensions and studied the progress of other anticolonial movements, looking for external support and examples of successful struggle strategies.

Transitions to independence typically required the complete military withdrawal of the colonial power. Metropolitan powers elected to withdraw for many reasons: the financial and other costs of long-lived colonial wars, as in the French withdrawal from Algeria in 1962; cataclysmic military defeat, as in the French disaster at Dien Bien Phu in 1954; the transfer of power to moderates after the defeat of insurgent forces, as in Malaya in 1957; the collapse of the metropolitan government, as in Portugal in 1974; and international isolation and condemnation, as in South Africa's withdrawal from Namibia in 1989. Although negotiations between colonial authorities and insurgent leaders gave the latter political legitimacy, anticolonial leadership structures often fractured after hostilities ended, plunging newly independent states into extended civil wars.

MILITARY ACHIEVEMENT

Although few colonial wars produced clear military results for either party, there are important examples of decisive battlefield victories that prefigured political change. Colonial powers thoroughly suppressed mid-twentieth century armed rebellions in both Madagascar and Malaya, allowing gradual transitions to independence in each case. Similarly, certain nationalist forces were able to force colonial administrations to withdraw after inflicting military defeat upon colonial troops. This occurred in Indochina, where Vietnamese forces engineered the collapse of the fortified French position at Dien Bien Phu and in Algeria, after a less disastrous but equally costly six-year conflict (1954-1962).

For both colonial and nationalist militaries, one of the great challenges of anticolonial conflict lay in asserting cohesive command over multinational and multicultural troops. Where anticolonial commanders failed in this project, as the Chinese-dominated Malayan Communist Party did, broad popular support proved elusive. Where they succeeded, as in ethnically diverse Guinea-Bissau under the political leadership of Amilcar Cabral (1921-1973), the shared experience of colonial occupation became a unifying factor that promoted nation-building. Colonial powers, on the other hand, routinely utilized troops and bureaucrats from other colonies in colonial wars. In Malaya, for example, the British used Gurkhas from India, whereas the French employed Moroccans in Indochina and Senegalese in Algeria. Coordination of these international forces underpinned cooperative bilateral relations between colonial powers and the donor colonies: India (1947), Morocco (1956), and Senegal (within the Federation of Mali, 1960) all achieved political independence with relatively little anticolonial violence.

WEAPONS, UNIFORMS, AND ARMOR

In almost all colonial wars, nationalist forces initially armed themselves with crude weapons fashioned from local materials by local manufacturers. Knives, machetes, and small bombs filled with bits of wire or glass were devised for urban conflicts. In jungle and bush terrain camouflaged pits concealed sharpened *punji* sticks, often soaked in snake venom or human waste in order to inflict both injury and infection. Similarly, vines and jute laid across footpaths and in streams served as triggers for swinging spikes, bombs, and falling rocks or nets. Such traps were especially valuable because they required little matériel, could be constructed by noncombatants, and remained viable without maintenance.

In Southeast Asia arms stored by anti-Japanese guerrillas during World War II supplied anticolonial insurgents in the late 1940's. Weapons were also purchased in neutral Thailand and smuggled to insurgent units in unguarded coastal areas in Indochina, Malaya, and Indonesia. Later, more advanced armaments were captured from colonial forces and received from external allies. Colonial wars in central and sub-Saharan Africa in the 1950's were characterized by insurgents' use of antiquated and in some cases primitive weaponry, deployed against European forces wielding automatic guns, explosives, and aircraft. In Guinea-Bissau, for example, the earliest guerrilla units organized by the Partido Africano pela Independencia da Guinea-Bissau e Cabo Verde (PAIGC), or the African Party for the Independence of Guinea-Bissau and Cape Verde, were armed with

traditional spears and shields, supplemented by stolen or smuggled handguns. Arms smuggling proliferated during the 1960's and increasingly included heavier weapons such as light artillery, mortars, and rocket launchers. In the 1970's superpower weapons deliveries to African fighters introduced greater weapons standardization. In Angola and Namibia, Soviet and Cuban military advisers oversaw combat operations, and in Indochina Soviet and Chinese advisers were sporadically present from the early 1950's until the early 1970's.

Anticolonial forces typically had greater difficulty obtaining ammunition for their varied weapons stock than in obtaining the guns themselves. As a result self-activating weapons such as explosives were particularly valued. Plastic explosives were preferred because of their stable state, easy detonation, and amenability to cutting and shaping to meet specific operational demands. Land mines were of similar utility because of their destructive capabilities against both personnel and vehicles. Lightweight shoulder-launched rockets were prized for their effectiveness against aircraft, particularly slow-moving helicopters.

Asian and African anticolonial forces' uniforms were seldom standardized but usually consisted of dark-colored cotton shirts, trousers, and rubber-soled shoes with cotton uppers, or sandals. Exceptionally, PAIGC forces in Guinea-Bissau in 1964 received shipments of lightweight khaki camouflage uniforms made of Chinese cotton sewn in Cuba. Colonial troops were universally better clothed and equipped that their anticolonial counterparts. Typical uniforms were European summer-weight issue, with mosquito netting, wide-brimmed cotton hats, and rubberized boots as appropriate for deployments into jungle, desert, or riverine environments. In Kenya white combatants blended into the local African population by staining their skin, wearing native dress, and adopting rebel practices such as oiling their skin with animal fat to avoid detection by tracking dogs. Elsewhere equipment innovations proved vital. In Malaya British paratroopers were regularly injured in treetop landings and in climbing to the jungle floor; new safety equipment was introduced to reduce the weight of jump kits, and in 1950 paratroopers were issued newly developed abseil, or rappelling, devices.

Conventional equipment and weaponry found new uses in colonial wars, and new weapons were introduced. British troops used explosives and mechanical saws to prepare landing "pads" for helicopters, because drooping rotors and steep descent angles made extensive foliage removal essential. Airborne delivery of high explosives and new small fragmentation bombs was common. Napalm, or jellied petroleum, bombs were widely used in Indochina, Malaya, and Guinea-Bissau to attack villages and storehouses and to clear deep jungle growth. Airplanes and helicopters sprayed toxic defoliant chemicals to destroy jungle cover and food cultivation sites. Airplanes dropped whistles and bottles known as "screamers" in conjunction with resettlement programs to intimidate civilians without causing physical harm.

In 1950 helicopters were introduced by Britain in Malaya for troop transport, reconnaissance, and liaison where mountainous terrain interrupted wireless communications. Despite functional problems caused by heat, humidity, and high-altitude operations, the helicopter's utility was fully demonstrated in Malaya. Helicopters were used by the British in Cyprus and Kenya, by the French in Indochina and Algeria, and by the Portuguese in Guinea-Bissau, Mozambique, and Angola. In each case only colonial troops deployed helicopters, guaranteeing their forces important mobility, reconnaissance, and tactical advantages.

MILITARY ORGANIZATION

The maintenance of political control over armed activists was critical for the coherent management of independence movements. In Malaya, the Malayan Communist Party (MCP) controlled its guerrilla organization, the Malayan Races Liberation Army (MRLA), through a political commissariat attached to guerrilla units. Commissars were charged with assuring the political allegiance of armed units and transmitting political directives from the Communist leadership. A commissariat system was also estab-lished by the PAIGC within its military wing in Guinea-Bissau. There, however, commissars conducted political instruction and oversaw non-operational problems such as health care, literacy, and complaints within armed units.

Escalating levels of armed conflict required insurgent forces to broaden their recruitment efforts and adopt more complex organizational schemes. In Cyprus, the armed struggle of the Ethnikí Orgánosis Kypriakoú Agónos (EOKA), or National Organization of Cypriot Fighters, began with a handful of armed operatives trained by a single commander. As EOKA's goal of unifying Cyprus with Greece gained popularity, it formed auxiliary nonmilitary groups including a youth organization and civilian support networks, which in turn yielded new recruits for the armed struggle that began in 1955. The EOKA guerrilla organization itself developed cells with differentiated tasks including terrorist attacks, patrol ambushes, and assassinations. In Algeria refugees and political exiles throughout North Africa provided military recruits for the Front de Libération Nationale (FLN) or National Liberation Front. As armed units proliferated in the mid-1950's commanders organized geographical divisions, known as *wilayāhs*, within the guerrilla organization. When propaganda and persuasion failed to produce sufficient manpower for the expanding armed struggle in Mozambique, operatives of the Frente de Libertação de Moçambique (Frelimo), or Mozambique Liberation Front, initiated conscription campaigns; women as well as men were given weapons training and inducted into Frelimo-controlled military units.

Auxiliary noncombat organizations could play key roles in the success of guerrilla operations. In Malaya insurgent forces depended upon material support from a civilian network, the Min Yuen, or People's Movement, which provided food, clothing, medical supplies, cash, and local intelligence. The Min Yuen had its own comprehensive district and branch organizational scheme and functioned under the direction of the Malayan Communist Party, which also controlled the guerrilla forces. As Min Yuen networks became the targets of British counterinsurgency operations in 1952, many Min Yuen operatives took up arms, but they remained organizationally distinct from the movement's military wing.

Cohesive command systems were also crucial to the success of anticolonial armed struggles. Lack of central organization by insurgent forces in Madagascar allowed French troops to completely rout 4,000 anticolonial fighters in 1947. In contrast, in Southeast Asia relatively small nationalist forces based on well-organized guerrilla units active against the Japanese during World War II were able to conduct successful military operations for several years against British and Dutch main-force troops in Malaya (1948-1960) and Indonesia (1945-1948). In Malaya the MRLA was divided into eight regional commands with companies of from 50 to 80 fighters as the basic operational units. Smaller guerrilla cells known as Blood and Steel Corps conducted specialized intelligence, terrorist, and demolition operations.

A similarly organized insurgent force was developed by Algerian partisans. The armed struggle originated with the small Special Organization, a radical paramilitary wing of the nationalist Mouvement pour le Triomphe des Libertés Démocratiques (MTLD), or the Movement for the Triumph of Democratic Liberties. From this beginning the anticolonial insurgent force grew after 1954 into tens of thousands of fighters, but it retained its small-scale organizational model. The *ferka*, a unit of about thirty-five active combatants, remained the principal operational unit. In Guinea-Bissau in the mid-1960's PAIGC guerrillas were grouped into units of twenty-six men each, including a commander and a commissar. These units, operating in pairs, were deployed by regional military commanders who coordinated the activities of each pairing with those of others in the same region.

Some insurgent organizations

developed larger armed units to confront colonial main-force troops. In response to the influx of thousands of Portuguese troops, the PAIGC in Guinea-Bissau reorganized its guerrilla fighters into main-force troops and created a system of regional "fronts," or interzonal command centers, to replace the small autonomous zones that had been previously occupied by its guerrillas in 1964. In Indochina in the late 1940's the Communist-led Viet Minh pursued a two-track program of force enlargement, building small guerrilla units in southern and central Vietnam and regular battalions in northern Vietnam.

The Mau Mau Rebellion (1952-1956) was organized against British rule in Kenya by the Kikuyu and Meru tribes, led by the Kikuyu Central Association (KCA). Mau Mau forces included two wings: large units operating under seven regional commands on

Hulton Archive/Getty Images

Men suspected to be Mau Mau rebels are retained in a barbed-wire compound in Kenya, circa 1955.

A Turkish army tank rolls through the Turkish section of Nicosia, Cyprus, in July, 1974, part of an invasion sparked by an abortive coup by supporters of union with Greece.

the coastal plan, and loosely organized bands of guerrillas operating in the forested foothills of Mount Kenya. Within one year of the arrival of British regular troops, the KCA launched a general offensive in the low country (1953). In a rare organizational innovation by colonial forces, the British military authorized the creation of special units of white Kenyan settlers known as pseudos, which included captured Mau Mau operatives and defectors. From them pseudos learned local techniques for tracking guerrilla fighters through the jungle, as well as the locations of rallying points and supply caches. The 1956 arrest of the elusive guerrilla commander Dedan Kimathi, which effectively terminated the Mau Mau Rebellion, was made by a pseudo unit. In general,

however, colonial military commanders used standard troop configurations against anticolonial forces, relying on superior numbers, weapons, and the administrative tools of the colonial administration to counter armed rebels.

DOCTRINE, STRATEGY, AND TACTICS

In the pursuit of independence and self-government, anticolonial movements cultivated the support of the general populations. The KCA-led Mau Mau Rebellion, for example, exploited long-standing resentment about the British seizure of land from local people and its distribution to white settlers.

Such popular support was not always forthcoming. In Guinea-Bissau the PAIGC was led by formally educated civil servants with few links to the peasantry, yet its armed forces required food, equipment, shelter, and recruits from peasants to fight the Portuguese. PAIGC leaders looked to the Chinese Civil War for doctrinal direction, embracing Mao Zedong's prescriptions for the political mobilization of the peasantry and a rural-based revolutionary struggle. They also borrowed Mao's concept of a "people's war," in which all nationalist classes banded together against colonial occupation, making colonial rule too costly for the metropolitan power. These Maoist perspectives also shaped the anticolonial wars in Indonesia, Indochina, Malaya, Cyprus, Algeria, and Kenya. Colonial wars in Africa were also shaped by a widespread belief in Uhuru, a concept that combined pan-African unity and the political independence of the whole continent from European colonialism.

Most colonial wars began with a political decision by nationalist leaders to confront colonial power with local violence. Small-scale, low-intensity violence was then directed against targets of symbolic importance. As the metropolitan power responded, isolated instances of violence expanded into an insurgency, with more and better-armed guerrilla units operating over wider areas and attacking larger targets, often of administrative or military importance to colonial authorities. The transition to widespread insurgency often required new tactics to supplement the armed struggle. In Cyprus a broad program of boycotts and passive resistance to British authority developed under EOKA guidance. In both Guinea-Bissau and Kenya, tribal customs, such as the Kikuyu tribe's complex oath rituals, were incorporated into the nationalist forces' recruitment process. In the early 1970's small arms were distributed to the civilian population as part of Frelimo's popular mobilization effort to counter the Portuguese military's distribution of weapons to white settlers.

In certain independence struggles guerrilla warfare escalated into the deployment of conventional main-force units. In Indochina, for example, the use of regular infantry divisions in northern Vietnam in the early 1950's dominated the Communists' antico-

lonial military strategy, culminating in a series of positional battles against French troops and the surrender of the French redoubt of Dien Bien Phu. Vietnamese guerrilla forces in southern and central Vietnam remained relatively quiescent in favor of the main-force battles. The situation was reversed in Mozambique and Angola, where, under the guidance of Soviet and Cuban military advisers, anticolonial military organizations developed some main-force units that confronted Portuguese regulars, but small-scale guerrilla operations remained the primary engine of the insurgent movements.

Many anticolonial military organizations sought tactical advantages over metropolitan forces by utilizing military base areas located outside colonial borders, and thus beyond the operational theater of the colony itself. FLN forces in Algeria received weapons, supplies, and reinforcements from cross-border camps in Tunisia from 1956 to 1957. Frelimo forces from Mozambique operated bases in Tanzania. Angola's Movimento Popular de Libertação de Angola (MPLA), or Popular Movement for the Liberation of Angola, received aid from the Congo. In Namibia from 1966 to 1990 the South West Africa People's Organization (SWAPO) operated its guerrilla organization largely from bases in southern Angola.

Elsewhere guerrilla organizations made tactical decisions to concentrate their operations in terrain that offered them operational advantages over colonial regular forces. In Cyprus EOKA guerrillas concentrated in the mountains on the western end of the island, where British troops' mobility was impaired. In Malaya MRLA guerrillas retreated into deep mountainous jungle territory to avoid British air reconnaissance and "sweep" operations. Upland Mau Mau guerrillas led by Dedan Kimathi eluded British troops for years.

Colonial powers' military planning was influenced by such strategic concepts as the "domino theory," which posited that a Communist "takeover" of one colony would cause the successive collapse of other pro-Western governments in Asia and Africa. Thus for Britain to protect its naval facilities in Singapore it had to extinguish the insurgency in Malaya. The domino metaphor retained its cachet into the

1960's: To retain its access to Kuwaiti oil, Britain committed troops against insurrectionist tribesmen in Yemen from 1958 to 1961.

Colonial powers saw as a strategic imperative the separation of guerrilla forces from their civilian sources of supply. In Malaya British commanders implemented a "food denial" campaign that combined strict food rationing, identity registration, and air strikes against crop cultivation. Similar tactics were used in Kenya. Mass arrests, interrogations, and trials of suspected sympathizers were conducted in Indonesia, Malaya, Kenya, Algeria, and Cyprus.

"Area domination" also segregated insurgents from their civilian sources of food, supplies, and recruits. Troops and aircraft were used to clear known guerrilla strongholds, and a police presence was established. The British Briggs Plan (1950) in Malaya followed this approach, forcing MRLA units from the south to the north of the peninsula. In Kenya British troops established guerrilla-free "exclusion zones," creating mile-wide clearings that prevented insurgents from crossing and a 50-mile-long ditch around the foothills of Mount Kenya. In Algeria from 1954 to 1956 the French used "quadrillage" tactics, developing fortified areas free of insurgents.

Another common segregation tactic was population resettlement. As part of the Briggs Plan in Malaya civilians were forcibly removed from their villages and located in access-controlled "strategic hamlets." Similar projects were undertaken in Indochina, Guinea-Bissau, Kenya, and Algeria.

The elimination of cross-border bases was a key colonial military objective. In 1958 French forces in Algeria built a 200-mile-long controlled barrier, known as the Morice line, along the border with Tunisia to interdict the flow of weapons and reinforcements. The Morice line included electrified fences, machine gun nests, and land mines; it was patrolled by 80,000 French troops including mechanized units, armored trains, paratroopers, helicopters, and mobile infantry. In 1975 South African troops concentrated in northern Namibia to attack SWAPO bases in southern Angola and continued these military incursions until an international settlement was reached in 1989.

In deploying the helicopter in counterinsurgency warfare, colonial forces developed new troop movement and air-support tactics. Small payloads, slow airspeeds, and exposed fuel tanks made helicopters vulnerable to ground attack, and rapid approach and departure protocols were developed for battlefield landings. The helicopter was, however, the vehicle of choice for rapid troop deployments in difficult terrain. In one 14-day operation in Malaya in 1953, 415 helicopter sorties moved 1,600 troops and their equipment on counterinsurgency patrols through high-altitude jungle that prevented rapid deployment by foot.

CONTEMPORARY SOURCES

Most insurgent movements made extensive use of radio broadcasts to deliver political instructions, propaganda, and military directives. Many of the publicized analyses of anticolonial military campaigns produced by their leaders were prepared for use by other combatants, and thus were broadcast rather than printed for general circulation. An important exception to this rule was the promulgation by Abel Djassi, a pseudonym for Amilcar Cabral, the political leader of the anticolonial movement in Guinea-Bissau, of "The Facts About Portugal's African Colonies" (1960), a pamphlet that outlined nationalists' complaints about Portuguese political and military policies in their colonies. Djassi drew attention to the brutality of Portuguese colonial forces, and appealed to the United Nations for military assistance in restraining Portuguese troops in Guinea-Bissau.

General Georgios Grivas (1898-1974), leader of the Cypriot insurgency against the British, published a treatise on small unit tactics entitled "Agon EOKA kai Antartiopolemos: Politikostratiotike" (1962; "General Grivas on Guerrilla Warfare," 1965), in which he extolled the psychological and political uses of terrorist attacks on colonial targets. He endorsed the tactic of drawing metropolitan forces into ambushes and unfamiliar terrain. He urged insurgents to wear down colonial forces' strength with hit-and-run attacks, which forced colonial forces to commit manpower to guarding potential targets. He encouraged military leaders to incorporate political activities into their tactical plans by coordinating guerrilla actions with protests and demonstrations by civilians.

Political leaders and other combatants have also published polemical tracts and memoirs on colonial warfare. Among polemicists, one of the most important was socialist lawyer and Indonesian nationalist Sutan Sjahrir (1909-1966), the principal negotiator with the Dutch (1946) and prime minister in the earliest Indonesian nationalist government (1945-1947). Sjahrir's tract entitled "Perdjuangan Kita" (1945; "Our Struggle," 1945), outlined the nationalists' political rationale for violent opposition to a return to Dutch colonial rule and the general strategy for postcolonial unification of the geographically dispersed islands of the Indonesian archipelago.

Participant memoirs of colonial warfare constitute a growing literature. Vietnamese Communist leader Hoàng Van Hoan's *Tsan Hai i Su* (1988; *A Drop in the Ocean: Hoàng Van Hoan's Revolutionary Reminiscences*, 1988) emphasizes the Communist Party's oversight and management of the anti-French conflict and reveals the importance of Chinese military assistance to the Communists' prosecution of the anti-French war. K'tut Tantri, a female resistance fighter and intelligence operative who fought against Japanese, British, and Dutch forces in Indonesia in the 1940's, described her experiences in her book *Revolt in Paradise: One Woman's Fight for Freedom in Indonesia* (1960).

Few journalistic accounts convey the full scope of anticolonial armed conflict, but the works of two exceptional reporters merit study. A French specialist on revolutionary warfare, Gerard Chaliand, published a firsthand account of PAIGC guerrillas' daily life and operational activities in *Lutte Armée en Afrique* (1969; *The Armed Struggle in Africa: With the Guerrillas in Portuguese Guinea*, 1969). The prolific journalist and former British intelligence officer Basil Davidson has produced a body of work detailing anticolonial warfare in Africa, including *In the Eye of the Storm: Angola's People* (1973), *The People's Cause: A History of Guerrillas in Africa* (1981), and *The Liberation of Guinea: Aspects of an African Revolution* (1969). The latter volume includes a foreword on revolutionary politics by PAIGC leader Amilcar Cabral, as well as detailed statements on political and military tactics by Cabral and by the Chinese-trained PAIGC commander in northern Guinea-Bissau, Osvaldo Vieira.

BOOKS AND ARTICLES

Ansprenger, Franz. *The Dissolution of the Colonial Empires*. London: Routledge and Kegan Paul, 1989.

Chabal, Patrick, et al. *A History of Postcolonial Lusophone Africa*. Bloomington: Indiana University Press, 2002.

Clayton, Anthony. *Frontiersmen: Warfare in Africa Since 1950*. London: UCL Press, 1999.

DeFronzo, James. "The Vietnamese Revolution." In *Revolutions and Revolutionary Movements*. 3d ed. Boulder, Colo.: Westview Press, 2007.

Foran, John. "The Closest Cousins: The Great Anti-Colonial Revolutions." In *Taking Power: On the Origins of Third World Revolutions*. New York: Cambridge University Press, 2005.

Gander, Terry. *Guerrilla Warfare Weapons: The Modern Underground Fighters' Armory*. New York: Sterling, 1990.

Goodwin, Jeff. *No Other Way Out: States and Revolutionary Movements, 1945-1991*. New York: Cambridge University Press, 2001.

Horne, Alistair. *A Savage War of Peace: Algeria, 1954-1962*. Rev. ed. New York: Viking Penguin, 1987.

Lawrence, Mark Atwood, and Fredrik Logevall, eds. *The First Vietnam War: Colonial Conflict and Cold War Crisis*. Cambridge, Mass.: Harvard University Press, 2007.

Lord, Cliff, and David Birtles. *The Armed Forces of Aden, 1839-1967*. London: Helion, 2000.

Meredith, Martin. *The Fate of Africa: A History of Fifty Years of Independence*. New York: Public Affairs, 2005.

Peluso, Nancy Lee. *Rich Forests, Poor People: Resource Control and Resistance in Java*. Berkeley: University California Press, 1992.

Postgate, Malcolm. *Operation Firedog: Air Support in the Malayan Emergency, 1948-1960*. London: H.M.S.O., 1992.

Robie, David. *Blood on Their Banner: Nationalist Struggles in the South Pacific*. London: Zed Press, 1989.

Shrader, Charles R. *The First Helicopter War: Logistics and Mobility in Algeria, 1954-1962*. Westport, Conn.: Praeger, 1999.

FILMS AND OTHER MEDIA

The Battle of Algiers. Feature film. Magna, 1966.

Le Crabe-tambour. Feature film. AMLF, 1977.

French Foreign Legion. Documentary. History Channel, 1998.

Guns at Batasi. Feature film. Twentieth Century-Fox, 1964.

Simba. Feature film. Group Film Productions Limited, 1955.

Laura M. Calkins

WARFARE IN VIETNAM

Dates: 1945-1975

POLITICAL CONSIDERATIONS

As the conclusion of World War II liberated Southeast Asia from Japanese domination, Indochinese Communist Party leader Ho Chi Minh (1890-1969) swiftly moved ahead with his political goal of a unified and independent Vietnam, proclaiming a Democratic Republic of Vietnam on September 2, 1945. At the same time, however, France began reasserting its colonial rule in Indochina. Ho, previously allied with the United States—especially through its Office of Strategic Services (OSS), the forerunner of the Central Intelligence Agency (CIA), against the Japanese, looked for support in his goal from the United States.

However, with a Cold War developing between the United States and the Soviet Union, U.S. president Harry S. Truman (1884-1972) chose not to risk a break with France and adopted a policy of what has been called "guarded neutrality." The United States accepted France's return to Indochina but required that aid to France not be used in Vietnam. As war in Korea threatened in 1950, the United States recognized the French-supported government of Emperor Bao Dai (1913-1997), the last emperor of the Nguyen Dynasty, and made available both economic aid and military supplies.

The Geneva Conference (1954), which ended the war between France and Ho's Viet Minh, called for a partition of Indochina into four countries—North Vietnam, South Vietnam, Laos, and Cambodia—and for an election no later than 1956 to unify the two Vietnams. The United States, however, assumed political control of South Vietnam from the French in 1955, when the American choice for president, Ngo Dinh Diem (1901-1963), replaced Bao Dai. Diem proclaimed the Republic of Vietnam, and both he and the United States refused to be bound by the call for a reunification election, knowing that the popular Ho Chi Minh would win.

North Vietnam, determined to conquer the South, had the political, financial, and technological support of the Soviet Union and China. The South Vietnamese government sought, with the support of the United States, to maintain its rule in the South. The United States government feared a so-called "domino effect"; if South Vietnam fell to communism, it reasoned, so would other nations in Asia, including India. Both North and South Vietnam were now markers in the Cold War conflict between the three superpowers—the United States, the Soviet Union, and China. During its long struggle in Vietnam, the United States remained hampered by Cold War concerns and the desire to avoid pushing either of the other superpowers into active engagement in the fighting.

MILITARY ACHIEVEMENT

The crushing defeat of the French at Dien Bien Phu in northern Vietnam in 1954 essentially brought the First Indochina War (1946-1954) to an end. However, Ho Chi Minh controlled only the northern half of Vietnam, and although the French had been forced out, the Americans had replaced them. Now the North Vietnamese turned their attention to undermining the South Vietnamese government and extracting such a high price for American involvement that the United States would withdraw.

The date often given for the beginning of the Second Indochina War, or what Americans call the Vietnam War, is 1956, the year in which the United States and Diem rejected the Geneva-mandated reunification elections. In 1959, North Vietnam's Central Executive Committee formally changed the country's approach from political to armed struggle. Remnants of the Viet Minh who had stayed in the South (the Viet Cong) were activated by the North Vietnamese Politburo.

VIETNAM CONFLICT, 1954-1975

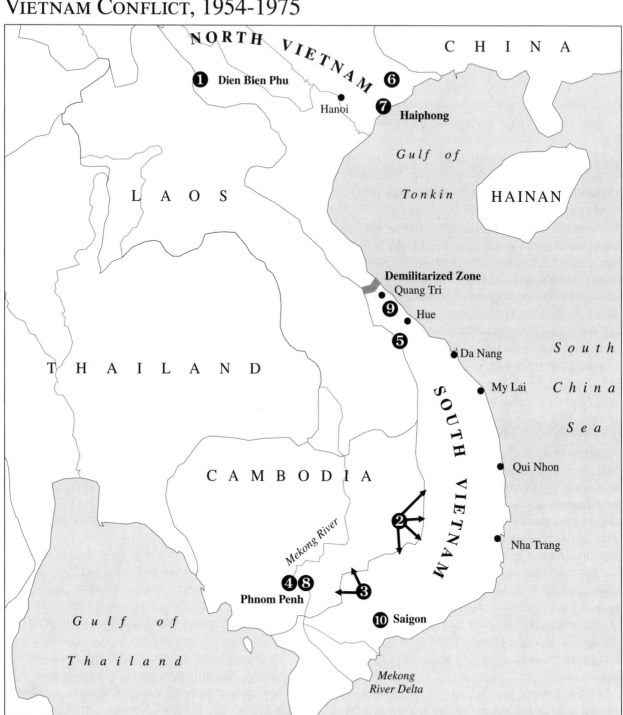

(1) France falls, 1954. (2) Tet Offensive, January, 1968. (3) Cambodian invasion, April-May, 1970. (4) Sihanouk falls, April, 1970. (5) Laotian incursion, February, 1971. (6) Areas of U.S. bombing, 1972. (7) Mining of Haiphong Harbor, May, 1972. (8) Lon Nol falls, April, 1975. (9) North Vietnamese offensive, spring, 1975. (10) South Vietnam surrenders, April 30, 1975.

The Viet Cong specialized in terrorist warfare against U.S. soldiers and South Vietnamese loyal to the Diem government. Their largest campaign was the Tet Offensive of 1968, which ended in the almost complete destruction of the Viet Cong infrastructure and the end of the Viet Cong as a significant military threat. From that point on, the war to unify the country was carried out primarily by traditionally organized North Vietnamese military forces.

U.S. president Richard M. Nixon (1913-1994), taking office in 1969, implemented the policy of Vietnamization, whereby the war effort would be turned over gradually to the South Vietnamese. The final American fighting forces withdrew from Vietnam in late March, 1973, following a January 27 peace agreement. The South Vietnamese were given some breathing room by many American victories, including the decimation of the Viet Cong forces and the disruption of Communist staging areas and transportation routes in Cambodia by means of a 1969 bombing (Operation Menu) and a 1970 invasion. Nonetheless, Saigon eventually fell, on April 30, 1975.

WEAPONS, UNIFORMS, AND ARMOR

The French army in the First Indochina War was highly mechanized and had the support of such artillery pieces as 105-millimeter howitzers, 75-millimeter recoilless rifles, and heavy mortars. Quad-50 machine guns, consisting of four .50-caliber machine guns mounted together, were capable of great destruction. France also had fighters, fighter-bombers, and bombers, but only about one hundred planes all together. The Viet Minh began its military efforts against the French with a ragtag collection of arms given them by the United States during World War II or captured from the French. Land mines proved useful against the French, as they would later against the Americans.

As the Korean War (1950-1953) neared its end, arms and other equipment began to flow into North Vietnam from the Soviets and Chinese. Russian heavy-duty Molotova trucks proved invaluable for transporting arms and supplies. Russia provided rifles, machine guns, and a variety of heavier weapons, including 120-millimeter mortars, recoilless cannons, and bazookas.

Effective additions to Viet Minh uniforms were two large wire-mesh disks, one over the helmet, the other hanging from the back. The wire mesh was filled with foliage to hide the troops from both aerial and ground observation.

In the Second Indochina War, or the Vietnam War, the most powerful aerial weapon for the United States was the Air Force B-52 Stratofortress strategic bomber, modified to carry thirty tons of conventional bombs and with a range of 7,500 miles. Leading fighter-bombers were the Air Force F-105 Thunderchief and the Navy and Marine Corps A-4 Skyhawk. The top fighter plane was the F-4 Phantom, flown by the Air Force, Navy, and Marines. Napalm, a jellied gasoline, was widely employed by the United States and South Vietnam in aerial bombs. The South Vietnamese Air Force, trained and supplied by the U.S., flew F-5 Freedom Fighters and A-37 Dragonfly fighter-bombers.

The North Vietnamese essentially had no air force until the mid-1960's when China and the Soviet Union started supplying the North with MiG-15, MiG-17, MiG-19, and MiG-21 jet fighters.

The United States relied heavily on helicopters. The Huey utility helicopter (UH-1) was used to transport troops and supplies, evacuate wounded, and even attack the enemy when modified with heavy armaments. The primary attack helicopter was the AH-1 Cobra gunship, armed with a grenade launcher, machine guns, and rockets.

The U.S. Navy's Seventh Fleet deployed attack carrier strike forces consisting of carriers, cruisers, destroyers, and other vessels. American forces also had access to amphibious ships, swift inland boats to patrol rivers, and air-cushioned hovercraft (PACVs) and airboats for marshy areas.

U.S. artillery included 105-millimeter towed artillery, 105-millimeter and 155-millimeter self-propelled howitzers, 175-millimeter guns, and 8-inch howitzers. The portable, shoulder-fired M72 light antitank weapon (LAW) was used by Americans and South Vietnamese against tanks and bunkers. North Vietnam began to use medium and heavy artillery in the South during the 1970's. Their artillery pieces ultimately included 76-millimeter, 85-millimeter, 100-millimeter, 122-millimeter, and 130-millimeter guns and howitzers.

Communist forces in the South had only machine guns and rifles to use against planes early in the war but near the end had Soviet SA-7 antiaircraft missiles and Soviet SA-2 surface-to-air missiles (SAMs), the latter able to reach 85,000 feet. Another SAM, the Soviet SA-7, could be shoulder-fired.

Americans switched in 1967 from the heavy M-14 rifle to the lighter and shorter M-16, which used a smaller, 5.56-millimeter cartridge and could be fired either one shot at a time or fully automatically. The United States also armed the South Vietnamese with

the new rifle. The most effective sniper weapon was a carefully modified version of the M-14, the M-14 National Match rifle (M-14NM) with the Limited War Laboratory's adjustable ranging telescope (ART), possessing a range of more than 1,000 yards. North Vietnamese and Viet Cong used the Soviet AK-47 rifle, which was similar to the M-16.

Less conventional weapons included mines and booby traps. The United States and its allies used the antipersonnel Claymore mine, which could be detonated at a distance by closing an electrical circuit, and also did extensive mining from the air. The Viet Cong made widespread use of booby traps, ranging from sharpened bamboo stakes called pungi stakes to a variety of mines including the Bouncing Betty, which would bounce into the air when triggered and explode around waist height.

Military uniforms of generally standard types were worn by the regular forces. Although Viet Cong are associated with the black pajamas and sandals they sometimes wore in combat, they often mingled during the day with other South Vietnamese, wearing no uniform or other clothing that would set them apart.

Despite the often inhospitable terrain, the United States and South Vietnamese troops used tanks throughout the war, including the diesel-powered M48A3 Patton tank and the M42 Duster tank. North Vietnamese, beginning in 1968, utilized Soviet-made T-34, T-54, and T-59 medium tanks as well as PT-76 amphibious tanks.

The United States made wide use of armored personnel carriers (APCs), especially the M-113 APC. The APCs were often altered to carry weapons and other cargo as well as troops, and, with the addition of gun shields, extra armor, and machine guns, served as attack vehicles.

NARA

U.S. F-105 Thunderchiefs drop bombs over Vietnam in 1966.

TURNING POINTS

1945	As World War II concludes, Indochinese Communist Party leader Ho Chi Minh proclaims a Democratic Republic of Vietnam, and France begins reasserting its colonial rule in Indochina.
1954	The Geneva Conference calls for a partition of Indochina into four countries—North Vietnam, South Vietnam, Laos, and Cambodia—and for an election within two years to unify the two Vietnams.
1955	The United States assumes political control of South Vietnam from the French.
1956	The United States and the U.S.-backed South Vietnamese president, Ngo Dinh Diem, reject the Geneva-mandated reunification elections, knowing that the popular Ho Chi Minh would win.
1959	North Vietnam begins armed struggle against U.S. soldiers and South Vietnamese loyal to the Diem government.
June, 1961	Washington conferences lead to the assignment of training specialists and increased military funding for the South Vietnamese army.
Aug. 5, 1964	Tonkin Gulf Resolution by the U.S. Congress authorizes President Lyndon Johnson to "take all necessary measures . . . to prevent further aggression" by North Vietnam.
Mar. 2, 1965	Beginning of systematic U.S. bombing campaign (Operation Rolling Thunder) of North Vietnam.
1968	North Vietnamese and Viet Cong launch the Tet Offensive, which, although unsuccessful, contradicted U.S. reports that a decisive end to the war was near at hand.
1969	U.S. President Richard Nixon institutes "Vietnamization" policy designed to transfer military responsibilities gradually to the South Vietnamese government.
May-June, 1970	U.S. invasion of Cambodia in pursuit of North Vietnamese troops.
1973	The final American fighting forces withdraw from Vietnam in late March, following a January 27 peace agreement.
1975	Saigon finally falls to the North Vietnamese forces, and Vietnam is united under Communist rule.

MILITARY ORGANIZATION

Both the French and Communist forces used traditional patterns of organization such as battalions, regiments, and divisions. However, Viet Minh general Vo Nguyen Giap (born 1911) gave his commanders considerable flexibility regarding strategy and tactics, thus permitting quick decision-making. French control remained more centralized along World War II models to coordinate armor, infantry, airpower, and parachute drops.

During the Second Indochina War, or Vietnam War, American decision making was fragmented, split along various vectors that included the president of the United States as commander in chief, the secretary of defense, the joint chiefs of staff, and the commander in chief of the Pacific Command (CINCPAC), the latter stationed in Honolulu and responsible for prosecution of the war.

The United States/Vietnam-based command and control entity after 1962 was MACV (U.S. Military Assistance Command Vietnam). As a "subordinate unified command," MACV was required to seek approval from the Honolulu-based CINCPAC headquarters. Virtually all military control for the North Vietnamese was unified under Giap, who was a member of the ruling Politburo, minister of defense, and commander in chief of the armed forces. The United States divided South Vietnam into four tactical zones numbered, from north to south, I, II, III, and IV Corps. Air Force operations, except for Strategic Air Command B-52 actions, were carried out by the Seventh Air Force, with Naval operations conducted by the Seventh Fleet, both ultimately under CINCPAC.

The basic units of the U.S. Army were the squad, platoon, company, battalion, brigade, division, and corps, with minor differences in the Artillery and

Marine Corps. Below the Seventh Air Force in Vietnam was the 834th Air Division, divided into wings, squadrons, and flights. A flight included about five aircraft. Marine and Naval air units were similarly organized.

The South Vietnamese Armed Forces were organized largely in the image of the United States but under the South Vietnam National Armed Forces (SVNAF) Joint General Staff, which increasingly took direction from MACV. The South Vietnamese Regional Forces and Popular Forces, both civilian militias, also were under the Joint General Staff. The Civilian Irregular Defense Groups (CIDGs), primarily Montagnards, were trained and usually led by U.S. Army Special Forces.

The North Vietnamese and Viet Cong were organized generally along the same lines as the U.S. forces, starting with divisions but including regiments rather than brigades. The Viet Cong had a party secretary and various supply, social welfare, and propaganda units. After Tet, remaining Viet Cong were organized into cadres under North Vietnamese control.

DOCTRINE, STRATEGY, AND TACTICS

The primary doctrines that drove the First and Second Indochina Wars were colonialism, nationalism, communism, and democracy. At the conclusion of World War II, France sought to reestablish its colonial rule over Indochina. Ho Chi Minh, widely seen within his country and by the Americans as more of a nationalist than a communist, a perception the validity of which continues to be debated, sought to assert his vision of a unified and independent Vietnam. Ho's triumph over the French in 1954 removed one colonial ruler but failed to unite all of Vietnam.

The Second Indochina War, or the Vietnam War, achieved Ho's nationalist goal of unifying all of Vietnam, but as a Communist nation. The United States throughout adopted the moral high ground of eschewing colonial domination while attempting to help South Vietnam secure permanent freedom as a democratic state, thus containing the spread of communism. These basic tenants led, affected by a variety of misconceptions, to the strategies and tactics adopted by the various warring parties.

The French tried to fight a war of attrition, believing they could wear down the Viet Minh. The French implemented this strategy by constructing hundreds of forts and pillboxes in northern Vietnam, which the Viet Minh simply went around whenever they chose. The French finally decided to adopt a more active strategy, which included cutting supply lines and luring the enemy into face-to-face battles. In the climactic manifestation of this policy, the French began in November, 1953, to establish a "mooring point" for French troops in a valley in northwestern Vietnam near the village of Dien Bien Phu. There the French established a defense perimeter, built two landing strips, and sent out patrols to cut supply lines to the enemy forces in Laos and engage the enemy in direct combat. Giap used Russian-supplied trucks and large numbers of construction workers to enlarge a winding mountain road to permit transportation of heavy artillery into the surrounding mountains and began his assault on March 13, 1954. The battle, and effectively the war, ended on May 7.

The United States, during its Vietnam War, fused a war of attrition with both a limited war to contain communism and a misjudgment that the Viet Cong were engaged in an insurgency that could be opposed with counterinsurgency tactics. Because the United States never fully recognized that North Vietnam was the true enemy and that the Viet Cong were an arm of the North, its primary goals, which included supporting the South Vietnamese government and rooting out insurgent elements in the South, at best addressed only parts of the problem.

President Lyndon B. Johnson (1908-1973), given a free hand by the Gulf of Tonkin resolution (1964), began a steady buildup of American forces in Vietnam that numbered about 550,000 by 1968. The United States had thus abandoned its earlier advisory role and taken over primary direction and prosecution of the war.

To weaken the enemy's resolve, the United States bombed the North in a campaign called Operation Rolling Thunder that lasted from 1965 until 1968. The bombing stopped in 1968 to encourage peace discussions but resumed in 1972 to push the Communists toward serious negotiations. The United States also steadily bombed the Ho Chi Minh Trail in fruitless efforts to halt infiltration of men and materials into the South.

Airpower never achieved the major goals the United States set for it, but it did help win many battles in the South with bombing and close support for ground operations. Helicopters proved extremely effective in transporting men and supplies and evacuating the wounded. In addition, the bombing of Cambodia in 1969 and 1970 bought time for the South Vietnamese armed forces to try to improve their war capabilities.

On the ground, American forces attempted to en-gage the enemy in direct combat operations, which first occurred in the fall of 1965 in the Ia Drang Valley. Like most such encounters, the short-term effect was a victory for the Americans.

Counterinsurgency tactics included such pacification efforts as educational, medical, and economic-development programs and search-and-destroy operations such as Cedar Falls (1967) and Junction City (1967) to deny the Viet Cong access to the countryside and its people. The hammer-and-anvil tactic caught Viet Cong between forces already in place (the anvil) and forces sweeping in from the sides (the hammer). These operations cleared the land for a time, but the Viet Cong inevitably moved back in.

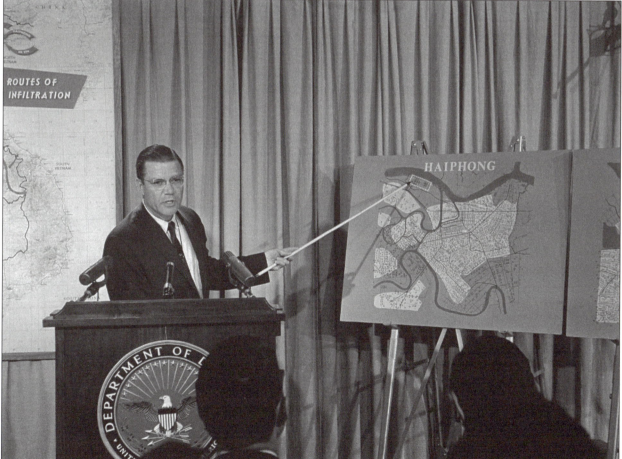

AP/Wide World Photos

U.S. Secretary of Defense Robert S. McNamara discussing strikes on North Vietnam during a 1966 Pentagon news conference.

A Vietnamese and a U.S. paratrooper drop from a helicopter during a battle with the Viet Cong. Helicopters were the key transport vehicles during the war.

hamlets, North Vietnamese and Viet Cong launched attacks on January 31, during the Vietnamese Tet holiday. In all locations, the Communist forces were ultimately driven back. Although the Viet Cong suffered massive losses and ceased to be a major player in the war, Americans were unaware of the magnitude of their defeat. Instead, seeing attacks all across South Vietnam convinced Americans that the war was going badly. In 1969 President Nixon instituted a new strategy called Vietnamization, which meant getting the United States out of the war and turning the fighting over to the South Vietnamese.

With a plan to capture as much territory as possible before a final peace agreement, the North Vietnamese army launched attacks against provincial and district capitals throughout much of South Vietnam in the spring of 1972. Like Tet, the offensive was a military defeat for the North but a psychological victory, demonstrating how dependent the South Vietnamese were on U.S. support.

By 1975 the North Vietnamese army had twice as many tanks as did the South Vietnamese, and the more than 25,000 North Vietnamese troops in the Central Highlands were easily reinforced from the North. The U.S. failure to recognize North Vietnam as the central enemy had led to peace with the supply lines along the Ho Chi Minh Trail still functioning and the war production effort in the North unimpeded after 1973. The strategic definition of the war as counterinsurgency and the principle of containment, along with fear that movement of U.S. forces into the North might trigger a war between superpowers, meant there would be no invasion by U.S. forces. The United States had by

As a guerrilla force, the Viet Cong used such tactics as mines and booby traps with deadly effectiveness. They dug elaborate tunnel complexes that served as supply depots, hiding areas for troops, even field hospitals.

The Tet Offensive of 1968 was the result of the change in strategy on the part of the North Vietnamese to a wider armed struggle. In cities, towns, and neither force nor negotiation been able to drive the Communists out of the South. The United States had the military might but not the strategy, and therefore not the tactics, to defeat the enemy.

With the expectation that the March, 1975, offensive would be both a prelude to a final triumph the following year and a test to see whether the United States would intervene, the North began its military push on March 11 with a victory at Ban Me Thuot in the Central Highlands. South Vietnamese president Nguyen Van Thieu (born 1923) decided to abandon the Central Highlands, and the North Vietnamese drove to the sea, cutting South Vietnam in half. The northern provinces fell, Thieu resigned on April 21, and on April 30, the new president, General Duong Van Minh (born 1916), surrendered.

CONTEMPORARY SOURCES

Historians who expressed insights during the Indochina Wars included Joseph Buttinger, author of *The Smaller Dragon: A Political History of Vietnam* (1958) and *Vietnam: A Dragon Embattled* (1967); and George Coedès, author of *Histoire ancienne des états hindouisés d'Extrome-Orient* (1944; *The Indianized States of South-east Asia*, 1968). French colonialism was analyzed in John T. McAlister's *Vietnam: The Origins of Revolution, 1885-1946* (1968) and David G. Marr's *Vietnamese Anticolonialism, 1885-1925* (1971).

Bernard Fall's important *Street Without Joy: Indochina at War, 1946-1954*, first published in 1961, was followed by a string of other important critiques of French and American policy in Vietnam: *The Two Viet-Nams: A Political and Military Analysis* (1963), *Viet-Nam Witness, 1953-1966* (1966), and *Hell in a Very Small Place: The Siege of Dien Bien Phu* (1967).

The Pentagon Papers (1971), including official statements and Defense Department memos, depicts, in some 7,000 pages written between 1967 and 1969, the actions and policies of the United States in Vietnam starting in 1945.

Americans would have better understood the enemy by examining a variety of books published by North Vietnamese, including General Vo Nguyen Giap, commander of the People's Army of Vietnam (1946-1972). He published a book on the battle that earned him lasting fame, *Dien Bien Phu* (1959; *Dien Bien Phu*, 1962).

BOOKS AND ARTICLES

Arnold, James R. *Tet Offensive, 1968: Turning Point in Vietnam*. Botley, Oxford, England: Osprey, 1990. Reprint. Westport, Conn.: Praeger, 2005.

Cash, John A. *Seven Firefights in Vietnam*. New York: Bantam, 1993.

Dunn, Peter M. *The First Vietnam War*. New York: St. Martin's Press, 1985.

Ha, Mai Viet. *Steel and Blood: South Vietnamese Armor and the War for Southeast Asia*. Annapolis, Md.: Naval Institute Press, 2008.

Harder, Robert O. *Flying from the Black Hole: The B-52 Bombardiers of Vietnam*. Annapolis, Md.: Naval Institute Press, 2009.

Herring, George C. *America's Longest War: The United States and Vietnam, 1950-1975*. New York: Alfred A. Knopf, 1986.

Karnow, Stanley. *Vietnam: A History*. 2d rev. ed. New York: Penguin, 1997.

Lawrence, Mark Atwood, and Fredrik Logevall, eds. *The First Vietnam War: Colonial Conflict and Cold War Crisis*. Cambridge, Mass.: Harvard University Press, 2007.

Moore, Harold G., and Joseph L. Galloway. *We Were Soldiers Once . . . and Young: Ia Drang, the Battle That Changed the War in Vietnam*. New York: Random House, 1992.

Moyar, Mark. *Triumph Forsaken: The Vietnam War, 1954-1965*. New York: Cambridge University Press, 2006.

Neville, Peter. *Britain in Vietnam: Prelude to Disaster, 1945-6*. New York: Routledge, 2007.

Olson, James Stuart, and Randy Robert. *Where the Domino Fell: America and Vietnam, 1945-1995*. Rev. 5th ed. Malden, Mass.: Blackwell, 2008.

Palmer, Dave Richard. *Summons of the Trumpet: A History of the Vietnam War from a Military Man's Viewpoint*. San Rafael, Calif.: Presidio Press, 1978.

Summers, Harry G., Jr. *On Strategy: A Critical Analysis of the Vietnam War*. Novato, Calif.: Presidio Press, 1995.

Van Staaveren, Jacob. *The United States Air Force in Southeast Asia: Interdiction in Southern Laos, 1960-1968*. Washington, D.C.: Center for Air Force History, 1993.

Wiest, Andrew, ed. *Rolling Thunder in a Gentle Land: The Vietnam War Revisited*. Botley, Oxford, England: Osprey, 2006.

Windrow, Martin. *The Last Valley: Dien Bien Phu and the French Defeat in Vietnam*. Cambridge, Mass.: Da Capo Press, 2004.

FILMS AND OTHER MEDIA

Apocalypse Now. Feature film. United Artists, 1979.

The Battle of Dien Bien Phu. Docudrama. , 1992.

Born on the Fourth of July. Feature film. Universal, 1989.

Chopper Wars. Documentary. Video Treasures, 1987.

The Deer Hunter. Feature film. EMI/Universal, 1978.

The Fog of War. Documentary. Sony Pictures Classics, 2003.

Full Metal Jacket. Feature film. Natant, 1987.

The Green Berets. Feature film. Warner Bros.-Seven Arts, 1968.

Hamburger Hill. Feature film. RKO Pictures, 1987.

Hearts and Minds. Documentary. Rainbow Pictures, 1974.

Jacob's Ladder. Feature film. TriStar, 1990.

Indochine. Feature film. Sony/Roissy, 1992.

Platoon. Feature film. Hemdale Film, 1986.

Ulzana's Raid. Feature film. Universal, 1972.

Vietnam: A Television History. Documentary. Public Broadcasting Service, 1983.

The War at Home. Feature film. Touchstone Pictures, 1996.

We Were Soldiers. Feature film. Icon Entertainment, 2002.

Winter Soldier. Documentary. Winterfilm Collective, 1972.

Edward J. Rielly

WARFARE IN AFGHANISTAN
THE SOVIET-AFGHAN CONFLICT
Dates: 1979-1989

POLITICAL CONSIDERATIONS

The war in Afghanistan was the last major conflict of the twentieth century involving a superpower, the Soviet Union, and a regional actor, Afghanistan. The Soviet invasion of Afghanistan in 1979 was precipitated by a premeditated series of events that took place in Kabul and were rooted in the milieu of domestic Afghan politics. In the preceding years, following the coup d'état that had toppled President Mohammed Khan Daoud, the Khalq faction within the People's Democratic Party of Afghanistan (PDPA) seized power and began implementing sweeping reforms that included eradicating illiteracy, eliminating women's dowries, and changing the land tenure system, which alienated the traditional, conservative rural society where 90 percent of the population resided. The PDPA's reform program was hugely unpopular in the countryside.

A spontaneous rural insurgency followed, which the government was unable to control. Between July, 1978, and the autumn of 1979, the Afghan government lost two-thirds of Afghanistan. Complicating the situation was the murder of Soviet citizens in February, 1979, by angry mobs in Herāt. Then in March, 1979, the accession of Hafizullah Amin, also of the Khalq faction, to the post of prime minister marked a steady disintegration in the countryside that culminated in the September assassination of President Nur Mohammed Taraki by bodyguards of Amin, who then assumed the presidency. Amin was killed three months later, shortly after the invasion of the Soviet forces in December, and replaced by Barbak Karmal.

Two patterns emerged from the 1979 Soviet invasion. The first was the Soviets' lack of preparedness to fight, and the second was that their decision to invade was improvised and poorly conceived. Instead of gaining support for the moderate regime, the Soviets encountered a mounting backlash, as thousands of government soldiers and their officers defected to the Islamic guerrillas, or the Mujahideen, as they called themselves, seizing government outposts and their arsenals of weapons and ammunition.

The turning point in the Soviet invasion of Afghanistan came in 1986, when the Mujahideen began to receive large amounts of weapons and technical support through covert programs conducted by the U.S. Central Intelligence Agency (CIA). Mujahideen acquired Stinger surface-to-air missiles, 120-millimeter mortars, and communications equipment that allowed for the coordination of attacks on a broad scale.

MILITARY ACHIEVEMENT

The military conflict in Afghanistan can be characterized as static, with the Soviets retaining control of the cities and towns and the transportation infrastructure, while the Mujahideen retained control of the countryside.

The Soviets established garrisons at strategic points, such as cities, villages, and valleys, from which the army could carry out offensives. Spetsnaz (special forces) units were dispatched into the Mujahideen-controlled countryside to gather intelligence, ambush Mujahideen guerrilla units, and create confusion and chaos among the populace. This tactic effectively divided the Afghan resistance and rendered the Mujahideen incapable of challenging the Soviet army. Even with the introduction of covert military aid from the CIA, the Mujahideen were incapable of sustaining prolonged attacks on Soviet positions.

TURNING POINTS

Apr. 27, 1978	Military officers sympathetic to the People's Democratic Party of Afghanistan (PDPA) overthrow President Mohammed Daoud, who is killed during a *coup d'état*.
Apr. 30, 1978	Nur Mohammad Turaki is appointed Chairman of the Revolutionary Government and Prime Minister.
Dec. 5, 1978	While in Moscow Nur Mohammad Turaki signs a treaty aligning Kabul with Moscow and setting the stage for later Soviet involvement in Afghanistan.
Dec. 27, 1979	Soviet forces enter Afghanistan ostensibly to overthrow the government of Prime Minister Hafizullah Amin and install a puppet government loyal to Moscow.
Jan. 9, 1980	President Babrak Karmal gives a press conference justifying Soviet intervention in Afghanistan.
Jan. 23, 1980	U.S. president Jimmy Carter declares that the United States will consider any threat against the Persian Gulf a threat against its vital interests and will react, if necessary, with military force.
Mar., 1981	Soviets launch their first well-planned offensive in Afghanistan.
Aug. 20, 1985	The Soviet-Afghan troops launch their second offensive of 1985.
July 28, 1986	Soviet leader Mikhail Gorbachev announces a limited withdrawal of Soviet troops from Afghanistan.
Autumn, 1986	Stinger missiles are first used by the Mujahideen to counter the Soviets' overwhelming air superiority.
Feb., 1989	The Afghan Interim Government (AIG) is established, and the Soviet Union completes its withdrawal from Afghanistan.
Oct., 1989	Soviet foreign minister Edvard Shevardnadze publicly condemns the 1979 Soviet invasion of Afghanistan.

WEAPONS, UNIFORMS, AND ARMOR

The Soviet army was ill-equipped for combat in Afghanistan. Although the Soviets had overwhelming military superiority, they were ill-suited for anti-insurgent warfare. In the air, the Soviets used MiG-23's and SU-24 fighter-bombers for carpet bombing and refined the use of the MI-24 helicopter gunship to support motorized rifle units. Troops were issued AK-47's and AK-74's, which were of little use against an invisible enemy.

Uniforms were bulky, clumsy, camouflage overalls. Soldiers were issued crudely made uniforms and greatcoats of khaki, grey, or brown. They carried no body armor but wore vintage 1940's-style steel helmets.

At the onset of the war in Afghanistan the Mujahideen used whatever weapons were available: AK-47's looted from police posts, British-style .303 Enfields, FN-FALS supplied by Pakistan, and leftovers from the colonial wars. Soon thereafter frontline units began to carry DShK machine guns, 82-millimeter mortars, grenade launchers, AK-47's, and AK-74's either looted or bought from government soldiers and garrisons. Then in 1985, the United States began to funnel SAM-7 surface-to-air missiles to the Mujahideen units. Unlike their Soviet counterparts, the Mujahideen boasted no uniform. They wore their traditional tunics and blended into the civilian population.

MILITARY ORGANIZATION

The Soviet military was a modern, centralized military structure, but in order to counter the resistance they encountered, the Soviets continually introduced changes in the size, equipment, and organizational structure of their forces. The occupational forces consisted of three motorized rifle divisions, two independent rifle brigades, one airborne division, one independent air brigade, and three Spetsnaz brigades. These Soviet units were deployed carrying their full equipment, including antitank weaponry and antiaircraft batteries, both of which were poorly geared toward anti-insurgency warfare.

Mujahideen units were organized along ethnic or tribal lines, which dictated the composition of the guerrilla unit. Often the Mujahideen operated in small mobile units of ten to twenty men that lacked an overall command structure. Overall, the Mujahideen were a conglomeration of some three hundred guerrilla units operating in all twenty-eight provinces of Afghanistan.

Although some of the units were affiliated with political parties, the majority were led by autonomous local commanders. The guerrilla units themselves were composed of untrained, disorganized local recruits who were organized by *qawm*, or tribe, and thus limited to hit-and-run operations.

DOCTRINE, STRATEGY, AND TACTICS

The so-called Brezhnev Doctrine undergirded the Soviet invasion of Afghanistan, during which aiding "democratic" forces consolidated revolutionary gains threatened by "foreign supported subversion." The Soviets had developed the Brezhnev Doctrine as a means of maintaining and defending the Communist bloc countries against internal and external threats, thus reinforcing Soviet dominance over Warsaw Pact nations. The first test of the Brezhnev Doctrine had been the 1968 Soviet intervention in Czechoslovakia, where the Soviets had ruthlessly crushed the Prague Spring liberalization movement. Although Afghanistan was not a member of the Communist bloc, the Soviets justified their use of the Brezhnev Doctrine with a friendship agreement they had made with Afghanistan.

Unlike their Soviet counterparts, the Afghan Mujahideen did not have an overarching military doctrine on which to base their resistance. Historically, warfare was used to improve one's social standing vis-à-vis the other qawm.

Initial Soviet military strategy in Afghanistan was in line with traditional operational strategy: the rapid

AP/Wide World Photos

Mounted Afghan guerrillas ready for combat with Soviet and government forces in western Afghanistan, January, 1980.

deployment of large numbers of armor and troops was intended to strengthen Afghanistan's faltering government. Once the Soviets had become ensconced in the capital of Kabul, little thought was given to strategic and security concerns. Soviet strategy evolved to consolidate control over the country without long-term commitment. Soviet aircraft and heavy artillery would first lay down heavy bombardment, while helicopter transports ferried troops to nearby ridges where they would lay down covering fire. Tanks and combat vehicles could then plough through what was left of the villages.

Initial Soviet tactics, using ground forces supported by tanks, were similar to those used in the 1968 invasion of Czechoslovakia. Following initial consolidation in and around Kabul, the Soviets deployed motorized rifle units to support the Afghan army waging classic large-scale armored warfare.

The well-planned Soviet offensives deployed motorized rifle divisions that used tactics based on warfare in the European theater. These motorized rifle units suffered heavy casualties owing to their lack of training in mountain and counterinsurgency warfare.

Beginning in June, 1980, the Soviets changed their strategy from the centrally controlled high-intensity mechanized operations to antiguerrilla warfare. As Soviet tacticians realized they had to adapt to the geographic and topological conditions of Afghanistan, they reorganized the Red Army itself, sending home antiaircraft missile brigades and artillery brigades and combining army ground forces and supporting them with MI-24 helicopter gunships. They also realized the importance of airborne assaults and covering air support in mountain warfare.

Initially lacking a central command, the Mujahideen never had an overall anti-Soviet strategy, instead adopting localized hit-and-run tactics such as bombings, assassinations, and attacks on supply convoys and military barracks. Over time, the Mujahideen began developing a strategy to counter the Soviets' anti-insurgency measures, attacking isolated military garrisons. Mujahideen tactics were localized and hindered by the lack of communications, properly organized command structures, and clear orders.

CONTEMPORARY SOURCES

By all accounts the Soviet-Afghan War was particularly vicious in nature. Atrocities were committed by both sides. Alex Alexiev, in *Inside the Soviet Army in Afghanistan* (1988), chronicled the individual experiences of individual Soviet soldiers in Afghanistan. Svetlana Aleksievich wrote *Tsinkovye malchiki* (1991; *Zinky Boys: Soviet Voices from the Afghanistan War*, 1992), a harrowing account of the lives of men and women who lived and served in Afghanistan, many of whom carry deep psychological scars from the devastation they witnessed there. Artyom Borovik's *The Hidden War: A Russian Journalist's Account of the Soviet War in Afghanistan* (1990) is a journalistic account of the Soviet-Afghan War. Each book chronicles Afghanistan's deadly descent into near-anarchy, as each battle brought vicious reprisals against the enemy. The Soviets used the terror of carpet bombing and forced migration to depopulate entire villages in hopes of depriving the Mujahideen of their support. The Mujahideen were also guilty of wartime atrocities, as they often shot their Soviet prisoners.

Mujahideen also terrorized Soviet-controlled towns and villages, bombing and killing civilians. In the Soviet-Afghan conflict, the use of terror became the norm. Little has been written about the real victims of the war, the people of Afghanistan, who endured ten years of civil war and forced migration, as the Soviets depopulated huge areas of the countryside. Although, as in Rasul Bakhsh Rais's *War Without Winners: Afghanistan's Uncertain Transition After the Cold War* (1994), attempts have been made to examine the factors that account for the Afghan tragedy and the fragmentation of the country, until the people of Afghanistan can tell their own stories, the full scope and nature of the Soviet-Afghan War will not be known.

FILMS AND OTHER MEDIA

The Beast of War. Feature film. Columbia Pictures, 1988.

Charlie Wilson's War. Feature film. Universal Pictures, 2007.

Guns of Afghanistan. Documentary. History Channel, 2002.

Inside Afghanistan. Documentary. Multi-Media, 1988.

The Kite Runner. Feature film. DreamWorks, 2007.

Shadow Warriors. Documentary. History Channel, 2005.

The Taliban. Documentary. History Channel, 2007.

Keith A. Leitich

WARFARE IN THE GLOBAL AGE

WARFARE IN IRAQ

Dates: Since 1990

POLITICAL CONSIDERATIONS

Although conflict between Iraq and the United States and its allies did not begin until 1990, in order to understand the political situation that led to the conflict, it is necessary to start with a review of U.S.-Iraqi relations from 1980 to 1990. In 1979, a group of Islamist Iranian revolutionaries occupied the American embassy, taking fifty-three Americans hostage as a protest against U.S. support of the regime of Mohammad Reza Shah Pahlavi. In this pivotal episode in the history of U.S.-Iranian relations, the hostages were held for more than a year, through a failed U.S. rescue attempt, and released only after the intervention of Algeria just as President Ronald Reagan took office. As the Iranian hostage crisis wore on into 1980, American and Saudi leaders looked for a bulwark against the spread of Islamic revolution throughout the Middle East. The most likely candidate seemed to be Iraq, led by President Saddam Hussein. More than willing to invade Iran, Hussein quickly became an ally of the West, keeping both Iran and his own nation mired in an eight-year-long war of attrition.

By the end of the Iran-Iraq War in 1988, however, Hussein was embittered toward the Arab and American leaders, who he felt had led him into a self-defeating conflict. Additionally, he was particularly angry at Kuwait, his neighbor to the south, which he accused of slant drilling across the border into Iraqi oil fields and, at the same time, refusing to extend credit to Hussein's regime. U.S. ambassador April Glaspie's ambiguous response to Hussein's explanation of his frustration with Kuwait gave Hussein the impression that the United States would not oppose his planned invasion. He could not have been more wrong.

On August 2, 1990, Iraqi forces crossed the border into Kuwait, easily seizing control of the small nation. Within less than a week, the United States, led by President George H. W. Bush (the first Bush presidency), began Operation Desert Shield, massing troops in Saudi Arabia, ostensibly to prevent a further Iraqi invasion. The United Nations Security Council condemned Iraq's invasion, giving the American buildup international backing. By November, the U.N. Security Council had voted to place a deadline of January 15, 1991, on Iraq to remove all troops from Kuwait. After waiting one extra day, American forces, along with those of other allied countries, began the softening of Iraqi forces through a massive bombing campaign, and on February 24, 1991, Operation Desert Storm began when coalition ground forces engaged the Iraqis, beginning an extended period of conflict.

MILITARY ACHIEVEMENT

By the time Operation Desert Storm began, the United States was engaged in a "War on Terror," even though it was not yet called that. The holding of the fifty-three American hostages for 444 days in the U.S. embassy in Iran had turned the Middle East from a troubled but far-off region to a clear and present danger in the American mind. The 1983 bombing of the U.S. embassy in Beirut, Lebanon, and, later that same year in the same city, the deaths of 241 Marines in another bombing only intensified fears. Terrorist attacks, such as the 1988 bombing of Pan Am flight 103 over Lockerbie, Scotland, continued throughout the decade. These attacks were directed against the West and nationals from Arab states, such as Saudi Arabia and Kuwait, who were friendly with the West. When Hussein's attitudes toward the West changed during the late 1980's, he quickly went from being a friend of the United States to becoming an enemy, and he was consequently painted with the same brush as terrorist groups such as Hezbollah, Islamic

Jihad, Hamas, and the recently established al-Qaeda.

The stated primary goal of American actions in the Persian Gulf War (1991), the interwar period, and the Iraq War (beginning in 2003), was to limit Iraqi participation in the terrorists' *jihad*, or holy struggle, against the West, particularly the United States, Israel, and America's Arab allies. The immediate goal of the Persian Gulf War, as most of the American public understood it, was the removal of Hussein as a threat. However, the United Nations' mandate was only for the reestablishment of the status quo, that is, the removal of Iraq from Kuwait. By that limited definition of the Persian Gulf War's aim, the war was a success. However, if the Persian Gulf War is viewed as one incident in a larger War on Terror, with the longer-term goal of removing Hussein as a threat, the Persian Gulf War was a dismal failure, a failure that would haunt the rest of the first Bush presidency and impact the way his son, George W. Bush, would view

the region during the second Bush presidency (2001-2009). As a part of the agreement that ended the Persian Gulf War, Hussein agreed to the presence of U.N. weapons inspectors and an American patrolled "no-fly zone" over much of Iraq. These measures placed the United States and the United Nations in Iraq for the long term, which only exacerbated anti-Western feeling both in Iraq and throughout the Middle East.

For much of the interwar period, the United Nations Special Commission on Iraq conducted no-notice inspections on sites throughout Iraq, uncovering clandestine programs to create weapons of mass destruction (WMDs). Though sporadic incidents of airborne conflict continued throughout the 1990's, it was not until after the terrorist attacks against the World Trade Center and the Pentagon on September 11, 2001, and the second Bush presidency that Iraq once again came to be seen as a primary threat in the

GULF WAR, 1991

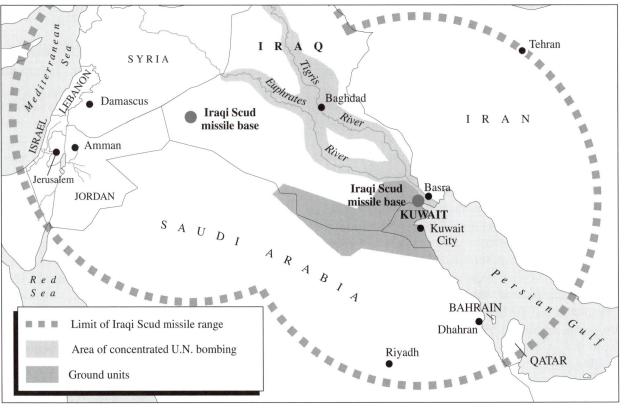

War on Terror. Although the Central Intelligence Agency (CIA) repeatedly asserted that there was no connection between Iraq and al-Qaeda, the terrorist group headed by Osama Bin Laden that carried out the 9/11 attacks, the American people wanted someone to pay for the thousands of Americans who had died, and Iraq was a convenient and immediate target. Those who opposed the war speculated that the second conflict, known as the Iraq War, or Operation Iraqi Freedom, was more about finishing the job begun by the first President Bush and protecting American oil interests than actually fighting against world terrorism. The final assessment of the achievement of goals will have to wait until years after the Iraq War concludes, but members of the second Bush administration, notably Vice President Dick Cheney, have repeatedly asserted that the Iraq War, and the larger War on Terror, have been successes, as evidenced by the fact that there have been no further terrorist attacks on American soil after 9/11.

WEAPONS, UNIFORMS, AND ARMOR

As warfare in Iraq has extended for twenty years, the number of different weapons used by Iraqi and coalition forces is vast and has evolved over the course of the conflict. However, two generalizations are possible. First, the Iraqi military, though the fourth largest standing army in the world in 1991, was using relatively outdated Soviet military hardware. Second, and this flows from the first, the United States and its allies enjoyed overwhelming superiority in terms of both the number and quality of its weapons.

Listing the staples of Iraqi weaponry is relatively simple. The main infantry rifle was the Soviet-made AK-47. The primary tank fielded was the Soviet T-72, which was introduced in 1974. Though vastly outnumbered by American air forces, the Iraqi Air Force utilized a number of Soviet aircraft, including the MiG-21, MiG-23, MiG-25, and MiG-29. However, the best-known Iraqi weapon of the Persian Gulf War has to be the SS-1 Scud missile. Though few in number and relatively inaccurate, these Scuds were used by the Iraqis to strike terror into Israeli and Saudi civilians, by firing a few mis-

siles during the conflict, resulting in about thirty deaths. At the end of the first conflict, the weaponry allowed to what remained of the Iraqi military was severely curtailed. Almost all of the Scuds were destroyed, and the Iraqi Air Force basically ceased to exist. Therefore, by the beginning of the Iraq War in 2003, the Iraqi military was at an even greater disadvantage, while the American forces were even better equipped.

Although the coalition forces fielded a much wider variety of weapons, their workhorses are also easily listed. The infantry rifle used was the M16A2 semiautomatic rifle. The main battle tanks of the conflicts were the M1 and M1A1 Abrams tanks, though the venerable M60 Patton also saw action. In the air, the F-14, F-15, F-15E, F-16, and F/A-18S fighters saw heavy action in the first conflict, being joined by the F-117 Stealth fighter during the second. The Patriot and Tomahawk missiles were the weapons that struck fear into Iraqi civilians, as the Scuds did for the Saudis and Israelis. Among the vast numbers of weapons wielded by the West that the Iraqis did not have were the strategic bombers, including the B-52, B-1B, and B-2 Stealth bombers. The might of the U.S. Navy stood unchallenged by the few small Iraqi patrol boats.

MILITARY ORGANIZATION

During the Persian Gulf War, the command of the coalition forces was divided between the Western armies, under the leadership of U.S. general Norman Schwarzkopf, and allied Arab nations' forces, under the leadership of Saudi general Khaled Bin Sultan. This division was seen as necessary to avoid the perception that the offensive into Iraq was a case of a Western nation invading and occupying an Arab nation. The two separate commands coordinated very closely—thanks to the efforts of the Coalition Coordination, Communications, and Integration Center— and no problems arose because of the division. It was clear to all that Schwarzkopf had the final word. The Iraqis operated under a unified command structure with approval from Baghdad necessary for nearly every military action. The practical ramifications of

M-1A1 Abrams tank in Iraq during Operation Desert Storm.

this were that when the United States began its bombing missions in anticipation of the invasion, the centers of authority for the Iraqi military were primary targets, which were hit with regularity. The ensuing confusion played directly into the coalition's hands. Although the Iraqi military was said to have been the fourth largest standing army in the world, it was an army that had recently finished a grueling eight-year war with its neighbor, Iran. Although it fielded sixty divisions, many units were undermanned and many commanders were inexperienced, due to Hussein's purges of military leaders. What did concern coalition leaders were the elite Republican Guard and other special forces units, who were battle-hardened.

The end of the Persian Gulf War, however, was not the end of conflict. The cease-fire agreement that ended the war called for Iraq to allow U.N. weapons inspectors to enforce a ban on offensive weapons systems and allowed the coalition air forces (those of the United States, the United Kingdom, and France) to enforce so-called no-fly zones over northern and southern Iraq. Although defeated in the Persian Gulf War, Iraq bristled under the restrictions and actively engaged coalition air forces with antiaircraft weap-

ons. This situation continued, and began to intensify, in the months following the 9/11 attacks, eventually seeing Hussein expel U.N. weapons inspectors from the country.

The coalition put together for the Iraq War was much smaller than the broad, multination, U.N.-based coalition during the Persian Gulf War. Essentially consisting of the United States, the United Kingdom, Canada, and Australia, American primacy in the prosecution of the war was even more complete. General Tommy Franks, as head of U.S. Central Command (CENTCOM), the unified American command in charge of American interests in the countries of the Middle East, was the supreme commander as the United States invaded Iraq once again. If the command structure of the Iraqi military had been centralized during the Persian Gulf War, it was even more concentrated during the Iraq War. All Republican Guard and Special Republican Guard units reported directly to Hussein and his son Qusay. All key military posts were given to hand-picked, dedicated supporters of Hussein, so it is not a stretch to say that he exercised complete and nearly direct control over all military units in Iraq. Hussein's loyalists manned all four Air Command Sector Operations Centers, which were set up to coordinate defense on a regional level.

Just as in the Persian Gulf War, the aerial bombardment of Iraq was effective, this time even more so as the technology behind the smart bombs had evolved dramatically during the twelve years between the conflicts. Though Iraq fielded a larger army and more tanks than did the coalition, Iraqi tanks were even more outdated and their army much more poorly trained and led. In addition, the superiority of American air forces was complete.

DOCTRINE, STRATEGY, AND TACTICS

A simple way of looking at the guiding doctrines of the three phases of the conflict is to look at the presidents who were commanders in chief at those times. President George H. W. Bush oversaw the Persian Gulf War, and his working with a large coalition to enforce a U.N. mandate fit with his overall way of pursuing foreign policy. President William J. Clinton governed during most of the interwar period, and his use of the no-fly zone rules and food-for-oil programs fits with his ideas of using less direct means of increasing diplomatic pressure on Saddam Hussein. George W. Bush became president about eight months before 9/11, and his Bush Doctrine of preemptive war guided the American buildup to and prosecution of the Iraq War.

The Western powers believed that the doctrine guiding Saddam Hussein's 1990 invasion of Kuwait was a desire to dominate the oil supply in the Persian Gulf. This, then, raised fears of a further invasion of Saudi Arabia, one of the nations Hussein blamed for goading him into the Iran-Iraq War. Further, by opposing the United States, Israel's most important ally, he hoped to take a leadership position in the Arab world.

The U.S. doctrine going into the Persian Gulf War was simple. President Bush hoped to liberate Kuwait in fulfillment of the United Nations' mandate, defend the world's oil supply, and emasculate the Iraqi military's capabilities and pursuit of WMDs.

Whereas Iraq followed the strategy of an entrenched, defensive war, the coalition followed the strategy set out in the Army AirLand Battle Doctrine. This set out the idea that gaining and maintaining total air superiority and overwhelming, but carefully targeted, bombing were the keys to success. Hussein, for his part, did not believe that the bombing campaign would weaken his defenses significantly, and he did believe that the U.S. strategy would mean a long, costly land war, which he could either win or force into a stalemate. However, what he was not prepared for was a new generation of weapons that allowed the coalition forces to target military installations precisely and hit them with massive force. As former Air Force chief of staff Michael Dugan said: "Technology has caught up with doctrine."

During the interwar period, the U.S. strategy on the militarily diminished but not destroyed Iraq rested on two ideas: economic sanctions and the no-

U.S. Navy

Sailors aboard the USS Abraham Lincoln *in San Diego on May 2, 2003, announcing "Mission Accomplished" in Iraq. The war would actually continue for several more years.*

fly zones. President Clinton's goal was to diminish Hussein's influence in the region through diplomatic means and the threat of military force. Iraq was allowed to sell oil only to buy food, which was used as a means of keeping Iraq from recovering economically. As effective as that might have been, it was not the military in Iraq that suffered but the people. Hussein was able to rebuild his military capability, though not to the level he had in 1990. The army was approximately 40 percent smaller. The same tanks he had in 1990 were fewer in number and twelve years older. His air force was practically nonexistent.

As George W. Bush took office in 2001, Iraq already occupied a prominent place on his agenda. Though Iraq was diminished, the Bush administration feared that Hussein was succeeding in acquiring weapons of mass destruction that could be launched against Saudi Arabia or, worse yet, Israel. When the 9/11 attacks happened, Bush administration officials immediately attached their agenda on Iraq to the newly declared War on Terror. Though there was no evidence that Iraq played any role in fomenting or supporting the attacks, Vice President Cheney and Defense Secretary Donald Rumsfeld led a massive public opinion campaign to transform the resurgence in patriotism spurred by 9/11 into support for a war in Iraq. Ignoring world opinion and leading a small coalition consisting of only America's closest allies, U.S. forces under the command of General Tommy

Franks quickly defeated the Iraqi army, leading Bush to declare, infamously, "Mission accomplished."

Of course, the mission was not accomplished but was just beginning, as the Iraq War went from a conflict between the American and Iraqi military forces to a long, bloody insurgent war, much more reminiscent of Vietnam than any other conflict in which the United States had engaged since. As the war became increasingly unpopular with the American public, a new strategy known as the "surge" was implemented in January, 2007, serendipitously coinciding with what would become known as the Anbar Awakening: a Sunni revival movement that sought to expose Shia insurgents. An additional 29,000 American troops were deployed, mostly in Baghdad, and violence declined, although American public opinion remained strongly opposed to the war, as the presidential election of 2008 demonstrated.

Antiwar feeling certainly contributed to Barack Obama's victory, as he promised to bring the troops home within eighteen months. However, even before he took office, the Bush administration began to draw back the number of troops in Iraq, in many cases redirecting them to the growing conflict in Afghanistan. Once in office, President Obama followed through on his campaign promise, implementing strategies designed to transfer responsibility for maintaining order in Iraq to the Iraqi military and police forces.

CONTEMPORARY SOURCES

Over the course of the interwar years, many of the policy makers and commanders during the Persian Gulf War wrote memoirs. A number of memoirs by the chief policy makers during the first Bush administration are among them, including Secretary of State James A. Baker III's *The Politics of Diplomacy: Revolution, War, and Peace, 1989-92* (New York: Putnam, 1995) and Joint Chiefs of Staff chairman Colin Powell's *My American Journey* (New York: Random House, 1995). Both the Western and Arab commanders during the conflict have written as well: H. Norman Schwarzkopf's *It Doesn't Take a Hero* (New York: Bantam, 1992) and Khaled Bin Sultan's *Desert Warrior* (New York: HarperCollins, 1995). Numerous assessments of the Persian Gulf War have also been published, including the House Armed Services Committee's *Defense for a New Era: Lessons of the Persian Gulf War* (Washington, D.C.: Government Printing Office, 1992). A good memoir of the interwar period was written by Hans Blix, the chief U.N. weapons inspector in Iraq: *Disarming Iraq* (New York: Pantheon, 2004). Over the course of both conflicts, numerous soldiers wrote accounts of their time in Iraq, and embedded journalists during the Iraq War also wrote extensively. There are not as many "insider" memoirs on the Iraq War, as the conflict is ongoing, though some hearings have proven fruitful for firsthand opinions about the conflict. A prime example is a Senate Armed Services Committee hearing with the American commander Tommy R. Franks and Secretary of Defense Donald Rumsfeld, entitled *"Lessons Learned" During Operation Enduring Freedom in Afghanistan and Operation Iraqi Freedom, and Ongoing Operations in the United States Central Command Region* (Washington, D.C.: Government Printing Office, 2004).

BOOKS AND ARTICLES

Atkinson, Rick. *Crusade: The Untold Story of the Persian Gulf War*. New York: Houghton Mifflin, 1993.

Collins, Joseph J. *Choosing War: The Decision to Invade Iraq and Its Aftermath*. Washington, D.C.: National Defense University Press, 2008.

Cordesman, Anthony H. *The Iraq War: Strategy, Tactics, and Military Lessons*. Westport, Conn.: Praeger, 2003.

Karsh, Efraim. *The Iran-Iraq War, 1980-1988*. New York: Osprey, 2002.

Loges, Marsha J. "The Persian Gulf War: Military Doctrine and Strategy." Research paper. Washington, D.C.: Industrial College of the Armed Forces, National Defense University, 1996.

Mahnken, Thomas G., and Thomas A. Keaney, eds. *War in Iraq: Planning and Execution*. New York: Routledge, 2007.

Marston, Daniel, and Carter Malkasian. *Counterinsurgency in Modern Warfare*. New York: Osprey, 2008.

Mockaitis, Thomas R. *The Iraq War: Learning from the Past, Adapting to the Present, and Planning for the Future*. Carlisle, Pa.: Strategic Studies Institute, U.S. Army War College, 2007.

Rottman, Gordon L. *Armies of the Gulf War*. New York: Osprey, 1993.

Schlesinger, Robert. "Iraq, the Surge, and the Sunni Awakening: Not So Fast, Jack." *U.S. News and World Report*, September 25, 2008.

Summers, Colonel Harry G. *On Strategy II: A Critical Analysis of the Gulf War*. New York: Dell, 1992.

Triumph Without Victory: The Unreported History of the Persian Gulf War. New York: Times Books, 1992.

FILMS AND OTHER MEDIA

Frontline: Bush's War. Documentary. WGBH Boston, 2008.

Frontline: The Gulf War. Documentary. WGBH Boston, 1996.

Green Zone. Universal Studios, 2010.

Iraq in Fragments. Documentary. Daylight Factory, 2006.

Jarhead. Feature film. Universal, 2005.

Three Kings. Feature film. Warner Bros., 1999.

Steven L. Danver

WARFARE IN AFGHANISTAN
THE UNITED STATES
Dates: Since 2001

POLITICAL CONSIDERATIONS

The attacks by al-Qaeda against the United States on September 11, 2001, led to the war in Afghanistan, also known as Operation Enduring Freedom. Since 1996, Osama Bin Laden had been granted sanctuary in Afghanistan by the Taliban, a militant Islamic group (led by Mullah Mohammad Omar) that seized power that same year. Because both al-Qaeda and the Taliban were hostile to the United States and the West, espousing a militant and violent interpretation of Islam, they quickly became allies. One month after the attacks of 9/11, the United States, Allied forces (primarily those of Britain), and anti-Taliban forces known as the Northern Alliance invaded Afghanistan with the stated aim of overthrowing the Taliban government and ending Afghanistan's role as a terrorist sanctuary for al-Qaeda. Suffering heavy casualties from U.S. and Allied air strikes and ground combat assault by U.S. and Allied special forces and Northern Alliance forces, al-Qaeda and Taliban forces retreated toward the eastern mountains of Afghanistan along the Pakistan border. Despite the swift collapse and defeat of the Taliban and al-Qaeda, Bin Laden and Mohammad Omar eluded capture or death, presumably fleeing during the December, 2001, Battle of Tora Bora into the lawless border areas of Pakistan (the North-West Frontier Province and Federally Administered Tribal Areas).

On December 20, 2001, the United Nations Security Council (UNSC) established the International Security Assistance Force (ISAF), led primarily by members of the North Atlantic Treaty Organization (NATO) but including nonmembers as well. ISAF was given the dual responsibility of assisting the United States in securing Afghanistan against al-Qaeda and the Taliban and also of promoting economic reconstruction of that devastated country after more than twenty years of civil war. ISAF was originally tasked with defending the capital city of Kabul and surrounding areas, but on October 13, 2003, the UNSC authorized ISAF to expand its presence throughout Afghanistan and in 2006 began to operate throughout the country. Until August, 2003, command of ISAF rotated among different nations on a six-month basis, but thereafter NATO assumed responsibility for appointing a commander, and ISAF was commanded by generals from Germany, Canada, Turkey, Italy, Britain, and the United States.

As of May, 2009, ISAF forces numbered more than 58,000 troops from forty-two different countries, including the United States, NATO-European countries, Australia, New Zealand, and Jordan. The ISAF force comprised 25,000 U.S. troops along with 30,000 troops from non-U.S./NATO countries. Another 17,000 U.S. troops operated independently of ISAF in training the Afghan National Army (ANA) and battling al-Qaeda and Taliban forces in eastern and southern Afghanistan along the lawless border regions of Pakistan used by al-Qaeda and the Taliban as a sanctuary. After the United States, Great Britain had the second largest presence in Afghanistan, with a total of 8,300 troops, the vast majority serving in Helmand Province, the heartland of the al-Qaeda and Taliban insurgency; Canada had 2,830 troops stationed in Kandahar—the former capital of the Taliban when it ruled Afghanistan—in the dangerous south; France had 2,800 troops deployed in Kabul; Germany had 3,500 troops stationed in the relatively peaceful north and northeast of the country; the Netherlands had almost 2,000 troops deployed in dangerous southern Afghanistan; and Italy had 2,350 troops in relatively peaceful western Afghanistan. A total of 159 British, 118 Canadian, 27 French, 31 German, 19

Dutch, and 14 Italian troops died in Afghanistan between 2001 and mid-2009.

The bulk of ISAF forces were in the insurgency-wracked south and east of the country, especially in the provinces of Helmand and Kandahar; elsewhere, ISAF troops were involved in peacekeeping and reconstruction instead of combat, according to the decisions of particular countries not to commit their forces to combat. By mid-2009, ISAF had deployed twenty-five provincial reconstruction teams to different parts of the country to rebuild damaged schools and hospitals and restore water supplies and damaged infrastructure in order to establish the conditions in which Afghans could enjoy a stable and inclusive democratic government to meet their needs and, in so doing, delegitimize and marginalize al-Qaeda and the Taliban. At the same time, however, continuing attacks by al-Qaeda and Taliban delayed progress in reconstruction. ISAF forces were also backed up by 80,000 troops of the Afghan National Army (ANA) and 30,000 Afghan policemen. The ANA conducted operations alongside U.S. and ISAF forces but were still unable to conduct combat operations independently, relying instead on Allied forces for logistics, artillery, and air support. In 2003, the Taliban and al-Qaeda had started regrouping and began launching attacks against U.S. and ISAF forces in Afghanistan.

The security situation worsened over the next five years, for a variety of reasons. First, the Afghan government of President Hamid Karzai remained weak, corrupt, and unable to govern effectively; its authority did not extend to large areas of the country and remained incapable of providing essential services to most of the people of Afghanistan. Second, as the security situation in Iraq dramatically improved in 2008-2009, al-Qaeda terrorists fled from Iraq to Afghanistan. Third, political instability and rising suicide bombings and attacks by al-Qaeda and the Taliban in Pakistan consumed that country and sapped its willingness to confront Taliban and al-Qaeda terrorists in Pakistan, leading to concern that Pakistan's pro-Western government might collapse as large parts of Pakistan remained under de facto control of al-Qaeda and Taliban militants.

On May 9, 2009, General David Petraeus, commander of U.S. forces in Iraq and Afghanistan, stated that Pakistan's lawless frontier border regions had become the headquarters of al-Qaeda's senior leadership, having displaced Afghanistan as al-Qaeda's main stronghold, and served as a sanctuary for the planning of attacks and for fund-raising and recruiting of members. Fourth, many Americans, including U.S. president Barack Obama, also attributed the deterioration of security in Afghanistan to the administration of President George W. Bush (2001-2009), which, by deciding that U.S. troops should invade Iraq in March, 2003, allegedly became distracted by that war, ignored Afghanistan, and failed to devote sufficient resources to the military effort there.

In any case, as American military deaths in Afghanistan rose in 2008 by 35 percent (to 155 soldiers killed) and were on track to exceed that rate in 2009, President Obama announced on March 27, 2009, that "urgent attention and swift action" were required because "the Taliban is resurgent in Afghanistan, and al-Qaeda . . . threatens America from its safe-haven along the Pakistani border." Pledging to "disrupt,

AP/Wide World Photos

Brigadier Tim Radford (right) speaks with the district governor in Gereshk, Afghanistan, in July, 2009.

dismantle, and defeat al-Qaeda and the Taliban," Obama dispatched an additional 17,000 combat troops to Afghanistan, as well as 4,000 military trainers from the Eighty-second Airborne Division to train that country's army—bringing the total number of U.S. troops in Afghanistan to some 60,000. Of these 17,000 additional troops, 10,000 were to be Marines stationed in the south; 3,800 were to be with an Army Stryker Brigade; 1,000 were to be Special Operations Force trainers; and 3,200 were to be force enablers.

MILITARY ACHIEVEMENT

After the defeat in Afghanistan of al-Qaeda and the Taliban in the fall of 2001, fighting continued on a sporadic basis, with occasional real battles, and control of the country largely reverted to the regional warlords who had held power before the Taliban. Britain, Canada, France, the Netherlands, and other NATO nations provided forces for various military, peacekeeping, and humanitarian operations. By the end of 2002, some stability, though tenuous, had been achieved in Afghanistan, but sporadic, generally small-scale fighting continued, particularly in the southeast, with the Taliban regaining some strength and even control in certain districts. In August, 2003, NATO assumed command of the international security force in the Kabul area. In early 2004, the United States and NATO both announced increases in the number of troops deployed in the country, and these increases continued into 2005. The U.S. troop increase coincided with new operations against an increasingly resurgent Taliban and al-Qaeda, and the spring of 2005 was marked by an increase in attacks by these militants.

Tensions with Pakistan escalated in early 2006, as members of the Afghan government increasingly accused Pakistan of failing to control Taliban and al-Qaeda camps in areas bordering Afghanistan; by the end of the year, President Karzai had accused elements of the Pakistani government of directly supporting the Taliban. In January, 2006, a U.S. air strike destroyed several houses in eastern Pakistan where al-Qaeda leaders were believed to be meeting. May

saw the U.S.-led coalition launch its largest campaign against Taliban forces since 2001; some 11,000 troops undertook a summer offensive in four southern Afghan provinces where the Taliban had become stronger and more entrenched. In July, NATO assumed responsibility for peacekeeping in southern Afghanistan. NATO troops subsequently found themselves engaged in significant battles with the Taliban, particularly in Kandahar Province, the birthplace of the Taliban. NATO took command of all peacekeeping forces in the country, including some 11,000 U.S. troops, in October; some 13,000 U.S. troops remained part of Operation Enduring Freedom, assigned to fighting Taliban and al-Qaeda forces in the rugged mountainous areas bordering Pakistan. In the second half of 2006, as casualties mounted, NATO commanders encountered difficulties when their call for reinforcements failed to raise the necessary number of troops and resources. NATO leaders also joined Afghan leaders in criticizing Pakistan for failing to end al-Qaeda's and the Taliban's use of areas bordering Afghanistan, especially in Baluchistan, as safe havens. By the end of 2006, 98 U.S. soldiers and 93 Allied soldiers had been killed.

In March, 2007, NATO forces launched a new offensive in Helmand Province against the Taliban and al-Qaeda. Around the same time, Pakistan's construction of a fence along the border with Afghanistan led to protests from Afghanistan and sparked several border clashes between the forces of the two countries, as Afghanistan disputed the border with Pakistan. In May, NATO forces killed the top Taliban field commander, Mullah Dadullah, but Taliban forces mounted some guerrilla attacks as deep as the outskirts of the capital, Kabul, and in the north during 2007. Also in 2007 and particularly in 2008, as Afghanistan suffered the worst violence since the overthrow of the Taliban in 2001 with more than 4,000 killed—perhaps as many as one-third estimated to be civilians—Afghan civilian casualties during U.S. air strikes increasingly became a source of anger and concern among Afghans, which in turn not only put immense pressure on the Karzai government but also made it unpopular.

Afghan civilian casualties from U.S. air strikes continued to be a problem in 2008, straining relations between Afghanistan and the United States. Significant fighting with insurgents continued through 2008, as the Taliban mounted some of their most devastating attacks ever. As the year progressed, U.S. forces mounted strikes against insurgent sanctuaries across the Pakistan border, leading to tensions with Pakistan. In April, President Karzai escaped an assassination attempt unhurt, and in July, he accused Pakistani agents of being behind insurgent attacks in Afghanistan, among them a suicide bombing of the Indian embassy in Kabul. By the end of 2008, 155 American and 139 Allied soldiers had died in combat that year, compared to 117 and 155, respectively, in 2007.

In 2009, as President Obama deployed additional U.S. troops to confront a resurgent al-Qaeda and Taliban, General Petraeus reported that these militants were planning a "surge" by moving weapons and forces into areas where the United States was adding troops. As the militants relocated across the border into Pakistan, the United States used unmanned Predator drones to fire missiles at dozens of militant targets inside Pakistan, killing several top al-Qaeda figures, but U.S. officials acknowledged that al-Qaeda's senior leadership had survived these attacks and that they continued to plot counterattacks, recruit fighters, and raise funds.

Al-Qaeda's resurgence in Pakistan, thus, posed a policy dilemma for the Obama administration: Pakistan's government would not allow U.S. military forces into that country, preventing the U.S. military from confronting these militants in ground combat to deny them sanctuary. Instead, without "boots on the ground," the United States was forced to strike either at targets from a distance (a tactic with limited military effect, even when it worked) or instead rely on Pakistan's military (which proved reluctant to venture into al-Qaeda's and the Taliban's sanctuaries). Pakistan's reluctance to confront al-Qaeda and the Taliban in its own country was said to stem from fear by the Pakistani government that this might lead to either (1) a collapse or even a mutiny among its military, which in addition to being trained to fight a conventional war against India was unwilling to confront its own Muslim countrymen, or (2) a civil war that could bring down the nuclear-armed Pakistani government. The Pakastani government seemingly alternated between trying to fight and trying to appease the militants. Indeed, in late April, 2009, while consolidating their control over two northwestern districts after Pakistan's government agreed to the Taliban's demand for Islamic law to be applied in the Swat valley, Taliban forces moved to within 60 miles of Pakistan's capital, Islamabad, before withdrawing. This move prompted Pakistan to launch a military offensive in the North-West Frontier Province, allegedly to rid the region of al-Qaeda and the Taliban; such operations in the past, however, had failed in their objectives.

After complaints in private failed to diminish or end the practice, President Karzai in 2009 demanded an end to U.S. air strikes in Afghanistan because of the allegedly high number of innocent civilians being killed. The U.S. and Allied forces, in turn, blamed the Taliban and al-Qaeda for hiding among innocent civilians and continued the air strikes.

American dead and casualties between 2001 and mid-2009 in Afghanistan were 610 killed and at least 2,766 injured. The total number of Allied casualties for that period was 452 dead. In April, 2009, six NATO soldiers, all Canadian, were killed in a roadside blast, bringing to 118 the total killed for Canadian troops alone. Although President Obama decided to send 17,000 more U.S. combat troops and 4,000 more training personnel, European NATO allies such as Britain, Canada, France, and Holland declined his request to send additional combat forces, although Australia announced it was deploying 450 additional troops to Afghanistan (bringing the total number of Australian troops to 1,550, of whom 10 had already died in the conflict). On Monday, May 11, as President Obama tried to turn around what by all accounts was a stalemated war, it was announced that he was replacing the top general in Afghanistan, David McKiernan, with Army Lieutenant General Stanley McChrystal. With national elections scheduled in Afghanistan for August, 2009, al-Qaeda and the Taliban were expected to continue and escalate their attacks.

Because al-Qaeda and the Taliban lack the firepower, particularly in terms of artillery and air power as well as night-vision equipment, of U.S. and Allied forces, they generally avoid open and direct, prolonged engagements and prefer ambush, hit-and-run attacks, and suicide bombings to frustrate and demoralize their adversaries by denying them a decisive victory. These tactics significantly prolong the conflict and, in so doing, make the conflict seem endless and thus unwinnable. Based on events between 2006 and 2009, the militants had succeeded in turning the war in Afghanistan into a stalemate, with the momentum on their side.

WEAPONS, UNIFORMS, AND ARMOR

As al-Qaeda is a most unconventional "army," their weapons, uniforms, and armor are equally unconventional. Conventional arms have little place with al-Qaeda, because the movement's combatants do not participate in conventional attacks. Their weapons have run the gamut from car bombs, boat bombs, and bombs attached to suicide bombers to—in their most notable attacks, perpetrated in the United States on September 11, 2001—jet airliners used as massive bombs.

The Taliban, as a ruling authority for part of its existence, had the Afghan military at its disposal, but in more recent years it has become the province of local warlords, whose forces are neither organized nor standardized either in uniforms or in arms.

MILITARY ORGANIZATION

As it did in Iraq, the United States appointed one supreme commander for the Afghanistan theater. In May, 2009, Lieutenant General Stanley McChrystal took over for General David McKiernan as head of the nearly 30,000 U.S. troops in Afghanistan, headquartered at Bagram Air Base, Afghanistan. Reporting to the U.S. commander were the Combined Joint Task Force 101, which handled specific missions throughout Afghanistan, and the Combined Security Transition Command-Afghanistan, which worked directly with the Afghan National Army and the Afghan National Police to train them for an eventual takeover of security operations.

Under separate, NATO-led command were approximately 65,000 troops (including approximately an additional 30,000 U.S. troops, along with troops from Australia, Canada, the Czech Republic, Denmark, Estonia, France, Finland, Germany, Hungary, India, Italy, Latvia, the Netherlands, New Zealand, Norway, Poland, Portugal, Romania, Spain, Turkey, and the United Kingdom), which form the ISAF. The ISAF was led by the Joint Force Command Brunssum in Brunssum, Netherlands. The ISAF commander reported to the Joint Force Command Brunssum and had five regional commanders who reported to him.

The opposing forces, usually given the umbrella term "Taliban," really were made up of several distinct groups, all fighting against the Afghan government and U.S. and NATO forces. The official Taliban leadership, headed by Mullah Omar, was strongest in the Kandahar and Helmand provinces. Some insurgent forces operated under the jurisdiction and with the approval of the Taliban central authority, but many acted independently of any authority and sometimes were no more than local criminal elements using the Taliban name as a means of legitimization.

DOCTRINE, STRATEGY, AND TACTICS

Al-Qaeda and the Taliban developed significant combat experience fighting the Soviet Union in Afghanistan from 1979 to 1989, and those experiences served as the basis for their insurgency campaign against U.S. and Allied forces, including NATO forces, in Afghanistan. Hit-and-run and ambush attacks, suicide attacks, and improvised explosive devices (IEDs) such as roadside bombs killed hundreds of American and Allied, including NATO, troops. In 2008, the U.S. military reported 3,800 suicide and roadside bomb attacks against Allied forces, killing 127 Allied troops, and in the first five months of 2009, there was a 25 percent increase in such attacks, killing a total of 53 U.S. and 52 Allied soldiers.

The terrain in Afghanistan is dotted with high mountains and deep valleys and caves, along with treacherous weather, especially in the winter. As a result, combat with al-Qaeda and the Taliban often oc-

Blocks of TNT explosives used for improvised explosive devices (IEDs) and other weapons, confiscated from insurgents in August, 2009.

curred in close quarters in remote and inhospitable areas, undermining, if not negating, the effectiveness of armor, artillery, and even aerial firepower. In addition to difficult terrain, the lack of a national system of roads made travel exceedingly difficult; where roads existed, they were dirt roads. Compounding the problems faced by the United States and its allies was the issue of national identity among the Afghan people: Although al-Qaeda and the Taliban were not necessarily popular with most Afghans, their lack of a sense of national identity or unity and their tendency to see themselves instead as members of a tribe or clan made it difficult for the Afghan government to enjoy the support of either the people or local clans and tribes. Furthermore, the presence of a porous mountainous border with Pakistan to the east and the vast, essentially anarchic Pakistan border regions of the North-West Frontier Province and Federally Administered Tribal Areas, autonomous from Pakistani government control, gave al-Qaeda and the Taliban sanctuary.

President Obama continued the policy of the predecessor Bush administration of sending unmanned Predator drones to strike both along the Afghan-Pakistan border and inside both of these Pakistani provinces—much to the anger of local residents, who not only sympathized with (if not supported) al-Qaeda and the Taliban but also claimed that these strikes killed innocent civilians. The Pakistani government, too, objected to these strikes as a violation of its sovereignty, which also fanned anti-American sentiment.

Complicating the war in Afghanistan, the weak, corrupt, and unstable Pakistani government was paralyzed from both a series of political disputes and a surge of attacks and acts of terrorism by al-Qaeda and the Taliban. There was also much tension between the United States and its NATO allies regarding Afghanistan. The U.S. resented having to shoulder most of the military burden in Afghanistan and hoped Europe could do more to help in the fight against al-Qaeda and the Taliban. Except for the British, Canadians, and Dutch, most European countries either did not permit their forces in Afghanistan to engage in combat or limited combat to defense against attack; this caused tension between European NATO countries as well. Moreover, the Iraq War had strained U.S.-European relations, and most European governments came to regard the war in Afghanistan as unwinnable. Hence, they objected to the single-minded military focus of the American war effort, arguing that instead the best way to blunt the appeal and strength of al-Qaeda and the Taliban was to rebuild the country's economy and infrastructure.

Despite his immense popularity in Europe, President Obama failed during his April, 2009, European trip to garner pledges for additional support for the war in Afghanistan from European members of NATO. Withdrawing or abandoning Afghanistan would not, however, make the United States safe from al-Qaeda, the Taliban, and future terrorist attacks but would only embolden these groups and once again turn Afghanistan into the terrorist safe haven it was during the 1990's.

On February 9, 2009, Frederick W. Kagan, a noted military historian and influential scholar behind the successful "surge" strategy used in Iraq, in an article entitled "Planning Victory in Afghanistan," published in the *National Review*, criticized the current U.S. strategy in Afghanistan for conducting effective counterterrorism operations against al-Qaeda and the Taliban without simultaneously protecting the population from the militants and using economic and political programs to build popular support for the Afghan government (which would promote popular resistance to al-Qaeda and the Taliban). The U.S. focus exclusively on defeating al-Qaeda and the Taliban without simultaneously working to win over the Afghan people had delegitimized and marginalized both groups.

CONTEMPORARY SOURCES

The war in Afghanistan is an ongoing conflict, and much of the primary source information on the Afghanistan War is current and available online, including the U.S. Department of Defense's annual Narcotics Control Reports (Afghanistan section) and the U.S. Department of State's South and Central Asia Reports.

Most of the book-length primary sources take the form of memoirs that are just beginning to appear. *At the Center of the Storm: My Years at the CIA* (New York: HarperCollins, 2007) is a memoir by former director of the Central Intelligence Agency George Tenet, in which he discusses all aspects of the U.S. response to the September 11, 2001, terrorist attacks, the War on Terror, the Afghanistan War, and the Iraq War. Douglas Feith, former undersecretary of defense for policy, in *War and Decision: Inside the Pentagon at the Dawn of the War on Terrorism* (New York: Harper, 2008), gives an insider's view of the history of the early years of the War on Terror, including the Afghanistan and Iraq Wars. His book also includes facsimiles of U.S. government memos and other documents from the period.

BOOKS AND ARTICLES

Combs, Cynthia. *Terrorism in the Twenty-first Century*. Upper Saddle River, N.J.: Prentice Hall, 2008.

Jacobson, Sid, and Ernie Colón. *After 9/11: America's War on Terror, 2001-*. New York: Hill and Wang, 2008.

Maley, William. *Afghanistan's Wars*. 2d ed. New York: Palgrave Macmillan, 2009.

FILMS AND OTHER MEDIA

Afghanistan: The Forgotten War. Documentary. Public Broadcasting Service, 2008.

The History Channel Declassified: The Taliban. Documentary. The History Channel, 2007.

The Road to 9/11. Documentary. Kunhardt Productions, 2005.

Suicide Killers, Documentary. City Lights Entertainment, 2007.

The War Against Al Qaeda. Documentary. The History Channel, 2008.

Stefan M. Brooks

THE WAR ON TERROR

Dates: Since 1988

POLITICAL CONSIDERATIONS

Though the name "War on Terror" was invented by the administration of U.S. president George W. Bush (2001-2009), the conflict between the Western powers (and their allies) and the usually less organized and therefore more difficult-to-track terrorist groups long predates the 2000's. The constant conflict between Israel and its Arab neighbors, not to mention its Palestinian residents, made terrorism a concern of the United States, as Israel's staunchest ally. During the late 1970's, the birth of the Islamic revolutionary movement in Iran provided the United States with its longest involvement with Arab groups bent on America's destruction, when fifty-three hostages were held in the U.S. embassy in Iran for 444 days. Further attacks, such as the 1983 bombings of the U.S. embassy and Marine Corps encampment in Beirut, Lebanon, and the 1988 bombing of Pan Am Flight 103 over Lockerbie, Scotland, continually kept terrorism near the top of the evening newscasts.

The 1990's witnessed a rise in the frequency and lethality of international terrorism, principally from the Middle East, perpetrated by Islamic religious fanatics and culminating in the attacks against the United States on September 11, 2001. This tragic, three-pronged attack—in which hijacked airlines were deliberately crashed into the World Trade Center towers, the Pentagon, and (after heroic action on the part of passengers) a field in Pennsylvania—was followed by bombings in Bali, Indonesia, in 2002; Madrid, Spain, in 2004; London, England, in 2005; and Mumbai, India, in 2008.

After the 9/11 attacks, the United States' efforts under President Bush to combat international terrorism—particularly from al-Qaeda and its associates and affiliates—was called the War (or Global War) on Terror. Taking office in 2009, President Barack Obama dropped this controversial phrase in favor of

"Overseas Contingency Operation." Nevertheless, the United States and Europe, as President Obama announced during his April, 2009, trip to the Continent, continued to face the very real threat of international terrorism.

Terrorism is not a new phenomenon—the 1960's and 1970's witnessed terrorism—nor has it been limited to foreign perpetrators. However, the decline and subsequent collapse of the Soviet Union in 1991, the rise of Islamic fundamentalism and its radicalization of the Middle East and Arab politics, the status of the United States as the sole remaining world superpower (along with the envy and hatred this created), the development of a truly global economy, and a growing interdependence among states in terms of communications, trade, and travel have all contributed to make terrorism more far-reaching and lethal to nation-states. The threat of nuclear war between the United States and the Soviet Union during the Cold War years (1945-1991) was replaced by international terrorism, and while that threat was disrupted and even weakened by the actions taken by the United States and its allies, it has yet to be eliminated, as demonstrated by the November, 2008, attacks on a hotel in Mumbai, India, which killed more than 170 people and injured some 300.

Initially, the world, including the United States, was slow in realizing—much less confronting—the growing danger posed by Islamic terrorism. Indeed, the National Commission on Terrorist Attacks upon the United States (the so-called 9/11 Commission), which investigated the events leading up to and during the September 11 attacks, cited a "failure of imagination" on the part of U.S. intelligence services, the Central Intelligence Agency (CIA) and the Federal Bureau of Investigation (FBI), as well as Congress for insufficient oversight of these and other agencies. Instead of recognizing the grave threat posed by al-Qaeda and like-minded groups, throughout the 1990's the American intelligence services were operating from a Cold War mind-set. In addition, American law prohibited the sharing of intelligence between the CIA and the FBI, and outdated laws crippled efforts to track suspected terrorists in the United States.

Historically, the United States has suffered few terrorist incidents and thus on September 11, 2001, had little experience dealing with terrorism, such that the federal government was slow and unprepared to confront this growing threat. Even Western Europe, which had suffered acts of terrorism over the preceding few decades, seemed to have failed to appreciate the growing threat posed by Islamic terrorism. For example, as a brutal civil war raged in the former French colony of Algeria throughout the 1990's, pitting the army-run government against the terrorist organization known as the Islamic Armed Group (or GIA, Groupe Islamique Armée, for the French name of the group), the GIA launched terrorist attacks in France in retaliation against France's alleged sympathy (if not also covert support) for the army-backed Algerian government. GIA attacks in France included the 1994 hijacking of an Air France flight from Algiers to Paris with the aim of flying the plane into the Eiffel Tower or blowing up the plane over Paris to inflict mass casualties; the plane was recaptured by French commandos in Marseille, France, while being refueled. The GIA also launched a series of bombings in the Paris metro in 1995 that killed eight people and injured more than one hundred. These attacks by the GIA—particularly the attempt to use a commercial aircraft as a bomb, as would be done on 9/11—seem neither to have alerted European nations that Islamic terrorists were starting to direct their attacks toward Europe nor to have signaled the increasing reach and operational capability of these groups. Even the February 26, 1993, World Trade Center and April 19, 1995, Oklahoma City bombings in the United States seemed to have been treated by the U.S. government as almost aberrant acts—perhaps because of the successful arrest and prosecution of those responsible for both attacks: Ramzi Yousef (a member of al-Qaeda) in the case of the 1993 World Trade Center attacks and Timothy McVeigh and Terry Nichols (anarchist opponents of the federal government) in the Oklahoma case.

Preoccupied with events in Europe as the Cold War came to an end, the breakup of Yugoslavia and the ensuing civil wars in Bosnia and Croatia, the building of a "new world order," the push to expand the North Atlantic Treaty Organization (NATO) into Eastern Europe, and the outbreak of the 1990-1991 Persian Gulf War (which precipitated the decades-long confrontation with Iraqi leader Saddam Hussein), the world failed to appreciate not only that terrorism was growing but also, more ominously and for the first time, that terrorist groups, particularly Arab Islamic groups, had begun to develop an international character in terms of presence and reach, finance and support. Disparate Islamic Sunni groups that had fought together against the Soviet Union in Afghanistan (1980-1988) developed a sense of identity that transcended nationality and were organized between the late

TURNING POINTS

1988	After Pan American Flight 103 explodes over Lockerbie, Scotland, killing hundreds, state terrorism mounted by Libya is suspected as cause.
1993	A bomb attack on New York's World Trade Center kills 6 people and injures more than 1,000.
1995	The April bombing of a federal office building in Oklahoma City, Oklahoma, by one or more individuals allegedly affiliated with militia groups kills 168. Within the same week, a Japanese religious cult mounts a gas attack in a Tokyo subway, hospitalizing 400.
1996	Millionaire Islamic extremist Osama Bin Laden issues a declaration of war against United States.
1998	The simultaneous bombings of U.S. embassies in Kenya and Tanzania in August kill 224, and Bin Laden group supporters are suspected. United States conducts counterattack shortly thereafter against Bin Laden training base in Afghanistan.
2000	The October 12 suicide bombing of the USS *Cole* in the Persian Gulf kills 17 sailors.

1980's and early 1990's by the exiled Saudi Arabian Osama Bin Laden into al-Qaeda (Arabic for "the base").

Bin Laden, like countless other Muslims, had gone to Afghanistan to wage jihad (holy war) against the Soviet Union and used his inherited family fortune and organizational skills to recruit, arm, train, and organize the mujahideen (Arabic for "holy warriors of jihad"), thereby developing a favorable reputation among the mujahideen community. Shortly after forming al-Qaeda, Bin Laden met fellow mujahideen Ayman al-Zawahiri in Afghanistan, merging al-Qaeda with al-Zawahiri's Egyptian Islamic Jihadist followers in the early 1990's. Announcing that America had declared war on God and Islam, in February, 1998, Bin Laden and al-Zawahiri arranged for an Arabic newspaper in London, England, to publish a fatwa (or religious edict) calling it the duty of every Muslim to kill Americans. In a May, 1998, interview with ABC News reporter John Miller, Bin Laden said the defeat of the Soviet Union in Afghanistan and its subsequent collapse convinced him that "we shall—with the grace of Allah—prevail over the Americans and the Jews." In the same interview, he also warned that unless the U.S. government stopped catering to "the interests of Jews," al-Qaeda would "inevitably move the battle to American soil, just as Ramzi Yousef and others have done"—a direct threat to commit terrorist attacks in America. By 1992, al-Qaeda had begun launching terrorist attacks, first in the Middle East and then, as the organization and its members' competence expanded, in other parts of the world, including Africa, the United States, and Europe.

MILITARY ACHIEVEMENT

Before the mass casualties inflicted by the attacks of 9/11, the United States and the rest of the world regarded terrorism as a problem for law enforcement rather than the military, emphasizing the arrest and prosecution of terrorists, such that where military force was used, it was limited to missile or air strikes designed to punish rather than destroy the terrorists and their safe havens. Until 9/11, despite several attacks overseas, the United States did not view terrorism as an act of war, and consequently airport security was lax and ineffective. Not until after 9/11 did President Bush declare a War on Terror, announcing to the world on November 6, 2001, that "you are either with us [the United States] or against us" in the global war on terrorism. Until 9/11, neither President Bill Clinton nor President Bush regarded terrorism as much of a threat to the United States. For that matter, the world was as surprised and horrified as Americans were at the ability of al-Qaeda to inflict such death and destruction (more than twenty-seven hundred people died in New York alone) on 9/11.

Despite the 1993 World Trade Center bombing, which had killed six people and injured more than one thousand, and the 1996 bombing of the U.S. Air Force's Khobar Towers barracks in Saudi Arabia, which killed nineteen airmen, not until August 7, 1998, and the American embassy bombings in Kenya and Tanzania, which killed twelve Americans and more than two hundred Africans, did President Clinton launch cruise missile strikes (on August 20) against al-Qaeda targets in Sudan and Afghanistan. These strikes, however, failed to kill al-Qaeda's leadership, including Bin Laden and al-Zawahiri, and, although destroying some al-Qaeda training camps (abandoned in anticipation of an American attack), had no effect on the organization; indeed, Bin Laden and al-Zawahiri promised more attacks against the United States. Although it is likely that any American response would have provoked additional al-Qaeda attacks, because America's response was ineffective and the use of missiles was interpreted by al-Qaeda as a sign of weakness (that the U.S. was unwilling to commit significant military forces and risk suffering casualties by committing ground troops to Afghanistan), Clinton's missile strikes probably only emboldened al-Qaeda.

It is worth remarking, however, that no political support existed among either Democrats or Republicans—or among the American people—for launching an invasion or even a limited ground campaign in Afghanistan, where the Taliban government had granted al-Qaeda sanctuary in 1996. In 1998, America still suffered from a false sense of invulnerability against terrorism, and therefore neither the will nor

The USS Cole, *after a terrorist attack in Yemeni waterways in October, 2000, possibly by the Aden-Abyan Islamic Army.*

the support existed for overthrowing the Taliban regime and depriving al-Qaeda of its sanctuary and bases in Afghanistan. In 2000, al-Qaeda terrorists attacked the U.S. Navy ship USS *Cole* in Yemen, killing seventeen sailors and severely damaging the ship, but failed in an attempt to bomb Los Angeles International Airport after the bomber—who apparently was under surveillance by Canadian intelligence—was arrested at the U.S.-Canadian border with explosives in his vehicle.

The attacks of 9/11, however, shattered America's sense of invulnerability and, tragically, literally brought home the threat posed by al-Qaeda. Like his

predecessor, it was not until faced with a crisis—this time, the 9/11 attacks—that President Bush took decisive action against al-Qaeda and international terrorism, launching the War on Terror with the stated aim of destroying al-Qaeda and states sponsoring or supporting terrorism. There was a strong outpouring of sympathy and support for the United States from most of the world as the 9/11 attacks united much of the world in solidarity with the Americans against al-Qaeda and terrorism. One month after 9/11, the United States, along with Britain, invaded Afghanistan, and two months later they overthrew the Taliban regime, inflicting heavy casualties on both Taliban and al-Qaeda forces as U.S. and British troops and their Afghan allies in the Northern Alliance pursued fleeing militants. However, despite the swift collapse and defeat of the Taliban and al-Qaeda, Bin Laden and al-Zawahiri eluded capture or death, presumably fleeing during the December, 2001, Battle of Tora Bora into the lawless tribal areas of northwestern Pakistan.

On March 20, 2003, the United States and Britain invaded Iraq to overthrow Saddam Hussein for his continued refusal to comply with sixteen U.N. resolutions stipulating that he account for and give up all of his weapons of mass destruction (WMDs)—namely, biological and chemical weapons—and thus prove that he no longer possessed them. President Bush alleged that Hussein's defiance of the United Nations, his continued efforts to develop WMDs (in defiance of the United Nations), his past use of WMDs, the brutality of his regime, and his links to terrorism (including, allegedly, to al-Qaeda) constituted a threat to the United States and the world. Bush believed that with Hussein redeveloping his WMDs and ties to terrorism, he might once again wage war against his neighbors (as he had done by invading Kuwait in 1990), form alliances with terrorist groups (including al-Qaeda), and even supply terrorists with WMDs. In the wake of 9/11, Bush argued that the specter of Hussein repossessing WMDs was intolerable. The March, 2003, invasion of Iraq, followed by the overthrow of Hussein's government one month later, killed about 150 American soldiers in two months of fighting. The post-invasion occupation of Iraq, however, proved to be an enormous challenge and a problem for the United States in terms of mounting casualties (4,277 as of April 19, 2009, according to the U.S. Pentagon), sustained and soaring costs (estimated at around $860 billion as of 2009), and loss of significant world support. The Iraq War not only preoccupied the Bush administration for the next six years but also proved to be the main factor in the six-year decline of Bush's approval ratings (to approximately 34 percent, according to Gallup) by the time he left office on January 20, 2009. By 2007, however, after a much-needed shift in U.S. strategy and tactics, the situation in Iraq had finally started to improve, and by 2008 violence in Iraq, including American casualties, had declined significantly and the country and its nascent democratic government had become much more stable.

Although the situation in Iraq improved, conditions in Afghanistan worsened as al-Qaeda terrorists fled from Iraq to Afghanistan, political instability consumed Pakistan and sapped its willingness to confront Taliban and al-Qaeda terrorists hiding in Pakistan, and the Taliban and al-Qaeda regrouped and launched an insurgency against U.S. forces and the democratic Afghan government of Hamid Karzai. As American military deaths in Afghanistan rose by 35 percent in 2008 (and to 113 soldiers killed in February, 2009), President Obama pledged to "disrupt, dismantle, and defeat al-Qaeda and the Taliban" and dispatched to Afghanistan an additional 17,000 combat troops and 4,000 military trainers from the Eighty-second Airborne Division to train that country's army, bringing the total number of U.S. troops to about 27,000.

WEAPONS, UNIFORMS, AND ARMOR

Al-Qaeda and its affiliates and associates have resorted to largely unconventional weapons to wage terrorism, using vehicles, boats (as in the case of the USS *Cole* attack), and airplanes (as on 9/11) to inflict mass casualties. In Afghanistan and Iraq, improvised explosive devices (IEDs), to say nothing of deadly ambush attacks, have killed hundreds of American and Allied, including NATO, troops. Al-Qaeda has also been known to rely on suicide bombings, as on 9/11 and in the Bali, Madrid, and London bombings.

Al-Qaeda and the Taliban lack firepower and technology, particularly the artillery, air power, and night-vision equipment used by U.S. forces. Therefore, they generally avoid open, prolonged engagements and favor ambushes and hit-and-run tactics. These serve to frustrate and demoralize their adversary, denying the enemy a decisive victory and thus prolonging the conflict. In so doing, the Taliban and al-Qaeda hope to win the psychological battle of wearing down the enemy by making the war seem endless and thus unwinnable.

MILITARY ORGANIZATION

The organization of forces in the war against terrorism is as nebulous and varied as it is vast. On the U.S. and Allied side, military organization comprises military and civilian departments within the U.S. government and the military forces and government offices of other Allied nations. Although the military structure and interrelationships of the myriad terrorist and extremist groups worldwide would take more than one volume to cover in detail, some rundown of the main players in the War on Terror is helpful.

Each terrorist group has a different structure, and often those structures change as soon as Western intelligence can classify them. Although al-Qaeda and the Taliban dominate the headlines, groups classified as current threats are not limited by geography. Other groups involved in the War on Terror include Colombia's National Liberation Army and Revolutionary Armed Forces of Colombia (both of whose members have carried out kidnappings of American citizens), Al-Jihad (whose members assassinated Egyptian president Anwar el-Sadat), al-Gama'a al-Islamiyya in Egypt, the National Liberation Army of Iran in Iraq, Aum Shinrikyo (Supreme Truth) sect in Japan (which carried out the 1995 Tokyo subway attack using sarin nerve gas), Hezbollah in Israel and Lebanon (which carried out the 1983 bombing of the U.S. Marine barracks), Hamas in Israel, Harakat ul-Ansar and Harakat ul-Mujahidin in Pakistan, the New People's Army in the Philippines, the Revolutionary United Front in Sierra Leone, the Liberation Tigers of Tamil Eelam in Sri Lanka, the Revolutionary People's Liberation Party in Turkey, and the Islamic Movement of Uzbekistan. Of course, the very nature of these transitory groups means that they are constantly and currently metamorphosing, as new groups are founded out of the remnants of old ones.

In the aftermath of the September 11, 2001, terrorist attacks, President Bush created the Department of Homeland Security, under whose auspices many previously independent federal bureaus and offices were consolidated, including the National Guard, the Federal Emergency Management Agency, the Coast Guard, Customs and Border Protection, Immigration and Customs Enforcement, Citizenship and Immigration Services, the Secret Service, the Transportation Security Administration, and the Civil Air Patrol. In addition, although the U.S. government has long called operations to quell terrorism and secure the country a "war," the varied and often unstructured nature of terrorist organizations has raised questions as to the status of their "soldiers." For its purposes, the United States has called them "unlawful combatants," which allows the United States to escape the provisions of the Geneva Conventions. However, such a characterization has not gone without criticism by the American public, as has been demonstrated by the backlash against the use of torture and the indefinite confinement, without being charged, of Iraqis and other nationals deemed to have been involved in international terrorism at the Joint Task Force's detention camps at Guantánamo Bay (Gitmo).

DOCTRINE, STRATEGY, AND TACTICS

Al-Qaeda and the mujahideen community in general developed significant combat experience fighting the Soviet Union in Afghanistan from 1979 to 1989, and those experiences served as the basis for their insurgency campaign against U.S. and Allied forces, including NATO forces, in Afghanistan and Iraq. In Iraq, the United States was able, under the leadership of U.S. Army general David Petraeus, then commander of U.S. forces in Iraq, to reverse most of the violence and terrorism plaguing Iraq. His strategy, known as the surge, changed the way the United States and its allies were battling al-Qaeda and other insurgents and terrorist groups in Iraq by denying them the ability to control territory, terrorize, and enjoy sanctuary among the local population. Under General Petraeus, the strategy of the United States was to clear and hold territory; instead of remaining ensconced in well-defended bases distant from violence, the U.S. military, along with Iraqi forces, took up residence inside the most violent areas of Iraq not only to eliminate insurgent activity but, just as important, to hold the territory, thereby denying the insurgents and terrorists sanctuary and support. As security improved (along with the competence of Iraqi forces), so did civil services, and the insurgents and terrorists lost much of their support and, at least temporarily, were rendered largely ineffective. In 2009, al-Qaeda no longer even mentioned Iraq in its propaganda broadcasts—a tacit admission it had failed to turn Iraq into a terrorist state.

In addition to the surge, al-Qaeda's killing of Muslim insurgents contributed to the improvement in Iraq's security, encouraging many Iraqis to turn against al-Qaeda through so-called awakening councils and enabling the United States to recruit former insurgents and terrorists to fight al-Qaeda.

Whether such a surge can succeed in Afghanistan is a different matter, since conditions in that country are very different from those in Iraq. Unlike Iraq, terrain in Afghanistan is dotted with high mountains and deep valleys and caves, along with treacherous weather, especially in the winter. There is little sense of a national identity or unity among the people of Afghanistan, and politics are based instead on ethnic (tribal, clan, and linguistic) identities. The country lacks a history of a centralized government and, in addition to its rough terrain, its lack of a national system of roads makes travel difficult. Furthermore, the presence of a porous mountainous border with Pakistan to the east—and vast, essentially anarchic border regions (the North-West Frontier Province and Federally Administered Tribal Areas), autonomous from Pakistani government control—gives al-Qaeda and the Taliban sanctuary.

In his first year in office, President Obama continued the Bush administration's policy of unmanned Predator drone strikes along the Afghan-Pakistani border and also inside both the North-West Frontier Province and Federally Administered Tribal Areas, much to the anger of local residents, who not only sympathized with al-Qaeda and the Taliban but also claimed that these strikes have killed innocent civilians. The Pakistani government also objected to these strikes as a violation of its sovereignty, because of the civilians killed as well as the effect that attacks had of fanning anti-American sentiment. Exacerbating these problems was

a weak and unstable Pakistani government, paralyzed from both a series of political disputes and a surge of terrorist acts fomented by al-Qaeda and its affiliates and associates. The tension and hostility between the United States and its NATO allies regarding Afghanistan was another factor contributing to the problems: The United States resented having to shoulder most of the military burden in Afghanistan and viewed Europe as not doing enough to help in the the fight against al-Qaeda and the Taliban; in addition, most European countries did not permit their forces in Afghanistan to engage in combat (or limited such engagements to responses to being attacked).

On the other side, the Iraq War strained U.S.-

U.S. Navy

A small portion of the destruction of the World Trade Center towers in Manhattan, a few days after the September 11, 2001, terrorist attacks.

European relations, and most European governments, regarding the war in Afghanistan as unwinnable, objected to the military focus of the American war effort, arguing that the best way to blunt the appeal and strength of al-Qaeda and the Taliban was to rebuild the country's economy and infrastructure. Despite President Obama's immense popularity in Europe, his April, 2009, European trip was notable for its lack of success in gaining pledges of additional support for the war in Afghanistan.

In any case, withdrawing or abandoning Afghanistan would not make the United States safe from al-Qaeda and future terrorism; such a course of action would only embolden al-Qaeda and Afghanistan would once again become the terrorist safe haven it was during the 1990's. It seems likely that the War on Terror will continue for a very long time, and the best-case scenario is that the United States will stop and maybe even reverse much of the surge in al-Qaeda and Taliban attacks.

CONTEMPORARY SOURCES

Despite President Obama's change in nomenclature, the War on Terror is an ongoing conflict, with new primary sources being generated almost daily. There are a few indispensable pieces, without which the War on Terror cannot be fully understood. *The 9/11 Commission Report: Final Report of the National Commission on Terrorist Attacks upon the United States* (New York: W. W. Norton, 2004), is a sort of manual for the War on Terror, outlining the context of the September 11, 2001, terrorist attacks, and the U.S. government's response to the attacks. Most of the book-length primary sources take the form of memoirs that are just beginning to appear. *At the Center of the Storm: My Years at the CIA* (New York: HarperCollins, 2007) is a memoir by former director of the Central Intelligence Agency George Tenet, in which he discusses all aspects of the U.S. response to the September 11, 2001, terrorist attacks, the War on Terror, the Afghanistan War, and the Iraq War. Douglas Feith, former undersecretary of defense for policy, wrote *War and Decision: Inside the Pentagon at the Dawn of the War on Terrorism* (New York: Harper, 2008), in which he gives an insider's view of the history of the early years of the War on Terror, including the Afghanistan and Iraq wars. The book also includes facsimiles of U.S. government memoranda and other documents from the period.

BOOKS AND ARTICLES

Combs, Cynthia. *Terrorism in the Twenty-first Century*. Upper Saddle River, N.J.: Prentice Hall, 2008.

"Homeland Security: Protecting Airliners from Terrorist Missiles." Congressional Research Service Report for Congress RL31741, February 16, 2006.

Jacobson, Sid, and Ernie Colón. *After 9/11: America's War on Terror, 2001-*. New York: Hill and Wang, 2008.

National Commission on Terrorist Attacks upon the United States. *The 9/11 Commission Report: Final Report of the National Commission on Terrorist Attacks upon the United States*. Thomas H. Kean, chair, and Lee H. Hamilton, vice chair. New York: W. W. Norton, 2004.

FILMS AND OTHER MEDIA

Afghanistan: The Forgotten War. Documentary. Public Broadcasting Service, 2008.

The Road to 9/11. Documentary. Kunhardt Productions, 2005.

Suicide Killers, Documentary. City Lights Entertainment, 2007.

The War Against Al Qaeda. Documentary. The History Channel, 2008.

Stefan M. Brooks

WARFARE AND THE UNITED NATIONS

Dates: Since c. 1990

POLITICAL CONSIDERATIONS

International law recognizes the right of states to defend themselves. The United Nations system requires all states to abide by Article 2.4 of the U.N. Charter, prohibiting threat and use of force while also requiring that states resort only to peaceful countermeasures when addressing a breach of their legal rights by another state.

Chapter VII of the U.N. Charter vests the U.N. Security Council with broad powers of forcible intervention. It can intervene whenever it determines, under Article 39, that there exists a threat to the peace, a breach of the peace, or an act of aggression. It can then decide, under Article 41, upon sanctions that do not involve the use of force of arms, or it can then decide, under Article 42, to take action by force of arms against the aggressor or the state threatening peace.

The basic rule about the unilateral use of force in international relations is that such use is forbidden. The only exception is in the "inherent right of individual or collective self-defense if an armed attack occurs." The term "armed attack" in this context means a "very serious onslaught" either on the territory of the injured state or on its agents or citizens, while they are at home or abroad, meaning in another state or in international waters or airspace. According to Article 51 of the U.N. Charter:

> Nothing in the present Charter shall impair the inherent right of individual or collective self-defence if an armed attack occurs against a Member of the United Nations, until the Security Council has taken measures necessary to maintain international peace and security. Measures taken by Members in the exercise of this right of self-defence shall be immediately reported to the Security Council and shall not in any way affect the authority and responsibility of the Security Council under the present Charter to

take at any time such action as it deems necessary in order to maintain or restore international peace and security.

States have the right to resort to collective self-defense in the case of aggression by arms, subject to the request or consent of the victim of aggression. The collective self-defense measures do not affect or prejudice the possible operation of the U.N. security system. The U.N. security system may authorize states to take forceful measures against the wrongdoer if the U.N. Security Council concludes that a gross violation of international community obligations amounts to a threat to the peace, a breach of the peace, or an act of aggression. The U.N. Security Council takes over when it faces an international wrongful act that it deems that Article 39 of the U.N. Charter covers.

The U.N. Charter also sets a number of limits upon the right of self-defense, which Article 51 enshrines. This provision, which has developed into a provision of general international law, allows the use of force only in self-defense in order to repel an "armed attack," and the defending State must immediately inform the Security Council of the action of using arms in self-defense. Article 51 envisages self-defense as a provisional measure by which the victim of an attack by force of arms may safeguard its rights until the security system, which centralizes this function, begins to work.

The basic deficiencies of the collective security system the U.N. Charter outlines include the assumption of continuing agreement among the permanent members of the Security Council: the United States, Russia, China, the United Kingdom, and France. This "P5" consensus was the basis for the proposal of a collective monopoly of force that they would hold accordingly. Dissent with the individual veto power that the U.N. Charter gives to each permanent member gives each the right to cripple the system. The Cold War gave the permanent members the incentive to exercise this veto against an adversary's draft resolutions proposed under Chapter VII. Consequently, a distinguishing tendency to the present has emerged among states to engage in war under the cloak of "self-defense" without having to fear any decisive hindrance from the United Nations. In a number of cases, states have resorted to unilateral force under the cover of self-defense, protection of nationals abroad, or preemptive self-defense.

MILITARY ACHIEVEMENT

The end of the Cold War with the 1991 dissolution of the Soviet Union led to an increase in Great Power cooperation. The net result has been an increase in the number of peacekeeping operations, as well as in their size and complexity. The United Nations established only fifteen peacekeeping operations before 1988. Since then, the United Nations has established approximately forty such operations.

Two other critical features of peacekeeping operations are consent of the territorial state and impartiality. In some cases, peacekeeping has proceeded on the basis of a partial consent, meaning that peacekeeping forces have lacked the consent of one or more of the parties in the conflict. This situation has jeopardized the impartiality requirements of the operation. In 1992-1995, the U.N. Operation in Somalia (UNOSOM I) underwent a radical transformation through action by the Security Council, when UNOSOM I became UNOSOM II. The Security Council endowed UNOSOM II with enforcement

powers under Chapter VII of the U.N. Charter (Resolution 814/1993). In Resolution 836 (June, 1993), the U.N. Security Council authorized the U.N. Protection Force (UNPROFOR) in the former Yugoslavia, "acting in self-defense, to take the necessary measures, including the use of force, to reply to bombardments against the safe areas by any of the parties."

The United Nations deployed forces in all three cases where no peace existed to keep, that is, in situations of ongoing conflict within states and in which a partial or nearly total breakdown of governmental authorities had taken place. This trend in entrusting peacekeeping forces with enforcement functions has, however, undergone strong criticism—nor has it developed to the point of creating a special category of U.N. peace-enforcement units, which U.N. Secretary General Boutros Boutros-Ghali envisaged in 1992 in his "Agenda for Peace."

On other occasions, the U.N. Security Council implicitly authorized regional or other organizations or arrangements to use force. The Security Council authorized, for example, maritime operations to enforce the embargo, as well as air operations to back up the peacekeeping forces (UNPROFOR) protecting safe areas. The implementation of the authorization was implicitly but obviously to occur through the West European Union (WEU) and the North Atlantic Treaty Organization (NATO). The Security Council authorized NATO to establish a multinational force in Bosnia-Herzegovina, the Implementation Force (IFOR), which subsequently became the Stabilization Force (SFOR) after the end of the war in 1995. Its mandate was to ensure, if necessary by the use of force, the implementation of the General Framework Agreement for Peace in Bosnia and Herzegovina (Dayton Agreement).

Yugoslavia was the conflict with the greatest degree of complexity that the United Nations had confronted since the end of the Cold War. The developments in the following years of war in the former Yugoslavia included unsuccessful diplomatic efforts to end the conflict, including the Vance-Owen plan, the establishment by the Security Coun-

TURNING POINTS

Feb., 1991	U.N. forces undertake a decisive ground assault on Iraqi positions in Kuwait.
Apr., 1991	No-fly zones are established and enforced in Iraq to prevent repression of Kurds in northern Iraq.
Jan., 1996	An international force composed largely of NATO troops is deployed in Bosnia to ensure the implementation of the Dayton Accords.

cil of an International War Crimes Tribunal with the jurisdiction to prosecute crimes that had occurred in the violent conflict in the former Yugoslavia, and the authorization of member states by the Security Council in Resolution 816 in 1993 to take "all necessary measures in the airspace of the Republic of Bosnia and Herzegovina, in the event of further violation, to ensure compliance with the ban on flights." On May 6, 1993, Security Council Resolution 824 declared the cities of Sarajevo, Tuzla, Zepa, Goražde, and Bihać in Bosnia-Herzegovina as safe areas, after the United Nations declared Srebrenica and its surroundings as a safe area in Resolution 819 of April 16, 1993. Between April, 1994, and February, 1995, NATO airplanes conducted nine limited attacks against Serbian targets on the ground. In March, 1995, the Security Council decided on the replacement of UNPROFOR by three separate but interlinked peacekeeping operations in Bosnia-Herzegovina (UNPROFOR), Croatia (U.N. Confidence Restoration Operation, or UNCRO), and Macedonia (U.N. Preventative Deployment Force, or UNPREDEP).

On August 28, 1995, thirty-eight people died in the Muslim part of Sarajevo by artillery fire, for which NATO held the Serbs responsible. This action led to Operation Deliberate Force on August 30, 1995, which lasted until September 14, 1995. It included heavy bombardment of troops, weapons, military installations, and production sites. The targets also included civilian traffic routes, intersections and bridges, and targets throughout the whole part of Bosnia-Herzegovina that the Serb forces controlled, going beyond the U.N. mandate to protect the safety zones.

The parties initialed the General Framework

AP/Wide World Photos

U.S. M-1A1 Abrams tanks enter Bosnia in 1995 as part of a U.N. peacekeeping force that would allow the United Nations to focus on humanitarian issues.

Agreement for Peace in Bosnia and Herzegovina on November 21, 1995, at a U.S. Air Force base near Dayton, Ohio. They signed this "Dayton Agreement" in Paris on December 14, 1995, with the five members of the "Contact Group" witnessing: the United States, Russia, France, Germany, and Britain. In accordance with the terms of the agreement, on December 15, 1995, the U.N. Security Council authorized the deployment of a 60,000-member multinational military Implementation Force (IFOR), having within it NATO and non-NATO forces, to replace

UNPROFOR as of December 20, 1995, and to ensure compliance with the Dayton Agreement. Apart from the air strikes, in the case of Yugoslavia the Security Council was reluctant to back up by military sanctions the decisions it had taken under Chapter VII following the initial Resolution 713 of September 25, 1991.

The 1999 Kosovo crisis put this post-Cold War system, which the international community had consolidated, at significant risk. NATO decided to attack the Federal Republic of Yugoslavia (Serbia and Montenegro) without any Security Council authorization because of the massive gross violations of human rights by de facto and de jure state agents who were perpetrating them against the Kosovar population. The response of some commentators is that the Security Council, acting through Resolution 1244/1999 (adopted after the end of the war), endorsed NATO's action ex post facto. A gradual alteration of the legal framework governing the use of force emerged as a consequence of the events of September 11, 2001, which focused world attention on terrorism. Which terrorist group had actually launched the attack was not clear on that day or for weeks afterward—nor was the answer clear as to whether or not one or more states had been instrumental in organizing and effecting the strike or at least harboring and assisting the terrorists.

The U.N. Security Council unanimously passed a resolution, 1368, on September 12, 2001. Its preamble "recognized" the right of individual and collective self-defense, plainly of the United States and other states willing to assist it, respectively. The resolution defined the terrorist acts of September 11 as a "threat to the peace" and, therefore, not as an "armed attack," which would legitimize self-defense under Article 51. A later U.N. Security Council resolution, 1373, which it adopted on September 28, 2001, expressed the Security Council's "readiness to take all the necessary steps to respond to the terrorist attacks . . . in accordance with its responsibility under the Charter of the United Nations." The U.N. Security Council declared itself, thereby, to be ready to authorize military and other action, if necessary. This resolution wavered between the desire to take matters into its own hands, on one hand, and resignation to unilateral action by the United States, on the other. The ambiguity of the resolution probably stems to a large extent from the will of the United States to manage the crisis by itself, though with the possible assistance of states of its own choice. It wanted to do so without having to go through the U.N. Security Council and regularly report to it.

On the same day, relying on Article 5 of the NATO Statute, the North Atlantic Council unanimously adopted a statement providing for the right of collective self-defense in case of attack on one of the (then) nineteen members of the Alliance. The NATO member states opted to base their solution on U.N. Charter Article 51, thereby referring to the right of self-defense as the avenue rather than collective use of force under the authority of the Security Council.

Practically all states took an attitude that implied a considerable departure from the legal system on the use of force in the matter of a few days, to the effect of broadening the notion of self-defense. States came to assimilate action by a terrorist group amounting to a "threat to the peace" with aggression by force of arms, thereby entitling the victim state to resort to individual self-defense and third states to act in collective self-defense at the request of the former state. The events following September 11, 2001, allowed the victim state of terrorism to resort to a delayed response, undertaking self-defense use of force after some lapse of time. Classic legal doctrine on self-defense requires that the state react immediately to a specific aggressor state. The international community held as admissible that the United States could establish by its own judgment which state had harbored, supported, and assisted the terrorists. The United States thereby became itself accountable and a legitimate target of military reaction. The traditional U.N. Charter system of self-defense implied that the state acting in self-defense may strike only at a specific state or group of states—that is, the aggressor or aggressors. In other words, the victim state could not choose the target; the victim state was to respond immediately to an act of aggression.

On October 7, 2001, the United States, with the initial assistance of the United Kingdom, initiated military action against Afghanistan, which it termed Operation Enduring Freedom. The United States alleged that its aim was to destroy the bases and infrastructure of the terrorist organization al-Qaeda in that country. It also intended to disrupt the incumbent Afghan authorities, the Taliban. The United States claimed that the Afghan authorities actively assisted, supported, and even used the terrorist organization. The United States invoked the right to individual self-defense, and the United Kingdom relied upon the right of collective self-defense. Both the United States and the United Kingdom claimed that they were responding to the terrorist attacks on the World Trade Center and the Pentagon, thereby acting to deter further terrorist attacks. The military action in Afghanistan lasted a few weeks. Only Iraq and Iran among the community of states openly and expressly challenged the legality of resort to force by the United States, with initial British help. Later, in a letter to the U.N. Security Council, the United States asserted its right to use force not only against Afghanistan but also against other organizations and countries that it claimed were supporting terrorism. Later, the United States mentioned Iran, Iraq, and North Korea. The United States acted forcibly through the United Nations in Iraq in 1990-1991, in Somalia in 1992, and in Bosnia-Herzegovina, 1992-1995, but when the U.N. support was not forthcoming, it acted through NATO in Kosovo in 1999. In other instances, the United States refrained from taking action because it did not have a sufficiently intense interest to intervene (Rwanda in 1994, Sierre Leone in 2000), or it engaged in military operations without any U.N. authorization (Iraq, 2003-2004).

WEAPONS, UNIFORMS, AND ARMOR

National ground-force contingents participating in U.N. peacekeeping operations are typically characterized by their distinctive, white-painted armored vehicles, designed to facili-tate their identification as a neutral force. Military personnel typically paint their helmets the distinctive U.N. sky blue. The United Nations also awards its own military decorations for meritorious service in peacekeeping operations.

MILITARY ORGANIZATION

The founders of the United Nations never envisaged the formation of an "army" that was to be at the disposal of the U.N. proper, exclusively dependent on the U.N. Security Council. Originally, the various member states were to place forces at the disposal of the Security Council as military contingents. Special agreements would determine the number and type of forces and their readiness. The U.N. Security Council would exercise its authority over national forces. These national forces would act under the strategic and military direction of the Security Council's Military Staff Committee. The Charter did not envisage that a state sending a contingent would continue to exercise command and control over it, but by the same token it did not clearly exclude national control,

AP/Wide World Photos

The U.N. Security Council in 1999, voting to allow one more month for the Taliban, which controlled Afghanistan, to hand over Osama bin Laden for trial.

U.N. peacekeepers with clearly marked vehicles drive toward Kibati in eastern Congo in November, 2008.

leading to the dangerous possibility of a "dual allegiance" paralyzing these units. However, with the polarizing effect of the Cold War, the attempt at centralizing the use of force failed.

DOCTRINE, STRATEGY, AND TACTICS

The framers of the U.N. Charter envisaged a different Chapter VII regime governing the use of force in international relations other than the role that U.N. peacekeeping operations fulfill, just as the "authorizations regime" giving complete control to individual member states when using force to enforce the will of the U.N. Security Council also differs. Nevertheless, Chapter VII has become one of the most important U.N. tools, and often the only available one. According to Antonio Cassese (Italian jurist and first president of the International Criminal Tribunal for the former Yugoslavia), the international community universally recognizes it as consistent with the Charter.

The intent of peacekeeping operations is not actually to compel the parties to accept a solution that the U.N. imposes but rather to help put into practice, on the spot, the solution upon which the contending parties agree. U.N. peacekeepers can be very helpful in facilitating the fulfillment of complex peace processes in which the parties are willing to cooperate and build for the future. They of course must serve the first task of stopping the parties from fighting. They also, however, have come under criticism for being counterproductive, in that they freeze the situation without providing a real solution to the basic problems lying at the root of the conflict. An example of a successful U.N. peacekeeping operation includes the United Nations Interim Force in Lebanon (UNIFIL), which assisted in making possible, and less dangerous, the Israeli withdrawal from Lebanon in May and June of 2000. UNIFIL helped stabilize the situation there.

The notion of anticipatory self-defense is a controversial one, with prominent legal scholars disputing and qualifying it. The main concern is that antici-patory self-defense becomes a justification for any use of force. Nuclear weapons, and arguably other forms of weapons of mass destruction (WMDs), have added a new dimension to this argument. Many reject the principle of anticipatory self-defense as legally valid, arguing that it has no legal basis in Article 51 of the U.N. Charter or in customary international law.

CONTEMPORARY SOURCES

For the U.N. report on the sequence of events and causes escalating to UNOSOM II combat with Somali militia, leading to numerous Somali and many UNOSOM II casualties in Mogadishu in 1993, see the "Report of the Commission of Inquiry Established Pursuant to Security Council Resolution 885 (1993) to Investigate Armed Attacks on UNOSOM II Personnel Which Led to Casualties Among Them" (U.N. Security Council, S/1994/653, June 1, 1994). For a U.N. summary and critical analysis of U.N. military peacekeeping operations in Bosnia and Herzegovina leading up to the Srebrenica massacre in the former Yugoslavia, see "Report of the Secretary-General Pursuant to General Assembly Resolution 53/35, the Fall of Srebrenica" (U.N. General Assembly, A/54/549, November 15, 1999). For a U.N. summary and critical analysis of U.N. peacekeeping operations in Rwanda, see "Report of the Independent Inquiry into the Actions of the United Nations During the 1994 Genocide" (U.N. Security Council, S/1999/1257, December 16, 1999). All U.N. Security Council resolutions are available at http://www.un.org/Docs/sc.

BOOKS AND ARTICLES

Cassese, Antonio. *International Law*. New York: Oxford University Press, 2005.
Falk, Richard A. *The Costs of War: International Law, the U.N., and World Order After Iraq*. New York: Routledge, 2008.
Lowe, Vaughan, et al., eds. *The United Nations Security Council and War: The Evolution of Thought and Practice Since 1945*. New York: Oxford University Press, 2008.
Malone, David M., ed. *The U.N. Security Council: From the Cold War to the Twenty-first Century*. Boulder, Colo.: Lynne Rienner, 2004.
Silber, Laura, and Allan Little. *Yugoslavia: Death of a Nation*. New York: Penguin, 1996.

FILMS AND OTHER MEDIA

Black Hawk Down. Feature film. Columbia, 2001.
Crisis in Kosovo. Documentary. ABC News, 1999.
Ghosts of Rwanda. Documentary. Public Broadcasting Service, 2004.
Hotel Rwanda. Feature film. Lions Gate Entertainment, 2004.
The Peacekeepers. Documentary. BFS Entertainment, 2005.
Sometimes in April. Television film. HBO Films, 2005.
Welcome to Sarajevo. Feature film. Miramax, 1997.
Yugoslavia: Death of a Nation. Documentary. Discovery Channel, 1996.

Benedict E. DeDominicis

GLOBAL MILITARY CAPABILITIES

Dates: 2010

OVERVIEW

The military capabilities of 2010 are not goals for the future but the functions of our militaries today. Indeed, some militaries today seem to be militaries of tomorrow, with robots, drone airplanes, and other high-tech weapons. Speed and communication are considered the most valuable traits in a modern army, the high cost of which has led to an incredible diversity in military capabilities. The level at which a nation can conduct warfare has many measurements. Is it strong enough to protect itself from aggressive neighbors? Can it project power beyond its own borders? How far can it project and how much of its forces can be mobilized? How quickly can its army move its forces?

SIGNIFICANCE

Throughout the ages, armies have used superior speed and mobility to gain an advantage, and the armies of today must be faster than ever before. Beyond conventional warfare, a modern military must also be able to compete with asymmetric warfare—to deal with guerrilla tactics, kidnappings, terror bombings, and fighting in close proximity to civilians. Like conventional warfare, asymmetric warfare has evolved. Insurgents and malcontents make excellent use of mass communications to strike at civilians around the globe.

DEFINITIONS OF GLOBAL MILITARY CAPABILITIES IN 2010

The complications mentioned above create benchmarks by which the military capabilities of a nation can be assessed. Few nations are able to excel in all areas. The strata of modern militaries can be broken down into innumerable subcategories of those who are able to meet certain challenges but lack the capabilities to meet others, but for simplicity's sake can be divided into three groups. Those in the top tier are, unsurprisingly, those nations with high military budgets, nuclear weapons, and a hand in the direction of global politics. The second-tier nations all have respectable conventional militaries, capable of protecting their borders, but lack the resources to project that power in other parts of the world. The third tier consists of nations that lack advanced military technology and use archaic weapons and weapon systems. This analysis will address the soldiers of asymmetric warfare, or "fourth-generation warfare," as it is heralded by some. These soldiers are known by many names: guerrilla, insurgent, terrorist, and freedom fighter among them. Although it is difficult to gauge the capabilities of these forces with accuracy, any study of upcoming armed conflict, and military capability, would be remiss to exclude them.

It is generally those nations with the strongest economies and highest military budgets that have the most advanced militaries. In 2010, the nations on this exclusive list were the People's Republic of China (referred to herein as China), the Russian Federation, the United States, France, the United Kingdom, India, Pakistan, Israel, and North Korea. These nations have sophisticated machines, cutting-edge electronics, and huge numbers of troops, planes, and tanks. It is important to note that not all of the world's major powers seek to project military force globally. Many are simply concerned with national security. Currently North Korea, Israel, India, and Pakistan are mainly interested in national security. China is evolving from a period of defense to one of interest in global affairs. In fact, only the member nations of the North Atlantic Treaty Organization (NATO) seem mainly concerned about projecting their military

U.S. president Barack Obama at the Group of Eight (G8) meetings in Italy during July, 2009, where he expressed "serious concern" over post-election violence against demonstrators in Iran.

might across the planet. Therefore, as different as each of these nation's military goals are, their nuclear weapons tie them together.

Some individuals and organizations argue that nuclear weapons have, to a great extent, lost their place in battle and have become purely political tools. The invasion of Israel in 1947-1948 illustrates that nuclear weapons do not necessarily prevent attack. Nuclear weapons give negotiating power, but they do not win wars or protect any nation completely. For rival nuclear powers like India and Pakistan, the possibility of nuclear war is very real, held off only by a fragile peace. Here nuclear weapons produce the same circumstances that they did in the Cold War. The theory of mutual assured destruction (MAD) has brought the nations to the negotiating table.

Hence, the major asset of a nuclear arsenal remains the defensive advantage gained by the threat of large-scale destruction. An excellent example is the newest member to the nuclear club. In 2006, North Korea conducted its first successful nuclear test. The result was that Western powers were forced to see North Korea in a new light; once admitted to the club, "nuclear" nations are given a new respect. Even before North Korea started its nuclear weapons program, it had built a substantial military. In fact, having the enormous amount of money that is necessary to develop nuclear weapons, as all of these nations have, means there is a great deal of money available for investment in building an excellent conventional army. Let us take a closer look at the military capabilities of the United States and China.

U.S. MILITARY CAPABILITIES

Strategic capabilities are what make the U.S. armed forces such a powerful military. The United States has the ability to project military power to almost any part of the globe and can do so very quickly. The American military has bases throughout Europe—in Germany, Italy, and the United Kingdom. It has bases in the Pacific—in Alaska, Hawaii, Singapore, Japan, and Australia. It even has permanent bases in the Middle East—in Kuwait, Oman, Qatar, and Saudi Arabia. Beyond bases, it has forces abroad in Bosnia, Egypt, Ethiopia, Hungary, Turkey, Kyrgyzstan, Tajikistan, Uzbekistan, and the former Yugoslavia. Even that is not a complete list of known bases and deployments. This worldwide presence gives the United States its unmatched ability to deploy troops far and wide; it is strategic planning at the highest level.

How fast can the American military respond to international threats? Unfortunately, that information is not readily available. The U.S. military is understandably cautious about disclosing response times to international threats; however, some of the U.S. ability to deal with domestic threats has been announced. The U.S. government has stated that the Marine Corps is capable of deploying two platoons of soldiers anywhere in the United States within twenty-four hours, and then is able to support those Marines with another thousand soldiers within three days. Considering the size of the continental United States, twenty-four hours is quite a short amount of time. The use of this type of accelerated deployment domestically is a response to new threats.

AP/Wide World Photos

A robot designed to detect improvised explosive devices (IEDs), used by terrorists and other insurgents, in Afghanistan in 2005.

The shock of the terrorist attacks on September 11, 2001, sent a devastating message to the United States. Americans realized that, although they had little to fear from most conventional armies, they were still vulnerable. As in the case of the special unit of Marines mentioned above, the U.S. has invested heavily in research and development of tactics to deal with asymmetric warfare. In the search for viable counterstrategies to terrorism, the United States has developed ideas such as "network-centric warfare" and has invested billions in robotics and information technology.

One pursuit of the United States and other top-tier nations has been robotics. Used commonly in manufacturing, robots (robotic devices) have been examined by the military for their use in warfare. The wars in Iraq and Afghanistan have finally brought these science-fiction dreams into reality. Drone airplanes, controlled by soldiers thousands of miles away, are a perfect example of the type of warfare one can expect to be increased in the future. Drone airplanes, and the robotic aides that accompany ground troops, mark a very interesting turning point in warfare. Many of the robots in service now are used to do jobs that are considered too dirty, too dangerous, or too demanding (the "three D's") for human soldiers. In using robots to locate and disarm improvised explosive devices (IEDs), for example, robots have become human proxies; they are being used to limit the discomfort and danger of warfare. The impact of robots in the near future has not yet been fully conceived, however, and tough questions are already being asked. How do robots identify targets? What if the robot's program fails to work and it attacks a friendly target? What if it sees a child with a gun? Although we are a long way from automated tanks and electronic super soldiers taking over for humans, the presence of robots on the battlefield increases daily, and their impact on warfare is changing the way that militaries assess threats.

CHINA'S MILITARY CAPABILITIES

In stark contrast to the United States, China's military seems powerful but slow. This is not a failing of the Chinese military People's Liberation Army (PLA) but is in fact adherence to China's central international policy: noninvolvement. Despite that ideology, China is beginning to emerge from its shell and is enhancing its capabilities for power projection. In mid-April of 2009, China celebrated its navy's sixtieth anniversary. To mark the occasion, it brought out a great deal of its fleet on maneuvers. The fleet is composed of modern destroyers, submarines, and frigates. Although many Chinese citizens flocked to the highly publicized event, the maneuvers were not for the people's entertainment; they were intended as a spectacle for the rest of the world to see.

China has the largest land army in the world, but it is still in the process of modernization. China announced that during the 2010's it will focus on closely integrating its various military branches—a prerequisite for developing advanced strategic capabilities. China's two international focuses are acquiring sources of oil and the reintegration of Taiwan (the latter is considered a domestic issue by the People's Republic). Although the United States pledges its continued support to Taiwan's independence, if China decided to invade Taiwan, the conflict would be short and likely end in China's favor, since China is fully capable of quickly pacifying the tiny nation. American support, however, keeps Taiwan's independence a political and not a military issue. In January of 2007, China shot one of its own satellites out of space. The action was a show of China's military advances. Along with its own program to put more satellites into space, the satellite strike suggested that China is moving to become a player in the game of information warfare.

NETWORK-CENTRIC WARFARE

The greatest technological advances have been in information-gathering technology, not robotics. Since 1991, a great deal of the information and communication technology that the United States used to overpower Iraqi forces has become commercial technology: the Global Positioning System (GPS), night-vision goggles, thermal imaging cameras, and satellite photographs of anywhere on Earth available over the Internet. Since these technologies are now widely available, advanced nations seek to gain further control over the flow of information. This information advantage forms the basis for network-centric warfare (sometimes referred to as "net-war").

Freed from constant military threats, advanced nations like the United States, Russia, and China have turned their focus to dominating their opponents' communications. Because of the incredible amount of information that is available from satellites, spy planes, and long-distance detection devices, a battle can be fought over hundreds of miles in multiple locations. The modern theater of engagement could include offshore batteries from miles away, tactical bombing and missile attacks from aircraft, indirect fire from mobile batteries, and enfolding tactics from soldiers behind enemy lines (deep striking). With modern technology, attacks can be synchronized and coordinated across an entire country.

The key theory in net-war is that the army that has the most information, and that is able to make best use of that information, is unbeatable—or, as stated in a report by the Center for Strategic and International Studies, "[to be] able to penetrate the enemy's decision making system and react so quickly that the opponent cannot compete." In ages past, if a battlefield commander could find a key spot in battle from which to gain the advantage, that commander was said to have an "eye" for the battlefield. Now battlefields are so large that the only "eye" of any use is one from a satellite or aircraft.

FOURTH-GENERATION WARFARE AND NONCONVENTIONAL THREATS

The capability for power projection via strategic warfare is what stands between many modern nations and a world-class army. Although some nuclear powers are not actively projecting power, they have the capabilities to do so. The second-tier nations listed above lack the resources or motivation to project power outside their region. These nations build up their militaries mainly for defense. Outside the major powers there are many large and powerful mil-

itaries. Most European countries are proud of their armed forces, as are nations like Turkey, Egypt, and South Korea.

Not everyone, however, is convinced that the robot revolution and net-centric warfare are the keys to modern military dominance. Fourth-generation warfare, or 4GW for short, is a theory that focuses on the changing nature of warfare. 4GW states that in the modern era we have passed the days of centralized warfare between well-organized armies, having moved into an era of warfare when armies fight against small cells of armed civilians. Fourth-generation warfare has its own critics, however, who point out that a new theory is not needed to explain guerrilla war tactics—which have been used for thousands of years. What the theory of fourth-generation warfare identifies is that we are moving into a period when conflicts between ideologies and inequalities are championed (or taken advantage of) by militant groups. Using modern technology, these militants are able to move quickly and communicate secretly. Military analysts point to conflicts like those in Vietnam, the wars in Afghanistan (both the 1979-1989 Soviet and the current U.S. attempts to pacify the area), and the current conflicts in Israel and Iraq to show the weakness of conventional armies. Therefore, modern militaries must adapt; they must become more flexible, more covert, and better able to handle a range of different threats. Instead of using a platoon of tanks to accomplish a mission, for example, they must use covert operations ("black ops").

One great benefit of the 4GW theory is that it takes into account a wide range of capabilities and combatants. In fact, that range is the whole point of 4GW—it covers militants from African warlords to the Sri Lankan Tamil Tigers. They are usually either loosely connected or not connected to traditional armies and fight for ideology, resources, or family or tribal groups instead of a national military. These groups are so small that they are infuriatingly difficult to pin down by conventional militaries. However, like traditional militaries, these sideline groups have evolved.

The West holds some stereotypes of nonconventional combatants: that they all use AK-47 machine guns, old Soviet RPG launchers (rocket-propelled grenades), and the infamous IEDs, or homemade bombs, to harass invaders. Due to constant news coverage and stories from the Middle East, most Americans would connect this type of warfare to extremist Muslim groups. The tales of suicide bombers have become all too commonplace on the nightly news. However, this type of fighting neither is confined to the Middle East nor represents the extent of these groups' capabilities.

In *The New Face of War* (2003), Bruce Berkowitz describes a friend, a reporter, who bought a computer from a pawnshop while covering the conflict in Afghanistan. The pieces for his new computer had all come from a PC that was looted when al-Qaeda forces were routed and pushed into the mountainous areas near the Afghanistan-Pakistan border. Recognizing his luck, the reporter sent the hard drive to a computer specialist to crack and retrieve the information. What he found on the hard drive was a plethora of plans and communications of incredible complexity. It should be understood that the terrorists who owned that computer represent the majority, and not the minority, of modern nonconventional threats. Antulio J. Echevarria, in her work *Fourth-Generation War and Other Myths* (2005), debunks the legitimacy of the 4GW theory, although she concedes that it is tempting to see new, nontraditional combatants as a brand-new and trendsetting threat simply because they are so far from the cave-dwelling nomads with AK-47's that many believed they were.

Asymmetric soldiers have access to such a wide range of technology and are so mobile that they are able to strike almost anywhere. In his award-winning research on nuclear disarmament, Ward Wilson argues that nuclear weapons are most useful to those (perhaps useful only to those) aiming to spread terror. Governments are justifiably worried about terrorist groups acquiring weapons of mass destruction. In the 1960's the United States was forced to fight asymmetric warfare against national communists in Vietnam; however, the Vietnamese were incapable of striking at the American people. The situation has changed: In 2010, militaries and governments must prepare to fight a new breed of nonconventional opponent who is globally mobile and capable of massive attacks on civilians.

Militaries of today face the constant pressure of modernization and preparation. If there is any single military truth that has made its way through history and is unlikely to change soon, it is that militaries must constantly evolve. Not only are traditional militaries expanding their capabilities; even nonconventional military forces are expanding and adapting their strategies to gain the upper hand. This element adds a new level to an already difficult and expensive competition. Today the threat from the nonconventional opponents is perhaps the most pressing.

To meet these threats, foreign and domestic militaries will continue to adapt. They will buy more robots, build more ships, acquire new long-range cameras, piece together new tanks, and develop new tactics and technologies. The militaries will continue to evolve—as they must. The militaries of 2010 are our militaries of today; however, with phenomena like global reach, network-centric warfare, airplane drones, and combat robots, the capabilities of some advanced militaries embody our ideas of the future.

BOOKS AND ARTICLES

Berkowitz, Bruce. *The New Face of War: How War Will Be Fought in the Twenty-first Century.* New York: Free Press, 2003. Investigates how information in warfare has changed the nature of combat in the twenty-first century.

Burke, Arleigh A. *The Asian Conventional Military Balance in 2006: Overview of Major Asian Powers.* Washington, D.C.: Center for Strategic and International Studies, 2006. Presents detailed profiles of major Asian nations, as the region has become increasingly vital in the early twenty-first century.

Echevarria, Antulio J., II. *Fourth-Generation War and Other Myths.* Carlisle, Pa.: Strategic Studies Institute, United States Army War College, 2005. Discusses the idea of fourth-generation war: an insurgency that uses political, economic, social, and military pressure to convince an opponent nation that victory will cost more than it is worth.

Langton, Christopher. *The Military Balance, 2002-2003*. New York: Oxford University Press, 2002. The major source book, presenting the relative strengths of the world's armed forces, rebel groups, and other military forces.

Wilson, Ward. "The Myth of Nuclear Deterrence." *Nonproliferation Review* 15, no. 3 (2008): 422-439. Investigates whether the strategy of nuclear deterrence actually was the preventive factor during the Cold War and whether or not it can work in the modern age, with the slow but steady proliferation of nuclear weapons.

Bryan Buschner

WITHDRAWN